RECLAIMING AMERICAN CATHOLICISM

RECLAIMING AMERICAN CATHOLICISM

Faith, Politics, and the Future of the Catholic Church

JOHN GEHRING

Foreword by E. J. Dionne Jr.

GEORGETOWN UNIVERSITY PRESS / WASHINGTON, DC

Cataloging-in-Publication Data is on file with the Library of Congress.

ISBN 9781647126049 (hardcover)
ISBN 9781647126056 (paperback)
ISBN 9781647126063 (ebook)

∞ This paper meets the requirements of ANSI/NISO Z39.48-1992 (Permanence of Paper).

EU GPSR Authorized Representative
LOGOS EUROPE, 9 rue Nicolas Poussin,
17000, LA ROCHELLE, France
E-mail: Contact@logoseurope.eu

26 25 9 8 7 6 5 4 3 2 First printing

Printed in the United States of America

Cover design by Brad Norr
Interior design by Westchester Publishing Services

CONTENTS

FOREWORD

E. J. Dionne Jr.

When a Jesuit from Argentina named Jorge Mario Bergoglio became Pope Francis on March 13, 2013, it was not irrational to hope that this friend of the poor and champion of simple piety might bring together a divided church. He was chosen, after all, because the Cardinals who elected him sensed a crisis in the church and the need for a new departure. The Holy Spirit moved in a surprising way.

In the United States, where the Catholic leadership often found itself to the right of the global church, Francis's election was greeted, initially at least, with thunderous enthusiasm among the faithful across political lines. In a time of great hurt and difficulty around the world, his description of the church as "a field hospital after battle" appealed beyond—or perhaps above—political divisions. He tossed away many of the trappings of showy piety and might, and he disdained the ornate regalia that appeal to so many prelates but distance them from the rank-and-file in the pews. The joke in Rome was that as priests got on board with the new program, many lacy surplices went on sale at steep discount on eBay. He gave up the papal apartments and treated the Vatican staff more as coworkers than employees.

There was also an infectious hopefulness and joy about him. *The Joy of the Gospel*, one of his first formal documents, captured how he thought Christians should approach the world. He spoke out against "querulous and disillusioned pessimists," and I always wanted to meet the English translator of *The Joy of the Gospel* who told us that Francis took people to task for being "sourpusses." It's hard to disagree with Francis on the sourpuss issue. My friend Michael Sean Winters, an important chronicler of contemporary Catholicism, got Francis exactly right when he said: "If you understand that preaching a God of mercy is central to his ministry, everything else falls into place."

But the prospect that he might bring the church together also rested on a careful balance he struck. Yes, Francis was—in some ways quite radically—changing the emphasis of church teaching. His priorities were global poverty, the unfairness of the economic system, the need to give sustenance and help to immigrants and refugees, and the imperative to protect the Earth by fighting climate change. Early on he insisted that he had a problem with the all-consuming emphasis so many Catholic leaders had placed on issues such as abortion and homosexuality. In an interview with *America* and other Jesuit journals around the world in the fall of 2013, Francis made this plain:

> We cannot insist only on issues related to abortion, gay marriage, and the use of contraceptive methods. This is not possible. I have not spoken much about these things, and I was reprimanded for that. But when we speak about these issues, we have to talk about them in a context. The teaching of the church, for that matter, is clear and I am a son of the church, but it is not necessary to talk about these issues all the time.

Notice the last sentence. Francis did not change church teaching on abortion or on many other questions. He made clear that he viewed "unborn children" as "the most defenseless and innocent among us." He defended the Catholic position on abortion by insisting that it was not "ideological, obscurantist, and conservative," but was rather "linked to the defense of each and every other human right." Maybe, just maybe, Francis could begin to bring warring factions of the church together, in the United States and elsewhere. By being cautious about changing doctrine he could reassure conservatives. But by being outspoken on issues related to social and economic justice, he could restore a balance for a church whose social teaching had emphasized a communitarian, pro-poor, and pro-worker worldview since Pope Leo XIII's 1891 encyclical *Rerum Novarum*. On economic matters, he went out of his way to offer frequent nods to his large areas of agreement on these issues with his predecessors (and heroes to church conservatives), Popes John Paul II and Benedict XVI.

In the United States a decade on, it's sadly clear that Francis's effort to create a new unifying center of gravity in the church has failed to win over Catholics on the right or to ease divisions in the church. On the contrary, as John Gehring concludes in this deeply thoughtful, passionate, and well-reported book: "The Francis papacy, an emboldened Christian right energized by Donald Trump, and the subsequent election of a pro-choice

Catholic president together stirred up something of a perfect storm of polarization in the US church."

It's true, as Gehring notes, that some of the divisions in American Catholicism are over issues specific to the church. These included a more than half-century-old argument over the meaning and import of the reforms of the Second Vatican Council and a related debate over the proper relationship between Catholicism and modernity. This second debate has of late taken on a new urgency in the face of a fierce and intellectually serious challenge to the new openness to liberal modernity in the Vatican II era. Pope John XXIII called upon Catholics to discern the "signs of the times" and upbraided "dis trustful souls" who saw in the modern era "only darkness burdening the face of the earth." The new antiliberal thinkers—Notre Dame's Patrick Deneen is one of the most prominent—think there is much to distrust in modernity and much darkness for which liberalism must be held to account.

But for those who take religious faith seriously, it is a depressing fact that so much of the discord is an import from American politics at its most raw. In a sense one could argue that Trump had a larger impact on parts of the American church than Pope Francis, and nowhere more so, as Gehring writes, than in the growing popularity of Christian nationalism in some Catholic circles. The "increasingly tribal nature of Catholicism in the United States today," Gehring writes, "can't be understood in isolation from the widening political and cultural chasms of society." He goes on: "The church has become more fractious and bitterly divided because there are larger forces reconfiguring and dividing American life more broadly."

Gehring makes a particularly important contribution to the conversation—and to future scholarship—by showing how closely the Catholic divisions over Francis's papacy and Joe Biden's presidency overlap. Biden, like Francis, might have been a source of unity. Only the second Catholic president in the nation's history, Biden was a quintessentially Catholic figure of the post–World War II era, Catholic to his bones down to his regular Mass attendance and the rosary he always carried with him. And Biden's commitment was not just to liturgy or old practices. As Gehring shows, Biden was also representative, in his worldview and in the policies he championed, of a longstanding Catholic commitment to social reform, embodied in the work of Father John A. Ryan (known during FDR's presidency as "Father New Deal") and the 1919 Bishops' Program of Social Reconstruction that laid out many of the New Deal's initiatives in advance. This all came naturally to "Scranton Joe," who grew up in a world in which the boundaries between the church, the party, and the union were thin to nonexistent—the church being Catholic and the party being Democratic.

Gehring is shrewd in analyzing the two large forces that undermined the world of Biden's Catholicism. The first is the decline of a Catholic subculture built around immigrant status or background, ethnic identification, and a powerful network of institutions rooted in the Catholic parish and the Catholic school. Although much is made of Vatican II's impact, the decline of the Catholic subculture owes far more to sociology: to upward and geographic mobility, the rise of the suburbs and exurbs, new forms of media, and the integration of older streams of Catholic immigrants—from Ireland, Italy, Poland, other parts of Europe, Lebanon, Quebec, and elsewhere—into the mainstream of American life. Newer immigrant groups from Latin America, Vietnam, and the Philippines have built latter-day versions of the old subculture, but they are building them in a more secular time.

But above all is the power of the abortion issue and the growing party polarization around it. It became the defining issue for a large part of the hierarchy, which inevitably pushed church institutions toward the Republican Party. For some it truly was a foundational issue. But for many conservative politicians—one thinks especially of Trump, whose positions have shifted with the polls—it was also an issue of convenience to move formerly Democratic white Christians, especially Catholics, toward the GOP. As Gehring shows, Francis's efforts to push the church toward a reengagement with the late Cardinal Joseph Bernardin's "Seamless Garment" approach linking life issues across the board—poverty, war and peace, the death penalty, access to health care—was a threat to conservative and right-wing politics. Here lies the bond between anti-Biden, anti-Democratic politics and the reaction against Francis. Since the *Dobbs* decision overturning *Roe v. Wade,* voters even in very red states have shown their support for keeping abortion broadly legal. This might open room for some cooperation between right-to-life and social justice groups in backing more help for women and families to bolster those who bring children into the world. Some in the right-to-life movement have shown an interest in this, but others remain committed to pushing back on abortion rights whenever and wherever they can. A less conservative hierarchy might want to rethink its political posture on the issue. This does not seem likely in the near term.

Gehring and I can both be fairly categorized, in the shorthand of these things, as social justice Catholics. Both of us remain grateful that the church we grew up in and to which we remain committed inclined us toward the broadly progressive views we now hold. There are millions of Catholics like us in parishes around the country, one of them being a recent occupant of the White House. But the developments Gehring describes here have had an important impact on who remains Catholic and will affect who joins the church in the future. Our conservative fellow Catholics should ponder that their success in identifying the church with the political right has pushed younger Catholics away from the church in large numbers.

A 2011 Pew Research Center study found that "one-in-ten American adults (10.1 percent) have left the Catholic Church after having been raised Catholic, while only 2.6 percent of adults have become Catholic after having been raised something other than Catholic." That is not a growth trajectory. Among former Catholics who are now religiously disaffiliated, 65 percent said they had stopped believing in Catholicism's teachings overall, 56 percent expressed dissatisfaction with Catholic teachings about abortion and homosexuality, and 48 percent cited dissatisfaction with church teachings about birth control.

Conservative and traditionalist Catholics might well say good riddance to those who do not share their view of what orthodoxy demands. But Catholicism is not supposed to be sectarian. And as Gehring suggests, so much of the acrimony in the church is political in the narrowest sense. He quotes Cardinal Blase Cupich of Chicago warning against a polarization that leaves people "living an isolated and siloed existence in their own spheres." Perhaps social justice Catholics in the United States are destined to fight a rearguard action to maintain the church as a broad and inclusive institution that welcomes progressives and conservatives alike—and will have to do so, for a while at least, with less support from the next generation as younger potential allies leave the church altogether. If that is their fate, progressive Catholics would do well to pay attention to Pope Francis and not become liberal versions of the "querulous and disillusioned pessimists" he described. They should embrace the struggle they face with the joy Francis recommends. They will certainly get nowhere if they become "sourpusses."

PREFACE

The author who sets out to explore contemporary issues at the intersection of faith and politics can often feel like someone sprinting to catch a speeding train that is already a mile down the track. Not long after submitting the last iteration of this manuscript for the final months of preparation before publication, the political news cycle kicked into overdrive. President Biden's disastrous debate performance on June 27, 2024, sparked growing calls for Biden to leave the race. Less than a month later, Donald Trump survived an assassination attempt during a campaign speech. The photograph of a bloodied former president pumping a defiant fist in the air before he was rushed off the stage by Secret Service agents became one of the most iconic images in American political history. Two days later Trump picked Senator JD Vance of Ohio, who converted to Catholicism in 2019 after attending Yale Law School, as his running mate. Reporters scrambled to understand the senator's close associations with Catholic intellectuals and authors who identify as "post-liberals" and Catholic "integralists." Leaders in this relatively small but vocal movement seek to leverage government and other institutional power to privilege conservative expressions of Christianity in public policies and society more broadly. I had already been documenting Catholic strains of Christian nationalism, as well as the role that integralism plays in conservative Catholic circles, before Vance's rapid political ascent. The reader will find an exploration of these themes in Chapter 4.

Amid rising demands from prominent Democrats urging the president to drop out of the race, Joe Biden became the first president since Lyndon Johnson to announce he would not seek a second term. "It has been the greatest honor of my life to serve as your President. And while it has been my intention to seek reelection, I believe it is in the best interest of my party and the country for me to stand down and to focus solely on fulfilling my duties as President for the remainder of my term," Biden wrote in a letter to the American people on July 21, 2024. In a speech from the Oval Office a few days later, the president displayed an authentic patriotism and humility rarely demonstrated by those who hold power. "I revere this office, but I love my country more," Biden said, adding that "nothing can come in the way of saving democracy, and that includes personal ambition." As I explore in the book, Biden's presidency put a white-hot spotlight on an increasingly polarized church in the United States. While the second Catholic president in American history is no longer making headlines, the struggle to define the public voice of Catholicism in political life will continue as divisions over abortion, gender, sexual identity, religious liberty, and LGBTQ rights roil bishops, elected officials, and Catholic activists on the left and right. "Despite institutional decline and internal conflict, Catholicism retains a surprising resonance in American life—especially in certain elite circles," the conservative Catholic writer Matthew Schmitz wrote in *The New York Times*. "It has emerged as the largest and perhaps the most vibrant religious group at many top universities. It claims six of the nine Supreme Court justices as adherents. It continues to win high-profile converts, and its social teaching exerts an influence (often unacknowledged) on public debates, inspiring political thinkers who seek to challenge both the cultural left and the laissez-faire right."

I'm writing this brief introduction three months before the 2024 presidential election. The political landscape of American Catholicism will undoubtedly be influenced by those results but not defined by them. By taking the long view and weaving historical context with reporting on contemporary issues, I hope this book offers readers a wide lens to view the interplay of politics, Catholic social teaching, theology, and grassroots Catholic activism.

John Gehring
August 14, 2024
Washington, DC

Pope Francis died on April 21, 2025, not long before publication of this book. The author dedicates these pages to his memory. May the spirit of Francis help rekindle our commitment to justice, mercy, and a politics of the common good.

ACKNOWLEDGMENTS

The publication of a book is always a collaborative process. I am sincerely grateful for E. J. Dionne Jr., an enthusiastic cheerleader for this project who introduced me to the team at Georgetown University Press. E. J. is not only an insightful commentator about the intersection of faith and politics but also a gracious and thoughtful fellow Catholic who cares deeply about the future of our church. Al Bertrand of Georgetown University Press provided a steady editing hand over the several years the book took shape. I met my wife Nneoma as the writing of this book started. When I felt overwhelmed or discouraged, you were always there with encouragement, smart editing advice, and a hot cup of tea. Your deep faith and spirituality are an inspiration to me. To my children Sophie and Leo, as you continue to write the stories of your lives, always know Dad loves you.

Introduction

THE FRANCIS EFFECT

Reform, Resistance, and a Church in Crisis

In those heady early days after Cardinal Jorge Mario Bergoglio of Buenos Aires, Argentina, became the 266th pontiff of the Roman Catholic Church, an ancient institution beset by scandal, emptying pews, and plummeting moral credibility suddenly felt energized and hopeful. A Jesuit with instincts for reform, little patience for the Vatican's monarchical trappings, and an impish sense of humor that disarmed and charmed, Pope Francis had managed to pull off the unlikely feat of reviving, at least for a time, a gloomy Catholic narrative long defined by dour doctrinal watchdogs and embattled culture warriors.

A Latin American outsider "from the end of the earth," as he described it in the moments after his election, Pope Francis used evocative language and powerful gestures to put justice, joy, and mercy at the center of the church's vision. The pope moved to break down barriers between the hierarchy and laity; strike a welcoming tone toward LGBTQ people; and urge clergy to find what he called "a new balance" when speaking about centuries of Catholic social justice teachings that don't end with opposing abortion. The first pope to take his name from St. Francis of Assisi said he dreamed of a "poor Church for the poor," led by pastors who have the "smell of the sheep," and a church that acts more like a "field hospital" for the wounded than a fortress against perceived threats gathering at the gates. This unlikely new pope seemed to move with the discerning style of an Ignatian spiritual retreat director—asking probing questions, upending certitudes, even inviting disagreement.

When I wrote my book about "the Francis effect" in 2015, there was a palpable buzz about a "springtime" for the Catholic Church in the United States. Those of us who had spent years trying to revitalize an eroded Catholic social justice vision in political debates, theologians who faced heavy-handed scrutiny by church authorities—and US Catholic sisters who only a year before Pope Francis's election were investigated for what the Vatican called "serious doctrinal problems"—felt optimistic, relieved, and perhaps even vindicated by the pope's refreshing style and priorities. As I chronicled in my book, the pre-Francis era in the US church was often defined by a generation of bishops appointed by Pope John II, men who embraced a muscular, countercultural Catholicism that flexed most conspicuously on matters of sexual morality. Catholic activists and conservative Catholic intellectuals such as the late Rev. Richard John Neuhaus, editor of *First Things*, also linked arms with evangelical Protestant leaders as the religious right became a potent force in American politics. Neuhaus had the ear of President George W. Bush, and along with his fellow Catholic neoconservatives, the late Michael Novak and George Weigel, broke with Pope John Paul II to rally behind the Iraq war and endorse a philosophy of free-market fundamentalism that clashed with traditional Catholic social teaching on labor, the limits of market fundamentalism, and the dignity of work. During Pope Benedict XVI's papacy, the US bishops' conference became more deeply invested, both in dollars and institutional energy, in political battles against abortion, LGBTQ rights, and contraception funding—even opposing the passage of historic health care reform—all as clerical sexual abuse and institutional coverup continued to devastate the hierarchy's moral credibility.

Pope Francis couldn't reverse the decades-long development of these entrenched forces with a simple snap of papal fingers. But it quickly became clear that his papacy represented a disruption to the prevailing forces that had long shaped American Catholicism. Along with modeling a servant leadership style that emphasized accompanying people through the complexity of life, the pope opened space for a more expansive conversation about what it means to be "pro-life." In particular, economic inequality and climate change, issues that his predecessor also took seriously, were elevated to urgent priorities under the Francis papacy. The lives of "the poor, those already born, the destitute," Pope Francis wrote, are as "equally sacred" as the unborn in the womb. Conservative Catholics who assumed they owned the narrative about Catholic identity in American politics—selectively cherry picking from and even distorting centuries of church teaching to endorse a narrow ideological agenda—now faced an unwelcome development: a Latin American pope who made it a lot harder, if not impossible, to brand Catholicism as simply a religious imprimatur for the Republican Party or a Catholic branch office of the US Chamber of Commerce.

But the spirit of reform and renewal in the air when Pope Francis was elected in March 2013 has fizzled. A decade after the pope's election, the

US hierarchy has mostly failed to embrace the pope's call for more pastoral leadership, continues to hunker down in fighting culture wars, and is at best indifferent, and at worst hostile, to his appeals for urgent action on economic inequality and the existential threat of climate change as pro-life priorities. The US bishops' conference announced major staffing cuts in the summer of 2024 to its Department of Justice, Peace and Human Development, which focuses on issues of environmental justice and domestic and international policy, and oversees grants that fund antipoverty campaigns. A younger generation of priests shows more resistance to Pope Francis than older priests, according to a 2021 research study from the Austin Institute that found that while nearly 80 percent of priests ordained before 1980 "approve strongly" of the pope, only 20 percent of those ordained in 2010 or later did.[1] Nearly half of the younger priests, the study found, disapprove of the pope, either "strongly" or "somewhat."

In many ways, the Catholic Church in the United States remains far more responsive to wealthy conservative donors who hold significant influence across a wide swath of Catholic institutions than to the pastoral and social justice priorities of the pope. The United States is the epicenter of a vocal, anti-Francis resistance movement—a fact that even the pope himself acknowledges. Not long after his election, Vatican ambassadors briefed Francis about an array of global issues and urged him to be cautious when appointing bishops and cardinals in the United States. "That is where the opposition is coming from," the pope said, a high-ranking Vatican official told the *New York Times* in 2017. Two years later, the pope candidly retorted that it is "an honor that the Americans attack me," when asked about a book from a French journalist that chronicles opposition to Francis from right-wing Catholics in the United States. Indeed, the pope's unsparing denunciations of "trickle-down" economic theories, and what he calls an "economy of exclusion and inequality" that "kills," are threatening to many conservative Catholics who hold influential positions in business and politics.

In retrospect, perhaps it was inevitable that a pope who has challenged so many comfortable certitudes on the right—and raised unrealistic expectations on the left for fundamental change in church teaching—would provoke both a backlash from reactionary conservatives and engender disillusionment from liberals. Even so, it would have been hard to predict the sustained opposition and sheer contempt hurled at a sitting pope from a vocal faction on the Catholic right. Conservatives who once accused liberal Catholics of heresy for even the most nuanced critiques of Pope Benedict XVI have no reservations maligning Francis in bracing terms. In particular, the pope's efforts to open a more pastoral conversation about church teachings on the family and reception of Communion for divorced Catholics—the Eucharist is not "a prize for the perfect, but powerful medicine and nourishment for the weak," the pope has said—are viewed by self-proclaimed traditionalists as dangerous breaks with orthodoxy that could lead the church to the brink of schism.

In a 2017 letter to Pope Francis from a former director of the US bishops' doctrine office, Fr. Thomas Weinandy told the pope he was "demeaning" the importance of doctrine, appointing bishops who "scandalize the faithful," and creating "chronic confusion" in his teachings. "To teach with such an intentional lack of clarity inevitably risks sinning against the Holy Spirit, the Spirit of truth," Weinandy wrote in stunning language more befitting a teacher scolding a wayward student than a priest addressing the successor of St. Peter. Overheated claims that Pope Francis was sowing doctrinal "confusion" among the faithful began to grow into a more emboldened anti-Francis movement—a network that includes various commentators featured on the global Catholic media outlet EWTN and the EWTN-owned *National Catholic Register* and *LifeSiteNews,* former St. Louis archbishop Cardinal Raymond Burke, and even Donald Trump's erstwhile political advisor Stephen Bannon, who has frequently criticized Pope Francis's advocacy on behalf of refugees and immigrants. Bannon even teamed up with Cardinal Burke in a failed effort to launch an academy in an 800-year-old monastery in Rome that would train what Bannon called "modern gladiators" committed to right-wing populist ideology.[2]

The opposition to Pope Francis exploded into mainstream news coverage in August 2018 when Archbishop Carlo Maria Vigano, the Vatican's former papal nuncio in Washington, released an unprecedented attack on a sitting pope from a church official. In an eleven-page letter, the archbishop called on Pope Francis to resign, accusing him and other senior church leaders of covering up the sexual abuse of former cardinal Theodore McCarrick of Washington. McCarrick became the first US prelate to resign his position in the College of Cardinals a few weeks before Vigano's letter was released. The archbishop also accused Pope Francis of giving support to what Vigano described as the Vatican's "homosexual current," a lobby "with the power of octopus tentacles."

The release of the manifesto offered a case study in church politics. Vigano consulted with conservative Vatican analyst Marco Tosatti in drafting the document, and coordinated its release in the American outlet *LifeSiteNews,* a publication that is frequently critical of the pope. Cardinal Joseph Tobin of Newark viewed the letter as part of a consistent campaign against Pope Francis. "I do think it's about limiting the days of this pope, and short of that, neutering his voice or casting ambiguity around him," the cardinal told *The New York Times*. Journalists quickly produced reporting that contradicted Vigano's claims and conspiratorial accusations. In the weeks following the letter's circulation, several bishops' conferences around the world released statements of solidarity with Pope Francis and specifically denounced Archbishop Vigano. The then-president of the US Conference of Catholic Bishops, Cardinal Daniel DiNardo of Galveston-Houston, said Vigano's letter raised questions that "deserve answers that are conclusive and based on evidence." More than two dozen US bishops issued statements of support for Vigano at the time, a move that helped legitimize anti-Francis sentiment in some dioceses and parishes across the country. Vigano, who during his years as papal representative in Washington used his power to help secure the appointments of several conservative bishops in the United States, emerged again in 2020—a few months before the presidential election—with another communication to a prominent recipient.

In an open letter to President Trump, also published by *LifeSiteNews*, the archbishop praised Trump for his strong leadership opposing "children of darkness whom we may easily identify with the deep state." Vigano also claimed that protest movements after the police killing of George Floyd were orchestrated by "deep state" operatives. (Trump and other conservatives frequently reference "the deep state" as a secret network inside the government that aims to undermine elected governments.) President Trump, quick to seize on what he viewed as an influential Catholic endorsement, tweeted that he was "honored" to receive Archbishop Vigano's support and urged his 82 million followers to read the letter. Prominent national media outlets, including the *Washington Post*, covered the archbishop's letter and Trump's response. After Trump's defeat in 2020, the archbishop accused Joe Biden of stealing the election and later called for the president to be excommunicated. In the summer of 2024, the Vatican's doctrinal office charged Vigano with schism. The archbishop, who refers to the pope by his original surname of Bergoglio rather than his papal name, has labeled Pope Francis a "false prophet." In a statement responding to the Vatican charges, the archbishop called it an "honor" to face the accusations. "Bergoglio is to the Church what other world leaders are to their nations: traitors, subversives, and final liquidators of traditional society," he wrote. The Vatican excommunicated Vigano two weeks later.

The symbiotic relationship between the Catholic far right's capitulation to Trumpism, the emboldened anti-Francis movement, and the campaign to demonize the faith of a Catholic president require a profound reckoning for the church in the United States.

RECLAIMING THE CATHOLIC NARRATIVE IN POLITICS AND PUBLIC LIFE

At a time when only the second Catholic president in American history speaks authentically about his faith, attends Mass, and affirms many themes of Catholic social teaching in his administration's policies, vocal church leaders and Catholic activists who gave Donald Trump a de facto Catholic blessing because of his antiabortion agenda decided to wage a single-issue culture war against President Biden. This stark contrast illuminates a deeper crisis at the heart of the church's participation in the public square. Drawing on reporting and analysis, this book will make an argument that reclaiming the Catholic narrative in politics and public life is vital for both the future of the church and the country.

Declining religious affiliation and distrust of institutions more broadly might prompt a skeptical reader to ask why the public voice of the Catholic Church even matters. A Pew Research Center study found that between 2007 and 2014, the Catholic Church lost more members than any other religious institution.[3] These losses are especially acute with younger Catholics, an exodus driven in part by alienation over the hierarchy's perceived alignment with the Republican Party and a right-wing political movement, especially on issues of reproductive rights and LGBTQ equality. This trend of religious decline and disaffiliation isn't limited to the Catholic Church. The percentage of Americans who no longer have an affiliation with any religious denomination is now about the same as those who identify as evangelicals or Catholics. A 2020 Gallup poll found that for the first time in the survey's eight-decade trend, less than half of all Americans (47 percent) said they belonged to a church, synagogue, or mosque.[4]

I'm not unsympathetic to those who think that Catholic leaders in the United States have lost the capacity to be viewed as a positive force for justice in the public square. I have spent more than a few hours ranting, and lamenting, in the company of other Catholics who love our church but find ourselves increasingly disillusioned and exhausted by many of our leaders. In recent years alone, Catholics watched a once beloved cardinal, the former archbishop of Washington, exposed as a sexual predator who used his influence to abuse children and prey on seminarians. A Pennsylvania grand jury report, released in 2018, provided another front-page reminder of the chilling scale of the clergy sexual abuse crisis. Seventy-six percent of Catholics said that clergy abuse has damaged the reputation of the church, according to a survey from the Center for Applied Research in the Apostolate. A third of Catholics even said they were "embarrassed" to tell others that they were

Catholics because of the crisis.[5] By the time of the 2020 presidential election, many Catholics had already reached a breaking point. When a small but vocal chorus of bishops—and a larger network of conservative Catholic activists and organizations—became cheerleaders for a president who embraced white Christian nationalism and used the politics of fear to stoke division, the church's already threadbare moral credibility felt lost.

The steady drip of dispiriting news—a Catholic school fires an unmarried pregnant teacher, the Vatican's doctrine office issues another document that leaves LGBTQ Catholics deeply pained—can leave me discouraged. I buck myself up with a reminder that Catholicism is much bigger than the hierarchy or the latest headline. The church is a messy institution—ancient, beautiful, and flawed. At my baptism, I inherited a faith tradition rich with the treasures of mysticism, the examples of fearless spiritual reformers, the inspiring stories of activists, a history of sinners, saints, and seekers. I also know that Catholics once silenced or vilified by the Vatican are sometimes welcomed back and make profound contributions. In 1950 the ideas that French Dominican Yves Congar had about church reform were deemed scandalous by Rome. Only a decade later, Congar's writings helped inspire the Second Vatican Council, and his thoughts are reflected in the Council's most influential documents. Being a member of a church that stretches back to the time of the Apostles imbues you with an appreciation for complexity and the long view. The late Cardinal Avery Dulles, a Jesuit who had converted to Catholicism as a young man after growing up in a family of diplomats and influential leaders, once described his unexpected move into the Catholic Church as that of a timid swimmer who "jumps into the roaring sea." The Catholic waters have been swirling for centuries. Our present era is not an exception.

This book is anchored in my belief that the best of Catholicism can still enrich culture, politics, and our collective search for justice. Along with institutional church leaders, the Catholic artists, advocates, and ordinary Catholics who live out an embodied faith in the shadow of scandal and hypocrisy are not blind to the flaws of our church. If authentic patriotism is never simply mindless obedience but always a "lover's quarrel" with your country, as the Rev. William Sloan Coffin put it, then I believe that an authentic faith is an engaged faith that questions and quarrels from a place of love. "I love America more than any other country in the world and, exactly for this reason, I insist on the right to criticize her perpetually," James Baldwin wrote in words that capture the spirit of anyone who wrestles with contradictions. Doubt and faith, challenge and commitment can be held together in creative tension. We Catholics who are still holding on despite it all search and struggle together, connected in spirit and memory to all those who did the same before us, and to future generations who will take up this pilgrimage long after we're gone.

The Catholic intellectual and social justice traditions are sources from which Catholic sisters, lay activists, clergy, and politicians shaped by their faith's teachings have made essential contributions to the nation. From the New Deal and the civil rights movement to contemporary advocacy to protect immigrants and end the death penalty, many Catholics have been at the forefront of social change. And even during an era when institutions are viewed skeptically or even with hostility, the Catholic Church remains a vital institution. In the United States, outside of the federal government, Catholic charity networks make up the nation's largest providers of social services. One in six hospital beds are in a Catholic facility. The US bishops' Migration and Refugee Services (MRS), the largest nongovernmental resettlement agency, has resettled more than a million refugees since 1975. The Catholic Campaign for Human Development (CCHD) is one of the nation's most important antipoverty grant-making institutions empowering secular and faith-based grassroots organizations.

Even if you long ago tuned out the public voices of bishops, the election narratives, policy agendas, and the laws of our nation are often shaped by Catholics. From President Biden to Supreme Court Justice Amy Coney Barrett, Catholics are often at the center of fractious debates and take center stage in contested questions over the role of faith in public life. Six justices on the Supreme Court are Catholic. Prominent politicians in both parties, from Rep. Alexandria Ocasio-Cortez and former House Speaker Nancy Pelosi to Sen. Marco Rubio and Florida Governor Ron DeSantis, are Catholic. "A good Catholic meddles in politics," Pope Francis has said, a quip that reflects the church's longstanding teaching that the aim of politics is ultimately dignity and human flourishing. In his encyclical *Fratelli Tutti*, the pope calls for a "better kind of politics, one truly at the service of the common good." He challenges right-wing populism and xenophobic nationalism. This political vision is grounded in the dignity of the person, radical solidarity with the most vulnerable, and a recognition that social change is most often driven by grassroots justice movements. As the pope said during a convening of the World Meeting of Popular Movements in Brazil, the future of humanity "does not lie solely in the hands of great leaders, the great powers and the elites. It's fundamentally in the hands of people and their ability to organize."

It's hard to observe the bitter divisions in both the Catholic Church and the country without recognizing the need for a better path forward. Catholics should bring humility to a diverse public square, even as we recognize how the centuries-old wisdom of our intellectual, theological, and social traditions can speak in timely ways to contemporary challenges. Catholic social teaching is uniquely situated to help connect values and issues often pitted against each other in political debates: rights and responsibilities, the immigrant child at the border and the child in the womb; the essential role of government and the importance of local civic institutions. The Catholic commitment to solidarity and the common good can be a powerful corrective to the radical individualism that poisons our culture and politics. Libertarian ideologies that make an idol of individual autonomy have been exposed more than ever in recent years as a dangerous form of social Darwinism that leaves the most vulnerable behind and weakens our capacity to confront collective challenges such as global pandemics and extreme climate change.

But to rescue the Catholic Church from culture wars and draw from this rich history to renew the public voice of Catholicism today, we need discernment and reform. In particular, the hierarchy must find a more effective and ultimately more Catholic way to express its laudable commitment to the sanctity of life. This challenge takes on even greater urgency now that the US Supreme Court has overturned a legal right to an abortion. By defining abortion as their "pre-eminent priority," US bishops have steadily eroded the church's commitment to a consistent ethic of life and aligned themselves with a political movement at odds with much of the church's social justice teachings. These trends coalesced in calamitous ways with the election of Donald Trump. The fact that so many Catholics—bishops, voters, priests, and well-funded advocacy groups—accommodated the former president's nativism and contempt for bedrock norms of democracy and basic decency in the transactional pursuit of "pro-life" judges underscores how distorted Catholic political engagement has become. This book will offer an analysis of Catholic politics during the rise of Donald Trump, which presents an opportunity to explore what lessons can be learned for the future. Even as the church must reckon with its failures in relationship with Trump, I will explore Catholic identity in the Biden era, years that in many ways seem to have only hardened reactionary political and ecclesial strategies, as evidenced by how conservative American bishops have clamored to deny Communion to a Catholic president and other pro-choice Catholics in elected office.

The hierarchy will also need to confront how its teachings on gender and sexuality are in stark tension with the church's own claims to seek justice and human dignity. A church that continues to marginalize women and LGBTQ Catholics is not a church capable of speaking with persuasive moral credibility to many in its own flock and beyond. While some might argue these neuralgic issues are exclusively internal, theological debates to be worked out by Catholics inside the church, they are also inextricably connected to how the church engages in a diverse public square. When the US bishops' conference opposes the Violence Against Women Act by citing the dangers of "gender ideology" and lobbies behind the scenes to oppose legislation for a national suicide hotline because it contains funding for vulnerable LGBTQ people, the church gravely wounds those it professes to love—and demonstrates an inability to prudently apply the tools of Catholic moral theology to contested issues in the political sphere.

While the most conservative clergy often garner disproportionate media attention, and leaders at the US bishops' conference in Washington have yet to embrace systemic reform and renewal, a growing number of "Francis bishops" do recognize the need for change. Many of these bishops, including San Diego Cardinal Robert McElroy, Chicago Cardinal Blase Cupich of Chicago, and Cardinal Joseph Tobin of Newark, New Jersey, have been more emboldened to speak out in recent years. They recognize the church must welcome LGBTQ people, de-escalate the abortion culture wars, and do more to amplify the church's teachings on environmental justice and economic inequality.

THE BROAD CANVAS OF AMERICAN CATHOLICISM

The Catholic hierarchy does not exist in a vacuum. The politics of the US church can only be understood in a broader context. I will analyze how a well-funded Catholic right has used conservative media outlets, networking spaces that draw in Republican politicians, and even Catholic business schools to advance an agenda that often aligns more with a right-wing political movement than the principles of Catholic social teaching. Organizations such as Catholic Vote, which spent nearly $10 million to help reelect Trump, and the Napa Institute, which brings together wealthy donors, GOP politicians, and conservative bishops for prayer and strategy sessions in exclusive settings, are part of a flourishing conservative Catholic ecosystem that wields disproportionate influence in the church. I will also examine why religious liberty—until recent years embraced as a bipartisan, core value in American life—is now one of the most contested issues in legislatures, courts, and public debates. From bishops to Supreme Court justices and attorneys at prominent religious liberty law firms, Catholics have played an outsized role in shaping these narratives.

In an information-saturated culture dominated by social media and a twenty-four-hour news cycle, it's also easy to lose sight of the fact that Catholicism transcends church politics or the latest Catholic controversy in the headlines. The church that Pope Francis envisions—"bruised, hurting and dirty because it has been out on the streets"—can be found every day among Catholic advocates working on the border; in the lives of young Catholics who question the church's teachings but who are active in parish and social justice campaigns; in creative efforts to bring together the disaffiliated "nones" with Catholic nuns; in the persistence of LGBTQ Catholics who carve out tenuous shelters in a church that often fails to respect their full humanity; and in the experiences of seminarians in Yakima, Washington, who spend time working in the fields with migrants as part of their religious formation. And while churches and Catholic schools are closing doors in places that once defined an immigrant American Catholicism (Boston, Philadelphia, Cleveland, Baltimore), Latino immigrants have made Catholic dioceses in the South and West the new epicenters of a vibrant, diverse church.

Throughout the book, I will incorporate snapshots of these Catholics, weave in on-the-ground reporting, and examine trends that are essential to understanding the Catholic experience in the United States. By illuminating these stories, I hope both to provide a richer portrait of American Catholicism than what most people see in the media, as well as offer living examples of prophetic Catholicism that can serve as inspiration for more institutional reform and renewal.

NOTES

1. Francis X. Roca, "U.S. Catholic priests are increasingly conservative as faithful grow more liberal," *The Wall Street Journal*, December 18, 2022, https://www.wsj.com/articles/u-s-catholic-priests-are-increasingly-conservative-as-faithful-grow-more-liberal-11671343608?st=5f2spmjsabjuvjm&reflink=desktopwebshare_twitter.
2. Richard Engel and Kennett Werner, "Steve Bannon and U.S. ultra-conservatives take aim at Pope Francis," *NBC News*, April 12, 2019, https://www.nbcnews.com/news/world/steve-bannon-u-s-ultra-conservatives-take-aim-pope-francis-n991411.
3. "America's Changing Religious Landscape," Pew Research Center, May 12, 2015, https://www.pewresearch.org/religion/2015/05/12/americas-changing-religious-landscape/.
4. Jeffrey M. Jones, "U.S. Church Membership Falls Below Majority for the First Time," *Gallup News*, March 29, 2021, https://news.gallup.com/poll/341963/church-membership-falls-below-majority-first-time.aspx.
5. The Editors, "Editorial: How you see the sexual abuse crisis," *American Magazine*, July 15, 2021, https://www.americamagazine.org/faith/2021/07/15/sexual-abuse-crisis-catholic-church-survey-america-241051.

1

DIVIDED NATION, DIVIDED CHURCH

A few hours before he would be sworn in as only the second Catholic president in American history, Joseph Robinette Biden Jr. went to church.

The Cathedral of St. Matthew the Apostle in downtown Washington is about four blocks from the White House. On several occasions when Biden served as the vice president, I watched him discreetly slip into a back pew for 5:30 p.m. Sunday evening Mass—a man in quiet prayer like the rest of us, participating in a comforting and familiar ritual. But sitting in the front pew on a cold morning in January 2021, anonymity was not an option. The eyes of the world were now on the man from Scranton who prays the rosary, grew up around priests and nuns, and was shaped by a white ethnic Catholic culture thick with feast days, union halls, and fish on Lenten Fridays. A few feet away from Biden's seat, an inlay on the floor of the cathedral memorialized the spot where, fifty-seven years earlier, the casket of John F. Kennedy, the nation's first Catholic president, rested during his funeral.

A day that began with Catholic prayer and ritual unfolded with more expressions of faith. At the Capitol, still encircled by barbed wire fencing after a bloody insurrection only two weeks earlier, Fr. Leo Donovan, a Jesuit priest, former president of Georgetown University and family friend of the Bidens, delivered the invocation by confessing "our past failures to live according to our vision of equality"[1] and summoned Pope Francis's call to "dream together." Amanda Gorman, the twenty-three-year-old poet laureate who grew up attending St. Brigid Catholic Church in Los Angeles, rallied the nation in a dark time with the lyrical hope that "the new dawn blooms as we free it, for there is always light if only we're brave enough to see it, if only we're brave enough to be it."[2]

After Chief Justice John Roberts swore Biden in as the nation's forty-sixth president at 11:50 a.m.—the first time in history a Catholic chief justice had asked a fellow Catholic to take the oath—the president delivered his inaugural address. Referencing a "saint of my church," Biden quoted St. Augustine that "a people are a multitude defined by the common objects of their love." To a country still reeling from the second impeachment of Donald Trump by the House of Representatives, the former president's attempts to overthrow the election, and a violent attack on the Capitol from Trump loyalists, the new president made a plea for unity. "My whole soul is in this, bringing America together, uniting our people, uniting our nation, and I ask every American to join me in this cause," Biden implored. While the president acknowledged that "speaking of unity can sound to some like a foolish fantasy these days," he insisted that "history, faith and reason show the way of unity."[3]

But not long after starting his day at Mass and urging the nation to come together, Biden was met with division and dueling reactions from leaders of his own church. In a lengthy inauguration day statement, the president of the US bishops' conference, Los Angeles Archbishop José Gomez, chose to emphasize disagreement and conflict. "I must point out that our new president has pledged to pursue certain policies that would advance moral evils and threaten human life and dignity, most seriously in the areas of abortion, contraception, marriage, and gender," Archbishop Gomez wrote. "Of deep concern is the liberty of the Church and the freedom of believers to live according to their consciences."[4] From Rome the message sounded very different. Pope Francis sent a telegram encouraging Biden to pursue common ground and policies "marked by authentic justice and freedom." Two months earlier, after the election results were announced, the pope had personally called Biden to congratulate him, and they discussed working together on migration and the environment. Pope Francis also sent the new president a signed copy of his book, *Let Us Dream*. In an unprecedented move, Chicago Cardinal Blase Cupich, a close advisor to Pope Francis, publicly criticized his own bishops' conference inauguration day statement, tweeting that Archbishop Gomez's words were "ill-considered."[5] The cardinal also questioned why the statement was released without wide consultation with other bishops. "The internal institutional failures involved must be addressed, and I look forward to contributing to all efforts to that end, so that, inspired by the Gospel, we can build up the unity of the Church, and together take up the work of healing our nation in this moment of crisis,"[6] the cardinal wrote. Vatican leaders were also displeased by the US bishops' hardline approach to the Biden presidency. The Jesuit magazine *America* quoted a Vatican official calling Archbishop Gomez's statement "most unfortunate."[7]

Ten months after Biden's inauguration, Archbishop Christophe Pierre walked toward a podium with a daunting assignment. The Vatican's point man in Washington stood before hundreds of masked Catholic bishops gathered in a hotel ballroom in downtown Baltimore to deliver a plea for church unity. Reporters from across the country were on hand to chronicle the hierarchy's ongoing, and increasingly contentious, debates over how to engage with the new president. An earlier proposed document on the Eucharist prepared by the bishops, ostensibly a pastoral reflection on what the church calls the "source and summit" of the Catholic faith, had turned into a bitter source of episcopal feuding over whether President Biden, House Speaker Nancy Pelosi, and other pro-choice Catholic elected officials should be denied the sacrament. Only a few weeks before the bishops gathered in Baltimore, President Biden met with Pope Francis in Rome. The photos of a smiling pope and president pledging to find common ground despite fundamental differences served as a stark visual reminder of how isolated culture warriors in the American church were from Rome. On a crisp November morning, in the first city to establish a Catholic diocese in the United States, the congenial French diplomat spoke to leaders of a divided church that increasingly felt as fractured as the nation.

"A church that teaches must be firstly a church that listens," Archbishop Pierre told the bishops. "It is true that the path forward is not always immediately clear," the archbishop said.[8] "Patience and discernment are necessary. Still, the path forward necessarily involves unity. A divided Church will never be able to lead others to the deeper unity desired by Christ. The Church needs this attentive listening more now than ever if she is to overcome the polarization afflicting this country." The archbishop used the word "listen" thirty-five times in his address, a *Washington Post* religion reporter noted in her coverage. Even as church leaders were divided among themselves, many people were clamoring for the bishops' attention. Outside the waterfront hotel in Baltimore, demonstrators provided a real-time snapshot of a church splintered over abortion, politics, the clergy abuse crisis, and a pandemic then more than a year old. Liberal Catholics held signs that read "Who would Jesus deny?" and "Communion is for all." Activists from progressive groups—the Women's Ordination Conference, FutureChurch, and DignityUSA, an LGBTQ Catholic organization—staked out space not far from a large rally hosted by the right-wing Church Militant, where protestors railed against coronavirus restrictions and blasted the bishops for not prioritizing abortion.[9] Speakers at the rally included Fr. James Altman, a rogue Wisconsin priest who three months earlier had been removed from his parish and restricted from ministry after making national headlines for a video referring to liberals as "left-wing fascist Nazis" and warning that Catholics who supported the Democratic Party could "face the fires of hell."[10]

The Francis papacy, an emboldened Christian right energized by Donald Trump's presidency, and the subsequent election of a pro-choice Catholic president together stirred up something of a perfect storm of polarization in the US church. This series of events underscored and exacerbated long-standing Catholic divisions. While there are divisions in Catholicism best understood by a discrete study of internal church politics, the increasingly tribal nature of Catholicism in the United States today also can't be understood in isolation from widening political and cultural chasms in society. The church has become more fractious and bitterly divided because there are larger forces reconfiguring and dividing American life more broadly.

* * *

Americans don't simply disagree over politics or policy. We live in different realities. Where we live, go to school, and attend church; who we date; even what we eat and binge watch on television are increasingly segmented by ideological leanings and partisan affiliation. "We have built a country where everyone can choose the neighbors (and church and news shows) most compatible with his or her lifestyle and beliefs," Bill Bishop wrote in his 2008 book, *The Big Sort: Why the Clustering of Like-Minded America Is Tearing Us Apart*. "And we are living with the consequences of this segregation by way of life: pockets of like-minded citizens that have become so ideologically inbred that we don't know, can't understand, and can barely conceive of 'those people' who live just a few miles away."[11] In the decade and a half since Bishop wrote about this sorting, major cultural disruptions—especially over race, religion, and national identity—metastasized these divisions and fueled a politics of backlash. As Robert P. Jones documents in his book *The End of White Christian America*, the swift decline in the number of Americans who are white Christians has challenged the cultural, religious, and political hegemony of white Protestantism, a demographic trend that leads to what Jones calls "nostalgia voters," many of whom voted for Donald Trump as a perceived bulwark against these changes.[12] (I will explore Trump's 2016 election and Catholic politics in the following chapter.) A national reckoning over racism and police brutality, galvanized by the police killing of George Floyd and other Black Americans, is playing out against the backdrop of wider debates over how history is taught in school and what voices have been marginalized or ignored in the telling of those stories.

Suspicion and hostility toward those outside our identity groups run high. A Pew Research Center survey found that more than half of all Republicans and nearly half of all Democrats believe their political opponents to be "immoral."[13] More than 70 percent of Republicans and Democrats told

Pew in 2019 that both parties can't even agree on "basic facts." Compared to people in seventeen countries in Europe, Asia, and North America, the research center found that Americans were most likely to say our country was divided along partisan, racial, and ethnic lines. In recent years, political scientists have also tracked a rise in "negative partisanship," a term used to describe voting behavior and partisan identity fueled by hostility toward opposing parties.

While the divisions of our era have ample historical precedent, there is evidence that by some measures polarization is growing. Trump voters in red states are more likely to say they would be personally "better off" (33%) than "worse off" (29%) if their state seceded from the United States and "became an independent country," according to a Yahoo News/YouGov poll conducted in July 2022.[14] Fewer than half of Americans said there were "very strong conflicts" between Democrats and Republicans in 2012. By 2020, that number had soared to 70 percent.[15] Scholars have found that people's attachment to political parties is stronger than identification with their race and religion. Political identity is also reinforced by physical distance. Harvard University researchers have used geolocation data and addresses of registered voters in the United States to map where Democrats and Republicans live in relation to each other in every town, city, and state in the country. Most Democrats and Republicans, the study found, live in places where levels of partisan segregation exceed what scholars of racial segregation consider highly segregated.[16] This means that Americans are not only living in virtual media echo chambers, where we consume news sources that usually confirm our own political views, but we are also living in actual geographical bubbles where we rarely meet or talk to someone from a different political party.

The coronavirus pandemic only poured more gasoline on the fires of polarization. Mask and vaccine mandates quickly became politicized. In a seventeen-country Pew survey, about 60 percent of people on average say their countries are more divided than before the pandemic. But that number jumps to 88 percent for Americans.[17] A Marquette University Law School poll in 2021 found that 70 percent of Democrats said they considered Covid a "serious problem," compared to only 30 percent of Republicans.[18] Elizabeth Kolbert recounts in a *New Yorker* article, "How Politics Got So Polarized," that the day after the World Health Organization declared Omicron a "variant of concern," Rep. Ronny Jackson, a Texas Republican, labeled the new strain a Democratic ploy to justify absentee voting. "Here comes the MEV—the Midterm Election Variant," Jackson tweeted.[19] Divisions over Covid also split the Catholic Church into factions. While Pope Francis said in an interview that "morally everyone must take the vaccine" and described getting vaccinated as "an act of love," other church leaders sent different messages.[20] Bishop Joseph Strickland, whom Francis removed from his post in Tyler, Texas, in 2023, tweeted that he had "spoken out against these mandates and will continue to do so."[21] San Francisco Archbishop Salvatore Cordileone publicly acknowledged that he chose not to receive a Covid vaccination, telling reporters in 2021 that his "immune system is strong."[22] In particular, disagreement over the ethics of taking vaccines with links to cells derived from aborted fetuses also divided Catholic leaders. "U.S. bishops splinter on the morality of taking coronavirus vaccines," the *Washington Post* reported in the spring of 2021.[23] The Vatican's doctrine office in 2020 declared it "morally acceptable" to take vaccines that used cell lines from aborted fetuses in their research and production "when ethically irreproachable Covid-19 vaccines are not available."[24] But when a vaccine from Johnson & Johnson hit the market, the Archdiocese of New Orleans called it "morally compromised" because it used cells from tissue taken from an elective abortion in the 1980s.[25] The US Conference of Catholic Bishops said Catholics should avoid taking the Johnson & Johnson vaccine if possible. The Diocese of Bismarck, North Dakota, went further, calling it "unacceptable for any Catholic physician or health care worker to dispense and for any Catholic to receive due to its direct connection to the intrinsically evil act of abortion."[26] San Diego Cardinal Robert McElroy argued that Catholic moral theology is more complex. In a letter to his diocese, he wrote that "in the current pandemic moment, with limited vaccine options available . . . it is entirely morally legitimate to receive any of these four vaccines, and to recognize, as Pope Francis has noted, that in receiving them we are truly showing love for our neighbor and our God."[27] In contrast, the president of the National Catholic Bioethics Center, Joseph Meaney, released a statement in July 2021 defending people who refused to get vaccinated because they are "unwilling to compromise their ethics or consciences." While Pope Francis stressed the moral duty to receive a vaccination, Meaney argued "there is freedom on this matter and no strict moral obligation one way or the other."[28]

DIVIDED PARISHES

Churches and other houses of worship have in many cases become more politically divided in recent years. Trump's election, the proliferation of social media echo chambers that reinforce more extreme views, the politicization of Covid, and the decline of parish boundaries as the traditional markers for where Catholics choose their parish have all contributed to this trend. "I've been studying religion and religious congregations for thirty years," Michael O. Emerson, a sociologist at the University of Illinois at Chicago, told Bloomberg News in 2021. "This is a level of conflict that I've never seen. What is different now? The conflict is over entire worldviews—politics, race, how we are to be in the world, and even what religion and faith are for."[29]

The Shrine of the Most Blessed Sacrament is a Catholic parish in a leafy section of northwest Washington, DC, close to the Maryland line. The surrounding neighborhood attracts lawyers, lobbyists, established journalists, and government officials for its ample homes and strong schools only a few miles from the power centers of institutional Washington. Over the years Blessed Sacrament has managed to bring together an ideologically diverse congregation, including an unlikely mix of prominent parishioners spanning the political spectrum. The fiery right-wing populist Pat Buchanan, the Reagan-era secretary of education Bill Bennett, and liberal political commentators Mark Shields and Chris Matthews have all worshiped together. In the 1980s and 1990s the parish became something of a model for how Catholic Republicans and Democrats in a divided town could set aside differences and worship together. "It was a different time and there was still kind of a hold the Catholic Church had writ large over a generation of Catholics," recalled longtime parishioner Jim Zogby, a prominent liberal advocate for Palestinian rights in the Middle East, president of the Arab American Institute and longtime Democratic party advisor. "The idea that you just wouldn't go to church or that you would not go to your neighborhood parish was not even considered back then."[30] Zogby, who is 75, recalls inviting Pat Buchanan back to his house after Mass one day for coffee on the porch. The progressive activist and the former Richard Nixon advisor, who ran for president in 1992 vowing to "make America first again" and fight "a religious war" against secular America, had little in common but their shared Catholic faith. The two disagreed sharply that day over politics, but the conversation was cordial.

The late Blessed Sacrament pastor Msgr. Tom Duffy led his congregation of power brokers with an understated, pastoral style. A homilist with a scholarly bent, he would quote from the poetry of the Jesuit priest Gerald Manley Hopkins and T.S. Eliot, and sprinkle in occasional references from newspaper editorials. "He really held the parish together in magnificent ways," said Zogby, whose children were altar boys at the church and attended the parish school. "I'm sure conservatives didn't always agree with him, but it didn't matter what your political stripe was, you found comfort in him."[31] Things began to change in the fall of 2018 when Donald Trump nominated a Blessed Sacrament parishioner, Brett Kavanaugh, to fill a vacancy on the US Supreme Court after the death of Ruth Bader Ginsburg. When Christine Blasey Ford accused Kavanaugh of sexually assaulting her at a party when he was a student at Georgetown Preparatory School in suburban Maryland, the parish began to split into de facto camps that mirrored larger cultural and political divides. The accusations of sexual assault against someone who was the product of an all-male, elite Catholic institution sparked national conversations about power, privilege, and toxic masculinity. At Blessed Sacrament, those issues were personal. Parishioners who knew Kavanaugh as a neighbor, a good father, and a popular girls basketball coach defended him. Another group of parishioners, some of them graduates of all-girls Catholic schools in the area who socialized with boys from Georgetown Prep as adolescents, believed Ford and recalled their own discomfort at parties with students at the school.

The controversy came at a raw time for Catholics. Three months before the allegations against Kavanagh, the Archdiocese of New York announced a credible allegation of abuse against Cardinal Theodore McCarrick of Washington, one of the Catholic Church's most influential leaders. Two months later, a Pennsylvania grand jury report found that more than 300 Catholic priests had abused children over seven decades across the state. Clergy abuse was once again back in the headlines. Blessed Sacrament parishioners were angry. Zogby recalls a well-attended meeting at the church where people spoke up to vent their anger. But now that one of their own faced sexual assault charges, parishioners who had come together united in outrage over clergy abuse were torn over how to respond to Kavanagh. "It really divided us at a time when we were coming together on the pedophilia issue," Zogby said. "The tensions were very sharp."[32] For Zogby and his late wife Eileen, who served as a Eucharistic minister at the church, the sadness over divisions at Blessed Sacrament ran alongside a deeper sense of disaffection with the rightward lurch of the church's hierarchy. Zogby organized a parish sign-on letter in 2012 expressing concern that the US bishops' religious liberty "Fortnight for Freedom" campaign had become politicized and too closely connected to the bishops' opposition to former President Obama's efforts to pass health care reform, which included contraception coverage for women. "We have been through trying times together—war, civil strife, scandals in the church, terrorist attacks on our nation, contested elections, and controversial legislation—but we have remained a community, with our parish serving as our refuge," the letter from more than two dozen parishioners read.

> For all of us, whatever our political philosophy, our church has been a welcoming home. This, we fear, may be changing. We are deeply concerned that, under cover of a campaign for religious liberty, the provision of universal health care—a priority of Catholic social

> teaching from the early years of the last century—is being turned into a wedge issue in a highly-charged political environment and that our parish, and indeed the wider church, is in danger of being rent asunder by partisan politics.[33]

The Zogbys, who have a gay daughter, also watched with sadness as Catholic bishops teamed with up evangelical and Mormon leaders to spend millions of dollars on high-profile campaigns against same-sex marriage. The couple stopped sending donations to Catholic Charities in Washington, DC, after the charity responded to the city's legalization of same-sex marriage in 2009 by shutting its doors on its adoption services rather than place children with same-sex couples. Even after the Supreme Court legalized same-sex marriage in 2015, church leadership continued to frame its opposition to LGBTQ rights as a religious liberty issue—firing gay and lesbian teachers at Catholic schools and even lobbying behind the scenes to oppose legislation that created a suicide prevention hotline because some funding was targeted to at-risk LGBTQ people. "The politics of the church became a genital theology," Zogby lamented:

> It's all about sex. And the gay issue. And the obsession over abortion at the expense of everything else. It felt like the bishops became a cheerleading squad for the GOP. The church is increasingly irrelevant in the lives of our kids and many of the kids who grew up at Blessed Sacrament. That became a huge topic of conversation for families at the parish. Our children are all Christian. It's their moral grounding and how they live their lives. Some of my kids still go to Mass, but the church became more problematic and isn't seen as a place of refuge anymore. They didn't leave the church. The church left them.[34]

Even as research shows that Catholics, especially young people, are becoming less connected to parishes, Tricia Bruce says a parish community remains a "microcosm for Catholics in America and a laboratory for understanding social life." The sociologist of religion and director of the Springtide Research Institute notes that while the old ethnic parishes that defined the Catholic immigrant experience through the middle part of the twentieth century were insular, provincial, and reflected the exclusionary racism of the broader society, they were also settings where people of different classes, professions, and political views could have shared experiences. Parishes are still one of the few remaining places in a divided public square that at least have the potential to put disparate groups of people in contact with each other.

"Part of the beauty of the parish model, and the sociological effect of that model, is that it brings people together who would not otherwise be meeting," said Bruce, the author of *Parish and Place: Making Room for Diversity in the American Catholic Church* and coeditor of *Polarization in the U.S. Catholic Church: Naming the Wounds, Beginning to Heal.* "This helps create empathy and a respect for the common good. That's the ideal, of course. It's a lot harder to find in practice."[35] While the geographical boundaries of neighborhoods historically determined which parish a Catholic family would attend, Bruce said that Catholics today are more likely to "hop and shop" for a parish that is tailored to their liturgical, ideological, ethnic, or racial preferences. She notes that despite growing diversity in the church, driven in large part by Latino Catholics, there are still few truly multiracial and multicultural parishes in the United States. "Catholic parishes can look more diverse on paper than in practice," she said. "When you have multiple Masses in different languages, sometimes people at the same church never even see each other."[36]

Catholics who disagreed over politics a century ago still often shared a unifying solidarity that came from being part of parishes and immigrant subcultures at a time when Catholicism was viewed with hostility by the dominant Protestant society. This embattled mindset of outsiders began to change during World War II as Catholics proved their patriotic bona fides. If the ties of the Catholic subculture began to fray in the postwar years as Catholics moved from urban immigrant enclaves to the suburbs and ascended the socioeconomic ladder, the Catholic subculture disintegrated dramatically in the 1960s. A historic series of meetings at the Vatican catapulted the Catholic Church into uncharted territory at the center of American culture. These tectonic shifts, which occurred at the same time the sexual revolution challenged traditional mores, opened new opportunities for Catholic leaders to speak out boldly on some of the most searing political issues of the time. It also set the stage for an era of dissent and discord, presaging today's contentious debates over episcopal authority, Catholic identity, LGBTQ rights, and the role of the church in public life. "It used to be this attitude of Catholics against the world," Bruce observed. "Now the divisions are *within* Catholicism."[37]

THE SECOND VATICAN COUNCIL: A CONTESTED REVOLUTION

To understand the contemporary landscape of American Catholicism, it's necessary to look back. The Second Vatican Council (1962–1965) provoked a revolution in how the Catholic Church related to the modern world.

A monarchical institution that had a Holy Office of the Inquisition and condemned what it considered the evils of modernism and liberalism late into the nineteenth century would now—as Pope John XXIII described it in convening the unexpected gathering of more than two thousand bishops from around the world—"throw open the windows of the church and let the fresh air of the spirit blow through." In a series of meetings over three years, the Council produced landmark documents that called on all "people of God," not simply the hierarchy, to respond to the "signs of the times." The Council prioritized interfaith dialogue with Jews. It transformed the liturgical experience of Catholics by having priests face the congregation and offer Mass in the vernacular, not in Latin as the church had done for centuries. The American Jesuit priest and theologian John Courtney Murray, who had faced Vatican censure for his writings only a decade earlier, became the architect behind the Council's affirmation of religious freedom and freedom of conscience in secular society. Vatican II embodied a renewal that grew from a vision of *ressourcement,* a return to the sources of Scripture and the early church—fertile ground for applying the best of the church's tradition to contemporary realities. The Council also sparked opposition from Catholics who viewed changes in liturgical style and other reforms as assaults on tradition.

Nearly sixty years since its conclusion, the Council's legacy remains a fault line running through the church. Many conservative Catholics and self-styled restorationists believe the Council went too far in accommodating modernity. The seventy-eight-year-old "Good Pope John," the oldest pope elected in two centuries when he convened the Council, wanted a church that looked to the future "without fear" and challenged what he called "prophets of gloom."[38] This attitude doesn't describe some American Catholics leaders today who are anxious, defensive, and fixated on threats real or imagined in ways that can nurture an identity of victimhood. "These are dark times," Denver Archbishop Samuel Aquila warned at the conservative Napa Institute conference in 2021. "I often tell my seminarians some of you may become martyrs if our country continues in the direction it's going."[39] If Vatican II sought, in part, to lower the barricades that had built up a fortress mentality in the church over the centuries, some want the ramparts reinforced. "We're in a season in which we need to rebuild the walls of the church," R.R. Reno, editor of the conservative Catholic journal *First Things,* said during a panel discussion at the Napa conference. "We're in a Nehemian moment in the 21st century where we rebuild the walls of the church so the world sees we are a fundamentally distinct institution that lives in accord with its own laws and principles, and not the principles and laws of the world."[40] In a 2022 article, "Is Vatican II Spent?," Michael Pakaluk, a professor at the Busch School of Business at The Catholic University of America, opined: "We need another Council that diagnoses, indeed, but also anathematizes, brings to an end an implicit schism by drawing lines as to who belongs and who does not."[41] Pope Francis is blunt in his response to how the Council has been weaponized. "Either you are with the church and therefore follow the Council, or you interpret it in your own way—and you do not stand with the church," the pope told members of the National Catechetical Office of the Italian Bishops' Conference in 2022.[42] "Restorationism has come to gag the Council," the pope told editors of Jesuit journals in Europe. "The number of groups of 'restorers'—for example, in the United States there are many—is significant."[43] A former top official at the US bishops' conference responded indignantly to that assertion. "Someone has to say it publicly: The Holy Father does not understand the Catholic Church in the United States and he is doing her great harm," Jayd Hendricks, who served as the executive director of government relations for the US Conference of Catholic Bishops, wrote in *First Things*.[44]

At an invitation-only conference in Chicago in 2022, about seventy cardinals, bishops, and theologians gathered for two days to examine US opposition to Pope Francis in the context of resistance to the Council. The event, entitled "Pope Francis, Vatican II, and the Way Forward," was organized by Loyola University Chicago's Hank Center for the Catholic Intellectual Heritage, Boston College's Boisi Center for Religion and American Public Life, and Fordham University's Center on Religion and Culture. "We have this what they call 'opposition' to the pope," Honduran Cardinal Oscar Rodriguez Maradiaga, one of the conference attendees, told the *National Catholic Reporter*. "It's trying to build walls, going backwards—looking to the old liturgy or maybe things before Vatican II."[45] In a keynote address at the meeting, church historian and theologian Massimo Faggioli of Villanova University argued that "there is a parallel between the rejection of Vatican II and the relationship between the church in the United States and Pope Francis." The opposition to Pope Francis, Faggioli underscored, is rooted in the opposition to Vatican II—a theological crisis that did not begin with this pontificate. This is a problem that is not just theological but also ecclesial; that is, it has a profound consequence for the ways in which all Catholics experience their life of faith in the church." Faggiloi continued:

> What we have seen during the last nine years in the Church in the U.S., in terms of opposition to Pope Francis, defies imagination and has also distorted our expectations about the church in dangerous

> ways. We have witnessed unprecedented, rebellious challenges—sometimes coming from members of the clergy—to the legitimacy of the bishop of Rome that are clearly incompatible with the *sensus ecclesiae*. It's a phenomenon not limited to social media. It's something fundamentally different from the "dissent" against some aspects of papal teaching that we have seen under Paul VI, John Paul II and Benedict XVI. And it's something that must be denounced for what it really is, without tactical silences and without complacency.[46]

While the intensity of Catholic opposition to Pope Francis is highly unusual, the divisions over Vatican II that continue to animate disputes inside the church were there from the start. "The drama of the Council itself sensitized Catholics, as never before, to the behind-the-scenes maneuvering and to subtle shifts in church policy," Peter Steinfels wrote in his essential book, *A People Adrift: The Crisis of the Roman Catholic Church in America*.

> Since those who had opposed the conciliar decrees remained entrenched in the Vatican, they were suspected of stubbornly sabotaging, or at least contesting, each effort to implement the Council. And rather than clearly seize the lead of the postconciliar momentum, Pope Paul VI preferred to take two steps forward, one backward, always trying to moderate the pace of change and maintain unity by placating contending factions. It was not an unreasonable strategy. But the fear that the Council's work was being undermined and might ultimately be reversed was never dissipated. Mounting distrust fed harsher, more radical critiques, and more radical criticism fed greater resistance. Stir in the highly political, questioning, confrontational mood of the 1960s and early 1970s. Soon every Vatican pronouncement, every new theological proposal or pastoral intervention, every critical observation from left or right was scrutinized through the lens of suspicion, interpreted as a shift toward one or another extreme.[47]

* * *

In the days after the Council ended in 1965, many Catholics embraced social action and took steps to institutionalize its ideals. In *Gaudium et spes*, the Pastoral Constitution on the Church in the Modern World, a landmark document of the Council, bishops were called on to create national or regional conferences. These were not intended to be toothless associations that would simply rubber-stamp orders from Rome, but robust episcopal bodies that could enhance the church's voice on key moral issues in public life. US bishops, at the time largely focused on local and diocesan matters, moved to beef up their national operations. The hierarchy's existing National Catholic Welfare Conference in Washington was not designed for the new challenge. Bishops were not required to be members in this voluntary association, official statements were rare, and it lacked an authoritative voice. In 1966, a year after Vatican II ended, the National Conference of Catholic Bishops was officially designated as the hierarchy's collective body. In addition, bishops established the US Catholic Conference, which would serve as the church's policy arm in the nation's capital. "The bishops really began to think of themselves differently after the Council," said Fr. Bryan Hehir, a key architect behind many of the bishops' national pastoral letters when he was an influential advisor to the US bishops' conference during the 1970s and 1980s. "They now had a psychology of collegiality, and the idea that they were responsible for speaking out on issues for the wider church."[48] Hehir, a professor at Harvard University's John F. Kennedy School of Government, has a long view when it comes to church politics and division. As a top aide to the late Cardinal Joseph Bernardin, one of the most consequential leaders in American Catholicism over the past century, Hehir was often called on to help bishops navigate thorny political questions. If Vatican II propelled the church into taking a more visible role in public life, an early test awaited. In 1976, only three years after the US Supreme Court legalized abortion in *Roe v. Wade*, Jimmy Carter challenged the incumbent Gerald Ford in the presidential election.

On a late summer day in 1976, at the Mayflower Hotel down the street from the White House, Carter met with a delegation of Catholic bishops, including Archbishop Bernardin, president of the bishops' conference. A born-again evangelical who taught Sunday school and easily quoted the Bible, Carter was comfortable around faith leaders. Carter expected and received tough questions about his views on abortion when he sat down with bishops that day in Washington. Over the next two decades, Archbishop Bernardin would become the nation's most influential Catholic leader and proponent of a consistent-ethic-of-life, "seamless garment" framework that situated abortion as part of a broad pro-life witness that included issues such as economic justice, capital punishment, and nuclear disarmament. But for now abortion dominated the discussion inside the Mayflower. While Carter assured the bishops of his personal opposition to abortion, he didn't commit to supporting a constitutional amendment on the issue. When the bishops issued a statement after the meeting expressing their "disappointment," national media outlets reported the news as a blow to the Carter campaign.[49] Commentators blasted the bishops for what critics called a de facto endorsement of Ford.

Hehir feared the bishops were in danger of letting principled opposition to abortion become subsumed by partisan politics. In a memo to Bernardin on September 5, 1976, only a few days after the Carter meeting and less than a week before a similar meeting with Ford would take place at the White House, the priest warned that bishops were in "a precarious position." "This has nothing to do with our right to speak forcefully and consistently to the abortion issue or to any other question in the political process," Hehir wrote in his memo.[50] "The delicacy of our position relates to how we speak. How the Church speaks is as important as what it says. We are now deeply involved in the most specific level of political choice. The public perception is that we are partisan protagonists not moral teachers. The stress here is on the public perception: it exists apart from our intentions, plans or desires." Those words were prescient, if not prophetic. Four decades before the US bishops' conference boxed itself into a political corner by declaring abortion its "preeminent priority" before the 2020 presidential race between Joe Biden and Donald Trump, Hehir saw the trap awaiting church leaders. "You have correctly held that abortion is not a Catholic issue," he wrote. "In moral terms, this is true, but the way we have placed the political-legal dimension of the issue (the amendment) up front in the argument is making it a Catholic issue. To say this is the *only* way to solve the moral dilemma is to speak with more specificity and authority than either ecclesial or moral argument allows." If the bishops sent a message to Catholic voters that they could not support a presidential candidate who didn't specifically endorse a pro-life constitutional amendment, Hehir predicted a "*Humanae Vitae* dynamic will begin as soon as it is perceived that our specific position is becoming a substantial force in the campaign—creating a swing constituency."

His reference to the 1968 encyclical *Humanae Vitae* (On Human Life) was a potent warning about the potential for widespread dissent and division in the church if the bishops overreached on how they addressed abortion in an electoral context. Only eight years earlier, Pope Paul VI had reaffirmed the church's teaching against birth control as an "intrinsic evil," even for married couples. In issuing such an absolutist proclamation, the pope ignored the guidance of his own theological commission. Catholic theologians around the world criticized the encyclical. Cardinal Patrick O'Boyle of Washington suspended nineteen priests in the archdiocese for refusing to endorse *Humanae Vitae*. Fr. Charles Curran, a moral theologian at Catholic University in Washington, criticized the encyclical in a statement that was eventually signed by more than 600 theologians. The Vatican later prohibited Curran from teaching Catholic theology. Drawing on this example, Hehir used his memo to implore Bernardin "to avoid provoking organized dissent in the church. . . . I for one don't want to see you presiding over organized blocs of opposing Catholics swirling around the abortion issue and the election."[51] Given the fallout from the Carter meeting, Bernardin heeded Hehir's advice and made sure to put more distance between the bishops and Ford. After meeting with Ford, Bernardin said the bishops were "encouraged" but "not totally satisfied" with the president on the abortion question.[52] The archbishop also told reporters the conference was vigorously opposed to the Ford administration's acceleration of federally funded abortions. But the optics of bishops meeting with a president at the White House during a campaign drowned out their carefully calibrated statement. The *New York Times* called the bishops' meeting with the president "a clear asset to Mr. Ford in his attempt to win the support of Catholic voters in battleground industrial states of the Northeast and Middle West."[53] Russell Shaw, a spokesperson for the bishops' conference at the time, described the fallout. "All hell broke loose," Shaw said. "The bishops took a pounding for sticking their noses in the presidential election. Conference staff threatened to resign. Bernardin got chewed out by some of his brother bishops."[54]

CALL TO ACTION: THE LESSONS AND LIMITS OF A LISTENING CHURCH

Even as the US bishops stumbled during that foray into presidential politics, they were not giving up on putting into practice the ideals of Vatican II. The year 1976 was not only a presidential election year; it was also the bicentennial of the country's founding. Celebrations and events were planned in Washington and around the nation. The Catholic hierarchy found its own way to observe the anniversary by involving the faithful in a historic series of listening sessions on critical issues facing the church and nation. The Call to Action conference became one of the most ambitious efforts to engage with lay Catholics ever undertaken by American bishops. The initiative's success provides a window into how church leaders can marshal formidable institutional capacity to amplify a Catholic voice on social justice issues. Its failures are a case study in how divisions among the hierarchy, and the disconnect between the priorities of bishops and the laity, continue to hamstring efforts to reform and renew the church.

Four decades before Pope Francis called for a more synodal, "listening" church, the two-year Call to Action sought to live out the stirring opening words in the Second Vatican Council's Pastoral Constitution on the Church in the Modern World: "The joys and the hopes, the griefs and the anxieties of the men of this age, especially those who are poor or in any way afflicted, these are the joys and hopes, the griefs and anxieties of the followers of Christ."[55] Cardinal John Dearden of Detroit, who directed the commission at the Council that drafted those words, was the driving force behind Call to Action. An outspoken national leader on issues of poverty and racial justice, Dearden gave a powerful speech to open the conference. His words still carry wisdom for the church today.

> All of us in this hall are against racism and war and hypocrisy and violence; all of us are committed to the Gospel of Jesus, a Gospel of peace and justice and love and brotherhood and sisterhood; the tough part is translating all that into action. Translating it into a community of faith which conducts worship and prayer and education and works of charity and social service. Translating it into a moral position on questions of public significance, impacting on the processes by which legislation and public policy are made, because it is there that the basic work of justice is done in modern society. Both the pastoral task of building the Church, and the political task of building the world, involve choices, concrete and specific choices of how to spend our money, make our decisions, allocate our resources, direct our personal and collective allocation of time, treasure, and talent. None of us knows for sure how best to do these things, none of us can be certain that our program of reform is exactly what the Lord intends for us today. So we have no choice, if we are to be a community of both faith and freedom, except to meet, debate and make some decisions. That is what we are trying to do here. We are trying to begin a new way of doing the work of the Church in America. We may fail but let us try and let people in the nation say of us that they cared enough to try.[56]

What Dearden describes as a "new way of doing the work of the Church in America" illuminates how much Vatican II influenced a generation of bishops who were rethinking the old clerical mindset that expected lay Catholics to fall quietly in line behind their shepherds.

Only four months after returning from Rome at the conclusion of the Council, the cardinal coordinated a three-year mobilization involving tens of thousands of Detroit Catholics in a grassroots effort that he now wanted to replicate on a national scale. Dearden was a leader, but a servant leader who wanted the laity to speak up, stand beside him, even at times lead the way. Debate and disagreement would not be shut down or feared during the meetings. Criticism, even of the church's positions, could be aired with mutual respect. "Bishops were not running away at that point," said Frank Butler, then a congressional staffer with a newly minted degree in theology who left Capitol Hill to become director of the Call to Action conference. "Bishops were really listening and became pastors right in front of you," he recalled. "It was quite gripping. There had never been this kind of face-to-face candor."[57] In the planning stages, Butler recommended that the gatherings be modeled on congressional hearings and town hall meetings. "We built on a democratic town hall model and adopted it for church use," he said. "I told Cardinal Dearden that this is discerning the signs of the times using an American device. It all made sense to him." Before a culminating event convened in Detroit, Catholics from across the country met over a three-week period. In Texas immigration was a top issue. In Minneapolis and St. Paul delegates talked about the church's relationship with Native American communities. Labor rights and the dignity of work took center stage in Sacramento, where the famed farmworker organizer Cesar Chavez took part. Dorothy Day attended the Newark, New Jersey, meeting. Butler recalls an especially lively gathering in Atlanta. "It was like a tent revival. We had sugar cane workers from Louisiana, coal miners, a lot of community organizers," he said. At the same time discussion guides were mailed to every diocese in the country. The bishops were asking for feedback and ideas. They got it. Replies came pouring into the bishops' conference. "We have in many ways become a more divided and clericalized church, but in the nineteen seventies we were still pretty euphoric about this notion of a church where we had equality through our baptism and shared discipleship," Butler said. "That was the prevailing ethos."[58]

In Detroit more than 1,300 delegates debated and voted on more than a hundred recommendations to send the bishops. The gathering attracted attention far outside Catholic circles. The *New York Times* described Call to Action as an "extraordinary meeting" and "the most far-reaching experiment in democratic process that the Catholic church in this country has ever experienced."[59] Contentious issues were not ignored. Calls to discuss and potentially reform the church's positions on divorced and remarried Catholics, along with recommendations to study ordaining women and married men, passed overwhelmingly. Cardinal Dearden tried to calm the nerves of some bishops who had grown anxious that the gathering was too democratic in its posture toward church authority and established Catholic teaching. The results from the conference "may at this point seem hasty, untidy, careless, even extreme," Dearden wrote in a concluding report. "But on closer examination, it seems to me that far more often the working papers and conference resolutions demonstrate a warmth and sympathy for the problems of church leadership on the part of our people, their enthusiastic affirmation of the Christian faith and hope, their sincere willingness to share in building a stronger church. No one expects us to endorse all that transpired at Detroit. People do expect us to continue the process by responding with decisive action where it is called for and with honest disagreement where that seems necessary."[60]

But an archbishop in a powerful position was nervous. Joseph Bernardin, president of the US bishops' conference, had been a protege of Dearden. While Bernardin supported the broad goals of Call to Action, when bishops from around the country met for their semiannual meeting that November and reporters asked about the effort, he had already been chastened by the Ford–Carter abortion debacle earlier that year. Bernardin was trying to hold the bishops' conference together at a fraught political moment. The prospect of open debate over church teaching on issues of birth control, married priests, women's ordination, and lay participation in the selection of bishops wasn't an appealing prospect for him. Call to Action was frequently attacked by conservative Catholic publications and high-profile activists on the right such as Phyllis Schlafly. Cardinal John Krol of Philadelphia, a powerful conservative and former president of the bishops' conference, told the media he was disappointed that "the overwhelming thrust of the conference was to tell the institutional church what to do."[61]

At the conclusion of the Call to Action conference, Bernardin issued a statement charging that "special interest groups" had played "a disproportionate role" in crafting recommendations that "were not representative of the church in this country."[62] Looking back, Frank Butler said the bishops' conference reception of Call to Action was "an injustice" and that nervous bishops "hit the panic button." While church leaders were willing "to listen to the candor and wisdom of the Catholic people, the response was not what people expected," he said.[63] Writing in *America* magazine in 2021, Butler described the convenings as "a kind of beta version of the process of synodality now advanced by Francis' papacy." And he wondered what might have happened if church leaders had moved from listening to lay Catholics to implementing more of those ideas.

> Imagine what a difference it would have made over these past four and half decades if synodal processes like those inspired by Cardinal Dearden's leadership had been continued. Would we have had

> to wait for the *National Catholic Reporter* or the *Boston Globe* to uncover decades of clergy sexual abuse if listening forums had been regular features of church life? Would the massive numbers of parish closures, and consolidations of parishes and parochial schools, have reached epidemic levels had there been a governance structure reflective of accountability, transparency and vigorous engagement from all Catholics? Further, the long and severe decline in vocations and the exodus of young people from the church over decades are trends exacerbated by an aging church culture of rigid resistance to change. Had there been a more candid way for ordinary Catholics to make church leaders understand the deleterious impact of their one-way communications, might Catholicism in the United States have avoided losing more members than any other religious faith? We will never know for sure, but chances are that processes of mutual listening would have led us down a path of greater solidarity, honesty and unity.[64]

Despite its limitations, Call to Action still proved a success in many ways. Until they heard painful testimony from divorced Catholics in town hall meetings and other venues, many bishops didn't even know, or were indifferent to the fact, that the Third Baltimore Council of 1884 decreed that divorced and remarried Catholics were automatically excommunicated. The bishops removed the penalty of excommunication. While divorced Catholics were still not permitted to receive Communion, it opened the door to participation in other church worship. In broader terms, Call to Action instilled in American Catholics a deeper sensibility that they should not be passive spectators in either church matters or in the civic life of the nation. "It put social justice front and center in the American church," Butler said. "As an experiment in listening there was great value in personalizing the church and breaking down the walls of clerical bureaucracy."[65] Only a few years later, as the Reagan era dawned, leaders at the bishops' conference would use a similar model of consultation and dialogue with a cross-section of leaders and experts to produce an influential national pastoral letter on the nuclear arms race. This effort would once again put Archbishop Bernardin in the media spotlight and set the stage for his innovative, and still frequently contested, framework for rescuing the church's position on abortion from partisan politics. Despite his best efforts, divisions inside the church would become even more pronounced and bitter.

THE CONSISTENT ETHIC AND THE FAILURE OF COMMON GROUND

By the time Archbishop Bernardin stood to deliver the Gannon Lecture at Fordham University on December 6, 1983, he was already the public face of the Catholic Church in the United States. A year earlier, *Time* magazine featured him on the cover. "God and the Bomb—Catholic Bishops Debate Nuclear Morality," read the headline. The archbishop had steered a complex, often contentious three-year drafting process of a landmark national pastoral letter on nuclear weapons as the Reagan administration sought to outgun the Soviet Union in a Cold War arms race. The bishops' conference consulted widely with policy experts, ethicists, and church officials in Europe and the Vatican as part of a public process that provoked heated debate between bishops and the Reagan administration, as well as sparking a round of detailed public criticism from conservative Catholics. In "The Challenge of Peace: God's Promise and Our Response," the bishops wrote that "the whole world must summon the moral courage and technical means to say 'no' to nuclear conflict; 'no' to weapons of mass destruction; 'no to an arms race which robs the poor and the vulnerable."[66] The *New York Times* described it in Bernardin's 1996 obituary as "a theologically and militarily sophisticated document that has become a standard resource for study and discussion in military circles."[67]

Seven months after the peace pastoral, Bernardin visited Fordham to propose what he called a "consistent ethic of life," an expansive pro-life vision that defined the church's defense of life in the womb as part of "a seamless garment" bearing on "the multiple ways in which human life is threatened today." In front of a packed crowd of church leaders, theologians, and national media, the archbishop argued that the bishops' opposition to abortion and to nuclear war were "specific applications of this broader attitude." Bernardin wanted to both reclaim the church's antiabortion stance from the machinery of partisan politics that had damaged the bishops' reputation during the Ford–Carter race and attempt to reconcile divisions inside the church between "pro-life" and "social justice" factions. Noting that he had just been elected to the US bishops' committee on pro-life activities, the cardinal said he was committed to "shaping a position of linkage among the life issues."

> When one carries this principle into the public debate today, however, one meets significant opposition from very different places on the political and ideological spectrum. Some see clearly the application

> of the principle to abortion but contend the bishops overstepped their bounds when they applied it to choices about national security. Others understand the power of the principle in the strategic debate but find its application on abortion a violation of the realm of private choice. I contend the viability of the principle depends on the consistency of its application. . . . If one contends, as we do, that the right of every fetus to be born should be protected by civil law and supported by civil consensus, then our moral, political and economic responsibilities do not stop at the moment of birth. Those who defend the right to life of the weakest among us must be equally visible in support of the quality of life of the powerless among us: the old and the young, the hungry and the homeless, the undocumented immigrant and the unemployed worker. Such a quality-of-life posture translates into specific political and economic positions on tax policy, employment generation, welfare policy, nutrition and feeding programs, and health care. Consistency means we cannot have it both ways. We cannot urge a compassionate society and vigorous public policy to protect the rights of the unborn and then argue that compassion and significant public programs on behalf of the needy undermine the moral fiber of the society or are beyond the proper scope of government responsibility.[68]

Despite offering a nuanced, well-crafted synthesis of how various strands of Catholic teaching could be applied to public policy debates, over the next two decades of Bernardin's life secular and church politics became even more polarized. As the archbishop was advocating for a consistent life ethic that could help depoliticize the church's position on abortion, Ronald Reagan's 1984 reelection campaign put Catholic bishops and abortion on the front pages again.

Archbishop John O'Connor, newly appointed by Pope John Paul II to lead the Archdiocese of New York, was engaged in a testy public battle with high-profile Catholic politicians. Democrats had nominated a pro-choice Catholic woman, Queens assemblywoman Geraldine Ferraro, as Walter Mondale's vice-presidential candidate. "I do not see how a Catholic in good conscience can vote for an individual expressing himself or herself as favoring abortion," the archbishop said during a televised news conference.[69] Asked by a reporter if he might excommunicate New York Governor Mario Cuomo, a pro-choice Catholic, O'Connor demurred but also didn't rule it out. At a convention in Altoona, Pennsylvania, O'Connor again plunged into the political fray, telling a crowd at the Pennsylvania Pro-Life Federation that Ferraro had misrepresented Catholic teaching on abortion. Before the archbishop spoke, a seven-minute message from President Reagan was aired. "For this fight, God will bless you," the president told the convention. "The time has come for Congress to act and pass a human life amendment. Abortion is a tragedy that can't wait."[70] After the president's message, Archbishop O'Connor quipped, "I didn't tell you to vote for Ronald Reagan, did I?"[71] Archbishop O'Connor told reporters that "Pope John Paul II has said the task of the church is to reaffirm that abortion is death." Geraldine Ferraro "doesn't have a problem with me," the archbishop added. "If she has a problem, it's with the pope." O'Connor praised Reagan as "a friend of the unborn."[72]

Another archbishop appointed by Pope John Paul II, Bernard Law of Boston, also tried to make the election a referendum on abortion. At a press conference in his stately residence, Law called abortion "the critical issue in this campaign" and released a statement signed by seventeen other Catholic bishops from Maine, Vermont, New Hampshire, and Massachusetts that called it "irresponsible" to downplay the centrality of abortion in the presidential election. The bishops acknowledged that "nuclear holocaust is a future possibility," but said that "the holocaust of abortion is a present reality."[73] Law, who resigned in 2002 after the *Boston Globe* uncovered a pattern of priests who sexually abused children being moved from church to church in his archdiocese, insisted he was not endorsing any candidate. "This statement is directed at all the candidates and all voters," he said, before slyly adding: "I think Geraldine Ferraro is a candidate."[74] A year later, after Reagan's landslide victory, Archbishop O'Connor and Archbishop Bernardin spoke on WPIX-TV radio in New York. "You got caught in an eggbeater," O'Connor told Bernardin. "Some people feel you softened the position against abortion because of your 'seamless garment' view for a consistent ethic about life." Bernardin responded that it "strengthened our position" by helping people to recognize the "linkage of all life issues."[75]

For conservatives in the hierarchy and Catholic activists on the right, the US bishops' conference in the 1980s was too closely aligned with liberal issues most associated with Democrats. After the bishops' national pastoral letter on nuclear weapons in 1983 and Bernardin's high-profile push for a consistent-ethic-of-life framework at Fordham University that same year, the conference released another national letter, "Economic Justice for All," in 1986. The bishops consulted widely with economists, labor leaders, workers in various fields, and experts across the ideological spectrum in producing the letter. At a time when the Reagan administration was eviscerating social welfare programs and fighting unions, the bishops offered a moral critique of the conservative movement's embrace of free-market fundamentalism. "Economic Justice for All" called for a more progressive system in which "those with relatively greater financial resources pay a higher rate of taxation," affirmed the importance of unions as tools to help "workers resist exploitation," and articulated a vision for the common good rooted in traditional Catholic social teaching.[76] In the same way that conservatives organized counter statements to challenge the bishops' letter on nuclear weapons, the economic pastoral prompted a coordinated response from the Catholic right. William Simon, a former Treasury secretary under Nixon, led a committee of high-profile Catholics to take on the letter. The group released their own analysis that touted limited government and market solutions. Five years after the bishops' letter on economic justice, Pope John Paul II released *Centesimus Annus,* an encyclical conservatives cheered as the most market-friendly reflection ever written by a pope. Prominent conservatives who had the ear of Vatican officials were ready. Writing in the *Wall Street Journal* the day after its release, Fr. Richard John Neuhaus, the editor of *First Things,* argued that the US bishops' economic pastoral "must now be recognized as unrepresentative of the church's authoritative teaching." Under the headline, "The Pope Affirms the 'New Capitalism,'" Neuhaus even blessed capitalism as "the economic corollary of the Christian understanding of man's nature and destiny." He argued that the encyclical should bring a "rethinking of conventional wisdoms about Catholic social teaching."[77] The response conveniently ignored the pope's frequent challenges to unbridled capitalism. The same conservatives now rallying around the pope and selectively using his words in commentaries that made the Reagan administration gush were only a few years earlier taking issue with John Paul's assertion of "the priority of labor over capital."[78]

The backlash to Archbishop Bernardin's effort to elevate a consistent-ethic approach to life issues was also framed by the Catholic right as a defense of Pope John Paul II's prioritization of abortion. "In spite of Bernardin's intentions, the broadening of the pro-life position enabled the Catholic Conferences to back away from the abortion issue and distance themselves from pro-life activists who were demanding more action from the bishops," Deal Hudson, who led Catholic outreach for President George W. Bush, wrote in his book *Onward, Christian Soldiers: The Growing Political Power of Catholics and Evangelicals in the United States.* "The election of Reagan may have alarmed the conference staff in Washington, DC, and led to a series of anti-Reagan pastoral letters, but the election of Karol Wojtyla as pope in late 1978 had consequences they could not thwart."[79] When John Paul II released his encyclical *Evangelium Vitae* (The Gospel of Life) in 1995, he offered a stark image of a "culture of death." The pope spoke out strongly against a broad spectrum of threats to life and human dignity, including euthanasia and capital punishment, as well as what he called "disgraceful working conditions, where people are treated as mere instruments of gain."[80] But with his emphasis on abortion, the encyclical quickly became a seminal text for the pro-life movement. Six months after its publication in 1995, the pope visited the United States. "Resist the pressures and temptations of a world that too often tries to ignore a most fundamental truth: that every life is a gift from God," the pope told a crowd estimated at 120,000 people who gathered on the Great Lawn in Central Park for an outdoor Mass.[81] After praying the rosary with three thousand invited guests at St. Patrick's Cathedral, the pontiff waved off his drivers and started walking down Fifth Avenue and then east on 50th Street to Madison Ave., where he entered Cardinal O'Connor's residence. While other popes had condemned abortion, John Paul II's papacy in many ways elevated antiabortion advocacy to be the lynchpin of Catholic identity in the public square. His countercultural and prophetic posture became the model for a generation of priests, bishops, and Catholic pro-life activists. In politics, the lines of debate hardened as the increasingly uncompromising rhetoric of the Democratic Party and the influence of pro-choice advocacy organizations that made abortion rights a litmus test for liberal orthodoxy clashed with an energized antiabortion movement.

Inside the church, divides deepened over the consistent-ethic-of-life framework. Liberal theologians and conservative Catholic writers battled over issues of gender, sexuality, and episcopal authority. The politics of abortion inflamed nearly every debate over Catholic identity. Cardinal Bernardin and his advisors surveyed this landscape and wanted a ceasefire in the Catholic culture wars. In 1996, a year after the pope's visit to the United States, the cardinal launched a common-ground initiative with the goal of encouraging constructive dialogue between different factions in the church. The Catholic Common Ground Project's foundational document—*Called to Be Catholic: Church in a Time of Peril*—didn't downplay the fractured state of American Catholicism:

> A mood of suspicion and acrimony hangs over many of those most active in the church's life; at moments it even seems to have infiltrated the ranks of the bishops. One consequence is that many of us are refusing to acknowledge disquieting realities, perhaps fearing that they may reflect poorly on our past efforts or arm our critics within the church. Candid discussion is inhibited. Across the whole

> spectrum of views within the church, proposals are subject to ideological litmus tests. Ideas, journals, and leaders are pressed to align themselves with preexisting camps, and are viewed warily when they depart from those expectations. There is nothing wrong in itself with the prospect that different visions should contend within American Catholicism. That has long been part of the church's experience in this nation, and indeed differences of opinion are essential to the process of attaining the truth. But the way that struggle is currently proceeding, the entire church may lose.[82]

The statement accurately read the signs of the times when it bluntly stated that "many of the church's leaders, both clerical and lay, feel under siege and increasingly polarized." The project included a committee of nearly two dozen prominent Catholics who would host discussions on topics that included women's roles in the church, human sexuality, the responsibility of theology, and Catholic identity in education. Charter members included the prominent conservative Mary Ann Glendon, a Harvard law professor the Vatican named to lead the Vatican's delegation to the 1995 World Conference on Women in Beijing; Sister Elizabeth Johnson, a noted feminist theologian; and the conservative Michael Novak, a leading Catholic champion of free-market capitalism who often clashed with statements from the US bishops' conference. Along with Cardinal Bernardin, the committee included seven other bishops from across the ideological spectrum. The balanced makeup of the committee and the modest goal of addressing obvious fissures in the church made the instant blowback against the initiative from powerful forces in the hierarchy even more shocking. Within hours of its release several cardinals denounced the effort in stinging language. "The church already has common ground," Cardinal Law of Boston bristled in a statement. "It is found in sacred Scripture and tradition. . . . Dissent from revealed truth or authoritative teaching of the church cannot be 'dialogued away.'"[83] The next day Cardinal James Hickey of Washington declared that "we cannot achieve church unity by accommodating those who dissent from church teaching."[84] Cardinal Bevilacqua of Philadelphia and Cardinal Adam Maida of Detroit weighed in with similar statements that appeared in their diocesan newspapers. The pushback reflected a coordinated effort to kill the common ground initiative before it ever got off the ground. Bernardin was personally stung by the reaction. He offered detailed and thoughtful responses to the criticism. It was a lost cause. The power dynamics inside the church had shifted.

Only three months after Bernardin launched the common ground project, he died of cancer at sixty-eight. Over the next decade and a half the church became even more divided and often demoralized. Common ground proved elusive. The clergy abuse crisis exploded into national consciousness in 2002 after the *Boston Globe* uncovered extensive abuse and coverup in the Boston archdiocese. The hierarchy was reeling from severe damage to its credibility at the same time the US bishops' conference in Washington began to shift rightward as a new generation of younger conservatives assumed leadership roles once occupied by post–Vatican II progressives and moderates. During the 2004 presidential election, the most conservative bishops declared they would deny pro-choice Catholic Sen. John Kerry the Eucharist because of his support for abortion rights. Rifts between Catholic sisters and bishops became front page news in 2010 when the Leadership Conference of Women Religious, the Catholic social justice lobbying group Network, and Sister Carol Keehan, then president of the Catholic Health Association, supported President Obama's historic health care reform package while the bishops' conference opposed the final bill because of concerns it would subsidize coverage of abortions. Only two years after the Catholic sisters' advocacy for Obama's health care law, the Vatican's doctrine office, led by future pope Cardinal Joseph Ratzinger, cracked down on the Leadership Conference of Women Religious, citing its "silence on the right to life from conception to natural death," and calling the conference's disagreement with bishops as "not compatible with its purpose."[85]

Cathleen Kaveny, a prominent theologian and legal scholar at Boston College, argues that the common ground initiative Bernardin launched in the mid-1990s never took root because in subsequent years there have been few, if any, organized efforts to address even more challenging issues in the church beyond division and polarization. In her 2021 article, "Anger, Lamentation, and Common Ground," published in the journal *Theological Studies*, she praises many aspects of the original "Called to be Catholic" statement that launched the common ground project but now describes it as "significantly dated and incomplete." Most strikingly, Kaveny says, at no point does the statement ever describe American Catholics as angry. "In fact, the word does not even appear in the document," she writes. "And yet, when I think about the attitude of American Catholics today, that is the word that first comes to mind. American Catholics are angry. We are angry at the bishops and angry at one another as fellow Americans and fellow worshippers. And our anger undermines our efforts to find common ground in ways that the founding document of Catholic Common Ground Initiative did not anticipate."[86] Kaveny proposes a model of reparation where "sorrow and lamentation" are acknowledged, honored, and given space for expression.

> The Catholic Common Ground Initiative, in my view, has been stymied by its focus on trying to find agreement about disputes through structured dialogue. Rituals of lamentation avoid this problem by changing the subject; they focus on expressing common grief rather than exploring common rational commitments. But they do not do so by papering over rational disagreements. A ritual of lamentation can allow people to set aside their moral, political, and theological differences without relativizing those differences, so they may confess their experiences of loss, hope, and deep dependence on God. Lamentation offers us the possibility to name, decry, and mourn our losses, and to experience the first humble stirrings of hope together as a community.

The need for a new paradigm to rethink common ground today is especially important, Kaveny argues, now that the papacy itself is a lightning rod among "contesting segments of the American church."[87]

A NEW CATHOLIC CIVIL WAR?

Mike Lewis has watched with sadness and plenty of anger as some corners of a conservative Catholic culture where he once felt at home became rife with hostility toward Pope Francis. He has lost friends and is frequently attacked online by self-styled traditionalists who react to his popular blog, *Where Peter Is*. Most painfully, the anti-Francis sentiment spreading through American Catholicism in recent years infected his own family. When Lewis's mother, a lifelong Catholic who loved Pope John Paul II and Pope Benedict XVI, began consuming a steady diet of right-wing Catholic media, she grew convinced that Pope Francis represented a threat to her faith. Her friends at church and members of her Catholic book club sent articles branding the pope a heretic. She watched videos from the now-defunct extremist group Church Militant, which relentlessly attacked liberal Catholics and accused the pope of "tearing the Body of Christ apart."[88] As his mother spent more time bedridden during the final months of her life, the Catholic network EWTN was constantly on the television. She was a devotee of the network's signature program, "The World Over," a weekly talk show hosted by Raymond Arroyo that often features critics of Pope Francis. When Lewis tried to offer counterpoints, the conversations with his mother only provoked defensiveness and tension. "Not being able to talk about God and the church with the person who gave me my faith as she was dying was agonizing," Lewis recalled.[89]

A former staffer in the publishing department of the US bishops' conference, the father of four was once responsible for preparing to disseminate church documents, including the pope's encyclicals. "I could see we were not really reaching and connecting with people in the pews," he said. "People were being influenced by EWTN, *First Things* and the *National Catholic Register,* all of these outlets spreading negative ideas about the pope."[90] After he left the bishops' conference in 2017, Lewis became increasingly alarmed by the steady deluge of anti-Francis content he was seeing on Facebook, especially the bitter animosity toward the pope in some traditionalist Catholic circles. "There was no consistent voice out there coming from an orthodox Catholic perspective that was addressing these attacks on the pope," Lewis said. He started his blog to fill the vacuum.

Resistance to Pope Francis became evident early in his papacy. The pope drew critical responses from some arch-conservative bishops and lay commentators for his more inclusive tone toward LGBTQ people and his frequent challenges to clergy fixated on a legalistic reading of doctrine. When Francis removed Cardinal Raymond Burke, a leading American culture warrior, from a key Vatican committee tasked with helping the pope to appoint new bishops—and later pulled the cardinal from his post as the leader of the Vatican's highest court—self-identified traditionalists were furious. A few days before his demotion, the cardinal gave an exclusive interview to Breitbart, a nationalist alt-right propaganda outlet, where he warned of "a risk of schism" if the faithful perceived church leaders to be overturning "unchanging and unchangeable truths."[91] The pope's 2015 landmark encyclical on the environment and ecology, *Laudato Si,* also provoked a campaign on the right to downplay the magisterial significance of the document and refute its calls for specific policy action to address climate change. In the lead-up to the encyclical's release, the prominent conservative legal scholar and political philosopher Robert George of Princeton University, an influential advisor to US bishops, wrote that the pope "does not know whether, or to what extent, the climate changes (in various directions) of the past several decades are anthropogenic—and God is not going to tell him."[92] But the most significant backlash to Pope Francis began in earnest with the publication of his 2016 apostolic exhortation *Amoris Laetitia,* which called for the church to take a more pastoral approach to dealing with difficult family issues involving divorced and remarried Catholics. The document was the product of intense dialogue and debate, released only after a two-year series of at times contentious meetings at the Vatican that brought bishops from around the world to Rome for a Synod on the Family. "Many people feel that the Church's message on marriage and the family does not clearly reflect the preaching and attitudes of Jesus, who set forth a demanding ideal yet never failed to show compassion and closeness to the frailty of individuals like the Samaritan woman or the woman caught in adultery," the pope wrote.[93]

While Francis did not create a new church policy that would offer a blanket dispensation for divorced and remarried Catholics to receive the Eucharist without an annulment, he called for "pastoral discernment" in specific situations and urged clergy to apply "the logic of pastoral mercy." A pastor, Francis added, can't simply "apply moral laws to those living in 'irregular' situations, as if they were stones to throw at people's lives."[94] Even before the apostolic exhortation was published, writing as disagreements escalated during the synod meetings, *The New York Times* columnist Ross Douthat, a conservative Catholic, warned of a potential "schism." The orthodox faithful, he argued, "have done the most to keep the church vital in an age of institutional decline," and did not "deserve a theological betrayal."[95] On his diocesan website, Bishop Thomas Tobin of Providence, Rhode Island, warned that the church was at risk of losing "its courageous, counter-cultural, prophetic voice," and scoffed that "the concept of having a representative body of the church voting on doctrinal applications and pastoral solutions strikes me as being rather Protestant."[96] In an unusual public challenge to a sitting pope, four cardinals wrote to Francis and the prefect of the Vatican's doctrine office with several *dubia* (doubts) and questions about the apostolic exhortation. The letter expressed concern that the document had unleashed "uncertainty, confusion, and disorientation among the faithful."[97] It was signed by Carlo Caffarra, the former archbishop of Bologna; the American archbishop Raymond Burke; Walter Brandmüller, the former president of the Pontifical Committee for Historical Sciences; and Joachim Meisner, the former archbishop of Cologne, Germany.

The animus toward Pope Francis that grew among traditionalist Catholics after the synod on the family reached new heights during a three-week Vatican synod in 2019 focused on the Amazon. The gathering highlighted a wide range of issues in the nine-nation region, including environmental devastation, economic inequality, and corporate exploitation of indigenous land. Pope Francis also emphasized the importance of integrating and showing greater respect for local cultures in the life of the church, a process of "inculturation" that he frequently addresses. But conservatives quickly balked at discussions—supported by most bishops in the region—to allow married Catholic men in the Amazon to become priests to address the severe clergy shortage in the area. "It is in moving forward that makes the church loyal to its true tradition," the retired Brazilian Cardinal Claudio Hummes, the synod's lead organizer, said at the opening of the convening. "We must not fear newness, we must not fear Christ, the new. This synod is in search of new pathways."[98] It was exactly this "newness" that conservatives opposed. The presence of an indigenous man wearing a feathered headdress at the gathering's opening Mass raised consternation on the Catholic right. After indigenous leaders presented Pope Francis with a two-foot-high wooden carving of a naked pregnant woman they called "Our Lady of the Amazon" during a tree-planting ceremony at the Vatican Gardens, traditionalists were apoplectic. The synod suddenly became news around the world after the far-right Catholic websites LifeSiteNews and Church Militant showed video of two men stealing the statues from Santa Maria Traspontina Church and tossing them into the Tiber River. A 26-year-old Australian, Alexander Tschugguel, later released a video claiming credit for the theft. He quickly became a hero to many in traditionalist Catholic circles. Tschugguel was invited to the United States for a victory lap hosted by Taylor Marshall, a former Episcopal priest from Texas who has become a celebrity in far-right Catholic circles with his videos, podcast, and book *Infiltration: The Plot to Destroy the Church from Within*. While the synod approved a proposal to allow some married Catholic men in Amazonian regions to be ordained as priests, the pope ignored the issue in his follow-up document, *Querida Amazonia*.

When Pope Francis reimposed restrictions on celebrating the Latin Mass in 2021, which Pope Benedict XVI had relaxed fourteen years earlier, the decision further inflamed animosity among traditionalist Catholics. The pope explained that he took action because the rite had become a source of division and even a cudgel used by Catholics opposed to the Second Vatican Council. Under the new law, delivered by Francis in the motu proprio *Traditionis Custodes*, clergy must obtain explicit permission from bishops to celebrate the Latin Mass. "Pope Francis is Tearing the Catholic Church Apart," the headline read for a *New York Times* commentary by Michael Brendan Dougherty, a senior writer at the *National Review*. "To stamp out the old Latin Mass, Pope Francis is using the papacy in precisely the way that progressives once claimed to deplore: He centralizes power in Rome, usurps the local bishop's prerogatives and institutes a micromanaging style that is motivated by paranoia of disloyalty and heresy," Dougherty wrote.[99] In the journal *First Things*, George Weigel called the pope's action "a sorry example of the liberal bullying that has become all too familiar in Rome recently."[100] The popular traditionalist blog Rorate Caeli responded with particular fury. "Francis HATES US," the group tweeted. "Francis HATES Tradition. Francis HATES all that is good and beautiful."[101]

Mike Lewis watched his blog grow to more than a million page views as resistance to the pope continued to roil the church. Catholics frequently send him parish bulletins and homilies from pastors questioning the pope's statements. While Pope Francis remains broadly popular in the United States, many embittered traditionalists, conservative commentators, and far-right bishops are more emboldened than ever to attack the pope as church politics increasingly mirrors the smash-mouth style of secular politics today. "This is a battle," Lewis said, "for the soul of the church."[102] Lewis often thinks about how his mother's descent into the far-right Catholic echo chamber was not a unique experience. "Since I began writing and speaking publicly about this phenomenon, I have heard from hundreds of Catholics who have seen their families and communities divided over Pope Francis," Lewis wrote in *America* magazine in 2020. "In some parishes—and even some diocesan seminaries—negativity toward Francis has become so commonplace that those who support him feel compelled to keep their views to themselves. One priest told me that several seminarians referred to their seminaries as 'Francis-free zones.' Francis' less reactionary critics have done little to stem the rise of their much more vicious counterparts."[103]

RED AND BLUE CATHOLICISM

Over three early summer days in 2018, a hundred prominent and emerging Catholic leaders huddled at Georgetown University in Washington, DC, to address division in the Catholic Church, politics, and public life. Presidents of Catholic universities, diocesan directors, national leaders of the church's social service agencies, pollsters, and a handful of Catholic political commentators met for an ambitious gathering that veteran Catholic journalist John Allen called "the most serious effort to address divisions in the American Church in a long time." The conference, *Through Many, One: Overcoming Polarization Through Catholic Social Thought*, took place inside the stately Riggs Library. The dome of the US Capitol was visible in the hazy distance.[104] A Supreme Court decision handed down as the meeting kicked off, a ruling that sided with a Christian Colorado baker who refused to prepare a wedding cake for a gay couple, only underscored escalating divisions in the nation and the church. "Catholics in the United States can be seen as a microcosm of what is happening in the broader culture," Greg Smith, a senior researcher at Pew Research Center, told the assembled group. "On issue after issue, Catholics are divided over partisan lines even on issues in which you would think Catholics would have a distinctive Catholic approach. Catholic partisans often resemble their fellow partisans more than they do their fellow Catholics."[105] From views on abortion to social safety net programs for the poor to climate change, Catholic Republicans and Catholic Democrats are far apart.

Mark Gray, a senior research associate at the Center for Applied Research in the Apostolate, described Catholics as "somewhat politically homeless" because there are "two parties and neither of them fit the faith or Catholic social teaching very well." Catholic voters, he said at the gathering, are forced to make "very constrained choices." Despite the stark contrasts between Catholic Republicans and Catholic Democrats, Gray noted that 42 percent of Catholics say they don't belong to either party and that most Catholics don't identify as either liberal or conservative. "There are divides but also potential for bridges," he told the attendees.[106] Scott Appleby, a Catholic historian and dean of the Keough School of Global Affairs at the University of Notre Dame, also expressed hope that "the Catholic middle" can find opportunities for ways to come together around shared values of faith and justice. Since the 1960s, he said, "change has been rapid, often traumatic and hard to absorb so it's not surprising, and historically understandable, we're so divided."[107] But Appleby noted that compared to white evangelicals, who now vote in lockstep with the Republican Party, "Catholics have attempted to hold the center." Cardinal Blase Cupich of Chicago and Los Angeles Archbishop José Gomez, often viewed as leaders representing progressive and conservative camps inside the church, both spoke about the perils of polarization. While civil debate is healthy for the church and essential in a democracy, Cupich said in his address, entrenched polarization leads to people "living an isolated and siloed existence in their own spheres, depending on different sources of information, and distrustful, if not dismissive, of the other group and their sources of information." Archbishop Gomez urged leaders at the conference to remember that Catholics are not meant to represent sides in a debate but are called to be saints. "That is why there is no polarization in the community of saints; and there are no single-issue saints," Gomez said.[108] For all the important symbolism of the two archbishops coming together in a sign of episcopal unity, neither adequately addressed how bishops and other clergy have inflamed divisions in recent years by mirroring the style and tone of partisan political leaders, especially by using the virtual pulpit of social media in ways that reinforce the proliferation of ecclesial echo chambers where like-minded Catholics congregate.

Rev. James Martin, a popular author and advisor to Pope Francis who has been a leading voice for LGBTQ dignity in the church, encouraged participants "to encounter the person rather than the Twitter handle." Martin is relentlessly attacked on social media by right-wing Catholics. He participated in a panel discussion with Robert George, the Princeton political philosopher and Catholic *The New York Times* magazine once called "this country's most influential conservative thinker."[109] "The divisions between the social justice and pro-life crowds might be more perception than reality," Martin said, pointing to the civil dialogues at the event and the common concern expressed by participants for the unborn, undocumented immigrants, and the poor.[110]

John Carr, who for several decades led the US bishops' social justice advocacy and helped organize the polarization conference, sees hope in younger Catholics who are not as defined by the old post-Vatican battles. "This new generation doesn't carry the baggage that people like me carry," Carr acknowledged.[111] Elise Italiano, a Catholic millennial who has been involved in various church projects and identifies as a pro-life feminist, echoed that message. "For many in this room who are emerging leaders in the academy, ministry, and apostolates, it's really hard to ignore the polarizing attitudes and language that many of our mentors and guides have embraced," she said. "While the intra-ecclesial debates about Pope Francis, continued culture wars and fights over how exactly we're supposed to implement Vatican II take place, our peers are being carried out in spiritual body bags in front of our eyes."[112] For all the civil conversation at Georgetown, and the bonhomie between church leaders often at odds in public debates, even some participants were skeptical. "It is harder to really detest someone you just had breakfast with, but the hard work of discerning the sources of polarization remains to be done," *National Catholic Reporter* political columnist Micheal Sean Winters wrote after the conference.

> Mostly, people pulled their punches; they were on their best behavior, so the root causes of polarization were not really reached. . . . Although the organizers repeatedly said the goal was not to sing "Kumbaya" and paper over differences, the one or two times the tension in the room came to the surface, we all moved on. True, a discussion of the abortion vote in Ireland, for example, might have become a rabbit hole, but if polarization happens in rabbit holes, that is where those who wish to heal it must go.[113]

By 2022 Kim Daniels looked back at the conference with some wistfulness. She helped organize the event as codirector of Georgetown's Initiative on Catholic Social Thought and Public Life, which she now leads. "It was a sign of hope for all of us to come together around shared principals with a language of respect," Daniels said, noting that since the initiative's founding in 2013, more than 300,000 participants have been involved in more than 150 dialogues and other gatherings. "There is a real hunger for the kind of conversations we provide. People want principled and candid dialogue."[114] But she acknowledged Catholic polarization has only grown worse since the summer conference at Georgetown in 2018. "You look back now and the conference kind of feels like a moment in time," she said. "A lot has changed." A religious liberty attorney and antiabortion advocate, Daniels has spent plenty of time in conservative Catholic circles. For a brief period she was the spokesperson for Cardinal Timothy Dolan of New York when he was president of the US bishops' conference. Daniels watched with growing frustration as vocal Catholic leaders on the right, a few of them friends and onetime allies, became more radicalized in their opposition to Pope Francis and their enthusiastic embrace of Donald Trump. "The anti-Francis voice has become shriller and stronger over the years," said Daniels, whom the pope named as a member of the Vatican's Dicastery for Communication in 2016. "We have a new Catholic right that has admiration for authoritarians and that defines itself by their enemies."[115] After Trump's election Daniels spoke on a panel at a Catholic Women's Forum event sponsored by the Ethics and Public Policy Center, a conservative Washington think tank. She acknowledged the opportunities the new administration presented for antiabortion policies but also warned that Trump's views clashed with traditional Catholic teaching on many issues, including his positions on immigrants and refugees. At the end of the panel an audience member stood up and shouted that she wasn't a real conservative. "It was a wakeup call for me," Daniels said. "Trump undermined the credibility of Catholic leaders and others who would not push back against the president." Many antiabortion Catholics were afraid to "poke the bear," in her reading, because Trump vowed to appoint justices who would roll back abortion rights and overturn *Roe v. Wade* given the opportunity. What should have been in Daniel's words a "clarifying moment" for many Catholics never came to pass.[116]

While the media fixated on Trump's dominant 2016 election showing with white evangelical voters, his ability to win 60 percent of white Catholics—and emerge as an improbable hero for many pro-life Catholics—played a key role in his success. How did a formerly pro-choice reality television host who boasted about groping women, mocked a disabled reporter, rarely darkened the door of a church, and demonized immigrants and refugees in ways that energized white nationalists become the clear choice for Catholics who claim to care about life and human dignity? Why did some clergy and bishops provide a de facto or explicit political blessing for Trump? What lessons can be learned from Catholic political engagement with Trump? Those questions raise often uncomfortable but essential issues that church leaders, Catholic voters, and anyone who cares about the future of Catholicism in public life must confront with clear eyes.

NOTES

1. Fr. Leo Donovan, "The Invocation at the Inauguration of President Joe Biden," *America*, January 20, 2021, https://www.americamagazine.org/faith/2021/01/20/invocation-joe-biden-inauguration-leo-odonovan-239769.
2. Amanda Gorman, "The Hill We Climb," *The Hill*, January 20, 2021, https://thehill.com/homenews/news/535052-read-transcript-of-amanda-gormans-inaugural-poem/.
3. President Joe Biden, "Inaugural Address," The White House, January 20, 2021, https://www.whitehouse.gov/briefing-room/speeches-remarks/2021/01/20/inaugural-address-by-president-joseph-r-biden-jr/.
4. Archbishop Jose Gomez, "Statement on the Inauguration of Joseph R. Biden, Jr., U.S. Conference of Catholic Bishops," January 20, 2021, https://www.usccb.org/news/2021/usccb-presidents-statement-inauguration-joseph-r-biden-jr-46th-president-united-states.
5. Cardinal Blase Cupich (@CardinalBCupich), "Today, the U.S. Conference of Catholic Bishops issued an ill-considered statement on the day of President Biden's inauguration," Twitter, January 20, 2021, 5:29 p.m., https://twitter.com/CardinalBCupich/status/1352020541285216257.
6. Michael J. O'Loughlin, "In Rare Rebuke, Cardinal Cupich Criticizes USCCB President's Letter to President Biden," *America*, January 20, 2021, https://www.americamagazine.org/politics-society/2021/01/20/biden-cupich-gomez-bishops-239779.
7. Gerard O'Connell, "Pope Francis Sends Greeting to President Biden, Contrasting with Sharper Message from Head of US Bishops," *America*, January 20, 2021, https://www.americamagazine.org/faith/2021/01/20/pope-francis-message-joe-biden-prayer-239772.
8. Michelle Boorstein, "Pope's Emissary Urges U.S. Bishops to Listen and Unite as They Ready to Vote on Communion Document," *Washington Post*, November 16, 2021, https://www.washingtonpost.com/religion/2021/11/16/bishops-catholic-pope-communion-biden-/.
9. Jack Jenkins, "As Catholic Bishops Gather, So Do Protestors on Right and Left," *Religion News Service*, November 12, 2021, https://religionnews.com/2021/11/12/bannon-protests-planned-ahead-bishops-gathering/.
10. Todd Richmond, "Father James Altman, Who Said Democrats Would Burn in Hell and Called Covid Restrictions 'Nazi-esque,' Removed by His Bishop," *Associated Press*, July 9, 2021, https://www.americamagazine.org/faith/2021/07/09/father-james-altman-removed-wisconsin-bishop-241015.
11. Bill Bishop and Robert G. Cushing, *The Big Sort: Why the Clustering of Like-Minded America Is Tearing Us Apart* (Boston, New York: Houghton Mifflin Company, 2008).
12. Robert P. Jones, *The End of White Christian America* (New York: Simon & Schuster, 2016).
13. Elizabeth Kolbert, "How Politics Got So Polarized," *The New Yorker*, December 27, 2021, https://www.newyorker.com/magazine/2022/01/03/how-politics-got-so-polarized.
14. Andrew Romano, "Poll: Many Red-State Trump Voters Say They'd Be 'Better Off' If Their State Seceded from U.S.," *Yahoo News*, July 15, 2022, https://news.yahoo.com

/poll-many-red-state-trump-voters-say-theyd-be-better-off-if-their-state-seceded-from-us-160454042.html?

15. Katherine Shaeffer, "Far More Americans See 'Very Strong' Partisan Conflicts Now Than in the Last Two Presidential Election Years," Pew Research Center, March 4, 2020, https://www.pewresearch.org/short-reads/2020/03/04/far-more-americans-see-very-strong-partisan-conflicts-now-than-in-the-last-two-presidential-election-years/.
16. Christina Pazzanese, "Democrats and Republicans Do Live in Different Worlds," *The Harvard Gazette*, March 16, 2021, https://news.harvard.edu/gazette/story/2021/03/democrats-and-republicans-live-in-partisan-bubbles-study-finds/.
17. Kat Devin, "People in Advanced Societies Say Their Society Is More Divided Than Before Pandemic," Pew Research Center, June 23, 2021, Ihttps://www.pewresearch.org/global/2021/06/23/people-in-advanced-economies-say-their-society-is-more-divided-than-before-pandemic/.
18. Marquette University News Center, "New Marquette Law School Poll Finds Strong Partisan Divisions on Afghanistan, Covid Policies, and Election Results," *Marquette University News Release*, September 23, 2021, https://www.marquette.edu/news-center/2021/new-marquette-law-poll-finds-strong-partisan-divisions-on-afghanistan-covid-policies-election.php.
19. Elizabeth Kolbert, "How Politics Got So Polarized," *The New Yorker*, December 27, 2021, https://www.newyorker.com/magazine/2022/01/03/how-politics-got-so-polarized.
20. Joshua J. McElwee, "Pope Francis Suggests People Have Moral Obligation to Take Coronavirus Vaccine," *National Catholic Reporter*, January 11, 2021, https://www.ncronline.org/vatican/pope-francis-suggests-people-have-moral-obligation-take-coronavirus-vaccine.
21. Bishop J. Strickland (@BishStrickland), "I have spoken out against these mandates and will continue to do so," Twitter, November 21, 2021, 5:27 p.m., https://twitter.com/BishStrickland/status/1462548183112839170?s=20&t=TC6ErLsuJOd1usN8euu3bQ.
22. Michael J. O'Loughlin, "San Francisco Archbishop's Reasons for Not Getting Vaccinated Don't Add up, Public Health Experts Say," *America*, December 9, 2021, https://www.americamagazine.org/faith/2021/12/09/vaccine-religious-archbishop-cordileone-242007.
23. Jaclyn Peiser and Michelle Boorstein, "U.S. Bishops Splinter on the Morality of Taking Coronavirus Vaccines," *Washington Post*, March 3, 2021, https://www.washingtonpost.com/nation/2021/03/02/archdiocese-new-orleans-johnson-vaccine/.
24. Vatican News, "Vatican CDF Says Use of Anti-Covid Vaccines "Morally Acceptable," *Congregation for the Doctrine of the Faith*, December 21, 2020, https://www.vaticannews.va/en/vatican-city/news/2020-12/vatican-cdf-note-covid-vaccine-morality-abortion.html.
25. Jessica Williams, "Archdiocese Calls Johnson & Johnson Vaccine 'Morally Compromised' Due to Abortion Ties," *New Orleans Times-Picayune*, March 1, 2021, https://www.nola.com/news/archdiocese-calls-johnson-johnson-vaccine-morally-compromised-due-to-abortion-ties/article_652ae29e-7aaf-11eb-ad0b-33a248664219.html.
26. Bismarck Diocese, "Covid Vaccine Announcement Update," statement from Bismarck Diocese, March 2, 2021, https://bismarckdiocese.com/news/vaccine-announcement-update.

27. Diocese of San Diego, "Statement from San Diego Bishop," March 3, 2021, https://sdcatholic.org/news-release/san-diego-bishop-issues-statement-says-it-is-entirely-morally-legitimate-for-catholics-to-receive-all-approved-covid-19-vaccines/.
28. Joseph Meaney, "The Rhetoric of 'Vaccine Hesitancy,'" The National Catholic Bioethics Center, July 30, 2021, https://www.ncbcenter.org/messages-from-presidents/hestitancy.
29. Francis Wilkinson, "America's Churches Are Now Polarized, Too," *Bloomberg*, February 21, 2021, https://www.bloomberg.com/opinion/articles/2021-02-21/after-trump-america-s-churches-are-more-polarized-than-ever.
30. James Zogby, interview with author.
31. James Zogby, interview with author.
32. Zogby, interview with author.
33. Blessed Sacrament Families United in Faith and Action, "Religious Liberty, Health Care, and the Catholic Faithful," June 19, 2012, http://familiesunitedinfaith.blogspot.com/2012/06/.
34. Zogby, interview with author.
35. Tricia Bruce, interview with author.
36. Bruce, interview with author.
37. Bruce, interview with author.
38. Richard McBrien, "Pope John XXXIII's Opening Address to the Second Vatican Council," *National Catholic Reporter*, November 5, 2012, https://www.ncronline.org/blogs/essays-theology/pope-john-xxiiis-opening-address-second-vatican-council.
39. John Gehring, "Napa Institute Expands to Fight the Culture War," *National Catholic Reporter*, August 4, 2021, https://www.ncronline.org/news/people/napa-institute-expands-fight-culture-war.
40. John Gehring, "Napa Institute Expands to Fight the Culture War," *National Catholic Reporter*, August 4, 2021, https://www.ncronline.org/news/people/napa-institute-expands-fight-culture-war.
41. Michael Pakaluk, "Is Vatican II 'Spent?'" February 16, 2022, https://www.thecatholicthing.org/2022/02/16/is-vatican-ii-spent/.
42. Cindy Wooden, "Pope Francis: Vatican II Must Be Taught as Part of Church Teaching, or 'You Are Not with the Church,'" *Catholic News Service*, February 1, 2021, https://www.americamagazine.org/faith/2021/02/01/pope-francis-vatican-ii-council-second-church-teaching-239892.
43. Christopher White, "Pope Francis: 'Significant" Numbers of U.S. Catholics Want to 'Gag' Vatican II Reforms," June 14, 2022, https://www.ncronline.org/news/vatican/pope-francis-significant-number-us-catholics-want-gag-vatican-ii-reforms.
44. Jayd Henricks, "Pope Francis Does Not Understand the American Church," *First Things*, June 16, 2022, https://www.firstthings.com/web-exclusives/2022/06/pope-francis-does-not-understand-the-american-church.
45. Joshua J. McElwee, "Cardinals, Theologians Gather to Plan How U.S. Church Can Support Pope Francis," *National Catholic Reporter*, March 29, 2022, https://www.ncronline.org/news/people/cardinals-theologians-gather-plan-how-us-church-can-support-pope-francis.
46. Massimo Faggioli, "Opposition to Pope Francis Is Rooted in Rejection of Vatican II," *National Catholic Reporter*, April 4, 2022, https://www.ncronline.org/news/opinion/opposition-pope-francis-rooted-rejection-vatican-ii.

47. Peter Steinfels, *A People Adrift: The Crisis of the Roman Catholic Church in America* (New York: Simon & Schuster, 2004).
48. Fr. Bryan Hehir, interview with author.
49. Kenneth A. Briggs, "Carter and the Bishops," *New York Times*, September 3, 1976, https://www.nytimes.com/1976/09/03/archives/carter-and-the-bishops-struggle-could-affect-abortion-bills-and.html.
50. J. Brehn Hehlr to Joseph L. Bernardin, memorandum, Cincinnati, Ohio, September 5, 1976, National Conference of Catholic Bishops, Box no. G3, Ad Hoc Committee on Pro Life Activities, Jul-Sept, 1976, The American Catholic History Research Center & University Archives, Washington, DC.
51. Hehlr to Bernardin, Cincinnati, Ohio, September 5, 1976.
52. James M. Naughton, "Bishops 'Encouraged' by Ford on Abortion," *New York Times*, September 11, 1976, https://www.nytimes.com/1976/09/11/archives/bishops-encouraged-by-ford-on-abortion-but-they-arent-totally.html.
53. James M. Naughton, "Bishops 'Encouraged' by Ford on Abortion," *New York Times*, September 11, 1976, https://www.nytimes.com/1976/09/11/archives/bishops-encouraged-by-ford-on-abortion-but-they-arent-totally.html.
54. John Gehring, *The Francis Effect: A Radical Pope's Challenge to the American Catholic Church* (Rowman & Littlefield, 2015).
55. Pope Paul VI, "*Gaudiem Et Spes*: Pastoral Constitution on the Church in the Modern World," December 7, 1965.
56. John Dearden, Call to Action Conference, Detroit, Michigan, October 21, 1976.
57. Frank Butler, interview with author.
58. Frank Butler, interview with author.
59. Kenneth A. Briggs, "Catholic Bishops Stirred to Debate by the Proposals of 'Call to Action,'" *New York Times*, November 11, 1976, https://www.nytimes.com/1976/11/11/archives/catholic-bishops-stirred-to-debate-by-the-proposals-of-call-to.html.
60. Briggs, "Catholic Bishops Stirred."
61. Briggs, "Catholic Bishops Stirred."
62. Kenneth A. Briggs, "Catholic 'Call to Action,'" *New York Times*, October 27, 1976, https://www.nytimes.com/1976/10/27/archives/catholic-call-to-action-a-diversified-group-of-delegates-took-full.html.
63. Butler, interview with author.
64. Francis J. Butler, "Cardinal John Dearden Wanted to Give Lay Catholics Influence After Vatican II. Pope Francis' Vision for Synods Could Finally Do It," *America*, October 8, 2021, https://www.americamagazine.org/faith/2021/10/08/cardinal-dearden-1976-synodality-vatican-241578.
65. Butler, interview with author.
66. US Conference of Catholic Bishops, "The Challenge of Peace: God's Promise and Our Response: A Pastoral Letter on War and Peace by the National Conference of Catholic Bishops," May 3, 1983, https://www.usccb.org/upload/challenge-peace-gods-promise-our-response-1983.pdf.
67. Peter Steinfels, "Cardinal Bernardin Dies at 68; Reconciling Voice in Church," *New York Times*, November 15, 1996, https://www.nytimes.com/1996/11/15/us/cardinal-bernardin-dies-at-68-reconciling-voice-in-church.html.

68. Richard McBrien, "Seamless Garment' Marks 25th Anniversary," *National Catholic Reporter*, December 22, 2008, https://www.ncronline.org/blogs/essays-theology/seamless-garment-marks-25th-anniversary.
69. Peter Steinfels, *A People Adrift: The Crisis of the Roman Catholic Church in America* (New York: Simon & Schuster, 2004).
70. Associated Press, "O'Connor Critical of Ferraro Views," September 9, 1984, https://www.nytimes.com/1984/09/09/nyregion/o-connor-critical-of-ferraro-views.html.
71. Associated Press, "O'Connor Critical of Ferraro Views," September 9, 1984. https://www.nytimes.com/1984/09/09/nyregion/o-connor-critical-of-ferraro-views.html.
72. Peter Steinfels, "Death of a Cardinal; Cardinal O'Connor, 80, Dies; Forceful Voice for Vatican," *New York Times*, May 4, 2000, https://www.nytimes.com/2000/05/04/nyregion/death-of-a-cardinal-cardinal-o-connor-80-dies-forceful-voice-for-vatican.html.
73. Fox Butterfield, "Archbishop of Boston Cites Abortion as 'Critical" Issue," *New York Times*, September 6, 1984, https://www.nytimes.com/1984/09/06/us/archbishop-of-boston-cites-abortion-as-critical-issue.html.
74. Butterfield, "Archbishop of Boston."
75. George W. Cornell, "Archbishop O'Connor and Cardinal Bernardin Spar over Abortion Issue," *Associated Press*, March 9, 1985, https://www.latimes.com/archives/la-xpm-1985-03-09-me-23495-story.html.
76. U.S Conference of Catholic Bishops, "Economic Justice for All: Pastoral Letter on Catholic Social Teaching and the U.S. Economy," November 1986, https://www.usccb.org/upload/economic_justice_for_all.pdf.
77. Acton Institute, "Initial Reactions to *Centesimus Annus*," July 20, 2010, https://www.acton.org/pub/religion-liberty/volume-1-number-3/initial-reactions-centesimus-annus.
78. Pope John Paul II, *Laborem Exercens*, September 14, 1981, https://www.vatican.va/content/john-paul-ii/en/encyclicals/documents/hf_jp-ii_enc_14091981_laborem-exercens.html.
79. Deal Hudson, *Onward, Christian Soldiers: The Growing Political Power of Catholics and Evangelicals in the United States* (Simon & Schuster, 2008).
80. Pope John Paul II, *Evangelium Vitae*, March 25, 1995, https://www.vatican.va/content/john-paul-ii/en/encyclicals/documents/hf_jp-ii_enc_25031995_evangelium-vitae.html.
81. Pope John Paul II, "Eucharistic Celebration for the Young People," Apostolic Journey to the United States of America. October 7, 1995, https://www.vatican.va/content/john-paul-ii/en/homilies/1995/documents/hf_jp-ii_hom_19951007_central-park.html.
82. Catholic Common Ground Initiative, *Called to Be Catholic: Church in a Time of Peril*, August 12, 1996, https://catholiccommonground.org/called-to-be-catholic-church-in-a-time-of-peril/.
83. Steinfels, *A People Adrift*.
84. Steinfels, *A People Adrift*.
85. Congregation for the Doctrine of the Faith, *Doctrinal Assessment of the Leadership Conference of Women Religious*, April 18, 2012, https://www.vatican.va/roman_curia/congregations/cfaith/documents/rc_con_cfaith_doc_20120418_assessment-lcwr_en.html.

86. Cathleen Kaveny, "Anger, Lamentation, and Common Ground," *Theological Studies* 82, no. 4 (November 27, 2021), https://journals.sagepub.com/doi/abs/10.1177/00405639211053648.
87. Cathleen Kaveny, "Anger, Lamentation, and Common Ground," *Theological Studies* 82, no. 4 (November 27, 2021), https://journals.sagepub.com/doi/abs/10.1177/00405639211053648.
88. The Vortex, "Church Militant Statement on the Pope," August 27, 2018. https://www.churchmilitant.com/video/episode/vort-cm-statement-on-the-pope.
89. Mike Lewis, interview with author.
90. Lewis, interview with author.
91. Cardinal Raymond Burke, "Cardinal Burke: Church Risks Serious Tensions in Months Ahead," *Breitbart News,* November 5, 2014, https://www.breitbart.com/national-security/2014/11/05/exclusive-cardinal-burke-church-risks-serious-tensions-in%20months-ahead/.
92. Robert George, "Four Things to Remember about the Pope's Environment Letter," *First Things,* January 3, 2015, https://www.firstthings.com/blogs/firstthoughts/2015/01/four-things-to-remember-about-the-popes-environment-letter.
93. Pope Francis, *Amoris Laetitia,* March 19, 2016, https://www.vatican.va/content/dam/francesco/pdf/apost_exhortations/documents/papa-francesco_esortazione-ap_20160319_amoris-laetitia_en.pdf.
94. Pope Francis, *Amoris Laetitia,* March 19, 2016, https://www.vatican.va/content/dam/francesco/pdf/apost_exhortations/documents/papa-francesco_esortazione-ap_20160319_amoris-laetitia_en.pdf.
95. Ross Douthat, "The Pope and the Precipice," *New York Times,* October 25, 2014, https://www.nytimes.com/2014/10/26/opinion/sunday/ross-douthat-the-pope-and-the-precipice.html.
96. Globe Pulse Staff, "U.S. Bishop Causes Furor with Outspoken Criticism of Pope," *La Croix International,* October 27, 2014, https://international.la-croix.com/news/world/us-bishop-causes-furor-with-outspoken-criticism-of-pope/230.
97. Joshua J. McElwee, "Four Cardinals Openly Challenge Francis over *Amoris Laetitia,*" *National Catholic Reporter,* November 14, 2016, https://www.ncronline.org/blogs/four-cardinals-openly-challenge-francis-over-amoris-laetitia.
98. Joshua J. McElwee, "Francis, Cardinals Urge Amazon Synod to Consider New Ideas, Including Married Priests," *National Catholic Reporter,* October 7, 2019, https://www.ncronline.org/vatican/francis-cardinals-urge-amazon-synod-consider-new-ideas-including-married-priests.
99. Michael Brendan Dougherty, "Pope Francis Is Tearing the Catholic Church Apart," *New York Times,* August 12, 2021, https://www.nytimes.com/2021/08/12/opinion/pope-francis-latin-mass.html.
100. George Weigel, "Liberal Authoritarianism and the Traditional Latin Mass," *First Things,* July 21, 2021, https://www.firstthings.com/web-exclusives/2021/07/liberal-authoritarianism-and-the-traditional-latin-mass.
101. Rorate Caeli (@RorateCaeli), "Francis HATES US," the group tweeted. "Francis HATES Tradition. Francis HATES all that is good and beautiful." Twitter, July 16, 2021, https://twitter.com/RorateCaeli/status/1415984736099618821.
102. Lewis, interview with author.

103. Mike Lewis, "Pope Francis' Critics are Dividing the Church and Families—Including Mine," *America*, August 13, 2020.
104. Georgetown University, *Through Many, One: Overcoming Polarization Through Catholic Social Thought*, June 4, 2018, https://catholicsocialthought.georgetown.edu/events/though-many-one-overcoming-polarization-through-catholic-social-thought.
105. Georgetown University, *Through Many, One.*
106. Georgetown University, *Through Many, One.*
107. Georgetown University, *Through Many, One.*
108. Georgetown University, *Through Many, One.*
109. David Kirkpatrick, "The Conservative Christian Big Thinker," *New York Times*, December 16, 2009, https://www.nytimes.com/2009/12/20/magazine/20george-t.html.
110. Mark Zimmermann, "Gathering Looks at How to Overcome Polarization by Using Social Teaching," *Catholic News Service*, June 13, 2018, https://catholicphilly.com/2018/06/news/national-news/gathering-looks-at-how-to-overcome-polarization-using-social-teaching/.
111. Georgetown University, *Through Many, One.*
112. Georgetown University, *Through Many, One.*
113. Michael Sean Winters, "Ending Polarization Takes Getting into Rabbit Holes," *National Catholic Reporter*, June 8, 2018, https://www.ncronline.org/opinion/distinctly-catholic/ending-polarization-takes-getting-rabbit-holes.
114. Kim Daniels, interview with author.
115. Daniels, interview with author.
116. Daniels, interview with author.

2

TRUMP, CATHOLICS, AND THE MORAL PERILS OF TRANSACTIONAL POLITICS

Neil Young's "Rockin' in the Free World" played as Donald J. Trump rode a golden escalator down to the lobby of Trump Tower on June 16, 2015, to announce his bid for the presidency. Most pundits and the professional political class watched with a mix of surreal bemusement and scorn as the real estate mogul and "hair icon," as one reporter described him, settled in behind the podium. "We are going to make our country great again," Trump declared in a forty-five-minute speech that touted his personal fortune and prophesied that he would be "the greatest jobs president that God ever made." Trump boasted that "the American dream is dead, but if I get elected president, I will bring it back bigger, and better, and stronger than ever before."[1]

The grandiose pronouncements and gaudy optimism clearly borrowed themes from Ronald Reagan, who first used the slogan "make America great again" during his 1980 campaign for president. But if Reagan was prone to using somewhat more subtle and coded appeals to stoke white grievance, Trump wielded a megaphone to say the quiet part out loud. "The U.S. has become a dumping ground for everybody else's problems," Trump said during his announcement speech.[2] "When Mexico sends its people, they're not sending their best. They're not sending you. They're sending people who have lots of problems. They're bringing drugs. They're bringing crime. They're rapists. And some, I assume, are good people." The man who had once built casinos and an airline that went bankrupt—and later moved on to constructing a race-baiting "birther" lie that Barack Obama was not an American citizen—then cast himself in the part of savior to the chaos he had conjured. "I would build a great wall. And nobody builds walls better than me, believe me. . . . I will build a great, great wall on our southern border and I will have Mexico pay for that wall."[3]

His announcement speech provoked and offended people in ways that Trump surely intended and relished. "I can never apologize for the truth," he told Fox News in the face of growing calls that he apologize to the immigrant community. "I said tremendous crime is coming across. Everybody knows that's true. So, why, when I mention, all of a sudden, I'm a racist. I'm not a racist. I don't have a racist bone in my body."[4] Six months after announcing his candidacy by demonizing Mexicans as rapists, Trump used a tragic shooting that killed fourteen people in San Bernardino, California, to call for "a total and complete shutdown of Muslims entering the United States." Muslims' "great hatred" of the United States, Trump added, justified drastic measures, including surveillance in American mosques.[5] The candidate was not a newcomer to using fear opportunistically to cultivate a tough-on-crime image. When a twenty-eight-year-old white woman was beaten and raped while jogging in Central Park in 1989, the case became national news. A group of African American and Latino teenagers, who became known as the Central Park Five in the media, were charged in the case. Trump took out a full-page advertisement in *The New York Times*, the *Daily News*, the *New York Post*, and *New York Newsday* with a massive headline printed in capital letters: "BRING BACK THE DEATH PENALTY. BRING BACK OUR POLICE!"[6] The teenagers served prison sentences from six to thirteen years before their convictions were overturned in 2002 after a man whose DNA matched evidence from the scene confessed to the crime.

"Build the wall!" chants quickly became a staple of Trump rallies in 2016, a signature battle cry that gained energy as Trump steadily separated himself from the pack in a crowded GOP field. As the campaign progressed and it became clear that Trump's run for the White House had traction, a clash between two of the most visible people in the world played out in extraordinary fashion. When Pope Francis was asked by reporters for his reaction to Trump's allegation that the pope's decision to celebrate Mass in Ciudad Juarez near the US–Mexico border made him a political pawn of Mexico, Francis didn't equivocate. "A person who thinks only about building walls, wherever they may be, and not building bridges, is not Christian. This is not in the Gospel," the pope said. "I'll only say that this man is not Christian if he says this."[7] Trump called the comment "disgraceful" and fired back. "If and when the Vatican is attacked by ISIS, which as everyone knows is ISIS's ultimate trophy, I can promise you that the Pope would have only wished and prayed that Donald Trump would have been President because this would not have happened," Trump said in a statement released by his campaign.[8] The pope wasn't the first prominent Catholic leader to challenge the candidate's anti-immigrant rhetoric. A year earlier, Cardinal Timothy Dolan of

New York, writing in a *New York Daily News* op-ed, clearly had Trump in mind even though he never specifically used the candidate's name. "I wish I were in the college classroom again, so I could roll out my 'Trump card' to show the students that I was right. Nativism is alive, well—and apparently popular!" the cardinal wrote.[9] Dolan contrasted nativists "who see the unwashed, ignorant, bothersome brood as criminals and misfits who threaten 'pure America,'" to those who recognize immigrants "as a gift to our nation, realizing that the only citizens whose ancestors were not immigrants are the Native Americans." The cardinal wrote that he was "not in the business of telling people what candidates they should support or who deserves their vote," but noted that "as a Catholic, I take seriously the Bible's teaching that we are to welcome the stranger, one of the most frequently mentioned moral imperatives in both the Old and New Testament."[10] Getting into a high-profile tussle with the pope might have seemed like a political death knell for a candidate who needed Catholic voters to win the election. But despite the church's biblically inspired, centuries-old advocacy for refugees and immigrants, Trump clearly knew that many Catholic voters were more in line with him than Pope Francis. Less than half of white Catholics (44 percent) believe immigrants strengthen the country, according to a 2015 Public Religion Research Institute poll released a year before Trump and Pope Francis squared off.[11] The same survey found that more than four in ten white Catholics say immigrants threaten traditional American customs and values.

Breitbart Media, the right-wing outlet whose former chairman Steve Bannon, a Catholic, went on to run Trump's campaign, blasted Dolan's commentary as a "political hit piece" and found a Catholic priest willing to defend Trump. "As a Catholic priest, I can only say it is embarrassing to have a Cardinal so blatantly and unfairly trying to associate Mr. Trump with the worst kinds of racism imaginable," Fr. Marcel Guarnizo wrote in a commentary that warned of the "social unrest that lax immigration laws" are causing in Europe.

> It is not Catholic or Christian to advocate for irresponsible immigration. Immigration to be of any help to immigrants and the host country, requires order, knowledge and balance. If Dolan were to say something sensible about politics to Catholics he should perhaps state the obvious: no Catholic in good conscience can vote for the Democratic party, a party that supports funding Planned Parenthood, opposes marriage, and is seen to be devastating the social fabric of this nation while bringing economic ruin to a once prosperous country.[12]

Trump's religion problem wasn't limited to Pope Francis. Many conservative Christian leaders were initially wary of the twice-divorced New Yorker who had long supported abortion rights, rarely attended church, and once appeared on the cover of *Playboy* magazine. While Trump managed to secure the endorsement of Jerry Falwell Jr. after a speech at Liberty University, where he vowed to "protect Christianity," antiabortion leaders were dubious. A week before the Iowa caucuses, where evangelical Christians historically flex their electoral muscles, pro-life women leaders from Iowa and national pro-life organizations circulated an open letter to voters with the headline: "Pro-Life Women Sound the Alarm: Donald Trump is Unacceptable."

> As pro-life women leaders from Iowa and across the nation, we urge Republican caucus-goers and voters to support anyone but Donald Trump. On the issue of defending unborn children and protecting women from the violence of abortion, Mr. Trump cannot be trusted and there is, thankfully, an abundance of alternative candidates with proven records of pro-life leadership whom pro-life voters can support. We have come to this conclusion after having listened patiently to numerous debates and news reports, but most importantly to Donald Trump's own words. The next president will be responsible for as many as four nominations to the Supreme Court. Mr. Trump has given us only one indication about the type of judges he would appoint, and it does not bode well for those who would like to see the court overturn *Roe v. Wade*. Mr. Trump has said his sister, Judge Maryanne Trump Barry, who struck down the Partial Birth Abortion Ban in New Jersey, would be a "phenomenal" choice for the court. Earlier this month, Mr. Trump also said he thought pro-choice Senator Scott Brown would make a "very good" Vice President. If one truly believes, as we do, that abortion is the taking of an innocent human life and is committed to the pro-life priorities of ending abortion after five months, and defunding the nation's largest abortion business, Planned Parenthood, it would be a disaster to have a vice president who disagrees.[13]

The letter also went on to criticize Trump's treatment of women. "He has impugned the dignity of women, most notably Megyn Kelly, he mocked and bullied Carly Fiorina, and has through the years made disparaging public comments to and about many women," it said. "Further, Mr. Trump has profited from the exploitation of women in his Atlantic City casino hotel, which boasted the first strip club casino in the country. America will only be a great nation when we have leaders of strong character who will defend both unborn children and the dignity of women. We cannot trust Donald Trump to do either." The letter was signed by, among others, Jennifer Bowen, executive director of Iowa Right to Life; Beverly LaHaye, founder of Concerned Women for America; and arguably the most prominent Catholic in the antiabortion movement, Marjorie Dannenfelser, president of the Susan B. Anthony List, an influential organization that works to elect antiabortion candidates. Sen. Ted Cruz of Texas won the Iowa caucuses. "To God be the glory," Cruz told his supporters. "Tonight is a victory for the grassroots. Tonight is a victory for courageous conservatives all across Iowa and our great nation."[14] It would be a fleeting moment of celebration for Cruz. A few days later Trump captured the New Hampshire primary, and a week after that strong support from white evangelicals powered his victory in the important South Carolina primary.

Even as Trump's campaign gained energy, conservative Catholics remained a significant part of the "Never Trump" contingent, which on the evangelical side was led by prominent Southern Baptist Russell Moore. As president of the Southern Baptist Convention's political and policy arm, Moore faced backlash from many Southern Baptist leaders for calling Trump "an awful candidate" and criticizing "the old-guard religious right political establishment" for supporting him despite what he called Trump's "serious moral problems."[15] Less than a month after Trump's primary win in South Carolina, George Weigel and Robert George, Catholics long involved with social conservative movements in the Republican Party, spearheaded "An Appeal to Our Fellow Catholics." Published in the conservative journal *National Review*, the statement was a blunt critique. "Donald Trump is manifestly unfit to be president of the United States," they wrote.

> His campaign has already driven our politics down to new levels of vulgarity. His appeals to racial and ethnic fears and prejudice are offensive to any genuinely Catholic sensibility. He promised to order U.S. military personnel to torture terrorist suspects and to kill terrorists' families—actions condemned by the Church and policies that would bring shame upon our country. And there is nothing in his campaign or his previous record that gives us grounds for confidence that he genuinely shares our commitments to the right to life, to religious freedom and the rights of conscience, to rebuilding the marriage culture, or to subsidiarity and the principle of limited constitutional government.[16]

The letter commended the Republican Party in recent decades as "a vehicle—imperfect, like all human institutions, but serviceable—for promoting causes at the center of Catholic social concern in the United States." These causes, the authors listed, included "providing legal protection for unborn children," "defending religious freedom," "rebuilding our marriage culture," and "re-establishing constitutional and limited government." But Trump's ascent in the Republican Party threatened those values, they argued, and the writers urged voters to see the dangers posed by Trumpism.

"We urge our fellow Catholics and all our fellow citizens to consider, however, that there are candidates for the Republican nomination who are far more likely than Mr. Trump to address these concerns, and who do not exhibit his vulgarity, oafishness, shocking ignorance, and—we do not hesitate to use the word—demagoguery," the appeal stated. "Mr. Trump's record and his campaign show us no promise of greatness; they promise only the further degradation of our politics and our culture. We urge our fellow Catholics and all our fellow citizens to reject his candidacy for the Republican presidential nomination by supporting a genuinely reformist candidate." Along with coauthors George Weigel and Robert George, the open letter was signed by notable conservative Catholic writers, academics, and politically minded activists, including Ryan Anderson, then a research fellow at the Heritage Foundation; Mary Eberstadt of the Ethics and Public Policy Center; Gerard Bradley, University of Notre Dame law professor; Brian Burch, president of CatholicVote.org; and Joe Cella, founder of the National Catholic Prayer Breakfast.

But Trump had already piqued the interest of a more powerful Catholic ally than those dissenters. The same month as the open letter made the rounds in conservative Catholic circles, Trump met with Leonard Leo at the Washington law firm Jones Day. One of the most influential operators in Washington, Leo led the Federalist Society, a conservative legal organization, and has played a key role in building a network of advocacy organizations dedicated to reshaping the judiciary with conservative judges who oppose abortion and same-sex marriage and who promote what they consider to be an "originalist" interpretation of the Constitution. During the George W. Bush administration, Leo led campaigns supporting Supreme Court nominees John Roberts Jr. and Samuel Alito. A 2019 *Washington Post* investigation found that he helped raise $250 million from mostly undisclosed, dark money sources in recent years to promote conservative judges.[17] Leo is a member of the Knights of Malta, a Catholic lay religious order founded in the eleventh century known for both its charitable work and wealthy patrons. At various times, he has served on the board of The Catholic University of

America, the Catholic Information Center, an Opus Dei affiliated bookstore in downtown Washington, the National Catholic Prayer Breakfast, and the Catholic Association, a conservative lay organization focused on religious liberty issues. In 2016 the Catholic Association paid him $100,000 for management consulting, according to the *Washington Post* investigation. Leo and his wife were named stewards of St. Peter by the Papal Foundation, an honor given to those who pledge to donate $1 million or more to Vatican projects and initiatives around the world. Leo met Trump in downtown Washington only a few weeks after the death of Supreme Court Justice Antonin Scalia, a hero in the conservative legal movement. All eyes were on the court. Leo later told reporters that he briefed Trump about the composition of the court and the ideology of the sitting justices. He later gave Trump a list of possible Supreme Court nominees. In an unusual move two months after their meeting, Trump released the list publicly to help convince skeptical Republicans to support his candidacy.

As the 2016 campaign headed into summer, Trump ramped up his effort to woo Christian conservatives and found more receptive audiences. At a high-profile meeting in New York with hundreds of leaders on the Christian right, Trump promised to make religious liberty and the appointment of antiabortion judges the centerpieces of his agenda. The candidate drew a standing ovation. Some anti-Trump Catholics were now beginning to back away from their earlier denunciations. Brian Burch of Catholic Vote, who just a few months earlier signed the appeal that described the candidate's "appeals to racial and ethnic fears and prejudice" as "offensive to any genuinely Catholic sensibility," began striking a friendlier tone. After helping the Trump campaign organize the meeting with Christian leaders, Burch told the *National Review* he was pleased that "both the Federalist Society and Heritage (the Heritage Foundation) have helped guide him in thinking about potential judicial nominations."[18] Another Catholic with influence in the pro-life movement also attended the meeting and soon began distancing herself from earlier criticism of Trump. Marjorie Dannenfelser, president of the Susan B. Anthony List, had helped spearhead the letter released before the Iowa Caucus that blasted the candidate for his treatment of women and warned antiabortion voters that he "cannot be trusted." But after meeting with Trump in New York, Dannenfelser sounded more like a cheerleader than a critic. "I believe that he came across very well as a messenger for everybody in the room, not just as a beneficiary of evangelical votes but as a fellow traveler," she told the *Washington Post*. "He made no missteps. There were no explosions." Dannenfelser was impressed that Trump specifically promised to appoint "pro-life justices," a phrase that she noted most presidential candidates avoid. "They usually couch it in other words, like "constitutional," she said.

Aimee Murphy watched with a sickness in her stomach as many of her fellow pro-life activists moved from principled opposition to a transactional embrace of Trump. Murphy had signed the same letter from pro-life women raising red flags about the candidate that Dannenfelser did. Many of the women who had signed the letter were now starting to rally behind Trump. "Our movement was being dragged behind the Republican Party slavishly and bowing at the feet of the Republican golden elephant, rather than the golden calf," the thirty-three-year-old founder of Rehumanize International and *Life Matters Journal* told me in an interview.[19] Murphy describes herself as a Catholic pro-life feminist who opposes abortion. She also opposes war, torture, the death penalty, abusive treatment of migrants, and any policy that degrades human life. She wanted *Roe v. Wade* overturned but also supports universal health care and a universal basic income for families. Pro-choice and an atheist as a teenager, Murphy became active in pro-life circles after she was raped by her boyfriend at sixteen. He threatened to kill her and himself if she didn't have an abortion. Raised Catholic, Murphy started to explore her faith more seriously as her pro-life advocacy took root. She was drawn to the church's consistent-ethic-of-life teachings and "womb-to-tomb" defense of human life. Trump may have been antiabortion, but for Murphy that was not the same as being pro-life.

Murphy observed a generational divide in how the movement responded to Trump. Pro-life activists in their forties and fifties, Murphy found, were more willing to make concessions for Trump than advocates in their twenties and thirties. "People were trying to get me on board the Trump train and insist he was the lesser of two evils, but for me the lesser of two evils is still evil, and I don't want to support evil," Murphy said. "People thought I was an idealist. No, I just have my standards. I think younger people are turned off by political hypocrisy." While Murphy is glad that Trump appointed antiabortion judges and laid the groundwork for ending Roe, she laments the costs to the pro-life movement's credibility. "Trump is incredibly toxic for the pro-life movement," said Murphy, the author of *Rehumanize: A Vision to Secure Human Rights for All.*

> I think he brought open racism and xenophobia into the movement. I've seen so many friends and peers who have told me they are not pro-life anymore because of his influence. They just can't do it anymore. His legacy is tearing people away from this work. The pro-life movement is so tied to a Republican Party that is dedicated to this

individualistic, boot-strap culture, and it doesn't understand the systemic nature of poverty, pregnancy discrimination, or the history of systemic racism. No movement for human rights should ever be beholden to a political party.[20]

Another Catholic pro-life activist, who requested anonymity so she could speak candidly, said she felt "whiplash" at watching how quickly antiabortion leaders who had been openly critical of Trump changed their tune once it was clear he would be the Republican nominee. "At first there was a lot of confusion in the pro-life movement about Trump and people were in different camps, but once he had success there was this very big shift," the advocate who worked in communications for national pro-life groups said.[21] "It was very concerning to me that you saw so many people jump into his camp. It felt like all they cared about was winning. Everyone seemed to forget about the questions and concerns they had about him. It was like that movie *Men in Black,* where they shine the light in your eyes and you forget what you saw." As Trump continued to rebrand himself from someone who said he was "pro-choice in every respect" during a 1999 *Meet the Press* interview to a president who would do everything he could to end abortion rights, the shifting politics of the Democratic Party were also giving him an assist. The 2016 Democratic platform for the first time specifically advocated for federal tax dollars to cover abortion by repealing the Hyde Amendment, a bipartisan effort passed in 1976 that blocks federal funding of abortion. Over four decades, Hyde had been generally accepted as a compromise by many antiabortion and pro-choice politicians. The change to the party platform before the 2016 election infuriated antiabortion Democrats and felt like a poke in the eyes to many Catholic moderates. It was also not lost on some critics of the move that President Obama's historic health care reform achievement, the Affordable Care Act, by the president's own acknowledgment never would have passed without the support of antiabortion Democrats and Catholic sisters who helped push the legislation across the finish line in the face of opposition from the US bishops' conference.

Sister Simone Campbell, who spoke at the 2012 Democratic National Convention and served as the executive director of Network, a lobbying group of Catholic sisters, told *America* magazine that the change to the platform was "a political mistake and a policy mistake. . . . It's a political mistake because some I know in the Democratic Party think it's not possible to lose this election, and quite frankly, traveling around the country, I've come to another conclusion: that it is possible and this is not the time to move your agenda to the far left," she said.[22] Steve Krueger, president of Catholic

Democrats, called the draft language of the Democratic Party platform "one of the least faith-friendly abortion planks that the Democratic Party has ever considered."[23] The Democratic Party of 2016 was not the party of Bill Clinton, who famously campaigned in 1992 on a "safe, legal and rare" approach to abortion, or even the party of Barack Obama. In a 2009 commencement address at the University of Notre Dame, the newly elected president said, "let us work together to reduce the number of women seeking abortions."[24] While the Democratic Party was moving left on abortion, changes to the 2016 Republican Party platform underscored the party's lurch to the right. This push-and-pull effect between the two parties reflected the influence of activists and donors more than the positions of most voters. The Republican platform cited Planned Parenthood by name and even specifically referenced discredited allegations that were made against the organization in a series of undercover videos that alleged Planned Parenthood sold fetal tissue. While no state or federal investigations, even inquiries led by states with antiabortion governors, ever found evidence to support those allegations, the attacks on Planned Parenthood became a potent weapon for the Republican Party and Trump's campaign.

Trump's decision to select Indiana Governor Mike Pence as his vice-presidential nominee energized Christian conservative voters and helped mollify lingering doubt about Trump in pro-life circles. As a member of Congress, Pence sponsored the first bill to defund Planned Parenthood in 2007, and he was one of the most visible antiabortion politicians in the country. Raised Catholic in a family of Democrats, Pence became an evangelical in college but worked as a youth minister at a Catholic parish, met his wife at Mass, and in a 1994 interview described himself as a "born-again evangelical Catholic."[25] Pence called *Roe v. Wade* "the worst Supreme Court decision since Dred Scott," an 1857 decision that held enslaved people were property and could never be citizens.[26] At the Republican National Convention, Pence accepted his nomination and told the audience that "for the sake of the sanctity of life, for the sake of our Second Amendment and for the sake of all our other God-given liberties, we must ensure that the next president appointing justices to the Supreme Court is Donald Trump."[27]

In his convention speech Trump vowed "to appoint justices to the United States Supreme Court who will uphold our laws and our Constitution." The "replacement of our beloved Justice Scalia," Trump said, "will be a person of similar views, principles and judicial philosophies. Very important. This will be one of the most important issues decided by this election." Trump also returned to his familiar themes of division and fearmongering. He painted a dark picture of an America besieged by crime, illegal border crossings, violent immigrants, and the killing of police officers. Trump promised to restore "law and order" and put "America First," a slogan once used by Nazi sympathizers in the United States. Contrasting "Americanism" with "globalism," Trump praised "the forgotten men and women of our country" and declared: "I am your voice."[28] As the campaign entered the fall, Trump was easily shoring up the conservative white evangelical vote, but his favorability with other Christians, especially the critical Catholic swing vote, showed serious vulnerabilities. One of the more intriguing religion storylines in the 2016 race was the apparent weakening of the so-called "God gap," the tendency for those attending church weekly or more regularly to vote for Republicans in higher numbers.[29] A Pew Research Center survey released four months before the election found that for the first time in several decades the overall gap was narrowing significantly. Registered voters who attended religious services at least weekly, Pew found, leaned to Trump by a 49–45 percent margin over Clinton, a much smaller advantage than the 55–40 percent difference that Republican Mitt Romney held over President Obama at the same time in 2012.[30] And most notably Clinton enjoyed a nineteen-point margin over Trump with Catholics who attended Mass weekly. In contrast, Romney led Obama by 3 points among that same group, a twenty-two point shift for Clinton. The selection of Sen. Tim Kaine—a Jesuit-educated Catholic who once served as a missionary in Honduras—was also seen as a potential boon for her campaign's Catholic outreach.

The Trump campaign announced a Catholic advisory team made up of thirty-three Catholics that included a mix of politicians, antiabortion activists, a Catholic priest, and two former Vatican ambassadors. Joseph Cella, a Detroit-based consultant and a founder of the National Catholic Prayer Breakfast, led the group. Held each year in Washington, DC, the Catholic Prayer Breakfast is ostensibly a nonpartisan event, but in practice the gathering has long been a venue where Republican leaders, including presidents, find a warm welcome from conservative donors, activists, and other leaders on the right. The event frequently awards honors to Catholic politicians who have taken positions on the death penalty, war, and the environment that clash with church teaching. Only five months earlier, Cella had signed the appeal from conservative Catholics in the *National Review* calling Trump "manifestly unfit to be president of the United States" and denouncing his "demagoguery" and "vulgarity." Now that Trump was the Republican nominee, appeals to character or high ideals proved politically inconvenient. Cella told *America* magazine that he had a "sincere change of heart and mind." He cited Trump's pledge to appoint judges who oppose abortion and his decision to pick Mike Pence as critical. "Mr. Trump has promised to appoint justices in the mold of great Catholic jurist and thinker Antonin Scalia," he said. "Hillary Clinton has promised to do just the opposite, and that will have far reaching and long-lasting implications for the Catholic Church and the lay faithful, on everything from pro-life issues to religious liberty to health care in ways we can't fathom."[31] While several bishops and Pope Francis had challenged Trump's demonization of immigrants and rhetoric about the border wall, Cella was already trying to give the campaign's talking points a Catholic gloss. "It's really an opportunity to address the safety and security of our country, of our communities and civil order, and that's something consistent with Catholic social teaching," he said.

A month before the election, Denver Archbishop Samuel Aquila used his diocesan newspaper to effectively tell Catholic voters that supporting Hillary Clinton and the Democratic Party would be morally unacceptable. Without using the name of either candidate and applying the caveat that "both are disliked, lack credibility, and have made comments that make the hair on the back of your neck stand up," the archbishop then proceeded to condemn the Democratic Party platform as "aggressively pro-abortion, not only in funding matters, but in the appointment of only those judges who will support abortion and the repealing of the Helms Amendment, which prevents the U.S. from supporting abortion availability overseas."[32] He praised the Republican platform for being "supportive of the Hyde Amendment" and "its support for life by calling for the defunding of Planned Parenthood, banning dismemberment abortion and opposing assisted suicide." The archbishop then railed against what he called "the attempt by President Obama to force a transgender agenda onto public schools" and caricatured the Obama administration as an enemy of religious liberty.[33] What about the two candidates' positions on immigrants, health care, living wages for workers, or social policies that help women and families support children after they are born? While the archbishop spent several paragraphs blasting the Democratic Party and excoriating President Obama by name, he was conspicuously silent about the many ways Republican Party orthodoxy clashes with Catholic teaching when it comes to the role of government and pro-family economic policies the church supports. On the topic of Republican politicians who claim to be pro-life but fail to back up that rhetoric with policies that build a consistent ethic of life, Aquila had nothing to say. Abortion must be the defining issue for Catholic voters. "There are some issues that can legitimately be debated by Christians, such as which policies are the most effective in caring for the poor, but the direct killing of innocent human life must be opposed at all times by every follower of Jesus Christ," he wrote. "There are no legitimate exceptions to this teaching."[34]

The Trump campaign saw an opportunity in the archbishop's de facto support. On the same day Archbishop Aquila's column was published, Trump wrote a letter to Catholic leaders from across the country attending a conference in Denver that week. "I have a message for Catholics: I will be there for you. I will stand with you. I will fight for you. I am, and will remain, pro-life," Trump wrote to the Catholic Leadership Conference, an event for heads of national Catholic organizations, including Eternal World Television Network (EWTN), Fellowship of Catholic University Students (FOCUS), the Catholic Scripture Study International, and Priests for Life, led by Fr. Frank Pavone, who served as a Catholic advisor to the Trump campaign. "I will defend your religious liberties and the right to fully and freely practice your religion, as individuals, business owners and academic institutions."[35] Trump also claimed that "Hillary Clinton supports forcing The Little Sisters of the Poor who have taken care of the elderly poor since 1839, pay [*sic*] for contraceptives in their health care plan (even though they have never wanted them, never used them and never will), and having the government fine them heavily if they continue to refuse to abide by this onerous mandate." He added that Clinton "has been hostile to the core issues and policies of greatest concern to Catholics: life, religious liberty, Supreme Court nominations, affordable and quality healthcare, educational choice and home schooling." The candidate then homed in on Tim Kaine, the Democratic vice-presidential candidate, describing him as having "a 100 percent voting record from the National Abortion Rights Action League," and noting his support for same-sex marriage, "despite professing to be Catholic."[36]

Three days after writing to Catholic leaders gathered in Denver, Trump faced a bombshell that appeared likely to doom his candidacy. The *Washington Post* reported on a video it obtained of the candidate bragging in vulgar terms about kissing, groping, and trying to have sex with women during a 2005 conversation caught on a hot microphone. "And when you're a star, they let you do it," Trump boasted on the tape to Billy Bush, an *Access Hollywood* host. "You can do anything. Grab them by the p—y," Trump says. "You can do anything."[37] Trump tried to brush over the comments as "locker-room banter, a private conversation that took place many years ago." He also attempted to shift the focus to Bill Clinton, accusing him of abusing women, and Hillary Clinton, whom Trump said "bullied, attacked, shamed and intimidated his victims." Joseph Cella, who led Trump's Catholic advisory team, described the video as "repulsive and undignified." But it was clear that boasting about sexual assault could be at least tolerated by many Catholic political activists intent on using the candidate as a means to an ends. "Donald Trump and Mike Pence remain the only candidates in this election who will bring jobs back home where they belong, keep our families and communities safe, defend the right to life, the right to fully and freely exercise our religious freedom, and other issues of great importance to Catholics—and most importantly, they will appoint Supreme Court Justices who will do the same for future generations," Cella said.[38] Marjorie Dannenfelser of the Susan B. Anthony List also wasn't wavering in her support. While Trump's comments were "absolutely outrageous and unacceptable," she essentially told *National Public Radio* that Trump's xenophobia, nativism, and sexism could be stomached for larger goals. "Well, I am still with Trump, and you know why? You look at a Supreme Court that will last for generations and be changed one way or the other. And you look at taxpayer funding of abortion, which is an issue that we don't believe in and that she does, which will be 50,000 more kids a year," Dannenfelser said.[39]

As Dannenfelser and Cella publicly defended their continued support of Trump, a publication not exactly known for its liberal positions drew a line in the sand. *Christianity Today* offered a stinging moral critique of the hollow transactional politics that defined much of the public Christian support for the candidate. In an editorial, "Speak Truth to Trump," the executive editor Andy Crouch wrote:

> Most Christians who support Trump have done so with reluctant strategic calculation, largely based on the president's power to appoint members of the Supreme Court. Important issues are indeed at stake, including the right of Christians and adherents of other religions to uphold their vision of sexual integrity and marriage even if they are in the cultural minority. But there is a point at which strategy becomes its own form of idolatry—an attempt to manipulate the levers of history in favor of the causes we support. Strategy becomes idolatry, for ancient Israel and for us today, when we make alliances with those who seem to offer strength—the chariots of Egypt, the vassal kings of Rome—at the expense of our dependence on God who judges all nations, and in defiance of God's manifest concern for the stranger, the widow, the orphan, and the oppressed. Strategy becomes idolatry when we betray our deepest values in pursuit of earthly influence. And because such strategy requires capitulating to idols and princes and denying the true God, it ultimately always fails.[40]

Joseph Cella, Marjorie Dannenfelser, and other public Catholic apologists for Trump who prioritized appointing Supreme Court nominees and overturning *Roe* were surely relieved to pivot away from disclosures of the candidate's crude sexual boasting when, less than a week after the tape's disclosure, WikiLeaks released a series of emails that included one with the subject line "Conservative Catholicism." In the email chain from 2011, Jennifer Palmieri, a Catholic who would become Clinton's communications director, and John Halpin, a fellow at the Center for American Progress, discussed Rupert Murdoch—then the CEO of News Corp, the media conglomerate that includes Fox News—and *Wall Street Journal* managing editor Robert Thompson, baptizing their children as Catholics. "Many of the most powerful elements of the conservative movement are all Catholic—many converts. It's an amazing bastardization of the faith," Halpin wrote in an email to Palmieri and John Podesta, a Catholic who was Hillary Clinton's campaign chairman and who served as a chief of staff to President Bill Clinton and an advisor to President Obama.[41] "They must be attracted to the systematic thought and severely backwards gender relations and must be totally unaware of Christian democracy." Halpin added: "I imagine they think it is the most socially acceptable politically conservative religion. Their rich friends wouldn't understand if they became evangelicals."[42] Cella fired back as the point man for Trump's Catholic team. The emails, he said, proved "the open anti-Catholic bigotry" of a Clinton campaign that would "turn the clock back to the twentieth century 'No Catholics Need Apply' type of discrimination."[43] Charles Chaput, then the archbishop of Philadelphia, wrote about the emails in his diocesan newspaper, describing them as "contemptuously anti-Catholic." "Of course, it would be wonderful for the Clinton campaign to repudiate the content of these ugly WikiLeaks emails. All of us backward-thinking Catholics who actually believe what Scripture and the Church teach would be so very grateful," Chaput wrote.[44] A *Wall Street Journal* editorial, under the headline "Anti-Catholics for Clinton," used the leaks to pounce: "It's no secret that progressive elites despise religion," it declared. "This disdain for people of faith helps explain today's political polarization and why so many people are willing to support a blunt, avenging force like Donald Trump."[45]

A few days later, the campaign narrative shifted back to the Supreme Court at the final debate before the election. "I am pro-life," Trump said when asked if he wanted *Roe v. Wade* overturned. He pledged that "will happen, automatically" if he was elected. After Clinton articulated her support for abortion rights, Trump claimed she approved of procedures that would "rip the baby out of the womb . . . just prior to birth," a widely criticized comment that turned the anguished complexity of late-stage pregnancy medical decisions into a blunt political attack.[46] Two days after the debate, Trump attended the usually jovial Al Smith Dinner, a quadrennial white-tie event that brings together the presidential candidates, the archbishop of New York, national media, and a roomful of donors for a Catholic Charities fundraiser at the Waldorf Astoria Hotel. "Here she is tonight, in public, pretending not to hate Catholics," Trump sniped at Clinton during his time at the podium.[47] The evening was a sad spectacle as it unfolded in real time, and even more so in retrospect. Trump's swift ascent to securing the Republican nomination and eventually the White House was enabled, in part, by the normalization and Catholic mainstreaming of someone who thrilled white supremacists, publicly demeaned women, and had contempt for basic civility. What message did it send to voters who saw images of Cardinal Dolan chuckling alongside a candidate who called Mexican immigrants rapists, proposed a ban on all Muslims entering the country, mocked a disabled reporter at a campaign rally, and called Pope Francis "disgraceful"?

The gregarious cardinal who enjoys rubbing shoulders with the powerful did face a tricky predicament. A decision not to invite Trump would have come with its own complications. Every four years New York archbishops are under pressure from antiabortion Catholics who object to giving a platform to a pro-choice presidential candidate. In 2012, Cardinal Dolan took heat from Fr. Frank Pavone of Priests for Life for not excluding then-candidate Barack Obama from the banquet. Pavone argued that "the polite putting aside of differences for a while amounts to scandal," adding that "there comes a time when enough is enough and we can no longer give people a reason to doubt our position as a church."[48] There was precedent, however, for withholding invitations. In 1996 Cardinal John O'Connor didn't give the pro-choice Bill Clinton a platform. In 2004 Cardinal Edward Egan made the same decision because John Kerry, the Democratic nominee and a Catholic, supported abortion rights. Trump's nativism, cruel rhetoric, and worship of money—"you have to be wealthy in order to be great" he declared that spring—amounted to a walking contradiction of authentic Christian values. A prominent Catholic bishop should have been wary of giving Trump a platform or even the slightest appearance of support.

Less than two weeks before the election, Trump enjoyed free Catholic advertising when he appeared on the global Catholic media network EWTN for a softball interview from its popular host Raymond Arroyo. "Religious liberty in this country is in tremendous trouble," Trump declared in what had become a common theme of depicting Christians as under siege. "People that are faith-based are not having, you know, they're just not having, they're not being accepted. It's almost like they're not being accepted in our country anymore. Obama has been a disaster, in terms of religious liberty."[49] Arroyo predictably didn't challenge the candidate on his promise to ban refugees from predominantly Muslim countries as a religious liberty issue or bring up the many ways Catholic agencies serve undocumented immigrants and refugees. Instead the host teed it up for Trump with a comment that "WikiLeaks revelations have offended a lot of evangelicals and Catholics." Trump relished the opportunity to play arbiter of Catholic values. "Frankly, if any Catholic votes for Hillary Clinton, you know, I would say, if I were a Catholic, I wouldn't be talking to them anymore. She's been terrible in what she said and her thoughts towards Catholics and to evangelicals."[50]

In a speech delivered at the Vatican three days before the election, Pope Francis never mentioned the candidates by name, but his message amounted to a timely repudiation of many themes Trump emphasized during the race. The pope urged grassroots activists representing social justice organizations from sixty countries to build bridges, not walls, and never give in to the politics of fear. "Because fear—as well as being a good deal for the merchants of arms and death—weakens and destabilizes us, destroys our psychological and spiritual defenses, numbs us to the suffering of others," the pope said. "All walls fall," Francis told the group, stressing that "mercy is the best antidote against fear" and that it "is much more effective than walls, than barbed wire fences."[51] In contrast to Trump's demands that US borders be shut down, the pope urged nations to welcome migrants and recognize the urgency of the global refugee crisis, which Francis said had roots in "an unjust socioeconomic system and wars." The pope specifically referenced the hundreds of thousands of migrants who had died in the Mediterranean Sea attempting to enter Europe. "No one should be forced to flee their homeland," he said.[52]

* * *

Heading into election day, Hillary Clinton had reason to be confident. National polls had her leading by solid margins. While everyone knew Trump would easily capture the white evangelical vote, several polls in the final months of the race showed Clinton up big with Catholics, a bellwether for the election. Catholics have voted for the winning ticket in every presidential election except once since 1976. "Donald Trump has a massive Catholic problem," a *Washington Post* headline read on August 30.[53] The article cited a Public Religion Research Institute survey from that week showing Trump's support with Catholics down twenty-three points, and a *Washington Post*–ABC News Poll from earlier that month that found his Catholic numbers falling by twenty-seven points. In the end, the pundits, polling, and prognosticating were wrong. Donald Trump shocked almost every political and media observer by earning 304 electoral votes and winning the presidency. Clinton won the popular vote by nearly 2.9 million votes. Only two other presidents besides Trump have been elected with smaller popular vote margins since records began in 1824. The conventional wisdom among Democratic Party operatives and progressive analysts that an increasingly diverse electorate, which had elected Barack Obama twice, would overpower a mostly older white Trump coalition didn't hold. The winning formula could not be replicated. Clinton failed to fire up the Obama coalition and earned nearly 5 million fewer votes than the former president. Early exit-poll results from *The New York Times* found that Trump won 52 percent of the Catholic vote to Clinton's 45 percent. *CNN* reported a similar tally with Trump winning 50 percent of Catholic voters compared to 46 percent for Clinton. Five months after the election, according to an analysis of American National Election Studies data by Georgetown University's Center for Applied Research in the Apostolate, Catholic voters overall narrowly favored Clinton, 48 percent to 45 percent. "I don't think we will ever really definitively know," Mark Gray, CARA's director of polling, told *America* magazine, suggesting that the Catholic vote was likely a "toss up" between the two candidates.[54] Gray noted that American National Election Studies data is more reliable than exit polls because political scientists gather it both before and after the election, and exit polls are often plagued by a number of limitations.

White Catholics supported Trump over Clinton by a wide, twenty-three-point margin (60 percent to 37 percent), rivaling Romney's nineteen-point favor with white Catholics in 2008. Trump won the highest percentage of white Catholics in the past five elections. Latino Catholics heavily turned out for Clinton (67 percent to 26 percent), but that represented a loss of eight percentage points compared to Obama's 2012 performance.[55] While Trump and Clinton essentially split the Catholic vote overall nationally, white Catholics in the key battleground states of Pennsylvania, Michigan, and Wisconsin had a decisive role in paving Trump's path to victory. For Clinton, losing those heavily Catholic Rust Belt states, considered a "blue wall" for Democratic candidates, sealed her fate. Wisconsin, Michigan, and Pennsylvania were only each decided by about one percentage point. In Wisconsin, a state Clinton didn't even visit during the general election campaign, she won voters under thirty years old by only four points. Obama won those voters by twenty-three points four years earlier. The state voted for a Republican presidential candidate for the first time since 1984. In Pennsylvania, where Catholics outnumber evangelicals by a two-to-one margin, places such as Scranton and Wilkes-Barre that Obama won delivered for Trump. "Youngstown, Ohio, where Mr. Obama won by more than 20 points in 2012, was basically a draw," *The New York Times* reported.[56] "Mr. Trump swept the string of traditionally Democratic and old industrial towns along Lake Erie. Counties that supported Mr. Obama in 2012 voted for Mr. Trump by 20 points." Clinton's lukewarm faith outreach contrasted with the Obama campaign's robust religious efforts in 2008 and 2012. Clinton staff, headquartered in Brooklyn, New York, made a strategic and ultimately flawed calculation that white Catholics were not a priority. According to one national media account, the campaign turned down a request from a prominent group of supporters that Clinton address a prestigious St. Patrick's Day gathering at the University of Notre Dame, an invitation that previous presidential candidates quickly accepted.[57] Given longtime political trends of white voters favoring the GOP, Clinton was never going to win white Catholics—Mitt Romney outperformed Barack Obama with that group 59 percent to 40 percent—but by failing to chip into Trump's margins, she lost ground with those voters compared to Obama.

Easy explanations for why a national election turned a certain way risk oversimplifying complex realities. Voters often have multiple, often contradictory motivations. The fact that Trump easily won counties that Obama carried underscores the array of factors at work in 2016—an election that included a polarizing female candidate long demonized by the right, the Clinton campaign's failures in the Midwest, Russian interference in the race, and the media fury sparked by the letter FBI Director James Comey sent to the House Judiciary Committee less than a week before the election announcing the discovery of new emails that appeared relevant to its closed investigation of Clinton. But it's impossible to evaluate the 2016 election without understanding the role that race, religion, and identity played in voters' views about an increasingly diverse, less Christian nation. Between Barack Obama's 2008 election and 2016, the United States underwent a little noticed but profound shift by transforming from a majority white Christian nation (54 percent) to a minority white Christian nation (43 percent).[58] "But on Election Day, paradoxically, this anxious minority swarmed to the polls to elect as president the candidate who promised to 'make America great again' and warned that he was its 'last chance' to turn back the tide of cultural and economic change," Robert Jones, a prominent religion pollster and author of *The End of White Christian America,* wrote two days after the election.

> Hillary Clinton's final campaign ad featured Katy Perry's song 'Roar,' but the loudest voices of this election turned out to be not the 'new America' demographic groups of Latinos, African-Americans and millennials, but Mr. Trump's aging and raging white Christian

> supporters. The waning numbers of white Christians in the country today may not have time on their side, but as the sun is slowly setting on the cultural world of white Christian America, they've managed, at least in this election, to rage against the dying of the light.[59]

Trump's ability to appeal to country-club Republicans with ample stock holdings, disaffected working-class whites in swing states devastated by free-trade deals that sent jobs overseas, and conservative Christians who saw him as their best chance to overturn *Roe* made for a potent combination.

A leitmotif running through this cultural and economic big-tent Trumpism was the promise to restore the traditional values of white Christian America. But those conservative white Christians who had raised alarms about Trump from the beginning as lonely voices in the political wilderness were not going away. "If the Trump campaign foreshadows his presidency, America under Trump will be fundamentally different than it has been—coarser, less temperate and civilized, more inward and resentful," Peter Wehner, a senior fellow at the Ethics and Public Policy Center who served in three Republican administrations, wrote in *The New York Times*. "The Republican Party will fundamentally change, from a conservative party to one that champions European-style ethnic nationalism. . . . What happened on Nov. 8 was a mystery that may lead to a calamity. I hope to God it won't."[60] Perhaps accustomed to the mainstreaming of the newly elected president by some Catholic leaders and others, the outgoing US ambassador to the Vatican, Ken Hackett, seemed more sanguine. Leading a nation, the former CEO of Catholic Relief Services told a Catholic news outlet in Rome, "calls you to be your best, to weigh decisions, to listen to advice, to play the role on the world's stage that the United States has played and is capable of playing." It was unclear what candidate Hackett had been watching on the campaign trail when he expressed optimism that "good will prevail" and Trump will "take the best advice offered to him."[61]

In the weeks leading up to inauguration, New York Cardinal Timothy Dolan, who read a brief scripture passage at the ceremony, struck a similar tone. "Many people may have reservations about the president-elect and I certainly do, as with any incoming president," Dolan said. "But in the great American tradition, we look at the time of an incoming president as a time of hope . . . a way to give a man a chance and try to fulfill some of the promises he made."[62] Another American cardinal sounded more jubilant about Trump's win. Speaking two days after the election to the Italian conservative daily *Il Giornale*, Cardinal Raymond Burke, the former archbishop of Saint Louis, said he believed the election result reflected a long-running crisis in the United States and hoped the country would find the "right path to follow." The cardinal praised Trump for his "defense of human life" and desire to "put in place every action possible to fight abortion."[63] Burke also told the *National Catholic Register* that he had no concerns about the incoming president's views on migrants and refugees. "I don't think the new president will be inspired by hatred in his treatment of the immigration issue," Burke said. "These are prudential questions—of how much immigration a country can responsibly sustain, also what is the meaning of immigration, and if the immigrants are coming from one country—questions that principally address that country's responsibility for its own citizens." The cardinal added a coda with a suspicious Trumpian flavor. "Charity is always intelligent," he said. "It demands to know: Exactly who are these immigrants? Are they really refugees, and what communities can sustain them?"[64]

Trump picked up where he left off on the campaign trail during his inaugural speech. "We must protect our borders from the ravages of other countries making our products, stealing our companies, and destroying our jobs," Trump said. "This American carnage stops right here and stops right now."[65] The president's angry nationalism and insistence that immigrants and other perceived outsiders posed a dangerous threat to the country contributed to a wider climate that made people of color less safe. Reported hate crimes with racial or ethnic bias jumped the day after President Trump won the 2016 election, from ten to twenty-seven, according to an analysis of FBI hate crime statistics by the *Washington Post* in 2018. There were more reported hate crimes on November 9 than any other day in 2016, the newspaper reported.[66] The trend continued throughout Trump's term. Hate crimes surged almost 20 percent during his administration, according to an FBI report on hate crime statistics.[67] Hate-crime murders, largely committed by white supremacists, spiked to their highest levels in twenty-eight years. While the president was falsely depicting a nation threatened by dark-skinned immigrants, the real victims were people of color and religious minorities targeted by white extremists, many of them Christian.

* * *

A week after the inauguration, the nation's largest antiabortion rally commenced in Washington. The March for Life, an annual event held in January to protest the 1973 Supreme Court *Roe v. Wade* decision that legalized abortion, draws thousands for several days of speeches, prayer vigils, and lobbying visits on Capitol Hill. While the event is not officially Catholic or exclusively religious, Catholics make up a large percentage of organizers and participants. Catholic high schools bus in students from across the country.

The National Shrine of the Immaculate Conception in Washington draws up to 20,000 Catholics for a fourteen-hour vigil that starts the night before the march. The crowd, peppered with priests in Roman collars and nuns in traditional habits, filled Constitution Avenue and rallied at the Supreme Court building across from the US Capitol. Trump's election had energized these activists. The presence of Mike Pence—the first vice president in history to speak at the event—was viewed as a sign that the new administration didn't take pro-lifers for granted. "We will not rest until we restore a culture of life in America for ourselves and our posterity," Pence told the crowd during a ten-minute address. "Life is winning again in America."[68] He added that Trump asked him to speak at the rally. "That is evident in the historic election of a president who I proudly say stands for the right to life." Next week, he said to applause, "President Donald Trump will announce a Supreme Court nominee who will uphold the God-given liberty enshrined in our Constitution in the tradition of the late and great Justice Antonin Scalia." Presidential advisor Kellyanne Conway, the highest-ranking woman in the White House and a graduate of an all-women's Catholic college only a few miles away from the rally, told the marchers: "I am a wife, a mother, a Catholic, a counselor to the president of the United States of America, and yes, I am pro-life. This is a new day, a new dawn, for life."[69]

Only a few hours after the march concluded, Trump signed an executive order that banned foreign nationals from seven predominantly Muslim countries from visiting the country for 90 days, suspended entry to the country of all Syrian refugees indefinitely, and prohibited any other refugees from coming into the United States for 120 days. An extreme, sweeping measure that drew immediate protests across the country and a flurry of lawsuits from civil-rights organizations, the Muslim travel ban highlighted the tensions between Trump's religious supporters and the nation's largely faith-based refugee resettlement agencies. The announcement of the ban on the same day as the March for Life only underscored the contrast. In fact, a night before the march, Cardinal Dolan told those attending the vigil Mass at the basilica that "refugees and immigrants continue to believe that this nation is still a sanctuary, as they arrive with relief and thanksgiving. We pray they are never let down!"[70] A few months before Trump announced the executive action, Pope Francis told a gathering of Catholics and Lutherans in Germany that people can't defend Christianity by being "against refugees and other religions." The pope offered a blunt assessment. "It's hypocrisy to call yourself a Christian and chase away a refugee or someone seeking help. . . . If I say I am Christian, but do these things, I'm a hypocrite."[71] Catholic leaders quickly denounced the executive order.

Chicago Cardinal Blase Cupich called it a "dark moment in U.S. history. We know that history well, for, like others, we have been on the other side of such decisions."[72] In a statement from the US bishops' conference, Bishop Joe Vásquez pledged that church leaders would "continue to engage the new administration, as we have all administrations for the duration of the current refugee program, now almost forty years. We will work vigorously to ensure that refugees are humanely welcomed in collaboration with Catholic Charities without sacrificing our security or our core values as Americans, and to ensure that families may be reunified with their loved ones."[73] Not every Catholic bishop responded with urgency. "Since Inauguration Day critics of Donald Trump have marched, rioted, verbally abused and in some cases viciously assaulted their opponents on a scale previously unseen," then Philadelphia Archbishop Charles Chaput wrote in a column published the same day as the Muslim travel ban. "Mr. Trump is now President Trump, and curiously, some of the harshest, ongoing fury directed at him has nothing to do with his personal character," he continued. "Rather, it's a very special brand of 'progressive' intolerance for the approach his administration may take toward a range of difficult social decisions, including abortion."[74] The archbishop went on to suggest that the University of Notre Dame, which has a long history of inviting presidents from both parties to give the commencement address, should welcome Trump. Asked by a *Washington Post* reporter if the archbishop was going to comment on Trump's Muslim ban, Chaput's senior advisor Francis Maier responded: "The archbishop will be writing about immigration this week and will probably touch on it, but he does not think it wise to engage in some of the frantic protests so far. This requires a reasoned response, not an anxiety attack."[75] The fact that a prominent archbishop of a major American city with a platform to speak on timely moral issues seemed more disturbed by progressive critics of Trump than an executive order that targeted Muslims or the alarming rise in hate crimes offered a window into an embattled Catholic subculture often animated by similar cultural grievances that Trump tapped into so effectively.

Three days after signing the travel ban, Trump sparked a furor in Washington when he abruptly fired his acting attorney general for refusing to defend the executive order. The president declared that Sally Yates had betrayed the administration by announcing to Justice Department lawyers that she was not convinced the order was lawful and would not defend Trump's order against legal challenges. "Ms. Yates is an Obama administration appointee who is weak on borders and very weak on illegal immigration," a statement from the White House read.[76] A day after firing Yates, President Trump began making good on his promises to transform the Supreme Court when he nominated Neil Gorsuch, at forty-nine years old the youngest nominee in twenty-five years. The announcement resurfaced outrage among Democrats after Senate Republicans refused to even consider President Obama's nominee, Merrick Garland, a year earlier during the presidential campaign. One of the most influential Catholics in Washington, the judicial activist Leonard Leo of the Federalist Society, who had met with Trump during the campaign to advise him on Supreme Court nominations, loomed large over the Gorsuch nomination. Leo rose to prominence more than a decade earlier when he served as the national cochair for Catholic outreach for the Republican National Committee and as a Catholic strategist for George W. Bush's 2004 presidential campaign.

Buried in the Senate's sixty-eight-page questionnaire of Judge Gorsuch, the nominee was asked to describe how he had come to President Trump's attention. "I was contacted by Leonard Leo," Gorsuch wrote. In a speech at the Conservative Political Action Conference a few weeks after the nomination, the prolific fundraiser and architect of Republican judicial strategy stressed that "how we deal with this vacancy now, the strength that we as the pro-Constitution movement demonstrate in this fight, will determine the extent to which we are able to both nominate and confirm pro-Constitution judges as we move forward."[77] Conservative Catholic advocacy groups and antiabortion organizations cheered the nomination of Gorsuch, who was raised Catholic and now worships in an Episcopalian church. Catholic Vote praised Gorsuch for his "outstanding track record of faithfully applying the law and defending the Constitution—including in two cases where he ruled in favor of Hobby Lobby and the Little Sisters of the Poor—upholding religious liberty for all." The organization quickly launched a campaign to support the nominee. "This is the fight we have been waiting for!" the group said in a fundraising email to supporters.[78] Marjorie Dannenfelser of the Susan B. Anthony List called the nomination "the swift fulfillment of President Trump's commitment to appoint pro-life Supreme Court justices," and a "tremendous win for the pro-life movement."[79] Ashley McGuire of the Catholic Association, which paid Leo $100,000 in consulting fees in 2016 according to the *Washington Post,* touted Gorsuch's record upholding "the Constitutional right to free exercise of religion without government bullying."[80]

Leo took a leave of absence from the Federalist Society to lead the Trump administration's nomination process for Gorsuch, who was confirmed by the Senate on a mostly party-line vote a little over two months after his nomination. The following year, Gorsuch's influence on the court was visible when he voted with the narrow 5–4 majority on decisions upholding Trump's travel ban and in the court's ruling that a California law requiring crisis pregnancy centers to provide information about abortion likely violated the First Amendment. Religious and social conservatives felt vindicated in their support for Trump. "These 5–4 decisions remind us of the key role Justice Neil Gorsuch plays on the Supreme Court and why 81 percent of evangelicals voted for President Trump," said Penny Nance, president of the Concerned Women for America.[81] The Susan B. Anthony List's Dannenfelser called the ruling on pregnancy centers "wind in the sails for President Trump's overall pro-life agenda," and stressed the importance of the Supreme Court for her organization's strategy for the midterm elections. "There could be one or several vacancies on the Supreme Court in the next two years," she said. "President Trump is committed to nominating pro-life justices, but in order to confirm them, we must have a pro-life majority in the Senate."[82] A year later, Trump again had the opportunity to shift the court to the right for decades to come when he nominated fifty-three-year-old Brett Kavanaugh, a federal appeals court judge, to replace the retiring Justice Anthony Kennedy. Kavanaugh graduated from the same all-male Jesuit high school, Georgetown Preparatory School, that Supreme Court Justice Neal Gorsuch did. Kavanaugh highlighted his Catholic faith during an announcement ceremony at the White House. "The motto of my Jesuit high school was 'men for others,'" he said at a White House announcement ceremony. "I am part of the vibrant Catholic community in the D.C. area. The members of that community disagree about many things, but we are united by a commitment to serve. Father John Enzler is here. Forty years ago, I was an altar boy for Father John. These days, I help him serve meals to the homeless at Catholic Charities."[83]

In *America* magazine, the influential Jesuit publication, the editors took a surprisingly direct and controversial position on the justice's nomination. "At this juncture, anyone who recognizes the humanity of the unborn should support the nomination of a justice who would help return this issue to the legislative arena," the editors wrote. "Overturning *Roe* would save lives and undo a moral and constitutional travesty."[84] But the nomination quickly became explosive after Christine Blasey Ford, a Palo Alto University professor, accused Kavanaugh of sexually assaulting her at a high school party. Ford's painful, riveting testimony—and Kavanaugh's emotional, at times angry denials—became part of a broader national debate over male privilege and sexual assault at a time when the #MeToo movement had punctured the silence often surrounding these issues in the past. The hearings surfaced tensions not only along traditional ideological lines but also within the highly politicized Catholic community in the nation's capital. "Brett Kavanaugh's nomination is dividing his DC Catholic Church," read a *Washington Post* headline. "The tension today, some members say, has been fueled in part by partisanship but perhaps even more so by differences in class and social associations that Kavanaugh represents, and ideas about what the Catholic faith requires of its adherents," the *Post* reported. "Those whose children attend the Blessed Sacrament school and belong to nearby elite country clubs are more apt to support Kavanaugh, who travels in the same circles, than are those whose children attend local public schools and lead somewhat more modest lives, they say. Perhaps the biggest dividing line is between those who see no connection at all between clergy abuse accusers and Kavanaugh's accusers, and those who view the topics as inextricably bound together."[85] Two months after endorsing Kavanaugh's nomination, *America* magazine withdrew its support. "If Dr. Blasey's allegation is true, the assault and Judge Kavanaugh's denial of it mean that he should not be seated on the U.S. Supreme Court," the editors wrote. "But even if the credibility of the allegation has not been established beyond a reasonable doubt and even if further investigation is warranted to determine its validity or clear Judge Kavanaugh's name, we recognize that this nomination is no longer in the best interests of the country."[86] If Senate Republicans proceeded with his nomination, the editors added, "they will be prioritizing policy aims over a woman's report of an assault. Were he to be confirmed without this allegation being firmly disproved, it would hang over his future decisions on the Supreme Court for decades and further divide the country." Kavanaugh was confirmed to the Supreme Court by one of the narrowest margins in history.

CATHOLIC ACTIVISM IN THE TRUMP ERA

Catholic divisions over Trump were not only relegated to Supreme Court battles and the fight to overturn *Roe*. The Trump era was barely a month old when I traveled to Modesto, California, to report on a unique three-day gathering that brought together an eclectic mix of Catholic advocates, ecumenical faith-based organizers, immigrants, a cardinal representing the Vatican, secular activists, and more than a dozen US bishops. Nearly 700 people packed into Central Catholic High School for the first US gathering of the World Meeting of Popular Movements, a global effort launched by Pope Francis as a convening space for grassroots organizers in the church and civil society. The meeting in California was organized by PICO National Network (now called Faith in Action), the US bishops' signature antipoverty initiative, the Catholic Campaign for Human Development, and the Vatican's office for Promoting Integral Human Development.

When I arrived, twenty-five chairs in front of the gym stage sat conspicuously empty, T-shirts draped over them with "*Presente!*" written on each. The seats should have been filled by participants, all undocumented immigrants, but they decided the travel risk was too great. Planning for the Modesto gathering began long before Donald Trump entered the White House. But the fear, anxiety, and anger his administration had provoked were palpable during the panel discussions, raw personal testimonies, and small break-out sessions in classrooms spread across the school's campus. Modesto is not a high-profile spot on the media, financial, or political map. Organizers chose the location because the city brought into sharp focus core themes on the meeting's agenda: economic inequality, high rates of incarceration for young people of color, the disproportionate impact environmental degradation has on the poor, and the myriad challenges faced by a large population of undocumented immigrants.

Cardinal Joe Tobin of Newark, New Jersey, didn't tip-toe around the charged political backdrop during a video message he sent on the first day of the meeting. "As we look around our beloved country, we can see dark clouds gathering," Tobin said. "Your work of building community and calling all of us to truly 'see' one another is needed now more than ever." The powerful, Tobin continued, "demonize excluded groups—people who look, sound, or believe differently from the dominant group. This act of misdirection—channeling the anger of anxious people toward 'the other' rather than toward the architects of the economy of exclusion—is a classic tactic of a populist leader."[87] In another speech at the event, Archbishop José Gomez of Los Angeles noted that more than forty languages are spoken in his city, which is home to a million undocumented immigrants. "People are afraid," Gomez said. "Our brothers and sisters are hurting. Children are terrified. Any day they can come home and find their parents deported. It isn't right. Even if they broke the law, they are still human beings and have rights. . . . I don't like the tone coming out of the administration. The bishops are making clear we oppose the executive orders put out by President Trump." Gomez urged the group to study the farmworkers movement and what he called "the beautiful example of Cesar Chavez." "At the heart of activism," the archbishop said, "is the Beatitudes."[88]

The strong words were not enough for Andrea Mercado, the campaign director for the National Domestic Workers Alliance. "With all due respect to Archbishop Gomez and his work in LA, but we do not hear the Catholic church speaking out enough," said Mercado, who took part in a 100-mile pilgrimage from an immigrant detention center in Pennsylvania to Washington when Pope Francis visited the United States in 2015. "Be bold! Take action! Offer sanctuary to immigrants!"[89] The delegates were on their feet, cheering loudly. During a small break-out group session inside a classroom with pictures of Jackie Robinson, Abraham Lincoln, and Martin Luther King Jr. hanging on the walls, a dozen participants squeezed into undersized desks. Frustration bubbled to the surface. Catalina Morales, twenty-five, was raised in a proud Catholic family and is an organizer in Minnesota for ISAIAH, a faith-based organizing network that includes hundreds of congregations around the state. "She is saying what people need to hear," Morales remarked about the speaker from the National Domestic Workers Alliance who challenged the Catholic Church to be bolder in defending immigrants. Tears welled up in her eyes, and her voice crackled with emotion. In her work with nearly two dozen congregations in Minnesota, Morales has found that Catholic churches are the most cautious about becoming a sanctuary parish that would provide refuge for undocumented immigrants. Some priests and parish leaders have confided to her that the caution around not joining other Christian denominations embracing sanctuary comes, in part, from not wanting to alienate white, conservative parishioners who contribute the most financially to the parish. "You have churches choosing money over the lives of human beings," Morales said.[90]

When San Diego Bishop Robert McElroy took the stage, he began by reminding the diverse audience, not all of whom were Catholic or Christian, that Catholics have long been at the forefront of social-justice activism. From "worker movements of Catholic action in France, Belgium, and Italy to Pope John XXIII's call to restructure the economies of the world in *Mater et magistra*, to the piercing missionary message of the Latin American church, the words 'see,' 'judge' and 'act' have provided a powerful pathway for those who seek to renew the temporal order, in the light of the Gospel and justice," he said. But at this "pivotal moment as a people and a nation," the bishop warned, "our very ability to see, judge and act on behalf of justice is being endangered by cultural currents which leave us isolated, embittered and angry." McElroy's pace and energy picked up.

> President Trump was the candidate of disruption. He was "the disruptor." Well now, we must all become disruptors. We must disrupt those who would seek to send troops into our streets to deport the undocumented, to rip mothers and fathers from their families. We must disrupt those who portray refugees as enemies rather than our brothers and sisters in terrible need. We must disrupt those who train

> us to see Muslim men, women and children as forces of fear rather than as children of God. We must disrupt those who seek to rob our medical care, especially from the poor. We must disrupt those who would take even food stamps and nutrition assistance from the mouths of children.[91]

Many in the overflow crowd of organizers, immigrants, and clergy in the stuffy Catholic high school gymnasium rose to their feet. "But we, as people of faith, as disciples of Jesus Christ, as children of Abraham, as followers of the Prophet Muhammad, of people of all faiths and no faith, we cannot merely be disruptors, we also have to be rebuilders," the bishop continued.

> We have to rebuild this nation so that we place at its heart the service to the dignity of the human person and assert what that flag behind us asserts is our heritage: Every man, woman and child is equal in this nation and called to be equal. We must rebuild a nation in solidarity, what Catholic teaching calls the sense that all of us are the children of the one God, there are no children of a lesser god in our midst.[92]

For three minutes, the bishop received a standing ovation. I noticed people wiping away tears. In a meeting filled with progressive activists, some of whom openly expressed frustration with the Catholic hierarchy's lack of urgency to confront Trump, McElroy's speech did what too few Catholic leaders had managed to do since the election. He used the gospels and Catholic social teaching to draw a bright moral line in the sand. "I was sad and embarrassed that so many Catholics voted for Trump," Ellie Hidalgo, at the time a pastoral associate at Dolores Mission Church, a Jesuit parish in East Los Angeles, told me after the speech. "But listening to Bishop McElroy gave me hope and made me proud to be Catholic. It helped me reconnect with the great history of Catholic social teaching. We stand on the shoulders of giants. Other Catholics have struggled for justice and gave us this rich heritage. It's now our moment."[93]

Even as progressive Catholic activists and a handful of bishops spoke out directly against Trump, other Catholics energized by his election were also organizing. A month after I returned from Modesto to my home in Washington, DC, I heard that a group of well-heeled, politically active conservative Catholics planned to meet at the Trump International Hotel in Washington for a two-day, $1,250-a-person symposium. Billed as an exclusive gathering of "Catholic leaders, clergy and important DC insiders," the event didn't sound like your typical religious conference. I coughed up the hefty registration fee. The gathering in downtown Washington was a long way from that crowded Catholic school gymnasium in Modesto. Over three-course dinners, wine receptions, and panel discussions, the symposium featured a mix of networking, liturgies, wonky policy discussions, and political chattering. Timothy Busch, a prominent Catholic philanthropist who owns several luxury hotels and the Napa-based vineyard Trinity Cellars, helped organize the meeting for the Napa Institute. Cofounded in 2010 by Busch and then Philadelphia Archbishop Charles Chaput, the institute was established to respond to what the archbishop lamented was "the next America," a time of growing secularization and perceived hostility toward traditional religious believers. Busch set the tone at the conference by praising Trump at a National Press Club dinner attended by Supreme Court Justice Samuel Alito. "We were headed down a path that was pretty dark with a Supreme Court decision redefining marriage," he told a crowd of about a hundred business leaders, clergy, religious liberty attorneys, and conservative activists.[94] While acknowledging that President Trump's policies and rhetoric toward immigrants didn't align with Catholic teaching, he spoke in buoyant terms about the new political potential in Washington. "In the early weeks of this administration more has been done to address the biggest tragedy, the biggest catastrophe, and that is abortion," said Busch, an attorney in Orange County, California, whose firm specializes in estate planning and other services for wealthy clients. "More has been done to benefit the causes of life, which is more important than anything we have in our society. . . . Everything else is trumped by this issue of life." Busch raised the case of the Little Sisters of the Poor, who sued the Obama administration over contraception-coverage requirements in the Affordable Care Act. Trump, he said, would work to dismantle those requirements. "I told one of the sisters today that it's over for the devil. It is over for evil. It is over for that compromise of religious liberty," Busch said to loud applause.[95] The next morning, in a Trump hotel conference room with chandeliers and gold-trimmed mirrors, the praise for the president continued to flow. "What this administration represents is freedom," Busch told the gathering. "The cabinet appointments and Supreme Court appointments have been stellar. It may be that the personality of the president is not to our liking, but it may be the only personality that can change the government and the status quo."

During one panel session, Carter Snead, a law professor and director of the de Nicola Center for Ethics and Culture at the University of Notre Dame, praised then Health and Human Services Secretary Tom Price as a "pro-life" physician who could take steps to allow states to defund Planned Parenthood. Snead also described key presidential adviser Stephen K. Bannon and

Attorney General Jeff Sessions as "pro-life." Trump, he said, gave an "important cultural symbol to the pro-life movement" by sending Vice President Pence and adviser Kellyanne Conway to the annual March for Life. "The pro-life movement is back at the White House," Snead declared.[96] The meeting also included time for prayer and religious observance. Before a Mass in the crypt of the Basilica of the National Shrine of the Immaculate Conception, participants prayed a "Patriotic Rosary for the Consecration of our Nation" that included readings from George Washington and John Adams. I was most unsettled by a reading in the rosary booklet from General Robert E. Lee that appealed to God "in the defense of our homes and our liberties, thanking Him for His past blessings, and imploring their continuance upon our cause and our people."[97] In 1863 "the cause" was slavery, and the defense of southern homes was armed resistance to the North. Mixing Lee and the southern cause with the rosary—especially at a time when the "alt-right" and white Christian nationalism were basking in the glow of renewed attention and proximity to power—was cringeworthy.

Allies of Pope Francis in Rome were paying close attention to the reinvigorated Catholic activism on the right as Trump settled into power. In an essay in the Vatican-vetted journal *La Civiltà Cattolica,* published in July 2017, two close associates of Pope Francis offered a blistering critique of the way conservative Catholics and Christian evangelicals in the United States had teamed up on some issues at the heart of Trump's agenda. The authors, Fr. Antonio Spadaro, the journal's editor, and Marcelo Figueroa, an Argentine Presbyterian minister who is a longtime friend and collaborator with Pope Francis, took particular issue with President Trump's chief strategist, Steve Bannon, whom they described as a "supporter of an apocalyptic geopolitics" and someone who has thwarted action on climate change and exploited fears of migrants and Muslims with calls for what the authors described as "walls and purifying deportations."[98] Bannon, a Catholic, has long touted right-wing nationalism and cultivated relationships with conservative bishops in Rome who have clashed with Pope Francis. He has also sought alliances with reactionary populist leaders in Europe such as Marine Le Pen, the National Front leader in France. "Let them call you racist, let them call you xenophobes, let them call you nativists," Bannon said in a 2018 speech to a National Front conference. "Because every day we get stronger and they get weaker."[99] In a 2014 speech delivered via Skype to a conference at the Vatican organized by the conservative Institute for Human Dignity, Bannon declared there was a "global tea party movement," praised European far-right political parties, and framed the future as a fight between the "Judeo-Christian" West and what he called "jihadist Islamic fascism." "We're at the very beginning stages of a very brutal and bloody conflict, of which if the people in this room, the people in the church, do not bind together and really form what I feel is an aspect of the church militant, to really be able to not just stand with our beliefs, but to fight for our beliefs against this new barbarity that's starting, that will completely eradicate everything that we've been bequeathed over the last 2,000, 2,500 years," Bannon told the conference.[100]

Two months after the Vatican journal challenged Bannon and warned about the Catholic–evangelical alliance on the Christian right, hundreds of white supremacists—some clearly emboldened by the president's nationalist, anti-immigrant rhetoric—marched on Charlottesville, Virginia. Holding torches and chanting, "You will not replace us! Jews will not replace us!," the group of neo-Nazis, white Christian nationalists, and their supporters—several wearing "Make America Great Again" hats—clashed with counter-protestors at a "Unite the Right" rally at a park once named for Confederate General Robert E. Lee. James Alex Fields Jr., a former teacher who later said he was fascinated by Nazism and Hitler, drove his car into the crowd and killed thirty-two-year-old Heather Heyer. Dozens of others were injured. In his initial televised remarks, President Trump condemned the "egregious display of hatred, bigotry and violence on many sides" and called for the "swift restoration of law and order." Speaking with reporters a few days later, the president drew a false equivalence between the white supremacists and counterprotestors. "What about the alt-left that came charging at, as you say, at the alt-right?" Trump asked in the lobby of Trump Tower. "Do they have any semblance of guilt? I've condemned neo-Nazis. I've condemned many different groups. But not all of those people were neo-Nazis, believe me. You had many people in that group other than neo-Nazis and white nationalists. The press has treated them absolutely unfairly. You also had some very fine people on both sides."[101] The president then questioned the removal of Confederate statues by equating them with other monuments. "Many of those people were there to protest the taking down of the statue of Robert E. Lee," Trump said. "This week it is Robert E. Lee. And I notice that Stonewall Jackson is coming down. I wonder, is it George Washington next? And is it Thomas Jefferson the week after? You know, you have to ask yourself, where does it stop?[102]

A month after the white nationalist violence in Charlottesville, Trump ended an Obama-era program that had protected nearly 800,000 young undocumented immigrants from deportation. Often called "Dreamers," the immigrants were brought to the United States as children by their parents. "I do not favor punishing children, most of whom are now adults, for the actions of their parents," the president announced in a statement about taking a position that would do exactly this. "But we must also recognize that we are a nation of opportunity *because* we are a nation of laws."[103] Catholic and other religious leaders widely denounced the move. "The President of the United States presents himself as pro-life and if he is a good pro-lifer, he understands that family is the cradle of life and its unity must be protected," Pope Francis said when asked about Trump's action. A policy that would hurt immigrant youth, the pope added, "isn't something that bears fruit for either the youngsters or their families."[104] The US bishops' conference called it "reprehensible," "heartbreaking," and "the opposite of how Scripture calls us to respond."[105] New York Cardinal Timothy Dolan said the president had turned young immigrants into "political hockey pucks" and that ending the program "is certainly not Christian."[106] Even Steve Bannon, who joined the administration from Breitbart, an online media outlet that he once described as "the platform for the alt right," publicly disagreed with the president.[107]

But the Catholic, who played a key role in shaping many of Trump's anti-immigrant, "America First" policies as the White House's chief strategist during his one year with the administration, also went on the attack after Catholic leaders denounced the president's order. "The Catholic Church has been terrible about this," Bannon told CBS in an interview. "The bishops have been terrible about this. . . . Because they're unable to really—to come to grips with the problems in the church, they need illegal aliens. They need illegal aliens to fill the churches. It's obvious on the face of it. They have an economic interest. They have an economic interest in unlimited immigration, unlimited illegal immigration." Bannon continued: "As much as I respect Cardinal Dolan and the bishops on doctrine, this is not doctrine. This is not doctrine at all. I totally respect the pope, and I totally respect the Catholic bishops and cardinals on doctrine. This is not about doctrine. This is about the sovereignty of a nation. And in that regard, they're just another guy with an opinion."[108] A person who liked to style himself as a defender of Judeo-Christian values was content with ignoring biblical commands to "love the alien as yourself." Bannon's real endgame was clear. He understood that an increasingly diverse Catholic Church that uses its institutional weight to speak out for immigrants represents a political threat to the mainstreaming of nationalism. Trump's ascent to the presidency, built in part on the backlash politics of inflaming white fear, was evidenced in Bannon's vision of a fortress nation that kept out immigrants, refugees, and anyone deemed a threat to white Christian culture. Bannon wanted to drive a wedge between Catholic voters and church leadership—keeping the white Catholics who were pivotal to Trump's victory afraid and politically mobilized—while also trying to dampen the power of an emerging generation of Latino Catholics who threatened the nationalists' endgame.

The Trump administration dramatically escalated its targeting of immigrants in 2018. At the beginning of that year, the president ended Temporary Protected Status (TPS) for more than 200,000 people from El Salvador. The humanitarian and historically bipartisan program had allowed Salvadorans to live and work legally in the United States since a pair of devastating earthquakes struck the country in 2001. The change of policy, announced during the US bishops' annual National Migration Week, came just weeks after more than 45,000 Haitians lost protections that were offered to them after a 2010 earthquake struck their country. Sister Donna Markham, CEO of Catholic Charities USA at the time, described the president's action as "devastating not only for the 250,000 Salvadorans who have established themselves in this country as trusted employees, neighbors and members of the community but also for the nearly two-hundred thousand children who are citizens of this country and face either being separated from their families or leaving the only country they have ever known."[109] While many Catholic leaders decried the administration's moves, one of the most influential Catholics on Trump's team drew attention for his demeaning depiction of young immigrants. Commenting on the administration's roll-back of the Deferred Action for Childhood Arrivals (DACA), White House chief of staff John Kelly said many undocumented immigrants were either "too afraid" or "too lazy to get off their asses" and apply for legal protections under the Obama-era program, according to an audio recording obtained by the *Washington Post.*[110] Criticized by immigrant rights groups, Kelly didn't back down, saying more immigrants should have "probably gotten off the couch and signed up."[111] Kelly's rhetoric evoked the long history of Republican leaders using coded or explicit language to fuel stereotypes about people of color as lazy and dependent—whether Ronald Reagan taking aim at so-called "welfare queens," Newt Gingrich calling Barack Obama the "food stamp President," or former Rep. Paul Ryan's description of "makers and takers" to pit hard-working Americans against welfare recipients. An Irish American Catholic from Boston, Kelly was trafficking in a familiar style of pernicious caricature. Irish Catholic immigrants were similarly demonized in the nineteenth century when they fled the potato famine. Like the parents of today's young immigrants, these migrants took considerable risks in search of a better life for their families. The Irish Catholics were viewed as so alien to the Anglo-Saxon Protestant majority they were not even regarded by many as white. "In the popular press, the Irish were depicted as subhuman," the *Boston Globe* noted in a 2016 article.

"They were carriers of disease. They were drawn as lazy, clannish, unclean, drunken brawlers who wallowed in crime and bred like rats."[112]

Working in tandem with a broad coalition of interfaith religious activists, Catholic social justice leaders found renewed purpose and energy responding to the Trump administration's attacks on Muslims, immigrants, and other vulnerable groups. Trump's presidency brought an urgency to progressive religious organizing not found since the civil rights movement. A part of that revived tradition included the use of nonviolent civil disobedience. Frustrated that statements denouncing Trump's policies were not making a difference or attracting only coverage in the religious press, Catholic justice leaders mobilized for a "National Catholic Day of Action for Dreamers" on February 27, 2018. Two hundred Catholic advocates marched on Capitol Hill to challenge President Trump's anti-immigrant policies and risk arrest. I also joined the protest. "We have to insist that it's not a time to wait around anymore—our Dreamers have heard plenty of false promises, but their lives are on hold," said Bishop John Stowe of Lexington, Kentucky, addressing the crowd on the Capitol lawn.[113] Rev. Thomas Reese, a Jesuit priest and prominent Catholic writer, singled out House Speaker Paul Ryan, who frequently referenced his Catholic faith during his political career. Reese criticized what he saw as Ryan's failure to pass legislation restoring protection for young immigrant Dreamers and invoked a passage from the Book of Acts where the Apostle Paul is asked by God why he persecutes Christians.

"Speaker Paul Ryan needs to hear those words, so let's tell him: 'Paul, why do you persecute me?!'" Reese shouted as the crowd took up the chant and headed into the rotunda of the Russell Senate Office Building.[114] "I have never been arrested in my life, but with the blessing of my community, I am risking arrest today as an act of solidarity with our wonderful Dreamers," Sister Elise Garcia of the Adrian Dominican Sisters, who traveled from Michigan to participate, told a reporter. "To our leaders in Congress and in the White House, I say: Arrest a nun, not a Dreamer!"[115] Inside the rotunda the demonstrators stood in a circle singing "Amazing Grace" and praying the rosary. Some held signs with "Catholics for Dream Act" on a poster board with an image of the Virgin of Guadalupe. Bishop Stowe followed the procession to the Senate office building. As congressional staff watched from the balcony and television cameras angled for close-ups, the bishop stood in the sun-streaked center of the rotunda and blessed those of us about to get arrested for peacefully congregating. "We stand with the Dreamers. We are one with the Dreamers," the bishop said, extending his hand over the group. "And now I ask God's blessing upon those who are acting in civil disobedience, part of a longstanding tradition of not supporting unjust laws."[116]

Capitol Police warned us to disperse three times. We continued our Hail Marys as police handcuffed us and slowly led us out to police vans to be arrested, fingerprinted, and released after paying a fine. Forty Catholics, many of them older nuns, were arrested that day. The peaceful protest and solidarity march attracted national media attention.

Similar acts of faith-based activism in response to President Trump's policies were also happening at the state level. Fr. Chris Wadelton, pastor of a largely Hispanic congregation in Indianapolis, decided to participate in civil disobedience for the first time to dramatize the threats immigrants faced under Trump. "If your letters and rallies and talks don't seem to be working, civil disobedience is the natural next step," Wadelton told me at the time.[117] When Sister Tracey Horan, an organizer with Faith in Indiana—a network with more than sixty congregations from various denominations across the state—called for blocking a downtown street to call attention to the plight of Dreamers, the priest eagerly participated. A few hundred activists shut down the corner of Pennsylvania and Ohio Street, near the offices of the state's US senators. Nineteen people, including Wadelton, were arrested. "It's a strong public statement," he said. "It shows you're willing to put yourself out there. We have complete control over whether we get arrested or not. But immigrants can go to work in the morning and end up in detention by the afternoon. It's intolerable. We need to respond." A month after the Catholic day of action in Washington, I sat in a nondescript conference room on Capitol Hill. "Please hear the stories of immigrants," Bishop Mark Seitz of El Paso, Texas, one of the most vocal Catholic leaders on the border, implored about seventy-five congressional staff members during a briefing at the Capitol. "Don't let the political morass in Washington take you over. Stand for something. Listen to your conscience," he said.[118] At the briefing the El Paso–based Hope Border Institute released a report—"Sealing the Border: The Criminalization of Asylum Seekers in the Trump Era"—that detailed human-rights violations by immigration-enforcement agencies against migrants and asylum seekers.[119]

Dylan Corbett, executive director of the Hope Border Institute, explained that the militarization of the border has come at both a human and fiscal cost. President Trump's insistence on more fencing on the border to stop crime and violence, he told the congressional staffers, is a solution in search of a problem. According to FBI data, El Paso and other border communities have been ranked as some of the safest cities in the country. "The wall is not addressing an actual policy problem," Corbett said. "It's political theater." While border fencing is usually talked about as a simple security issue, the reality is more complicated, he explained. The original wall in El

Paso, constructed in the 1990s between El Paso and Ciudad Juarez, Mexico, was built at the same time as the North American Free Trade Agreement (NAFTA), which became a boon to US corporations even as hundreds of thousands of factory workers just across the border in Mexico faced dire conditions. "The motivations for putting up that wall are economic," Corbett said. "It ensures the flow of capital, but poor people, brown people, can't travel freely. We are morally complicit in many of the root causes that drive migration—free trade deals, our drug consumption. We are involved. To build a wall is to close our eyes to our ethical responsibilities."[120]

The Trump administration continued announcing more draconian immigration enforcement measures. Attorney General Jeff Sessions explained perhaps the most cruel and inhumane policy shift in early May 2018 when the administration decided on a "zero-tolerance" policy that would separate immigrant children from their parents when they were apprehended crossing the border. "Today we're here to send a message to the world that we are not going to let the country be overwhelmed," Sessions said in a speech. "People are not going to caravan or otherwise stampede our border. . . . If you are smuggling a child then we will prosecute you, and that child will be separated from you as required by law."[121] The US bishops' conference and even some conservative evangelical Christian leaders swiftly denounced the policy. But the nation's largest pro-life organizations, incapable of summoning any critique of Trump, were silent. "We refrain from public comment on immigration and many other topics, including other policies that impact families," the Susan B. Anthony List's Marjorie Dannenfelser told reporters.[122] David O'Steen, executive director of National Right to Life Committee, said the organization was busy enough "trying to stop the killing of babies." "There are many policies on which we have no stand, for or against," O'Steen said. "We're not on either side of this issue."[123] The nation's leading pro-life organizations were again willing to accommodate the worst of Trumpism. Charles Camosy, an antiabortion advocate and a Catholic professor of theology, highlighted the hypocrisy in a *New York Times* op-ed entitled "You Can't Be Pro-Life and against Immigrant Children." Camosy wrote:

> Where is National Right to Life? Where is the Susan B. Anthony List. . . . In standing by President Trump and his administration—and, indeed, in now honoring him as their standard-bearer—traditional pro-life leaders have put short-term and uncertain political gain ahead of consistent moral principle. Because of their support of the president and general silence on his administration's actions, the major players in the pro-life movement are now tethered to his

> horrific border policies. This presents a real threat to the broader movement's capacity to be taken seriously by young people and people of color. The silence on the border policies is not a simple question of groups keeping a focus solely on abortion. Many pro-life organizations also do extensive work opposing euthanasia. There is nothing in principle compelling such organizations to ignore anti-life and anti-family border policies. If the traditional pro-life movement is to regain credibility as something other than a tool of the Trump administration, it must speak out clearly and forcefully against harming innocent children as a means of deterring undocumented immigration.[124]

Attorney General Sessions faced challenges from a range of religious leaders, including lay leaders from his own denomination, after he shamelessly tried to justify the family separation policy and the Trump administration's broader anti-immigrant policies by citing the Bible. "I would cite you to the Apostle Paul and his clear and wise command in Romans 13, to obey the laws of the government because God has ordained the government for his purposes," the nation's top law enforcement official said in a speech defending the policies. "Orderly and lawful processes are good in themselves. Consistent, fair application of the law is in itself a good and moral thing, and that protects the weak and protects the lawful."[125] More than six hundred members of the United Methodist Church filed a formal complaint against Sessions in a letter that accused him of "dissemination of doctrines contrary to the standards of doctrine of the United Methodist Church." Sessions's support and advocacy for "holding thousands of young children in mass incarceration facilities with little to no structured educational or socio-emotional support" and for "directing employees and staff members to kidnap children from their parents" falls in violation of the Methodists' Book of Discipline, the Methodists argued in the letter.[126]

Reports from the border were gut-wrenching. Federal authorities took a child from her mother as she was breastfeeding, an attorney with the Texas Civil Rights Project told reporters. Journalists and human rights advocates toured an old warehouse in McAllen, Texas, where hundreds of children were being kept in a series of cages made of metal fencing. The *Associated Press* reported that overhead lighting stayed on around the clock, children slept under "large foil sheets," older children were forced to change the diapers of toddlers, and children had no books or toys.[127] The Pulitzer Prize–winning investigative outlet *ProPublica* published audio clips of Central American children separated from their parents sobbing in cages and shouting for their parents.[128] Between April 19 and May 31 of 2018, nearly two thousand children were sent to mass detention centers or foster care.[129] "I appreciate the need to enforce and protect our international boundaries, but this zero-tolerance policy is cruel," former First Lady Laura Bush wrote in a *Washington Post* commentary. "It is immoral. And it breaks my heart. Our government should not be in the business of warehousing children in converted box stores or making plans to place them in tent cities in the desert outside of El Paso. These images are eerily reminiscent of the internment camps for U.S. citizens and noncitizens of Japanese descent during World War II, now considered to have been one of the most shameful episodes in U.S. history."[130]

While the Obama administration deserved the persistent criticism it received from immigration reform advocates for deporting more than two million undocumented immigrants during his presidency, President Trump gave Immigration and Custom Enforcement (ICE) vast power to detain and deport migrants that previous administrations did not view as a threat. Parents who had lived in the United States for many years, held jobs, paid taxes, and were raising their children were swept up in the Trump administration's intensified enforcement regime. I interviewed Edith Espinal, a Catholic mother, who was targeted for deportation back to her native Mexico in the fall of 2017. Soft-spoken and prayerful, Espinal did not fit the profile of the "bad hombres" Trump promised to deport during the campaign. Instead of complying with her deportation order and leaving her children behind in the United States, Edith sought sanctuary at Columbus Mennonite Church, where she lived for more than three years during Trump's presidency. "I'm a mother and I'm fighting to keep my family together," Espinal told me in 2020.[131] "This is the country where my children were born, and it's the only country they know. I want my children to have opportunities for a better future. The truth is I can't even imagine going back to Mexico. My family is here." (Espinal was able to leave the church in 2021 and reunite with her children in Columbus after Biden administration policy changes meant she was no longer considered an enforcement priority.) Espinal told me that during the hardest days of isolation, she turned to her Catholic faith and a prayer, the Magnificat, drawn from the Gospel of Luke: "He has shown might with His arm, He has scattered the proud in the conceit of their heart, He has put down the mighty from their thrones, and has exalted the lowly, He has filled the hungry with good things, and the rich He has sent away empty."

The detention of immigrant children continued to galvanize faith-based responses. On a steamy July day in 2019, Catholic advocates again mobilized in Washington. Hundreds of Catholics, organized by a coalition of groups including the Sisters of Mercy and the Leadership Conference of Women Religious, gathered outside the Capitol to urge the Trump administration to end its inhumane detention policies. "We hope that by being here and putting our bodies on the line, we can give people, members of Congress, courage to do the right thing," Sister Marge Clark, from the Sisters of Charity of the Blessed Virgin Mary, told a reporter.[132] "It's important to go beyond words, to put your body where your words are, where your beliefs are." Demonstrators carried photographs of migrant children who died in federal custody into the Russell Senate Office Building, where more than thirty senators have offices. As five protesters lay on the floor of the rotunda to make the shape of a cross with their bodies, the group recited the children's names: "Darlyn," protestors chanted in unison. "Jakelin. Felipe. Juan. Wilmer. Carlos." Seventy Catholic clergy, sisters, and other advocates were arrested for failing to disperse. "We are here today because of our faith. The gospel compels us to act," Sister Ann Scholz from the Leadership Conference of Women Religious told the crowd.

A week after Catholic activists were being led away from the Capitol in handcuffs, a high-profile Catholic in the Trump administration announced the federal government would resume capital punishment after a nearly two-decade lapse. The president had picked William Barr to lead the Justice Department a year earlier in the wake of firing his previous attorney general, Jeff Sessions. The decision to bring back federal executions was another reminder that Catholic enablers of Trump who viewed themselves as orthodox defenders of the faith were content to ignore church teaching when it inconvenienced their own political ideology. Both John Paul II and Benedict XVI were vocal opponents of the death penalty. In the summer of 2018, a year before Barr became attorney general, Pope Francis announced that the Catechism of the Catholic Church would be officially updated to reflect that the death penalty would in all cases be considered "inadmissible" under church teaching because it is "an attack on the inviolability and dignity of the person."[133] When I interviewed Sister Helen Prejean, the renowned anti-death penalty advocate and author of *Dead Man Walking*, she underscored its historic nature. "Pope John Paul II said that the times when the death penalty could be justified were so rare they would practically be nonexistent. But this did reserve the use of the death penalty in cases of absolute necessities," Prejean told me. "Pope Francis has now established a foundational principle that no matter the severity of the crime, it's never legitimate."[134]

Barr was not simply any Catholic. The attorney general was one of the most influential leaders in the country, revered by many conservative Catholic activists and scholars as a staunch defender of pro-life values. As the head of the Justice Department, he now had direct authority over the federal government's role in overseeing a punishment that his own church teaches is an attack on the dignity of life. Barr never shied away from connecting his faith and politics. In fact, he seemed to relish the culture wars and often depicted traditional believers as victims of a hostile secularism. The public dissonance created by his role in overseeing federal executions despite church teaching on capital punishment didn't cause Barr to back away from speaking about the intersection of religion, values, and politics. Three months after he announced the federal government would resume implementing the death penalty, the attorney general gave a widely covered speech at the University of Notre Dame. Barr railed against "militant secularists" and said secularism could be blamed for "virtually every measure of social pathology," including "the wreckage of the family," "soaring suicide rates," "alienated young males," and a host of other social ills. "Suffice it to say that the campaign to destroy the traditional moral order has brought with it immense suffering, wreckage, and misery," the attorney general said at an event hosted by Notre Dame's Law School and the de Nicola Center for Ethics and Culture.[135] Barr lamented what he called the "macro-morality" of the welfare state and of "collective action to address social problems." In contrast he argued that Christianity "teaches a micro-morality" where "we transform the world by focusing on our own personal morality and transformation"—an observation that distorts traditional Catholic teaching about the role of government, the common good, and the collective nature of addressing social sins such as systemic racism, greed, inequality, and an economy of exclusion. While Barr expressed moral outrage at secularists' perceived attacks on traditional religion, he had nothing to say about his own role in promoting a system of punishment that his church had called an attack on human life. "It's profoundly disappointing and even infuriating," Krisanne Vaillancourt Murphy, executive director of the Catholic Mobilizing Network, a national organization that works to end the death penalty, told me when I interviewed her for a profile of Barr published in the *National Catholic Reporter*. "We were hopeful that someone who takes their faith seriously would uphold the sanctity of all life."[136]

IMPEACHMENT AND COVID PANDEMIC

By the fall of 2019, President Trump faced growing scrutiny over allegations that he invited foreign interference in the presidential election and took steps to conceal that activity. Democratic calls for impeachment grew louder. When special counsel Robert Mueller III earlier that spring released a four-hundred-page redacted report examining whether there was coordination between the Trump campaign and Russian operatives, it did not accuse the president of criminal wrongdoing. But the report also did not clear the president of obstructing justice. "If we had confidence after a thorough investigation of the facts that the president clearly did not commit obstruction of justice, we would so state," the report said. The *Wall Street Journal* published a story on September 20 alleging that President Trump in a July phone call repeatedly pressured the president of Ukraine to investigate Joe Biden's son, Hunter, who held a seat on the board of a Ukrainian oil and gas company.[137] It was the first time the public heard details of the call. When the Trump administration released a rough transcript of the conversation, which took place shortly after the president withheld nearly $400 million in aid to the country, there was no direct evidence of a *quid pro quo*, but the context was clear. After reminding the Ukrainian president that the United States had "been very, very good to Ukraine," Trump told the president, "I would like you to do us a favor," and proceeded to say: "There's a lot of talk about Biden's son, that Biden stopped the prosecution, and a lot of people want to find out about that so whatever you can do with the Attorney General would be great."

House Speaker Nancy Pelosi, citing the president's "breach of his Constitutional responsibilities," announced an official impeachment inquiry. "The president must be held accountable," Pelosi said. "No one is above the law." Trump blasted the announcement on Twitter as "a total Witch Hunt!" After public impeachment hearings in the House Intelligence Committee and Judiciary Committee hearings over two months, Pelosi announced in early December that articles of impeachment would be drawn up against the president for abusing the power of his office and obstructing Congress. At a tense press conference, a reporter asked if the speaker hated President Trump. "I don't hate anybody," Pelosi said. "I was raised in a Catholic house. We don't hate anybody, not anybody in the world. Don't accuse me of hate. As a Catholic, I resent your using the word 'hate' in a sentence that addresses me. I don't hate anyone."[138] The House Judiciary Committee spent more than fourteen hours in often emotional debate on December 12 and on the following day approved articles of impeachment. Donald Trump became the fourth president in American history to be impeached by the House. The chamber voted 230–197 to charge the president with abuse of power and 229–198 to charge him with obstruction of justice.

Once again Trump would rely on a loyal cadre of conservative Catholics to defend him, both in legal terms and in the media. Presidential advisor Kellyanne Conway went on EWTN and tried to position the president as a lofty figure who "wants prayers for healing."[139] Bishops remained mostly silent on the impeachment proceedings with the exception of Bishop Thomas Tobin of Providence, Rhode Island, who tweeted that impeachment had "become so very partisan that it's just a political sideshow."[140] The most vocal sycophants for Trump on the Catholic right parroted the president's talking points. After the House voted to impeach, Trump tweeted: "In Reality, They're Not After Me, They're After You. I'm Just in the Way." Fr. Frank Pavone of Priests for Life, one of Trump's Catholic advisors during the campaign, told the far-right Church Militant that "they are after us, not simply the president."[141] Pavone quickly pivoted to the upcoming election. "The choice in this election is between the Culture of Life and the Culture of Death, between America and globalism, between free trade and socialism, between secure borders and open borders, between prosperity and poverty, between security and chaos, between religious freedom and religious oppression, between the Constitution and mob rule," he said. "This is war, and for those who haven't noticed, it's a war the Democrats have declared on people of faith and people who love America."[142] Sister Simone Campbell, then the executive director of NETWORK, framed the showdown differently. "This constitutional crisis is also a spiritual crisis," Campbell said. "Our democracy is in tatters, and the people are divided. The evidence is clear that the President broke the law when he sought the Ukrainian President's support for his presidential campaign. This violates the law. The remedy for such criminal action is impeachment. But this impeachment is also a moral action to reclaim our national integrity."[143]

Trump named his White House counsel, Pat Cipollone, to lead his defense in the Senate impeachment trial. A fifty-three-year-old father of ten, Cipollone was part of a well-connected circle of Catholics wielding power in Washington. Along with Leonard Leo, he helped start the Republican-friendly National Catholic Prayer Breakfast and spent time as a board member of the Catholic Information Center on K Street. In a 2020 interview with the *Washington Post*, Leo said Cipollone cares about "religious freedom, the culture of life."[144] Cipollone, a former corporate lawyer who worked as a speechwriter for William Barr when Barr was attorney general in the first Bush administration, had also served as the general counsel for the Knights of Columbus. The Catholic fraternal organization, historically known for its charitable work, in more recent years had garnered as much attention for its well-funded campaigns against Obamacare and pro-choice Catholic politicians and its major funding of the US bishops' efforts to stop same-sex marriage. At the Knights, Cipollone filed a brief in a Supreme Court abortion case in support of a Nebraska law that outlawed a procedure critics called "partial birth" abortion. The Fox News host Laura Ingraham, a frequent critic of Pope Francis, credits Cipollone with helping her decide to become a Catholic. The first attorney to take the podium to debate the proposed rules for the trial, Cipollone called the proceedings a "partisan impeachment" and urged senators to "end this ridiculous charade" so we can "go have an election."[145]

Utah Senator Mitt Romney, the only Republican who voted to impeach the president, gave an emotional floor speech that frequently cited his Mormon faith. "I am profoundly religious. My faith is at the heart of who I am," Romney said at the end of nearly three weeks of proceedings. "I take an oath before God as enormously consequential. Were I to ignore the evidence that has been presented, and disregard what I believe my oath and the Constitution demands of me for the sake of a partisan end, it would, I fear, expose my character to history's rebuke and the censure of my own conscience."[146] Senators voted largely along party lines to acquit Trump. Two-thirds of the Senate was required to convict the president and remove him from office, which has never happened in American history. The day after his acquittal, Trump attended the National Prayer Breakfast. After walking on stage, the president held up a copy of the *USA Today* front page with a headline "ACQUITTED" in large font. He then held up a copy of the *Washington Post*, showing off its "Trump acquitted" banner headline. Keynote speaker Arthur Brooks, a prominent social scientist and conservative Catholic who writes frequently about faith and values, tried his best to convince the political crowd that something in our country was deeply askew.

"I am here today to talk about what I believe is the biggest crisis facing our nation—and many other nations—today. This is the crisis of contempt—the polarization that is tearing our society apart," the former president of the conservative American Enterprise Institute told the crowd assembled at the Washington Hilton.

> To start us on a path of new thinking to our cultural crisis, I want to turn to the words of the ultimate original thinker, history's greatest social entrepreneur, and as a Catholic, my personal Lord and Savior, Jesus. Here's what he said, as recorded in the Gospel of Saint Matthew, chapter 5, verse 43–45: You have heard that it was said, 'Love your neighbor and hate your enemy.' But I tell you, love your enemies and pray for those who persecute you, that you may be children of your Father in heaven.
>
> Love your enemies! Now *that* is thinking differently. It changed the world starting two thousand years ago, and it is as subversive and counterintuitive today as it was then. But the devil's in the details. How do we do it in a country and world roiled by political hatred and differences that we can't seem to bridge?[147]

When Trump stepped up to the podium after Brooks's speech, the embittered president had a different motive in mind than bridging divides or loving enemies. There were scores to settle. The fact that doing so at a prayer breakfast was crass and unseemly didn't give him pause. "Arthur, I don't know if I agree with you. . . . I don't know if Arthur is going to like what I'm going to say. As everybody knows, my family, our great country, and your president, have been put through a terrible ordeal by some very dishonest and corrupt people," Trump said as House Speaker Pelosi sat a few feet away on the dais. "They have done everything possible to destroy us and by so doing, very badly hurt our nation." In an obvious swipe at Pelosi and Romney, the president said: "I don't like people who use their faith as justification for doing what they know is wrong. Nor do I like people who say, 'I pray for you,' when they know that that's not so."[148]

On the same day Trump lashed out at his political opponents at the prayer breakfast, the US Center for Disease Control and Prevention announced that coronavirus test kits were being shipped to state labs across the country. A new era was beginning. The president initially downplayed the risks of the virus. Reporting by journalist Bob Woodward later revealed the president knew Covid was far more serious.[149] "By April, you know, in theory, when it gets a little warmer, (the coronavirus) miraculously goes away," Trump said at a political rally in New Hampshire on February 10.[150] "The Coronavirus is very much under control in the USA," he tweeted two weeks later. While any presidential administration would have struggled to respond effectively to the outbreak, the United States was less prepared than it should have been after Trump, in the spring of 2018, closed the federal government office responsible for preparing for pandemics. In a primetime Oval Office address on March 11, Trump announced travel restrictions for foreign nationals coming to the United States from Europe's Schengen area. He described the risk of coronavirus as "very, very low" for most Americans even as the World Health Organization on the same day declared the coronavirus outbreak to be a pandemic. Days after Trump addressed the nation, most businesses, bars, restaurants, churches, and workplaces shut down. Schools quickly transitioned to online learning. In what would become an iconic image from the Vatican, Pope Francis walked alone in the rain to a white canopy on the steps of St. Peter's Basilica for a special prayer service on March 27. The somber pope spoke to an eerily empty square that usually drew thousands of people. "We have realized that we are in the same boat, all of us fragile and disoriented, but at the same time important and needed, all of us called to row together, each of us in need of comforting the other," Pope Francis said in an address that praised doctors, nurses, and essential workers still on the job.

The pope urged the world to "reawaken and put into practice that solidarity and hope capable of giving strength, support and meaning to these hours when everything seems to be floundering."[151]

As the deadly virus spread across the globe, the pandemic deepened political divides, exacerbated inequality, and often pitted public health experts against vocal Christian conservatives who argued religious liberty rights were being infringed by lockdown precautions. The world seemed to be spinning into a harrowing and surreal future. But amid the existential dread, there was still the matter of conducting an election campaign. The previous spring Joe Biden announced his presidential bid, joining a crowded field of more than twenty Democrats vying for the nomination. Framing the 2020 election as a "battle for the soul of this nation," Biden would be a different candidate than Hilliary Clinton when it came to religion. The former vice president frequently referenced his Catholic faith in speeches, name dropped Pope Francis, and would make a targeted play for moderate white Catholics whom Clinton mostly overlooked. The president was not going to concede any ground with Catholics. A month after the pandemic drove the nation into lockdown in the middle of March, the Trump campaign launched a "Catholics for Trump" event to officially kick off its Catholic outreach. The president is "trying to protect the right to life," Fr. Frank Pavone told the Associated Press, adding without any concern for the truth that the Trump administration's policies were "completely consistent with Catholic teaching." The group's senior political adviser, former Republican Rep. Tim Huelskamp, criticized Biden for failing to be a faithful Catholic while "you've got a non-Catholic in Donald Trump who's delivering on Catholic social teaching and principles."[152]

A few weeks after the launch of Trump's Catholic outreach initiative, the Catholic news outlet *Crux* reported that the president used a call with a group of religious leaders, officially billed as a discussion about when houses of worship might reopen amid the pandemic, to solicit political support for his reelection. Trump described himself as the "best president in the history of the Catholic Church," according to a recording of the call obtained by *Crux*.[153] He repeatedly touted his commitment to pro-life and religious liberty issues, along with his support for school choice and Catholic education. "I hope that everyone gets out and votes and does what they have to do," he told the group, which included New York Cardinal Timothy Dolan and then US bishops' conference president Archbishop José Gomez of Los Angeles. "You're going to have a very different Catholic Church," he warned the leaders, if Biden was elected. Trump praised Cardinal Dolan as a "great gentleman" and a "great friend of mine." Dolan reciprocated. "The feelings are mutual sir," the cardinal said, adding that the two had been on the phone so often in recent months that his ninety-year-old mother said he called Trump more than he called her. Dolan focused on the dire state of Catholic schools during the pandemic. "Never has the outlook financially looked more bleak, but perhaps never has the outlook looked more promising given the energetic commitment that your administration has to our schools," the cardinal told the president. "We need you more than ever."[154] The president responded by reminding the leaders of the "situation coming up on November 3, the likes of which have never been more important for the Church." Trump told the faith leaders that Democrats "want abortion and they want it now and they want it to go up to the end of the ninth month and beyond." The president referenced the final debate of the 2016 race, where he challenged Hillary Clinton for supporting late-term abortion. "We did very well defending that during our last race with Hillary Clinton because she had it right up until the time at birth," Trump said. "We probably helped out the pro-life [cause] more than anything you can imagine." A few days after the call, Cardinal Dolan appeared on "Fox & Friends" and gave Trump a boost in front of a large national audience. "I really salute his leadership," Dolan said. "Everybody has really come through, but the president has seemed particularly sensitive to the, what shall I say, to the feelings of the religious community."[155] Amid criticism from Catholic social justice leaders that the cardinal was crossing a line by giving the appearance of political support for the president, Dolan defended his engagement with Trump as part of what he called the "sacred enterprise of accompaniment" during a Facebook Live event with *America* magazine.[156]

It was an insufficient response from a cardinal with a powerful pulpit and media reach. Dolan's public coziness with the president helped burnish Trump's brand with Catholics at a precarious political moment. The president faced a Catholic opponent and had to contend with a pope who consistently prioritized economic justice, climate change, and the dignity of immigrants in ways that highlighted how Trump's ideology and policies clashed with traditional Catholic teaching. Meanwhile the worsening pandemic continued to expose and exacerbate racial and economic disparities. Black and Latino Americans were dying at higher rates than whites from the virus. Rising unemployment and the stress of parents struggling to work while caring for children at home brought renewed attention to our nation's woeful lack of paid parental leave, paid sick days, and other social safety net programs. Another epidemic prompting justified rage—the deaths of Black men and women at the hands of police—was captured in horrific detail on video when a white Minneapolis police officer knelt on the neck of an unarmed Black man for more than nine minutes. The police killing of George Floyd, only three months into the beginning of the pandemic, sparked mass protests across the country as thousands took to the streets calling for racial justice. "My friends, we cannot tolerate or turn a blind eye to racism and exclusion in any form and yet claim to defend the sacredness of every human life," Pope Francis said in the wake of Floyd's killing. During his weekly general audience at the Vatican, the pope joined the faithful in Minneapolis and across the US "in praying for the repose of the soul of George Floyd and of all those others who have lost their lives as a result of the sin of racism."[157] Archbishop José Gomez, president of the bishops' conference, also condemned Floyd's death. "How is it possible that in America, a black man's life can be taken from him while calls for help are not answered and his killing is recorded as it happens?" he asked in a statement. "It is true what Rev. Martin Luther King, Jr. said, that riots are the language of the unheard. We should be doing a lot of listening right now."[158]

While the vast majority of protestors were nonviolent, Trump used examples of sporadic demonstrators who threw bricks and clashed with police to escalate his "law-and order" rhetoric with an even more authoritarian tone. After thousands of demonstrators gathered outside the White House, the president tweeted a warning that if protestors had breached the fence, they would "have been greeted with the most vicious dogs, and most ominous weapons, I have ever seen."[159] Trump implored Democratic mayors and other leaders to crack down more forcefully on protestors or he warned that the federal government "will step in and do what has to be done, and that includes using the unlimited power of our Military and many arrests." A week after Floyd's death, Trump walked out of the White House gates flanked by a military officer in camouflage fatigues, Attorney General William Barr, and other administration officials. Less than an hour before, mounted police had used tear gas to clear out peaceful protestors from Lafayette Park. Trump walked the short distance to St. John's Episcopal Church. The boarded-up building had been damaged the day before in a fire during protests over Floyd's killing. As reporters jockeyed for position, the president stood in front of the church and held a Bible in his hand as the surreal photo-op played out live on television. "We have the greatest country in the world. We are going to keep it nice and safe," Trump said in a brief statement before walking back to the White House.[160] The brash display of Christian nationalism was an attempt to send a message to protestors. The president used a holy book as a political prop. A clergy member who was driven from St. John's Church described the scene to *Religion News Service*. "They turned holy ground into a battleground," said the Rev.

Gini Gerbasi, who was dressed in clerical garb as police approached. "I was suddenly coughing from the tear gas," she said. "We heard those explosions and people would drop to the ground because you weren't sure what it was."[161]

The next day the president and First Lady Melania Trump traveled across town to visit the Saint John Paul II National Shrine near The Catholic University of America. In front of a statue of Pope John Paul II outside the shrine, the Trumps stood silently for a few minutes and again posed for photographs. The visit was another manufactured display of faith and strength that used a religious site as a backdrop. Wilton Gregory, the first Black cardinal of Washington, quickly issued a sharp response. "I find it baffling and reprehensible that any Catholic facility would allow itself to be so egregiously misused and manipulated in a fashion that violates our religious principles," the cardinal said in a statement. Noting the treatment of peaceful protestors preceding the president's appearance at Saint John's Episcopal Church the day before, the cardinal said that John Paul II would "certainly not condone the use of tear gas and other deterrents to silence, scatter, or intimidate for a photo opportunity in front of a place of worship."[162] Brian Burch, president of Catholic Vote, an organization playing a leading role in Trump's reelection, called the archbishop's statement "a partisan attack on the president."[163] A petition on LifeSiteNews encouraged Catholics to ask the archbishop to "apologize for, and withdraw, these churlish, hurtful and unspiritual remarks." Edward Peters, a canon lawyer and professor at Sacred Heart Major Seminary in the Archdiocese of Detroit, tweeted that the cardinal's condemnation was "devoid of any sense of Christian sentiment."[164] Archbishop Carlo Maria Viganò, the former apostolic nuncio to the United States who two years earlier had called for Pope Francis to resign, wrote in a letter to priests and laity of the Archdiocese of Washington that "the Catholic Church is led by many false pastors."[165]

Four days later Viganò moved from blasting a fellow archbishop to playing footsie with Donald Trump. In a bizarre open letter to the president published in LifeSiteNews, the archbishop said the Black Lives Matter protests that drew thousands of Americans after George Floyd's killing, and the ongoing Covid lockdowns, were part of an apocalyptic battle between "the children of darkness" and "the children of light." Viganò wrote that "on the one hand there are those who, although they have a thousand defects and weaknesses, are motivated by the desire to do good, to be honest, to raise a family, to engage in work, to give prosperity to their homeland, to help the needy, and, in obedience to the Law of God, to merit the Kingdom of Heaven." On the other hand, he wrote, "there are those who serve themselves, who do not hold any moral principles, who want to demolish the family. . . . In society, Mr. President, these two opposing realities co-exist as eternal enemies, just as God and Satan are eternal enemies." The archbishop, who also praised the president for attending the March for Life earlier in the year, said "it is quite clear that the use of street protests is instrumental to the purposes of those who would like to see someone elected in the upcoming presidential elections who embodies the goals of the deep state."[166]

The recipient of the letter took notice. "So honored by Archbishop Viganò's incredible letter to me," Trump tweeted to his 82 million followers, with a link to the letter. "I hope everyone, religious or not, reads it!"[167] Trump was nothing if not a shrewd opportunist. He would happily take advantage of the internal divisions inside the Catholic Church and ally himself with a Catholic leader who had become the de facto face of opposition to Pope Francis. Archbishop Viganò may have been something of a fringe figure, unrepresentative of mainstream Catholic thought, but as the former Vatican ambassador in Washington, he was an extremist with a resume and a loyal following among self-styled traditionalists on the Catholic right. The *National Catholic Reporter* noted that some Catholic priests and parishes in the United States shared the letter with their congregations. "The Prelate is not in good standing with the current mob in Vatican City and has for a long time lived in hiding, in fear for his own life," Fr. Ronald Antinarelli, pastor of Our Lady of Victory in Rochester, New York, wrote on the parish website's homepage. He included a link to Viganò's letter. "I urge you to read it and to send copies to all the people you know. Remember this: The gates of hell shall not prevail against it."[168]

"MAGA CATHOLICISM": THE TRUMP EFFECT IN CATHOLIC PARISHES, SCHOOLS, AND COMMUNITIES

In many ways it's not surprising that Archbishop Viganò's pro-Trump, anti-Francis, apocalyptic ravings were echoed, with varying degrees of fervor, in some Catholic parishes across the country during the Trump years. Obama's presidency not only intensified the decades-old Catholic culture wars against abortion, contraception, and LGBTQ equality; his presidency also radicalized elements of the Catholic right into a more identitarian, fundamentalist, antigovernment movement convinced that secular elites want to drive religion from the public square. This embattled psychology of white Christian victimhood, ripe for paranoia and conspiratorial explanations, found a wider audience under Trump as the president stoked cultural fears, anxieties, and animosities for maximum effect. The fact that Trump's opponent was a pro-choice Catholic from the Obama administration who spoke frequently about his faith and admiration for a Jesuit pope from South America only made the battle more urgent and the enemy clearer. In states across the country, I interviewed Catholics who described, in anger and pained sadness, the ways their Catholic parishes and communities were overtaken by a pro-Trump fervor during his presidency and ramped up even more as the 2020 election grew closer. In this surreal upside-down subculture, Pope Francis was a socialist, and his papacy threatened the church. Joe Biden wasn't a real Catholic. And a president who had spent years attacking migrants, stoking white grievances, and wielding power to help the most powerful was all that stood between the end of Christian values and secular tyranny. Trump himself tapped into this worldview whenever he could. Biden was not simply a fellow American and Christian who shared a different vision for the future. Instead, as the president declared at a campaign rally in Ohio, Biden would "take away your guns, destroy your 2nd Amendment, no religion, no anything, hurt the Bible, hurt God. He's against God."[169]

Ed Overell grew up in what he calls "my Catholic bubble." The forty-four-year-old attended Catholic school from kindergarten until graduate school. Growing up in the San Francisco area, his Catholic experience mostly leaned progressive and focused on social justice. After college Overell moved to Minnesota, where he became a Catholic school middle teacher for a decade and spent fourteen years as a youth minister in various parishes before returning to teach in a Catholic school. When Trump was elected, he worked at a parish that welcomed LGBTQ Catholics and that took racial and economic justice seriously. "We were all in mourning," Overell said about the mood at the parish after Trump's victory. On a Sunday not long after the election, his family went to Mass at the parish where his children attended school. Fr. John Echert, the pastor of Holy Trinity Catholic Church in South Saint Paul Minnesota, was known to be conservative, but Overell was horrified by what he heard in the homily that day. "I will never forget it was the weekend when Trump put out his anti-Muslim ban and there were protests at airports all over the country, but the priest's homily was all about abortion," Overell said. "The pastor used the phrase 'Make America Great Again' twice, and he explicitly said thank goodness we have a true pro-life president who will be the most pro-life president we have ever seen. I was furious but a lot of people were lapping it up."[170]

Overell saw Catholics in his community become increasingly outspoken about abortion, which was frequently paired with a willingness to rationalize Trump's bullying and often racially tinged denunciations of social justice protests. "Trump gave permission for some Catholics to say the quiet part out loud," Overell told me.

> I think he allowed Catholics to link the church to the MAGA movement and helped them justify supporting so many policies that were explicitly anti-Catholic. I remember asking a Catholic mom I knew, a really wonderful person who was very pro-Trump, where she drew the line with the president, and she said we need Supreme Court justices, and she said she would put up with almost everything to get those justices. I watched on Facebook as she slowly started to support more of Trump's policies after George Floyd's murder.

As the protests in the wake of Floyd's killing grew, Overell reflected on the fact that even for white Catholics living only a few miles from where the brutal assault took place, the Black Lives Matter movement was viewed with deep suspicion and even hostility. "People were making 'all lives matter' arguments to me," he said. "And they were couching it in religious language by saying things like 'Jesus doesn't care what color you are.'"[171]

The Catholic pastor, whom Overell watched give a "Make America Great Again" homily after Trump's election, only became more emboldened as Trump's presidency unfolded. Fr. Echert of Holy Trinity was particularly enraged by Covid restrictions and the closure of churches after the pandemic spread across the country. Holding Mass in the parking lot with congregants lined up in cars, the pastor delivered a Memorial Day weekend homily in 2020 that compared the president to Moses. "I also want to acknowledge someone else who went to war and he is not in the military," the priest told his congregation.

> President Donald Trump, more broadly than anyone else, any political leader or even church leader for that matter, went to war and refused to negotiate or take prisoners. This past week he publicly declared and demanded that churches throughout the nation were to be open to the faithful. I think of a biblical figure when I think of President Trump. I think of Moses. I think of Moses. Remember Moses went to Pharaoh multiple times and he said, "let my people go!" That is what Donald Trump, our president, said to the pharaohs of the states who were oppressing their people in a lockdown. Unreasonable, ungodly lockdowns. Let my people go to worship. I have no doubt that even though Donald Trump is not Catholic that was the work of the Holy Spirit as well.

A month before Trump vied for reelection, the pastor delivered a homily in which he twice referred to "the false religion" of Islam, warned that Europe was being overrun by Muslims, and framed the upcoming election in apocalyptic terms.

> It is that element, very strong in our nation, but still a minority, which seeks to destroy our sovereignty, which seeks to tyrannize us and which seeks to subdue or eliminate or at least control the Holy Catholic Church. Thirty days from now we are facing a battle, a battle such as our spiritual ancestors faced. We don't have to set sail. We don't have to risk our lives in the way those sailors did to go to war, but we do need to go to the ballot box and we do need to do what we can physically and spiritually. This can not be just a physical battle. Physically and spiritually to defeat these forces that seek to collapse our nation, to give way to a godless, godawful globalism. A new order in the world. An order that controls the world, that tyrannizes the world, that crushes true religion. Our friend Archbishop Vigano has written extensively not only to our own president, for whom we need to keep up our prayers, but to the American people, warning us that our nation might be the last bastion to be conquered by these forces that seek to globalize government and establish a one-world religion that is not authentic. Ultimately, it is guided, governed by the Evil One himself. If the battle of Lepanto had been lost, Europe would have become Islamic, subject to a false religion centuries ago. If we lose this battle at the ballot box, rest assured the sovereignty of our nation will go down, we will find ourselves enslaved, and we will find a world that is given over to Satan itself in its government and in its religion.[172]

Janis Bork, who taught in Catholic schools for nearly twenty-five years in Macomb County, Michigan, never heard a homily anywhere close to that extreme, but she described Trump's election as "an ugly pivot point at my school."[173] As a Catholic Democrat, Bork felt like an outsider in a community where Catholic enthusiasm for Trump ran high. Growing up, Bork remembers Macomb County as heavily Democratic and filled with working-class union members. When Ronald Reagan won the area in his 1984 election by a two-to-one margin, the suburb of Detroit achieved national attention when a pollster coined the term "Reagan Democrats" to describe Macomb voters who supported Reagan despite their usual loyalty to the Democratic Party. When Trump entered the picture in 2016, she found herself driving past "Catholics for Trump" signs on her way to work and surrounded by neighbors and colleagues who were absorbing an all-or-nothing political mentality fueled by Fox News and the Trump juggernaut. "When Trump got elected it was like all Democrats became bad people," she said. "It wasn't that we looked at the world differently or had political differences. We were bad people." Bork tried to keep a low profile and stifle her reactions when a fellow teacher at school would praise Trump. She was worried the atmosphere would become so uncomfortable she would need to leave her job. "I felt like I had to hide or shut up and not say anything. People excused a lot of Trump's behavior because they thought he would end abortion and end *Roe v. Wade*." At church it was the silence of the priests that began grating on her. Even when Trump's rhetoric and policies could be described as cruel and un-Christian, she never heard a homily raising any objection. "I felt like the clergy didn't speak out because they didn't want to offend people," she said. "But Jesus was an instigator! I wanted more from my faith."

Her Catholic school's response to the pandemic was also demoralizing and connected to Bork's broader sense of alienation with the church during Trump's presidency.

> All the public schools were closed because they couldn't social distance and lacked proper ventilation, but our church was going back full bore. They were not protecting teachers and families. They were packing classrooms to the maximum and our pastor was giddy about it. The church had lost lots of money. They needed that money to pay the bills. When I talked to the assistant principal about it, he said this is how we evangelize. I was disgusted and furious. I walked away and resigned.

Looking back, she recognizes how much Trump's presidency, the Catholic enthusiasm for the president in her community, and her Catholic school's response to the pandemic all made it harder for her to maintain strong ties to her faith. "I never left Jesus and I carry him with me," Bork said, growing emotional and tearing up. "But I couldn't look at him through the lens of Catholic faith anymore." She has not been to Mass since she resigned from her job in August 2020, a loss that weighs on her. "I drive by Catholic churches and I do think maybe I could go to Mass and just sit with Jesus but I haven't. I feel like my faith was a call to community and I don't know if I can be in community there anymore."[174]

Less than an hour down the road in another suburb of Detroit, José De Nigris couldn't make sense of what he saw happening at his children's

Catholic school. He struggled as Catholics he knew in the community fully embraced Trump with no reservations. A forty-nine-year-old immigrant from Mexico who grew up in a pious Catholic family, De Nigris works in the car industry. His political views lean moderate. He has voted for Democrats and Republicans. "This was a conservative Republican community, but the MAGA mentality really contaminated the water," De Nigris said. "Trump's election, the 2020 campaign, and then Covid was a perfect storm that changed everything. A big percentage of the people I know socially went from being conservative Republicans to seeing Trump as some sort of semigod. It was very hard to see how conspiracy theories and Trump's rhetoric simply replaced any basic understanding of the Catholic faith."[175] De Nigris and his wife grew increasingly uncomfortable. Questioning the president would be met with disapproval and a feeling of being ostracized socially.

The parents stopped sending their children to the school-sponsored March for Life. "It turned into Trump rallies after his election," he said. "You would see kids wearing MAGA hats. For these families, it was the pro-life issue that really got them to jump on the Trump train. You would hear people say, 'if you vote for Biden, you can't be a Catholic.'" As an immigrant from Mexico, De Nigris acknowledged how painful it was to see so many Catholics he knew embrace a president for being pro-life when Trump ran for election demonizing immigrants from his birth country as violent rapists. "It was very ugly, and it hurt to see people accept that stuff at face value," he said. "I would hear people say Trump is the most Catholic president we've ever had. It was ridiculous." While Trump was almost viewed as someone to venerate, Pope Francis was talked about in a different way. "It was kind of like an unofficial truth and is well known that Pope Francis is not well perceived in the school. He is viewed as too liberal and the antithesis of Trump. People had a very difficult time contradicting or challenging Trump, but not the Pope." The couple eventually wrote a letter to school administrators expressing their concerns about how the excessively pro-Trump political atmosphere surrounding the school clashed with Catholic values and expressed their dismay that the school had joined a lawsuit filed by religious schools in the state challenging Covid protocol restrictions. School leaders, De Nigris said, never took their concerns seriously. "Radicalized Catholics we could no longer recognize drove us out," he said.[176]

Rural central Virginia is deep in the heart of Trump country. Lisa Haertel, a fifty-two-year-old Catholic convert who was drawn to the faith in part by her admiration for Pope John Paul II, lives thirty minutes from Liberty University, the bastion of white evangelical conservatism founded by Rev. Jerry Falwell. As Haertel explored Catholicism in the 1990s, eventually converting from the Methodist faith, she found a home in conservative Catholic circles. Her politics followed that journey. While she had some reservations, Haertel voted for Trump in 2016. "I thought he would be a breath of fresh air," the public high school English teacher said. "He didn't come from a political background and had savvy financial skills. I thought he could go to Washington and get something done."[177] Haertel began to lose her political faith in Trump after the police killing of George Floyd. "I was appalled at his behavior during Black Lives Matter protests and his use of the Bible as a piece of propaganda," she said, referring to Trump's staged moment in front of St. John's Episcopal Church across the street from the White House.

> Having grown up in the South, I have always detested racism. Even as a child, I found it wrong. I have a lot of Black students. We all know we have a problem with racism in this country. Black Lives Matter helped bring racism to the fore. People were talking about these problems. Trump handled it so poorly. He didn't even try to create a dialogue. He just tried to grandstand and take the side of white people. When I saw him walk to that church with the Bible, it was all about white evangelical voters. It was all propaganda.

Haertel knew from experience how easy it was for people to live in an echo chamber where the information they consumed was filtered through an ideological lens that confirmed their own worldview. During her conversion to Catholicism, her reading came from conservative Catholic websites and newsletters that focused on traditional liturgical practices, articles about Marian apparitions, and an aggregate of news stories from conservative perspectives. Social justice or Catholic social teaching was not in the mix. But as Haertel began questioning Trump's leadership and reading more broadly, her Catholic and political identity was changing. The evolution was stressful. "The 2020 election really tested my faith, my marriage and my friendships," she said. Abortion became a consistent point of contention with a friend who viewed herself as pro-life and supported the president.

> As I watched the election progress and saw Trump and other Republicans waive the abortion flag to get voters, I began to think Trump doesn't care about abortion and that he didn't really care about Christians. My friend and I began to disagree about Trump. I started to say I'm not sure I can vote for this man anymore. We had some very strong arguments. We don't talk about politics anymore or we

> have to just tiptoe around it. The same thing happened with my husband who supported Trump. There were a lot of arguments. We don't talk about politics now.

There were also heated conversations about Trump with her prayer partner. Haertel still attends a conservative Catholic church but finds herself struggling with homilies that focus on abortion or LGBTQ issues at the expense of broader justice issues. Watching Catholics and other Christians embrace Trump affected her own faith identity in ways she never expected. "Will I stay in the Catholic Church? I would have never asked this question of myself in 2019," Haertel said. "Now I'm not sure."[178]

Against the backdrop of surging Covid cases and racial tension, Trump's reelection campaign heated up over the summer of 2020. For his first indoor rally since lockdown measures had been implemented in the spring, the president chose Tulsa, Oklahoma, the site of the infamous 1921 Tulsa Race Massacre. White residents killed, looted, and burned to the ground a prosperous section of town often called Black Wall Street in what is considered one of the worst acts of racial terrorism in American history. While the president didn't make a reference to that history or acknowledge its legacy, he wasn't shying away from race. "Virtually every policy that has hurt Black Americans for half a century, Joe Biden has supported or enacted," Trump said at the rally. "I have done more for the Black community in four years than Joe Biden has done in 47 years." In a cavernous 19,000-seat Bank of Oklahoma Center that was more than half empty, the president told his supporters who had ignored public health officials' concerns about the indoor rally: "I stand before you today to declare the Silent Majority is stronger than ever before!"[179]

When a virtual Republican National Convention opened in Orlando at the end of the summer, the Trump campaign showcased several Catholics as part of its silent majority sales pitch. The legendary University of Notre Dame football coach Lou Holtz used his time at the podium to draw contrasts between the president and Biden on abortion. "Nobody is a stronger advocate for the unborn than President Trump," the retired coach said. "The Biden-Harris ticket is the most radically pro-abortion campaign in history. They and other politicians are Catholics in name only and abandon innocent lives. President Trump protects those lives. I trust President Trump."[180] The following day, Notre Dame's president, Fr. John Jenkins, issued a statement distancing the university from Holtz's endorsement and challenging the former coach's depiction of Biden as a "Catholic in name only." Jenkins wrote that Holtz's remarks "must not be taken to imply that the university endorses his views, any candidate or any political party," and added that "we Catholics should remind ourselves that while we may judge the objective moral quality of another's actions, we must never question the sincerity of another's faith, which is due to the mysterious working of grace in that person's heart."[181] Standing behind a podium with a sign that read "Trump 2020," Sister Deidre Byrne delivered a Catholic blessing for the president at the convention as a prime-time audience watched her speech on television. "Donald Trump is the most pro-life president this nation has ever had, defending life at all stages," the retired army officer, missionary, and surgeon said.

> His belief in the sanctity of life transcends politics. President Trump will stand up against Biden-Harris, who are the most anti-life presidential ticket ever, even supporting the horrors of late-term abortion and infanticide. Because of his courage and conviction, President Trump has earned the support of America's pro-life community. Moreover, he has a nation of religious standing behind him. You'll find us here with our weapon of choice, the rosary. Thank you, Mr. President, we are all praying for you.[182]

While Catholics at the Republican National Convention were rallying behind Trump before a national television audience, the president could also depend on a devoted cadre of grassroots Catholic boosters. A priest from Wisconsin released a slickly produced election video that went viral. "Here's a memo for clueless, baptized Catholics out there," Fr. James Altman, who then served as pastor of St. James the Less Catholic parish in Lacrosse, Wisconsin, said in a video that sparked news coverage around the country and quickly racked up more than a million views. "You cannot be Catholic and be a Democrat. Period."[183] The video flashes photos of Biden and House Speaker Nancy Pelosi while Altman rages against "godless politicians." Catholics who vote for Democrats will face eternal damnation, Altman said. He singled out Fr. James Martin, a Jesuit priest and bestselling author who has been commended by Pope Francis for his ministry to LGBTQ Catholics. (Martin offered a general prayer at the Democratic National Convention but did not endorse the candidate or reference Biden by name.) "So just quit pretending that you're Catholic and vote Democrat," Fr. Altman says. "Repent of your support of that party or face the fires of hell."[184] Bishop Joseph Strickland of Tyler, Texas, amplified the message on Twitter. "As the Bishop of Tyler I endorse Fr Altman's statement in this video," the bishop wrote. "My shame is that it has taken me so long. Thank you Fr Altman for your COURAGE. If you love Jesus & His Church & this nation . . . please

HEED THIS MESSAGE."[185] A few weeks later, Fr. Ed Meeks, the pastor of Christ the King Church in Towson, Maryland, preached a homily, also uploaded to YouTube, called "Staring into the Abyss," in which he declared the Democratic Party the "party of death."[186] The video, which has been viewed more than two million times, was again shared by Bishop Strickland, who tweeted it to his 40,000 followers with the message: "Every Catholic should listen to this wise and faithful priest."[187]

The Trump campaign circulated a Fox News interview with Cardinal Raymond Burke in which the former St. Louis archbishop declared that "no devout Catholic, no practicing Catholic" can vote for a pro-choice politician. In a snarky tweet, Bishop Thomas Tobin of Providence, Rhode Island, wrote: "The first time in a while that the Democratic ticket hasn't had a Catholic on it. Sad."[188] A Catholic pastor in Greenville, South Carolina, with a large social media following, Fr. Dwight Longenecker, called Biden a "fake Catholic" in a tweet to his nearly 40,000 Twitter followers.[189] Fr. Kevin Cusick, the pastor of St. Francis de Sales Parish in Benedict, Maryland, wrote: "Joe Biden is not a practicing Catholic. And practicing Catholics cannot vote for Biden for president in good conscience."[190] Fr. David Miller, the pastor of St. Dorothy's Parish in North Carolina, said in a homily posted on YouTube that if "[Mr. Biden] dies the way he is now, unrepentant for his years of denying Christ . . . before repentance . . . you and I know where he will go: He will be damned to hell for all eternity."[191]

A month before the election, the rector of St. Peter in Chains Cathedral in Cincinnati, Fr. Jan Kevin Schmidt, used his weekly column in the church's bulletin to criticize what he called "politicians on the left" and to remind Catholics that abortion is the "preeminent" issue. "Much is on the line as we approach Nov. 3 and for Catholics there is only one party upholding life," the priest wrote. "The other party has degraded itself so terribly with its embrace of that which is fundamentally about death, be it abortion or euthanasia, or the slide towards the embrace of socialism and the evils that lead from it."[192] Around the same time, another Catholic pastor in Ohio, Fr. Shawn Landenwitch of St. Patrick's Church in Bellefontaine, northwest of Columbus, used his homily on "Respect Life Sunday" to defend the white nationalist group the Proud Boys, claiming that the group is entitled to its "good name" and that those who accuse it of white supremacy are committing "a mortal sin." Fr. Landenwitch told his congregation: "The Proud Boys were labeled as white supremacists. This is a group, I don't support them, but they've publicly renounced white supremacy, and they're led by an African Latino. And yet they're accused of being white supremacists. You know, these charges that are just unfounded and ridiculous, and people are just labeling anyone who doesn't agree with them as a racist."[193] The priest seemed to be echoing President Trump, who less than a week earlier during a presidential debate was equivocal when he was asked by moderator Chris Wallace if he would clearly condemn the Proud Boys. After initially sidestepping the question, Trump gave a less than resounding answer. "Sure, I'm prepared to do that. But I would say almost everything I see is from the left wing, not from the right wing. . . . Proud Boys, stand back and stand by. But I'll tell you what: Somebody's got to do something about antifa and the left."[194]

Characterizing Biden as a "bad Catholic" and implicitly, or explicitly, depicting Trump as the only responsible choice for Catholic voters became a message amplified by social media and a flourishing ecosystem of conservative Catholic media that is often more partisan than journalistic. While several million people watched Sister Byrne's speech at the Republican National Convention—and viewed pastors' messages that went viral on YouTube—far fewer Catholics actually read the US Catholic bishops' election-year reflection document, *Faithful Citizenship*. The document provoked objections from some US bishops most in line with Pope Francis's more expansive pro-life vision by referring to abortion as the church's "preeminent priority"—an issue I will take up more thoroughly in a later chapter—but the full scope of *Faithful Citizenship* challenges the kind of partisan, single-issue framing that many Catholics hear before elections. *Faithful Citizenship* does not endorse a party or any candidate, underscores that neither party completely reflects Catholic social teaching, and recognizes that Catholics can vote for a candidate who doesn't share church teaching on abortion. "There may be times when a Catholic who rejects a candidate's unacceptable position even on policies promoting an intrinsically evil act may reasonably decide to vote for that candidate for other morally grave reasons," the bishops write.[195] There were several "morally grave reasons" for why a Catholic in good conscience—and in keeping with church teaching—would choose Biden over Trump.

A few bishops and a former top official at the US bishops' conference did speak out publicly to challenge Trump. Bishop John Stowe of Lexington, Kentucky, offered the most direct assessment. "For this president to call himself pro-life, and for anybody to back him because of claims of being pro-life, is almost willful ignorance," the bishop said on a webinar hosted by the International Catholic Movement for Intellectual and Cultural Affairs, or ICMICA-Pax Romana, a global lay community of Catholic intellectuals. "He is so much anti-life because he is only concerned about himself, and he gives us every, every, every indication of that," Stowe said.[196] Bishop Mark Seitz of El Paso, Texas, challenged the reduction of Catholic teaching to abortion. While Seitz lamented what he called "the deepening dogmatism of the Democratic Party on abortion," he wrote in *America* magazine that "Catholics also need to recognize that we are living out the collateral effects of a misbegotten decades-long settlement between certain groups of political and religious leaders on the right." For far too long, the bishop said, "in pursuit of 'single-issue' strategies to end abortion, many Christians have scandalously turned a blind eye to real breakdowns in solidarity and dehumanizing policies, including crackdowns on worker rights and voting rights, the slashing of social support for the poor and sick, racism and the exploitation of immigrants and the environment."[197] John Carr, who for more than two decades was a top domestic policy advisor to the US bishops' conference and helped draft *Faithful Citizenship* for many years, used core themes from the bishops' election document to articulate his opposition to Trump. "I believe Mr. Trump's character, lack of integrity and record on racism and Covid-19, among other matters, constitute 'morally grave reasons' to oppose his re-election," he wrote in *America* magazine.[198] "I believe Mr. Biden has the 'character [and] integrity' to lead our nation and is 'more likely to pursue other authentic human goods.' I will vote for Mr. Biden for what he can do to help us recover and heal, lift up those left behind, ensure health care for all and treat immigrants and refugees with respect. I will not vote for him to support his position on abortion, but in spite of it." Carr added:

> Mr. Trump demonizes immigrants, fans the flames of race and division, refuses to denounce racist groups or actions and seeks to divide the country by overt appeals to racial fears. Mr. Biden condemns racism and seeks national healing, speaks for voting rights and against systemic racism. At this moment of national reckoning on racial injustice and clear disparities in the impact of the coronavirus crisis, electing a president who will fight racism, not exacerbate it, is a moral imperative for me.

* * *

The relatively few Catholic leaders with a platform who were willing to directly critique Trump and challenge the coordinated Catholic campaign against Biden lacked the funding and organizing muscle of the right. In the last few months of the election, CatholicVote launched a $9.7 million effort to reach Catholic voters in key battleground states. The push, which included full-time staff in six states and thousands of volunteers, reached voters through digital advertising, parish-by-parish canvassing, direct mail, and get-out-the-vote efforts aimed at five million Catholic voters. The message focused on warning voters about what the organization called Biden's "anti-Catholic record and policy agenda." Biden's record, warned CatholicVote's president Brian Burch, "makes clear he will not protect our Catholic values or defend our way of life. For Catholics who cherish the Faith and their freedom to live it, a Biden presidency represents an existential threat."[199] The group spent $350,000 on advertisements in Michigan and Pennsylvania describing how Biden "would force American Catholics to pay for abortions, sacrificing his Catholic values to kneel before the leftist mob." The clip featured Sister Dede Byrne from the Republican National Convention. The organization also used cutting-edge technology called "geofencing" to capture data from the cellphones of Catholics attending church so that advertisements and tailored political messages could be sent to them. "We are already building the largest Catholic voter mobilization program ever," Burch boasted in a blog post. In Wisconsin, a battleground state that Trump won by only 22,748 votes in 2016, CatholicVote organized a "ground team" to encourage registration and voting among the Catholics identified through geofencing. "With this mobile targeting, we are able to reach our fellow Catholics in the pews. And we can ensure that our fellow Catholic voters get the facts and hear the truth—not the latest lies peddled by the media," he wrote. "Catholics will decide the 2020 elections. It's up to us to make it happen."[200]

The 2020 National Catholic Prayer Breakfast, held virtually in September because of coronavirus restrictions, also became another tool in the Trump campaign's Catholic operation. The president was billed as a "special guest." The event showcased how some of the most influential political power brokers in Washington's Republican circles and in the Trump administration were deeply connected to the conservative Catholic movement. Leonard Leo, the point person for Supreme Court nominations who over several decades had built a formidable advocacy and fundraising machine that pushed the judiciary to the right, introduced Trump as the president who has defended the sanctity of human life "more than any other president in my lifetime."[201] In a prerecorded address from the White House, Trump pledged that he would "always defend the sacred right to life" and announced that he would sign the Born-Alive Executive Order to "ensure that all precious babies born alive, no matter their circumstances, receive the medical care that they deserve."[202] One of the most powerful Catholics in the Trump administration, Attorney General William Barr, received a "Christifidelis Laici" award for service to the church. It was an audacious display of hypocrisy and selective orthodoxy. Barr had played a key role in reviving the federal death penalty, which the church teaches is always morally unacceptable.

Two years earlier Pope Francis had built on clear condemnations of the death penalty by previous popes and officially revised the Catechism of the Catholic Church to declare the church's opposition to the practice in every circumstance because government-sanctioned killing is "an attack on the inviolability and dignity of the person." For decades, conservative Catholic leaders had argued that Catholics who supported abortion rights should never be honored or given platforms to speak at Catholic institutions. In church parlance such honors would bring "scandal" to the faithful and sow confusion. But there was Leonard Leo introducing Barr as "truly a Catholic public servant" who embodies "integrity, honesty, humility, sincere and wise counsel." Barr delivered a ten-minute speech decrying "militant secularists" and a "new orthodoxy that is actively hostile to religion."[203]

Sister Helen Prejean, the prominent anti-death-penalty activist, tweeted: "I raise my voice in fervent opposition to the National Catholic Prayer Breakfast's scandalous offer of an award to Attorney General Barr for his 'exemplary Christlike' behavior. . . . What is Christlike about a Catholic believer using his discretionary power as Attorney General to undertake a series of speedy federal executions?" The US Conference of Catholic Bishops released a statement the day before the event. "In the last sixty years, before the Trump administration restarted federal executions, there were only four federal executions," the bishops wrote. "Since July, there have been five, which is already more federal executions than were carried out in any year in the last century. There are two more federal executions scheduled this week. We say to President Trump and Attorney General Barr: Enough. Stop these executions."[204] The executions did not stop. Krisanne Vaillancourt Murphy, the executive director of the Catholic Mobilizing Network, called the National Catholic Prayer Breakfast "a twisted halftime show between executions."[205]

Three days after the breakfast, President Trump nominated Amy Coney Barrett to the Supreme Court. A conservative Catholic who had taught in the law school at the University of Notre Dame, Barrett was tapped to fill a seat left vacant by the liberal icon Ruth Bader Ginsburg. The justice had died a week earlier. Barrett was only forty-eight years old. The opportunity to place another conservative on the court who could push the institution even further to the right over the next several decades was an opportunity Trump relished. The fact that Barrett was a Catholic mother with seven children, shortlisted by Leonard Leo and well known in a conservative legal movement populated by many Catholics, was an added bonus for a president whose polling numbers with Catholics were flagging. "Among white Catholic voters, a survey this week showed Trump's lead over Biden narrowing to just five percentage points—an alarming development for the candidate who carried this group by a 23-point margin in 2016," *Politico* reported at the end of September, less than two months before the election. "But in the death of Justice Ruth Bader Ginsburg, a fierce champion of women's rights and left-wing legal icon, Trump and his conservative allies believe they've found a political Hail Mary."[206] At a campaign rally in Pennsylvania a few hours after nominating Barrett, the president played his card. "I just came from the Rose Garden of the White House," Trump said, pausing while the crowd chanted "Fill That Seat!" "This is our third nomination. We have Justice Gorsuch, Justice Kavanaugh—and now we have Amy."

Barrett was the perfect nominee for a president who had mastered stoking the politics of religious and cultural grievance. In the case of Barrett, Trump and the conservative movement had a helpful assist from a Democratic senator. During a 2017 Senate confirmation hearing for her appointment as a judge to the US Circuit Court of Appeals, Barrett was grilled about her faith and membership in the charismatic group People of Praise. During questioning, Sen. Dianne Feinstein of California told Barrett that "the dogma lives loudly within you."[207] The phrase quickly became a rallying cry and proud mantra for conservative Catholics who plastered the phrase on coffee cups or added it to their Twitter bios as a badge of honor. "Joe Biden knows that if he gets a majority of the Catholic vote he's going to be elected president, so there's been a very aggressive effort by his campaign to underscore his faith," Republican lobbyist Matt Schlapp, whose wife Mercedes helped lead Catholic outreach for the Trump campaign, told *Politico*. "But if the president's choice for the Supreme Court is a Catholic mother who, because she believes deeply in her faith, is considered disqualified for the job by Democrats, that puts Biden in a pickle."[208] Barrett was confirmed by the Senate on a 52–48 vote a month after her nomination.

Less than a month before the election, a Catholic media outlet gave a final push for the president. Michael Warsaw, the CEO of EWTN and publisher of the *National Catholic Register*, wrote an editorial framing the contest between Trump and Biden as a choice between "two completely different views of America." Clearly recognizing that Trump's personal character was difficult to defend from a Catholic perspective, Warsaw pivoted. "You are casting your vote this year for a long-term vision of America, not for a person," he wrote.

> One campaign has built itself on the notion that America is a great country, with much to offer. It embraces a vision that sees religious practice and belief in God as central to the country's private and

> public life. In this understanding of America, faith is not something to be defended against with a "wall of separation" designed to keep Christians out. Instead, faith—and Christianity itself—are seen as critical to the flourishing of our country in a perspective shared by many of our Founding Fathers. It believes in equality of opportunity, opposes violent riots, and stands against the revisionist historians who would undermine everything in America in order to so taint the country's heritage as to make it anathema.[209]

Against this idealized and even illusory depiction of Trump as a standard bearer for traditional Christian values and defender of democratic ideals, Warsaw caricatured Biden as part and parcel of a left that has contempt for religion and patriotism. "Against it is rising a progressive view that is increasingly popular in many colleges and universities and the news media and with protesters and rioters and even in political circles, including one of the presidential campaigns. In this telling of our history, America has much to atone for and little to be proud of. Traditional religious and Christian values are seen as a form or vehicle for discrimination, not a central element of the country. Abortion isn't just celebrated; its export with taxpayer dollars is an article of faith for them." The editorial had not a single line challenging Trump's demagoguery or taking issue with one of his administration's many policies that clashed with church teaching. In that regard it was at least consistent with the uncritical pro-Trump propaganda the president had grown accustomed to from his most vocal Catholic apologists.

ELECTION, INSURRECTION, AND CONFRONTING CATHOLIC COMPLICITY

The 2020 election would, in many ways, come down to whether Trump could repeat his success in Michigan, Wisconsin, and Pennsylvania. Trump narrowly edged out Clinton in these heavily Catholic states in 2016, landing a major blow in states Democratic party leaders call the "blue wall." A repeat would not happen. Biden won all three states. His ability to chip into Trump's appeal with white Catholics in Rust Belt states and across the country was evident. Nationally, Trump won white Catholics by a fifteen-point margin, according to AP VoteCast, a major decline from his thirty-three point margin of victory over Clinton four years earlier.[210] While President Trump dominated with white evangelicals as expected—winning eight out of ten of those voters and even improving his performance with white evangelicals from the last election—overall the Catholic vote was roughly split down the middle. Fifty percent of Catholics backed Trump, according to AP VoteCast, while 49 percent favored Biden, a decline from the president's 2016 performance with Catholics, when he won 52 percent of Catholics compared with 44 percent for Hillary Clinton. The real divide among Catholic voters fell along race and ethnic lines. Sixty-seven percent of Hispanic Catholics backed Biden, compared to 32 percent who supported Trump.[211]

Biden turned to faith in striking a conciliatory tone in his victory speech. "The Bible tells us that to everything there is a season," the president-elect said in an address from Wilmington, Delaware. "Now, let's give each other a chance. It's time to put away the harsh rhetoric. To lower the temperature. To see each other again. To listen to each other again. To make progress, we must stop treating our opponents as our enemy. We are not enemies. We are Americans." He concluded by citing a popular Catholic hymn, "On Eagles Wings," a song inspired by Psalm 91. "In the last days of the campaign, I began thinking about a hymn that means a lot to me and my family, particularly my deceased son Beau," Biden said.

> It captures the faith that sustains me and which I believe sustains America. And I hope it can provide some comfort and solace to the 230,000 Americans who have lost a loved one through this terrible virus this year. My heart goes out to each and every one of you. Hopefully this hymn gives you solace as well. It goes like this. And he will raise you up on eagle's wings, bear you on the breath of dawn, make you to shine like the sun, and hold you in the palm of his hand.[212]

Donald Trump never accepted the results of the election. He hurled accusations of voter fraud without evidence, promoted conspiracy claims, and tried to intimidate state election officials. It was a brazen abuse of power from a sitting president. In an audio recording of an hour-long phone call obtained by the *Washington Post,* Trump pressured Georgia's Republican secretary of state to find enough votes to overturn the election. "I just want to find 11,780 votes, which is one more than we have," Trump said during the conversation, according to the recording. The president also implied on the call that Georgia election officials could be prosecuted for "a criminal offense" if they didn't follow the president's instructions.[213] As Trump dug in for a fight, a small but vocal cadre of familiar Catholics rallied behind him. The day after the election, Archbishop Viganò, the former Vatican ambassador to Washington, again proved his loyalty to the president and his penchant for promoting conspiracy theories. In a "Letter to American Catholics and Americans of Good Will," the archbishop wrote: "We have seen the deep state organize itself, well in advance, to carry out the most colossal electoral fraud in history, in order to ensure the defeat of the man who has strenuously opposed the establishment of the New World Order that is wanted by the children of darkness."[214] In an interview with the president's onetime advisor Steve Bannon, Viganò cited what he called the "overwhelming evidence of irregularities that has emerged in several states" and said that "a president who is simply proclaimed as such by the mainstream media affiliated with the *deep state* would be deprived of all legitimacy." The archbishop praised the Trump administration for "the traditional values that it holds in common with those of Catholics" and contrasted the president with "the deep state of the self-styled Catholic Joe Biden, who is subservient to the globalist ideology and its perverse, anti-human, antichrist, infernal agenda."[215]

Archbishop Viganò joined Bishop Joseph Strickland of Tyler, Texas, and Fr. Frank Pavone of Priests for Life in what became known by Trump supporters as the "Stop the Steal" movement. Their video messages were featured in a "Jericho March" that promoted the president's lie that the election had been stolen. Viganò was listed as the headliner for the rally, along with retired Lt. Gen. Michael Flynn, a former national security advisor Trump had pardoned. The archbishop appeared on a jumbo video screen on the National Mall. "We are the silent army of the children of light, the humble ranks who overthrow evil by invoking God, the praying army that walks around the walls of lies and betrayal in order to bring them down," Viganò told the crowd.[216] Bishop Strickland was filmed standing in front of an altar. "We pray in a special way for our nation in a time of darkness, confusion, this time of too much corruption and doubt," he said. "Lord, you have given President Trump victory over all these enemies and we ask you to give him and us victory once again," Fr. Frank Pavone said in his message. "Bless his campaign as it fights voter fraud."[217] In Madison, Wisconsin, Fr. John Zuhlsdorf, who blogs as "Father Z," had conducted an exorcism, broadcast on YouTube, for those who were involved in counting votes, who he said were engaged in "fraud," "sin," "lying," "cheating," and "stealing" and "put their souls in terrible mortal peril."[218]

Bishops and clergy who promoted false claims that the election was illegitimate, demonized Biden as a God-hating globalist, declared that Catholics would go to hell if they voted for a Democrat, and used apocalyptic language to frame the election as a battle between good and evil all contributed to an environment that eventually turned violent on January 6, 2020. Protesters who breached the US Capitol that day carried Trump 2020 signs, "Jesus is My Savior" banners, and the Christian flag, an ecumenical white flag with a blue field and a red Latin cross. A gallows was set up outside the Capitol. Capitol police officers were attacked as they tried to stop the mob. Members of Congress huddled in fear during several hours of lockdown. It took three hours to secure the building. More than a hundred law enforcement officers were assaulted. In the end, four protestors died, thirteen were wounded, and a police officer died several days later from his injuries. "I couldn't believe my eyes, there were officers on the ground, they were bleeding, they were throwing up," US Capitol Police officer Caroline Edwards, told the House panel investigating the events in 2022. "I was slipping in peoples' blood."[219] A week after the siege on the Capitol, the House of Representatives voted to impeach President Trump for inciting the violent insurrection. He became the first president in US history to be impeached twice.

On the Sunday morning after the Capitol was stormed, Fr. William Corcoran stood to deliver his homily at St. Elizabeth Seton Catholic Church in the Chicago suburb of Orland Hills. The early morning Mass was filled with more than a hundred masked parishioners. Fr. Bill, as he is known at the parish, was about to wade straight into the kind of turbulent waters many pastors avoid. "On this Feast of the Baptism of the Lord, we drink in the last goodness and glories of the Christmas season, and begin ordinary time on Monday," he began.

> Goodness and glory are not two words that we would use to describe our past week when we saw an angry and violent mob seize our United States Capitol and interrupt Congress in its duty of certifying the State Elector votes for President and Vice-President. Such an action has left many of us angry and hurt. Since then we have entered a typical moment of finger pointing, blame, and holding people responsible for what happened. Such finger pointing is not new. . . . I too want to engage in finger pointing and point to myself, and accept personal responsibility in part for what happened in the Capitol this past Wednesday.[220]

This would not be an ordinary homily. The priest went on to accept responsibility for staying silent about Trump's crude behavior—mocking a disabled reporter, demeaning Sen. John McCain for getting captured in Vietnam, boasting about sexually assaulting women. He talked about the

German Catholic Church's failure to condemn Adolf Hitler and US church leaders' complicity in protecting priests who abused children. "As President Trump has lied about so many things," he told his congregation, "I have never spoken out, and fear we are teaching the young that truth and facts do not matter."[221] It almost felt like on that early January morning, a mild-mannered priest in his mid-sixties was taking on the collective failure of so many in the Catholic Church who had remained silent about Trump. A dozen people walked out of Mass that morning, and nearly two dozen more did during the 9:30 Mass. Even more left during the 11:30 a.m. Mass. The sight of people walking out during his homily was shocking. Corcoran never preached about the election because he didn't want to divide his parish along partisan lines. But something changed after January 6. "I guess I was naive because I didn't expect people to walk out," Corcoran told me. "What I saw at the Capitol was so outrageous and something beyond my imagination. I had maintained my silence about the president and many things that he did that bothered me, but this violence crossed the line."[222] As he reflected on how many Catholic leaders remained silent during Trump's presidency, the priest now saw the costs of inaction. "We had allowed so much of what was abnormal to be framed as normal," he said. "There was an instinct to normalize what was wrong." While a handful of people never returned to the parish after his homily, Corcoran also received many emails from people thanking him. The hundreds of messages came from Ireland, England, France, Australia, New Zealand, and Abu Dhabi. "What struck me is you had so many people waiting for someone from the Catholic Church to say something about Trump," he said. "They had only heard the message that if you vote for Biden you are a baby killer and you will go to hell. They were waiting for their local pastor to say something about Trump and they heard crickets."

Fr. Bill's willingness to critique what he considered his own small role in mainstreaming and normalizing Donald Trump offers a lesson for the Catholic Church in the United States. While some clergy and a handful of bishops spoke with moral clarity by specifically naming how much of Trump's rhetoric and policies were hostile to church teaching about human dignity and a consistent ethic of life, many were silent or spoke only in tepid generalizations. For some the fear of being perceived as "divisive" or "political" prevented them from speaking out. In particular, priests under the authority of conservative bishops could see the writing on the wall and likely chose the safe path. The loudest pro-Trump Catholics filled this void with viral YouTube videos, homilies, tweets, messages in parish bulletins, and voter mobilization efforts that reached millions of Catholics.

The messages were simple, clear, and in many cases untethered from Catholic moral theology and church teaching. It's perhaps reassuring, but ultimately a mistake, to dismiss clergy who delivered pro-Trump homilies or claimed election fraud as only fringe figures. While it's true they didn't represent official church positions, pro-Trump clergy were amplified and echoed by similar messages across a broad spectrum of conservative Catholic media, in right-wing nationalist outlets like Breitbart, and in a parallel Catholic subculture where Trump is far more popular than Pope Francis. Perhaps church leaders, not unreasonably, didn't want to draw attention to Trump's more extreme Catholic apologists. But when the president of the United States is tweeting out the de facto political endorsement and loony conspiracy theories of an archbishop who once served as the Holy See's ambassador to Washington, silence can be too easily interpreted as complicity.

If bishops, clergy, and other Catholic pro-life leaders are willing to engage in discernment about their role in enabling Trump, they will need to grapple with the costs of a nearly fifty-year campaign to make ending a legal right to an abortion the preeminent Catholic value in public life. When a conservative majority on the US Supreme Court overturned *Roe v. Wade* on June 24, 2022, in the case of *Dobbs v. Jackson Women's Health Organization*, the historic decision was hailed as a landmark victory by church leaders who had spent decades organizing for this moment. Catholic bishops, pro-life activists, and influential Catholic power brokers from the conservative legal movement who helped Republican presidents shift the court to the right all played complementary roles in the ultimately successful campaign. But the road to overturning *Roe* was littered with moral compromises and alliances that damaged the credibility of the antiabortion movement and underscored the perils for the church of narrowly defining Catholic pro-life engagement by a single issue. A specific political and judicial strategy on abortion had been framed by the loudest voices on the Catholic right as the ultimate test of pro-life Catholic identity.

"The culture wars have distorted the Catholic tradition. The tradition has been weaponized to achieve certain ends," M. Therese Lysaught, a professor at the Neiswanger Institute for Bioethics and Health Care Leadership and the Institute for Pastoral Studies at Loyola University Chicago, told me.[223] In Texas, a state law that preceded the Supreme Court's overturning of *Roe* banned abortion after six weeks of pregnancy and allowed private citizens to sue an abortion provider or anyone who helps a patient obtain an abortion. A successful lawsuit came with a $10,000 reward. "Those who claim to be pro-life are acting in ways that are violent and vicious and dehumanizing toward women," Lysaught said. "They are turning neighbor against neighbor. This is what happens when one issue becomes preeminent. It's an idolatry of a particular issue and agenda. Once you turn something into an idol, you sacrifice everything to it: your tradition, your faith, your well-being and other people's lives." In the year after *Roe* was overturned, despite a significant drop in abortion in the seventeen states with total or six-week bans in effect, the number of abortions increased nationwide overall as more people had abortions in the thirty-three states where it remained legal.[224]

Even as Catholic bishops and pro-life leaders achieved a long-sought victory at the Supreme Court with *Roe*'s demise, the same court that Trump drove to the right with his appointment of three justices undermined efforts to protect life more broadly by making it harder for the federal government to regulate toxic air pollution and—even after a string of mass shootings—ruled New York state's century-old law placing limits on carrying guns in public was unconstitutional. The specter of Trumpism continues to haunt the pro-life movement. The former president quickly took credit for the court's abortion ruling, saying it was only possible "because I delivered everything as promised, including nominating and getting three highly respected and strong Constitutionalists confirmed to the United States Supreme Court."[225]

Trump's presidency provides a stark reminder that Catholic engagement in politics and public life becomes corrupted when those who speak in the name of defending human life are willing to ally with or refuse to challenge leaders, ideologies, and movements that threaten the common good and actively seek to undermine our democracy. Trump's contempt for bedrock democratic principles, his willingness to spread lies and stoke anger, and his crude denigration of public discourse are legacies that too many Catholics were complicit in condoning. The election of only the second Catholic president in American history elevated a new set of opportunities and challenges for the church.

NOTES

1. ABC News, "Donald Trump Announces 2016 Presidential Campaign: 'We Are Going to Make Our Country Great Again,'" June 16, 2015, https://abcnews.go.com/Politics/donald-trump-announces-2016-presidential-campaign-make-country/story?id=31799741.
2. *Time* staff, "Here's Donald Trump's Presidential Announcement Speech," *Time*, June 16, 2015, https://time.com/3923128/donald-trump-announcement-speech/.

3. *Time* staff, "Donald Trump's Presidential Announcement."
4. Michelle Ye Hee Lee, "Donald Trump's False Comments Connecting Immigrants and Crime," *Washington Post*, July 8, 2015, https://www.washingtonpost.com/news/fact-checker/wp/2015/07/08/donald-trumps-false-comments-connecting-mexican-immigrants-and-crime/.
5. Jessica Taylor, "Trump Calls for 'Total and Complete Shutdown of Muslims Entering' U.S." *National Public Radio*, December 7, 2015, https://www.npr.org/2015/12/07/458836388/trump-calls-for-total-and-complete-shutdown-of-muslims-entering-u-s.
6. Jan Ransom, "Trump Will Not Apologize for Calling for Death Penalty over Central Park Five," *New York Times*, June 18, 2019, https://www.nytimes.com/2019/06/18/nyregion/central-park-five-trump.html.
7. Gerard O'Connell, "Pope Responding to Question on Trump: 'A Person Who Only Thinks about Building Walls, and Not Building Bridges, Is Not Christian," *America*, February 18, 2016, https://www.americamagazine.org/content/dispatches/aboard-plane-home-mexico-pope-francis-responds-questions-donald-trump.
8. Chris Cillizza, "Donald Trump Just Went Negative on Pope Francis," *Washington Post*, February 18, 2016, https://www.washingtonpost.com/news/the-fix/wp/2016/02/18/donald-trump-just-went-negative-on-pope-francis/.
9. Catholic News Service, "Cardinal Dolan in Op-ed Criticizes Trump's Anti-Immigrant Rhetoric," July 31, 2015, https://www.ncronline.org/blogs/immigration-and-church/cardinal-dolan-op-ed-criticizes-trumps-anti-immigrant-rhetorıc.
10. Catholic News Service, "Cardinal Dolan in Op-ed Criticizes Trump's Anti-Immigrant Rhetoric," July 31, 2015, https://www.ncronline.org/blogs/immigration-and-church/cardinal-dolan-op-ed-criticizes-trumps-anti-immigrant-rhetoric.
11. Betsy Cooper, Daniel Cox, Rachel Lienesch, and Robert P. Jones, "How Americans View Immigrants, and What They Want from Immigration Reform: Findings from the 2015 American Values Atlas," Public Religion Research Institute, March 29, 2016, https://www.prri.org/research/poll-immigration-reform-views-on-immigrants/.
12. Fr. Marcel Guarnizo, "With Apologies to Donald Trump for the Crazy 'Nativist' Rant on Cardinal Dolan," *Breitbart*, July 30, 2015, https://www.breitbart.com/politics/2015/07/30/with-apologies-to-donald-trump-for-the-crazy-nativist-rant-of-cardinal-dolan/.
13. Susan B. Anthony Pro-Life America, "Pro-Life Women Sound the Alarm: Donald Trump Is Unacceptable," January 26, 2016, https://sbaprolife.org/home/pro-life-women-sound-the-alarmdonald-trump-is-unacceptable.
14. Ted Cruz Caucus Night Speech, *C-Span*, February 1, 2016, https://www.c-span.org/video/?404055-1/ted-cruz-caucus-night-speech.
15. Tom Gjelten, "Evangelical Leaders Under Attack for Criticizing Trump Supporters," *National Public Radio*, December 20, 2016, https://www.npr.org/2016/12/20/506248119/anti-trump-evangelical-faces-backlash.
16. Robert P. George and George Weigel, "An Appeal to Our Fellow Catholics," *National Review*, March 7, 2016, https://www.nationalreview.com/2016/03/donald-trump-catholic-opposition-statement/.
17. Robert O'Harrow Jr. and Shawn Boburg, "A Conservative Activist's Behind-the-Scenes Campaign to Remake the Nation's Courts," *Washington Post*, May 21, 2019,

https://www.washingtonpost.com/graphics/2019/investigations/leonard-leo-federalists-society-courts/.

18. CatholicVote, "CV President Brian Burch Interviewed about Meeting Trump, Asked What Did You Learn?" *National Review*, June 27, 2016, https://catholicvote.org/cv-president-brian-burch-interviewed-about-meeting-trump-asked-what-did-you-learn/.
19. Aimee Murphy, interview with author.
20. Aimee Murphy, interview with author.
21. Anonymous, interview with author.
22. Michael J. O'Loughlin, "Platform Proposal on Hyde Amendment Challenged by Pro-Life Democrats," *America*, July 5, 2016, https://www.americamagazine.org/politics-society/2016/07/05/platform-proposal-hyde-amendment-challenged-pro-life-democrats.
23. O'Loughlin, "Platform Proposal."
24. *Time* staff, "Read President Obama's Commencement Address at Notre Dame," *Time*, June 2, 2016, https://time.com/4336922/obama-commencement-speech-transcript-notre-dame/.
25. Michelle Boorstein, "What It Means that Mike Pence Called Himself an 'Evangelical Catholic,'" *Washington Post*, July 8, 2016, https://www.washingtonpost.com/news/acts-of-faith/wp/2016/07/15/what-it-means-that-mike-pence-called-himself-an-evangelical-catholic/.
26. Monica Davey and Michael Babaro, "How Mike Pence Became a Conservative Hero: Unwavering Opposition to Abortion," *New York Times*, July 16, 2016, https://www.nytimes.com/2016/07/17/us/politics/mike-pence-conservative-abortion.html.
27. The American Presidency Project, "Address Accepting the Vice Presidential Nomination at the Republican National Convention in Cleveland, Ohio," July 20, 2016, https://www.presidency.ucsb.edu/documents/address-accepting-the-vice-presidential-nomination-the-republican-national-convention-0.
28. CBS News New York, "Donald Trump: I Am Your Voice," July 21, 2016, https://www.cbsnews.com/newyork/news/donald-trump-speech-rnc/.
29. David Gibson, "Analysis: Can Hillary Clinton Finally Close the 'God Gap?'" *Religion News Service*, July 26, 2016, https://archive.sltrib.com/article.php?id=4159505&itype=CMSID.
30. Gibson, "Analysis."
31. Michael J. O'Loughlin, "Trump's Catholic Advisers Focus on the Supreme Court, Not Immigration," *America*, September 23, 2016, https://www.americamagazine.org/content/dispatches/head-trumps-catholic-advisory-group-its-all-about-judges.
32. Archbishop Samuel J. Aquila, "Voting as a Catholic in 2016," *Denver Catholic*, October 5, 2016, https://denvercatholic.org/voting-catholic-2016/.
33. Aquila, "Voting as a Catholic."
34. Aquila, "Voting as a Catholic."
35. Brian Roewe, "Trump's Pledge to Catholics: 'I'll Be There for You," October 7, 2016, https://www.ncronline.org/trumps-pledge-catholics-ill-be-there-you.
36. Roewe, "Trump's Pledge to Catholics."
37. *New York Times* staff, "Donald Trump's Taped Comments about Women," October 8, 2016, https://www.nytimes.com/2016/10/08/us/donald-trump-tape-transcript.html.

38. Michael J. O'Loughlin, "Catholic Republicans Have Mixed Reactions to Trump's Crude Talk," *America*, October 9, 2016, https://www.americamagazine.org/politics-society/2016/10/09/catholic-republicans-have-mixed-reactions-trumps-crude-talk.
39. Steve Inskeep, "Conservative Female Voters Disagree on Trump Tape Fallout," *National Public Radio*, October 12, 2016, https://www.khsu.org/regional-interests/2016-10-12/conservative-female-voters-disagree-on-trump-tape-fallout.
40. Andy Crouch, "Speak Truth to Trump," *Christianity Today*, October 10, 2016, https://www.christianitytoday.com/ct/2016/october-web-only/speak-truth-to-trump.html.
41. Julie Asher, "WikiLeaks Hack Exposes Clinton's Staff Past Catholic Conversations," *Catholic News Service*, October 13, 2016, https://www.ncronline.org/wikileaks-hack-exposes-clinton-staffs-past-catholic-conversations.
42. Asher, "WikiLeaks Hack."
43. Asher, "WikiLeaks Hack."
44. Charles J. Chaput, "About Those Unthinking, Backwards Catholics," *First Things*, October 13, 2016, https://www.firstthings.com/blogs/firstthoughts/2016/10/about-those-unthinking-backwards-catholics.
45. *Wall Street Journal*, "Anti-Catholics for Clinton," editorial, October 13, 2016, https://www.wsj.com/articles/anti-catholics-for-clinton-1476315156?mod=rss_opinion_main.
46. Danielle Paquette, "'Rip the Baby Out of the Womb,': What Donald Trump Got Wrong about Abortion in America," October 20, 2016, https://www.washingtonpost.com/news/wonk/wp/2016/10/20/rip-the-baby-out-of-the-womb-what-donald-trump-got-wrong-about-abortion-in-america/.
47. Eric Bradner, "Trump Delivers Harsh Remarks on Clinton at Charity Dinner," *CNN*, October 21, 2016, https://www.cnn.com/2016/10/20/politics/al-smith-dinner-hillary-clinton-donald-tump/index.html.
48. David Gibson, "Guess Who's Coming to Dinner?" *Commonweal*, August 6, 2012, https://www.commonwealmagazine.org/guess-whos-coming-dinner.
49. Catholic News Agency Staff, "Here's the Full Text of Donald Trump's Interview with EWTN," October 28, 2016, https://www.catholicnewsagency.com/news/34829/heres-the-full-text-of-donald-trumps-interview-with-ewtn.
50. Catholic News Agency Staff, "Here's the Full Text of Donald Trump's Interview."
51. Michael J. O'Loughlin, "Days Before the U.S. Election, Pope Francis Warns about the Politics of Fear," *America*, November 6, 2016, https://www.americamagazine.org/faith/2016/11/06/days-us-election-pope-francis-warns-against-politics-fear.
52. O'Loughlin, "Days Before the U.S. Election."
53. Aaron Blake, "Donald Trump Has a Massive Catholic Problem," *Washington Post*, August 30, 2016, https://www.washingtonpost.com/news/the-fix/wp/2016/08/28/donald-trump-has-a-massive-catholic-problem/.
54. Michael J. O'Loughlin, "New Data Suggests Clinton, Not Trump, Won Catholic Vote," *America*, April 6, 2016, https://www.americamagazine.org/politics-society/2017/04/06/new-data-suggest-clinton-not-trump-won-catholic-vote.
55. Jessica Martinez and Gregory A. Smith, "How the Faithful Voted: A Preliminary 2016 Analysis," Pew Research Center, November 9, 2016, https://www.pewresearch.org/short-reads/2016/11/09/how-the-faithful-voted-a-preliminary-2016-analysis/.

56. Nate Cohn, "Why Trump Won: Working-Class Whites," *New York Times*, November 9, 2016, https://www.nytimes.com/2016/11/10/upshot/why-trump-won-working-class-whites.html.
57. Amy Chozick, "Hillary Clinton's Expectations, and Her Ultimate Campaign Missteps," *New York Times*, November 9, 2016, https://www.nytimes.com/2016/11/10/us/politics/hillary-clinton-campaign.html?referringSource=articleShare.
58. Robert P. Jones, "The Rage of White, Christian America," *New York Times*, November 10, 2016, https://www.nytimes.com/2016/11/11/opinion/campaign-stops/the-rage-of-white-christian-america.html.
59. Jones, "The Rage of White, Christian America."
60. Peter Wehner, "When the Decent Drapery of Life Is Rudely Torn Off," *New York Times*, 2024, https://www.nytimes.com/interactive/projects/cp/opinion/election-night-2016/when-the-decent-drapery-of-life-is-rudely-torn-off.
61. Elise Harris, "Outgoing Vatican Ambassador Predicts Trump Will Drop Campaign Rhetoric," January 13, 2017, https://cruxnow.com/interviews/2017/01/outgoing-vatican-ambassador-predicts-trump-will-drop-campaign-rhetoric.
62. Dennis Sadowski, "Cardinal Dolan Has a Minute to Read from Book of Wisdom at Inauguration," *Catholic News Service*, January 12, 2017, https://www.ncronline.org/cardinal-dolan-has-minute-read-book-wisdom-inauguration.
63. Josephine McKenna, "Cardinal Burke: Trump Will Defend Human Life from Conception," *Religion News Service*, November 10, 2016, https://www.ncronline.org/blogs/ncr-today/cardinal-burke-trump-will-defend-human-life-conception.
64. Edward Pentin, "Cardinal Burke: Trump's Victory a Wake-Up Call to U.S. Political Leaders," *National Catholic Register*, November 9, 2016, https://www.ncregister.com/news/cardinal-burke-trump-s-victory-a-wake-up-call-to-us-political-leaders.
65. "Full Text: 2017 Donald Trump Inauguration Speech Transcript," *Politico*, January 20, 2017, https://www.politico.com/story/2017/01/full-text-donald-trump-inauguration-speech-transcript-233907.
66. Aaron Williams, "Hate Crimes Rose the Day after Trump Was Elected, FBI Data Show." *Washington Post*, March 23, 2018, https://www.washingtonpost.com/news/post-nation/wp/2018/03/23/hate-crimes-rose-the-day-after-trump-was-elected-fbi-data-show/.
67. Daniel Villarreal, "Hate Crimes Surged Nearly 20 Percent Says FBI Report," *Newsweek*, November 16, 2020, https://www.newsweek.com/hate-crimes-under-trump-surged-nearly-20-percent-says-fbi-report-1547870.
68. Julie Zauzmer and Sarah Pulliam Bailey, "March for Life: Pence Speaks as Thousands Assemble at Washington Monument," *Washington Post*, January 27, 2017, https://www.washingtonpost.com/local/march-for-life-thousands-assemble-at-washington-monument/2017/01/27/7d880d52-e40a-11e6-ba11-63c4b4fb5a63_story.html.
69. Zauzmer and Bailey, "March for Life."
70. Cardinal Timothy Dolan, "Opening Mass, 2017 National Prayer Vigil for Life," January 26, 2017, https://www.usccb.org/committees/pro-life-activities/cardinal-timothy-m-dolan-opening-mass-2017-national-prayer-vigil.
71. Cindy Wooden, "Christians Who Reject All Refugees Are 'Hypocrites,' Pope Says," *Catholic News Service*, October 13, 2016, https://www.ncronline.org/christians-who-reject-all-refugees-are-hypocrites-pope-says.

72. Cardinal Blase J. Cupich, "Statement of Cardinal Blase J. Cupich, Archbishop of Chicago, on the Executive Order on Refugees and Migrants," January 29, 2017, https://www.archchicago.org/statement/-/article/2017/01/29/statement-statement-of-cardinal-blase-j-cupich-archbishop-of-chicago-on-the-executive-order-on-refugees-and-migrants.
73. Bishop Joe S. Vasquez, "USCCB Committee on Migration Chair Strongly Opposes Executive Order Because It Harms Vulnerable Refugee and Immigrant Families," February 6, 2017, https://www.usccb.org/news/2017/usccb-committee-migration-chair-strongly-opposes-executive-order-because-it-harms.
74. David Gibson, "Archbishop Chaput Slams Trump Critics, Says Notre Dame Should Honor the President," *Religion News Service*, January 27, 2017, https://religionnews.com/2017/01/27/archbishop-chaput-slams-trump-critics-says-notre-dame-should-honor-the-president/.
75. *Washington Post* Staff, "Some of the U.S.' Most Important Catholic Leaders Are Condemning Trump's Travel Ban," *Washington Post*, January 30, 2017, https://www.twincities.com/2017/01/30/some-of-the-u-s-most-important-catholic-leaders-are-condemning-trumps-travel-ban/.
76. Alex Johnson, "Trump Fires Acting Attorney General over Immigration Directive," *NBC News*, January 30, 2017, https://www.nbcnews.com/news/us-news/acting-attorney-general-bars-justice-department-defending-immigration-order-n714451.
77. Eric Lipton and Jeremy W. Peters, "In Gorsuch, Conservative Activist Sees Test Case for Reshaping the Judiciary," *New York Times*, March 18, 2017, https://www.nytimes.com/2017/03/18/us/politics/neil-gorsuch-supreme-court-conservatives.html.
78. CatholicVote, "Gorsuch Is an Absolutely Superb Choice," January 31, 2017, https://catholicvote.org/gorsuch-superb/.
79. Matt Hadro, "Pro-Life, Religious Freedom Leaders Cheer Confirmation of Neil Gorsuch," *Catholic News Agency*, April 7, 2017, https://www.catholicnewsagency.com/news/35795/pro-life-religious-freedom-leaders-cheer-confirmation-of-neil-gorsuch.
80. Hadro, "Pro-Life, Religious Freedom Leaders."
81. Elizabeth Dias and Sydney Ember, "Abortion and Travel Ban Rulings Are Victory for G.O.P. Tactics on Gorsuch," *New York Times*, June 26, 2018, https://www.nytimes.com/2018/06/26/us/politics/travel-ban-donald-trump.html.
82. Dias and Ember, "Abortion and Travel Ban Rulings."
83. Sarah Mervosh, "Kavanaugh and Gorsuch Both Went to the Same Elite Prep School," *New York Times*, July 10, 2018, https://www.nytimes.com/2018/07/10/us/kavanaugh-gorsuch-georgetown-prep.html?smid=nytcore-ios-share&referringSource=articleShare.
84. "The Editors: Anyone Who Recognizes the Humanity of the Unborn Should Support the Nomination of Judge Kavanaugh," *America*, July 9, 2018, https://www.americamagazine.org/politics-society/2018/07/09/editors-anyone-who-recognizes-humanity-unborn-should-support-nomination.
85. Michelle Boorstein, "Brett Kavanaugh's Nomination Fight Is Dividing His D.C. Catholic Church," *Washington Post*, October 5, 2018, https://www.americamagazine

.org/politics-society/2018/09/27/editors-it-time-kavanaugh-nomination-be-withdrawnhttps://www.washingtonpost.com/religion/2018/10/05/brett-kavanaughs-nomination-fight-is-dividing-his-dc-catholic-church/.

86. "The Editors: It Is Time for the Kavanaugh Nomination to Be Withdrawn," *America*, September 27, 2018, https://www.americamagazine.org/politics-society/2018/09/27/editors-it-time-kavanaugh-nomination-be-withdrawn.
87. John Gehring, "Disrupters and Rebuilders: What a Meeting in Modesto Says about the Francis Church," *Commonweal*, May 15, 2017, https://www.commonwealmagazine.org/disrupters-and-rebuilders.
88. Gehring, "Disrupters and Rebuilders."
89. Gehring, "Disrupters and Rebuilders."
90. Gehring, "Disrupters and Rebuilders."
91. Gehring, "Disrupters and Rebuilders."
92. Gehring, "Disrupters and Rebuilders."
93. Gehring, "Disrupters and Rebuilders."
94. John Gehring, "Here's What I Saw When I Attended a Conservative Catholic Gathering in DC's Trump Tower," *Washington Post*, March 17, 2017, https://www.washingtonpost.com/news/acts-of-faith/wp/2017/03/17/heres-what-i-saw-when-i-attended-a-conservative-catholic-gathering-in-dcs-trump-tower/.
95. Gehring, "Here's What I Saw."
96. Gehring, "Here's What I Saw."
97. Gehring, "Here's What I Saw."
98. Jason Horowitz, "A Vatican Shot across the Bow for Hard-Line U.S. Catholics," *New York Times*, August 2, 2017, https://www.nytimes.com/2017/08/02/world/europe/vatican-us-catholic-conservatives.html.
99. Tracy McNicoll, "Wear 'Racist' Like a Badge of Honour, Bannon Tells French Far-Right Summit," *France 24*, November 3, 2018, https://www.france24.com/en/20180311-france-usa-bannon-le-pen-national-front-racist-badge-honour-populist-pep-talk-lille-trump.
100. J. Lester Feder, "This Is How Steve Bannon Sees the Entire World," *BuzzFeed News*, November 15, 2016, https://www.buzzfeednews.com/article/lesterfeder/this-is-how-steve-bannon-sees-the-entire-world#.yky2v0dLgo.
101. Rose Gray, "Trump Defends White Nationalist Protestors: 'Some Very Fine People on Both Sides,'" *Atlantic*, August 15, 2017, https://www.theatlantic.com/politics/archive/2017/08/trump-defends-white-nationalist-protesters-some-very-fine-people-on-both-sides/537012/.
102. Eli Watkins, "Trump: Taking Down Confederate Memorials Is 'Changing History.'" *CNN*, August 15, 2017, https://www.cnn.com/2017/08/15/politics/donald-trump-robert-e-lee/index.html.
103. Vanessa Romo, Martina Stewart, and Brian Naylor, "Trump Ends DACA, Calls on Congress to Act," *National Public Radio*, September 5, 2017, https://www.npr.org/2017/09/05/546423550/trump-signals-end-to-daca-calls-on-congress-to-act.
104. Delia Gallagher, "Pope Francis Says Rescinding DACA Is Not 'Pro-Life,'" *CNN*, September 12, 2017, https://www.cnn.com/2017/09/11/politics/pope-daca-trump/index.html.
105. Kevin Clarke, "Catholic Church Leaders Condemn Trump Administration's Decision to End DACA," *America*, September 5, 2017, https://www.americamagazine

.org/politics-society/2017/09/05/catholic-church-leaders-condemn-trump-administrations-decision-end-daca.

106. David Hinckley, "Cardinal Dolan Calls DACA Termination 'Not Christian' and 'Not American,'" *Huffington Post*, September 5, 2017, https://www.huffpost.com/entry/cardinal-dolan-calls-daca-termination-not-christian_b_59af16c4e4b0c50640cd62c0.
107. Louis Nelson, "Bannon Breaks With Trump on DACA: Conservatives 'Are Not Happy with This,'" *Politico*, September 7, 2017, https://www.politico.com/story/2017/09/07/steve-bannon-trump-daca-242430.
108. Adam Edelman, "Bannon: Catholic Church Backed DACA Because 'It Needs Illegal Aliens,'" *NBC News*, September 7, 2017, https://www.nbcnews.com/politics/immigration/bannon-catholic-church-backed-daca-because-it-needs-illegal-aliens-n799441.
109. John Gehring, "Resist & Be Not Afraid," *Commonweal*, January 11, 2018, https://www.commonwealmagazine.org/resist-be-not-afraid.
110. *Washington Post* Staff, "Kelly: 'Dreamers' Who Didn't Sign Up for DACA Were 'Too Afraid' or 'Too Lazy,'" February 6, 2018, https://www.washingtonpost.com/video/politics/kelly-dreamers-who-didnt-sign-up-for-daca-were-too-afraid-or-too-lazy/2018/02/06/01172cf6-0b66-11e8-998c-96deb18cca19_video.html.
111. Erica Pandey, "John Kelly Doubles Down on 'Lazy' Dreamers Comments," *Axios*, February 7, 2018, https://www.axios.com/2018/02/07/john-kelly-doubles-down-dreamers-should-have-gotten-off-the-couch-and-signed-up-1518022202.
112. John Gehring, "Heavy on Bluster, Thin on Facts," *Commonweal*, February 8, 2018, https://www.commonwealmagazine.org/heavy-bluster-thin-facts.
113. Jack Jenkins, "Dozens of Nuns, Other Catholics Arrested Advocating for Immigrants," *Religion News Service*, February 28, 2018, https://www.deseret.com/2018/2/28/20640780/dozens-of-nuns-other-catholics-arrested-advocating-for-immigrants.
114. Jenkins, "Dozens of Nuns."
115. Rhina Guidos, "Dozens of Catholic Protestors Arrested as They Ask Congress to Help 'Dreamers,'" *Catholic News Service*, March 1, 2018, https://www.chicagocatholic.com/u.s./-/article/2018/03/01/dozens-of-catholic-protestors-arrested-as-they-ask-congress-to-help-dreamers-.
116. Guidos, "Dozens of Catholic Protestors Arrested."
117. John Gehring, "Traditional Disobedience: Renewing the Legacy of Catholic Activism," *Commonweal*, May 22, 2018, https://www.commonwealmagazine.org/traditional-disobedience.
118. John Gehring, "A Bishop against Border Fences," *Commonweal*, March 8, 2018, https://www.commonwealmagazine.org/bishop-against-border-fences.
119. Hope Border Institute, *Sealing the Border: The Criminalization of Asylum Seekers in the Trump Era*, January 2018, https://www.hopeborder.org/sealing-the-border.
120. Gehring, "A Bishop against Border Fences."
121. Department of Justice, Office of Public Affairs, "Attorney General Sessions Delivers Remarks Discussing the Immigration Enforcement Actions of the Trump Administration," May 7, 2018. https://www.justice.gov/opa/speech/attorney-general-sessions-delivers-remarks-discussing-immigration-enforcement-actions.
122. CBS News staff, "Some Pro-Family Groups Silent, While Others Speak Up on Family Separations," June 22, 2018, https://www.cbsnews.com/news/some-pro-family-groups-quiet-on-child-separations/.
123. CBS News staff, "Some Pro-Family Groups Silent."

124. Charles C. Camosy, "You Can't Be Pro-Life and Against Immigrant Children," *New York Times*, June 16, 2018, https://www.nytimes.com/2018/06/16/opinion/sunday/pro-life-immigrant-children-separation.html.
125. Julie Zauzmer and Keith McMillan, "Sessions Cites Bible Passage Used to Defend Slavery in Defense of Separating Immigrant Families," *Washington Post*, June 15, 2018, https://www.washingtonpost.com/news/acts-of-faith/wp/2018/06/14/jeff-sessions-points-to-the-bible-in-defense-of-separating-immigrant-families/.
126. Daniel Arkin, "Over 600 United Methodist Clergy, Laity File Church Complaint against Sessions, a Methodist," *NBC News*, June 19, 2018, https://www.nbcnews.com/storyline/immigration-border-crisis/600-united-methodist-clergy-file-church-complaint-against-attorney-general-n884726.
127. Associated Press/CBS staff, "Inside Look at Border Patrol Facility in Texas Housing Hundreds of Children," June 17, 2018, https://www.cbsnews.com/news/inside-united-states-border-patrol-facility-mcallen-texas-tour-today-2018-06-17/.
128. Ginger Thompson, "Listen to Children Who've Just Been Separated from Their Parents at the Border," *ProPublica*, June 18, 2018, https://www.propublica.org/article/children-separated-from-parents-border-patrol-cbp-trump-immigration-policy.
129. Aline Barros, "A Timeline of Migrant Family Separations," *VOA News*, https://projects.voanews.com/family-separation/.
130. Laura Bush, "Separating Children from Their Parents at the Border Breaks My Heart," *Washington Post*, June 17, 2018, https://www.washingtonpost.com/opinions/laura-bush-separating-children-from-their-parents-at-the-border-breaks-my-heart/2018/06/17/f2df517a-7287-11e8-9780-b1dd6a09b549_story.html.
131. John Gehring, "Mothers in Sanctuary, Living in Churches for over Two Years, Endure Isolation," *National Catholic Reporter*, May 8, 2020, https://www.ncronline.org/opinion/guest-voices/mothers-sanctuary-living-churches-over-two-years-endure-isolation.
132. Marissa J. Lang, "70 Catholics Arrested in D.C. Protest over Trump Immigration Policies," *Washington Post*, July 18, 2019, https://www.washingtonpost.com/local/70-catholics-arrested-in-dc-protest-over-trump-immigration-policies/2019/07/18/1f3b2bd6-a973-11e9-86dd-d7f0e60391e9_story.html.
133. Chico Harlan, "Pope Francis Changes Catholic Church Teaching to Say Death Penalty Is Inadmissible," *Washington Post*, August 2, 2018, https://www.washingtonpost.com/world/pope-francis-changes-catholic-church-teaching-to-say-death-penalty-is-inadmissible/2018/08/02/0d69ef5e-9647-11e8-80e1-00e80e1fdf43_story.html.
134. John Gehring, "What Pope Francis Did Is Just Huge," *Commonweal*, August 7, 2018.
135. Office of Public Affairs, US Department of Justice, "Attorney General William P. Barr Delivers Remarks to the Law School and the de Nicola Center for Ethics and Culture at the University of Notre Dame," October 11, 2019, https://www.justice.gov/opa/speech/attorney-general-william-p-barr-delivers-remarks-law-school-and-de-nicola-center-ethics.
136. John Gehring, "William Barr, Nation's Top Lawyer, Is a Culture Warrior Catholic," *National Catholic Reporter*, July 23, 2020, https://www.ncronline.org/news/william-barr-nations-top-lawyer-culture-warrior-catholic.
137. Alan Cullison, Rebecca Ballhaus, and Dustin Volz, "Trump Repeatedly Pressed Ukraine President to Investigate Biden's Son, *Wall Street Journal*, September 21, 2019,

https://www.wsj.com/articles/trump-defends-conversation-with-ukraine-leader-11568993176.
138. Michael D. Shear, "Pelosi Denies 'Hate' for Trump, Who Accuses Her of Having a 'Nervous Fit,'" *New York Times*, December 5, 2019, https://www.nytimes.com/2019/12/05/us/politics/nancy-pelosi-dont-mess-with-me.html.
139. Lauretta Brown, "Impeachment: Catholic Experts Weigh In," *National Catholic Register*, December 20, 2019, https://www.ncregister.com/news/impeachment-catholic-experts-weigh-in.
140. Brown, "Impeachment."
141. Martina Moyski, "Trump Impeachment: Catholics Weigh in," *Church Militant*, December 19, 2019, https://www.churchmilitant.com/news/article/president-trump-posts-chilling-meme-after-dems-vote to impeach-him-catholics-weigh-in.
142. Moyski, "Trump Impeachment."
143. Sister Simone Campbell, "Catholic Lobby Supports Impeachment of President Trump," *Network*, December 18, 2019, https://networklobby.org/news/catholic-lobby-supports-impeachment-of-president-trump/.
144. Manuel Roig-Franzia and Josh Dawsey, "Trump Lawyer Pat Cipillone Was a Camera-Shy Washington Everyman—Until Impeachment Made Him a Star," *Washington Post*, January 30, 2020, https://www.washingtonpost.com/lifestyle/trump-lawyer-pat-cipollone-was-a-camera-shy-washington-everyman—until-impeachment-made-him-a-star/2020/01/30/97e00354-3ece-11ea-8872-5df698785a4e_story.html.
145. Roig-Franzia and Dawsey, "Trump Lawyer Pat Cipillone Was a Camera-Shy Washington Everyman."
146. *New York Times* staff, "Full Transcript: Mitt Romney's Speech Announcing Vote to Convict Trump," February 5, 2020, https://www.nytimes.com/2020/02/05/us/politics/mitt-romney-impeachment-speech-transcript.html.
147. Arthur C. Brooks, "America's Crisis of Contempt," *Washington Post*, February 7, 2020, https://www.washingtonpost.com/opinions/2020/02/07/arthur-brooks-national-prayer-breakfast-speech/?arc404=true&itid=lk_inline_manual_2.
148. President Donald Trump, "Remarks by President Trump at the 68th Annual National Prayer Breakfast," February 6, 2020, https://trumpwhitehouse.archives.gov/briefings-statements/remarks-president-trump-68th-annual-national-prayer-breakfast/.
149. Tara Submaraniam and Christopher Hickey, "Timeline: Charting Trump's Public Comments on Covid-19 vs. What He Told Woodward in Private," *CNN*, September 16, 2020, https://www.cnn.com/interactive/2020/09/politics/coronavirus-trump-woodward-timeline/.
150. Amanda Terkel, "Trump Said Coronavirus Would 'Miraculously' Be Gone by April, Well, It's April," *Huffington Post*, April 1, 2020, https://www.huffpost.com/entry/trump-coronavirus-gone-april_n_5e7b6886c5b6b7d8095959c2.
151. Claire Giangrave, "Pope Francis Says 'We Are All in the Same Boat' during Urbi et Orbi Ceremony," *Religion News Service*, March 27, 2020, https://religionnews.com/2020/03/27/pope-francis-only-together-we-can-do-this-during-extraordinary-indulgence-ceremony/.
152. Elana Schor, "Trump Campaign Kicks Off Catholic Voter Outreach Project," *Associated Press*, April 3, 2020, https://apnews.com/general-news-b71c87e148e45bff372dda88467f669b.

153. Christopher White, "Trump Says He's 'Best President in History of the Church' in Call with Catholic Leaders," *Crux*, April 26, 2020, https://cruxnow.com/church-in-the-usa/2020/04/trump-says-hes-best-president-in-history-of-the-church-in-call-with-catholic-leaders.
154. White, "Trump Says He's 'Best President.'"
155. Michael J. O'Loughlin, "On Fox News, Cardinal Dolan Praises Trump's Sensitivity to 'Feelings of the Religious Community,'" *America*, April 27, 2020, https://www.americamagazine.org/politics-society/2020/04/27/fox-news-cardinal-dolan-praises-trumps-sensitivity-feelings-religious.
156. Michael J. O'Loughlin, "Cardinal Dolan Defends Comments about Trump, Argues He Has Critics on Both Sides," *America*, May 1, 2020, https://www.americamagazine.org/politics-society/2020/05/01/cardinal-dolan-defends-comments-about-trump-argues-he-has-critics-both.
157. Gerard O'Connell, "Pope Francis on the Death of George Floyd: We Cannot Tolerate Racism and Claim to Defend Life," *America*, June 3, 2020, https://www.americamagazine.org/faith/2020/06/03/pope-francis-death-george-floyd-we-cannot-tolerate-racism-and-claim-defend-life.
158. US Conference of Catholic Bishops, "Statement of U.S. Bishops' President on George Floyd and the Protests in American Cities," May 31, 2020, https://www.usccb.org/news/2020/statement-us-bishops-president-george-floyd-and-protests-american-cities.
159. Alex Rogers, "Trump's Response to Police Killing Threatens to Further Deepen Unrest in America, Democrats and Republicans Say," *CNN*, May 31, 2020, https://www.cnn.com/2020/05/31/politics/trump-george-floyd-protests/index.html.
160. Jill Colvin and Darlene Superville, "Tear Gas, Threats for Protesters before Trump Visits Church," *Associated Press*, June 2, 2020, https://apnews.com/article/donald-trump-ap-top-news-dc-wire-religion-politics-15be4e293cdebe72c10304fe0ec668e4.
161. Jack Jenkins, "Ahead of Trump Photo op, Police Forcibly Expel Priest from St. John's Church Near White House," *Religion News Service*, June 2, 2020, https://religionnews.com/2020/06/02/ahead-of-trump-bible-photo-op-police-forcibly-expel-priest-from-st-johns-church-near-white-house/.
162. John Gehring, "Necessary Bluntness," *Commonweal*, June 9, 2020, https://www.commonwealmagazine.org/necessary-bluntness.
163. CatholicVote, "Statement by CV President on Trump Visit to JPII Shrine," June 2, 2020, https://catholicvote.org/trump-visit-jpii-shrine/.
164. Edward Peters (@canonlaw), "I don't plan to debate the point, but will simply say, I find Archbishop Wilton Gregory's condemnation of the National Shrine devoid of any sense or Christian sentiment," June 2, 2020, https://twitter.com/canonlaw/status/1267880430721695746.
165. Gehring, "Necessary Bluntness."
166. Caitlin Dixon, "A Global Conspiracy against God and Humanity: Controversial Catholic Archbishop Pushes QAnon Themes in Letter to Trump," *Yahoo News*, October 31, 2020, https://news.yahoo.com/a-global-conspiracy-against-god-and-humanity-controversial-catholic-archbishop-pushes-q-anon-themes-in-letter-to-trump-134003985.html.
167. Michelle Boorstein, "Trump Praises Italian Archbishop Who Urges Him to Fight 'Deep State' Protests," *Washington Post*, June 10, 2020, https://www.washingtonpost.com/religion/2020/06/10/trump-archbishop-vigano-letter-deep-state/.

168. Christopher White, "Priests, Parishes Share Vigano's Letter to Trump," *National Catholic Reporter*, June 18, 2020, https://www.ncronline.org/news/priests-parishes-share-vigan-s-letter-trump.
169. Lisa Lambert, "Trailing in Polls, Trump Says Rival Biden Opposes God and Guns," *Reuters*, August 6, 2020, https://www.reuters.com/article/us-usa-election-trump-god/trailing-in-election-polls-trump-says-rival-biden-opposes-god-and-guns-idUSKCN25237A/.
170. Ed Overell, interview with author.
171. Ed Overell, interview with author.
172. Homily of Fr. John Echert, Gloria TV, May 27, 2020, https://gloria.tv/post/uBR4QQ73bYQi4owiEV2ASpAzt#30.
173. Janis Bork, interview with author.
174. Janis Bork, interview with author.
175. Jose De Nigiris, interview with author.
176. Jose De Nigiris, interview with author.
177. Lisa Haertel, interview with author.
178. Lisa Haertel, interview with author.
179. Dartunorro Clark, Susan Kroll, and Monica Alba, "With Low Turnout, Trump Delivers Routine, Rambling Speech in Tulsa as Nation Grapples with Race," *NBC News*, June 20, 2020, https://www.yahoo.com/now/trump-tulsa-holds-first-rally-231719009.html.
180. NBC News, "Holtz: Trump Is a 'Consistent Winner,'' https://www.youtube.com/watch?v=ePB_k-3lm9s.
181. Tribune Staff Report, "Notre Dame Distances Itself from Lou Holtz Comments at RNC," *South Bend Tribune*, August 28, 2020, https://www.southbendtribune.com/story/news/local/2020/08/28/otre-dame-distances-itself-from-lou-holtz-comments-at-rnc/116061256/.
182. Catholic News Agency staff, "Full Text: Sister Dede Byrne's Speech at the 2020 Republican National Convention," August 26, 2020, https://www.catholicnewsagency.com/news/45617/full-text-sister-dede-byrnes-speech-at-the-2020-republican-national-convention.
183. Kenosha News staff, "Video: La Crosse Catholic Priest Says Democrats in Church Are 'Godless' and Imposters in Video," September 8, 2020, https://kenoshanews.com/html_2495c280-82f9-52de-b1de-76d9728c47ac.html.
184. Kenosha News staff, "Video: La Crosse Catholic Priest."
185. Bishop J. Strickland (@BishStrickland), "As the bishop of Tyler I endorse Fr. Altman's statement in this video. My shame is that it has taken me so long. Thank you Fr Altman for your COURAGE. If you love Jesus & His Church & this nation . . . please HEED THIS MESSAGE," September 5, 2020, https://twitter.com/BishStrickland/status/1302293048659935232.
186. Fr. Edward Meeks, "Staring into the Abyss," October 11, 2020, https://www.youtube.com/watch?v=Pi1pHExl6Ug.
187. Bishop J. Strickland (@BishStrickland), "Every Catholic should listen to this wise and faithful priest," October 21, 2020, https://twitter.com/BishStrickland/status/1318974720977571841.
188. Jack Perry, "Bishop Tobin Stirs Up Twitter with Biden Tweet," *Providence Journal*, August 12, 2020, https://www.providencejournal.com/story/news/coronavirus/2020/08/12/bishop-tobin-stirs-up-twitter-with-biden-tweet/113796798/.

189. Fr. Dwight Longenecker (@dlongeneker1), "Joe Biden: fake hair, fake teeth, fake tan, fake working class, fake face job, fake empathy, fake Catholic," August 12, 2020, https://twitter.com/dlongenecker1/status/1293542486594519040?lang=en.
190. Fr. Kevin M. Kusick, "A Leaven in the World . . . Biden Is Not a Practicing Catholic," *The Wanderer*, August 19, 2020, https://thewandererpress.com/catholic/news/our-catholic-faith/a-leaven-in-the-world-biden-is-not-a-practicing-catholic/.
191. Fr. David Miller, Homily, https://www.youtube.com/watch?v=QRDwxHwMq9A.
192. RNS Press Release Distribution Service, "Priests Behaving Badly: Election Edition," October 29, 2020, https://religionnews.com/2020/10/29/priests-behaving-badly-election-edition/.
193. RNS Press Release Distribution Service, "Priests Behaving Badly."
194. Sarah McCammon, "From Debate Stage, Trump Declines to Denounce White Supremacy," *National Public Radio*, September 30, 2020, https://www.npr.org/2020/09/30/918483794/from-debate-stage-trump-declines-to-denounce-white-supremacy.
195. US Conference of Catholic Bishops, *Forming Consciences for Faithful Citizenship*. https://www.usccb.org/issues-and-action/faithful-citizenship/forming-consciences-for-faithful-citizenship-part-one.
196. Lucy Grindon, "Bishop John Stowe Rebukes Trump as 'Anti-Life,'" *National Catholic Reporter*, August 7, 2020, https://www.ncronline.org/news/bishop-john-stowe-rebukes-trump-anti-life.
197. Mark J. Seitz, "Bishop Seitz: Single-Issue Voting Has Corrupted Christian Political Witness," *America*, September 30, 2020, https://www.americamagazine.org/politics-society/2020/09/28/bishop-seitz-el-paso-catholics-single-issue-voting-election-2020-biden-trump.
198. John Carr, "I Helped Write the Bishops' First Document on Catholics and Voting, Here's Why I'm Voting Biden, Not Trump," *America*, September 17, 2020, https://www.americamagazine.org/politics-society/2020/09/17/catholic-biden-trump-faithful-citizenship-election.
199. Mairead McCardle, "Catholic Group Launches $9.7 Million Anti-Biden Campaign in Battleground States," *National Review*, September 15, 2020, https://www.nationalreview.com/news/catholic-group-launches-9-7-million-anti-biden-campaign-in-battleground-states/.
200. Brian Burch, "Peek at These Numbers," CatholicVote, November 11, 2019, https://catholicvote.org/peek-at-these-numbers/.
201. Christopher White, "Trump Courts Catholic Voters at Conservative-Run National Catholic Prayer Breakfast," *National Catholic Reporter*, September 23, 2020, https://www.ncronline.org/news/trump-courts-catholic-voters-conservative-run-national-catholic-prayer-breakfast.
202. White, "Trump Courts Catholic Voters."
203. White, "Trump Courts Catholic Voters."
204. US Conference of Catholic Bishops, "Statement of U.S. Bishop Chairmen on Federal Executions Scheduled this Week," September 22, 2020, https://www.usccb.org/news/2020/statement-us-bishop-chairmen-federal-executions-scheduled-week.
205. Catholic Mobilizing Network, "Catholics Decry Federal Executions as A.G. Barr Receives Award," September 25, 2020, https://catholicsmobilizing.org/posts/catholics-decry-federal-executions-ag-barr-receives-award.

206. Gabby Orr, "Trump Attempts a Fall Turnaround: Reclaiming His Catholic Base," *Politico*, September 24, 2020, https://www.politico.com/news/2020/09/24/donald-trump-catholic-vote-court-fight-420935.
207. *New York Times* staff, "The Dogma Lives Loudly in You: Revisiting Barrett's Confirmation Hearing," September 26, 2020, https://www.nytimes.com/2020/09/26/us/politics/the-dogma-lives-loudly-within-you-revisiting-barretts-confirmation-hearing.html.
208. Gabby Orr, "Trump Attempts a Fall Turnaround: Reclaiming His Catholic Base," *Politico*, September 24, 2020, https://www.politico.com/news/2020/09/24/donald-trump-catholic-vote-court-fight-420935.
209. Michael Warsaw, "Voting for a Vision, Not a Person," *National Catholic Register*, October 17, 2020, https://www.ncregister.com/commentaries/voting-for-a-vision-not-a-person.
210. Elana Schor and David Crary, "APVoteCast: Trump Wins White Evangelicals, Catholics Split," *Associated Press*, November 6, 2020, https://apnews.com/article/votecast-trump-wins-white-evangelicals-d0cb249ea7eae29187a21a702dc84706.
211. Schor and Crary, "APVoteCast."
212. The American Presidency Project, "Address in Wilmington, Delaware Accepting Election as the 46th Presidency of the United States," November 7, 2020, https://www.presidency.ucsb.edu/documents/address-wilmington-delaware-accepting-election-the-46th-president-the-united-states.
213. Michael D. Shear and Stephanie Saul, "Trump, in Taped Call, Pressured Georgia Official to 'Find' Votes to Overturn Election," *New York Times*, January 3, 2021, https://www.nytimes.com/2021/01/03/us/politics/trump-raffensperger-call-georgia.html.
214. Preborn Jesus, "Message of Archbishop Carlo Maria Vigano to American Catholics," November 5, 2020, https://prebornjesus.com/news/message-of-archbishop-carlo-maria-vigano-to-american-catholics.
215. Stephen K. Bannon, "EXC—The Great Reset: Bannon Interviews Archbishop Vigano—'Biden an Irreparable, China-Complicit Disaster,'" *The National Pulse*, 2021, https://thenationalpulse.com/archive-post/the-great-reset-bannon-vigano-biden/.
216. Paul Moses, "The Renegade Catholic Clerics Who Shamefully Backed Trump's Big Lie," *CNN*, January 19, 2021, https://www.cnn.com/2021/01/19/opinions/catholic-clerics-who-backed-trump-big-lie-moses/index.html.
217. Moses, "Renegade Catholic Clerics."
218. James Martin, "How Catholic Leaders Helped Give Rise to Violence at the U.S. Capitol," *America*, January 12, 2021, https://www.americamagazine.org/faith/2021/01/12/capitol-riot-congress-trump-catholic-bishops-james-martin-239697.
219. Mike Dorning and Bill House, "'Slipping in People's Blood': Capitol Police Officer Edwards Recalls Fight with Jan. 6 Mob," *Bloomberg*, June 9, 2022, https://www.bloomberg.com/news/articles/2022-06-10/-slipping-in-people-s-blood-cop-recalls-fight-with-jan-6-mob.
220. Mary Schmich, "Column: A Catholic Pastor Speaks Out about Trump. Some Parishioners Walk Out," *Chicago Tribune*, January 16, 2021, https://www.chicagotribune.com/2021/01/16/column-a-catholic-pastor-speaks-out-about-trump-some-parishioners-walk-out/.
221. Schmich, "Column: A Catholic Pastor Speaks Out About Trump."

222. Fr. William Corcoran, interview with author.
223. M. Therese Lysaught, interview with author.
224. Deidre McPhillips, "Abortions Increased Overall in the Year Post-Dobbs, but There Are Stark Inequalities State-to-State," *CNN*, October 24, 2023, https://www.cnn.com/2023/10/24/health/abortion-access-inequality-one-year-post-dobbs-wecount/index.html.
225. Lauren Feiner and Dan Mangan, "Trump Takes Credit for End of *Roe v. Wade* after His 3 Supreme Court Justice Picks Vote to Void Abortion Rights," June 24, 2022, https://www.cnbc.com/2022/06/24/roe-v-wade-decision-trump-takes-credit-for-supreme-court-abortion-ruling.html.

3

JOE BIDEN AND THE BATTLE OVER CATHOLIC IDENTITY IN POLITICS

When John F. Kennedy became the first Catholic to win the presidency in 1960, his narrow victory over Richard Nixon came only after overcoming organized opposition from Protestant leaders who feared a Catholic in the White House would take his marching orders from the pope. A group of Protestant clergy, representing more than two dozen denominations and led by Norman Vincent Peale—a preacher who later presided over the church Donald Trump attended in his youth—warned that a Catholic president would be "under extreme pressure by the hierarchy of his church."[1] Ignoring the advice of his political advisors, the young Massachusetts senator gave a pivotal speech on September 12, 1960, to the Greater Houston Ministerial Association in an effort to convince those clergy and anxious voters that he would remain independent of Vatican control.

"I believe in an America that is officially neither Catholic, Protestant nor Jewish," Kennedy said, "where no public official either requests or accepts instructions on public policy from the Pope, the National Council of Churches or any other ecclesiastical source; where no religious body seeks to impose its will directly or indirectly upon the general populace or the public acts of its officials."[2] Sixty years later, after Biden's election as only the second Catholic president in American history, the kind of intentional distance Kennedy put between himself and the Catholic Church was no longer culturally necessary. President Biden put a picture of Pope Francis in the Oval Office and praised the pope as "the most significant warrior for peace I've ever met."[3] In one of his first speeches as president-elect, Biden addressed the Jesuit Refugee Service on its fortieth anniversary. He vowed to meet his campaign promise to increase the number of refugees resettled in the United States after years of massive cuts during the Trump administration.[4] Earlier that day, the president-elect spoke with Pope Francis on the phone. The conversation focused on their shared goals of protecting immigrants and refugees and fighting climate change.[5]

The historical arc from Kennedy to Biden reflects the trajectory of a striving immigrant faith taking its place in the American mainstream as well as the shifting politics of the church over the past six decades. While Kennedy's religious opposition came from Protestant ministers—he never had to navigate thorny debates over abortion or LGBTQ rights in relation to Catholic teaching—Biden's faith has been relentlessly questioned by bishops from his own church. As Pope Francis and Vatican leaders accentuate common ground with the president on a range of issues that align with Catholic social teaching, the most reactionary US bishops blithely ignored frequent admonishments from Rome not to give the impression the Catholic Church is a single-issue interest group. These leaders have tried to selectively weaponize Communion against Biden and other pro-choice Catholic elected officials and even question their right to call themselves Catholic. "The politicization of the leadership of the Catholic Church in the U.S. today is very clear," said Shaun Casey, author of *The Making of a Catholic President: Kennedy vs. Nixon 1960* and a former director of the Office of Religion and Global Affairs at the U.S. Department of State. "In Kennedy's era, Catholic leaders were still struggling to carve out legitimacy in the culture. In many ways now, Catholic bishops are struggling to recover the legitimacy they have lost in the culture wars."[6]

BIDEN, BISHOPS, AND COMMUNION POLITICS

Less than a week after the president-elect spoke with Pope Francis and later in the same day delivered a speech to the Jesuit Refugee Service, where he vowed to "restore America's historic role in protecting the vulnerable and defending the rights of refugees everywhere," the president of the US bishops' conference announced a special working group focused on Biden. The president's support for abortion rights presented a "difficult and complex situation," Archbishop José Gomez of Los Angeles said in a statement. "When politicians who profess the Catholic faith support [abortion rights], there are additional problems. Among other things, it creates confusion among the faithful about what the Catholic Church actually teaches on these questions."[7] It's not surprising that bishops would challenge Biden on abortion. Church teaching holds that life is sacred from the moment of conception until natural death. The Catechism of the Catholic Church defines abortion as a "moral evil."[8] Biden and the Democratic Party's shift to the left on abortion (a theme I will address later in the chapter) has also heightened tensions between pro-choice Catholic politicians and church leaders. But to argue the president was creating "confusion" among Catholics about what the church teaches strains credulity. You would be hard pressed to find many people, whether they are Catholic or not, who don't know that the Catholic Church opposes abortion. Bishops and Catholic activists have been some of the most visible leaders in the antiabortion movement for decades. As detailed in the previous chapter, conservative Catholic political activists made abortion, and the appointment of Supreme Court justices who would overturn *Roe*, the lynchpin of Catholic support for Trump. If Catholic social teaching is often called Catholicism's "best kept secret," the church's high-profile campaigns against abortion are organized, well-funded, and widely covered by the media. Pope Francis, who strongly condemns abortion, addressed the subject in a 2013 interview shortly after his election when he urged church leaders to embrace a more expansive pro-life ethic. "We cannot insist only on issues related to abortion, gay marriage, and the use of contraceptive methods," the pope said. "We have to find a new balance."[9]

The problem for Archbishop Gomez and other bishops seemed not so much to be the purported confusion Biden creates for other Catholics but the fact that the nation's most prominent Catholic represents a vivid reminder of the church's own inability to convince most Catholics of the church's position that abortion should always be criminalized, even in the cases of rape and incest. The president's position that one of the most personal, often anguished decisions a woman can make should not be decided by the government is hardly an outlier belief. High percentages of Christians across different denominations, with the exception of white evangelicals, believe that abortion should be legally accessible.[10] While polling data finds that Catholics' views on the legality of abortion differ depending on political party and frequency of Mass attendance, the majority of Catholics say abortion should not be prohibited in all cases. A Pew Research Center survey in 2022, released a month after the US Supreme Court overturned *Roe*, found that 60 percent of Catholics in the United States said abortion should be legal in all or most cases. The end *of Roe*, in fact, seems to have solidified some Catholics' views.[11] A 2022 survey from the Public Religion Research Institute taken after the Court's decision found that 75 percent of Latino Catholics believe that abortion should be legal in most or all cases, a significant increase from 2010 when 51 percent said the same.[12] It's also true that while the loudest activist voices garner the most media attention, Americans' views on the legality of abortion can be relatively nuanced and don't always fall along neat political lines. Overall, about one-third of Americans who identify as Republican or as Republican-leaning independents do not agree with their party on abortion, while three in ten Democrats and Democratic-leaning independents do not agree with their party on abortion, according to a 2020 Pew study. "As is true on many other political issues, sizable minorities of Republicans and Democrats say they do not agree with the dominant position on abortion of the party they identify with or lean toward," the research center noted.[13]

Church leaders should not be expected to use polling to determine their position on abortion or any other issue. At the same time, the bishops' tone and style of public engagement should not happen in a vacuum—especially when there is no consensus among Catholics or other Americans that making abortion illegal is the only, or most effective, way of building a culture where women and children are valued. The late Archbishop John Quinn of San Francisco, who served as the president of the US bishops' conference from 1977 to 1980, spoke candidly to the risks the church faces. In an essay written in *America* magazine after President Obama gave the 2009 commencement address at the University of Notre Dame, which provoked outrage among many bishops and conservative Catholic leaders, Quinn articulated the important distinction between holding a foundational moral principle (all life is sacred) and applying that principle in the contested arena of politics and public life. "There is no disagreement within this conference about the moral evil of abortion, its assault upon the dignity of the human person, or the moral imperative of enacting laws that prohibit abortion in American society," Quinn wrote. "But there is deep and troubled disagreement among us on the issue of *how* we as bishops should witness concerning this most searing and volatile issue in American public life. And this disagreement has now become a serious and increasing impediment to our ability to teach effectively in our own community and in the wider American society. The bishops' voice has been most credible in the cause of life when we have addressed this issue as witnesses and teachers of a great moral tradition, and not as actors in the political arena." Quinn continued:

> For most of our history, the American bishops have assiduously sought to avoid being identified with either political party and have made a conscious effort to be seen as transcending party considerations in the formulation of their teachings. The condemnation of President Obama and the wider policy shift that represents signal to many thoughtful persons that the bishops have now come down firmly on the Republican side in American politics.[14]

Nearly a decade and a half later, many church leaders have still not learned the lessons Archbishop Quinn sought to impart. As bishops prepared to meet for the first time as a group after Biden's election, a proposal to draft a statement about the Eucharist that would include taking a position on whether pro-choice Catholics should be prohibited from receiving the sacrament attracted a buzz of national media attention. The fact that US bishops were even considering a statement that could possibly recommend denying Communion to Catholic elected officials was another dramatic sign of how adrift the American hierarchy had grown from Pope Francis and Vatican leaders. The Eucharist, Pope Francis wrote in *Evangelii Gaudium*, is "not a prize for the perfect but a powerful medicine and nourishment for the weak."[15] As the debate over Biden, bishops and Communion politics heated up, reporters asked the pope for his opinion. Francis answered carefully and said he didn't know enough about the US context, but he issued a pointed warning, one that echoed what Archbishop Quinn told his fellow bishops more than a decade earlier. "Whenever the church, in order to defend a principle, didn't do it pastorally, it has taken political sides," the pope said. "If the pastor leaves the pastorality of the church, he immediately becomes a politician." In contrast, Francis urged priests and bishops to demonstrate "the style of God" and accompany the faithful with "closeness, compassion and tenderness." "And what should pastors do? Be pastors and not go condemning." The pope told reporters he had never denied Communion to anyone.[16]

Church leaders viewed as more conservative than Francis have also been wary of using Communion to sanction elected officials. Pope John Paul II, a hero in the antiabortion movement, gave Communion to Rome's mayor Francesco Rutelli, a Catholic who led his party's campaign for liberalized abortion laws. When Pope Benedict XVI visited the United States in 2008, John Kerry and Pelosi both received Communion during a papal Mass at Nationals Park. New York Cardinal Timothy Dolan, who Donald Trump saw as an ally during the 2020 election, said he would not have denied Biden Communion after the presidential candidate was turned away by a South Carolina priest during the campaign. A month before bishops met for their annual spring meeting to discuss whether to move forward with drafting a document on the Eucharist, key Vatican leaders urged the conference to back down. In a letter to the US bishops' conference president, the prefect of the Vatican's Congregation for the Doctrine of the Faith, outlined his concerns. Cardinal Luis Ladaria warned that without unanimity on the issue, any national policy could "become a source of discord rather than unity within the episcopate and the larger church in the United States." The cardinal also reminded bishops that any national policy cannot supersede the authority of individual bishops in their own dioceses. And, perhaps most notably, Ladaria reminded the US bishops that it would be "misleading" to present abortion and euthanasia as "the only grave matters of Catholic moral and social teaching that demand the fullest level of accountability on the part of Catholics."[17] Despite those red flags from the Vatican, the proposal was added to the agenda. The conference meeting, held over Zoom for Covid precautions, revealed a deeply divided American hierarchy.

"The proposal before us presents us with a stark and historic choice," Cardinal Joseph Tobin of Newark, New Jersey, told his fellow bishops during the meeting. "Voting in the affirmative will produce a document, not unity. Voting against it will allow us to work together in dialogue to forge a broad agreement on the serious questions embedded in the issue of eucharistic worthiness." The "categorical exclusion of Catholic political leaders from the Eucharist based on their public policy positions," Tobin warned, would force the bishops' conference "into the very heart of the toxic partisan strife, which has distorted our own political culture."[18] At the time the cardinal was one of only two Americans on the Vatican's Congregation for Bishops, a body that advises the pope on which clergy to appoint as bishops around the world. Wilton Gregory of Washington, DC, the newest American bishop to be elevated to a cardinal by Pope Francis a year before—and the first Black cardinal in the United States—also urged caution. "The choice before us at this moment is either we pursue a path of strengthening unity among ourselves or settle for creating a document that will not bring unity, but may very well further damage it," he said. "The strength of our voice in advancing the mission of Christ has been seriously weakened," he acknowledged.[19] As a cardinal in the nation's capital, Gregory gave an early signal he had no interest in denying the president Communion when he told a reporter shortly after Biden's election that he wanted to work through disagreements civilly and seek common ground. "I don't want to go to the table with a gun on the table first," Gregory told *Religion News Service*.[20]

Bishop Kevin Rhoades, chair of the bishops' doctrine committee, insisted that the goal of the proposal was not political or about pro-choice Catholic politicians at all. The claim was a stretch. Even as Rhoades tried to distance the effort from politics, several bishops made frequent references to Biden and House Speaker Nancy Pelosi during the open floor discussions at the meeting. "It's not the bishops that have brought us to this point, it's really, I think, some of our public officials," said Kansas City, Kansas, Archbishop Joseph Naumann, who chaired the bishops' pro-life committee at the time. "Our president talks about it [abortion] as a right," he said. "This is a Catholic president that is doing this."[21] (In 2008 Naumann told then

Kansas Governor Kathleen Sebelius not to receive Communion.) Bishop Liam Cary of Baker, Oregon, endorsed the proposed document because, he noted, "we've never had a situation like this where the executive is a Catholic president who is opposed to a teaching of the church."[22] San Francisco Archbishop Salvatore Cordileone had already released his own detailed pastoral letter on Communion to Catholics in his archdiocese, which included House Speaker Nancy Pelosi. "Those who reject the teaching of the church on the sanctity of human life and those who do not seek to live in accordance with that teaching should not receive the Eucharist," the archbishop wrote in that document.[23] The message coming from Rome was sharply different. "The concern in the Vatican," Antonio Spadaro, a Jesuit priest and close confidant of Pope Francis told *The New York Times*, "is not to use access to the Eucharist as a political weapon."[24]

As the bishops deliberated, political leaders in Washington were not passive observers. A group of sixty Catholic Democrats in the House of Representatives, including Reps. Rosa DeLauro and Alexandria Ocasio-Cortez, released a "statement of principles" that called on church leaders to avoid "weaponizing" the Eucharist. Lawmakers asked the bishops to "heed the words of Our Holy Father Pope Francis, who wrote in his Apostolic Exhortation, 'The Joy of the Gospel,' that 'the Eucharist although it is the fullness of sacramental life, is not a prize for the perfect but a powerful medicine and nourishment for the weak.'" The representatives also noted their role in a pluralistic democracy. "As legislators, we too are charged with being facilitators of the Constitution which guarantees religious freedom for all Americans," the lawmakers wrote. "In doing so, we guarantee our right to live our own lives as Catholics but also foster an America with a rich diversity of faiths."[25] Despite warnings from the Vatican, a proposal to draft a document on "Eucharistic consistency" passed 168 to 55. Bishops would reconvene at their fall meeting to vote on a draft document. A month before bishops gathered in Baltimore for the vote, House Speaker Nancy Pelosi met Pope Francis for a private meeting at the Vatican. Pelosi called the meeting a "spiritual, personal and official honor" and praised the pope's advocacy for the environment, immigrants, and refugees.[26] The Vatican announced the meeting in its daily bulletin but gave no details. A few weeks later, only days before the US bishops' assembly, Biden met with Pope Francis at the Vatican for more than seventy-five minutes. Reporters who cover the Vatican noted it was the longest meeting between Francis and any world leader. According to a Vatican communique, climate change was the top issue discussed, along with the Covid pandemic and the plight of refugees. Biden later told reporters that Francis called him a "good Catholic" and encouraged him to "keep receiving Communion."[27] The Vatican did not dispute the president's account of the meeting.

The optics of Pope Francis's meeting with Pelosi and Biden as some American bishops were trying to bar them from the Eucharist sent a clear signal from Rome and provoked strong reactions from conservative church leaders. "I fear that the Church has lost its prophetic voice," tweeted Bishop Thomas Tobin of Providence, Rhode Island. "Where are the John the Baptists who will confront the Herods of our day?"[28] Tobin had earlier tweeted that Biden's "persistent support of abortion is an embarrassment for the Church and a scandal to the world." The American Cardinal Raymond Burke asked his 39,000 Twitter followers to pray "for the Church in the USA and in every nation, that she will be faithful and clear in defending the sanctity of the Holy Eucharist and safeguarding the souls of Catholic politicians who would grievously violate the moral law."[29] After a year of fierce debate and media attention, the bishops' conference ultimately backed down from directly taking on Biden and other Catholic politicians in the controversial document. The Vatican's representative in Washington, Archbishop Christophe Pierre, kicked off the bishops' national assembly warning that "a divided Church will never be able to lead others to the deeper unity desired by Christ."[30] The Communion text, approved 222–8, was largely a reiteration of church teaching about the Eucharist. The 30-page document made only a generic reference to lay Catholics who "have a special responsibility to form their consciences in accord with the Church's faith and the moral law, and to serve the human family by upholding human life and dignity." *Washington Post* columnist E. J. Dionne Jr. summed up the anticlimactic document as "more of a truce than a resolution" in the Catholic culture wars.[31]

Indeed, those church leaders most determined to take on Biden and other pro-choice Catholic elected officials were not about to go quiet. Archbishop Joseph Naumann, chairman of the bishops' committee on pro-life activities, used his homily at the annual National Prayer Vigil for Life to keep pressure on the president. "Sadly, President Biden is the perfect example of the religiously and ethically incoherent straddle: claiming to believe that human life begins at conception and personally opposing abortion, while doing everything within his power to promote and institutionalize abortion not only in the USA but also around the world," he said three months after the bishops' meeting.[32] A few weeks later, the archbishop told *The Catholic World Report* that "the president should stop defining himself as a devout Catholic."[33] Naumann knew that his certainty over the state of Biden's soul and his policing of the president's Catholic identity was not a perspective shared by Pope Francis. The archbishop had a conveniently tidy answer for that friction. "I think the pope doesn't understand the U.S., just as he doesn't understand the Church in the U.S.," the archbishop told the German newspaper *Die Tagespost.* "His advisers and the people surrounding him have completely misinformed him on this," Naumann added.[34] San Francisco Archbishop Salvatore Cordileone sparked an even more intense round of national media coverage over Communion politics in the spring of 2022 when he announced that he would bar House Speaker Nancy Pelosi from receiving the sacrament in his archdiocese.

> After numerous attempts to speak with her to help her understand the grave evil she is perpetrating, the scandal she is causing, and the danger to her own soul she is risking, I have determined that the point has come in which I must make a public declaration that she is not to be admitted to Holy Communion unless and until she publicly repudiate her support for abortion 'rights' and confess and receive absolution for her cooperation in this evil in the sacrament of Penance.

Cordileone wrote in a letter to Catholics in his archdiocese, "I assure you that my action here is purely pastoral, not political."[35] Despite that caveat, the public sanctioning of one of the most prominent Catholics in the nation would, with good reason, be viewed as decidedly political.

* * *

Hypocrisy does not seem to trouble the most ardent proponents of using Communion as a political cudgel. As noted in the previous chapter, Donald Trump's former Attorney General William Barr, a Catholic who has been outspoken about his faith, played a key role in reviving the federal death penalty in 2019. The Catholic Church teaches that executions are always morally unacceptable. The Catechism describes the death penalty as "an attack on the inviolability and dignity of the person." Simply put, the state-sanctioned killing of a human being on death row is a pro-life issue for the church. But instead of threats to deny Barr communion, the National Catholic Prayer Breakfast honored him in 2020 with an award dedicated to lay Catholics whose work "exemplifies" service and "fidelity to the Church."[36] On the day Barr received the award, former Archbishop Charles Chaput of Philadelphia praised him and gleefully added that Barr is "disliked by all the right people."[37] Many bishops denounced the University of Notre Dame when the university gave President Obama an honorary degree. But many bishops were silent when the most influential Catholic in the Trump administration, who advanced a policy directly at odds with church teaching on human life, was honored for his service and fidelity to the church. Deploying the Eucharist into political fights is wrong whether it's directed at those who support abortion rights or the death penalty. But those starkly different reactions from the hierarchy illuminated the selective policing of Catholic identity in politics and also sent a clear message that church leaders were willing to stay quiet if speaking out would upset powerful Republican leaders and conservative donors.

Two days after San Francisco's archbishop issued his Communion-banning decree against Pelosi, which only has standing in his own archdiocese, the House Speaker attended Mass and received Communion at Holy Trinity Catholic Church, a Jesuit parish in the Georgetown neighborhood of Washington, DC, where President Biden sometimes attends Mass.[38] Pelosi speaks often about the importance of her Catholic faith, and it's not unusual for her to attend Mass. A month later, Pelosi also received Communion in Rome at a papal Mass in St. Peter's Basilica. During a homily at the Sunday Mass Pelosi attended, Fr. Benjamin Hawley, a priest at Holy Trinity, referenced the divisions roiling the church and politics. Hawley pointed to three things he called "weapons of mass destruction" that are "destroying our civic and church cultures"—exclusion, repression, and scorn. "Worst of all for culture, country and church are the election deniers and Vatican II deniers who would exclude, repress and scorn all of us to gain the authoritarian control of culture, country and church," he said.[39] A year earlier, another Holy Trinity priest offered a blunt critique of viewing the church's pro-life stance only through a single lens. "You may think that we are already a pro-life Church, but, my friends, we are not," Fr. William Kelley said in a homily as President Biden sat in the congregation. "We are only an antiabortion Church. . . . Our Church also falls short in its self-identification as pro-life because of our disproportionate concerns for life in the womb and our relatively scant concern for the quality of life after birth."[40]

Holy Trinity has a long history as a parish at the crossroads of religion and politics. Founded in 1787, Holy Trinity is the oldest parish and church in continuous operation in Washington. Fr. Francis Neale, the first pastor, knew George Washington. Abraham Lincoln attended a funeral at the church and visited wounded Union soldiers on church grounds when it served as a field hospital during the Civil War. John Kennedy was a parishioner for a decade. Today it is not uncommon to find Joe Biden, Nancy Pelosi, and the retired Sen. Patrick Leahy at Mass. Rev. Kevin Gillespie, Holy Trinity's pastor, told me that from its beginning more than two hundred years ago the parish has always been a place where "Catholics have asked, how does our church engage with democracy in a collaborative way and not with the animosities that characterized the church in Europe?"[41]

"In some ways we're ground zero when it comes to politics," Gillespie said. "We've had presidents, senators and cabinet members who are comfortable worshiping here, and people on both sides of the aisle come up for Communion. We want to be a welcoming community." Holy Trinity displays a Black Lives Matter banner in front of the church. An annual Pride Mass is held for the parish's active LGBTQ community. Gillespie acknowledges that the Catholic culture wars, the clergy abuse crisis, and divisions over abortion have left many Catholics demoralized. But he still believes Catholics have resources to draw from that can renew our church, culture, and public life today. "Issues have a context," he said. "We have a rich history and tradition, along with a global perspective as a church, that enable us to say there have been battles and crises before and we can learn from the past and move forward to the future."

Gillespie was president of St. Joseph's University in Philadelphia in 2013 when he first met Joe Biden. The vice president was attending his niece's engagement party. "I remember that he was ecstatic talking about the election of Pope Francis," Gillespie recalled. When the president attends Mass at Holy Trinity, the priest says he sees "a devoted, reverent Catholic" who tries to be a respectful and engaged member of the parish. "There is a real genuineness to his faith," the pastor remarked. One spring Sunday, when a young boy received his First Communion, Biden waited in the back of the church to congratulate him. "It was very moving and authentic," Gillespie said. On Christmas Eve, when Holy Trinity is packed, Biden knows the gauntlet of security vehicles outside the church would be an inconvenience, the pastor said, so he watches the Mass on livestream from the White House.

Gillespie has received more than 130 letters and emails from people outside the parish angry that he welcomes and gives Communion to Biden and Pelosi. "It comes with the territory," he told me. "I talk to Cardinal Gregory here and we are on the same page. The weaponization of Communion is wrong." Gillespie believes in the sanctity of life in the womb. He also understands many Catholics disagree with the church's position on abortion. It's a subject he handles delicately as a pastor because he recognizes the complexity and gravity of the subject. "Personally, I confess I'm sometimes reluctant to use the A word in a homily because I know there are probably people in the pews who have had an abortion or made a decision to have a child and all of these are personal and profound decisions." Gillespie also acknowledges that he is not often perceived to be a trusted messenger on the issue. "I'm a white, celibate man. We need to value the voices of women."[42]

FROM "SAFE, LEGAL, AND RARE" TO "SHOUT YOUR ABORTION"

Joe Biden and Nancy Pelosi are not the only Catholic elected officials to have faced public rebukes from the hierarchy over abortion. Even years before John Kerry's 2004 presidential run became mired in Communion politics after a handful of bishops told him not to receive the sacrament, New York Governor Mario Cuomo squared off with the Archbishop of New York, John O'Connor. "I do not see how a Catholic in good conscience can vote for an individual expressing himself or herself as favoring abortion," O'Connor, who would soon be made a cardinal by Pope John Paul II, said during a televised press conference in 1984.[43] Cuomo had signed legislation providing state funding of abortion. A reporter from a conservative Catholic newspaper stirred the pot even more when he asked whether O'Connor would excommunicate the governor. The archbishop said he would have to think about it. Cuomo, watching the press conference on television, was incensed. "This remark set off one of the biggest, most public, and most prolonged brawls between a Catholic politician and a leading Catholic prelate in memory," the longtime religion reporter and Catholic editor Peter Steinfels wrote.[44]

Cuomo was a well-read, intellectual Catholic. In an editorial on his death in 2015, *Commonweal* magazine noted that "his willingness to engage his critics and explain in some detail why he thought prohibition (of abortion) was not a realistic or prudent option set him apart from most pro-choice Catholic politicians." So did, the editors wrote, "his command of the church's social teaching and tradition of moral reasoning, especially on the complex relationship between morality and the law."[45] Only a few days before Archbishop O'Connor's provocation on live television, Fr. Richard McBrien, the chairman of the University of Notre Dame's theology department who had been reading Cuomo's published diaries, invited the governor to give a lecture "on your own personal journey as a Catholic" and "your abiding effort to make your political activity a faithful expression of your religious conviction."[46] On September 13, 1984, Cuomo delivered a widely anticipated lecture at the University of Notre Dame entitled "Religious Belief and Public Morality: A Catholic Governor's Perspective."[47] The nearly hour-long speech, which received front-page coverage in *The New York Times* and is still both widely lauded and criticized by church leaders and theologians today, made clear distinctions between personal belief, morality, and the law. The governor acknowledged his personal opposition to abortion but asked, "When should I argue to make my religious value your morality?"

He also argued that banning abortion is "not a plausible possibility and even if it could be obtained, it wouldn't work." Instead, Cuomo proposed, "we should provide funds and opportunity for young women to bring their child to term, knowing both of them will be taken care of if that is necessary; we should teach our young men better than we do now their responsibilities in creating and caring for human life."

"The hard truth is that abortion isn't a failure of government," Cuomo said. "No agency or department of government forces women to have abortions, but abortion goes on. Are we asking government to make criminal what we believe to be sinful because we ourselves can't stop committing the sin? The failure here is not Caesar's. This failure is our failure, the failure of the entire people of God." A Catholic elected official, the governor argued, "lives the political truth most Catholics through most of American history have accepted and insisted on: the truth that to assure our freedom we must allow others the same freedom, even if occasionally it produces conduct by them which we would hold to be sinful. We know that the price of seeking to force our beliefs on others is that they might someday force theirs on us." In a question-and-answer period after the lecture, Cuomo was asked by a student to distinguish between his opposition to capital punishment and his support for legal abortion. "This isn't killing," the governor replied. "It's giving you a choice." The remark "drew boos and hisses from some segments of the audience, but applause from others," the *Times* reported.[48]

Cuomo's formulation of personally opposing abortion while refusing to publicly outlaw it in many ways became the standard default position of pro-choice Catholic Democrats who sought to navigate the rocky shoals of abortion politics in relation to Catholic teaching. The story of Joe Biden's long, evolving, and at times seemingly anguished history with the issue reflects broader shifts in the Democratic Party's approach to abortion policy in recent decades. While divides over whether a woman should have a legal right to an abortion now largely fall along partisan lines, in 1973—the year the Supreme Court's landmark *Roe v. Wade* decision sparked a national political battle over the issue—that was not the case. Abortion was not a defining issue for either party. It was also not unusual to see Republican politicians who supported abortion rights and Democrats who opposed the legalization of abortion. Even four years after *Roe*, abortion had not yet become a rigid partisan issue for voters. In fact, 39 percent of Republicans said abortion should be allowed for any reason, compared to 35 percent of Democrats, according to The General Social Survey opinion poll in 1977.[49] Antiabortion activism in the early days was not simply a project of Republican politics. "For the most part, the public rhetoric of the (antiabortion) movement tended to be grounded in liberalism as seen through a mid-20th-century Catholic lens. It's New Deal, Great Society liberalism," the historian Daniel K. Williams, author of *Defenders of the Unborn*, noted in a 2016 interview with the *Atlantic* magazine entitled "The Progressive Roots of the Pro-Life Movement." Williams told the journalist Emma Green that "too many historians took for granted that the pro-life movement emerged as a backlash against feminism, and/or as a backlash against the Supreme Court's decision in 1973." But Green noted that Williams writes in his book that "the pro-life movement that we have always labeled 'conservative' was at one time much more deeply rooted in the liberal rights-based values than we might have suspected."[50]

When *Roe* legalized abortion in 1973, a thirty-year-old Biden had just entered the Senate only seventeen days before. He said the ruling went "too far."[51] In 1982, when he voted in favor of a constitutional amendment backed by Republicans to allow states to overturn *Roe v. Wade*—a decision he called "the single most difficult vote I've cast as a U.S. senator"—Biden obliquely referenced his Catholic faith. "I'm probably a victim, or a product, however you want to phrase it, of my background."[52] He was even more specific in a 2007 interview on "Meet the Press." "I'm a practicing Catholic," Biden said. "And it is the biggest dilemma for me in terms of comporting my religious and cultural views with my political responsibility."[53] In his memoir "Promises to Keep," the president wrote that his position on abortion had "earned me the distrust of some women's groups." He recounted a 1973 conversation with a senator who said his cautious approach was a "tough" one. "'Yeah, everybody will be upset with me,' I told him, 'except me. But I'm intellectually and morally comfortable with my position.'"[54] Biden's position would not stay the same. His views shifted over the years as Democratic party leaders and activists increasingly made abortion rights more central to the party's orthodoxy.

There was a time when pro-choice Democrats talked about making abortion "safe, legal and rare," as Bill Clinton phrased it in 1992. "We have to remind the American people once again that being pro-choice is very different from being pro-abortion," Clinton told the Congressional Women's Caucus that year.[55] The "rare" part of the equation underscored both a level of political and tonal sensitivity toward antiabortion voters in the party and sent an implicit, however vague, message that reducing the number of abortions could potentially be common ground between people on different sides of the issue. During Hillary Clinton's 2008 presidential run, she revived the message, even going as far as emphasizing that "by rare, I mean *rare*."[56] After Barack Obama's election, the president called for "open hearts, open minds and fair-minded words" to characterize debates over abortion during his 2009 commencement address at the University of Notre Dame. "Let us work together to reduce the number of women seeking abortions," the president said.[57] The Vatican newspaper, *L'Osservatore Romano*, praised the president for inviting "Americans of every faith and ideological conviction to 'work in common effort' to reduce the number of abortions."[58] Obama also tasked his White House Office of Faith-Based and Neighborhood Partnerships with exploring how to "support women and children, address teenage pregnancy, and reduce the need for abortion."[59] Reflecting the push for common ground, two Catholic Democrats in Congress, Rep. Rosa DeLauro of Connecticut, a member of the congressional pro-choice caucus, and Rep. Tim Ryan of Ohio, then a member of the congressional pro-life caucus, introduced a comprehensive abortion-reduction legislative package. At a press conference touting the bill in the summer of 2009, leaders from Planned Parenthood and NARAL Pro-Choice America stood side by side with moderate Catholics and theologically conservative evangelicals. "It may not be an end to the culture war," Amy Sullivan, a prominent religion commentator and evangelical, wrote at the time, "but it looks a lot like a cease-fire."[60]

But abortion reduction efforts and "safe, legal and rare" messaging became heterodox for many on the left in more recent years. By the time Hillary Clinton ran for president again in 2016, she dropped "rare" and spoke about abortion being "safe and legal." In a 2019 presidential candidates' debate, Rep. Tulsi Gabbard argued for a return to "safe, legal and rare." Gabbard met fierce resistance from abortion rights activists. "There's a fundamental notion of bodily autonomy that we've been fighting for as advocates and activists on this issue for years," Destiny Lopez, codirector of the All* Above All Action Fund, a nonprofit that works to expand abortion access, told *Vox*. Emphasizing that abortions should be rare "completely negates all the work that we've done to really make this about the ability to decide what's best for your body, for your family, for your community," she said.[61] "It places the blame on the person who's had an abortion," reproductive justice activist Renee Bracey Sherman told the media outlet, "as if they just did something wrong to need one, rather than addressing the systemic issue as to why someone might not be able to have access to consistent health care or contraception." Amelia Bonow, a cofounder of the pro-abortion-rights group Shout Your Abortion, said in 2019: "I cannot think of a less compelling way to advocate for something than saying that it should be rare. And anyone who uses that phrase is operating from the assumption that abortion is a bad thing."[62] Rachel Laser, a former Planned Parenthood lawyer, helped advise Democrats in Congress to develop abortion-reduction legislation a decade ago in her previous role at Third Way, a centrist think tank in Washington. "It was never going to be a panacea, but we wanted to turn down the heat so we could make progress where there were shared values," Laser told me in 2013. "There are still elements on both sides of the divide who want to reduce the need for abortion, but the antiabortion side has taken an extreme approach."[63]

In the decade before the Supreme Court overruled *Roe* in 2022 and punted the issue back to the states, Republicans took control of many state legislatures in the South and Midwest. Between 2011 and 2017 half of the clinics in Arizona, Kentucky, Ohio, and Texas shut their doors. In 2017, 89 percent of counties had no abortion clinic, and six states had only one. Alabama Governor Kay Ivey signed a bill in 2019 that would outlaw abortion at any stage in a woman's pregnancy with no exceptions for pregnancies that result from rape or incest.[64] *USA Today* columnist and CNN commentator Kristin Powers, a Catholic who has argued that the Democratic Party should be more welcoming to antiabortion politicians, responded to the surge of antiabortion state laws at the time. "Am I still a 'pro-life' Christian? My faith is as strong as ever, but today I'd say I'm like many Americans who see themselves both as pro-choice and pro-life," Powers wrote.

> What I do know for sure is that I care about all lives, and that includes the lives of women contemplating abortion. The antiabortion movement pays lip service to caring for women, but what the recent spate of laws shows us is that in the end there is only one thing they care about: the embryo or fetus. The lives of young rape or incest victims are accepted as collateral damage, and women who want to protect their health are cast as sinister actors incapable of searching their own consciences for a way forward when a wanted pregnancy goes awry.[65]

As growing restrictions on abortion access in the states highlighted issues of racial and economic inequality, advocates and Democratic Party leaders increased their calls to repeal the Hyde Amendment. First passed by Congress in 1976, the amendment banned federal funding of abortion, with exceptions for rape, incest, and the life of the mother. Critics long argued that because it affects Medicaid funding of abortion, the amendment disproportionately impacts poor women, especially low-income women of color. For several decades Hyde had relatively broad bipartisan support in Congress. By 2016 the Democratic Party added a call to repeal Hyde in its official party platform. As a senator, Biden voted consistently to renew the Hyde

Amendment and even proposed his own amendment to prohibit foreign aid for biomedical research related to abortion. Even as Biden mulled a run for the presidency in 2019, abortion rights leaders expressed wariness of his support for Hyde and pressured him to "get with the times," as Ilyse Hogue, then president of NARAL Pro-Choice America, phrased it. "Anxiety is super high among women across the country," she told *The New York Times*. "Joe Biden is trying to carve out a space for himself as the middle, moderate candidate, and he's going to have to really get with the times and understand that standing with abortion rights is the middle, moderate position. I can't tell you if he's there or not."[66] For years after other national Democrats had switched their position on Hyde, Biden held firm. But after announcing his run for president, pressure from the left mounted. When his campaign confirmed he still supported Hyde, the backlash was immediate and vocal.

"The problem is, the Hyde Amendment affects poor women, women of color, black women, Hispanic women," Patti Solis Doyle, who served as Hillary Clinton's presidential campaign manager in 2008 and worked for Biden, told *The New York Times*. "And women of color will elect the next president of the United States."[67] Biden's opponents for his party's presidential nomination also responded swiftly. "Repealing the Hyde Amendment is critical so that low-income women in particular can have access to the reproductive care they need and deserve," Sen. Kristen Gillibrand of New York tweeted. "Reproductive rights are human rights, period. They should be nonnegotiable for all Democrats."[68] Vermont Senator Bernie Sanders wrote on Twitter: "There is #NoMiddleGround on women's rights. Abortion is a constitutional right. Under my Medicare for All plan, we will repeal the Hyde Amendment." And California Senator Kamala Harris, who Biden would name as his vice-presidential nominee, said "no woman's access to reproductive health care should be based on how much money she has. We must repeal the Hyde Amendment."[69]

Only a few days after his campaign confirmed he still supported restricting federal funding of abortion, Biden changed his position. "If I believe healthcare is a right, as I do, I can no longer support an amendment that makes that right dependent on someone's ZIP code," he said in a speech at a gala hosted by the Democratic National Committee in Atlanta. Efforts by Republicans to roll back abortion access in Georgia and other states, he noted, represented an extreme movement. "Folks, times have changed," Biden said. "I don't think these guys are going to let up." The Hyde amendment, he suggested in the speech, would be a barrier to his goals of "universal coverage" and providing the "full range of health services women need."[70] The switch didn't sit well with some antiabortion Catholics who supported

Biden. John Carr of Georgetown University, a former staffer at the US bishops' conference who opposes abortion and supports the Hyde Amendment but endorsed Biden in 2020, described the president as "a product of Catholic social teaching and Democratic orthodoxy" in an interview with *The New York Times*. "When the two go together, he's really comfortable with the way he talks, the way he acts. Where he is the least at home is where the two conflict."[71]

Sister Carol Keehen, the former president and CEO of the Catholic Health Association, has had a front-row seat to observe how Biden thinks about his faith in both his personal and public life. The two met while he was the vice-president, and they worked closely together to pass the landmark Affordable Care Act. She recalls traveling to Rome when Biden met Pope Benedict XVI for the first time. The vice president had brought several rosaries with him so the pope could bless them and he could give them to friends as gifts. "His faith means a lot to him," Keehan told me. "He is devoted to the sacraments and his faith really informs how he treats people." It saddened her to see Catholic bishops disparaging the president's faith and telling him he doesn't deserve Communion because of the abortion issue. "We are all unworthy to receive Communion," Keehan said. "There is a level of hypocrisy saying who should get Communion and who shouldn't. Denying someone Communion is a serious thing. You put yourself in the middle of an invitation from the living God. And, especially with a president, you would think we would want the president to have all of the spiritual resources he can for that job."[72]

Keehan is no stranger to public condemnation from bishops. Along with other Catholic sisters, she was critical to advocacy and policy efforts that led to the 2010 passage of the Affordable Care Act. "We would not have gotten the Affordable Care Act done had it not been for her," President Obama said about Keehan at a Catholic Health Association assembly in 2015.[73] The US bishops' conference opposed the legislation despite the church's long support for universal health care as a human right because of fears the law would fund abortion. Keehan received a letter at the time from Providence, Rhode Island, Bishop Thomas Tobin admonishing her for what he called "your enthusiastic support of the legislation, in contradiction to the position of the bishops of the United States." Keehan's backing of the bill, Tobin wrote, "misled the public and causes serious scandal for many members of the church." The bishop even asked that the Catholic Health Association remove his diocese's, St. Joseph Health Services of Rhode Island, from the organization's membership rolls. "Even the association with CHA is now embarrassing," Tobin wrote.[74]

While Keehan was disappointed that Biden reversed course on his previous support for the Hyde amendment, she lauded him for the times over his career when he worked to find common ground and navigate complicated policy disputes where he faced pressure from Catholic bishops on one side and progressive allies on the other. Keehan said that as vice president, Biden often cautioned Obama administration officials that rolling out regulations for contraception funding requirements as part of the health care law should be done in a way that respected Catholic institutions. The issue became a prickly policy and political challenge for the White House. "As a practicing Catholic, I am of the view that this can be worked out and should be worked out," Biden said at the time.[75] He argued for broad accommodations to protect Catholic institutions who objected to covering birth control. The question of how much to accommodate religious institutions divided senior leaders in the administration. When the first guidelines came out from the Department of Health and Human Services, Catholic churches were exempt from providing the coverage, but other Catholic institutions such as Catholic hospitals and charities were not. Biden had argued against that policy inside the White House and correctly predicted backlash that came not only from the US bishops' conference but also Obama's Catholic allies who helped pass health care reform. "I felt like he had made a really bad decision, and I told him that," Sister Keehan said of President Obama in 2012. "I told his staff that. I felt like they had made a bad decision on principle, and politically it was a bad decision. For me another key thing was that it had the potential to threaten the future of health reform."[76] The administration later consulted with Keehan, Catholic theologians, and others before issuing new guidelines offering a work-around that pleased the Catholic Health Association and other Catholic allies, even as bishops still opposed the plan. "I always found him respectful and sensitive to our concerns," Keehan told me about Biden. The president faced even more pressure from both the left and church leaders after the Supreme Court's *Dobbs* decision ended a constitutional right to abortion. Keehan expressed frustration with the substance and tenor of abortion debates.

"The Hyde amendment was born in an age when people talked to each other and tried to be reasonable in a pluralistic country," Keehan said. "This guerrilla warfare we are in now makes the potential for even reasonable compromise or even hearing each other utterly impossible." The Catholic sister, who has led several hospitals throughout her career and served on a special Vatican task force to educate people about Covid around the world, believes that abortion is a societal failure. But she notes the wide gap between pro-life rhetoric and the lack of substantive support for women and children. "If people were as passionate about mothers and children as we say we are, there would be quality maternity care for everyone, pediatric care, and daycare for every child. Why do we make having a child so incredibly expensive and challenging? Being a parent is so incredibly difficult, particularly for people who aren't well off. The abortion conversation is full of so much hypocrisy."[77]

BEYOND SLOGANS: ABORTION, MORAL THEOLOGY, AND ACTIVISM POST-*ROE*

Catholic moral theologians, Catholic health care ethicists, and Catholic women with lived experience who view themselves as pro-life have long argued that issues surrounding pregnancy and birth are complicated. Indeed, the Catholic moral tradition offers a set of sophisticated tools for evaluating what laws and policies respect or undermine life and dignity in ways that can't be reduced to simple bumper-sticker slogans or outrage tweets.

A Missouri lawmaker proposed a bill in 2022 that would have made it illegal to end a pregnancy even in the case of an ectopic pregnancy, when a fertilized egg is implanted outside the uterus. Ectopic pregnancies are not viable, and women are at high risk of dying if they are not addressed. When Fr. James Bretzke, a Jesuit priest and professor of theology at John Carroll University in Cleveland, tweeted in response to the proposal that Catholic health care ethics has long allowed for an ectopic pregnancy to be terminated to save the life of the mother, he found that some critical responses highlighted what he called "the problem of moral absolutism" when it comes to life issues. "Many of these legislative proposals are ultimately going to hurt women," Bretzke said. "We have to go back to Thomas Aquinas in his treatment of human life and be careful in formulating just laws. Human laws are almost always imperfect because they are incomplete and deal with circumstances that lawmakers don't foresee. Aquinas reminds us that human laws should be governed by prudence and aimed at the common good."[78]

Bretzke points to the stark language often used by the late Pope John Paul II, who spoke about a "culture of life" pitted against a "culture of death," as an unhelpful framework to evaluate the range of complex issues that always surround pregnancy and abortion. A generation of conservative US bishops appointed by the late pope, he noted, have embraced that binary view. Bretzke thinks the hierarchy has put a disproportionate amount of energy into making abortion illegal and launching campaigns against pro-choice Catholic politicians rather than working to address the root causes of why women have abortions, which he views as critical to shaping a culture where pregnant women and children are supported. "I'm against abortion and think it's a tragedy but using the principle of prudence I don't think the best approach is criminalizing abortion," said Bretzke, the author of *A Morally Complex World: Engaging Contemporary Moral Theology*.[79]

Cathleen Kaveny, a scholar at Boston College who focuses on the relationship of law, religion and morality, raises an important clarifying question. "How do we balance the legitimate autonomy and privacy rights of women against the interest of the unborn life? There is a lot of practicality that goes into making good laws and when you do that in a nation with different views on abortion, it's hard to employ a prophetic approach," Kaveny observed. She notes that "3-D ultrasounds have strengthened our perceptions of the unborn as 'one of us,'" while at the same time "the #MeToo movement has heightened our understanding of the radical vulnerability of women's bodily integrity."[80] Holding these two perspectives together, she said, means that abortion is "a unique legal and moral problem, because it does not fall neatly under one normative description." When it comes to public debates, who is heard frames the narrative. "People who have the loudest voices on abortion right now are conservatives," Kaveny said. "People who have a more nuanced view don't really have a platform to make the case without getting shot down by both sides."[81]

Mollie Wilson O'Reilly has explored those complexities and nuances Kaveny rightly notes are often missing from our debates about abortion. In an essay for *Commonweal* magazine, "When Abortion Isn't Abortion," O'Reilly offered a personal reflection on her own difficult pregnancies and miscarriages, along with a broader testimony about why she has grown disillusioned with the antiabortion movement. "I have learned over the course of six pregnancies and four births how inadequate pro-life rhetoric can be, and how lonely it is to find yourself in a place beyond the reach of slogans like 'Choose life!'," O'Reilly wrote. "The awful irony of restrictions on abortion is the way they put up barriers to basic health care, barriers that can be dangerous for women whose experience of pregnancy is not a smooth path to motherhood."[82] I asked O'Reilly why she wrote about such a searing personal issue and what she hoped people would take away from her essay. Her answer provides hard-earned practical wisdom for those who want to listen more, go deeper, and move beyond the "pro-choice/pro-life" binaries that limit more than they illuminate. "In the past, I had mostly avoided writing about abortion because I despaired of adding anything to the conversation, which seems so polarized and so hostile to nuance," O'Reilly told me. "But my experience of being hospitalized after a miscarriage, which happened just as the pro-life movement was having unprecedented success in restricting access to reproductive care, forced me to acknowledge how simplistic and inadequate the church's view of abortion policy is," she said.

> When the focus is only on protecting innocent babies, the very real risks to women that any pregnancy involves get left out of the conversation or treated as a distraction. I see that single-issue advocacy as deeply compromising to the church's broader witness. Just because a law restricts abortion doesn't mean it's something Catholics must or even should support. I am mostly hoping that Catholics who want to apply their pro-life principles in a thoughtful way will be encouraged to keep thinking for themselves about what that means in terms of politics and feel more comfortable pushing back against the expectation that they will fall in line and stop asking questions."[83]

Catholic women can play an important role in helping an all-male hierarchy understand these issues from a broader perspective. In many cases, only women who echo the most conservative bishops' messages and assumptions are listened to or viewed as credible inside the church. Susan Ross, a retired professor of theology at Loyola University Chicago and a past president of the Catholic Theological Society of America, served as a consultant to the US Conference of Catholic Bishops' doctrine committee from 2010 to 2013. "The bishops wanted theologians to be talking and writing more about abortion," Ross said. "In one of the meetings with them I said, 'don't you think it would make sense to find out why Catholic women have abortions at the same rate as other women?' It was as if I said the unthinkable. No one responded. You couldn't even say that. It was very frustrating. Except for a few bishops, they were pretty dismissive of us. We were treated with an attitude of contempt."[84] Therese Lysaught, a professor at the Neiswanger Institute for Bioethics and Health Care Leadership at Loyola University Chicago, observed that as the antiabortion movement and the Catholic hierarchy became politicized around a singular legal and political strategy, even many Catholic women who consider themselves pro-life grew alienated. The Supreme Court's *Dobbs* decision, she said, clarified that the pro-life movement's goal all along has more to do with "revoking women's agency" than building a culture that addresses the root causes of why people have abortions. "Catholic leadership in the United States has fomented a deeply problematic either–or understanding of a very complex issue," Lysaught said. "In their idolatrous focus on this one legal decision, they have supported astonishingly shoddy legal and historical reasoning. What they didn't realize—or maybe they did—was that Catholic anti-*Roe* activists have been complicit in the wider neoliberal project of dismantling governmental institutions."[85]

Even as the Democratic party's leftward shift on abortion created a charged climate that increased tensions between Catholic politicians and bishops, the almost fifty-year campaign to overturn *Roe* also required Catholic antiabortion leaders to link arms with a political movement hostile to much of what Catholic social teaching says about the dignity of life after a baby is born. This transactional marriage with Republicans who shredded social safety nets—and embraced a libertarian, antigovernment ideology anathema to Catholic teaching—left women and families to fend for themselves. Most conservative politicians who call themselves "pro-life" have been missing in action when it comes to supporting robust pro-family policies such as increasing the minimum wage, expanding Medicaid, improving the quality of pre- and post-natal health care, and providing paid parental leave after the birth of a child. Many of the same states that have raced to close abortion clinics and erect barriers to abortion access also have the worst outcomes on child poverty, maternal health, and health insurance enrollment. Mississippi—the state at the center of the Court's *Dobbs* decision—has some of the highest rates of infant mortality, maternal mortality, and preterm births in the nation.[86] The United States has the highest rate of maternal deaths in the industrialized world. Black women are three times as likely as white women to die of pregnancy-related complications. Researchers at the University of Colorado have estimated that rates of pregnancy-related deaths will rise significantly in the wake of *Roe* being overturned.[87]

M.T. Davila, a visiting associate professor of practice at Merrimack College and a past president of the Academy of Catholic Hispanic Theologians of the United States, points to how these disparities have disproportionate impacts. "Reproductive health care, which includes a range of care besides the termination of a viable pregnancy, will be significantly reduced in geographic areas where access and public attitudes toward women's and other gender minorities' health, especially for Black and Brown persons, follows the dehumanizing ideologies of our racist and sexist past," Davila said. In a post-*Roe* political climate, she urges Catholics who take different positions on the legality of abortion to forge relationships, alliances, and coalitions across diverse perspectives. "Reproductive justice can't be divorced from racial, gender, economic, migrant and other forms of justice," Davila said. "As we work to serve the common good, let's move beyond the simplistic binary of 'pro-life' and 'pro-choice' labels."[88] Any Catholic conversation about the need to better support women, children, and families also has to acknowledge the church often doesn't live up to its own professed values.

Many Catholic dioceses still don't provide full, paid parental leave after the birth of a child and lag behind some secular institutions when it comes to pro-family policies for employees.[89]

The US bishops' conference response to the *Dobbs* decision hailed the ruling as a "historic day in the life of our country." The bishops also included a call for "coming together to build a society and economy that supports marriages and families, and where every woman has the support and resources she needs to bring her child into this world in love."[90] While it's true that US bishops have issued statements and advocated over the years for a more robust social safety net, church leaders have put more political capital, organizing muscle, and financial resources into ending *Roe* than preparing for what happens afterward. Even the difference between how Vatican leaders and US bishops reacted to the *Dobbs* ruling was instructive. The Vatican's Pontifical Academy for Life praised the ruling but acknowledged that "the issue of abortion continues to arouse heated debate" and emphasized the importance of "developing political choices that promote conditions of existence in favor of life without falling into *a priori* ideological positions." The statement added that "this also means ensuring adequate sexual education, guaranteeing health care accessible to all and preparing legislative measures to protect the family and motherhood, overcoming existing inequalities."[91] Archbishop Vincenzo Paglia, who leads the academy, emphasized that being pro-life must also include efforts to reduce access to guns and ending the death penalty. Andrea Tornielli, editorial director of the Vatican's Dicastery for Communication, wrote in a post-*Dobbs* editorial that "being for life, always," includes not only supporting pregnant women but also defending life "against the threat of firearms."[92] Emilce Cuda, an Argentinian theologian appointed by Pope Francis as a member of the Pontifical Academy for Life in 2022, told the *National Catholic Reporter* after the Supreme Court ruling that "many Catholics fall into the temptation of confusing defense of life with defense of ideological positions."[93]

Less than two months after the Supreme Court reversed *Roe*, voters in Kansas dealt a surprising blow to an energized antiabortion movement—including Catholic bishops in the state—when they resoundingly defeated a proposed amendment that would have removed abortion rights from the state constitution. The amendment was defeated 59 percent to 41 percent in a deep red state where Donald Trump won by wide margins in 2020. Kansas City Archbishop Joseph Naumann led a vocal campaign to support the amendment, and his archdiocese spent more than $2 million on the effort. The dioceses of Wichita and Salinas combined to spend an additional $600,000. CatholicVote, the pro-Trump political action group, raised another half a million for an organization supporting the amendment.[94]

Even some conservative and moderate Christian voters in the state who have reservations about or oppose abortion viewed the proposal as too extreme. In one advertisement from an organization that worked to oppose the amendment, a Catholic grandmother says: "Growing up Catholic, we didn't talk about abortion. But now it's on the ballot. If I were my granddaughter, I wouldn't want the government making that decision for her." Another advertisement featured a Christian pastor. "As Christians, we are instructed to love one another," the woman says. "We do so when we respect and trust women as God does. I'm voting no because it replaces religious freedom with government control."[95] A few weeks before the vote, two Catholic sisters wrote a letter published in *The Kansas City Star* urging Kansans to reject the proposal. "A church sign said, 'Jesus trusted women.' the nuns wrote. "We do too. As Catholic women religious, we support Pope Francis and the social justice teachings of our Church. We respect all people and value life. In other states some doctors are afraid to provide lifesaving procedures for ectopic pregnancies or incomplete miscarriages. A child rape victim was further traumatized by having to travel across state lines to receive health care."[96] The sisters also noted that supporters of the amendment primarily focused resources on banning abortion and not policies that would help mothers, such as "healthcare, parental leave, Medicaid and other support for poor women." In the 2022 midterm election, five months after the *Dobbs* ruling, voters in Kentucky, another red state, rejected a proposed amendment to its state constitution that would have specifically stated its constitution does not protect the right to an abortion. Kentucky banned abortion immediately after the Supreme Court overturned *Roe*, and antiabortion activists hoped the amendment would have shielded the state's abortion ban from legal challenges. "Losing is never easy, especially when it comes to the lives of innocent babies," Brian Burch, president of CatholicVote, wrote after the midterms. His organization launched a $3 million advertisement campaign to help defeat pro-choice Catholics running in several states. "We're in a state-to-state brawl, and we will never surrender."[97]

* * *

Battles over Catholic identity in the Biden era have been largely defined by abortion. The bishops' threats to deny the president Communion and the influence of conservative Catholics on the Supreme Court in overturning *Roe* are important stories that deserve coverage. Yet even as abortion often defines the Catholic narrative in public life, the disproportionate attention it receives can obscure the fact that a Catholic president has in many ways prioritized a policy agenda that aligns with church teaching on the role of government, economic justice, labor rights, and climate change. Over his more than five decades in elected office, Biden has on many occasions spoken about his faith with depth and candor. The president's Catholicism was shaped by his parents, his Irish grandparents, and the priests and nuns he grew up around in blue-collar Scranton, Pennsylvania. It was a culture where family, union leaders, and clergy spoke a shared language of solidarity and human dignity.

Fr. Leo O'Donovan first met Biden when he was the vice president and O'Donovan served as president of Georgetown University. When Biden's son Hunter was a student at the university, O'Donovan invited the vice president to give a speech at Georgetown about how his faith shapes his political worldview and understanding of public service. O'Donovan said Biden told him it was "the toughest assignment he ever got."[98] The vice president worked for days on the speech. Over the years the Jesuit priest developed what he described as a "pastoral and personal relationship" with the president. After the president's son Beau died of brain cancer at the age of 46 in 2015, Biden called O'Donovan on an early Monday morning. "When I got on the phone I started to cry and the vice president began to comfort me," he recalled. O'Donovan presided at Beau's funeral Mass and gave the homily at St. Anthony of Padua Church in Wilmington, Delaware. When O'Donovan had open heart surgery in 2021, Biden called again. "I was very sick and he said, 'I just prayed the rosary for you and when this is over we will have lunch,'" he said. After Biden's election the president asked O'Donovan to give the invocation at the inauguration. Not long after the Jesuit sent the president a brief reflection during Advent that quoted from the German Jesuit Alfred Delp, who was executed by the Nazis for his resistance to Hitler, Biden integrated it into a speech. "I'm reminded of a quote about this season from the Jesuit priest Alfred Delp," the president said in December of 2020. "He wrote, 'Advent is the time for rousing.' Delp believed that first we are shaken to our depths. Then we're ready for a season of hope. As a nation, we have certainly been shaken to our depths this year. Now it's time to awaken, to get moving—for hope."[99] O'Donovan sees in Biden's presidency a strong commitment to addressing the climate crisis, protecting what Pope Francis calls "our common home," enacting policies that address economic inequality, and responding to the struggles of working and middle class-families. "I don't expect him to be quoting the gospels or encyclicals, but his policies do start with a focus on human dignity," the priest said. "When the president talks about the poor or the middle class it's not just a political slogan. It's the values he learned growing up."[100]

"The way I was raised and the social doctrine and the religious theology I was taught were totally consistent," Biden said in a lengthy 2015 interview with the Jesuit priest Matt Malone, then editor of *America* magazine.[101] "It was summed up best as I thought about it: all the things that animated my passions were all about what my father would say. My father would say, 'The cardinal sin of all sins, Joey, is the abuse of power. Whether it's a man raising a hand to a woman, whether it's economic power being invoked and asserted over someone else, whether it is the government abusing its power.' And that's how I look at what this is all about, why my faith is so consistent with the public policy." Later in the interview Biden called Pope Francis "the embodiment of the Catholic social doctrine I was raised with: The idea that everyone is entitled to dignity, that the poor should be given special preference, that you have an obligation to reach out and be inclusive." A president who quoted St. Augustine in his inauguration speech also cited the influence of the French Catholic philosopher Jacques Maritain on his views about social solidarity and the common good during a 2021 interview with *The New York Times* columnist David Brooks. "Like most of the major figures of Catholic social teaching, Maritain placed great emphasis on social solidarity, the organic interdependence of people and communities," Brooks wrote. "If you're drenched in Maritain, you believe we have serious responsibilities for one another."[102]

Despite this background and his cultivated image as "Amtrack Joe," a staunch defender of unions and advocate for the middle class, Biden the senator was also viewed as a centrist Democrat who often rankled progressives by championing legislation that benefited large financial institutions and credit card companies. But as president, Biden has responded to the challenges exacerbated by the Covid pandemic—economic inequality, extreme racial disparities, student debt, and a social safety net tattered by decades of antigovernment ideology—with some of the most significant government investments since Roosevelt's New Deal. Biden's American Rescue Plan, which passed Congress in 2021, made a historic expansion to the child tax credit. The law increased the benefit from $2,000 per child, per year, to a maximum of $3,600 per child, five years old or younger, and $3,000 for kids age six through seventeen.[103] The program was also changed to disburse half of the benefit in monthly payments rather than forcing families to wait for all of it to arrive as a lump sum at tax time. Congress also closed a gaping hole that had prevented about a third of the nation's children and half of all Black and Hispanic children from fully benefiting from the program because their families didn't earn enough income. Researchers from the Columbia University Center on Poverty and Social Policy found that the expanded child tax credit cut monthly child poverty by approximately 30 percent before Congress deadlocked, and the expansion was not renewed after six months.[104] While the president's original proposal, which among other things included raising the minimum wage to $15 per hour, was scaled back during congressional negotiations to appease Democratic senators Joe Manchin of West Virginia and Kyrsten Sinema of Arizona, the final package included extended unemployment benefits, direct economic impact payments to qualifying Americans, nearly $15 billion to help support child care facilities in high-needs areas, 4.5 billion for the Low Income Home Energy Assistance Program to help families with home energy bills, and $25 billion for emergency rental assistance.[105]

Along with the American Rescue Plan, the Biden administration also created a $2 trillion package called the Build Back Better Act. Kevin Appleby, a former staffer at the US bishops' conference, urged church leaders to put pressure on Republicans to support the legislation. "The bill contains many ideas that the U.S. bishops have long supported, at least as general principles, including paid family leave, tax credits for children and working families, expanded health care for the poor and elderly, child care support and climate initiatives," Appleby wrote in *America* magazine.[106] "From a Catholic teaching viewpoint, the legislation should be measured on how it supports and protects the most vulnerable among us, not by which party supports it. The budget reconciliation bill not only passes this test, but also addresses a significant portion of the church's social justice agenda." But Appleby told me he was disappointed in the response from church leaders. "It was an opportunity for the bishops to show some integrity and consistency," he said. "If you're going to beat Biden over the head on abortion then you should beat Republicans over the head to pass one of the most significant social justice bills in history. This was straight out of Catholic social teaching. They should have been shouting from the church rooftops. But they didn't bring the energy they do on abortion. The church almost seemed absent from the debate."[107]

In a *Politico* commentary headlined "Biden Is the Most Pro-Family President in Decades. So Why Is the Catholic Church Attacking Him?" Tom Perriello, a Catholic and former Democratic member of Congress from Virginia, also wondered why bishops were not putting more lobbying muscle into supporting proposals that reflect Catholic social teaching in action. "Americans are on the verge of benefiting from perhaps the most pro-family legislation in the nation's history. And the Catholic Church is nowhere to be seen," Perriello wrote, noting that Catholic leaders once played a major role in helping to develop America's social safety net.[108] The Build Back Better bill would provide "major assistance for child care, paid and family leave, health care and long-term care for seniors, a pathway out of the shadows for millions of immigrant families, and measures to move millions of children out of poverty," he wrote.

> However, with this sweeping pro-family measure hanging in the balance, the U.S. Conference of Catholic Bishops—whose support for major legislation historically has been crucial—has largely been silent. Church leaders, who enjoy guaranteed health care and housing for life, have mounted no public campaign to support it or lobbying of lawmakers to pass it. No pressure on Catholic Democratic Sen. Joe Manchin not to water down pro-family and anti-poverty provisions. No pressure on Catholic GOP senators like Susan Collins and Lisa Murkowski to provide bipartisan support for elderly and disabled care provisions. Their only advocacy so far has been to invent concerns about tax dollars funding abortion services that are not even included anywhere in the bill. This absence of moral leadership reflects a decades-long decline of the political relevance of the USCCB.

On a steamy August afternoon in 2022, I headed to Capitol Hill to ask a sitting Catholic lawmaker about these issues. The hallways of the Longworth House Office Building were mostly empty for summer recess. A few days earlier, Congress had passed major climate, tax, and health care legislation. The Inflation Reduction Act secured the largest-ever investment to address climate change through the promotion of green technology and curbing emissions, raised taxes on some billion-dollar corporations, and lowered prescription drug costs for seniors. Rep. Brendan Boyle, a graduate of the University of Notre Dame who represents the second district of Pennsylvania, was back in town for a few meetings before catching the Amtrak train home. Boyle, a boyish looking forty-five, was one of the youngest members of Congress when he was elected at the age of thirty-seven in 2014. He describes himself as a "Biden Democrat." He grew up in a row-house in a blue-collar neighborhood of Philadelphia, served as an altar boy at St. Helena Catholic Church, and attended Catholic schools as a kid. A framed photograph of Boyle meeting Pope Francis during the pope's 2015 visit to a Philadelphia prison hung on the wall in his office. After graduating from Notre Dame, Boyle studied at Harvard University, where he took a class taught by Rev. Jim Wallis, the founder of Sojourners.

"I was drawn to someone who was linking faith and politics from a progressive viewpoint," he said about Wallis. "Before the late 1970s, if you were religiously motivated and active in politics then it was more likely that you were liberal rather than conservative. That obviously changed with the religious right. Perhaps my greatest pet peeve about politics in my lifetime is the way 'religious voters' or 'values voters' became synonymous with conservatism. At long last I think that is changing," Boyle said. "There are many of us now on the left who are vocal about how our faith has motivated our political views."[109] As a pro-choice Catholic Democrat, Boyle thinks it's hypocritical for bishops who want to deny Communion to pro-choice Catholics like him. "For those of us in politics who are sincere Catholics and pro-choice and think it is not practical and wise to criminalize abortion, the fact that our Catholic faith gets called into question while those Catholics on the other side of the aisle get a free pass is enormously frustrating," he acknowledged. Boyle argues that the policies that he and the president have advocated for reflect Catholic values and are, in fact, pro-life. "If you read the teachings of Jesus from the gospels and you line them up with what we're trying to do here on health care and the minimum wage and the environment, I don't think there is any question that our policies align more with the social gospel," he said. Boyle recalls watching with disgust as Catholics praised former president Trump during the 2020 Republican National Convention. "The reality is the Trump administration was the most anti-life administration of my lifetime. But he cynically exploited the issue to act as if he was somehow more Catholic than the guy running who was actually Catholic and who embraced Catholic social justice."

Boyle said that in past decades Democrats were reluctant to talk about religion. "For a long time, we completely ceded the ground to the Republican side when it came to faith." But he noted that unlike John Kerry, who was reticent to discuss his faith during the 2004 election, the president has embraced his religion. "What Biden has done is show the connection between his faith and his policies. It's genuine," Boyle said. "It also reflects who I am. And I think it's a better political strategy as well." On abortion, Boyle would like to see more efforts to find common ground. Voters and lawmakers who disagree over the legality of abortion, he said, can still work together to promote public policies that "actually make it affordable to give birth and raise a child." But he worries that coming together to support a social safety net that values human life and dignity has become increasingly harder. "The abortion issue is so divisive and hate filled that it has infected how we approach other issues as well and that is part of the dysfunction and division we have in our country today. The public is actually much more nuanced in how they see this issue than our two political parties. We're at a very toxic moment where some folks who disagree see the other person as just plain evil. If you see your opponent as evil, it's very hard to find common ground and get things done."

A month after visiting Boyle, I returned to Capitol Hill to sit down with Rep. Juan Vargas. Vargas grew up as one of ten kids in a small house on a chicken ranch in San Diego. His father came to the United States from Jalisco, Mexico, as a farmworker under the Bracero program, which starting in 1942 allowed millions of Mexican men to work legally in the United States on short-term labor contracts. Vargas studied at Fordham University and entered the Jesuits. He was a priest for four years and spent time working with indigenous communities in the jungles of El Salvador. As we settled into his spacious office, he showed me a picture of himself as a young man with children at an orphanage where he worked that the Jesuits built and ran. "I love the Jesuit emphasis on social justice and their spirituality of finding God in all things. I was taught you have to put your faith into action," he said.[110] In El Salvador he got to know several Jesuits at the University of Central America before they were brutally killed on campus in a pre-dawn attack in 1989 during a civil war that left 75,000 people dead. Segundo Montes, one of the Jesuits killed in the raid, spent time as Vargas's spiritual advisor. The congressman, who described himself as a "Pope Francis Catholic," would like to see more of the pope's vision in American politics. He was thrilled when Pope Francis named his bishop in San Diego, Robert McElroy, the city's first cardinal in the late summer of 2022. The two met when they were seated next to each other on a plane. "When the bishops started talking about denying President Biden Communion, he called me up and said 'Juan, I know we don't agree on everything, but as long as I'm bishop here you will get Communion.'" Vargas is soft-spoken and gentlemanly even when he expresses frustration with how abortion is often viewed as the defining issue when church leaders assess a Catholic politician. "We need to be a big tent party and we should never alienate anyone who has a different view on abortion," he said. "Personally, I'm against abortion and in almost all cases I think it's the wrong decision to make, but women have a right to make a decision about their own body. We should not be weaponizing Communion. Communion connects us to Jesus." He recognizes that as a Catholic who supports a constitutionally protected right to abortion, some church leaders question his right to call himself a Catholic. Vargas is less defiant than quietly steadfast in his refusal to be marginalized by his own church or to allow one political party to claim a monopoly on religion. "The church formed me, and my faith is who I am," he said. "My mother always taught me to never be embarrassed by Jesus because you don't want Jesus to be embarrassed by you."

* * *

President Biden's efforts to bolster social safety nets and address economic inequality, disparities in health care, and the impacts of climate change are aligned with a long history of Catholic teaching about the common good and the vital role of government. While there is a celebrated American tradition of self-reliance and hyper-individualism, Catholicism offers a communitarian response to antigovernment ideologies and views libertarianism, both conservative and liberal strains, as a threat to the principle of social solidarity. For centuries, the Catholic tradition has emphasized the common good as a centerpiece of Catholic social teaching. Building on concepts articulated first by Aristotle, St. Thomas Aquinas spoke about the good sought by all as intertwined with the reality of God. Pope Leo XIII, in his encyclical *Rerum Novarum* (1891), was the first to make formal use of the common good as the starting point for the church's social analysis. According to the Vatican's *Compendium of the Social Doctrine of the Church*, published during Pope John Paul II's pontificate: "The principle of the common good, to which every aspect of social life must be related if it is to attain its fullest meaning, stems from the dignity, unity and equality of all people." The practical implications of serving the common good are hardly theoretical in church teaching. "The Church's social doctrine requires that ownership of goods be accessible to all," according to the Compendium. Even more, the church has "never recognized the right to private property as absolute and untouchable." Instead, the church teaches that the "universal destination of goods" is inextricably linked with a "preferential option for the poor" and that "any type of improper accumulation is immoral."[111] Imagine even a liberal Democrat running for office on those themes and you get a sense of how radically different Catholic teachings on government and economic principles are from mainstream American political discourse.

Most Catholic elected leaders, including Biden, are not directly thinking about the minutiae of Catholic social teaching as they develop policies and priorities. Even so, it's clear that the president's determination to promote policies that challenge the concentration of wealth in the hands of a few, his staunch support for unions, historic attempts to reduce students' debt burden, and policies that confront the climate crisis all reflect principles found in the church's social tradition. "I would actually argue that the Biden administration marks the most decisive turn against neoliberalism in the past five decades," said Anthony Annett, an economist who spent two decades as a speechwriter at the International Monetary Fund and serves as a senior advisor to the United Nations Sustainable Development Solutions Network.[112] The author of *Cathonomics: How Catholic Tradition Can Create a More Just Economy*, Annett has presented at several Vatican conferences focused on economics, development, and climate change. He points to Biden's "pro-family policies" such as the expanded child tax credit, paid leave, subsidized child care and universal pre-kindergarten as policies designed to provide the kind of robust support for workers and families that "gel with the economic rights laid out by Catholic social teaching." Annett noted that the $1,400 stimulus checks sent directly to people's bank accounts under the American Rescue Plan Act were a temporary experiment in a universal basic income (UBI). Pope Francis signaled his support for the idea in 2020 as part of a letter to popular movements and community organizations. "It would ensure and concretely achieve the ideal, at once so human and so Christian, of no worker without rights," the pope wrote at a time when the coronavirus pandemic was first beginning to ravage countries around the world.[113] Annett argues that as much as the president's economic and climate policies reflect core themes found in the church's social teachings, "the Catholic tradition is still more radical than Bidenomics." He notes that encyclicals and other church documents would endorse the principles of greater "workplace democracy," which include work councils, along with "more socialization of the means of production (profit-sharing, worker cooperatives)."

The president has long prided himself as a staunch ally of unions and the labor movement. Even if the church has sometimes failed to put its own principles into practice, Catholic teaching has affirmed the rights of workers to organize and supported paying workers a living wage since Pope Leo XIII's 1891 encyclical on labor and capital, *Rerum Novarum*. "You know, you've heard me say many times: I intend to be the most pro-union president leading the most pro-union administration in American history," Biden said in 2021.[114] While it doesn't make headlines, advocating for unions is another area of alignment between the Biden administration and Catholic bishops. The US Conference of Catholic Bishops filed a friend-of-the-court brief in the 2018 Supreme Court case *Janus v. AFSCME*. Church leaders argued that so-called "right-to-work" laws undermine workers' rights and that dues employees pay to unions are essential to collective bargaining.[115] In the first weeks of his presidency, Biden signed executive orders that raised the minimum wage to $15 an hour for federal workers and rescinded Trump-era rules that weakened protection for workers. In the spring of 2021, he signed an executive order creating a White House task force to promote labor organizing. The administration noted at the time that the National Labor Relations Act, the 1935 law governing federal labor rights, explicitly sought to encourage collective bargaining, but that the law had never been fully carried out. "No previous administration has taken a comprehensive approach to determining how the executive branch can advance worker organizing and collective bargaining," according to a White House statement.[116] The president has taken steps to make it easier for federal workers and employees of contractors to unionize. The White House also supported a $15 minimum wage in the president's pandemic relief package, but the Senate parliamentarian ruled it could not be included under budget reconciliation rules. As the pandemic continued to strain American workers, a surge in union organizing at Amazon, Starbucks, and other corporations drew national attention. Before a high-profile union vote at an Amazon facility in Bessemer, Alabama, Biden released a video expressing solidarity with the workers. "Today and over the next few days and weeks, workers in Alabama, and all across America, are voting on whether to organize a union in their workplace," Biden said. "There should be no intimidation, no coercion, no threats, no anti-union propaganda." The "choice to join a union is up to the workers—full stop," he emphasized. The *Washington Post* noted how unusual it was for a president to speak out before a union drive vote, calling it "a major break with historical precedent."[117]

"As a Catholic moral theologian, for me it represented a moment of hope, that Catholic social thought's commitment to economic justice might more strongly influence domestic U.S. policy, especially on the dignity of work and workers," Meghan Clark, an associate professor of moral theology at St. John's University in New York, wrote at the time.[118] The Biden administration has also supported the Protecting the Right to Organize Act, congressional legislation that would be the most significant overhaul of labor law in several decades.[119] The PRO Act would bar employers from retaliating against unionization efforts, permit independent contractors in the emerging "gig" economy to unionize, and expand labor protections to immigrant workers. It also allows for penalties up to triple an employee's wages when worker rights are violated. The Catholic Labor Network and The Interreligious Network for Worker Solidarity released a public statement supporting the legislation signed by nearly 400 religious leaders.[120] President Biden also took the unusual step of putting pressure on Gavin Newsom, the Democratic governor of California, to support legislation that would make it easier for farmworkers to organize and collectively bargain for better wages, benefits, and working conditions. Historically, farmworkers have been excluded from protections under US labor law. "Farmworkers worked tirelessly and at great personal risk to keep food on America's tables during the pandemic. In the state with the largest population of farmworkers, the least we owe them is an easier path to make a free and fair choice to organize a union," Biden said in a statement released by the White House. "Government should work to remove—not erect—barriers to workers organizing. But ultimately workers must make the choice whether to organize a union. And it's especially important today for Black and Brown workers whose voices have long been silenced through shameful race-based laws and policies. It is long past time that we ensure America's farmworkers and other essential workers have the same right to join a union as other Americans."[121] Joseph McCartin, a professor of history at Georgetown University and the executive director of the Kalmanovitz Initiative for Labor and the Working Poor, views Biden as "deeply influenced by Catholic social teaching on the issue of worker justice." McCartin said "the theme of solidarity, which is central to Catholic social teaching, is quite evident in Biden's labor agenda." Since the presidency of Franklin D. Roosevelt, he added, "a number of previous presidents have spoken favorably about the *right* to join a union, but no previous president has spoken so passionately about unions as a force for advancing the common good."[122] As examples, McCartin pointed to Biden's support for the PRO Act, which he said would "finally modernize the now ancient and decrepit national labor law that was shaped more than 80 years ago," and the president's economic stimulus package during the worst of the Covid outbreak that "saved many jobs, including union jobs." He also called the sweeping $750 billion health care, tax, and climate bill the president signed into law in August 2022 "a huge, pro-worker, pro-union bill." "Not only has he done more than any president to address the climate problem, he more than anyone has seen the potential of tackling climate change as intimately tied up with creating a socially sustainable economy as well, one that pays workers well and respects their rights to organize and bargain."

* * *

During another pandemic in 1919, Catholic leaders were at the forefront of making a bold case that the government should be a vehicle to protect workers' rights, distribute wealth more equitably, and provide Americans with basic economic security amid the vagaries and ravages of the market. Fr. John Ryan, a priest from Minnesota inspired by Pope Leo XIII's defense of workers and the right to organize, wrote his 1906 dissertation, *A Living Wage*, at The Catholic University of America in Washington.[123] Ryan's most influential book, *Distributive Justice*, released in 1916, drew from Catholic social teaching to examine industrial production, profits from enterprise, and the relationships between workers and owners. The *New Republic* magazine praised the book as "the most comprehensive and dignified existing treatise on the ethics of economic reform."[124] After the First World War, Catholic bishops formed the National Catholic Welfare Conference, marking the first time the US hierarchy had a coordinated body to address national issues. The bishops named Ryan as director of the Social Action Department, and in 1919 he drafted the *Bishops' Program for Social Reconstruction*.[125] The Catholic hierarchy threw its moral weight behind what at the time were viewed as radical social reforms: a minimum wage; public housing for workers; labor participation in management decisions; and insurance for the elderly, disabled, and unemployed that would be funded by a tax on industry. The bishops' proposals ended with a stern warning to the "capitalist."

> He needs to learn the long-forgotten truth that wealth is stewardship, that profit-making is not the basic justification of business enterprise, and that there are such things as fair profits, fair interest and fair prices. Above and before all, he must cultivate and strengthen within his mind the truth which many of his class have begun to grasp for the first time during the present war; namely, that the laborer is a human being, not merely an instrument of production; and that the laborer's right to a decent livelihood is the first moral charge upon industry. . . . This is the human and Christian, in contrast to the purely commercial and pagan, ethics of industry.[126]

The bishops' ambitious proposals, which the historian and Jesuit priest Joseph McShane credited with launching "the American Catholic search for social justice," never took root at the time they were written.[127] Americans elected three Republican presidents during the 1920s, and a bullish Wall Street left most political leaders in no mood for economic reform. But the 1929 stock market crash and the start of the Great Depression created a political climate ripe for the ideas Fr. Ryan had been writing and speaking about for two decades. Presidential candidate Franklin D. Roosevelt wrote to Ryan in 1932 and asked him to be an informal campaign adviser. A papal encyclical issued at the time, *Quadragesimo Anno* (In the Fortieth Year)—released four decades after Pope Leo XIII's labor encyclical—provided another round of sophisticated and timely Catholic thinking on questions of economic and social justice. In a section entitled "Reconstruction of the Social Order," the encyclical proposed a transformation of industrial capitalism by creating occupational councils made up of industry, labor, and government representatives who would together negotiate fair wages, hours, prices, and business practices. A year after the encyclical was released in 1932, Roosevelt gave a speech in Detroit sponsored by a key Catholic ally, Mayor Frank Murphy, where he sounded similar themes. "It is patent in our days that not alone is wealth accumulated, but immense power and despotic economic domination are concentrated in the hands of a few, and that those few are frequently not the owners but only the trustees and directors of invested funds which they administer at their good pleasure," Roosevelt said.[128]

Roosevelt won in a landslide. The social reforms Fr. John Ryan first proposed in his doctoral dissertation at Catholic University and later for the Bishops' Program for Social Reconstruction in 1919 now had a chance to move from theory into practice. Roosevelt appointed Ryan to the Federal Advisory Council of the US Employment Service, established by the progressive Wagner Act, which guaranteed workers the right to organize unions. He became a leading figure in the brain trust of Frances Perkins, the influential Secretary of Labor who led the charge for unemployment and elderly insurance, a massive public works program, and a minimum wage. At Roosevelt's second inauguration in 1937, Fr. Ryan gave the invocation. It was the first time a Catholic priest served in that role. Two years later, Frances Perkins toasted Ryan on his retirement from Catholic University. Supreme Court justices, members of Roosevelt's cabinet, and senators filed into the banquet room of the Willard Hotel in Washington to hear the labor secretary praise Ryan. "We have still not caught up with Father Ryan's thinking. . . . But we are coming closer to it," Perkins said. "Only lately has business begun to realize that economic policies are subject to ethics, and that a moral obligation to pay a good wage falls on the employer of labor as a consequence of his position of power over the fruits of the earth."[129] Nearly all of the recommended reforms in the US bishops' Program for Social Reconstruction were eventually enacted into law during Roosevelt's presidency. "Catholic social teaching had revolutionized the moral landscape of capitalism," wrote Lew Daly in his 2007 essay "In Search of the Common Good: The Catholic Roots of American Liberalism." "It was a turning point that made the welfare state morally necessary and, because of that, politically possible."[130]

Christine Firer Hinze, chair of the theology department at Fordham University, has studied Ryan's legacy of bringing Catholic social thought to the halls of power and thinks that Biden's presidency reflects a similar commitment. "I do see many resonances with Catholic social teaching in Biden's sensibilities about the role of government as serving the common good, and in his actions and proposed policies for advancing that aim," said Hinze, the author of *Radical Sufficiency: Work, Livelihood and a US Catholic Economic Ethic.*

> Biden is following a U.S. style, democratic party-version of advancing, at least indirectly, Catholic social principles whose lineage can be traced back to FDR and the New Deal with the active engagement and support at that time of Catholic leaders like John Ryan who found a way to successfully merge Catholic social teaching with an American democratic sensibility, and interpret Catholic social

> teaching into concrete policy directions for the U.S. context at that time. Biden is trying to do the same, though like FDR except in rare cases, he does not emphasize Catholic social teaching links explicitly in his public rhetoric.[131]

The symbiosis between US social and economic policy and Catholic social teaching principles that happened during the New Deal years, she observed, was born out of crisis and exceptional circumstances, especially the Great Depression. "Pulling oneself up by one's own bootstraps wasn't working, and this gave FDR and Ryan an opening to introduce and gain traction for (at least for a while) a much more communitarian political and economic agenda than Americans would normally have tended to embrace," Hinze said. The New Deal era, she noted, was "a time of a kind of 'golden confluence' between U.S. and Catholic social teaching sensibilities, one that after 1960 or so dissipated, as Catholic social teaching and U.S. culture (political and economic) went in different directions." Now that our nation again faces extraordinary challenges—the fallout from Covid, extreme inequality, and the intensifying effects of climate change—conditions are conducive for another radical rethinking of the status quo. Hinze wonders if a twenty-first century version of what Roosevelt and Ryan accomplished might be possible.

> I don't mean by this that public policy needs to be 'Catholicized' explicitly. What I mean—and what Ryan and FDR saw and I think Biden sees—is that the communitarian trajectories mapped by Catholic social thought point in directions that are shared in other corners, including among those who are non-religious, and that these are directions that have much to offer to our struggles for the health and even survival of the U.S. experiment, those who are poor and marginalized both within and beyond our borders, and our suffering environment.

IMMIGRATION, THE REFUGEE CRISIS, AND RELIGION IN GLOBAL AFFAIRS

While President Biden's commitment to addressing the ecological crisis and his support for economic, labor, and social safety net policies are widely praised by many Catholic advocates and scholars, his mixed record on immigration and refugee issues draws more fraught responses.

Joan Rosenhaur, who retired as the executive director of the Jesuit Refugee Service/USA in 2024, applauded the president for meeting his declared goal of raising the nation's annual refugee admission target to 125,000 and ending the Trump-era restrictions on people entering the United States from majority-Muslim countries, the so-called "Muslim ban." The swift reversal in tone and approach compared to the nativism and xenophobic policies that characterized the Trump years are welcome. However, she describes the administration's policies as "very much a mixed bag on issues related to migrants, refugees and asylum seekers."[132] Rosenhaur told me that Biden has "made some good policy decisions to protect and support refugees and migrants, but he has also made a number of bad decisions that are harming the world's most vulnerable people." "We continue to have an asylum system that is all but shut down," Rosenhaur, who spent sixteen years at the US bishops' conference and nearly a decade with Catholic Relief Services, said when we spoke in the summer of 2022. "The fact that has continued with the Biden administration is very surprising and disappointing. The attitude and the rhetoric from the administration are more positive, but we haven't seen the same commitment to funding and re-establishing the systems necessary to successfully have people entering the country. The politics of opening up opportunities for asylum seekers is very complicated and those political challenges often dictate the administration's approach."[133]

Along with those political optics, the Biden administration's approach to the US–Mexico border has also been shaped by a series of legal challenges and court decisions. On his first day in office, the president suspended the Trump-era Migrant Protection Protocols, which under the previous administration required thousands of migrants seeking asylum to remain in Mexico while awaiting review of their cases in court hearings. The policy was denounced by immigration experts and human rights advocates because of the violence migrants often face in the country while awaiting a ruling on their status. But after Biden's action, Republican officials in Texas and Missouri sued the administration. A federal judge in Texas sided with the states and ordered the administration to reinstate the Remain in Mexico policy. Jesuit Refugee Service/USA was part of a coalition of over ninety Catholic organizations that called on President Biden and Mexican President Andrés Manuel López, both Catholics, to finally end the policy. "It's shocking that the U.S. and Mexican government decided not only to reinstate but to expand the 'Remain in Mexico' policy to include additional Western-Hemisphere countries such as Haiti," Rosenhaur said. "Tens of thousands of potential newcomers are forced to remain in cartel-controlled areas, and are subject to human trafficking, domestic abuse, and destitute economic positions." The legal and policy fights over the policy reached the US Supreme Court, which ruled in June 2022 that the Biden administration could legally terminate the program. Some immigrant rights advocates criticized President Biden for not immediately ending the program after the ruling. Five weeks later, the US Department of Homeland Security announced that migrants placed in the program would be disenrolled at their next scheduled court date in the United States. Rosenhaur told me that regardless of who is in the White House, the task of rebuilding the broken asylum and refugee system must be a moral and political priority. "The number of people forced to flee their homes is incredible," she said. "There are over 100 million people forcibly displaced around the world. We have to support efforts to prevent displacement and respond to this displacement."

Dylan Corbett has a close-up view of migration. As executive director of the Hope Border Institute in El Paso, Texas, Corbett sees the impact that policies made in Washington have on real people. When I asked him for his assessment of the Biden administration, he was both reflective and direct. "It is difficult because it's complex," Corbett said.

> The way we talk about politics is all about angels and demons. There are lights and shadows and both are true at the same time. It is maddening and frustrating. I have had the opportunity to see the human impact of our laws. Here in El Paso, as I speak, there are several bodies at the morgue. We have pulled more bodies out of the river than ever before. Last year, we had record deaths on the border. These actions and policies have real human impact.[134]

The Trump administration's agenda of cruelty and punishment toward immigrants, he noted, caused so much damage that "the goal posts for success were moved and it's really hard to get back to the status quo never mind reforming the immigration system."

For decades, both Democrat and Republican presidents have contributed to what Corbett describes as "a hardening and militarization of the border." He notes the connection between the rise of so-called "tough-on-crime" laws in the 1990s and the increased enforcement approach at the border. "Biden is at the center of these trends," Corbett observed. "As a senator, he played a key role in passing the crime bill in 1994. The crackdown on crime through a militarized approach coincided with the crackdown on the border. Both Democrats and Republicans were implicated in those policies." Before moving to El Paso, Corbett worked in Washington, DC, for the US Conference of Catholic Bishops' flagship antipoverty initiative, the Catholic Campaign for Human Development (CCHD). During the Obama administration, he was inspired by the young immigrant activists known as Dreamers and worked with broad coalitions of church leaders and advocates to push Congress on passing comprehensive immigration reform. The experience of watching lawmakers come to the brink of passing immigration reform but ultimately failing was a painful experience. Corbett also grew disillusioned with President Obama, who immigration activists often clashed with because of his support for enforcement-heavy policies that led to major deportations of immigrants. Corbett left the nation's capital believing he could make more of a difference at a local and state level. At the Hope Border Institute, he often works closely with Bishop Mark Seitz, one of the nation's most outspoken Catholic leaders on immigration. When the Biden administration continued the "Remain in Mexico" policy initiated under Trump, Corbett traveled across the border to Juarez, Mexico with the bishop to deliver $40,000 in humanitarian aid to migrants and to see firsthand the harsh impacts of the policy.[135] When Vice President Kamala Harris made her first trip to the US–Mexico border in June 2021, Corbett was seated a few feet away from the vice president during a small, last-minute meeting with about seven faith and community leaders in El Paso. Harris had been tasked by President Biden to address the root causes behind the surge of migrants leaving Central America to seek refuge in the United States. Bishop Seitz spoke directly to the vice president during his opening remarks. "Borders are the places where the drama of human life—its suffering and aspirations—unfolds and they put squarely before us a moral choice—to build bridges of encounter or walls of fear," the bishop said.[136] Seitz urged the vice president to see beyond "foreboding walls of steel" and to experience "the suffering and aspirations that motivate people to leave family and homeland." The bishop also didn't shy away from uncomfortable truths.

> We must also avoid the danger of thinking the problem is only with *them: their* corruption, *their* underdeveloped economies, *their* widespread violence. This, too, is a form of "othering." We cannot ignore our historical complicity, our entanglement in an economy that kills, our inaction on climate change, our fueling of death-dealing violence with weapons of war and drug consumption,

> our obsession for power over the common good, our addiction to short-term results and eliminating opponents over the patient cultivation of social friendships, our indifference toward life, our racism. Addressing root causes means addressing these things, too.

Corbett said he was grateful for the vice president's visit, but "at the end of the day it was really more of a photo op." "It was an opportunity to reshape the narrative, but it was missed," Corbett told me. "She didn't want to be drawn into a discussion and there was little follow up." More broadly, Corbett worries that many in the Biden–Harris administration are so turned off by the loudest voices of the culture warrior bishops who want to deny the president Communion that there is a growing "breach" between the bishops' conference and the administration that can often hinder broader Catholic efforts to engage with the administration. "The bishops haven't been able to negotiate effective relationships and that can have a downstream effect on other groups," he noted. "Politics has served as a proxy for serving the broader culture, and the bishops are reacting to a culture that is less hospitable to traditional expressions of the Catholic faith. They have tried to engage that reality through politics. It's a flawed approach. They have tried to evangelize through a strategy of denunciation, and at a certain point you begin to burn bridges. You paint yourself into a corner."[137]

While President Biden has enjoyed a far warmer relationship with Pope Francis than with the US bishops' conference, some experts in religion and global affairs think his administration could be doing far more to leverage the practical expertise, diplomatic potential, and relationship-building capacity of religious institutions around the world. "I think the president views his relationships with global religious leaders primarily as personal, but he doesn't approach it from a more strategic or institutional perspective," said Shaun Casey, who served as the US special representative for religion and global affairs and director of the US Department of State's Office of Religion and Global Affairs in the Obama administration.[138] Casey's first-of-its-kind role at the State Department, he said, was made possible because former Secretary of State John Kerry understood the importance of religion in geopolitics. Trump shut the office down after his election. Biden did not reopen the office. "I'm not sure the president sees global religious communities strategically or wants to build a foreign policy apparatus that can engage these entities strategically," said Casey, the author of *Chasing the Devil at Foggy Bottom: The Future of Religion in American Diplomacy*. "That has been the norm historically in foreign policy. If you don't have a bureaucratic structure to maintain those ties it undermines the ability of senior leaders to speak to each other. You need the staff and policy structure around the president. It's a lack of a strategic view of how religion can be a powerful diplomatic force." Casey recalls that he was initially surprised when leaders of the US Catholic bishops' conference were eager to meet with him at the State Department after Kerry created his office. When Kerry ran for president in 2004, several bishops publicly rebuked him for his position on abortion rights and threatened to deny him Communion. There were also high-profile clashes between the bishops and the Obama administration over health care and contraception coverage in insurance plans. "The bishops were able to bracket that out because they still wanted to play a role in the foreign policy space," Casey said. His office worked closely with US bishops and Vatican officials on the Middle East, environmental justice issues leading up to the 2015 Paris climate agreement, highlighting Pope Francis's *Laudato Si* encyclical on ecology, and efforts to close the Guantanamo Bay detention camp in Cuba. But Casey lamented the current lack of institutional capacity at the State Department and throughout the Biden administration to engage religion seriously and worries that what he calls the "culture-war heartburn" between the administration and the US bishops on domestic issues has foreclosed opportunities in the international space.

Rev. David Hollenbach, a research professor in the Walsh School of Foreign Service and a senior fellow at the Berkley Center for Religion, Peace and World Affairs at Georgetown University, is a scholar who focuses on human rights, global humanitarian crises, refugees, and the role of religion in promoting international justice and peace. He also praised Kerry's efforts at the State Department during the Obama years to elevate religion and faith-based institutions as key actors in understanding geopolitical challenges. "It's unfortunate that effort has been left to drift," Hollenbach said about the Biden administration. "Kerry's initiative was quite remarkable and there was a lot of resistance to it even in the State Department at the time," he noted.[139] Hollenbach pointed to the important role religion has played in peacebuilding in West Africa, and how religion is central to the displacement of Rohingya in Myanmar and other conflicts around the globe. In particular, he cited the unique capacity of the Catholic Church to engage with governments and civil society organizations. "The Catholic community is in an important position to address global solidarity," Hollenbach said. "We are the largest international body in the world. There are no other associations or organizations that are more global than Roman Catholicism. The church is not just an international agency like the United Nations but is deeply connected to people and communities at the grassroots level." While Hollenbach commends bishops in the United States for their advocacy on behalf of migrants and refugees, he noted that compared to the 1980s—when church leaders spearheaded major efforts to address issues of economic justice and nuclear proliferation—their public witness today is more narrowly defined. "The culture wars over abortion have diverted the bishops' energy and focus from those broader concerns," he said. "Leading with a culture-war approach is a profound distortion of Catholicism. If Catholicism means anything it means we are not in favor of culture wars, but we always lead with dialogue and by persuasion, not by threats or exclusion from Communion."

The intersection of Catholicism and politics during Biden's presidency has been shaped by a complicated narrative of progress and conflict. A Catholic president's expressions of personal faith, evident in his deep connection to the rituals, traditions, and spiritual reserves of the church, are unquestionably sincere and resonate with many Americans. Biden's appreciation for Catholic social thought—in particular the principles of solidarity and the common good—are visible in the president's policy goals of honoring the dignity of work by providing more economic security to struggling families, defending the role of unions, and his efforts to expand the social safety net to reduce poverty. His significant investments in policies that address climate change and his halting but continued push to rebuild our country's tattered asylum and refugee system align with two of Pope Francis's most consistent priorities. For Catholics disillusioned by how Catholic identity in public life is often narrowly defined by self-styled traditionalists and single-issue advocates—including those who rallied behind Donald Trump—Biden's presidency has represented a welcome opening for a more social justice–inflected Catholicism. At the same time, a Catholic president's support for abortion rights and the US bishops' framing of ending abortion as the church's "preeminent priority" created a symbiotic dynamic of conflict that has further polarized the Catholic community and overshadowed other urgent life issues addressed by church teaching. A monumental challenge for the Catholic Church in the United States, during a time when most people of faith oppose the criminalization of abortion and support equality for LGBTQ rights, is to find a path out of the culture wars while still making a distinctively Catholic case for religious liberty, human life, and dignity in a pluralistic society. The ability to meet this challenge depends, in part, on whether lay Catholics and church leaders already attempting to navigate that course can succeed in reviving a consistent-ethic-of-life framework when addressing the most vital political and moral issues our nation faces today. How will lay Catholics and church leaders respond to an often-interconnected web of injustices that include threats to democracy and voting rights; rampant gun violence; deepening economic inequality; a refugee crisis at the border; climate change; the lack of social support for women and children highlighted by the end of *Roe*; a growing backlash to dismantling institutional racism; and an emboldened Christian nationalist movement? I will take up some of those questions in a subsequent chapter. But reclaiming a more expansive Catholic witness in public life and politics today will also require confronting the way in which a network of influential lay Catholics and the organizations they lead are using wealth, political connections, and close ties with the most vocal culture-warrior bishops to exert an outsized influence on American Catholicism.

NOTES

1. Karen Tumulty, "In Trying to Pressure Biden, the Catholic Bishops Forget the Lessons of JFK," *Washington Post*, June 20, 2021, https://www.washingtonpost.com/opinions/2021/06/20/trying-pressure-biden-catholic-bishops-forget-lessons-jfk/.
2. John F. Kennedy Presidential Library and Museum, "Address to the Greater Houston Ministerial Association," September 12, 1960, https://www.jfklibrary.org/learn/about-jfk/historic-speeches/address-to-the-greater-houston-ministerial-association.
3. Christopher White, "Biden Praises Pope Francis at Vatican as 'Most Significant Warrior for Peace,'" *National Catholic Reporter*, October 29, 2021, https://www.ncronline.org/news/francis-welcomes-biden-vatican-amid-tension-us-catholic-hierarchy.
4. Christopher White, "Against a Catholic Backdrop, Biden Vows Increase in Refugee Admissions," *National Catholic Reporter*, November 12, 2020, https://www.ncronline.org/news/against-catholic-backdrop-biden-vows-increase-refugee-admissions.
5. Christopher White, "Pope Francis Congratulates Biden on Election Win," *National Catholic Reporter*, November 12, 2020, https://www.ncronline.org/news/pope-francis-congratulates-biden-election-win.
6. Shaun Casey, interview with author.
7. Christopher White, "U.S. Bishops Issue Warning to President-Elect Joe Biden on Abortion," *National Catholic Reporter*, November 17, 2020, https://www.ncronline.org/news/us-bishops-issue-warning-president-elect-joe-biden-abortion.
8. U.S. Conference of Catholic Bishops, *Respect for Unborn Life: The Church's Constant Teaching*, 2024, https://www.usccb.org/issues-and-action/human-life-and-dignity/abortion/respect-for-unborn-human-life.
9. Antonio Spadaro, S.J., "A Big Heart Open to God: An Interview with Pope Francis," *America*, September 30, 2013, https://www.americamagazine.org/faith/2013/09/30/big-heart-open-god-interview-pope-francis.
10. Dalia Fahmy, "With Religion-Related Rulings on the Horizon, U.S. Christians see Supreme Court Favorably," March 3, 2020, https://www.pewresearch.org/short-reads/2020/03/03/with-religion-related-rulings-on-the-horizon-u-s-christians-see-supreme-court-favorably/.
11. Carrie Blazina, "Key Facts about the Abortion Debate in America," Pew Research Center, July 15, 2022, https://www.pewresearch.org/short-reads/2022/07/15/key-facts-about-the-abortion-debate-in-america/.

12. Alejandra Molina, "A New Survey Found Latino Catholics Overwhelmingly Support Abortion Rights. Here's Why," *Religion News Service*, July 18, 2022, https://religionnews.com/2022/07/18/a-new-survey-found-latino-catholics-overwhelmingly-support-abortion-rights-heres-why/.
13. Jeff Diamant, "Three-in-Ten or More Democrats and Republicans Don't Agree with Their Party on Abortion," Pew Research Center, June 18, 2020, https://www.pewresearch.org/short-reads/2020/06/18/three-in-ten-or-more-democrats-and-republicans-dont-agree-with-their-party-on-abortion/.
14. John R. Quinn, "The Public Duty of Bishops: Lessons from the Storm in South Bend," *America*, August 31, 2009, https://www.americamagazine.org/politics-society/2009/08/31/public-duty-bishops-lessons-storm-south-bend.
15. Pope Francis, Apostolic Exhortation *Evangelii Gaudium*, November 24, 2013. https://www.vatican.va/evangelii-gaudium/en/files/assets/basic-html/page40.html.
16. Nicole Winfield, "Pope: No Place for Politics in Biden Communion Flap," *Associated Press*, September 15, 2021, https://apnews.com/article/pope-francis-joe-biden-communion-d58f0eec9ac1a1ff576e38fb85bf532f.
17. Cindy Wooden, "Cardinal Ladaria Cautions U.S. Bishops on Politics and Communion," *Catholic News Service*, May 10, 2021, https://www.ncronline.org/news/cardinal-ladaria-cautions-us-bishops-politicians-and-communion.
18. Christopher White, "Ahead of Communion Document Vote, Pope Francis' U.S. Allies Urge Delay," *National Catholic Reporter*, June 17, 2021, https://www.ncronline.org/news/ahead-communion-document-vote-pope-francis-us-allies-urge-delay.
19. Christopher White, "Ahead of Communion Document Vote, Pope Francis' U.S. Allies Urge Delay," *National Catholic Reporter*, June 17, 2021, https://www.ncronline.org/news/ahead-communion-document-vote-pope-francis-us-allies-urge-delay.
20. Jack Jenkins, "D.C.'s Wilton Gregory, First African American Cardinal, on Joe Biden, Race, and COVID-19," *Religion News Service*, December 11, 2020, https://religionnews.com/2020/12/11/cardinal-wilton-gregory-on-joe-biden-race-and-covid-19/.
21. Jack Jenkins, "In Lengthy Debate, Bishops Wrangle over Politics and 'Eucharistic Consistency,'" *Religion News Service*, June 17, 2021, https://religionnews.com/2021/06/17/in-lengthy-debate-bishops-wrangle-over-politics-and-eucharistic-consistency/.
22. Jenkins, "In Lengthy Debate, Bishops Wrangle."
23. Archbishop Salvatore Cordileone, *Before I Formed You in the Womb I Knew You: A Pastoral Letter on the Human Dignity of the Unborn, Holy Communion, and Catholics in Political Life*, May 1, 2021, https://sfarchdiocese.org/inthewomb/.
24. Jason Horowitz, "Vatican Warns U.S. Bishops: Don't Deny Biden Communion over Abortion," *New York Times*, June 14, 2021, https://www.nytimes.com/2021/06/14/world/europe/biden-vatican-communion-abortion.html.
25. Jack Jenkins, "AOC, other Catholic Democrats Urge Bishops Against 'Weaponization' of Communion," *Religion News Service*, June 18, 2021, https://religionnews.com/2021/06/18/aoc-other-catholic-democrats-urge-bishops-against-weaponization-of-communion/.
26. Amy B. Wang, "Pelosi Meets Pope Francis in Private Audience at the Vatican," *Washington Post*, October 9, 2021, https://www.washingtonpost.com/politics/2021/10/09/pope-francis-meets-pelosi-private-audience-vatican/.

27. Kevin Liptak, "Biden Says Pope Told Him He's a Good Catholic and Should Continue Receiving Communion," *CNN,* October 29, 2021, https://www.cnn.com/2021/10/29/politics/good-catholic-joe-biden-pope-francis/index.html.
28. Brian Fraga, "U.S. Bishops Tweet Their Criticism of Pope Francis' Meeting with Biden," *National Catholic Reporter,* October 29, 2021, https://www.ncronline.org/news/politics/us-bishops-tweet-their-criticism-pope-francis-meeting-biden.
29. Fraga, "U.S. Bishops Tweet Their Criticism."
30. John Lavenburg and Ines San Martin, "Eucharist Focus of Archbishop's Remarks to U.S. Bishops; Nuncio Pushes Synodality," *Crux,* November 16, 2021, https://cruxnow.com/church-in-the-usa/2021/11/eucharist-focus-of-archbishops-remarks-to-u-s-bishops-nuncio-pushes-synodality.
31. E. J. Dionne Jr., "A Fragile Truce in Catholic Bishops' War over Biden," *Washington Post,* November 17, 2021, https://www.washingtonpost.com/opinions/2021/11/17/fragile-truce-catholic-bishops-war-over-biden/.
32. Archbishop Joseph F. Naumann, *Opening Mass 2021 National Prayer Vigil for Life,* January 28, 2021, https://www.usccb.org/prolife/archbishop-joseph-f-naumann-opening-mass-2021-national-prayer-vigil-life.
33. Jim Graves, "Abp. Naumann: Pres. Biden 'Should Stop Defining Himself as a Devout Catholic,'" *The Catholic World Report,* February 13, 2021, https://www.catholicworldreport.com/2021/02/13/archbishop-naumann-president-biden-should-stop-defining-himself-as-a-devout-catholic/.
34. AC Wimmer, "Archbishop Naumann Says He Is 'Sad' over Pope's Handling of Biden, Pelosi on Abortion," *Catholic News Agency,* July 18, 2022, https://www.thecatholictelegraph.com/archbishop-naumann-says-he-is-sad-over-popes-handling-of-biden-pelosi-on-abortion/82010.
35. Archbishop Salvatore Cordileone, *Letter to the Faithful on the Notification sent to Speaker Nancy Pelosi,* May 20, 2022, https://sfarchdiocese.org/letter-to-the-faithful-on-the-notification-sent-to-speaker-nancy-pelosi/.
36. Thomas J. Reese, "Catholics Are Divided over Award for William Barr at National Catholic Prayer Breakfast," *Religion News Service,* September 22, 2020, https://www.americamagazine.org/politics-society/2020/09/22/catholics-award-william-barr-national-catholic-prayer-breakfast.
37. Charles J. Chaput, "God Never Loses," *First Things,* September 21, 2020, https://www.firstthings.com/web-exclusives/2020/09/god-never-loses.
38. Jack Jenkins, "Banned by Cordileone in San Francisco, Pelosi Receives Eucharist in Washington," *Religion News Service,* May 23, 2022, https://www.ncronline.org/news/people/banned-cordileone-san-francisco-pelosi-receives-eucharist-washington.
39. Jack Jenkins, "Banned by Cordileone in San Francisco, Pelosi Receives Eucharist in Washington," *Religion News Service,* May 23, 2022, https://www.ncronline.org/news/people/banned-cordileone-san-francisco-pelosi-receives-eucharist-washington.
40. Peter Nicholas, "Biden the Sinner," *Atlantic,* October 29, 2021, https://www.theatlantic.com/politics/archive/2021/10/biden-pope-meeting/620513/.
41. Rev. Kevin Gillespie, interview with author.
42. Rev. Kevin Gillespie, interview with author.
43. Peter Steinfels. "Death of a Cardinal; Cardinal O'Connor, 80, Dies; Forceful Voice for Vatican," *New York Times,* May 4, 2000, https://www.nytimes.com/2000/05/04/nyregion/death-of-a-cardinal-cardinal-o-connor-80-dies-forceful-voice-for-vatican.html.

44. Peter Steinfels, *A People Adrift: The Crisis of the Roman Catholic Church in America* (Simon & Schuster, 2004).
45. The Editors, "Mario Cuomo, Politician," *Commonweal*, January 6, 2015, https://www.commonwealmagazine.org/mario-cuomo-politician.
46. Michael Oreskes, "Cuomo Drafts Talk on Theology and Politics," *New York Times*, September 9, 1984, https://www.nytimes.com/1984/09/09/nyregion/cuomo-drafts-talk-on-theology-and-politics.html.
47. Gov, Mario Cuomo, *Religious Belief and Public Morality: A Catholic Governor's Perspective*, University of Notre Dame Archives, September 13, 1984, https://archives.nd.edu/research/texts/cuomo.htm.
48. Michael Oreskes, "Cuomo Bids Catholics Persuade by Example, Not Impose Views," *New York Times*, September 14, 1984, https://www.nytimes.com/1984/09/14/nyregion/cuomo-bids-catholics-persuade-by-example-not-impose-views.html.
49. Andy Sullivan, "Explainer: How Abortion Became a Divisive Issue in U.S. Politics," *Reuters*, June 24, 2022, https://www.reuters.com/world/us/how-abortion-became-divisive-issue-us-politics-2022-06-24/.
50. Emma Green, "The Progressive Roots of the Pro-Life Movement," *Atlantic*, February 3, 2016, https://www.theatlantic.com/politics/archive/2016/02/daniel-williams-defenders-unborn/435369/.
51. Lisa Lerer, "When Joe Biden Voted to Let States Overturn *Roe v. Wade*," *New York Times*, March 29, 2019, https://www.nytimes.com/2019/03/29/us/politics/biden-abortion-rights.html.
52. Lerer, "When Joe Biden Voted to Let States Overturn *Roe v. Wade*."
53. Lerer, "When Joe Biden Voted to Let States Overturn *Roe v. Wade*."
54. Michae D. Shear, "Biden Is an Uneasy Champion on Abortion. Can He Lead the Fight in Post-*Roe* America?" *New York Times*, April 7, 2022, https://www.nytimes.com/2022/08/07/us/politics/biden-abortion-catholic-history.html?smid=nytcore-ios-share&referringSource=articleShare.
55. Anna North, "How the Abortion Debate Moved Away from 'Safe, Legal and Rare,'" *Vox*, October 18, 2019, https://www.vox.com/2019/10/18/20917406/abortion-safe-legal-and-rare-tulsi-gabbard.
56. North, "How the Abortion Debate Moved Away from 'Safe, Legal and Rare.'"
57. Michael Wear, "Obama's Forgotten Plan to Reduce Abortions," *Politico*, January 15, 2017, https://www.politico.com/magazine/story/2017/01/barack-obama-faith-adviser-book-abortion-reduction-214635/.
58. John Thavis, "Vatican Newspaper Says Obama Sought 'Common Ground' at Notre Dame," *Catholic News Service*, May 18, 2009, https://www.americamagazine.org/content/all-things/vatican-obama-sought-common-ground.
59. John Gehring, "Whatever Happened to Common Ground on Abortion Reduction?" *Religion & Politics*, April 16, 2013, https://religionandpolitics.org/2013/04/16/whatever-happened-to-the-common-ground-on-abortion-reduction/.
60. Amy Sullivan, "Finding Common Ground on an Abortion Bill," *Time*, July 23, 2009. https://content.time.com/time/nation/article/0,8599,1912284,00.html.
61. North, "How the Abortion Debate Moved Away from 'Safe, Legal and Rare.'"
62. Marie Solis, "Tulsi Gabbard's Stance on Abortion Is Stuck in the '90s," *Vice*, October 16, 2019, https://www.vice.com/en/article/43k5db/tulsi-gabbards-stance-on-abortion-is-stuck-in-the-90s.

63. John Gehring, "Whatever Happened to Common Ground on Abortion Reduction?" *Religion & Politics*, April 16, 2013, https://religionandpolitics.org/2013/04/16/what-ever-happened-to-the-common-ground-on-abortion-reduction/.
64. Debbie Elliot and Lauren Wamsley, "Alabama Governor Signs Abortion Ban into Law," *National Public Radio*, May 14, 2019, https://www.npr.org/2019/05/14/723312937/alabama-lawmakers-passes-abortion-ban.
65. Kristen Powers, "Heartbeat Bills Reveal Extremist Anti-Abortion View that Values Unborn over Women," *USA Today*, May 14, 2019, https://www.usatoday.com/story/opinion/2019/05/14/heartbeat-bills-anti-abortion-laws-late-term-women-christian-column/1190340001/.
66. Lisa Lerer, "When Joe Biden Voted to Let States Overturn *Roe v. Wade*," *New York Times*, March 29, 2019, https://www.nytimes.com/2019/03/29/us/politics/biden-abortion-rights.html.
67. Katie Glueck, "Biden Still Backs Hyde Amendment, Which Bans Federal Funds for Abortions," *New York Times*, June 5, 2019, https://www.nytimes.com/2019/06/05/us/politics/biden-hyde-amendment.html.
68. Glueck, "Biden Still Backs Hyde Amendment."
69. Glueck, "Biden Still Backs Hyde Amendment."
70. Katie Glueck, "Joe Biden Denounces Hyde Amendment, Reversing His Position," *New York Times*, June 6, 2019, https://www.nytimes.com/2019/06/06/us/politics/joe-biden-hyde-amendment.html.
71. Shear, "Biden Is an Uneasy Champion on Abortion."
72. Sister Carol Keehan, interview with author.
73. Patricia Zapor, "Obama in CHA Address Thanks Organization for Supporting Health Care Law," *Catholic News Service*, June 10, 2015, https://www.ncronline.org/news/politics/obama-cha-address-thanks-organization-supporting-health-care-law.
74. Nancy Frazier O'Brien, "St. Joseph Health Services Withdraws from CHA membership," *Rhode Island Catholic*, April 8, 2010, https://thericatholic.com/stories/st-joseph-health-services-withdraws-from-cha-membership3078?.
75. Jennifer Epstein, "Biden: Compromise on Contraception," *Politico*, February 9, 2012, https://www.politico.com/story/2012/02/biden-on-birth-control-furor-we-can-work-it-out-072701.
76. Helene Cooper and Laurie Goodstein, "Rule Shift on Birth Control Is Concession to Obama Allies," *New York Times*, February 10, 2012, https://www.nytimes.com/2012/02/11/health/policy/obama-to-offer-accommodation-on-birth-control-rule-officials-say.html.
77. Sister Carol Keehen, interview with author.
78. John Gehring, "Catholic Moral Tradition More Nuanced Than Anti-Abortion Slogans or Extreme Bills," *National Catholic Reporter*, March 31, 2022, https://www.ncronline.org/news/opinion/catholic-moral-tradition-more-nuanced-anti-abortion-slogans-or-extreme-bills.
79. Gehring, "Catholic Moral Tradition More Nuanced."
80. Cathleen Kaveny, "Could the Church Take a Risk," *Commonweal*, June 11, 2018, https://www.commonwealmagazine.org/could-church-take-risk.
81. Cathleen Kaveny, interview with author.
82. Mollie Wilson O'Reilly, "When Abortion Isn't Abortion," *Commonweal*, March 21, 2022, https://www.commonwealmagazine.org/when-abortion-isnt-abortion.

83. O'Reilly, "When Abortion Isn't Abortion."
84. Susan Ross, interview with author.
85. Faith in Public Life. 2022. "Catholic Scholars React to Supreme Court's *Dobbs* Ruling," *Press Release*, June 24, 2022, https://www.faithinpubliclife.org/news/catholic-scholars-react-to-supreme-courts-dobbs-ruling/.
86. Michael Goldberg, "Maternal Deaths and Disparities Increase in Mississippi," *Associated Press*, January 26, 2023, https://apnews.com/article/health-mississippi-state-government-e6d47374955e81342d325d4c790c1d42.
87. Lisa Marshall, "Study: Banning Abortion Would Boost Maternal Mortality by Double-Digits," *CU Boulder Today*, September 8, 2021, https://www.colorado.edu/today/2021/09/08/study-banning-abortion-would-boost-maternal-mortality-double-digits.
88. Faith in Public Life, "Catholic Scholars React to Supreme Court's *Dobbs* Ruling," *Press Release*, June 24, 2022, https://www.faithinpubliclife.org/news/catholic-scholars-react-to-supreme-courts-dobbs-ruling/.
89. Stephanie Clary, "Why Doesn't a Pro-Life Catholic Church Offer Paid Leave for New Mothers?" *National Catholic Reporter*, June 3, 2022, https://www.ncronline.org/news/opinion/ncr-connections/why-doesnt-pro-life-catholic-church-offer-paid-leave-new-mothers.
90. US Conference of Catholic Bishops, "USCCB Statement on U.S. Supreme Court Ruling in Dobbs v. Jackson," *Press Release*, June 24, 2022, https://www.usccb.org/news/2022/usccb-statement-us-supreme-court-ruling-dobbs-v-jackson.
91. Christopher White, "Reading between the Lines of Vatican Response to Supreme Court Overturning Roe," *National Catholic Reporter*, July 12, 2022, https://www.ncronline.org/news/reading-between-lines-vatican-response-supreme-court-overturning-roe.
92. White, "Reading between the Lines."
93. White, "Reading between the Lines."
94. Jack Jenkins, "Catholic Bishops Spent Big on Kansas Abortion Vote—and Maybe Lost Bigger," *Religion News Service*, August 5, 2022, https://www.washingtonpost.com/religion/2022/08/05/catholics-kansas-abortion-vote/.
95. Bill Scher, "The Ads That Won the Kansas Abortion Referendum," *Washington Monthly*, August 5, 2022, https://washingtonmonthly.com/2022/08/05/the-ads-that-won-the-kansas-abortion-referendum/.
96. Jack Jenkins, "Nuns Decry Kansas Abortion Amendment, Challenging Archbishop," *Religion News Service*, July 29, 2022, https://www.washingtonpost.com/religion/2022/07/29/kansas-abortion-amendment-catholics/.
97. Thomas Phippen, "CatholicVote Launches $3 Million Midterm Ad Campaign Aimed at Kicking Catholic Democrats Out of Office," *Fox News*, July 11, 2022, https://www.foxnews.com/politics/catholicvote-launches-midterm-ad-campaign-aimed-kicking-catholic-democrats-out-office.
98. Fr. Leo O'Donovan, S. J., interview with author.
99. The American Presidency Project, "Remarks by President-Elect Joe Biden in Wilmington, Delaware," December 22, 2020, https://www.presidency.ucsb.edu/documents/remarks-president-elect-joe-biden-wilmington-delaware-9.
100. Fr. Leo O'Donovan, interview with author.
101. Matt Malone, "Everyone's Entitled to Dignity,' A Conversation with Joseph R. Biden Jr." *America*, September 29, 2015, https://www.americamagazine.org/politics-society/2015/09/29/everyones-entitled-dignity-conversation-joseph-r-biden-jr.

102. David Brooks, "Has Biden Changed? He Tells Us." *New York Times*, May 20, 2021, https://www.nytimes.com/2021/05/20/opinion/joe-biden-david-brooks-interview.html.
103. US Department of Treasury, "Child Tax Credit: The American Rescue Plan Increased the Child Tax Credit and Expanded Its Coverage to Better Assist Families Who Care for Children," https://home.treasury.gov/policy-issues/coronavirus/assistance-for-american-families-and-workers/child-tax-credit.
104. Cory Turner, "The Expanded Child Tax Credit Briefly Slashed Child Poverty. Here's What Else It Did," *National Public Radio*, January 27, 2022, https://www.npr.org/2022/01/27/1075299510/the-expanded-child-tax-credit-briefly-slashed-child-poverty-heres-what-else-it-d.
105. Barabara Sprunt, "Here's What's in the American Rescue Plan," *National Public Radio*, March 11, 2021, https://www.npr.org/sections/coronavirus-live-updates/2021/03/09/974841565/heres-whats-in-the-american-rescue-plan-as-it-heads-toward-final-passage.
106. J. Kevin Appleby, "Catholic Groups—including the Bishops—Should Pressure Republicans to Support Biden's Spending Bill," *America*, October 20, 2021, https://www.americamagazine.org/politics-society/2021/10/20/biden-spending-bill-hyde-amendment-241684.
107. J. Kevin Appleby, interview with author.
108. Tom Perriello, "Biden Is the Most Pro-Family President in Decades. So Why Is the Catholic Church Attacking Him?" *Politico*, September 9, 2021, https://www.politico.com/news/magazine/2021/09/09/bishops-biden-catholic-church-perriello-510975.
109. Rep. Brendan Boyle, interview with author.
110. Rep. Juan Vargas, interview with author.
111. *Compendium of the Social Doctrine of the Church*, https://www.vatican.va/roman_curia/pontifical_councils/justpeace/documents/rc_pc_justpeace_doc_20060526_compendio-dott-soc_en.html.
112. Anthony Annett, interview with author.
113. Vatican News staff, "Pope Calls for Consideration of 'Universal Basic Wage' for Unprotected Workers," *Vatican News*, April 13, 2020, https://www.vaticannews.va/en/pope/news/2020-04/pope-letter-popular-movements-universal-basic-wage.html.
114. Ahiza Garcia-Hodges, "Biden's Vow to Be 'Most Pro-Union President' Tested in First Year," *NBC News*, January 20, 2022, https://www.nbcnews.com/business/economy/bidens-vow-union-president-tested-first-year-rcna12791.
115. Anthony R. Picarello, Jr., General Counsel, U.S. Conference of Catholic Bishops, "Brief of *Amicus Curiae* United States Conference of Catholic Bishops Supporting Respondents," January 19, 2018, https://www.usccb.org/about/general-counsel/amicus-briefs/upload/Janus-v-American-Federation-of-State-16-1466-bsac-usccb-amicus.pdf.
116. The White House, "Fact Sheet: Executive Order Establishing the White House Task Force on Worker Organizing and Empowerment," Press Release, April 26, 2021, https://www.whitehouse.gov/briefing-room/statements-releases/2021/04/26/fact-sheet-executive-order-establishing-the-white-house-task-force-on-worker-organizing-and-empowerment/.

117. Jay Greene and Eli Rosenberg, "Biden Hails Amazon Workers Pressing to Unionize in Alabama in Unusual Sign of Support," *Washington Post*, February 28, 2021, https://www.washingtonpost.com/technology/2021/02/28/amazon-biden-union-alabama/.
118. Meghan J. Clark, "Justice as Participation: Joe Biden and Catholic Social Thought on Workers' Rights," *Berkley Forum*, March 11, 2021, https://berkleycenter.georgetown.edu/responses/justice-as-participation-joe-biden-and-catholic-social-thought-on-workers-rights.
119. The White House, "Statement by President Joe Biden on the House Taking Up the PRO Act," *Press Release*, March 9, 2021, https://www.whitehouse.gov/briefing-room/statements-releases/2021/03/09/statement-by-president-joe-biden-on-the-house-taking-up-the-pro-act/.
120. The Catholic Labor Network, "400 Faith Leaders Say: PRO Act Now," *Press Release*, July 20, 2021, https://catholiclabor.org/400-faith-leaders-say-pro-act-now/.
121. The White House, "Statement by President Biden in Support of California's Agricultural Labor Relations Voting Choice Act," Press Release, September 4, 2022, https://www.whitehouse.gov/briefing-room/statements-releases/2022/09/04/statement-by-president-biden-in-support-of-californias-agricultural-labor-relations-voting-choice-act/.
122. Joseph McCartin, interview with author.
123. John Ryan, "A Living Wage, 1906," American Catholic History Classroom, The Catholic University of America, https://cuomeka.wrlc.org/exhibits/show/industrial/documents/cri-doc4.
124. Michael Sean Winters, *Left at the Altar: How the Democrats Lost the Catholics and How Catholics Can Save the Democrats* (Basic Books, 2008).
125. John Ryan, "Bishops' Program of Social Reconstruction," American Catholic History Classroom, The Catholic University of America, https://cuomeka.wrlc.org/exhibits/show/bishops/background/1919-bishops-reconstruction.
126. Ryan, "Bishops' Program of Social Reconstruction."
127. Lew Daly, "In Search of the Common Good," *Boston Review*, May 1, 2007, https://www.bostonreview.net/articles/in-search-of-the-common-good/.
128. Daly, "In Search of the Common Good."
129. Daly, "In Search of the Common Good."
130. Daly, "In Search of the Common Good."
131. Christine Firer Hinze, interview with author.
132. Joan Rosenhauer, interview with author.
133. Rosenhauer, interview with author.
134. Dylan Corbett, interview with author.
135. Julian Resendiz, "U.S. Catholic Groups Deliver $40K in Aid to Juarez Migrant Shelters," *Border Report*, December 20, 2021, https://www.borderreport.com/immigration/u-s-catholic-groups-deliver-40k-in-aid-to-juarez-migrant-shelters/.
136. J. D. Long Garcia, "Bishop Seitz Meets with Kamala Harris at the Border, Gives a Rosary Blessed by Pope Francis," *America*, June 25, 2021, https://www.americamagazine.org/politics-society/2021/06/25/harris-el-paso-border-visit-catholic-bishop-seitz-migrants-immigration.
137. Corbett, interview with author.
138. Shaun Casey, interview with author.
139. Rev. David Hollenbach, interview with author.

4

CATHOLIC CULTURE WARRIORS

When professors, academic deans, and bishops gathered inside a century-old gothic building at The Catholic University of America in the summer of 2022 to say farewell to departing president John Garvey, one of the most powerful men in Washington mingled among the crowd. Leonard Leo, the chief advisor to Donald Trump on Supreme Court nominations, listened alongside other guests that evening as one of the picks he helped secure on the bench, Justice Amy Coney Barrett, delivered remarks praising Garvey, her longtime mentor and former law professor at the University of Notre Dame. Leo and Barrett's presence together that night reflected the rising influence of conservative Catholics on the law, academia, and politics at a time when the Supreme Court's rightward transformation has reconfigured American jurisprudence on issues of abortion, voting rights, and religious liberty. The cochairman of the Federalist Society, Leo has spent nearly four decades helping to transform law schools and the federal judiciary by creating a pipeline of conservative lawyers and judges. He is also a key player in an increasingly deep-pocketed conservative Catholic movement that wields significant influence on the church in the United States.[1]

At Catholic University, the nation's only Vatican-chartered university, Leo has raised more than $20 million, primarily from anonymous donors, during his time on the board of trustees and on the business school's board.[2] Among those gifts, Leo directed $4.25 million from an anonymous donor last spring to establish the Project on Constitutional Originalism and the Catholic Intellectual Tradition at Catholic University's Columbus School of Law. Supreme Court Justice Samuel Alito delivered the initiative's inaugural lecture. Leo helped facilitate another $4 million in funding from an anonymous donor to establish an endowed chair for the project in partnership with the Knights of Columbus. He also brokered a $13 million donation from an anonymous donor in 2019 that supports the university's Institute on Human Ecology and the Busch School of Business. Catholic University's business school, which has also received more than $10 from the Charles Koch Foundation, is known for its libertarian-inflected economics and events that have featured GOP Sen. Marco Rubio of Florida and Charles Koch, a billionaire industrialist and longtime Republican donor.[3] Koch has used part of his fortune to fight policies that address climate change—a stark contrast to how Pope Francis has prioritized the need for urgent action and specifically called for "a global energy transition." "This whole crowd thinks of the church in terms of American politics and they really think they can buy the church and academic institutions with their money," said a Catholic University professor who spoke to me on the condition of anonymity. "There is nothing wrong with conservatism at a university. It's the ideology that often comes with it that can be problematic," the professor said.[4]

Leo has also been involved with ideologically motivated fundraising at George Mason University in Fairfax, Virginia. In 2016 the university announced a $30 million donation to its law school, which included $10 million from the Charles Koch Foundation and a $20 million gift from an anonymous donor facilitated by Leo. The anonymous donor's gift came with the stipulation that the law school be renamed after the late Supreme Court Justice Antonin Scalia, a conservative Catholic and close ally of Leo since their early days in the Federalist Society. In response to public record requests filed by an alumna of the law school, the administration of the donor money was traced back to the BH Fund, a company Leo helped lead. Email exchanges between the law school dean and Leo, disclosed after public record requests from student activists at George Mason and the activist group UnKoch My Campus, show Leo and the dean sharing detailed information about faculty hiring, judicial law clerk suggestions, allocations of the gift money, and communications about faculty taking leave to work in the Trump administration.[5]

Bethany Letiecq, an associate professor at George Mason, told me in an interview that the influence of Leo and Koch at her university should have been a "cautionary tale" for Catholic University. "We really saw how undue donor influence transformed our campus, especially in the law school and economics department," Letiecq said. "They had a strategy to start these centers and schools that were part of an effort to capture the university for their own political agenda. The faculty was rolled over and had so little power."[6] In response to questions about Leo's role at Catholic University, Daniel Drummond, the associate vice president of communications, said that "every single person on the Board is dedicated to the mission of the university and their service is central to its future as a research institution steeped in the Catholic tradition of education." While the university "welcomes donations and support from many different people, companies, and organizations," he added, "this support is not connected to any university policy making decisions, including hiring or tenure decisions."[7]

Nancy MacLean, a professor of history and public policy at Duke University, has chronicled the more than six-decade effort by conservative donors to mainstream libertarian ideologies and antigovernment philosophies in her book, *Democracy in Chains: The Deep History of the Radical Right's Stealth Plan for America.* Centers and institutes at universities that are backed by ideologically driven donors, MacLean said, provide beachheads for cultivating research, speakers, and faculty and developing a pipeline of students who will go on to other conservative networks. "These centers at universities often have innocuous sounding names, but they are really part of an integrated strategy on the right that is connected with think tanks and conservative state policy networks," MacLean said. Right-wing donors have been particularly successful at making inroads at universities and law schools by funding niche centers, she noted, including at Catholic universities where the church's social teachings clash with libertarian, market-oriented ideologies. "It gives these donors and causes tremendous legitimacy when they can invest in Catholic and other faith-based institutions that have a long history of social justice activism," she said. Compared to liberal donors who are often characterized by what MacLean described as driven by "causes that are often siloed," the right has "a more integrated strategy."[8]

INSPIRED BY FAITH, FLUSH WITH FUNDING

Leonard Leo has long been a fixture in the overlapping cultures of Republican politics and conservative Catholicism in Washington. The Opus Dei-affiliated Catholic Information Center—a K Street bookstore and chapel that describes itself as "the closest tabernacle to the White House"—awarded Leo a John Paul II New Evangelization Award in the fall of 2022. The center, where Leo sits on the board, is a popular gathering place for high-profile conservative Catholics in law, public policy, and politics. Former board members include Trump's White House counsel Pat Cipollone and his Attorney General William Barr. The center honored Leo as a "champion of the rule of law, advocate of global religious freedom, and committed leader of many Catholic organizations in Washington, DC and around the country."[9] The sold-out awards dinner at the Mayflower Hotel was closed to the press. Tickets for a "premium table" with ten seats cost $25,000 for a sponsorship. In a video of his speech released by the Catholic Information Center a month after the award's dinner, Leo described the work of Catholic evangelization as involving "every facet of life, including law, public policy and politics, which are the areas that I know best." He warned that this evangelization "faces extraordinary threats and hurdles" because "our culture is more hateful and intolerant of Catholicism than at any other point in our lives. It despises who we are, what we profess, and how we act." "Catholicism faces vile and immoral current-day barbarians, secularists and bigots," Leo said. "These barbarians can be known by their signs. They vandalized and burned our churches after the Supreme Court overturned *Roe v. Wade*. They show up at events like this one, trying to frighten and muzzle us. From coast to coast they are conducting a coordinated and large-scale campaign to drive us from the communities they want to dominate. . . . Our opponents are not just uninformed or unchurched. They are often deeply wounded people whom the devil can easily take advantage of."[10]

"I can't think of anyone who has lived his faith more powerfully than Leonard Leo," former Attorney General William Barr said in a video tribute produced by the center. "He does it quietly and unassumingly but with inhuman energy. It's particularly fitting that in the very year in which *Dobbs* was decided we are honoring Leonard Leo because no one has done more to advance traditional values, especially the right to life, than Leonard."[11] John Sniegocki, a professor of religious ethics at Xavier University in Cincinnati, countered that honoring Leo with an award named for the late pope is a prime example of how segments of the Catholic right continue to appropriate the Catholic tradition for ideological ends. "Many of the projects that Leo has been involved with support goals that run directly counter to the teachings of John Paul II," Sniegocki said.

> These projects have worked to undermine voting rights, hinder action on climate change and foster deregulation of corporate activities, whereas John Paul II called for the expansion of democracy, spoke of climate change as one of the most pressing ethical issues facing the modern world and supported strong regulation on behalf of the common good. The granting of this award appears to be another attempt by certain segments of the Catholic Church in the United States to hijack the name and reputation of Pope John Paul II to support a political agenda that runs deeply contrary to the actual teachings of John Paul II and the broader tradition of Catholic social teaching.[12]

After serving as a Catholic strategist for George W. Bush during the 2004 presidential campaign, Leo helped start the National Catholic Prayer Breakfast. For two decades, the event has been a destination for Republican politicians, conservative bishops, and Catholic lobbyists in the nation's capital. Leo is board president of the organization, which was cofounded by Joe Cella, an advisor on Catholic issues for Donald Trump's presidential campaigns. Leo is also a member of the Knights of Malta, a lay religious order of the Catholic Church dating back to the twelfth century. President George W. Bush appointed him to the US Commission for International Religious Freedom in 2007, and Leo later served as chairman. Robert George, a Princeton University professor and prominent Catholic conservative, first met Leo in the early 1990s when George received an award from the Federalist Society as a promising legal scholar under the age of forty. "We had a conversation about law and judicial politics in which I was impressed by his depth of understanding and his vision of the role of the Federalist Society," recalled George, who serves on the board of the Ethics and Public Policy Center in Washington with Leo. At Leo's urging, George accepted an appointment to the US Commission on International Religious Freedom, and George was later tasked with leading the commission. "Leonard is a person of deep faith," George told me in an interview. "He reads and thinks about the great religious questions and matters of theology. This deep faith moves and sustains him. It gives him strength when he comes under political attack or draws ideological fire."[13] Tom Carter, who served as Leo's media relations director when he was chairman of the US Commission on International Religious Freedom and later became a public critic of his former boss, told me that Leo was "a visionary" who "figured out 20 years before everyone else that Republicans couldn't win the culture wars at the ballot box so they had to stack the courts." Leo succeeded in that mission, Carter observed, even as white evangelical political activists received most of the media attention "The Christian right has been written about a lot, but hardly anyone talks about the Catholic right."[14]

Leo's three-decade effort to build the Federalist Society into a powerful pipeline for conservative legal talent is part of a broader organizing effort on the right. "Leonard Leo is fully integrated within a political infrastructure that seeks to radically transform the laws, the lawyers that litigate them, and the judges that interpret them," said Isaac Kamola, an associate professor of political science at Trinity College in Hartford, Connecticut, and author of *Free Speech and Koch Money: Manufacturing a Campus Culture War*. "Leo and the Koch network know that political ideas get legitimized in higher education so they have a sophisticated funding strategy for creating academic centers, influencing law schools and producing these ideologies and legal theories that are then used to justify policies like deregulation of corporations and denying climate science."[15] Cathleen Kaveny, a Boston College scholar who teaches in the theology department and the law school, said Leo has deftly used the Federalist Society to build a "coherent movement that stands for a certain view of constitutional interpretation that wants to enshrine conservative Christian values." But she argues that wasn't the intent of the founders and it doesn't align with a traditionally Catholic understanding of law and politics. "It's an approach that is far more evangelical and fundamentalist than Catholic," Kaveny told me. "If Catholics approached the Bible the way these originalists view the Constitution, we would be fundamentalists." A former law professor at the University of Notre Dame, Kaveny watched as the school transformed. She glimpses a potential similar effort taking place at Catholic University with Leo's influence. "At Notre Dame law school, they narrowed the notion of Catholic hiring to mean hiring a certain kind of Catholic who is committed to the culture wars," Kaveny said. "They hired very committed and talented people, and the money followed. It took thirty years, but they played the long game. And it was successful."[16]

"IN YOUR FACE CATHOLICISM" WITH A SIDE OF CIGARS

Tim Busch has the swaggering confidence of someone with a strategy and the money to ensure people in power listen. Tall and perpetually tanned, the owner of the Napa-based vineyard Trinitas Cellars is one of the most influential conservative lay Catholics in the United States. An attorney who specializes in high-net-worth estate planning and the CEO of a company that manages hotels and resorts in California, Busch cofounded the Napa Institute in 2010. Known for its high-priced conferences and networking events with bishops, Republican politicians, conservative donors, and business leaders, the institute was founded after the now retired Philadelphia Archbishop Charles Chaput warned in a 2010 essay, "Catholics and the Next America," that traditional religious believers would face increasing hostility from the secular culture. "If government now pressures religious entities out of the public square, or promotes same-sex 'marriage,' or acts in ways that undermine the integrity of the family, or compromises the sanctity of human life, or overrides the will of voters, or discourages certain forms of religious teaching as 'hate speech,' or interferes with individual and communal rights of conscience, well, why not?," the archbishop wrote. "In the name of tolerance and pluralism, we have forgotten why and how we began as a nation; and we have undermined our ability to ground our arguments in anything higher than our own sectarian opinions."[17]

The Napa Institute hosts an annual summer conference at Busch's Meritage Resort and Spa. Former Vice President Mike Pence delivered a keynote address at the 2023 summer gathering. "Men and women of the Napa Institute, you are the answer for America, not elected officials or conservative causes. They all follow your lead," Pence said. "When I look at the influential men and women in this room I have to tell you, don't underestimate the importance of your voice on behalf of your faith and your values."[18] Busch describes the role of the institute as "uniting Catholic leaders to transform the culture." Along with his position at Napa, Busch's $15 million donation to Catholic University in Washington in 2016 was the largest in school history. He served on the board of trustees for twelve years. The university's business school is named after him. During a $2,500-a-ticket conference at the business school in 2017 that headlined Charles Koch, Busch delivered opening remarks with his typically chummy rapport when talking about the Napa Institute's culture of rarefied networking. "Our events are open seating so you can pick your favorite bishop, priest, or businessman to sit next to," Busch told the audience before encouraging people to enjoy a cigar-bar reception on the eleventh floor of the Renaissance Hotel, where conference attendees stayed. "You don't have to smoke cigars, ladies. It's open bar. Great wine. Oh, it's our wine," he said to laughs from the audience. Busch praised Koch's financial support of the university—"he shares our values"—and also wasn't shy about taking his own credit. "We re-energized The Catholic University of America and made it great again," he said with Trumpian flair.[19] It wasn't the only time at the conference Busch used a line that echoed Trump's rhetoric. He also praised the global Catholic news outlet EWTN, whose board Busch has served on and a network that often features hosts and commentators critical of Pope Francis. "It's much better than this fake news you get elsewhere," Busch quipped. The businessman has ambitious goals for what his money and ideas for the university will mean moving forward. "We are the Catholic University of America and we have educated half of the bishops in this country," he said. "We can be the teaching pulpit for the American church, but also the teaching pulpit for the Vatican and for the global church. We can be that. And we will be that going forward, especially on the issues and topics of business."

Busch's money, influence, and relationships with prominent bishops and cardinals seem to insulate him from the scrutiny of church leaders when his views sound more like the US Chamber of Commerce than traditional

Catholic teaching. Even as he has praised "the compatibility of capitalism with Catholicism" in the *Wall Street Journal*,[20] he seems to pay little heed to what Pope John Paul II called "the priority of labor over capital." He opposes increases to the minimum wage, which he has called "an anti-market regulation that leads to unemployment" and causes "great harm" to workers.[21] And he supports so-called "right-to-work" laws that prevent unions from collecting fees from nonmembers that are used in collective bargaining negotiations that help all workers. In contrast the US bishops' conference filed an amicus brief with the US Supreme Court in 2018 that supported public-sector unions' right to collect dues from nonmembers for collective bargaining. When the former papal nuncio to Washington, Archbishop Carlo Maria Viganó, wrote an explosive letter in 2018 calling on Pope Francis to resign after falsely claiming the pope knew about the abuse committed by the former disgraced cardinal Theodore McCarrick, Busch was quoted in *The New York Times* praising Viganó as doing "a great service" and said Viganó's claims were "credible."[22] The letter was first released by several conservative Catholic news outlets, including the *National Catholic Register*, which is owned by EWTN. Busch served on EWTN's board. In a later communication to Napa supporters, Busch insisted that he "did not preview a copy of or in any way participate in drafting Archbishop Viganó's testimony, nor was I consulted in any capacity about his testimony."[23]

The Napa Institute has an ecclesiastical advisory board made up of nearly a dozen bishops, including the current president of the US bishops' conference, Archbishop Timothy Broglio, and the conference's past president, Los Angeles Archbishop José Gomez. Napa has also cultivated close ties with archconservative church leaders in Rome. Busch and Napa hosted a 2018 birthday soiree at the Rome residence of the American Cardinal James Harvey, according to *The New York Times*. At the bash, the German philanthropist-turned-conservative Catholic Princess Gloria von Thurn und Taxis mingled with American Cardinal Raymond Burke, another frequent foe of Francis, who "ate birthday cake in the shape of a red cardinal's hat, held champagne in one glass and blessed seminarians with the other, and watched fireworks light up the sky in his honor."[24] Princess Gloria also introduced the German Cardinal Gerhard Mueller, who Pope Francis ousted as the prefect of the Vatican's doctrine office and who sits on Napa's advisory board, to the former Trump advisor and right-wing media provocateur Steve Bannon. Bannon later invited the cardinal to his headquarters in Washington, according to *The Times*.

As the hierarchy's credibility continued to plummet in the wake of ongoing revelations that dioceses covered up clergy abuse, Busch and other conservative Catholics with ample checkbooks have moved quickly to fill that vacuum. "Catholic NGOs" (nongovernmental organizations) are at the heart of the Catholic Church's mission today," Busch has said. "The evangelization of our country is being done by private foundations, Catholic NGOs, like Napa and Legatus," Busch said at a 2017 conference at Catholic University.[25] (Legatus is an organization for wealthy Catholic businessmen and their spouses who promote Catholic evangelization in their professional and personal lives.) These nonprofits, he added, remain "tethered to the church through a bishop. . . . But they have access to capital that the church doesn't." Wealthy patrons have been privileged players in the church for centuries, but a new generation of conservative Catholic donors and philanthropists are not simply using their resources to support charitable causes. By funding networks of political advocacy organizations, nonprofits, academic centers at universities, think tanks, and media outlets, these conservative donors are fundamentally shifting the power structures of American Catholicism. It's not an exaggeration to say that an elite club of Catholics with deep wells of capital and a shared vision for advancing theological and political conservatism are now often more powerful than many bishops in shaping the direction of the church.

Tom Roberts, a veteran Catholic journalist and retired editor at the *National Catholic Reporter* who has reported on the church for decades, views these businessmen and philanthropists as related to but essentially distinct from the influential Catholics who defined conservative American Catholicism in the 1980s and 1990s. Roberts noted that while the late Rev. Richard John Neuhaus, who founded the journal *First Things*, John Paul II biographer George Weigel, and the late prominent Catholic social philosopher and author Michael Novak, all offered a series of intellectual arguments for their theological, philosophical, and political views that were part of vibrant public debates, this is not the case with Busch and other megadonors. "They are not really making intellectual arguments," he said. "They have an enormous amount of money and they are building an alternative structure of Catholic authority."[26]

These men (they are mostly white men) frequently sit on the same boards and host conferences that create strategic networking spaces for Catholic business leaders, clergy, religious liberty attorneys, and the occasional Republican politician. Their distinctly American brand of Catholicism is characterized by a preference for traditionalist religious rituals such as the pre-Vatican II liturgy, a preoccupation with fighting LGBTQ rights, and an unwavering faith in unfettered free markets. If Pope Francis dreams of a "poor church for the poor" and offers withering critiques of economic inequality, Catholic identity at Napa events is most conspicuously expressed by speakers who breathlessly warn about the dangers of secularism, "wokeism," and transgender rights while partaking in cigar bar receptions and wine tastings. While the Napa Institute has a larger footprint in California, the organization's profile in Washington, DC, is growing. Napa opened an office in the nation's capital a few blocks from the US Capitol in the spring of 2023. The office is housed in a newly renovated EWTN headquarters next to Union Station. Napa already had a Washington presence with its Napa Legal Institute office at the Ethics and Public Policy Center. Napa Legal provides consulting to faith-based nonprofits on corporate, tax, and philanthropic issues. The legal division launched what it calls its "flagship program," the Napa Legal League, at a 2019 event at Catholic University's business school. The league, according to the institute, seeks to become a "nationwide network of attorneys, accountants, and nonprofit professionals committed to Catholic culture-building in the 21st century."[27] A photograph posted on the Napa Institute's Facebook page in 2022 provided a snapshot of how wealthy Catholics with influence in law and politics have established close ties with the hierarchy and other clergy in leadership positions. The picture shows Busch dining at an Italian restaurant in Washington with a small group of lay Catholics and clergy, including Archbishop Timothy Broglio, who a month earlier had been elected as president of the US bishops' conference. Leonard Leo, the cochairman of the Federalist Society, is also seated at the table.

During a 2022 event in California where he made the announcement about Napa's new office in Washington, DC, Busch described the institute as "growing expansively" and touted a eucharistic procession through the streets of New York City that the Napa Institute organized. "Dolan was like, I've never seen anything like it since I've been here," Busch said, referring to Cardinal Timothy Dolan of New York. "We had a thousand people parading into St. Patrick's Cathedral. We shut down 7th Avenue, 6th Avenue and 5th Avenue, and the police were happy to do it."[28] Busch also thanked John Meyer, at the time Napa's executive director, for his work traveling "to all the Catholic fundraisers that go on in Washington, New York and even South Bend." The reference to South Bend, Indiana, points to one of Napa's newest projects at the University of Notre Dame. Napa, along with the Charles Koch Foundation and other donors, funds the Napa Institute Forum at the university's Center for Citizenship and Constitutional Government. The center, according to a news release, "plans to expand its focus on political leadership by bringing more national political figures to campus and hosting regular events in Washington, D.C., especially with established and aspiring Catholic politicians."[29] The Napa forum kicked off with an inaugural lecture from Supreme Court Justice Clarence Thomas at the university in 2021. I reported for the *National Catholic Reporter* that Napa's involvement at the university sparked challenges from several Notre Dame professors who objected to Busch's public criticism of the Black Lives Matter movement at Napa's 2021 summer conference, along with the presence of a speaker at the conference, veteran Republican activist L. Brent Bozell III, who signed a letter that called Donald Trump "the lawful winner of the presidential election."[30] The Black Lives Matter movement, Busch said in a speech at the livestreamed gathering, is "promoting racism, critical race theory, and destroying the nuclear family." This "neo-Marxist movement," he added, "operating under some discriminatory theory of Black Lives Matter, is attacking the American experiment, which is based on Judeo-Christian principles. We need to pray it will end or our country will be destroyed."[31]

Some faculty also objected to Napa's partnerships with Leonard Leo because of Leo's connection to organizations working to restrict voting rights. Leo and his wife Sally are among fifteen families that have pledged donations to Napa with the goal of raising $500,000 for the organization over the next five years. After Trump's defeat, the Judicial Education Project, a group tied to Leo, "has quietly rebranded itself as the Honest Elections Project, which subsequently filed briefs at the Supreme Court, and in numerous states, opposing mail-in ballots and other reforms that have made it easier for people to vote," the investigative reporter Jane Mayer wrote in a *New Yorker* article, "The Big Money Behind the Big Lie."[32] Mayer's reporting has uncovered a web of interlocking organizations on the right that have been powered by massive funding from the conservative donors. Leo's already prolific fundraising rocketed to new heights in the summer of 2022 when Marble Freedom Trust, one of Leo's nonprofit advocacy organizations, received a staggering $1.6 billion donation from Barre Seid, an electronics manufacturing mogul. The trust is a dark money group that can spend directly on elections as well as funding issue-advocacy groups, think tanks, religious institutions, and organizing campaigns. The Pulitzer Prize–winning investigative news outlet ProPublica described the gift as the "largest known donation to a political advocacy group in U.S. history."[33] ProPublica obtained tax documents in 2022 that show how Leo and his allied organizations have spent millions of dollars to influence efforts to restrict voting and impact some of the Supreme Court's most consequential cases.

"We should not accept money from organizations that undermine democracy," John Duffy, an English professor at Notre Dame who has taught at the university for more than two decades, told me in an interview.

"When we take money from those organizations, we're providing cover and legitimacy to those causes and we're saying those values align with our values."[34] The professor presented his concerns about the center's funding in an address to the university's Arts and Letters College Council, an advisory body to the dean of the College of Arts and Letters that reviews policies, practices, and procedures. Duffy warned that the university would be perceived to be, in his words, "throwing in our lot with the conspiracy theorists, the race baiters and the climate deniers," if it took funding from Napa and Koch. Major donors can have an influence on "shaping the ideological agenda," said Dianne Pinderhughes, a professor in the departments of Africana studies and political science. "The structural inequality in society gets reproduced in the university as well."[35]

CATHOLIC THREATS TO DEMOCRACY AND VOTING RIGHTS

Sean Fieler lives in a French chateau on four gated acres in Stamford, Connecticut. The fifty-two-year-old Catholic philanthropist and hedge fund manager of Equinox Partners has been named as one of the top political donors on Wall Street by *Business Insider*. In a 2019 interview with *Philanthropy Roundtable*, Fieler named Leonard Leo and Tim Busch of the Napa Institute as part of a "good network" he has learned from and worked with over the years.[36] Fieler is chairman of the American Principles Project, which calls itself the "only national pro-family organization engaging directly in campaigns and elections." The project was cofounded in 2009 by the Princeton University scholar and conservative Catholic Robert George. One of the nation's most prominent conservative constitutional law scholars, George coauthored the Manhattan Declaration in 2009. The manifesto, signed by leading conservative Catholics, bishops, and Christian evangelicals, named religious liberty, abortion, and same-sex marriage as the defining issues for religious voters.[37] The statement attracted widespread media attention when it was released at the National Press Club. Fieler sits on the board of the Manhattan Institute and has long been a major funder opposing same-sex marriage and LGBTQ rights more broadly.

Fieler is also on the board of the Susan B. Anthony List, a prominent antiabortion organization in Washington that funds pro-life candidates running for office. Marjorie Dannenfelser, a Catholic who was one of Donald Trump's most vocal advocates, leads the group. During the 2020 election cycle, the Susan B. Anthony List and its related entities committed to spend $52 million to reelect Trump and Republicans in the US Senate. In the wake of Trump's loss in the 2020 election—and the persistence of false claims that President Biden's victory was the result of election fraud—Fieler and other major Catholic funders and Catholic antiabortion leaders have turned their attention and checkbooks to voting issues. As Christopher White of the *National Catholic Reporter* documented in 2021, Catholic-led organizations have been key players behind efforts to limit voter access in several states and have spent millions of dollars on voter suppression efforts under the banner of "election integrity." After Trump's defeat, the Susan B. Anthony List teamed up with Fieler's American Principles Project to launch the Election Transparency Initiative, a $5 million voting reform campaign targeting states with "close 2020 margins and a pro-life GOP-controlled legislature."[38] Both organizations share an office space in Arlington, Virginia. Robert George is also on the board of the Heritage Foundation, which through its political advocacy arm, Heritage Action for America, has spent $24 million on voter restriction efforts.[39] Leading the joint effort by the American Principles Project and the Susan B. Anthony List, White reported, is Ken Cuccinelli, a Catholic who served as the director of US Citizenship and Immigration Services under Trump and is the former Virginia attorney general. In an interview with RealClearPolitics, Cuccinelli said conservative organizations "are clearly getting feedback from their members and their universe that is sort of questioning, 'Why should we put this much effort into a system that cheats us?' I'm not saying it does or doesn't, but that is the perception of many of them," he added. Chris Crawford, who led faith outreach during the 2020 election for the National Task Force on Election Crises, a cross-partisan group of experts promoting free and fair elections, told the *National Catholic Reporter* that Cuccinelli's response is emblematic of how a number of conservative Catholics have given a "wink and a nod" to the lie that the 2020 presidential election was rigged in order to advance particular partisan or ideological agendas. "As Catholics, everything we do, especially in public life, should be grounded in truth," said Crawford, who has also been active in the antiabortion movement for many years. "That is central to living out our public life to be grounded in the truth. You can't have a process that you say is fixing a problem when the problem didn't exist. You can't start from the position that the 2020 election was unfair and then say that you are on the side of building trust in our elections. And you can't build trust in our elections on the foundation of the former president's lie," he added.[40]

* * *

Conservative Catholic funders, activists, and the most reactionary bishops are fixated on LGBTQ issues and more recently seem consumed with fears about how "the trans movement is doing great damage to society"—as Oklahoma City Archbishop Paul Coakley described it during an Napa Institute gathering.[41] Yet there is almost complete silence when it comes to attacks on democracy and voting rights, even though Catholics have a vital role to play in expanding democracy protections for all Americans regardless of their race, religion, sexuality, or gender identity. Responding to unproven claims that the 2020 election was plagued by voting irregularities, Georgia Gov. Brian Kemp signed a controversial and widely criticized election law in 2021 that civil rights organizations warned would disproportionately impact voters of color. Republican-led legislatures across the country have enacted hundreds of new laws restricting access to the ballot box, according to the nonpartisan Brennan Center for Justice at New York University School of Law. These laws make it harder to vote by mail, expand proof of citizenship requirements, impose new photo ID requirements, and make it more difficult for individuals without traditional addresses to register to vote. All of these laws disproportionately impact Black voters. Religious leaders from diverse faith traditions in Georgia and other states were at the forefront of challenging these efforts. Pastors, rabbis, and imams lobbied lawmakers, wrote op-eds, and pressured corporations to denounce the voting restrictions. Catholic bishops were missing in action. The Archdiocese of Atlanta and the Georgia Catholic Conference, the public policy arm of the state's bishops, issued no statements. At a time when the US bishops' conference was publicly opposing the pro-LGBTQ Equality Act in Congress—and raising objections to the American Rescue Plan because of concerns over abortion funding—bishops failed to offer any public support for the John Lewis Voting Rights Advancement Act or the For the People Act, two legislative proposals to address the wave of state-level voting restrictions by expanding voting access and curbing partisan gerrymandering.[42]

Protecting democracy and expanding voting rights should unite Catholics on the left and right because strengthening the foundational pillars of our democracy is not a partisan cause. Catholics can disagree about many things in politics, but we should recognize that refusing to accept the results of a free and fair elections, increasing threats of political violence, conspiracy theories that undermine trust in democratic institutions, and systematic barriers to voting are all attacks on human dignity and the common good. David DeCosse, a religious studies professor at Santa Clara University, encouraged Catholic bishops to respond in timely ways to voter suppression during a 2018 address to the Catholic Theological Society of America. Church leaders could use theological teaching on conscience and an understanding of the church as the "people of God," DeCosse said, to address voting rights in its *Faithful*

Citizenship document issued every four years before presidential elections. “The document should pair its appropriate reluctance to tell the Catholic laity how to vote with an outspoken, prophetic advocacy for the right to vote,” DeCosse said. “There is no justification whatsoever for the voter suppression tactics now being practiced throughout the United States.”[43] Jonathan Rothchild, a professor of theological ethics at Loyola Marymount University in Los Angeles, noted how even past mechanisms to address racist voter disenfranchisement have been eroded in recent years. The Supreme Court’s 2013 decision in *Shelby County v. Holder,* which gutted key provisions of the Voting Rights Act of 1965, is a prime example. In a 2017 article in the *Journal of Law and Religion,* Rothschild wrote about the ruling by using key themes of Catholic social teaching—including subsidiarity, participation, solidarity, and the common good—to critique what he calls the decision’s prioritization of “states’ rights federalism.”[44] While conservatives often give preference to local and state rights over federal intervention, Rothchild argues that an authentically Catholic notion of subsidiarity can’t be reduced to a narrow ideological interpretation. “What we see in Georgia is not new, and it’s a deliberate attempt to disqualify and dissuade Black voters and communities of color,” Rothchild told me. “One of the roles the Catholic Church has to play here is calling all people of goodwill back to a common commitment to justice regardless of what political party is in power.”[45]

I asked Bishop John Stowe of Lexington, Kentucky, why so many Catholic leaders in the United States seem reluctant to speak out on these issues. “As much as I hesitate to state it, I think the silence on the part of bishops and church leaders about voting rights and the protection of democracy is directly linked to the uncritical preference for the Republican candidates because of the single-focus on abortion,” Stowe said.

> Of course, historically the church had been slow to embrace democracy, but since at least Vatican II we have seen how the church can flourish in a pluralistic and democratic society. The bishops in the United States were way ahead of Rome in embracing democracy, but do not seem to take the threat to democracy seriously at the present moment. When I mentioned the January 6, 2021 insurrection, one bishop audibly rejected the terminology of insurrection to describe the events at the Capitol that day.[46]

Cardinal Robert McElroy of San Diego has been a leader in calling for the church to play a more visible role on these issues. “We have just come through a period in which the most fundamental elements of our national democracy—the peaceful acceptance of election outcomes, boundaries for attacks upon the democratic institutions of our society, the safety of public officials and their families, and the search for essential truth and civility in our public dialogue—have been widely abandoned," the cardinal told me in 2022.

> We are witnessing a time in which the unthinkable has become real and, worse, justified, symbolized in insurrection and the invasion of the Capitol by a mob seeking to kill the vice president and the speaker of the House. This new anti-democratic culture must be vigorously and continually identified and rejected. But this will only happen if the major social and spiritual elements in our society speak clearly about the crisis we are facing and the need for a moral regeneration of our political institutions.[47]

The Catholic community, the cardinal emphasized, has "a broad and deep theological tradition that can enrich that regeneration, and any effort by the bishops of the United States to speak to the demands of Catholic social teaching in the present day must give wide scope and great depth to remedying the cancer that corrodes our democracy. Witnessing to this reality is the very core of faithful citizenship, not only for the bishops, but for the consciences of every Catholic in our nation."

The leaders of Catholic social justice organizations, scholars at Catholic colleges, and presidents of Catholic universities have warned that Christian nationalism and systematic efforts to undermine voting rights threaten our democracy. "Powerful institutions and political leaders are working to rig the system and erect racially discriminatory obstacles to voting and full participation in American life," the leaders wrote in a 2022 statement released by Faith in Public Life. "Voter suppression is a sin and silence is complicity."[48] The statement was endorsed by leaders representing the Sisters of Mercy of the Americas, the Leadership Conference of Women Religious, the Association of US Catholic Priests, the National Black Sisters' Conference, NETWORK, Pax Christi USA, the Franciscan Action Network, and the Maryknoll Office for Global Concerns. It was also signed by Rev. James Greenfield, the president of DeSales University in Pennsylvania, Sister Barbara Reid, president of the Catholic Theological Union in Chicago, and Patricia McGuire, president of Trinity Washington University.

"White Christian nationalism—an ideology heretical to authentic faith—represents a clear and present danger to building a multi-faith, multiracial democracy," the leaders wrote. Rev. Bryan Massingale, a professor of Christian ethics at Fordham University who also endorsed the statement, sees a throughline between past injustices and well-funded attacks on democracy today. "As a Black Catholic and an American, I believe we dishonor the legacy of courageous activists and faith leaders who were beaten and often killed fighting for the sacred right to vote when we fail to challenge those undermining our democracy today," he said. "The connected threats of Christian nationalism, political violence and racist voter suppression are not new, but they must be confronted again with moral clarity. I urge our bishops, my fellow priests and all Catholics to speak out more boldly."[49]

THE FALSE IDOL OF CHRISTIAN NATIONALISM

Christian nationalism is a topic that has attracted considerable interest and public visibility in recent years. The confluence of "America First" nationalism and white evangelical Christian identity politics during Trump's presidency sparked renewed scrutiny of how race and religion have long intersected in American life. The January 6, 2021, attack on the US Capitol, which as discussed in an earlier chapter included insurrectionists carrying Christian iconography, provided a chilling example of how Christian imagery and rhetoric can be deployed in the defense of violent and antidemocratic movements. The roots of white Christian nationalism run deep in our nation's history. In its most extreme manifestations, the ideology is intertwined with white supremacy and was used to rationalize genocide against Native Americans, slavery, and Jim Crow segregation. As the number of white Christians continues to decline and our nation becomes more diverse, the politics of anxiety and backlash are often animated by white Christians who fear this change represents a loss of their status and cultural privilege. Yale University sociologist Phil Gorski, coauthor with Samuel L. Perry of *The Flag and the Cross: White Christian Nationalism and the Threat to American Democracy*, defines white Christian nationalism as "an ideology based on a story about America that's developed over three centuries" and that "reveres the myth that the country was founded as a Christian nation by white Christians and that its laws and institutions are based on Protestant Christianity." Gorski continues:

> White Christian nationalists believe that the country is divinely favored and has been given the mission to spread religion, freedom, and civilization. They see this mission and the values they cherish as under threat from the growing presence of non-whites,

> non-Christians, and immigrants in the United States. This is one point at which white Christian nationalism overlaps with the Make America Great American narrative. It's the view that somebody has corrupted the country or is trying to take it away. White Christian nationalists want to take it back.[50]

Scholars who study Christian nationalism have found that the number of Americans who agree with the Christian nationalist statement—"the federal government should declare the United States a Christian nation"—has declined in recent years to about 19 percent (after growing slightly from 2010 to 2017). But raw numbers alone fail to capture the rising influence of Christian nationalism in the Republican Party and the conservative Christian movement more broadly, as the scholars Andrew Whitehead and Samuel Perry, authors of *Taking Back America for God: Christian Nationalism in the United States,* wrote in the *Washington Post* in 2022:

> But while fewer Americans say they agree with a core Christian nationalist tenet, its influence on our political life may nevertheless be expanding. The U.S. Census reports older Americans like those ages 65 to 74 vote at rates about 25 percent higher than Americans ages 18 to 24. Our research finds older Americans are also most likely to embrace Christian nationalism. And powerful people and lobbying groups like the Family Research Council, the National Association of Christian Lawmakers, and Florida Gov. Ron DeSantis (R) are working to promote Christian nationalist policy goals in government, the courts, and at the polls. According to political scientists Stella Rouse and Shibley Telhami, most Republicans support declaring the United States a Christian nation. And Christian nationalists are running for office at all levels of government, from local school boards to presumptive presidential candidates. Though the numbers of those who claim Christian nationalist beliefs may decline, Christian nationalism's influence in public life only continues to grow.[51]

Pope Francis has been vocal in his opposition to what he described in his encyclical *Fratelli tutti* as "myopic, extremist, resentful and aggressive nationalism."[52] Two days after a visit to Hungary in 2021, where Prime Minister Viktor Orbán has made the country's Christian roots and identity central to his nationalist political goals (Orbán is a darling of many conservative Catholic nationalists in the United States), the pope warned against what he called a "triumphalist Christianity" that dresses up nationalist ambitions with Christian rhetoric and symbols. "Let us not reduce the cross to an object of devotion, much less to a political symbol," Francis said. "How often do we long for a Christianity of winners, a triumphalist Christianity that is important and influential, that receives glory and honor?"[53] Christian nationalism is also a force in the pope's own backyard. In Italy Matteo Salvini, a Catholic politician who has played a leading role in promoting nationalist ideologies and antimigrant policies, often campaigned with rosary beads and kissed a crucifix at his European election night event. His far-right League party once proposed making it obligatory to display crucifixes in all public spaces. Salvini, who celebrated his European election victory next to a bookcase with an icon of Jesus and a "Make America Great Again" hat, has successfully courted relationships with cardinals critical of Pope Francis, including the American Cardinal Raymond Burke.

There is nothing authentically Catholic about Christian nationalism. Catholic social teaching emphasizes the principle of solidarity, and as a church with a presence in nearly every country in the world, Catholicism prioritizes the global common good. "Today the universal common good presents us with problems which are world-wide in their dimensions; problems, therefore, which cannot be solved except by a public authority with power, organization and means co-extensive with these problems, and with a world-wide sphere of activity," Pope John XXIII wrote in the encyclical *Pacem in Terris* in 1963.[54] Pope John Paul II, who expressed deep patriotism for his native Poland, also distinguished between love of country and what he called "narrow nationalism or chauvinism."[55]

The Covid-19 pandemic, climate change, and the largest number of refugees since World War II are ongoing reminders of the limits of nationalism to address challenges that transcend borders. As the visibility of ethnonationalist ideologies in the United States has grown in recent years, some vocal commentators on the Catholic right have emerged as enthusiastic proponents of nationalism. In some cases, they glibly gloss over the role that racism and xenophobia play in nationalist politics, even as they revel in deriding efforts to address racial injustice as so-called "wokeism." During a 2022 panel discussion at Catholic University in Washington entitled "Catholicism and Nationalism: Are They Compatible?" Michael Brendan Dougherty, a senior writer at *National Review,* pointed to international institutions as foes of traditional Catholicism. "A lot of conservative Catholics are looking to nationalism because international bodies like the European Union seem to set themselves up almost deliberately as enemies of the Church's causes," Dougherty said. "The EU deliberately left out Christianity as a basis for European civilization in its documents—referring only to its Roman and pagan inheritance—and these international bodies have been the vehicle for a rights revolution the Church generally opposes."[56] Dougherty praised nationalism for creating a "disruptive force in politics." He acknowledged its various manifestations are often built on "volcanic material" and can have "an angry emotive character" that "teem with powerful feelings about resentments and the deepest sense of your loyalties."

R.R. Reno, editor of *First Things* and author of *Return of the Strong Gods: Nationalism, Populism, and the Future of the West,* shrugged off any tensions between Catholicism and nationalism by asserting what he called the "protean character of the Catholic political imagination." The church, Reno claimed, "prefers no political form" and commented that "bureaucrats at the Vatican like to talk to bureaucrats in Brussels because like seeks like." He called nationalism "a project of recovery or restoration" that is a response to "the thirty-year project of globalization." Reno also advocated for putting prayer back in public schools. "If we reversed the Supreme Court cases from the early 1960s and school districts in North Dakota decided to open the school day with prayers, we should welcome this as an outcome," he said. "Our country would be better off if more people were Christian. The people themselves would obviously be better off if they were Christian."[57] Jennifer Frey, then a philosophy professor at the University of South Carolina and now the dean of the Honors College at the University of Tulsa, expressed frustration that none of the panelists grappled seriously with the fact that Catholic teaching strongly argues against nationalism and that nobody even mentioned the impact of white Christian nationalism in political life. "I don't understand this talk about repairing the civic bond with respect to nationalism," Frey commented. "Nationalism is indelibly caught up with Trumpism, and when I think about Trumpism I don't think about repairing the civic bond. That's not what that movement is all about." Reno responded that "the Trump phenomenon was helpful," and said that "the people who are running our country have gotten the message that we F-ed up with globalization and we need to correct course. One can have endless misgivings about Trump the man, but the phenomenon was a healthy wake up call to our ruling class."[58]

When the conversation turned to race, the tension escalated even more. An audience member asked why Christian nationalists have vocally opposed the Black Lives Matter movement. Michael Brendan Dougherty argued that Christian nationalists who oppose Black Lives Matter do so because of the movement's own statements about disrupting the nuclear family and support for socialism. "They are attacking it as a leftist movement not as a Black movement," he explained. But Frey countered. "It would be helpful for those who speak on behalf of nationalism to be more explicit and clear that they don't mean ethno-nationalism. One reason to be worried is the only real book we have making the case for Christian nationalism (*The Case for Christian Nationalism* by Stephen Wolfe) very explicitly says this is ethno-nationalism." Reno, who has dismissed the concepts of systemic racism and white privilege as "stock epithets" and once wrote that the Black Lives Matter movement is "largely a creature of the race industry,"[59] balked at the idea that nationalists should publicly distance themselves from ethnonationalists who traffic in racism and nativism. "Why do I have to sign some pledge?" he asked. "What evidence does anyone have that I am a white nationalist or a racist? Why do I have to sign some document pledging that I am not these things to avoid the charge that I am these things. I refuse to play that game."[60]

I spoke to Frey a few days after the panel. "Many Catholics forget that nationalism was weaponized against their own grandparents, and it's now being weaponized against fellow Catholics who are not European or not deemed European enough, or weaponizing it against Catholics from Africa," she said. "Ethno-nationalism stands against the gospel of Jesus Christ. If Catholic nationalists want to think seriously from within our own tradition on this topic, the burden is on them to explain how nationalism is not in tension with Catholic social teaching. And they will need to address what will stop twenty-first century nationalism from descending into the racist ethno-nationalism we saw in the 20th century."[61] Frey did acknowledge that nationalism holds an understandable appeal because it often diagnoses serious inequities with globalization and late-stage capitalism. "Those problems are real and those problems are first and foremost economic," Frey said. "But I'm not convinced that nationalism is a solution to any of these problems." Frey grew up in a Rust Belt city between Cincinnati and Dayton where manufacturing jobs vanished in the wake of neoliberal economic policies. "I understood Trump's appeal on some level," she said. "He was the only person who was willing to say free trade has been bad for so many Americans. My Dad was a forklift operator in a paper mill and lost his job. I lived through this and understand the appeal on an existential level. The trouble is this kind of nationalism is mixed up with toxic stuff."

CATHOLICS, NATIONAL CONSERVATISM, AND THE "NEW RIGHT"

Donald Trump shattered any notion that Reagan-style conservatism, interventionist in foreign policy and rooted in an unshakable faith in free markets, would continue to define the Republican Party. He turbocharged a populist, nationalist revival on the right that Pat Buchanan, a Catholic, presaged decades earlier when he entered the 1992 presidential race calling for "a new patriotism, where Americans begin to put the needs of Americans first."[62] Trump's denunciation of free-trade deals long supported by establishment Democrats and Republicans, along with his promises to protect Medicare and Social Security, were heretical departures from GOP orthodoxy. Conservatives who championed nationalism saw themselves as having a powerful advocate in the White House. But they also had a problem. Trump's crass political style, ideological unpredictability, and popularity with white nationalist groups like the Proud Boys didn't exactly contribute to a positive public image for those looking to forge wider mainstream support for nationalism.

The National Conservatism project, created in 2019 by the Edmund Burke Foundation, has emerged as the most ambitious and coordinated effort to reclaim nationalism as a vital component of the conservative movement. The project brought together scholars and writers affiliated with institutions, magazines, and think tanks such as the Claremont Institute, Hillsdale College, the Manhattan Institute, *First Things* magazine, and the Ethics and Public Policy Center. National conservatism describes itself as a movement "to recover and reconsolidate the rich tradition of national conservative thought as an intellectually serious alternative to the excesses of purist libertarianism, and in stark opposition to political theories grounded in race."[63] Despite the movement's high-minded claims to offer an intellectually sophisticated antidote to the most reactionary expressions of Trumpism, the separation can be tenuous. Steve Bannon was a featured speaker at the 2024 National Conservatism conference in Washington. Signatories on the project's ten-part statement of principles include the Manhattan Institute's Christopher Rufo, an activist who pioneered the right's messaging war against critical race theory, and Mark Meadows, a former chief of staff to President Trump who used a reference to Jesus (the "King of Kings") to defend the former president's efforts to overturn the election.[64] Others backing the statement of principles include R.R. Reno, the Catholic editor of *First Things*; Rod Dreher, a senior editor at *The American Conservative* and onetime Catholic turned Orthodox Chistian who praises Viktor Orbán and moved to Hungary; and Jim DeMint, the former Republican senator from South Carolina who used to lead the Heritage Foundation. The project is led by Yoram Hazony, an Israeli American philosopher and political theorist whose 2018 book, *The Virtues of Nationalism*, helped lay the intellectual groundwork for the national conservatism movement. "We want to make sure that the things that we stand for are not just reactive, but that they actually are constructive and leading to a restoration and reconstruction,"

Hazony said in a 2022 interview. "But I think we have to stop being afraid. You can't be afraid to use terms like nationalism or Christian nationalism. The haters have got the culture all lined up already."[65]

In its statement of principles, leaders of the National Conservatism project argue that religion is central to renewing what they view as traditional values threatened by secularization, globalization, and multiculturalism. "No nation can long endure without humility and gratitude before God and fear of his judgment that are found in authentic religious tradition," the statement reads.[66] While giving a nod to religious pluralism, it calls for a particular expression of Christianity to be given privilege of place in government and culture. The "Bible should be read as the first among the sources of a shared Western civilization in schools and universities, and as the rightful inheritance of believers and nonbelievers alike," the authors write. "Where a Christian majority exists, public life should be rooted in Christianity and its moral vision, which should be honored by the state and other institutions both public and private." The statement continues: "We believe the traditional family is the source of society's virtues and deserves greater support from public policy. The traditional family, built around a lifelong bond between a man and a woman, and on a lifelong bond between parents and children, is the foundation of all other achievements of our civilization." The statement criticizes "today's penchant for uncontrolled and unassimilated immigration" and argues that "restrictive policies may sometimes include a moratorium on immigration." Two dozen Christian intellectuals, including Catholic scholars, theologians, and pastors, responded to the National Conservatism principles with their own warnings. "In the 1930s many serious Christian thinkers in Germany believed they could manage an alliance with emergent illiberal nationalism," they wrote in a statement published in *Commonweal* magazine:

> Our situation in 2019 is surely different, but American Christians now face a moment whose deadly violence has brought such analogies to mind. Again we watch as demagogues demonize vulnerable minorities as infesting vermin or invading forces who weaken the nation and must be removed. Again we watch as fellow Christians weigh whether to fuse their faith with nationalist and ethno-nationalist politics in order to strengthen their cultural footing. Again ethnic majorities confuse their political bloc with Christianity itself. In this chaotic time Christian leaders of all stripes must help the church discern the boundaries of legitimate political alliances. This is especially true in the face of a rising racism in America, where non-whites are the targets of abominable

> acts of violence like the mass shooting in El Paso. . . . In charity and in hope, we urge our fellow Christians to repudiate the temptations and the falsehoods of nationalism. The politics of xenophobia, even when dressed up in high-minded social critique, can only be pursued in contradiction of the Gospel.[67]

The fraternal rebuke from their fellow Christians did not temper the movement. The National Conservatism conference in 2022 featured a speech from a political science professor entitled, "How I Learned to Stop Worrying and Love Christian Nationalism," and a keynote speech from Sen. Josh Hawley of Missouri entitled, "The Biblical Revolution." Governor Ron DeSantis of Florida, a Catholic who had a short-lived run for the 2024 Republican presidential nomination, addressed the gathering in a defiant tone. "We are not afraid to buck the discredited ruling class and elites in our country," he said, contrasting what he called "core American principles" with the "woke" ideologies of corporations and universities.[68] "We are not going to teach kids to hate each other or our country with your tax dollars," he said. "We are against critical race theory and against distorting American history. But what are we for? In Florida, we have launched an initiative to get American civics back in our schools. We need to be teaching kids about what it means to be an American. . . . We need to teach them that in the American system our rights come from God, not government." While DeSantis has called critical race theory "state sanctioned racism" and purged the teaching of racial justice history and books in Florida schools that he deems leftist indoctrination—including prohibiting material from the Pulitzer Prize–winning "1619 Project" published by *The New York Times*—he proposed overhauling higher education in the state by mandating courses in Western civilization. The governor also drew loud applause at the conference when he touted Florida as a state that bans "sanctuary cities" and pledged to send "illegal aliens" to states with liberal political leaders. A few days later, he sent two airplanes with fifty migrants, including four children ranging in age from three to eight years old, to Martha's Vineyard in Massachusetts.[69]

As his national profile grew, DeSantis took a page from Trump's religion playbook and began more frequently positioning himself as a fearless defender of Christian values who would not be intimidated. "Put on the full armor of God. Stand firm against the left's schemes. You will face flaming arrows, but if you have the shield of faith, you will overcome them, and in Florida we walk the line here," DeSantis told the audience at Hillsdale College, a Christian college in Michigan. "And I can tell you this, I have only begun to fight."[70] The governor was citing Ephesians 6, which calls on Christians to spiritually arm themselves against the "devil's schemes," but DeSantis replaced the "devil" with "the left." In a video shared on Twitter in the fall of 2022 from DeSantis's wife Casey, a narrator intones that on the eighth day: "God looked down on His planned paradise and said, 'I need a protector.' So God made a fighter." Images of the governor flash across the screen. DeSantis is billed as the fighter who will serve the people and "save their jobs, their livelihoods, their liberty, their happiness."[71]

Two years before DeSantis took the stage at the National Conservatism conference in his home state, another ambitious Catholic politician making waves on the right spoke at the project's 2020 event in Rome, Italy. Giorgia Meloni, now Italy's prime minister, gave a speech entitled "God, Homeland, Family" that evoked many of the same themes the Florida governor has emphasized in his challenges to LGBTQ rights, "woke" corporations, and other so-called progressive threats. "We do not need the ideological indoctrination manuals that are so dear to the left," said Meloni, a member of the Brothers of Italy, a nationalist party with neofascist roots that she helped create a decade ago.[72] She selectively deployed the late Pope John Paul II to offer an imprimatur on her vision for Christian nationalism. Referring to John Paul as "the patriot pope," Meloni said: "He never tired of repeating that there is no Europe without Christianity, a teaching that is more topical than ever today when the Christian identity of Europe is under attack by a distorted secularism that even attacks the symbol of Christian religion." Meloni, who as prime minister drew comparisons to DeSantis when she redirected humanitarian boats carrying migrants to embark in cities in Italy led by liberal mayors, also invoked the late pope's legacy to oppose what she called "mass immigration" and to support restrictive immigration policies. "Today John Paul II would be on the European Union's blacklist as a dangerous subversive," Meloni said.[73] The prime minister, in a 2022 speech, sounded like American politicians on the right when she said: "no to the LGBT lobby, no to gender ideology." Meloni is no stranger to cultivating ties with American conservatives and Republican politicians. She has strategized with Steve Bannon, praised Trump at the 2020 National Prayer Breakfast for his commitment to "God, fatherland and family," and spoke at the 2022 Conservative Political Action Committee in Orlando, Florida, along with Gov. DeSantis. "We have networks connecting us, our think tanks work with the International Republican Institute, with the Heritage Foundation, we do cultural exchanges, and many of their fights are about things we have talked about," she told the *Washington Post*.[74]

CATHOLIC "POST-LIBERALS" AND INTEGRALISTS

The National Conservatism movement includes self-declared "post-liberal" Catholic scholars, writers, theologians, and law professors. In a 2019 manifesto published in *First Things*, "Against the Dead Consensus," they argue that "any attempt to revive the failed conservative consensus that preceded Trump would be misguided and harmful to the right." Neoliberal faith in markets, free trade, technology, and a globalization that supersedes a nation's right to control immigration are named as destructive forces. The "old conservative consensus paid lip service to traditional values," it reads. "But it failed to retard, much less reverse, the eclipse of permanent truths, family stability, communal solidarity, and much else. It surrendered to the pornographization of daily life, to the culture of death, to the cult of competitiveness. It too often bowed to a poisonous and censorious multiculturalism."

> We embrace the new nationalism insofar as it stands against the utopian ideal of a borderless world that, in practice, leads to universal tyranny. Whatever else might be said about it, the Trump phenomenon has opened up space in which to pose these questions anew. We will guard that space jealously. And we respectfully decline to join with those who would resurrect warmed-over Reaganism and foreclose honest debate.[75]

Signatories included a number of prominent Catholics, including Patrick Deneen, a political science professor at the University of Notre Dame whose 2018 bestseller, *Why Liberalism Failed*, was widely read outside of academia and even made it on to Barack Obama's reading list; Chad Pecknold, a theology professor at Catholic University in Washington, DC; and Matthew Peterson, an editor at The Claremont Institute, a think tank in California that promoted Trump. A month before the 2020 presidential election, Peterson appeared on Glenn Beck's radio show and warned that "brownshirts on the left" were threatening to overturn the election. Peterson has defended Christian nationalism as "pro-Christian and pro-America." In a National Conservatism conference speech entitled "Catholicism in the Next America," he praised the now ousted Fox News host Tucker Carlson for his defense of traditional families. Carlson has promoted racist "great replacement" conspiracy theories that whites in the United States are being "replaced" by dark-skinned immigrants, has claimed that mass immigration makes the country "poor and dirtier," and used his massive audience of more than 3 million viewers to stoke white anger. "When Tucker Carlson starts talking about the family, it's some of the most powerful stuff coming from any thinker today," Peterson gushed. "I would like to hear that from the pulpit."[76] Sohrab Ahmari, an Iranian-born immigrant and prominent convert to Catholicism who is a former columnist for *The New York Post,* helped draft the "Against the Dead Consensus" statement. Ahmari has written that conservatives should "fight the culture war with the aim of defeating the enemy and enjoying the spoils in the form of a public square re-ordered to the common good and ultimately the Highest Good."[77] A visiting fellow at Franciscan University in Steubenville, Ohio, Ahmari was a lead organizer of a conference at the university, "Restoring a Nation: The Common Good in the American Tradition," held a few days before the 2022 midterm elections.

"Post liberalism is in the air and is perhaps the most talked about intellectual phenomenon in the Anglophone world," Ahmari said at the event. These post-liberal conservatives, often described as part of the "New Right," reject the antigovernment philosophy of establishment conservatism and view government power as an effective means to advance conservative policies and cultivate a culture oriented toward a restoration of Christian values. They can also sound like progressives in their critique of capitalism, globalization, and support for populist economic policies. Discussions at the gathering included panels entitled "The Post-Liberal Promise: Another World Is Possible" and "The Wisdom of the New Deal Tradition."[78] A headline speaker at the event was the Catholic convert, and author of *Hillbilly Elegy*, J.D Vance, a Republican who was elected a month later to the US Senate. "In some ways our task is to take the very corrupt American ruling class and replace it with something better," Vance said in his speech. Chad Pecknold of Catholic University told the conference attendees that the traditional conservatism of limited government and free markets could not counter a "left liberal materialism" because "you can't respond to left liberalism with liberalism." "Another world is possible, namely, Hungary," said Gladden Pappin, a University of Dallas political scientist and Catholic who has lauded the policies of Hungarian Prime Minister Viktor Orbán. During a 2022 interview with Tucker Carlson, Pappin pointed to Hungary as a model for recognizing "the importance of family, the identity of men and women, the strong borders of a country, the confidence in its national identity."[79] Orbán is a populist authoritarian who has turned Hungary into an "illiberal democracy" where press freedoms have been curtailed and dissident voices exiled. Orbán uses Christian ethnonationalist rhetoric and has called migration "the great European population replacement program."

His far-right Fidesz party has also prohibited the teaching of LGBTQ sexuality, blasted what he calls "gender madness," and has banned television stations from airing content "popularizing" LGBTQ identity during certain hours.[80]

Catholic post-liberals have a particular fondness for Orbán and other authoritarian leaders. The Hungarian government has noticed. After writing a *Newsweek* article[81] defending Hungary and Poland from then candidate Joe Biden's criticisms that the nations' leaders exhibited totalitarian proclivities, Pappin was invited to spend a year in Budapest as a visiting fellow at the Mathias Corvinus Collegium, a university Orbán founded to replace the liberal Central European University, which he forced out of Budapest. Pappin later moved to Budapest and is now the president of the Hungarian Institute of International Affairs. Patrick Deneen, the University of Notre Dame political philosopher, met with Orbán in 2022 after he was invited to speak at a three-day cultural festival in Hungary. Deneen has praised Orbán for his "remarkable analytic and even philosophical depth," and described him as a "genuine tour-de-force of political analysis and vision, a quality almost wholly absent in today's American political class."[82] When Deneen inveighs against "liberal totalitarianism," he points to Hungary as a model for American conservatives to move beyond "defeatism." "These political battles can be won if we prepare for them and fight them," he has said. "Hungary is a living example of this." In a 2021 essay, "Abandoning Defensive Crouch Conservativism," Deneen describes liberalism as a destructive force that leads to "the evisceration of all institutions that were originally responsible for fostering human virtue, family ennobling friendship, community, university, polity, church."[83] Deneen has been challenged by thoughtful interlocutors on the left and right for his reliance on abstract generalizations and tendency to create cartoonish boogeyman versions of liberalism and contemporary progressivism. Writing in *Commonweal,* Deneen's former student Matthew Sitman noted:

> It's easy to rail against an amorphous thing called "liberalism," to which you attribute much of what's wrong with the world; it's significantly harder to specify which features of liberalism we should reject and to grapple with the consequences of doing so. Which rights and freedoms associated with liberalism—or more precisely, *whose* rights and freedoms—should be curtailed? What sacrifices will have to be made, and by whom? Far safer to leave it all rather vague, expressing dismay about "the sexual revolution" or "multiculturalism" and "diversity," than to specify just who would bear the costs of finally

> putting liberalism behind us. We know who suffered in traditional communities, and the inequities and prejudices that the past can hand down to us. We should not forget the injustices that have been all too traditional. I wish more anti-liberals would think harder about what defending "tradition" against the claims of equality meant even just a few decades ago.[84]

If Sitman and other critics are rightly concerned about how today's post-liberals are indifferent to how their self-styled restorationist project could replicate the prejudices of the past, an increasingly vocal group of Catholic "integralists" amid the ranks of post-liberals are even more emboldened to use state power to achieve a government and culture defined by conservative Christianity. The Harvard University law professor and former Supreme Court clerk Adrian Vermeule, the most prominent Catholic integralist, challenged Deneen's book. In his view, Deneen is overly reliant on a cultural retreat to local communities as a response to liberalism's all-consuming ambitions. In contrast, Vermeule's 2018 essay, "Integration from Within," argues that Catholic integralists should endeavor to become "elite administrators" who occupy "the commanding heights of the administrative state."[85] Vermeule referenced Esther, St. Cecilia, and St. Paul as Christian figures who demonstrated "no hint of retreat into localism," but instead were "determined to co-opt and transform the decaying regime." Once ensconced in positions of government power, Christians would be able to achieve "integral restoration of Christendom" through "executive-type bureaucracies," as Vermeule described it in another essay.[86]

In an interview with *Hungarian Conservative* magazine, Vermeule praised Hungary for resisting what he called liberalism's tendency to "constantly celebrate the ritual of the overcoming of the past, the overcoming of darkness, the overcoming of repression in order to produce this perpetual liberation of the human person." Those who respect the separation of church and state in the United States, he argued, effectively believe that "all religious views and indeed all moral principles should be driven from the public sphere."[87] Vermuele has written that "atheists can't be trusted to keep an oath." Vermeule, who converted to Catholicism in 2016, wrote that his pro-immigration views would favor Catholics. "The principle is to give lexical priority to confirmed Catholics, all of whom will jump immediately to the head of the queue. Yes, some will convert in order to gain admission; this is a feature, not a bug. . . . As the superb blog Semiduplex observes, Catholics need to rethink the nation-state. We have come a long way, but we still have far to go—towards the eventual formation of the Empire of Our Lady of Guadalupe, and ultimately the world government required by natural law."[88] Vermeule's profile exploded into the national mainstream in 2020 when his essay in *The Atlantic*, "Beyond Originalism," sparked a raging debate in the conservative legal world. By taking on an originalist legal philosophy held sacrosanct by many on the right—the idea that modern interpretations of the Constitution should be based on the Founders' original intent—Vermeule challenged the powerful Federalist Society and conservatives on the Supreme Court when he wrote that originalism had "outlived its utility." Vermeule proposes an alternative called "common good constitutionalism" where leaders are "not ashamed of strong rule" and where "authority and hierarchy" are privileged. "Originalism has done useful work, and can now give way to a new confidence in authoritative rule for the common good," he writes.

> Common-good constitutionalism does not suffer from a horror of political domination and hierarchy, because it sees that law is parental, a wise teacher and an inculcator of good habits. Just authority in rulers can be exercised for the good of subjects, if necessary even against the subjects' own perceptions of what is best for them—perceptions that may change over time anyway, as the law teaches, habituates, and re-forms them. Subjects will come to thank the ruler whose legal strictures, possibly experienced at first as coercive, encourage subjects to form more authentic desires for the individual and common goods, better habits, and beliefs that better track and promote communal well-being.[89]

While he does not specify how constitutional law would change under this approach, Vermeule argues that "under a regime of common-good constitutionalism" the Court's jurisprudence on "free speech, abortion, sexual liberties, and related matters will prove vulnerable." He specifically takes aim at the Court's abortion rights opinion in *Planned Parenthood v. Casey*, arguing that ruling's reference to an individual's ability to "define one's own concept of existence, of meaning, of the universe, and of the mystery of human life" should "be not only be rejected but stamped as abominable, beyond the realm of the acceptable forever after." Vermeule says the same about "libertarian assumptions central to free-speech law and free-speech ideology." At the same time, he rattles those on the right when he rejects "libertarian conceptions of property rights and economic rights," asserts the power of governments to tackle climate change, defends workers' unions, and recognizes the legitimacy of the state to enforce vaccine requirements. Vermeule has also argued for expanded presidential powers to confront national security risks, including deferring to executive authority when it comes to "coercive interrogation," ethnic profiling, military trials, and indefinite detainment of enemy combatants.

President Trump appointed Vermeule to an independent federal agency focused on improving administrative procedures in the government. After the 2020 presidential election, Vermeule questioned the results of the race in a series of tweets and retweets.[90] "Lol the election isn't over until Team Joe fixes up your ballot for you," he wrote in one post. Eleven Harvard Law School student organizations signed a statement describing Vermeule's commentary on social media as "harmful to democracy" and called on law school administrators to condemn his "spread of inaccurate conspiracy theories about the election."[91] Jason Blakely, a political philosopher and professor of political science at Pepperdine University who has written frequently about Vermeule and other Catholic integralists, points out that Vermeule cites among his key influences the Catholic Nazi jurist Carl Schmitt, who once proclaimed the Catholic Church alone was politically capable of overcoming modern individualism. Vermeule has called Schmitt's book, *Roman Catholicism and Political Form*, his favorite work because "it offers both a grim vision of the spiritual and cultural wasteland of technological and economic liberalism, on the one hand, and a grand vision of the Church's eventual triumph and universal dominion, on the other."[92] For Blakely, "integralism exists in a complex relationship with darker elements on the right, and they overlap in two key ways: a fixation with reinstating 'Christian values' via executive rule and a visceral disgust for the liberal tradition."[93] But Catholic integralists' desire to reassert "a moral order," Blakely told Gloria Purvis during an *America* magazine podcast interview, often fails to grapple with abuses of power inherent in systemic racism, police brutality, and other injustices experienced by those on the peripheries. "Integralism is an elite movement that has very lofty and abstract, theoretical ideas, but it exists in the political world and is adjacent to a new ethnic nationalist right that has very disturbing racial and exclusionary dimensions," Blakely said.[94]

Liberals are not the only critics who warn that the newfound interest in Catholic integralism is worrisome. "There is nothing new under the sun, but some ideas do hide in the shadows for a time," Justin Dyer, the executive director of the Civitas Institute and a professor of government at the University of Texas at Austin, argued in a conservative case against integralism published in the *Washington Post* in 2023. "Resurrecting an old model of church-state relations would also resurrect old, dark answers to questions about citizenship, religious liberty and state power. Serious writers and scholars now envision the return of confessional states, religion-based citizenship, and a state powerful enough to enforce orthodoxy,"

Dyer wrote, adding that "combustible questions of religion and national citizenship once tore the West apart and fostered centuries of horrendous cruelty and injustice for Europe's religious minorities."[95] James Patterson, chairman of the politics department at Ave Maria University and contributing editor to the journal *Law & Liberty*, also regards the enthusiasm for integralism from an elite segment of Catholic academics, writers, and some traditionalist clergy as fundamentally driven by antidemocratic impulses. Integralists, he wrote in the conservative *National Review* in 2023, "revolt against the constant, low-level disorder typical of constitutional democracies," and "rather than enter the fray to persuade citizens, they instead wish to put their citizens under the control of a Catholic administrative state that degrades free associations of citizens into the solemn submission of subjects to their spiritual and temporal superiors."[96] He warns that historical precedents to this contemporary application of an old ideology can be found in "the reactionary Catholic theology that animated monarchist and clerico-fascist parties in Europe and Latin America." Patterson notes that today's "neo-integralists," as he calls them, "openly admire authoritarian regimes—including those in Iran, China, and Russia—that they regard as superior to America in crucial respects, and they embrace as well leaders of European parties with historical ties to fascism and contemporary ties to Russia's government."

The antidemocratic impulses woven into integralism's history and many of its modern manifestations are prevalent in what Patterson calls "the most important neo-integralist work to date." *Integralism: A Manual of Political Philosophy* (2020) by Father Thomas Crean and Alan Fimister is presented as aligning with Catholic doctrine. But as Patterson makes clear, the authors come to conclusions that are radically out of step with the seminal documents of the Second Vatican Council. "Since a citizen simply speaking is a subject endowed with certain rights and duties within a society because of his presumed willing of that society's common good, only someone who professes the Gospel, as taught by the Church, can be a citizen simply speaking in Christendom," Crean and Finister write. "Hence, baptism confers full citizenship." This position "runs directly contrary to *Nostra Aetate*, promulgated as part of the Second Vatican Council," Patterson responds:

> There the Council Fathers affirmed the principle of religious liberty for all people and, given the church's fraught historical relationship with Judaism, expressed particular concern for the rights of adherents of the elder religion. Vermeule, drawing on Schmitt, insists that politics rests on the friend–enemy distinction. No wonder, then, that

> Vermeule in the *Josias* recounts a question he received at a lunch: "In a fully Catholic polity, the sort you would like to bring about, what would happen to me, a Jew?" "Nothing bad, I assured him," Vermeule writes. I doubt that his colleague was reassured.[97]

Patterson also cites the landmark Second Vatican Council document on religious freedom, *Dignitatis Humanae* (1965), which affirmed the principle of religious freedom, as articulating a vision that is "precisely the opposite of integralism." He ends his essay with a challenge to understand the roots of this reactionary religious politics. "We must ascertain why so many young conservatives find neo-integralism and authoritarianism attractive," he writes. "We must make a new case for American constitutional republicanism, for a generation woefully misinformed about our own history and institutions—and refute a body of thought that would deform both politics and religion."

Massimo Faggioli, a Catholic theologian at Villanova University and prominent historian of the church, has argued that at a time "when the dangers to the public order of the conflating of religious ideology and ethnonationalism have become apparent," Catholics must recommit to values that the late Jesuit priest John Courtney Murray brought to the center of church teaching during the Council.[98] Murray, after years of being silenced by the Vatican for his scholarly work on the relationship between church and state, was invited to contribute to the Council as a theological advisor on the drafting of what became *Dignitatis Humanae*. His contributions were essential in moving the church from a position of condemning liberal democracy—rejecting the separation of church and state and viewing "Americanism" as a threat—to recognizing the importance of religious liberty and pluralism. Faggioli sees the resistance of integralists and the fundamentalism of Catholic culture warriors in the United States as a rejection of the Council's legacy. "A generation of Catholics has been trained to think exclusively in terms of 'non-negotiable values'—a notion that has been intellectually and spiritually a disaster, and on occasion a goad to extremism," he wrote in *America* magazine.[99]

* * *

The "goad to extremism" that Faggioli references is evident in a growing radicalization of some segments of the Catholic right in the United States. While often dismissed as fringe elements in the past, Donald Trump's 2016 victory, false claims of a stolen election in 2020, the insurrection at the US Capitol, and the aggressive backlash to Pope Francis from self-styled traditionalists gave far-right Catholics louder megaphones and increased visibility in recent years. The swift decline of Catholic diocesan newspapers, the shutdown of Catholic News Service at the end of 2022—a respected source for more than a century—and the growth of ideologically driven Catholic outlets and social media platforms have also created a communications landscape where extremism and disinformation now break through and reach bigger audiences than in the past.

A prime example is Church Militant, a Detroit-based multimedia outlet that has a national audience as a hub for Catholic resistance dedicated to what it calls reversing "the evil that has infiltrated our Church and culture." Mixing pious forms of Catholic devotion, Christian nationalism, conspiracy theories, and ugly witch-hunt campaigns that target individual Catholics and Catholic institutions they label as pro-LGBTQ, Church Militant uses "news" broadcasts, videos, social media, and interviews with far-right political leaders to reach an audience that views itself in an apocalyptic battle against godless liberalism in the church and society. In its content and sensationalist style, the website and video production are akin to a Catholic version of Breitbart News, the alt-right outlet founded by former Trump advisor and Catholic Steve Bannon. "We need a Church Militant to combat the evil that we confront," Bannon said in one of several interviews he has given to the group.[100] Michael Voris, a former television reporter and Emmy Award–winning producer, founded the organization after the Archdiocese of Detroit blocked his "Real Catholic TV" from using "Catholic" in its name. Despite not having an official Catholic status, Church Militant (which operates under St. Michael Media) reached nearly 290,0000 subscribers on YouTube and claimed more than one million page views a month through its website and social media accounts. Content is free, but premium users receive additional content. Voris has publicly repented for living most of his thirties in relationships with gay men and now rages against what he calls "sodomites" in the priesthood. Church Militant blames the clergy abuse crisis in the church on gay men. Voris promotes the conspiracy that Joseph Stalin planted more than a thousand homosexuals in Catholic seminaries in the 1920s and 1930s. "In fact, would any of you like to explain why the lay faithful should *not* think that some of you are the second generation of those original homosexual Communist infiltrators bent on the Church's destruction," Voris wrote in an article featured on Church Militant's website.[101]

After Cardinal Wilton Gregory, the first African American to lead the Archdiocese of Washington, publicly criticized then-President Trump for visiting a Catholic shrine in Washington a day after holding a Bible in a staged photo opportunity following the tear gassing of demonstrators, Voris lashed out in a video calling the cardinal an "accused homosexual," a "Marxist" and an "African Queen."[102] The Southern Poverty Law Center has named Church Militant a hate group for its frequent anti-LGBTQ content. Several of the most vocal critics of Pope Francis in the church hierarchy, including Bishop Joseph Strickland, whom Francis removed from his leadership in Tyler, Texas, in 2023, have aligned themselves with Church Militant. A prolific tweeter with a significant following on social media, Strickland once shared a video from his Twitter account entitled "Pope Francis, Nancy Pelosi and the Tyrannical Culture of Death" that made a reference to the pope as "a diabolically disoriented clown."[103] Church Militant prominently features "The Bishop Strickland Hour," an internet radio show, on its website. Voris described the 2016 election as "a spiritual war" and called Hillary Clinton "a tool of Satan" who is a "self-professed enemy of the Church." In contrast, he favorably compared Trump to the Roman Emperor Constantine, who in Voris's words "ended the persecution against the Church, and a year later elevated the Church to the level of preferred religion of the empire."[104] In a broadcast during the January 6 attacks on the US Capitol, Voris praised the insurrectionists as "American patriots" who were "fed up with the fraudulent election." On the day of the 2022 midterm elections, Voris released a video editorial where he called the election "a day of reckoning" and said that because of the "all-out war going on between the forces of darkness who have complete control of one political party and partial control over the other," Catholics might have "no choice but to fight back violently if needs be." Referencing the Crusades, Voris said that "sometimes violence must be unleashed to protect the innocent." While violence should not be the first resort, Voris acknowledged, the use of force "must always be an option."[105] During the violent storming of the US Capitol after Trump's defeat, Church Militant used its social media to cheer on the mob. In one post from the organization's Twitter account sent as the Capitol descended into chaos, they shared an iconic photograph of US Marines raising the American flag at Iwo Jima next to an image of a group of people raising a cross at a Trump rally. A senior producer at Church Militant tweeted that the mob consisted of "patriots furious at marxist media continually feeding them lies and ignoring 80 million votes for Trump."[106]

Church Militant acts as a bridge between far-right Catholics and the Christian nationalist movement. Voris has helped amplify messages from Trump's former national security advisor Michael Flynn, a Catholic and retired three-star army general who is now a leading figure in Christian nationalist circles. Flynn, who Trump pardoned after he was convicted for lying to the FBI about his contacts with the Russian ambassador, cofounded the ReAwaken America tour—a traveling road show that is part political pep rally and part spiritual tent revival where Christian nationalists and QAnon conspiracy theorists have found a home. "If we are going to have one nation under God, which we must, we have to have one religion," Flyn said at a megachurch conference in Florida. "We are in a spiritual war for the heart and soul of the United States of America," Flynn told Voris during a lengthy 2020 interview. "Right now the entire country needs to come back to its faith. The time to fight for your faith and family is now." Flynn, who cited "the election fraud of the 2020 election," called on Catholics to "put faith first, put family first, put America first."[107] During the interview, Voris described the Democratic Party "as a child killing machine that promotes sodomy, the destruction of the family, and open borders." He asked Flynn if US bishops should "disavow the Democratic Party" like they "should have done in Germany with the Nazi Party." Flynn agreed. "And this pope, Bergoglio, Pope Francis, is someone who is not helping the Catholic cause internationally," Flynn said. "I feel that very strongly. People who are Catholic need to look at this pope and say 'why is he saying these things?' Don't accept what he is saying. Just like our Constitution was written by men, this whole thing can be taken apart by men. The Catholic Church has lasted a long time but it can be destroyed at times."

Voris promoted Rep. Marjorie Taylor Greene of Georgia, a leading Christian nationalist in Congress, during an hour-long 2022 interview entitled "Marjorie for Pope" that was conducted in the congresswoman's house. The interview, which drew national media coverage, helped elevate Church Militant's reach beyond far-right Catholic circles. Greene, a former Catholic who is now an evangelical Protestant, has encouraged the Republican Party to embrace Christian nationalism, has expressed support for QAnon conspiracies, and posed with an AR-15 gun in her campaign ads. As Voris nodded along approvingly, Green criticized Catholic bishops and Catholic Relief Services for helping immigrants at the US–Mexican border and claimed that Christians who cite the biblical mandate to do so are "perverting" the Bible and the Constitution.[108] Writing in *Salon,* the investigative journalist Kathyrn Joyce reported that along with providing platforms for far-right Christian nationalist politicians, the activist arm of Church Militant—the Resistance network—has actively recruited from the racist, misogynist, and antisemitic "groypers" movement, led by the right-wing podcaster Nick Fuentes.[109] A white nationalist who has made jokes about the Holocaust and praised Hitler, the twenty-seven-year-old provocateur founded the advocacy group America First. During a livestream event in 2022, Fuentes advocated for a "Catholic Taliban rule in America" that would ban abortion, contraception, and same-sex marriage. His followers, known as groypers, are active in antivaccine and antiabortion rallies, where they often hold crucifixes and chant "Christ is king!" Fuentes' public profile grew significantly when he dined with Donald Trump and the rapper Ye, formerly known as Kayne West, at Mar-a-Lago in 2022.[110]

Paul Moses, a retired religion reporter and city editor for *Newsday* who is an emeritus professor of journalism, says that Church Militant, *LifeSite News*, and other Catholic outlets on the far right can elevate fringe voices in the church and politics in ways that distort the information stream reaching Catholics in the pews. "These outlets give power to marginal people but the average Catholic at home might think this is what the church teaches," Moses told me. "It's just so skewed who they choose to promote. Their coverage really sets a kind of tone where people can begin to reach extreme conclusions and feel justified in doing so in the name of their Catholic faith."[111] *LifeSiteNews* and Church Militant, Moses found in his reporting for *Commonweal* magazine, attracted nearly 10 million visits to their websites during the last three months of 2020. He described them as "a pair of powerful platforms that helped spread bogus election-conspiracy claims to a huge Catholic audience."[112] Moses compared Voris and Church Militant's attack-dog style to Fr. Charles Coughlin, a popular "radio priest" in the 1930s who spread conspiratorial and antisemitic messages. "You can trace Coughlin's style through McCarthyism and into Tucker Carlson and Church Militant today," Moses told me. Voris resigned from Church Militant at the end of 2023 for breaching the organization's morality clause, and the organization folded in 2024 after a defamation lawsuit.

Tony Spence, who for more than a decade served as the editor of Catholic News Service, knows how it feels to be on the receiving end of a Church Militant smear campaign. Church Militant and other right-wing Catholic sites, including The Lepanto Institute—which describes its mission as uncovering "heretics" and "traitors" who threaten the church—went after Spence in 2016 when the editor tweeted about how several religious liberty bills in state legislatures across the country would roll back rights for LGBTQ people. In a series of articles and videos, Church Militant accused Spence of promoting "a homosexual agenda" and essentially called for his ouster. Leaders at the US bishops' conference, who had management oversight over the more than centuries-old news service that they imprudently shut down at the end of 2022, forced the respected editor to resign not long after the tweets were sent.[113] Spence told me he was escorted from the conference's building and not allowed to speak with his staff before his forced departure. While Spence acknowledged some of his tweets were ill-considered given his position, he told me his firing underscored how Catholic groups on the radical fringe often have an outsized impact. “What blows my mind is these groups are given so much credibility and have influence,” Spence said. “They are destructive. We’re only talking about a few hundred people in a very big church, but church leadership sometimes doesn’t have confidence in its own voice and these shrill challenges make them jump for cover.”[114] The same groups that targeted Spence also launched a campaign to fire Rick Estridge, the former vice president for overseas finance at Catholic Relief Services (CRS), because he was in a same-sex marriage. The Lepanto Institute included screen grabs of Estridge’s Facebook page and published a copy of his Maryland marriage license. CRS consistently defended Estridge, who isn’t Catholic and worked in a specialized finance position. But in the wake of those attacks, he resigned after sixteen years at the agency.[115] Other church employees targeted by self-appointed Catholic watchdog groups include John Carr, who directed the US bishops’ domestic justice portfolio for more than two decades before leaving in 2012 to launch The Initiative on Catholic Social Thought & Public Life at Georgetown University. The American Life League denounced Carr for being part of “a systemic pattern of cooperation with evil” because he once served on the board of the Center for Community Change, which the American Life League views as a “pro-abortion” organization.[116]

While these groups are far to the right of mainstream conservative Catholic organizations, they are relentless and can succeed in rattling church leaders. A consistent target is the US bishops’ flagship antipoverty initiative, the Catholic Campaign for Human Development (CCHD). A “Reform CCHD Now” coalition, launched in 2009 by the American Life League, documents CCHD funding allegedly going to organizations that promote abortion, gay rights, and contraception. While the US bishops’ conference has dismissed these groups for having “clear ideological and ecclesial agendas,” the pressure campaigns have led to effective organizations losing church funding.[117] This is rarely because these organizations directly advocated for a cause at odds with church teaching; more often, they were faulted for being part of broad coalitions that included non-Catholic organizations that do oppose some church teachings. This kind of guilt by association hurts the church’s credibility in a pluralistic public square, undermines effective partnerships that help the poor, and erodes faith-based community organizing that has long been a powerful instrument for putting Catholic teaching into practice.

The bishops’ decision to close the US operations of Catholic News Service at the end of 2022 dealt a major blow to credible, professional Catholic journalism. The now-defunct wire service, widely respected for its accurate reporting and sober analysis, came as several diocesan newspapers closed their doors after struggling with an aging audience and tight finances over the last decade. Ideologically driven Catholic media outlets that are often more propaganda arms for a particular faction of the church than actual news gathering operations fill that vacuum. "These spurious news sources have been given a legitimacy they never should have been given," Spence, the former editor, told me in 2023. Spence died in 2024. As David Gibson, a veteran religion journalist and director of the Center on Religion and Culture at Fordham University observed in a column, the decision to shut down Catholic News Service "cedes the field to amateur and ideologically driven voices at a time when disinformation and division are threats not only to Catholicism but to our democratic institutions." The "growing number of bishops and cardinals who promote their personal brands at the expense of their church," Gibson added, "will come to be seen as the voice of Catholicism."[118]

Helen Osman watched bishops struggle with how to navigate a new media and communications landscape when she served as secretary of communications for the US bishops' conference from 2007 to 2015. "For a long time, the bishops assumed they drove the narrative and whatever came out in their diocesan newspaper was the reference point for the conversation, but that began to change with blogging and now with social media that's all been disrupted," said Osman, who has worked in Catholic communications for more than three decades and organized media preparations for Pope Benedict XVI's 2008 and Pope Francis's 2015 visit to the United States.[119] In 2022 Pope Francis appointed Osman to be a consultant to the Vatican's Dicastery for Communications, a five-year appointment to the body that oversees all aspects of the Vatican's communications efforts, including its radio, print, television, and digital platforms. "All of these changes in communications and media were happening at the same time the bishops were grappling with the abuse crisis, facing emptying church coffers, and struggling with vocations to the priesthood. So it became part of this larger crisis. Organizations like Church Militant began taking up too much oxygen in the room. Bishops were concerned that they were driving a narrative about the church they didn't see as accurate."

While Church Militant had an impact that belied its small size, the most influential Catholic media outlet in the world is Eternal Word Television Network (EWTN). Founded by Mother Angelica in 1981 as a station focused on devotional content such as televised daily Masses and Catholic catechesis, EWTN has grown increasingly more partisan—offering a friendly platform for Republican politicians courting Catholic voters—and is a favored venue for American critics of Francis's papacy. The network's most prominent anchor, Raymond Arroyo, conducted a friendly interview with Donald Trump before the 2016 election and has frequently promoted and interviewed Archbishop Carlo Maria Viganò, the former papal nuncio to the United States and Trump ally who has called for the pope to resign. On the network's flagship church and politics show, *The World Over*, Arroyo hosts a regular group of commentators known as the "The Papal Posse," which includes Fr. Gerald Murray, a priest in the Archdiocese of New York, and author Robert Royal of the Washington, DC–based Faith and Reason Institute, who are known for their anti-Francis views. When Pope Francis met with President Biden at the Vatican, Royal commented that the meeting "sends the wrong message" about abortion.[120] In the same episode, he called the pope's remarks about climate change during the COP26 summit "hysterical." After a school shooting in Uvalde, Texas, in the spring of 2022 left nineteen children and two adults dead, Pope Francis made a direct appeal for gun control: "It is time to say enough to the indiscriminate trafficking of arms," he said.[121] As journalist Molly Olmstead reported in *Slate*, the next day Arroyo brought Bill Donohue, president of the Catholic League, on his show to discuss the "sociological" reasons behind mass shootings. "It's not a matter of guns, per se," Donohue insisted. "No gun control is going to stop these men whatsoever. None."[122]

Arroyo is also a regular contributor to and occasional guest anchor for the Fox News opinion show, *The Ingraham Angle*, hosted by Laura Ingraham. Ingraham, who spoke at the 2016 Republican National Convention, has mocked Pope Francis for his teachings on climate change, described immigrant detention centers as "essentially summer camps," and lost advertisers after using Twitter to demean a Parkland High School shooting survivor who is now a gun control activist.[123] On Ingraham's show, Arroyo frequently jokes about President Biden being senile and rants at "woke" political correctness. Pope Francis offered a thinly veiled critique of EWTN in a meeting with Jesuits during a visit to Slovakia in 2021. "There is, for example, a large Catholic television channel that has no hesitation in continually speaking ill of the pope," Francis said. "I personally deserve attacks and insults because I am a sinner, but the church does not deserve them. They are the work of the devil. I have also said this to some of them."[124] In his 2020 book *The Outsider: Pope Francis and His Battle to Reform the Church*, British Vatican journalist Christopher Lamb reported that the apostolic nuncio to the United States, Archbishop Christophe Pierre, had expressed displeasure to EWTN CEO Michael Warsaw over the network's coverage of the papacy. Warsaw is a consultor to the Vatican's Dicastery for Communications. The network has a staggering reach. It's no exaggeration to call EWTN a multimedia communications empire. Along with its twenty-four-hour television broadcasting that airs in more than150 countries that reach nearly 400 million households, EWTN has a network of more than 500 radio affiliates around the world and a book publishing arm, and it operates the largest Catholic website in the United States. The nonprofit bills itself as "the largest religion-news organization in the world." "While secular alternatives to Fox News exist—from its counterpart on the left, MSNBC, to more centrist major network broadcasts—no alternatives are available to EWTN in the Catholic world," Heidi Schlumf wrote in a four-part investigative series for the *National Catholic Reporter* that examined the meteoric rise of the media conglomerate. "Once it overtook an early and flawed attempt by the U.S. bishops to form their own network, EWTN quickly became the only major Catholic voice on the television landscape in the United States—and that voice has gone global."[125] Across its various platforms, the network creates content in English, Spanish, German, French, Portuguese, Arabic, and Italian.

EWTN also owns the *National Catholic Register* newspaper and in 2014 acquired *Catholic News Agency*, which offers free content to dioceses, parishes, and Catholic websites. Both outlets rarely, if ever, strive for journalistic balance and instead amplify the voices of religious and political conservatives who express a one-sided version of Catholicism. Founded in 2004 in response to Pope John Paul II's call for a "new evangelization," Catholic News Agency describes its mission as covering "news related to the creation of a culture of life."[126] When Archbishop Viganó wrote an eleven-page treatise calling on Pope Francis to resign after claiming the pope knew about, and ignored, sexual abuse allegations against the now defrocked former cardinal of Washington, Theodore McCarrick, the statement first appeared in the *National Catholic Register.* Timothy Busch, the influential Catholic attorney who leads the Napa Institute, sits on EWTN's board of governors. Headquartered in Irondale, Alabama, EWTN has studios in Washington, DC, and a West Coast office in Orange County, California, where the studio is housed in Christ Cathedral. Busch served as cochair of the financial committee that helped the Diocese of Orange purchase the cathedral for $57 million after the previous owner, the famous evangelical televangelist Robert Schuller, had to sell the iconic glass-encased building (then named Crystal Cathedral) after filing for bankruptcy. EWTN reported a total revenue of $64 million on tax filings submitted to the Internal Revenue Service in 2021, and its board of governors include Archbishop José Gomez of Los Angeles, a former president of the US bishops' conference, and Archbishop Charles Chaput, the former Philadelphia archbishop. Major donors to EWTN include the powerful Knights of Columbus, which along with its global charitable work also spent millions of dollars in political advocacy trying to stop same-sex marriage and is a leading funder of religious liberty campaigns.[127]

At a conference cosponsored by EWTN and Franciscan University in Steubenville, Ohio, in 2023 entitled "Journalism in a Post-Truth World," the network's leaders and allies in the conservative secular press depicted the mainstream media as hostile to the church and traditional values. There was no self-scrutiny or reflection on the part of EWTN leaders. Instead, EWTN chairman Michael Warsaw credited Trump with introducing the term "fake news" into the nation's "political and media bloodstream." He described "fake news" as a symptom of the post-truth era. "Catholics only need to look around us to see the effects of the post-truth era in the discussions about abortion, gender, healthcare and religious liberty," Warsaw said in his keynote address at the meeting held at the Museum of the Bible in Washington, DC.[128] He offered a self-congratulatory explanation for why his network has come under increasing scrutiny. "Balancing our love for the Church, our mission to preach the Gospel, and our duty to help bring light to the darkness by accurate and truthful reporting has brought us much criticism, even from the highest levels of the Church," he said. "We have been attacked from both the left and the right. We have been denounced as reporting 'fake news' when we indeed reported facts. We have been criticized for pointing to centuries of doctrine and tradition when calling into question statements by prelates—and even cardinals—and conferences of bishops abroad."

Montse Alvarado, president and chief operating officer of EWTN News, offered a vision for the Catholic press that sounded more like unfiltered evangelization than actual journalism. She applauded the reporters and editors who contribute to the network for pursuing "the one truth that changes your entire life should you choose to accept it; the reality of Jesus Christ our Lord and Savior. The journalists for EWTN, they're not searching for the truth. They've found the truth, and they want to communicate it."[129] Pope Francis is not the only Catholic leader who has criticized the network. "There are also some bishops who are tied to a more conservative policy and the Holy Father himself has commented on the situation of EWTN, where many times the commentators are very critical of the Holy Father, at least of his ideas," Cardinal Sean O'Malley of Boston told an Argentinian journalist when asked about polarization among US bishops. "But I think the vast majority of Catholics are very much in favor. We have a young conservative clergy and sometimes they are very influenced by social media and that is a problem," the cardinal added.[130] Bishop John Stowe of Lexington, Kentucky, told the *National Catholic Reporter* that "there are blog sites and there are networks like EWTN that only teach about abortion, that do not present an entire view of the sanctity of human life and have even been hostile towards the teachings of Pope Francis."[131] Bishop Fernando Prado Ayuso of San Sebastian, Spain, made headlines for the most direct challenge to the Catholic media conglomerate in 2023 when only two days after being installed as bishop he banned his diocesan television station from carrying any content produced by EWTN.[132]

While EWTN prides itself on promoting a "pro-life" message, the network has a limited and not particularly Catholic way of understanding what that means. When EWTN's most prominent Black host started discussing police brutality as a pro-life issue in a segment of the radio show she had hosted for five years, the network canceled the program. Gloria Purvis, a Catholic commentator and vocal opponent of abortion, found herself out of a job. Only a month after George Floyd's murder at the hands of a police officer, Purvis and her cohosts were discussing police reform on EWTN's "Morning Glory" show. The US bishops' conference had released a statement advocating for reform. "I agree that there needs to be reforms, but they (bishops) should go on ride-alongs and see what these officers do every single day," Harold Burke-Sivers, a Black deacon and one of the hosts argued. "Amen," said Vincent De Rosa, another cohost and priest. "Jesus had 12 apostles, one was Judas, and we focus too much on Judas and not enough on Jesus," the deacon continued. "Jesus did not reason we should reform the apostles because of what Judas did."[133] Purvis recognized the faulty framing. "The better example, in my opinion, would be abortion," she said. "We call for reforms, right?" The deacon cut her off. "Abortion by nature is intrinsically evil," he said. "Policing is not intrinsic evil." "Let me finish," Purvis responded with growing impatience. "Police brutality by nature is evil." Purvis saw the police killings of Ahmaud Arbery, Breonna Taylor, George Floyd, and many other Black men and women not as isolated incidents perpetrated by a few rogue police officers but emblematic of systemic racism and deeper institutional injustices. Purvis could not stay silent as many Catholics in the church failed to accept, as Pope Francis said in the days after video of Floyd's horrifying final minutes were viewed around the world, that "we cannot tolerate or turn a blind eye to racism and exclusion in any form and yet claim to defend the sacredness of every human life."[134]

In this and preceding chapters, I have documented how well-funded movements—closely allied with some church leaders—use politics, media, and advocacy in ways that reduce Catholicism to a few issues most closely aligned with the conservative movement's political priorities. When opposing abortion and fighting efforts to achieve equality and dignity for LGBTQ people are viewed as *the* primary linchpins of Catholic identity, we risk turning a faith tradition with centuries of expansive social justice teachings into a narrow ideological cause stripped of its prophetic capacities. At a time when systemic racism, the epidemic of gun violence, extreme economic inequality, and the existential threat of climate change threaten so many lives, lay Catholics and church leaders must renew our traditional commitment to life and human dignity in ways that transcend a single issue or the binary categories of partisan politics. A major stumbling block to that effort is the US bishops' decision to narrowly define "the threat of abortion" as their "preeminent priority." Before the 2020 election the language was included in a letter introducing *Forming Consciences for Faithful Citizenship*, the bishops' teaching document for Catholic voters issued before every presidential election. Speaking in support of the proposed language, which drew public challenges from Chicago Cardinal Blase Cupich and San Diego Cardinal Robert McElroy—two of the pope's closest allies in the American hierarchy—at least one archbishop was not shy about couching his endorsement for the phrase in a decidedly political way. "We are at a unique moment with the upcoming election cycle to make a real challenge to *Roe v. Wade*, given the possible changes to the Supreme Court," Portland Archbishop Alexander Sample wrote during the editing process.[135] At their national meeting in the fall of 2023, the US bishops' conference again voted to affirm that abortion should be the "preeminent priority" for Catholic voters heading into the 2024 election.[136] Cardinal McElroy of San Diego told me in a 2022 interview that the framing of abortion as the "preeminent" issue leaves the church's message easily manipulated by partisan actors and has become "destructive in discussions of Catholic teaching and voting choices for Catholics."[137] The language, he said, "automatically and deliberately sends the signal that when it comes to voting by the light of the Gospel the whole of Catholic teaching is collapsed to a single issue." The cardinal emphasized that "an ethic of preeminence allows the warped partisan configuration of American politics to annul the most basic architecture of our faith as it is called to transform the world." We must not "allow the issues of racism, the protection of the earth and economic justice to be eclipsed by a focus on one element of Catholic teaching, no matter how important," Cardinal McElroy said.[138] A more expansive Catholic commitment to life and human dignity offers an opportunity to reclaim the public voice of American Catholicism. Catholics already involved in the pastoral and prophetic work of bringing the peripheries and broken places of our world to the center of our politics and moral imagination provide a model for this necessary renewal.

NOTES

1. John Gehring, "Leonard Leo Has Reshaped the Supreme Court. Is He Reshaping Catholic University Too?" *National Catholic Reporter,* December 15, 2022, https://www.ncronline.org/news/leonard-leo-has-reshaped-supreme-court-he-reshaping-catholic-university-too.
2. Gehring, "Leonard Leo Has Reshaped the Supreme Court."
3. John Gehring, "Koch Brothers Latest Target: Pope Francis," *American Prospect,* October 14, 2016, https://prospect.org/culture/koch-brothers-latest-target-pope-francis/.
4. Gehring, "Leonard Leo Has Reshaped the Supreme Court."
5. Gehring, "Leonard Leo Has Reshaped the Supreme Court."
6. Gehring, "Leonard Leo Has Reshaped the Supreme Court."
7. Gehring, "Leonard Leo Has Reshaped the Supreme Court."
8. Gehring, "Leonard Leo Has Reshaped the Supreme Court."
9. Gehring, "Leonard Leo Has Reshaped the Supreme Court."
10. Leonard Leo, "2022 John Paul II New Evangelization Award Leonard Leo Remarks," Catholic Information Center, November 30, 2022, https://www.youtube.com/watch?v=DtsXLstn77M.
11. Catholic Information Center, "2022 John Paul II New Evangelization Award Honoring Leonard Leo," October 28, 2022, https://www.youtube.com/watch?v=7M8sPOrbVJU.
12. Gehring, "Leonard Leo Has Reshaped the Supreme Court."
13. Gehring, "Leonard Leo Has Reshaped the Supreme Court."
14. Gehring, "Leonard Leo Has Reshaped the Supreme Court."
15. Gehring, "Leonard Leo Has Reshaped the Supreme Court."
16. Gehring, "Leonard Leo Has Reshaped the Supreme Court."
17. Charles J. Chaput, "Catholics and the Next America," *First Things,* September 17, 2010, https://www.firstthings.com/web-exclusives/2010/09/catholics-and-the-next-america.
18. John Gehring, "Mike Pence to Conservative Catholics at Napa Institute: 'You are the Answer for America,'" July 27, 2023, https://www.ncronline.org/news/mike-pence-conservative-catholics-napa-institute-you-are-answer-america.
19. John Gehring, "Bad Business: Why Would Catholic University Host Charles Koch," *Commonweal,* October 12, 2017, https://www.commonwealmagazine.org/bad-business.
20. Timothy Busch, "Teaching Capitalism to Catholics," *Wall Street Journal,* January 22, 2015, https://www.wsj.com/articles/tim-busch-teaching-capitalism-to-catholics-1421970676.
21. Timn Graves, "The Man behind Catholic U's Largest Donation Ever," *Catholic World Report,* May 19, 2016, https://www.catholicworldreport.com/2016/05/19/the-man-behind-catholic-us-largest-donation-ever/.
22. Elizabeth Dias and Laurie Goodstein, "Letter Accusing Pope Leaves U.S. Catholics in Conflict," *New York Times,* August 27, 2018, https://www.nytimes.com/2018/08/27/us/catholic-church-pope-francis-letter.html.

23. Jack Jenkins, "Catholic Donor Denies He Consulted on Vigano Allegations Against Pope Francis," *Religion News Service,* September 7, 2018, https://www.ncronline.org/news/catholic-donor-denies-he-consulted-vigan-allegations-against-pope-francis.
24. Jason Horowitz, "The 'It' 80s Party Girl Is Now a Defender of the Catholic Faith," *New York Times,* December 7, 218, https://www.nytimes.com/2018/12/07/world/europe/princess-gloria-von-thurn-und-taxis-francis.html.
25. Tom Roberts, "The Rise of the Catholic Right," *Sojourners,* March 2019, https://sojo.net/magazine/march-2019/rise-catholic-right.
26. Tom Roberts, interview with author.
27. John Gehring, "Catholic Conservative Napa Institute's Profile Grows in Washington, DC," *National Catholic Reporter,* December 13, 2022, https://www.ncronline.org/news/catholic-conservative-napa-institutes-profile-grows-washington-dc.
28. Gehring, "Catholic Conservative Napa Institute's Profile Grows."
29. John Gehring, "Napa, Koch Funding Sparks Backlash from Notre Dame Professors," *National Catholic Reporter,* December 16, 2021, https://www.ncronline.org/news/people/napa-koch-funding-sparks-backlash-notre-dame-professors.
30. Gehring, "Napa, Koch Funding Sparks Backlash."
31. John Gehring, "Napa Institute Expands to Fight the Culture War," *National Catholic Reporter,* August 4, 2021, https://www.ncronline.org/news/people/napa-institute-expands-fight-culture-war.
32. Jane Mayer, "The Big Money behind the Big Lie," *New Yorker,* August 2, 2021, https://www.newyorker.com/magazine/2021/08/09/the-big-money-behind-the-big-lie.
33. Andrew Perez, Andy Kroll, and Justin Elliott, "How a Secretive Billionaire Handed His Fortune to the Architect of the Right-Wing Takeover of the Courts," *ProPublica,* August 22, 2022, https://www.propublica.org/article/dark-money-leonard-leo-barre-seid.
34. Gehring, "Napa, Koch Funding Sparks Backlash."
35. Gehring, "Napa, Koch Funding Sparks Backlash."
36. Philanthropy Roundtable, "Interview with Sean Fieler," Winter 2019, https://www.philanthropyroundtable.org/magazine/interview-with-sean-fieler/.
37. Laurie Goodstein, "Christian Leaders Unite on Political Issues," *New York Times,* November 20, 2009, https://www.nytimes.com/2009/11/20/us/politics/20alliance.html.
38. Christopher White, "Major Catholic Funders and Powerbrokers Spearhead Voter Suppression Efforts," *National Catholic Reporter,* April 8, 2021, https://www.ncronline.org/news/major-catholic-funders-and-power-brokers-spearhead-voter-suppression-efforts.
39. Nick Corasaniti and Reid J. Epstein, "G.O.P. and Allies Draft 'Best Practices' for Restricting Voting," *New York Times,* March 23, 2021, https://www.nytimes.com/2021/03/23/us/politics/republican-voter-laws.html.
40. Christopher White, "Major Catholic Funders and Powerbrokers Spearhead Voter Suppression Efforts," *National Catholic Reporter,* April 8, 2021, https://www.ncronline.org/news/major-catholic-funders-and-power-brokers-spearhead-voter-suppression-efforts.
41. Gehring, "Catholic Conservative Napa Institute's Profile Grows."
42. John Gehring, "Vow of Silence: U.S. Bishops Are Quiet on Voting Restrictions," *Commonweal*, April 23, 2021, https://www.commonwealmagazine.org/vow-silence.
43. Gehring, "Vow of Silence."

44. Jonathan Rothchild, "Federalism, Subsidiarity and Voting Rights: Critiquing the Shelby County Decision through Johannes Althusius and Catholic Social Teaching," *Journal of Law and Religion* 32, no. 1 (March 2017):141–171, https://www.jstor.org/stable/26336696.
45. Jonathan Rothchild, interview with author.
46. Bishop John Stowe, interview with author.
47. Cardinal Robert McElroy, interview with author.
48. Michael J. O'Loughlin, 'We Are Increasingly Alarmed by the Signs of the Times': Catholic Leaders Urge Lawmakers to Protect Voting Rights," *America*, September 28, 2022, https://www.americamagazine.org/politics-society/2022/09/28/protect-voting-rights-christian-nationalism-jan-6-243860.
49. Faith in Public Life, "Catholic Leaders Challenge Attacks on Voting Rights and Democracy," Press Release, September 27, 2022. https://www.faithinpubliclife.org/news/catholic-leaders-challenge-attacks-on-voting-rights-and-democracy/.
50. Mike Cummings, "Yale Sociologist Phil Gorski on the Threat of White Christian Nationalism," *Yale News*, March 15, 2022, https://news.yale.edu/2022/03/15/yale-sociologist-phil-gorski-threat-white-christian-nationalism.
51. Andrew L. Whitehead and Samuel L. Perry, "Is Christian Nationalism Growing or Declining? Both," *Washington Post*, October 25, 2022, https://www.washingtonpost.com/politics/2022/10/25/republicans-christian-nationalism-midterms/.
52. Jason Horowitz, "Pope Criticizes Lack of Unity in World's Response to Coronavirus," *New York Times*, October 4, 2020, https://www.nytimes.com/2020/10/04/world/europe/pope-francis-coronavirus-response.html.
53. Philip Pullella, "Pope, in Slovakia, Says Don't Exploit Religion for Politics," *Reuters*, September 14, 2021, https://www.reuters.com/world/europe/pope-slovakia-says-dont-exploit-religion-politics-2021-09-14/.
54. *Pacem in Terris: Encyclical of Pope John XXIII on Establishing Universal Peace in Truth, Justice, Charity, and Liberty* (April 11, 1963), https://www.vatican.va/content/john-xxiii/en/encyclicals/documents/hf_j-xxiii_enc_11041963_pacem.html.
55. *Letter of His Holiness John Paul II to the People of Poland*, 1978, https://www.vatican.va/content/john-paul-ii/en/letters/1978/documents/hf_jp-ii_let_19781024_polacchi.html.
56. "Catholicism and Nationalism: Are They Compatible?" Institute for Human Ecology at The Catholic University of America, December 14, 2022, https://www.youtube.com/watch?v=9zaFFRbYghI.
57. "Catholicism and Nationalism: Are They Compatible?"
58. "Catholicism and Nationalism: Are They Compatible?"
59. R. R. Reno, "The Woke Script," *First Things*, October 2020, https://www.firstthings.com/article/2020/10/the-woke-script.
60. "Catholicism and Nationalism: Are They Compatible?"
61. Jennifer Frey, interview with author.
62. Pat Buchanan Presidential Campaign Announcement, *C-Span*, December 10, 1991, https://www.c-span.org/video/?23289-1/pat-buchanan-presidential-campaign-announcement.
63. National Conservatism, "Overview," https://nationalconservatism.org/about/.
64. Leigh Ann Caldwell and Dareh Gregorian, "January 6 Panel Has Text Messages between Ginni Thomas and Mark Meadows about Keeping Trump in Office," *NBC*

News, March 24, 2022, https://www.nbcnews.com/politics/donald-trump/jan-6-panel-text-messages-ginni-thomas-mark-meadows-keeping-trump-offi-rcna21482.
65. Albert Mohler, "Conservatism, Religion, Nationalism, and the Current Cultural Crisis—A Conversation with Yoram Hazony," June 15, 2022, https://albertmohler.com/2022/06/15/yoram-hazony.
66. National Conservatism, *A Statement of Principles,* https://nationalconservatism.org/national-conservatism-a-statement-of-principles/.
67. The Editors, "Open Letter: Against the New Nationalism—An Appeal to Our Fellow Christians," *Commonweal,* August 19, 2019, https://www.commonwealmagazine.org/open-letter-against-new-nationalism.
68. Gov. Ron DeSantis, "Florida Is a Model for America," speech at the National Conservatism Conference, September 2022, https://nationalconservatism.org/natcon-3-2022/presenters/gov-ron-desantis/.
69. Matt Adams, "DeSantis Defends Martha's Vineyard Migrant Flights after Texas Investigation Opens," National Public Radio, September 20, 2022, https://www.npr.org/2022/09/19/1123975684/texas-sheriff-criminal-investigation-desantis-migrant-flight-marthas-vineyard.
70. Anna Ceballos, "What Message Is DeSantis Sending with Religious 'Full Armor of God' Rhetoric?" *Tampa Bay Times,* September 12, 2022, https://www.tampabay.com/news/florida-politics/2022/09/12/what-message-is-desantis-sending-with-religious-full-armor-of-god-rhetoric/.
71. Jared Gans, "DeSantis Releases New 2022 Ad: 'God Made a Fighter,'" November 4, 2022, https://thehill.com/homenews/campaign/3720540-desantis-releases-new-2022-ad-god-made-a-fighter/.
72. Giorgia Meloni, "God, Homeland, Family," speech at the National Conservatism conference, February 3–4, 2020, https://nationalconservatism.org/natcon-rome-2020/presenters/giorgia-meloni/.
73. Meloni, "God, Homeland, Family."
74. Chico Harlan and Stefano Pitrelli, "Giorgia Meloni's interview with The Washington Post," *Washington Post,* September 13, 2022, https://www.washingtonpost.com/world/2022/09/13/giorgia-meloni-italy-interview/.
75. "Against the Dead Consensus," *First Things,* March 21, 2019, https://www.firstthings.com/web-exclusives/2019/03/against-the-dead-consensus.
76. Matthew Peterson, "Catholicism and the Next America," September 13, 2022, https://www.youtube.com/watch?v=Fy9xmhK9b8U.
77. Sohrab Ahmari, "Against David French-ism," *First Things,* May 29, 2019, https://www.firstthings.com/web-exclusives/2019/05/against-david-french-ism.
78. Brian Fraga, "'New Right' Academics Argue for Biblical Lawmaking at Steubenville Conference," *National Catholic Reporter,* October 17, 2022, https://www.ncronline.org/news/new-right-academics-argue-biblical-lawmaking-steubenville-conference.
79. Luke Larson, "Faith, Family and Fidesz—Why Some U.S. Catholics Are So Intrigued by Hungary's Populist Government," *National Catholic Register,* March 31, 2022, https://www.ncregister.com/news/faith-family-and-fidesz-why-some-us-catholics-are-so-intrigued-by-hungary-s-populist-government.
80. Marc F. Plattner, "Illiberal Democracy and the Struggle on the Right," *Journal of Democracy* 30, no. 1 (January 2019), https://www.journalofdemocracy.org/articles/illiberal-democracy-and-the-struggle-on-the-right/.

81. Gladden Pappin, "Biden and Big Tech Have Poland and Hungary in Their Crosshairs," *Newsweek*, October 20, 2022, https://www.newsweek.com/biden-big-tech-have-poland-hungary-their-crosshairs-opinion-1540063.
82. Patrick J. Deneen and Gladden Pappin, "Dispatch from Budapest," *Postliberal Order*, August 5, 2022, https://www.postliberalorder.com/p/dispatch-from-budapest.
83. The Ezra Klein Show, "What Does the 'Post-Liberal Right' Actually Want," interview with Patrick Deneen, May 13, 2022, https://www.nytimes.com/2022/05/13/opinion/ezra-klein-podcast-patrick-deneen.html.
84. Matthew Sitman, "Liberalism and the Catholic Left: A Response to Patrick Deneen," *Commonweal*, December 3, 2018, https://www.commonwealmagazine.org/liberalism-and-catholic-left.
85. Adrian Vermeule, "Integration from Within," *American Affairs Journal* 11, no. 1 (Spring 2018), https://americanaffairsjournal.org/2018/02/integration-from-within/.
86. Jason Blakely, "The Integralism of Adrian Vermeule," *Commonweal*, October 5, 2020, https://www.commonwealmagazine.org/not-catholic-enough.
87. "Hungary Resists the Disruptive Tendencies of Liberalism—An Interview with Harvard Professor Adrian Vermeule," *Hungarian Conservative*, December 2, 2023, https://www.hungarianconservative.com/articles/interview/adrian_vermeule_liberalism_conservatism_rule_of_law_neutrality_state_church_eu_von_der_leyen_morality_common_good/.
88. Adrian Vermeule, "A Principle of Immigration Priority," *Mirror of Justice*, July 20, 2019, https://mirrorofjustice.blogs.com/mirrorofjustice/2019/07/a-principle-of-immigration-priority-.html.
89. Adrian Vermeule, "Beyond Originalism," *Atlantic*, March 31, 2020, https://www.theatlantic.com/ideas/archive/2020/03/common-good-constitutionalism/609037/.
90. Mark Joseph Stern, (@mjs_dc), "Here is a sampling of the wildly irresponsible disinformation promoted by Harvard Law Professor Adrian Vermeule in the days following the election," Twitter, November 9, 2020, https://twitter.com/mjs_DC/status/1325880367220465665.
91. Emmy M. Cho and Isabella B. Cho, "Harvard Law School Organizations Petition to Denounce Professor Adrian Vermeule's 'Highly Offensive' Online Rhetoric," *The Harvard Crimson*, January 13, 2021, https://www.thecrimson.com/article/2021/1/13/harvard-law-school-petition-vermeule/.
92. Adrian Vermeule, "The Catholic Constitution," *First Things*, August 11, 2017, https://www.firstthings.com/web-exclusives/2017/08/the-catholic-constitution.
93. Jason Blakely, "The Integralism of Adrian Vermeule," *Commonweal*, October 5, 2020, https://www.commonwealmagazine.org/not-catholic-enough.
94. The Gloria Purvis Podcast, "Podcast: Catholic Integralism Rejects Liberalism. Should We Be Skeptical?" *America*, February 15, 2023, https://www.americamagazine.org/politics-society/2023/02/15/catholic-integralism-244729.
95. Justin Dyer, "The Catholic Right Wing Takes a Wrong Turn," *Washington Post*, February 21, 2023, https://www.washingtonpost.com/opinions/2023/02/21/catholic-integralism-wrong-republicans/.
96. James M. Patterson, "No to Neo-Integralism," *National Review*, January 5, 2023, https://www.nationalreview.com/magazine/2023/01/23/no-to-neo-integralism/.
97. Patterson, "No to Neo-Integralism."

98. Massimo Faggioli, "What Joe Biden (and all American Catholics) Owe Jesuit John Courtney Murray," *America*, January 19, 2021, https://www.americamagazine.org/faith/2021/01/19/joe-biden-john-courtney-murray-who-was-239757.
99. Faggioli, "What Joe Biden (and all American Catholics) Owe."
100. Exclusive Interview: Steve Bannon, October 20, 2021, *Church Militant*, https://www.churchmilitant.com/video/episode/intv-exclusive-interview-steve-bannon.
101. Michael Voris, "Episcopal Sodomy: Communist Homosexual Infiltrators," *Church Militant*, July 31, 2018, https://www.churchmilitant.com/news/article/news-episcopal-sodomy-communist-homosexual-infiltrators.
102. Jack Jenkins, "Conservative Catholic Group Denounced for Calling Black Archbishop 'African Queen,'" *Religion News Service*, June 11, 2020, https://religionnews.com/2020/06/11/church-militant-conservative-catholic-group-publishes-video-calling-black-archbishop-wilton-gregory-african-queen/.
103. Brian Killian, "Bishop Praises Video Calling Pope 'Diabolically Disoriented Clown,'" *Where Peter Is*, July 8, 2022, https://wherepeteris.com/bishop-praises-video-calling-pope-diabolically-disoriented-clown/.
104. The Vortex, "Donald 'Constantine' Trump?" *Church Militant*, September 21, 2016, https://www.churchmilitant.com/video/episode/vortex-donald-constantine-trump.
105. Kathyrn Joyce, "Political Violence 'Must Always Be an Option,' Says Far-Right Catholic Outlet," *Salon*, November 8, 2022, https://www.salon.com/2022/11/08/political-violence-must-always-be-an-option-says-far-right-catholic-outlet/.
106. Paul Moses, "Piety, Populism, and 'Patriots'—Right-Wing Catholic Media and the Capitol Riots," *Commonweal*, January 8, 2021, https://www.commonwealmagazine.org/piety-populism-and-patriots.
107. Michael Voris interviews Lt. Gen. Michael Flynn, *Church Militant*, January 31, 2022, https://www.churchmilitant.com/video/episode/vortex-fix-this-mess.
108. Michael Voris interviews Rep. Marjorie Taylor Greene, *Church Militant*, April 25, 2022, https://www.churchmilitant.com/video/episode/vortex-marjorie-for-pope.
109. Kathryn Joyce and Ben Lorber, "'Traditional' Catholics and White Nationalist 'Groypers' Forge a New Far-Right Youth Movement," *Salon*, May 13, 2022, https://www.salon.com/2022/05/13/trad-catholics-and-nationalist-groypers-forge-a-new-far-right-youth-movement/.
110. Joyce and Lorber, "'Traditional' Catholics and White Nationalist 'Groypers.'"
111. Paul Moses, interview with author.
112. Moses, "Piety, Populism, and 'Patriots.'"
113. John Gehring, "Two Steps Back: The USCCB & he Ouster of an Editor," *Commonweal*, May 3, 2016, https://www.commonwealmagazine.org/two-steps-back.
114. Tony Spence, interview with author.
115. Dennis Sadowski, "CRS Official Resigns Weeks after Report He Was in Same-Sex Marriage," *National Catholic Reporter*, June 3, 2015.
116. Nancy Frazier O'Brien, "Charges against Bishops' Official Called False, Ridiculous," *Catholic News Service*, February 5, 2010, https://www.ncronline.org/news/politics/charges-against-bishops-official-called-false-ridiculous.
117. Catholic Campaign for Human Development, "Memorandum to All Bishops," September 28, 2011, https://www.usccb.org/committees/catholic-campaign-human-development/soto-blaire-cchd-memo.

118. David Gibson, "In Closing Catholic News Service, U.S. Bishops Undermine Their Pastoral Work," *National Catholic Reporter*, May 12, 2022, https://www.ncronline.org/news/opinion/closing-catholic-news-service-us-bishops-undermine-their-pastoral-work.
119. Helen Osman, interview with author.
120. Molly Olmstead, "An Unholy Alliance," *Slate*, June 7, 2022, https://slate.com/human-interest/2022/06/ewtn-catholic-media-pope-francis-fox-news.html.
121. Lydia O'Kane, "Texas Shootings: Pope Condemns Indiscriminate Trafficking of Arms," *Vatican News*, May 25, 2022, https://www.vaticannews.va/en/pope/news/2022-05/pope-francis-heartbroken-at-latest-us-shooting.html.
122. Olmstead, "An Unholy Alliance."
123. Cleve R. Wootson Jr., "Fox News's Laura Ingraham Says Immigrant Child Detention Centers Are 'Essentially Summer Camps,'" *Washington Post*, June 19, 2018, https://www.washingtonpost.com/news/arts-and-entertainment/wp/2018/06/19/fox-news-laura-ingraham-says-immigrant-child-detention-centers-are-essentially-summer-camps/.
124. Christopher White, "Pope Francis Issues Thinly Veiled Criticism of EWTN, Comments on Gender Ideology," *National Catholic Reporter*, September 21, 2021, https://www.ncronline.org/news/vatican/pope-francis-issues-thinly-veiled-criticism-ewtn-comments-gender-ideology.
125. Heidi Schlumpf, "The Rise of EWTN: From Piety to Partisanship," *National Catholic Reporter*, July 16, 2019, https://www.ncronline.org/culture/rise-ewtn-piety-partisanship.
126. Catholic News Agency, "About Us," https://www.catholicnewsagency.com/about.
127. David Gibson, "Report: Knights of Columbus and Allies Are Leading Funders of Anti-Gay Marriage Drives," *Religion News Service*, October 18, 2012, https://www.washingtonpost.com/national/on-faith/report-knights-of-columbus-and-allies-are-leading-funders-of-anti-gay-marriage-drives/2012/10/18/ef4c2f16-196d-11e2-ad4a-e5a958b60a1e_story.html.
128. Brian Fraga, "EWTN-Sponsored Conference on Journalism Embraces Right-Wing 'Post-Truth' Narrative," *National Catholic Reporter*, March 14, 2023, https://www.ncronline.org/news/ewtn-sponsored-conference-journalism-embraces-right-wing-post-truth-narrative.
129. Fraga, "EWTN-Sponsored Conference on Journalism Embraces Right-Wing 'Post-Truth' Narrative."
130. Elise Ann Allen, "Spanish Bishop Bans EWTN from Diocesan Television Station," *Crux*, March 13, 2023, https://cruxnow.com/church-in-europe/2023/03/spanish-bishop-bans-ewtn-from-diocesan-television-station.
131. Facebook Live: "Building a Common Future," *National Catholic Reporter*, https://www.youtube.com/watch?v=okVH0dwjuxA.
132. Allen, "Spanish Bishop Bans EWTN."
133. Olmstead, "An Unholy Alliance."
134. Gerard O'Connell, "Pope Francis on the Death of George Floyd: "We Cannot Tolerate Racism and Claim to Defend Human Life," *America*, June 3, 2020, https://www.americamagazine.org/faith/2020/06/03/pope-francis-death-george-floyd-we-cannot-tolerate-racism-and-claim-defend-life.

135. Michael J. O'Loughlin, "U.S. Bishops: 'The Threat of Abortion Remains Our Preeminent Priority,'" *America,* November 12, 2019, https://www.americamagazine.org/faith/2019/11/12/us-bishops-threat-abortion-remains-our-preeminent-priority.
136. Brian Fraga, "U.S. Bishops Again Declare Abortion 'Preeminent Priority' for Catholic Voters," *National Catholic Reporter,* November 15, 2023, https://www.ncronline.org/news/us-bishops-again-declare-abortion-preeminent-priority-catholic-voters.
137. Cardinal Robert McElroy, interview with author.
138. Cardinal Robert McElroy, interview with author.

5

RECLAIMING A CONSISTENT ETHIC OF LIFE

The legacy of clergy abuse and coverup, along with decades of single-issue culture wars, has gravely damaged both the internal life of the church and the broader public perception of US Catholicism. The good news is there are powerful examples that point us toward healing, renewal, and institutionalizing a pro-life ethic that doesn't stop where the abortion culture wars begin. There is both resistance and progress happening at the same time. In this chapter, I provide a window into some of the Catholic resistance to engaging the wider culture on questions of social justice and spotlight Catholics who are expanding the pro-life witness to include racism, gun violence, and environmental degradation. I will also explore how Catholics are using the practices of restorative justice in different settings, including as a response to clergy sexual abuse and the church's long history of white supremacy.

"EQUALLY SACRED": WHAT DOES IT MEAN TO BE PRO-LIFE?

American political debates about what it means to be "pro-life" are usually reduced to predictable talking points and reactionary defenses of partisan agendas. An authentically Catholic approach to questions of life and human dignity challenges us to move past stale narratives and reject the false choices of rigid binaries. In remarks to US bishops during his 2015 visit to Washington, the pope specifically linked what he called "the innocent victim of abortion" to "children who die of hunger or from bombings," "immigrants who drown in the search for a better tomorrow," and "the environment devastated by man's predatory relationship with nature."[1] Francis has also framed extreme inequality as a life issue. An "economy of exclusion," in Francis' words, "kills" and "gives rise to new forms of violence." As San Diego Cardinal Robert McElroy wrote in 2013, the pope's efforts to revive and expand a consistent-ethic-of-life Catholicism "have enormous implications for the culture and politics of the United States and for the church in this country."[2] Those teachings, he emphasized, "demand a transformation of the existing Catholic political conversation." In his apostolic exhortation, *Gaudete et Exsultate* (Rejoice and Be Glad), Francis writes that along with "our defense of the innocent unborn," there must be a wider lens to view the defense of human life and dignity. "Equally sacred," the pope declares, "are the lives of the poor, those already born, the destitute, the abandoned and the underprivileged, the vulnerable infirm and elderly exposed to covert euthanasia, the victims of human trafficking, new forms of slavery, and every form of rejection."[3] The pope's use of the phrase "those already born" is illuminating because it acknowledges that Catholic pro-life narratives are too often reduced to abortion. Making his point even more explicit, Francis noted that the plight of migrants and refugees is often viewed as a "lesser issue" compared to "bioethical" concerns for some Catholics. The pope (and traditional Catholic teaching) rejects that position. "That a politician looking for votes might say such a thing is understandable, but not a Christian, for whom the only proper attitude is to stand in the shoes of those brothers and sisters of ours who risk their lives to offer a future to their children," he writes.[4]

When Cardinal Michael Czerny, S.J., prefect of the Vatican's Dicastery for Promoting Integral Human Development, delivered a 2022 keynote lecture at the Catholic Theological Union in Chicago, he grounded his call for a broader pro-life ethic in Pope Francis's encyclical *Fratelli tutti*. "Some seem to connect the idea of a consistent ethic of life and solidarity exclusively with biological life from conception to natural death," the cardinal observed.

> But to limit our understanding of the consistent ethic of life to mere bodily human life is a worrisome reduction of the full richness of the Church's teaching on the sanctity and dignity of human life. Consider, for example, how the global economy results in sweeping inequalities for life and for opportunities to live with dignity. Do not the shorter lifespans and higher infant mortalities of those in poverty cry to heaven for justice and mercy in the same way that deaths of unborn do? Are not the indignities and mistreatment of the lives of those marginalized and oppressed by the invisible hands of the market also contrary to what we should perceive as the consistent ethic of life?

The cardinal noted that *Fratelli tutti* "speaks of the unregulated market's anti-life attitude as 'throwing away' or 'discarding' others." Cardinal Czerny continued:

> A larger picture of what it means to be pro-life, of what we should understand to be the consistent ethic of life, begins to become clearer. It is certainly not enough to simply oppose abortion and euthanasia. Nor is it enough to recognize and tolerate the dignity of all lives, even with special tolerance for those who, unlike us, are marginalized or poor. No, Christ's garment is truly seamless and whole. To be genuinely pro-life also requires accompanying, welcoming and joining together with others as sibling children of God—especially those who, because of their difference, are hardest for us to love. A consistent ethic of life is also a consistent ethic of solidarity.[5]

A Catholic who responds to the signs of the times today with a consistent ethic of solidarity should seek ways that traditional Catholic social teaching and contemporary movements for justice and human dignity can find common cause. Pope Francis has lauded many social movements, both secular and religious, for challenging a status quo that perpetuates inequality and exclusion. "The future of humanity does not lie solely in the hands of great leaders, the great powers and the elites," Pope Francis has said. "It is fundamentally in the hands of people and their ability to organize."[6] The "antidote to populism and political showmanship," he insists, "lies in the efforts of organized citizens, particularly those who create in their daily lives—as is the case with so many experiences present in the movements—fragments of other possible worlds that fight to survive the darkness of exclusion."[7] After the police killing of George Floyd, the pope rooted his praise of racial justice movements in one of the most famous biblical narratives. "Do you know what comes to mind now when I think of the Good Samaritan?" the pope asked. "The protests over George Floyd. This movement did not pass by on the other side of the road when it saw the injury to human dignity caused by an abuse of power."[8] In contrast, some US Catholic clergy and conservative lay Catholic activists often view justice movements with hostility, fear, and even contempt.

INTERSECTIONALITY, CRITICAL RACE THEORY, AND CATHOLIC SOCIAL TEACHING

Los Angeles Archbishop José Gomez is a soft-spoken man who leads the largest Catholic archdiocese in the United States with a pastoral, even gentle style. But when the Mexican-born archbishop delivered a videotaped speech to the Congress of Catholics and Public Life in Madrid, Spain, in 2021, he charged headfirst into the culture wars. The archbishop, who at the time served as president of the US bishops' conference, criticized what he called "new social movements" that serve as "dangerous substitutes for true religion." He warned of "aggressive secularization" and "a deliberate effort in Europe and America to erase the Christian roots of society and to suppress any remaining Christian influences." Gomez took aim at what he called "cancel culture"—a common trope on the right—arguing that "often what is being canceled and corrected are perspectives rooted in Christian beliefs."[9]

While the archbishop noted that the police killing of George Floyd in Minneapolis was "a stark reminder that racial and economic inequality are still deeply embedded in our society," he also ignored centuries of white supremacy in the Catholic Church when he said, "the Church has been antiracist from the beginning." The archbishop argued that social justice movements that gained momentum in the wake of Floyd's murder serve as replacements for "traditional Christian beliefs," a statement that surely came as news to the many Christians and other religious Americans who are active in these movements. Because of "the breakdown of the Judeo-Christian worldview and the rise of secularism," the archbishop said, "political belief systems based on social justice or personal identity have come to fill the space that Christian belief and practice once occupied." "Whatever we call these movements—'social justice,' 'wokeness,' 'identity politics,' 'intersectionality,' 'successor ideology'—they claim to offer what religion provides."[10] Writing in a *National Catholic Register* editorial under the headline "Beware of the Woke!" publisher Michael Warsaw thanked the archbishop and argued that "these same secularist and anti-religious perspectives constituted the core of the Democratic Party's political vision during the 2020 election."[11]

The archbishop's speech provoked widespread criticism from Black Catholic leaders and Catholic social justice activists. "We are especially troubled by your comment 'the Church has been "antiracist" from the beginning,'" Sister Josita Colbert, president of the National Black Sisters' Conference, wrote in a pointed public letter to Gomez.

> With all due respect, Archbishop, do you not know the history of the Church's involvement with the slave trade, with the segregation of churches; with black people often being relegated to the back of churches and forced to receive Holy Communion after white parishioners; and the rejection of black men and women who desired to enter seminaries and religious communities? Over four hundred

> years of slavery, trauma, pain, disenfranchisement, and brutal violence have been a part of the fabric of this nation and the American Catholic Church. Black Lives Matter grew out of the frustration of seeing black lives struck down over and over again with no accountability. It is a racial justice movement, a gospel movement.[12]

By deriding what he called the "wokeness" and "intersectionality" of social justice movements, Gomez also missed an opportunity to articulate how those concepts—approached with respect rather than glib caricature—find support in the context of Catholic social teaching and within the broader Christian tradition. "The concept of 'waking up,' of having one's eyes opened to see more clearly what was hidden or ignored should sound familiar to Catholics," Pax Christi USA, a Catholic peace and justice organization, said in a statement responding to the archbishop's speech. "To lament 'becoming woke' is to miss the message of the gospel, the language of Jesus, John the Baptist, the apostles and the early Christian community for whom 'waking up' was a metaphor for an experience of transformation, the Christian concept of conversion, *metanoia*."[13]

Rather than simply provoke and denounce, the archbishop could have reached for points of connection and common ground. At its core to be "intersectional" is to recognize that issues and injustices are not siloed or separate. This should not be an alien or threatening concept for Catholics who find in church teaching on the common good and the consistent ethic of life a clear expression of overlapping values. "It cannot be emphasized enough how everything is interconnected," Pope Francis writes in his encyclical *Laudato Si.'* In the chapter on "integral ecology," Francis observed:

> Given the scale of change, it is no longer possible to find a specific, discrete answer for each part of the problem. It is essential to seek comprehensive solutions which consider the interactions within natural systems themselves and with social systems. We are faced not with two separate crises, one environmental and the other social, but rather with one complex crisis which is both social and environmental. Strategies for a solution demand an integrated approach to combating poverty, restoring dignity to the excluded, and at the same time protecting nature.[14]

The pope also quotes the Conference of Dominican Bishops: "Peace, justice and the preservation of creation are three absolutely interconnected themes, which cannot be separated and treated individually without once again falling into reductionism." Marcus Mescher, a professor of Christian ethics at Xavier University in Cincinnati and author of *The Ethics of Encounter: Christian Neighbor Love as a Practice of Solidarity*, observes that "intersectionality is consistent with a Catholic view of the human person in all its complexity."[15] Pope Francis is "shepherding the church toward a more nuanced consideration of what it means to be human today," he told me. "That includes an examination of the intersections and overlaps of privilege and power as a result of gender, race, sexual orientation, class, education, physical ability, and mental health, for example." An "intersectional lens," Mescher adds, also

> provides a clearer picture of how systems and structures inform and malform moral perception, reasoning, and agency. The church teaches that conscience formation is informed by scripture, tradition, reason, and human experience, which includes what we learn from the social sciences. So it betrays our own tradition to reject 'secular' sources of what is true, right, good, or just. Augustine drew from Plato and Aquinas engaged Aristotle. Today, scholars who employ an intersectional lens help us better understand the gifts and tasks of—as well as the threats against—human dignity, agency, and right-relationships.[16]

The term "intersectionality" was introduced and popularized by the legal scholar Kimberlé Crenshaw, a professor of law at Columbia University and the University of California, Los Angeles. Crenshaw first used the word in a 1989 article to describe how race, class, gender, and other individual characteristics intersect with each other and overlap. Because discrimination law historically failed to take this into account, she argued, civil rights violations of Black women were often ignored. "Intersectionality was a prism to bring to light dynamics within discrimination law that weren't being appreciated by the courts," Crenshaw told *Vox* in 2019. "In particular, courts seem to think that race discrimination was what happened to all black people across gender and sex discrimination was what happened to all women, and if that is your framework, of course, what happens to black women and other women of color is going to be difficult to see."[17] Crenshaw's work has also helped expand conversations about critical race theory beyond law school seminars into mainstream public discourse. Critical race theory (CRT) recognizes that racism is interwoven into our nation's institutions and structures in ways that impact the law, economy, housing policies, education, the criminal justice system, and health care, among other facets of American life. CRT was developed as a framework for legal analysis in the late 1970s and early 1980s by Crenshaw, Derrick Bell, Richard Delgado, and other legal scholars.

Republican politicians and conservative activists have used the banner of critical race theory to oppose a historically accurate examination of the central role race plays in American life. Donald Trump issued an executive order in 2020 that prohibited federal agencies from teaching what his administration described as "divisive concepts."[18] A year after the order, federal, state, and local governmental agencies introduced 250 measures to outlaw the teaching of critical race theory.[19] Even after President Biden revoked that executive order, efforts to ban critical race theory grew. In 2023 researchers in the Critical Race Studies Program at the UCLA School of Law found that between January 2021 and the end of December 2022, officials at the federal, state, and local levels introduced 563 anti-CRT measures. Nearly half of those measures were enacted. The study tracked legislation, executive orders, state attorney general letters, and statements by governors, and local school board officials. More than 90 percent of those efforts, the report found, targeted K–12 education.[20] Some Catholic leaders have also used their positions of influence to falsely depict any critical examination of structural racism as "fundamentally incompatible with Christianity," as Fr. Mathias Thelen, pastor of St. Patrick Catholic Parish in Brighton, Michigan, wrote in a 2021 letter to his parishioners. "We will not be teaching Critical Race Theory at St. Pat's School. We cannot subject our students to an unproven and divisive social theory that engages in historical revisionism and counterproductive activism around race."[21] *Catholic World Report* claims that CRT is "divisive and harmful to the minds and hearts of young people." Grazie Pozo Christie, a senior fellow for the Catholic Association, warned in the *National Review* that "the administrators of any Catholic school should recoil from" critical race theory because of its "tired atheist tropes of division and hopelessness."[22] In a 2021 letter from the president of the Catholic Medical Association to members of the association, Michael Parker wrote that "Marxist principles, in the guise of 'Critical Race Theory,' threaten the ideas that form the basis of our nation's founding principles, which protect the individual's rights." Parker added that "the language of 'social justice,' 'equity,' and 'diversity' distort the principles of Catholic social teaching. These terms have become a political tool to silence any opposition."[23] The letter ends with an alarmist call to action. "Please join me and other members to collaborate in the courageous fight to overcome ideologies opposed to Christianity and natural law." The Cardinal Newman Society, an organization that deems itself to be the arbiter of what constitutes faithful Catholic education, features an issue brief on its website with the headline "10 Ways Catholic Education and

Critical Race Theory Are Incompatible." Catholic education "teaches that sin is an individual fault that can have devastating social impact, but critical race theory imputes guilt for 'social sins' committed in the past," according to the group.[24] This explanation not only dismisses how centuries of white supremacy and its manifestation in specific public policies over time continue to impact current-day inequalities but also distorts how Catholic social teaching understands "social sin." In his encyclical *Sollicitudo Rei Socialis*, Pope John Paul II referred to "structures of sin" more than a dozen times and identified it as foundational to addressing past and present injustices.[25]

Catholic leaders need not accept every expression of critical race theory as seamlessly aligned with church teaching, but an unwillingness to show even basic humility and learn from scholars and others who have much to teach about the systemic nature of racism underscores a troubling resistance among some white Catholics to honestly grapple with racism. Reactionary responses that not only reject any engagement with CRT but demonize this framework of analysis as a "threat to Christianity" only proves that point. "There is a tendency to become immediately defensive when the issue of race is raised so people look for exit off ramps and say 'I don't want to confront these issues so I am going to find something that allows me to dismiss it completely,'" Vincent Rougeau, the former dean of Boston College law school and the first Black president of the College of the Holy Cross, said in a discussion about critical race theory on The Gloria Purvis Podcast. Critical race theory has been turned into "a bogeyman," Rougeau observed, and the idea that it is "a mind control mechanism that will destroy our children and make children feel terrible for being white is nonsense."[26] By using critical race theory, he added, "you come to some understandings about the law that you may or may not agree with, but it helps us understand more deeply the systems of racial injustice and racism. . . . How could it be the case that Catholics would not want to engage with an intellectual tool that deepens understanding?" In the wake of George Floyd's murder, Rougeau and other leaders at Boston College created a Forum on Racial Justice, an ongoing initiative that engages the Catholic university and the community in dialogues about systemic racism. "In the Catholic intellectual tradition there is a real understanding of the idea of structural injustice and structural sin," Rougeau said on the podcast.

> If we are thinking in terms of our own Catholic tradition, we have to let go of this notion that sin can only occur in the context of individual acts or omissions. That is not how our tradition understands sin or injustice. This idea that personal actions of goodwill alone are going to breakdown structures that have built up over centuries is

just naive. The Church itself, in its intellectual tradition, recognizes that and thinks in a much more complex way. If you are going to reject out of hand analytical tools designed to deeper understanding, that is anti-intellectual. It's like modern-day book burning.

BLACK LIVES MATTER AND THE FIGHT FOR RACIAL JUSTICE

Racism is a pro-life issue that US Catholic leaders must address with greater urgency, honesty, and institutional commitment. Black Americans have less access to quality health care, die at earlier ages, and are more likely to live in distressed communities where pollution and toxic industries leave them disproportionately at risk compared to white Americans. After decades of progress in reducing the life expectancy gap between white and Black Americans, the Covid pandemic has exacerbated longstanding inequalities in ways that underscore the persistent impact of systemic racism on health and life expectancy. "Decades of progress in extending human lives have been reversed," Matthew Thompson wrote in "The Elusive Quest for Black Progress," a 2023 article in *The New York Times* that examined a century of racial inequality.

> Life expectancy for Black and white Americans has diverged again, falling back to where it was in 1995. A gap of nearly five years of expected life now separates us. For Black Americans, this pattern—years of progress achieved and then erased—is common enough that the idea of racial progress in the U.S. is sometimes called a myth. Many of the indicators we use to track human advancement are particularly stuck for Black Americans, or are moving in the wrong direction.[27]

Despite persistent and growing inequalities, research shows that white Catholics are far less likely to hear church leaders address racism than Black Catholics. Four in ten Black Catholics said they had heard a discussion at church about race relations or racial inequality, compared with 29 percent of Hispanic Catholics and only 18 percent of white Catholics, according to 2021 data released as part of the Pew Research Center's "Faith among Black Americans" survey.[28]

Data from the Public Religion Research Institute (PRRI) has found that white Christians are *more likely* than whites who are religiously unaffiliated to deny the existence of structural racism.[29] "The United States has engaged in a long-overdue reckoning with the racist symbols of the past, tearing down monuments to figures complicit in slavery and removing Confederate flags from public displays," Robert Jones, the president of PRRI and author of *White Too Long: The Legacy of White Supremacy in American Christianity*, wrote in 2020.

> But little scrutiny has been given to the cultural institutions that legitimized the worldview behind these symbols: white Christian churches. A close read of history reveals that we white Christians have not just been complacent or complicit; rather, as the nation's dominant cultural power, we have constructed and sustained a project of perpetuating white supremacy that has framed the entire American story. The legacy of this unholy union still lives in the DNA of white Christianity today—and not just among white evangelical Protestants in the South, but also among white mainline Protestants in the Midwest and white Catholics in the Northeast.[30]

When white Catholic leaders do publicly name the church's own history of white supremacy, the reaction is particularly fraught when the Black Lives Matter movement comes up. Rob McCann, a white Catholic who serves as president and CEO of Catholic Charities of Eastern Washington, released a video in 2020 to staff and Catholic Charities' clients that set off a firestorm in the diocese. "Our primary job at Catholic Charities is to be an authentic Catholic voice on human dignity as we serve the poor and vulnerable," McCann said by way of introduction in the video. "Being an authentic voice sometimes means saying things that are hard to say and hard to hear." McCann acknowledged that as a white person, "every institution is geared to advantage people who look like me" and noted that "the bias of white people supports and feeds into powerfully racist systems in our country." He continued with an unusually frank and unflinching message:

> As a Catholic who believes in reconciliation, I must own my part in that and treat it like any other sin. I must know it, name it, speak it, ask for forgiveness for it, while trying to eliminate it from my life. In America, racism is no longer a question but rather the toxic water in which we all swim. My Catholic Church and my Catholic Charities organization is racist. How could they not be? Our Catholic faith tradition was built on the premise that a baby born in a manger in the middle east was a white baby. So how can we be surprised to know that we are a church that must still fight against racism even now?[31]

McCann spoke about the long history of the Catholic Church owning slaves and the abusive treatment of Indigenous youth in church-run schools, among other examples of what he called the "institutionalization of racism" in the church. "We can't avoid that reality until we speak it and ask for forgiveness with a love that takes action to repair," he said. McCann also noted that most of the leaders in his own Catholic Charities organization are white even as the majority of those they serve are Black or Hispanic. "The death of George Floyd and the Black Lives Matter movement is a watershed moment in our country's history and as such needs to be a watershed moment in the working future of Catholic Charities," McCann said. "Catholic Charities supports Black Lives Matter. We simply can't stand outside of something as significant as this movement even though we know full well there may be a price to pay for walking into it. We must walk in anyway now. In its purest, nonviolent form it is a Christ-like movement that honors the church's teaching that we must give a preferential option to those who are marginalized. Black lives have been marginalized for too long."[32]

Spokane Bishop Thomas Daly issued a response that was telling in its defensiveness. "No, not everybody is racist by sheer skin color," Daly told the *Spokesman-Review*. Daly said he received many calls and emails from Catholics who felt McCann spoke too broadly about racism and ignored positive things the church has done. In a statement posted on the diocesan website, the bishop criticized Black Lives Matter as "in conflict with Church teaching regarding marriage, family and the sanctity of life," and added that "it is disturbing that BLM has not vocally condemned the recent violence that has torn apart so many cities."[33] Despite the bishop's attempt to associate the Black Lives Matter movement with violence, research from the Carr Center for Human Rights Policy at Harvard University, among other organizations, has found that the vast majority of Black Lives Matter–led protests have been peaceful.[34] In contrast, the Department of Homeland Security has named white supremacists groups as a leading national security threat.[35] The controversy over the video became so intense that McCann was forced to issue a clarifying statement. "Though I meant the video to begin a humble examination of my role and Catholic Charities' role in systemic racism, it was perceived as an attack on the church," McCann wrote. "And though I meant the video to begin healing rifts within our community, it resulted in some people becoming further entrenched in their positions." McCann also said that Catholic Charities became the target of "violent and hateful language" in response to his video. "There also has now been violence committed against my wife and children at my home," McCann wrote. "For all of my best intentions, these past weeks have been marked by hurt and sadness from all involved."[36]

Along with his reprimand of McCann and negative comments directed at Black Lives Matter, Bishop Daly also asked Catholic Charities to "address the issue of abortion and its detrimental effects on the Black community." The bishop's quick pivot to abortion—an issue with no shortage of Catholic political lobbying, organizing, and media attention over the past four decades—was seemingly an attempt to move the conversation to more comfortable and familiar terrain for the church. But *discomfort* is precisely what white Catholics should feel as we grapple with the legacy of white supremacy and the enduring impact of institutional racism. Fr. Bryan Massingale, a Fordham University Catholic ethicist, theologian, and acclaimed writer on racism and the church, told me that when he speaks about racism in Catholic schools or parishes, he is often encouraged to do so "in a way that doesn't make white people uncomfortable."[37] But white discomfort should never frame the terms of discussion. The systemic racism inherent in police brutality, mass incarceration, the death penalty, the treatment of migrants, and the poisoning of Black and Hispanic communities impacted by polluting industries are all life-and-death issues that should make us all uncomfortable—and lead to action. The slain Archbishop Oscar Romero of El Salvador put it well when he asked: "A church that does not provoke crisis, a gospel that does not disturb, a word of God that does not rankle, a word of God that does not touch the concrete sin of the society in which it is being proclaimed—what kind of gospel is that?"

Olga Segura, author of *Birth of a Movement: Black Lives Matter and the Catholic Church*, has urged bishops—a leadership that is predominantly older, white, and all male—to understand why so many young people are inspired by a Black Lives Matter movement started by Black women. "This movement was born on Facebook and it used social media tools to teach people how to organize," Segura told me.

> It embraced social media when people were still trying to figure that out, and at a time when Millennials were coming of age. These women knew how to use these tools and resources, but they had also been organizing for more than fifteen years. They brought their own advocacy experience to the work. Because of the social media tools they used, I felt as if I could be a part of this conversation about the prison-industrial complex and police brutality. They really figured out how to talk to young people. Church leaders can learn from that and really jump into this work. A lot of bishops want to have an

auditing process first, to meet and vote. But when people are being killed by police violence, inequality, and the pandemic, there is no time for incrementalism. You have to meet people where they are.[38]

While the Black Lives Matter movement does not have as many official connections to religious institutions in the way that civil rights leaders of the past emerged from and organized in the Black church, Segura views the movement as having clear spiritual and moral underpinnings.

> There is spirituality and there are religious folks in the movement, especially after Ferguson. There was heavy church participation there, but it's so decentralized it means people are not necessarily telling these stories. I think religious media needs to take this movement more seriously. When I spoke with Alicia Garza [a co-founder of Black Lives Matter], she welcomed faith leaders getting involved. I can tell you this movement has made me a better Catholic. Imagine our faith leaders sitting down with the founders of Black Lives Matter and saying, 'We have messed up. Can you teach us?' That would say to me, a Black immigrant Catholic, that you finally care, you are finally listening, finally doing the accompaniment you like to talk about so much. The bishops are a body of mostly white men and to have them in dialogue with the Black women who started this movement would be extremely powerful.

Bishop Mark Seitz of El Paso, Texas, who leads a diocese on the border between the United States and Mexico, has been one of the most vocal antiracist Catholic leaders. Seitz made headlines around the world in 2020 when he knelt with twelve other priests from his diocese in a silent prayer vigil for 8 minutes and 46 seconds—the exact time a police officer took to choke George Floyd to death. The bishop and priests from the diocese all wore handwritten signs that read "Black Lives Matter."[39] Pope Francis called the bishop to thank him personally for his powerful display of solidarity. "Those who suffer racism need to know we're with them," Seitz told me in an interview.[40]

> We believe in a crucified God, after all. George Floyd died because someone we gave a badge and a gun knelt on his neck. And we all know he's not alone. That's scandalous. When Jesus was killed, the cross was a sign of shame at first. It smelled of torture and death. But it became a source of life and communion. As Paul said, 'God forbid that I should glory, save in the cross of our Lord Jesus Christ.' It was haunting to see how a people that were tired of injustice and

> death transformed a wretched image of asphyxiation into a rallying cry for justice and solidarity. On a human level, how could you not be moved by that? But on a spiritual level, how could you not hear the strains of the Gospel in their cries?

I asked the bishop why he embraced the Black Lives Matter movement even as other Catholic bishops and clergy often focus on how the movement's leaders hold views on marriage, gender, and sexuality that clash with church teachings: "There were those who thought it was indecent or somehow threatening to the Christian message because not everyone involved in the antiracism protests held all of our beliefs, but I don't agree," the bishop said. "The Scriptures say 'rejoice with them that rejoice, and weep with them that weep.' We need to recognize that when people have a deep thirst for justice and recognition of human dignity, even when some might think differently from us, it isn't without a holy foundation. And we might have something to learn."[41]

In 2019 Seitz released a powerful pastoral letter on racism and white supremacy, "Night Will Be No More," that should be required reading for every Christian.[42] One of the most important contributions the bishop makes in the letter is to frame multiple threats to life and human dignity—racism, gun violence, and dehumanizing treatment of migrants—as interconnected. The letter opens with a description of the 2019 mass shooting at a Walmart in El Paso that left twenty-two dead and dozens injured. The killer confessed to targeting Mexicans. "Hate visited our community and Latino blood was spilled in sacrifice to the false god of white supremacy," the bishop wrote in his reflection, published two months after the shooting. "Words like 'racism' and 'white supremacy' make us uncomfortable and anxious and I don't use these labels lightly. . . . Challenging racism and white supremacy, whether in our hearts or in society, is a Christian imperative and the cost of not facing these issues head on, weighs much more heavily on those who live the reality of discrimination." Only a few hours after the mass shooting in El Paso, a shooting in Dayton, Ohio, killed nine people. Bishop Seitz lamented how the "growing litany of deadly shootings in the United States . . . a list so long that each mass murder competes for our attention and memory."

GUN VIOLENCE AND THE CULTURE OF DEATH

Gov. Greg Abbott of Texas is widely regarded as a national leader in the antiabortion movement. In a 2015 speech at the National Catholic Prayer Breakfast, the governor, a convert to Catholicism, vowed his commitment to what he called "the never-ending battle to defend the unborn."[43] The Catholic governor's understanding of what it means to be pro-life often seems to end at birth, considering his support for the death penalty and the gun industry. As mass shootings have proliferated across the nation—and in Texas in particular—Abbott has remained a staunch opponent of gun reform. Two years after the mass shooting in El Paso, the governor pledged to keep Texas "a bastion of freedom." Surrounded by representatives from the National Rifle Association, he signed seven pieces of legislation that expanded gun rights, including allowing people to legally carry handguns without licenses. "Texas will always be the leader in defending the Second Amendment," Abbot boasted during the ceremony.[44] Less than a year later, nineteen children and two teachers were killed in a mass shooting at Robb Elementary School in Uvalde, Texas. Less than a year after that massacre, eight people—including two elementary school students—were shot at a crowded mall in an affluent Dallas suburb. The governor still resisted widespread calls to take significant legislative action to make it harder for people to access military assault weapons. At a Texas Rally for Life in 2023, the steady wave of killings by people wielding military-style assault weapons was never mentioned. The governor thanked hundreds of antiabortion advocates for their work in overturning the constitutional right to an abortion. "All of you are life savers, and thousands of newborn babies are the result of your heroic efforts," he said. "With your help, we made transformational changes in Texas law last session—life saving changes."[45] Abbott is not the only Catholic politician who touts his pro-life values in a selective way.

Two weeks after the massacre in Uvalde, Texas—the deadliest school shooting since the 2012 carnage at Sandy Hook Elementary in Newtown, Connecticut—Florida governor Ron DeSantis said he did not want to "knee cap the rights of law-abiding citizens" and warned that "leftists" want to "come after your Second Amendment rights."[46] Days after a former student killed three children and three adults at a Christian school in Nashville in March 2023, the Catholic governor signed a bill allowing Florida residents to carry guns without a permit—at the time making Florida the 26th state to give residents the right to carry concealed weapons without a permit. "You don't need a permission slip from the government to be able to exercise your constitutional rights," DeSantis said during a visit to a sporting goods store in Georgia that bills itself as the world's largest gun store.[47] His position on government overreach did not extend to pregnant women. Ten days later, the governor signed a ban on abortion after six weeks, a period when many women do not even know they are pregnant.[48]

In his 1995 encyclical *Evangelium Vitae* (Gospel of Life), Pope John Paul II describes how a "culture of death" is propped up by "a notion of freedom which exalts the isolated individual in an absolute way, and gives no place to solidarity."[49] This distorted understanding of personal autonomy, the pope writes, reflects "a completely individualistic concept of freedom which ends up by becoming the freedom of 'the strong against the weak.'" The pope's detailed attention to how this cultural attitude often underpins the philosophical and political support for abortion and euthanasia drew the most public attention when the encyclical was released. The document is viewed as a seminal text in the pro-life movement. But similar libertarian notions of freedom and personal rights drive much of the American idolatry of guns. In the wake of a 2022 mass shooting in Buffalo, New York, where ten people were shot to death in a racially motivated attack at a grocery store in a predominantly Black neighborhood, a poll conducted by CBS News and YouGov found that 44 percent of Republicans agreed that mass shootings are "unfortunately something we have to accept as part of a free society."[50] In a 2018 *Dallas Morning News* op-ed, Texas Sen. Ted Cruz wrote that "a free society" exists "only if its citizens have the means to defend themselves and their God-given rights." The senator argued that what he called "forced disarmament" is "a first step toward subjugation."[51]

The warped devotion to guns on the American right—reflected in distorted conceptions of personal liberty and freedom—has become so radical that the AR-15 and other assault weapons have been turned into surreal culture-war symbols of defiance. Rep. Thomas Massie, a Republican lawmaker in Kentucky, tweeted a photo of his smiling family holding rifles in front of their Christmas tree in 2021 with the message "Santa, please bring ammo."[52] Rep. Lauren Boebert of Colorado followed Massie's post with a tweet of herself standing with her four young sons, all of whom were holding rifles, in front of a Christmas tree. The pictures were posted only days after a fifteen-year-old in Oxford, Michigan, killed four students at a high school. Some members of Congress have even worn lapel pins in the shape of assault rifles on the House floor. Rep. Andrew Clay of Georgia took credit for the pins on Twitter, saying that he handed them out "to remind people of the Second Amendment of the Constitution and how important it is in preserving our liberties."[53] Some Catholics on the far right even fuse devotion to the rosary with a culture of gun militancy. "Just as the AR-15 rifle has become a sacred object for Christian nationalists in general, the rosary has acquired a militaristic meaning for radical-traditional (or 'rad trad') Catholics," Daniel Panneton wrote in a 2022 article, "How Extremist Gun Culture Is Trying to Co-Opt the Rosary," published in the *Atlantic*.[54]

"On this extremist fringe, rosary beads have been woven into a conspiratorial politics and absolutist gun culture," Panneton wrote. "These armed radical traditionalists have taken up a spiritual notion that the rosary can be a weapon in the fight against evil and turned it into something dangerously literal. Their social-media pages are saturated with images of rosaries draped over firearms, warriors in prayer, *Deus Vult* (God wills it) crusader memes, and exhortations for men to rise up and become Church Militants." Michael Diamond, a former military intelligence officer and Iraq war veteran, wrote about Catholicism, guns, and pro-life values in a 2021 commentary for NBC News. "Who's to blame for the lax gun laws that enable this shameful national embarrassment to continue?" Diamond asked. "Lawmakers and the gun lobby both come to mind. But frankly, I have also been part of the problem—because I am a Catholic who for decades has tacitly supported laws and policies that increase gun deaths through my pro-life vote."[55] Diamond noted that while most voters, including Republicans, support common-sense gun reforms such as background checks and limiting access to assault weapons, the National Rifle Association has stymied reform with its influence. "The NRA spent $1.6 million lobbying Congress during the 2019 fight to effectively make it easier for domestic abusers, fugitives and convicted felons to purchase a gun," he wrote. "Sadly, many of us pro-life Catholics have been propping up that dysfunction with our donations and our votes, telling ourselves that the issue of abortion holds a higher call on our partisan loyalties. The average Catholic voter has a lot of power in the Republican Party, something our immigrant forefathers would never have imagined. Catholics need to move beyond 'thoughts and prayers' for victims of gun violence and convert them to action." Diamond concludes with a reminder that an authentically Catholic pro-life witness in politics and public life must always make connections and understand the dignity of life in the broadest terms. Catholics "reject false dualisms," he wrote. "We are a 'both/and' Church, not an 'either/or' one. Jesus was both human *and* divine. We believe in faith *and* reason, Scripture *and* tradition. To be pro-life can't be about abortion *or* gun safety. It has to be both, along with other positions that protect and promote life. Within our bifurcated political system, we can push for responsible gun policy in a way that is aligned with, rather than contrary to, our Catholic values."

The American idolatry of guns should be challenged by any Catholics and clergy leaders who consider themselves pro-life. Gun violence is now the leading cause of death for children in the United States.[56] In 2023 alone there were more than six hundred mass shootings, according to the Gun Violence Archive, which defines a mass shooting as an incident in which four or more people are injured or killed.[57] When Pope Francis addressed a joint session of Congress in 2015, he asked: "Why are deadly weapons being sold to those who plan to inflict untold suffering on individuals and society? Sadly, the answer, as we all know, is simply for money: money that is drenched in blood, often innocent blood." Even as many self-identified pro-life Catholics in the United States still have not embraced gun reforms as a core part of their pro-life advocacy and voting choices, more US Catholics leaders are speaking out. "Gun violence is a pro-life issue when you start looking at the statistics and the impact that gun violence has on life and the destructive impact it has on society," Sister Mary Haddad, president and CEO of the Catholic Health Association, said during a Georgetown University panel discussion entitled "After Buffalo, After Uvalde, After Tulsa—Broken Hearts, Broken Nation, Faithful Action."[58] Less than two weeks after a gunman shot and killed nineteen elementary school students and two teachers in Uvalde, Texas, a gunman killed four people at a medical building on the campus of St. Francis Hospital in Tulsa, Oklahoma, before killing himself. The attack marked the 233rd mass shooting in 2022. St. Francis is a member of the Catholic Health Association. "The thought of such violence happening at a medical center really pushed me to the edge," said Sister Haddad, who urged Catholics to "hold our elected officials accountable and demand that action be taken to address gun violence in our country through sensible gun policies."[59]

After the Uvalde school shooting, Chicago Cardinal Blase Cupich framed gun violence in appropriately stark terms. "Who are we as a nation," he asked, "if we do not act to protect our children? What do we love more: our instruments of death or our future?"[60] The cardinal also didn't hesitate to challenge a common conservative myth that the rights of gun owners are absolute, unquestionable, and override other rights and responsibilities. "The Second Amendment, unlike the second commandment, did not come down from Sinai," Cupich told National Public Radio.[61] "There is an understanding that we all have in our hearts, engraved in our hearts, a natural law about the value of human life. And there is no amendment that can trump that." Bishop Daniel Flores of Brownsville, Texas, rejected another right-wing trope about firearms in unusually blunt language. "Don't tell me that guns aren't the problem, people are," the bishop tweeted. "I'm sick of hearing it. The darkness first takes our children who then kill our children, using the guns that are easier to obtain than aspirin. We sacralize death's instruments and then are surprised that death uses them."[62] In an interview with *The Pillar* a few days after his tweet, Bishop Flores said Catholics must "look with a wider lens" at protecting human life in ways that transcend conventional partisan arguments.[63]

The US Conference of Catholic Bishops also reiterated its decades-old appeals for more robust gun regulations after the string of mass shootings in 2022. In a letter to Congress signed by several bishops who chair leading committees at the conference—including Baltimore Archbishop William Lori, who chaired the bishops' pro-life committee—the conference called lawmakers to take concrete action that "addresses all aspects of the crisis, including mental health, the state of families, the valuation of life, the influence of entertainment and gaming industries, bullying, and the availability of firearms." The bishops again pressed for "the passage of reasonable gun control measures," and specifically cited legislation that would make improvements to background checks for gun owners. "This incomprehensible tragedy at Uvalde, Texas, comes as we are still grieving the loss of innocent lives in Buffalo, Dallas, Laguna Woods, and now Tulsa," the bishops wrote. "These tragedies can only bring us to one conclusion: we must unite in our humanity to stop the massacres of innocent lives." The conference letter laments that "in the ten years since the massacre of children at Sandy Hook, very little has been done by Congress to regulate these weapons and prevent another catastrophe."[64] In his own statement after the wave of mass shootings, the now retired Archbishop Michael Jackels of Dubuque, Iowa, not only addressed gun violence but also offered a surprisingly direct critique of how distorted the Catholic pro-life ethic has become in the United States. Bishop Jackels wrote:

> You've got to wonder about reasons for refusing reasonable limits on gun ownership, which are inspired by the common good and offering protection from harm. We readily identify things like abortion and capital punishment as life issues, which Catholic teaching identifies as absolutely wrong under any circumstance. But protecting the earth, our common home, or making food, water, shelter, education and health care accessible, or defense against gun violence . . . these are life issues too. Some people want to repair the scandal of pro-choice Catholic politicians by refusing them the Eucharist. But that's a misguided response for at least two reasons: As Jesus said, it's the sick people who need a doctor, not the healthy, and he gave us the Eucharist as a healing remedy; don't deny the people who need the medicine. Also, to be consistent, to repair the scandal of Catholics being indifferent or opposed to all those other life issues, they would have to be denied Holy Communion as well. Better, I think, to put the Eucharist in the hands of such Catholics in hopes that one day soon they would put their hands to work on behalf of life, in defense of all life.[65]

In the aftermath of the Uvalde shooting, Archbishop Gustavo García-Siller of San Antonio challenged political leaders to reform the nation's lax gun laws. "We have made guns an idol in this country," he said in an interview with MSNBC. "I believe with my whole heart that gun control has to take place in a more radical way."[66] In the days after the school shooting, the archbishop met frequently with victims' families, led evening Masses for the shattered community, and presided over funerals at Sacred Heart Church. When I interviewed the archbishop a year after the killings, he called gun reform a "pro-life" issue. I asked him why Texas Governor Greg Abbott, a Catholic, and other Catholic political leaders who define themselves as pro-life because of their support for outlawing abortion have opposed substantive efforts to restrict the sale of firearms. "Even though they proclaim themselves Catholics, they have other agendas," the archbishop told me. "This selfishness leads us to lose common ground. You start thinking in a very small way. Their vision is very short."[67] While breaking political stalemates on guns and other issues in a polarized environment seems increasingly hard at a national level, the archbishop pointed to the advocacy of faith-based community organizers in Texas and across the nation as hopeful signs that change can bubble up from the grassroots.

A "CHURCH IN THE STREETS": FAITH-BASED ORGANIZING

Josephine Lopez Paul grew up in a devout Catholic family in New Mexico. During her fifteen years as a public school teacher, Lopez Paul taught children from poor families who often came to school hungry. She watched her students carrying the weight of economic stress in ways that couldn't be easily walled off from the classroom. "I was always asking the principal what we could do for these kids," she told me. "I was told that was political and we don't do politics."[68] The answer never felt right. At the time her Catholic faith was lukewarm, and she wasn't particularly active in her parish. She eventually learned about Albuquerque Interfaith, an organization where people of diverse faith backgrounds work with low-income communities to build power and impact policy. She had no idea her church was even a member. "When I started to get involved with community organizing, I saw an outward expression of the Catholic faith in ways I had never experienced," Paul said. "This work brought me back to the church. It really turned church on its head for me." She volunteered for four years. Paul has a particular love for St. Francis of Assisi. During a spiritual retreat, she found herself meditating on the phrase, "rebuild my church," words that St. Francis was said to have heard from God while in prayer before a crucifix. She left teaching to become a full-time faith-based organizer in El Paso, Texas.

Paul worked to improve living conditions in the *colonias*, subdivisions in Texas border areas where migrants from Mexico and other countries went decades without basic infrastructure such as running water, sewage, electricity, and roads. Organizing in these communities reminded her of her own family history. Her grandfather did backbreaking labor in the mines of southern Colorado in the early twentieth century and lost his hands after a mining accident. His father died at the age of thirty-two from congestive heart failure caused by black lung. Faith and activism are in her blood. Paul's ancestors helped organize the first Catholic Church for Mexican Americans, Sacred Heart Parish in Durango, Colorado, and started a union that pushed for better wages and working conditions. After four years in El Paso, she was an organizer in Fort Worth and then moved to Dallas. For eight years she organized with Dallas Area Interfaith, part of the national Industrial Areas Foundation (IAF). Founded in 1940 by the community activist Saul Alinsky with support from Chicago auxiliary bishop Bernard Sheil, IAF is the nation's largest network of faith and community-based organizations. After a twenty-five-year-old Black military veteran shot and killed five police officers in Dallas during a racial justice demonstration protesting police shootings in 2016—turning what had been a peaceful gathering into a scene of carnage—Paul organized with clergy to host a forum at a Black church with Dallas police officers to help foster dialogue. Three years later, a twenty-one-year-old gunman killed twenty-three people in an El Paso Walmart shortly after posting a racist manifesto directed at Latinos on social media. She got in her car and drove nine hours south. Paul helped organize mental health teams in El Paso congregations and coordinated a public forum with elected officials, clergy, and community members. "I learned from these shootings that people need a public space to process what has happened to them collectively, and institutions become primal in the sense that a church is not just a place of worship but a place where people can make sense of what happened and also begin organizing a response," she told me.

After moving to San Antonio in 2022 to become the lead organizer for Communities Organized for Public Service (COPS) and the Metro Alliance—a coalition of congregations, schools, and unions—Paul responded to yet another mass shooting. For the first two days, she watched news reports out of Uvalde, a small town where most of the residents are Hispanic, with the familiar mix of grief and anger. COPS/Metro has a strong working relationship with Archbishop García-Siller, and officials at the archdiocese asked her to go. "We knew we needed an organized response in Uvalde even though we didn't have an organizational presence there," she said. Along with another organizer, Paul started walking the neighborhoods and listening to those reeling with unfathomable pain. The organizers helped community members with translation because police were not providing updates in Spanish. Sacred Heart Catholic Church, built more than a century ago, became a sacred space of refuge. People gathered at the church in the evening for Mass, prayer, and connection. The archbishop was a consistent presence at Sacred Heart, presiding at daily services and offering comfort to grieving families. When I spoke with Paul a few months before the one-year anniversary of the shooting, she acknowledged that achieving gun reform in Texas has been an uphill climb. "Guns are everywhere here, even in churches," she said, referencing the state's open carry law that allows people to carry firearms in public places. "This is a pro-life issue. The idolatry of guns is killing people." Her organization has focused on putting pressure on local political leaders in San Antonio and convening gatherings that give people venues to be heard. "It is our responsibility to shed light on those in power and there has to be an organized constituency that says your organized money will not win over us and our values," she said. This is very sacred work."

COPS/Metro organizes in thirty congregations in the predominantly Hispanic, low-income west and south side of San Antonio, where nearly one in three children grow up in poverty. Founded in 1974, it's the oldest Industrial Areas Foundation organization in the national network, and its success helped inspire the formation of congregational organizing throughout the West and Southwest. The late Patrick Flores, who became the first Mexican American archbishop in the United States when he was appointed to lead the San Antonio archdiocese, was a pioneering social justice bishop who as a child picked crops with his migrant farmworker parents. The activist-minded archbishop was a strong advocate for the organization. During a trip to Rome in 1974, he presented a COPS button to Pope Paul VI for a papal blessing. The organization puts considerable time and resources into breaking down racial and class barriers that divide many people across San Antonio. "If we want to be the body of Christ as a church that means we need to be in relationship with each other," Paul told me.

> North side parishes often have no clue about the lives of those on the south side. We take congregational development seriously. The training we're doing is with parish teams from the entire archdiocese so we're creating conversations and encounters across different parishes

and neighborhoods in the city. Organizing at its best puts people in relationships so there is a mutual conversion. Our work extends far beyond the four walls of the parish and that was the vision of Vatican II.

Over the past fifty years, COPS has helped raise wages for workers, worked to expand access to quality health care, and been a national leader in advocating for immigrant rights. In 2022 Paul and her fellow organizers played a key role in rallying voter support for a $1.2 billion municipal bond referendum that for the first time in San Antonio history dedicated $150 million toward affordable housing. COPS/Metro also works closely with Catholic bishops in Texas as part of a "Recognizing the Stranger" program funded by the US bishops' flagship social justice initiative, the Catholic Campaign for Human Development (CCCHD). The parish-based program identified, trained, and mentored immigrant leaders to build deeper connections with nonimmigrant communities. The program launched in 2016 in the Archdioceses of Los Angeles, Galveston-Houston, San Antonio, and the Dioceses of Las Vegas, Tucson, Dallas, and Brownsville. Four thousand people received organizing training during the five-year, $500,000 grant period that ended in 2023.[69] The potential of faith-based organizing is also evident in the way Catholic advocates can help clergy and other institutional leaders build a "listening church" that is informed by the experiences of those who are typically not heard in ecclesial or political halls of power. "We have been using synodality as organizers long before the pope called the Synod," Paul told me. "We have been doing this for fifty years. The way we organize is through synodality. We start where people are and we listen. When you hear someone's story and you hear their pain that becomes a part of you. We start from the bottom up. It is not sexy. It's not fast. But this is how you build the kingdom."

The US bishops' Catholic Campaign for Human Development (CCHD), a major funder of grassroots organizing that supports Paul's organization and others around the country, has long been a target of right-wing Catholic activists. As I documented in a 2010 report, "Be Not Afraid?: Guilt by Association, Catholic McCarthyism and Growing Threats to the U.S. Bishops' Anti-Poverty Mission,"—a report endorsed by nine retired bishops, including two former presidents of the US Conference of Catholic Bishops—the drumbeat to defund and delegitimize CCHD is a decades-old effort.[70] William Simon, a conservative Catholic and former Nixon administration treasury secretary, challenged the campaign in a 1989 letter to the Knights of Malta, an influential Catholic organization, calling it a "funding mechanism for radical left political activism." The late Fr. Richard John Neuhaus, editor of *First Things,* and other prominent conservative Catholic writers have at various times called for the bishops to eliminate the campaign. In more recent years the American Life League has targeted CCHD staff and pressured bishops to drop parish collections for the initiative. In contrast Pope Francis has praised faith-based grassroots organizers as "social poets" and views "popular movements" as essential to tapping into what he calls the "torrent of moral energy that springs from including the excluded in the building of common destiny."[71]

Pope Francis met with Josephine Lopez Paul and other COPS/Metro organizers who were part of a delegation of lay leaders, clergy, and professional organizers from the West/Southwest Industrial Areas Foundation invited to dialogue at his residence in 2022. During the ninety-minute conversation in Spanish, the organizers spoke about their work advocating for immigrants, fighting for living-wage jobs, and combating human trafficking. Pope Francis thanked the group for their persistence in confronting injustice and acknowledged the criticism they often face. "Surely, some call you communists or something similar," the pope told the group, according to Joe Rubio, the national codirector of the Industrial Areas Foundation West/Southwest Region, who attended the meeting and wrote about the gathering afterward.[72] "But when you read the standards by which we will be judged, these are the things: I was hungry and you gave me to eat, I was thirsty and you gave me drink, I was in prison and you visited me, I was sick and you cured me. This is the way." For Josephine Lopez Paul, the meeting with Pope Francis was a powerful validation. "There are days when you wonder why you are doing this work," Paul said as she fought back tears. "Organizers are sometimes viewed as the enemy by some people in the church, but to have the pope tell us that our work is what concrete love looks like was really incredible. He told us the church needs our work more than ever." Richard Wood, a sociologist who writes about faith-based organizing and has advised the bishops' Catholic Campaign for Human Development, agrees. He points to the clergy abuse crisis and the capture of segments of the American church by a sectarian Catholicism aligned with partisan interests as devastating forces that have left the church in need of authentic bottom-up renewal.

"Faith-based organizing offers a critical route for reclaiming Catholicism's public voice and moral authority," said Wood, president of the Institute for Advanced Catholic Studies at the University of Southern California, and author of *A Shared Future: Faith-Based Organizing for Racial Equity and Ethical Democracy*. "Rather than waiting for the church's hierarchy to define the public agenda, this is an expression of Catholics working together to really embody the church's rich ethical and moral teachings. Faith-based organizing is an extraordinary instrument for carrying the church's ideals and values into the world."[73] Wood sees both challenges and opportunities. Effective faith-based organizing should be woven into the fabric of parish life in ways that connect liturgy, catechetical teaching, and advocacy as an integrated framework. As more Catholics continue to drift away from the institutional church, deep connections with parish life are less frequent today. "Pastors and religious leaders have to articulate a vision of the church that isn't narrowly internal," Woods told me. "The Catholic faith is an incarnational faith that is embodied in the world. That is not preached very often or very well, and if we are not doing that it's hard for faith-based organizing to thrive." He notes that unlike a past generation of clergy who often came from working-class backgrounds and are steeped in labor and social justice activism, younger priests today are more rooted in expressions of personal piety and acts of charity than a commitment to organizing work that addresses structural injustice. Wood adds that traditional or conservative Catholic institutions have often done a better job of cultivating thick Catholic identity than more progressive Catholic networks. To fill that gap, Woods says that prayer groups, spiritual retreats, and liturgy should make more explicit connections between faith and justice. This requires educating clergy and lay leaders who teach the faith to see spiritual formation and justice formation as linked. Any expansion and scaling up of Catholic organizing will require training a new generation of leaders, institutionalizing justice advocacy more fully into the life of the church, and putting financial resources into these efforts. Successful social movements throughout history were often catalyzed by dramatic public events and prophetic actions that capture the public's imagination, but infrastructure and institutions are critical to sustainability. Rosa Parks didn't spontaneously ignite the Montgomery bus boycott. However courageous her personal action was on December 1, 1955, Parks had been trained for that moment at the Highlander Folk School, an interracial training center for labor and civil rights activists in Tennessee. The Southern Christian Leadership Conference tapped into the institutional and moral power of the Black church to provide a structure for the civil rights movement.

The US bishops' Catholic Campaign for Human Development, historically one of the most important funders for grassroots organizing across the country, should not only be defended and protected from right-wing pressure campaigns but provided the resources and prioritization to grow into a new era. As the Catholic Church grapples with questions of racial justice in particular, faith-based organizing provides a model for how to advocate on the peripheries, center the experiences of people of color, and build multiracial coalitions that can deepen solidarity across racial and class lines. "A lot of faith-based organizing is led by Black women," Wood said. "The church can learn from this dynamism."

ENVIRONMENTAL RACISM AND THE CLIMATE CRISIS

Sharon Lavigne never set out to become an activist or community organizer. The seventy-two-year-old retired teacher and grandmother wanted a quiet life on the flat stretches of Louisiana land her ancestors have lived on for generations. But the poison-spewing industries kept coming, and people kept dying. The industrial corridor between New Orleans and Baton Rouge, often called "Cancer Alley," is filled with more than 150 oil refineries and petrochemical plants. Cancer rates in the region are seven hundred times greater than the rest of the country. The *New Orleans Times-Picayune* and the investigative news outlet ProPublica released a 2019 report that described the corridor as "the largest hotspot of cancer-causing air in the country," noting that "predominantly Black and low-income communities are acutely affected."[74] A Black Catholic, Lavigne was baptized in St. James Church, a faith community that dates back 250 years. The church stands close to the Mississippi River. She has spent her life in St. James Parish, where there are more than thirty polluting plants concentrated in areas where most residents are Black and low-income. Lavigne founded Rise St. James, a faith-based organizing group that receives funding from the US bishops' Catholic Campaign for Human Development in the Diocese of Baton Rouge, after a 2018 meeting with a handful of residents in her house. The group began strategizing to stop a proposed $1.2 billion Chinese plastics manufacturing facility that would be built less than two miles from her home. "I was told you don't fight against this industry," said Lavigne, who has lost friends and family to cancer, including two people from the original group that first met in her house to plan a response. "If it wasn't for my faith, I wouldn't be doing this."[75]

In *Laudato Si'* Pope Francis highlights the reality that Lavigne and her community face every day. "Exposure to atmospheric pollutants produces a broad spectrum of health hazards, especially for the poor, and causes millions of premature deaths," he wrote.[76] Lavigne and members of Rise St. James, an organization led by Black women of faith, spoke out at town hall meetings and parish council events, organized marches, and partnered with other environmental justice organizations to build a campaign highlighting the damage another toxic plant in the area would cause to residents' health and the environment. Wanhua Chemical backed down and withdrew its land use application in 2019. Rise St. James also helped defeat a $2.2 billion development of land in the area owned by South Louisiana Methanol. Lavinge won the Goldman Environmental Prize, nicknamed "the Green Nobel," in 2021 and a year later was awarded the Laetare Medal, the oldest and most prestigious honor given to American Catholics. Lavigne was invited to the White House in the spring of 2023 to watch President Biden sign an executive order creating a White House Office of Environmental Justice. She invited the president to visit St. James Parish, where she told him "we have 12 industries within a 10-mile radius."[77]

Despite Rise St. James's success in stopping new petrochemical plants and Lavigne's growing national profile, the struggle for cleaner, healthier communities in her hometown is ongoing. Formosa Plastics, a Taiwanese company with a history of facing lawsuits and fines from the Environmental Protection Agency, began planning a $9.4 billion chemical plant near Lavigne's home. Formosa has been designated a "serial offender of environmental and human rights" by the Center for International Environmental Law. "This is a pro-life issue for us," Lavigne told me. "We want to live." She would like to see more commitment from the Catholic hierarchy. "Bishops speak out against abortion. Abortion kills a baby. Well, these industries are killing us!" she said. Since Pope Francis issued *Laudato Si'* nearly a decade ago, most US bishops have failed to prioritize environmental justice, according to a 2021 study from researchers at Creighton University, a Catholic, Jesuit university in Omaha, Nebraska. The report, published in *Environmental Research Letters*, was based on analysis of more than 12,000 official, written communications to parishioners by US bishops in the form of bishops' columns in diocesan newspapers over a five-year period.[78] Of these columns only ninety-three even mentioned climate change at all and even fewer (fifty-six) described climate change in terms that suggest it is real or currently happening. "The findings were stunning," Daniel DiLeo, an associate professor of theology at Creighton University who helped lead the research team, told me. "Bishops have a responsibility to teach the fullness of the faith and that includes climate justice. This is about fidelity to the church's own teachings."[79] As far back as 1990, DiLeo notes, Pope John Paul II warned that the "greenhouse effect has now reached crisis proportions," as the pope described it in his 1990 World Day of Peace message. Another indication of the lackluster reception given to *Laudato Si'* from American bishops is the fact that as of 2024 only one diocese (San Diego) has divested its financial portfolio holdings from fossil fuel companies. In contrast, Pope Francis in 2020 committed the Vatican to net zero carbon emissions by 2050. "Francis has called for specific and concrete action to decarbonize," DiLeo said. "It's not good enough to host a reading group or include a prayer of petition in Mass. It's necessary, but it's not sufficient." Catholic higher education is showing more leadership. DiLeo's own institution, Creighton University, announced in 2021 that it would phase out all investments in fossil fuels from its $587 million endowment within the next ten years and focus on new investments in sustainable energy.[80] In making that decision, the university cited a Vatican document on implementing *Laudato Si'*, which encourages Catholic institutions to "promote responsible investments in social and environmental sectors, for example by evaluating progressive disinvestment from the fossil-fuel sector." Along with Creighton, three other Catholic schools in the United States—the University of Dayton, Seattle University, and Georgetown University—have publicly committed to divesting their endowments from fossil fuels.

Sharon Lavigne views racial justice and climate justice as part of the same struggle. "The industry targets poor, Black communities," Lavigne said. "This is where they dump the poison. It's environmental racism. We used to have slaves and plantations here. Now we're still fighting for our lives. These industries are killing us. They buy out some white residents and those who have money. The poor people are still here and can't get out. It's a type of genocide."[81] History weighs heavy over these conversations. The historical thread connecting slavery, Jim Crow, and the current racism experienced by Black people in St. James Parish today is well documented in a 2023 federal lawsuit filed by Rise St. James, Inclusive Louisiana, and the Mount Triumph Baptist Church. The lawsuit, which names St. James Parish, St. James Parish Council, and the St. James Parish Planning Commission as defendants, sought a moratorium on the construction of new plants and protection of unmarked cemeteries of people once enslaved in the Parish. The Center for Constitutional Rights and Tulane University Law School collaborated with the community groups to file the lawsuit, which aimed to "remediate the ongoing effects of the Parish's environmental racism." "As a result of the vestiges of the slavery in Louisiana and in St. James in particular, plaintiffs' members reside in some of the most polluted, toxic—and lethal—census tracts in the country," the lawsuit stated. "The Defendants, obviously mindful of this historically segregated land distribution, have intentionally chosen to locate over a dozen enormous industrial facilities in the majority Black 4th and 5th Districts."[82] Lavigne is angry and wants accountability. But her voice also softens as she envisions a better future. "I want to breathe clean air, drink clean water, plant a garden again and play with my grandkids," she told me. "To love a community is to find ways to heal a community."

RESTORATIVE JUSTICE: A POWERFUL TOOL FOR REPAIR AND HEALING

Catholic leaders are increasingly turning to restorative justice to confront historic systems of oppression and heal institutional and individual wounds caused by racism, the trauma of clergy sexual abuse, and violence in communities. Rooted in Native American Indigenous practices, restorative justice uses storytelling, lament, and ritual to bring those who have been harmed and those who caused harm into a shared sacred space. In contrast to criminal justice models that are guided by a utilitarian view of individual punishment, restorative justice is anchored in communitarian values that resonate with traditional Catholic teaching and core Christian principles of atonement, reconciliation, and repair.

Fr. David Kelly moved to the Back of the Yards and Englewood neighborhoods of Chicago more than twenty years ago with a few other priests. Churches were closing across the city. The group of priests from the Missionaries of the Precious Blood didn't have a church or a parish, but they did have a vision for how to minister in a place where poverty, violence, and prison are routine parts of life for many residents. Catholics need to move out from the confines of walls enclosing a church and "enter the wounded spaces," as Kelly described it to me.[83] The priests spent two years getting to know and learning from their neighbors. Once populated by Irish, German, and other European immigrants who worked in the massive stockyards, the neighborhoods began changing in the 1940s as the Great Migration from the South brought waves of Black families to Chicago. Decades of underinvestment, racist housing policies such as restrictive covenants that excluded Black people from owning homes near middle-class white families, and mass incarceration fueled by lengthy prison sentences handed down during the war on drugs had devastated communities. Tensions between Black and Latino communities grew. Gang violence escalated. Fr. Kelly cofounded the Precious Blood Ministry of Reconciliation in 2004. "The idea was to work with and accompany young people impacted by violence, incarceration and structural inequity," Kelly explained. "The core of what we really see here is trauma."

The priest knew from prior ministry work in juvenile detention centers that the criminal justice system often exacerbates inequality, fails to restore grieving families, and leaves deeper pain unaddressed. "I would go to court and someone I knew very well would be sentenced to prison for decades and I would also know the person who got shot," Kelly recalled. "It was adversarial and cold. I always felt guilty because I struggled to embrace both the victim and the perpetrator. I said we can do better." His center began using "Restorative Justice Hubs" as a way to reduce youth violence, lower admissions into juvenile courts, and help youth, families, and communities heal. A common technique in restorative justice is a peacemaking circle where no individual sits above or below another person. The structure of the circle is intentionally designed to foster open communication and listening. "When I first started learning about restorative justice and the role of bringing ritual, storytelling and sacred objects into these circles, it felt very Catholic," Kelly said. "Restorative justice focuses on relationships. Before you get to the issues, first you talk about who is in that space. It humanizes people. You become empathetic when you hear about the harm you have caused, but you also learn that you are not the worst thing you have done." Fr. Kelly recalls conducting restorative justice sessions with a group of mothers whose children had been murdered. The mothers knew the priest also hosted restorative justice circles in prison. They couldn't understand why he would do this for convicted criminals. "I would invite them to come with me but they always resisted," he said. "But eventually they came. These were young people who had been sentenced as adults. You could see the mothers were guarded, but as the kids started to tell their stories the mothers began to lean in and listen. They could see these kids were not just thugs. The mothers kept coming back. It became such a powerful relationship. The mothers would even cook for them and celebrate their birthday. This work is about healing and community building."

Fr. Kelly's reconciliation ministry has grown over the years to thirty-five full-time staff, some of whom were previously incarcerated or lost a loved one to violence. Along with a prison ministry that provides spiritual care and accompaniment for people who are incarcerated, the center has comprehensive services for juveniles and adults who are released from prison, including help with job-skills training and housing. One of the ministry's loftier goals is to change the fundamental nature of the criminal justice system. Fr. Kelly has led restorative justice training for judges, and the practice is slowly making inroads in some cases where alternatives to incarceration can be mediated. The reconciliation ministry is also trying to develop alternatives to aggressive policing in predominantly Black and Latino communities. The priest knows that reforming big institutions and systems often requires reimaging the status quo. He sees similar opportunities and challenges for the Catholic Church, another institution that has over history both resisted change and shown the capacity to renew its mission. "The church grew in the United States because people saw needs and they responded creatively," he said. "So we get Catholic schools and hospitals and all of these incredible institutions. The church always needs to renew and grow. We can't just say 'this is how we've always done it.'"

Krisanne Vaillancourt Murphy, who has worked with Fr. Kelly over the years, views restorative justice as a hopeful pathway for renewal and healing in society and the church. The executive director of Catholic Mobilizing Network, Murphy partners with Catholics across the country to end the death penalty, transform the criminal justice system, and build the capacity of church leaders to use restorative justice practices. When I visited her in the network's Washington, DC, office in 2023, located across the street from Catholic University and next to the US bishops' conference, Murphy was in a reflective mood as she talked about what it means to lead a Catholic organization in the United States at a time of polarization in the church and politics. A few days earlier, the Attorney General of Maryland released a report detailing decades of sexual abuse by clergy within the Archdiocese of Baltimore that found over six hundred young people had suffered sexual abuse and "physical torture" by more than 150 clergy over six decades. "When you have the word Catholic in the name of your organization, you take a lot of heat for the sex abuse scandals and other abuses in the church," Murphy said. "Being women and lay-led as an organization, we are really working as a bridge in a wounded Catholic environment. This work isn't for everyone. But we have a decided positionality, which is to be inside the church and trying to heal and reform the church."[84] Murphy understands why so many people, especially young people and women, are often reluctant to have strong attachments to Catholic institutions. "The church has a lot of work to do around paternalism and polarization, its treatment of women, and valuing and learning from the laity," she said. "We are helping the church understand its role in restorative justice and in transformation." Murphy believes that the restorative justice practices of encounter, listening, and learning from those on the peripheries can also enrich Pope Francis's call for a more synodal church. "We're in a discernment period as a church and restorative justice has a lot to contribute to this process of synodal journeying," she said.

As a child growing up in a working-class family, Murphy would eagerly flip through the pages of her parents' *Maryknoll* magazines. The idea of a "church on mission" engaged with questions of justice and peace around the world always intrigued her. In her twenties she worked for a faith-based domestic service program advocating for and living alongside migrant farmworkers in Oregon. While at the Latin American Working Group, Murphy traveled throughout Central America in the 1990s meeting Catholic sisters and priests who awed her with their commitment to a theology of liberation in the face of poverty and violence. "I was captivated by Catholic social teaching, and I saw its witness through the church women who were killed in El Salvador, through the Jesuits, through Archbishop Romero," she said. "I understood the importance of grassroots organizing and addressing the root causes of injustice." The first time she watched the movie *Dead Man Walking*, which depicts the real-life story of Sister Helen Prejean accompanying a man to his execution on death row, she was captivated and knew if she ever had the opportunity to work on the issue, she would. Decades later, after earning her master's degree in theology and working for faith-based advocacy organizations in Washington, DC, focused on issues of hunger and global poverty, she found herself moved to tears by Pope Francis calling for an end to the death penalty during his 2015 speech before the US Congress. Two years later she was invited by Catholic Mobilizing Network's founder, Karen Clifton, to lead the organization. Clifton had worked closely with Sister Helen Prejean to start CMN (initially as a project of Prejean's religious community, the Congregation of St. Joseph). The Catholic Mobilizing Network is independent of the US bishops' conference but works closely with bishops around the country to end the death penalty and has a grassroots list of more than 50,000 Catholics it activates to drive letter and email campaigns to stop executions.

For Murphy, her work to end the death penalty and mass incarceration is rooted in a pro-life Catholic ethic, a belief in what she calls "the expansive range" of life issues. "The church is at our strongest when our commitment to life is consistent," she said. "Our tradition upholds the sanctity and interconnectedness of all human life. No current political party and few politicians adhere to a whole life or consistent ethic of life policy platform." When Donald Trump's Attorney General William Barr was scheduled to receive an award from the National Catholic Prayer Breakfast honoring him as a Catholic who serves the church—an accolade given only hours after authorizing the federal government's execution of William LeCroy—Murphy didn't shy away from responding. The prayer breakfast, she said in 2020, had "become a twisted halftime show between executions, and could mislead the public to believe the Catholic Church somehow condones the death penalty."[85] The church, Murphy added, "is unequivocal in its opposition to capital punishment because it is a violation of the dignity of the human person. The fact that Mr. Barr has led the federal government's relentless push to resume executions should preclude him from receiving any award said to honor 'those who serve the Church so well.'" In the weeks leading up to the breakfast, more than six thousand people signed the network's "National Catholic Petition against Federal Executions."

As part of its restorative justice advocacy, the Catholic Mobilizing Network also educates Catholics about how institutional racism in the criminal justice system has led to mass incarceration and death row populations that are disproportionately Black and Latino. Following the 2019 release of *Just Mercy,* the award-winning film that explores the role of racism on Alabama's death row, the network created a study guide that was ordered by more than 10,000 Catholics and hosted a webinar viewed by eight hundred church leaders. CMN organizes annual Lenten pilgrimages to Montgomery, Alabama, that provide Catholic ministry leaders from around the country with an immersion experience that explores the relationship between the nation's past and modern-day systems of oppression, particularly related to the criminal legal system.

Since 2022 participants from Catholic Relief Services, the Jesuit Conference, the Franciscan Mission Service, Network Lobby for Catholic Social Justice, the Society of St. Vincent de Paul, the US bishops' conference, the National Black Catholic Sisters Conference, and other Catholic organizations have explored the Equal Justice Initiative's *Legacy Museum: From Enslavement to Mass Incarceration.* Participants have also visited the initiative's National Memorial for Peace and Justice, which honors the more than four thousand Black people killed by lynching from 1877 to 1950. During the pilgrimages Catholic leaders have walked across the Edmund Pettus Bridge in Selma, Alabama, where freedom marchers were brutally beaten by police; met with civil rights activists; prayed the Stations of the Cross at historic sites in Alabama; and gathered in restorative justice peacemaking circles to reflect on ways to prioritize antiracism advocacy in their ministries. The trips are often intentionally timed during Lent, a liturgical season of reflection and repentance. CMN also organizes a biannual National Catholic Conference on Restorative Justice that brings together Catholic ministry leaders, academic and legal professionals, restorative justice practitioners, and directly impacted people for workshops and dialogue that often include racial justice. "Anti-racism work requires both learning and unlearning, listening and speaking up, confronting the harms of the past and present while creating a better future," Murphy said.

CONFRONTING CATHOLIC HISTORY: THE SINS OF SLAVERY AND WHITE SUPREMACY

Sr. Anita Baird stood before an audience of nearly all white Catholic sisters and began to speak hard truths. "In all of my life, I had never been confronted with such raw racism as I was working for the church," Baird told a group of women religious from the Sisters of Notre Dame USA and the

Ursuline Sisters of Cleveland who gathered in the spring of 2023 for an event on racism in the church and religious life at the Notre Dame Center in Chardon, Ohio. At seventy-six years old, Baird has a long view. She worked for thirty years in the corporate world. In 1997 she became the first Black person to serve as chief of staff to the archbishop of Chicago, the late Cardinal Francis George. That same year, three white teenagers, two from a Chicago Catholic high school and one a recent graduate, beat a Black 13-year-old unconscious. The incident drew national media attention and provoked soul searching in the archdiocese. In 2000 Cardinal George appointed Baird to be the founding director of the archdiocese's Office for Racial Justice, where along with a small team she led workshops and trainings for church agencies, departments, schools, and more than three hundred parishes. "It was a hard struggle, and I found the most resistance, believe it or not, from Catholic school teachers," Baird told the assembled sisters. "Their lack of education struck me. I realized as a nation we have failed to teach the truth about the founding of this country, and the impact it has had on people of color, beginning with our Indigenous brothers and sisters and those brought over in bondage from Africa." Only two months before the gathering, she noted in her speech, the Vatican officially repudiated the "Doctrine of Discovery." A series of papal "bulls," or decrees, developed in the fifteenth century effectively gave sanction to centuries of violent colonial subjugation of land and people. "Dum Diversas," a bull issued by Pope Nicholas V in 1452, explicitly granted Portuguese authorities the blessing of the church in reducing non-Christians to "perpetual slavery."[86] Because the history of the Catholic Church is so closely entwined with the sins of slavery and white supremacy, Baird argued, Catholics have an obligation to not only acknowledge that shameful history but also take action to address how the legacy of enslavement and segregation continues to impact our church and society. "Our history has taught us that slavery began in 1619, but it began with the Catholic Church," she told the sisters. "This is our work because we began this and we did it in the name of Christ, we did it in the name of the gospel, and it's our work to change it. It's our work to make reparations for it. To be pro-life, we have to address the issue of racism. As some religious congregations struggle to come to terms with their shameful history of owning and selling human beings during slavery, the majority of our religious communities in this country, while not having owned slaves, have practiced racism and segregation in their acceptance policies and in the operations of their sponsored institutions. Our congregations have to own that truth, acknowledge it, and repent for it, and we have to be reconciled not only through our words but our actions."

Georgetown University and Catholic Sisters Excavate the Past, Look to the Future

On an April morning in 2017, two days after Easter, Fr. Timothy Kesicki, SJ, then president of the Jesuit Conference of Canada and the United States, stood at a podium inside Georgetown University's ornate auditorium, Gaston Hall. His face was somber. A heavy silence filled the room. "Today the Society of Jesus, which helped to establish Georgetown University and whose leaders enslaved and mercilessly sold your ancestors, stands before you to say: We have greatly sinned, in our thoughts and in our words, in what we have done and in what we have failed to do."[87] The emotional public service, formally entitled a "Liturgy of Remembrance, Contrition, and Hope," brought together descendants of the men, women, and children the Maryland Jesuits enslaved and later sold in 1838 to pay off debts and keep the nation's first Catholic university financially viable. It was one of the largest sales of enslaved people recorded at the time, raising about $3.3 million in today's dollars. "When we remember that together with those 272 souls we received the same sacraments; read the same Scriptures; said the same prayers; sang the same hymns; and praised the same God; how did we, the Society of Jesus, fail to see us all as one body in Christ? We betrayed the very name of Jesus for whom our least Society is named."

Sandra Green Thomas, a descendant of one of the enslaved people sold by the Jesuits, honored the suffering and faith of those who were held in bondage. "Their pain was unparalleled," she said at the liturgy. "Their pain is still here. Penance is very important. Penance is required when you have violated God's law. The ability to transcend the realities of this life in this country has been a necessary tool in the survival kit of my people. For the 272, I believe that their Catholic faith enabled them to transcend. No matter how incongruous their existence was with the gospel of God's love and protection, they clung to their faith."[88]

Student activists at Georgetown played a key role in pushing university officials to grapple with the institution's painful history. Protests and sit-ins on campus in 2015 attracted media attention and gave urgency to the administration's fledgling efforts that began to take shape with President John DeGioia's convening of a Working Group on Slavery, Memory, and Reconciliation. The university removed the names of the Rev. Thomas Mulledy and Rev. William McSherry, Jesuits involved in the 1838 sale, from two campus buildings. Georgetown later renamed them for Isaac Hawkins, the first enslaved person listed in the 1838 sale document, and Anne Becraft Hall, a free woman of color who established a school in the town of Georgetown for

Black girls. A detailed public airing of the university's history with the slave trade landed on the front page of *The New York Times* in the spring of 2016. Under the headline, "272 Slaves Were Sold to Save Georgetown. What Does It Owe Their Descendants?," the article began with a chilling description. "The human cargo was loaded on ships at a bustling wharf in the nation's capital, destined for the plantations of the Deep South. Some slaves pleaded for rosaries as they were rounded up, praying for deliverance. But on this day, in the fall of 1838, no one was spared: not the 2-month-old baby and her mother, not the field hands, not the shoemaker and not Cornelius Hawkins, who was about 13 years old when he was forced onboard."[89] The high-profile article, written by Rachel Swarns, gave Georgetown's story international visibility at a time when the Black Lives Matter movement and broader calls for racial justice across the country were gaining more attention after the 2014 police killing of Michael Brown in Ferguson, Missouri. Swarns later turned her reporting about the Jesuits and Georgetown into a more comprehensive examination of the role slavery played in the expansion of the Catholic Church in the United States. "The priests in Maryland, who relied on the proceeds derived from slave labor and slavery built the nation's first Catholic college, the first archdiocese, and the first Catholic cathedral and helped establish two of the earliest Catholic monasteries," Swarns writes in *The 272: The Families Who Were Enslaved and Sold to Build the American Catholic Church.*[90] Profits from the selling of enslaved people not only helped Georgetown University but enabled Jesuits to establish other universities across the country. There are now twenty-seven Jesuit colleges and universities in the United States. "Without the enslaved," Swarns writes, "the Catholic Church in the United States, as we know it today, would not exist."

Adam Rothman, a history professor at Georgetown who served on the university's working group on slavery, describes the school's past as "a microcosm of the history of American slavery."[91] The spotlight on the university has helped provoke a long-delayed reckoning with uncomfortable truths. "The history of Georgetown and slavery was not a secret and some academics had been writing about it for a long time, but the real revelation was how few people really knew about all of this," said Rothman, who curates the Georgetown Slavery Archive and is coeditor of *Facing Georgetown's History: A Reader on Slavery, Memory and Reconciliation*. "That was a huge failure on the part of people like me who teach history, but we also saw it as an opportunity to do better." The university's Catholic identity is central to why Georgetown's story has drawn so much attention. While the University of Virginia, Brown University, and Harvard University have also examined their connections to slavery, Georgetown was the first Catholic university to do so and the first university with an enduring religious identity to grapple with this history. "That mattered a lot and why this case has been so important and compelling to a lot of people," Rothman told me. "Our institution's entanglement with slavery was so deep and involved Catholicism in some of the most troubling ways. So it was not just a question about history, but it was a question about Christianity." He pointed to the 2017 liturgy of remembrance at Georgetown, which involved prayer and religious atonement from Jesuit leaders, as an example of how powerful it can be to draw from a faith tradition. "Georgetown and the Jesuits have a language of religion and morality not available to more secular institutions wrestling with this history," he added. "Catholic rituals have been a part of the process of reconciliation."

Another important feature of Georgetown's reckoning with history, Rothman noted, is the role students continue to play. "One of the great things we've seen over the years with this work has been the persistent student engagement," said Rothman, who in 2023 was named founding director of the university's Center for the Study of Slavery and Its Legacies. "There has been an unwavering core of students who are interested in this history. The energy of students is constantly pushing the university to be accountable." What constitutes true accountability remains a fraught question. Disagreements between students and administrators, along with periods of tension between descendants and Georgetown leadership over reparations, have been part of a halting path forward. The university announced in 2016 that descendants of enslaved people owned by the Maryland Province of Jesuits would receive "preferential admission consideration" that "would be similar to the care and attention given to applicants who are descendants of faculty, staff or alumni."[92] In 2019 student activists frustrated with what they perceived as the university's slow response to taking concrete action, voted for a student fee that would raise $400,000 for a nonprofit led by a board of students and descendants that would donate to charitable causes benefiting descendants of the enslaved people sold by the university. Georgetown leadership agreed to raise the money through fundraising rather than from student fees. The Reconciliation Fund was "one way the university is reckoning with the legacies of slavery that have shaped our past and to respond by advancing justice and equity in our present," Georgetown President John DeGioia said in announcing the fund. Georgetown awarded $200,000 to five inaugural recipients in 2023.[93] The projects funded, located in Maryland and Louisiana, were directed to engaging young adults in rebuilding blighted homes in New Orleans, providing free legal services for those with severe mental illness, connecting members of the descendant community, launching a high school tutoring program co-organized by a descendant and Georgetown community members, and providing educational programming for children.

In 2021 leaders of the Jesuit conference also committed to raise $100 million to benefit the descendants and to promote racial justice initiatives across the country. Historians and church officials described the promise as the most significant effort by the Catholic Church to address its culpability in the buying and selling of enslaved people. Bishop Shelton J. Fabre, then chairman of the US Conference of Catholic Bishops' Ad Hoc Committee Against Racism, described the plan as the church's "largest financial commitment" to "heal the wounds" caused by its participation in slavery.[94] "This is an opportunity for Jesuits to begin a very serious process of truth and reconciliation," Fr. Timothy Kesicki, then president of the Jesuit Conference, said at the time. "Our shameful history of Jesuit slaveholding in the United States has been taken off the dusty shelf, and it can never be put back." Funds raised would be managed by a foundation established in partnership with a group of descendants and be distributed to organizations leading racial reconciliation projects and to support educational opportunities for descendants through grants and scholarships. The Jesuits made an initial $15 million investment. There are about five thousand living descendants of people enslaved by the Jesuits who have been identified by genealogists at the nonprofit Georgetown Memory Project, a private organization not affiliated with the university. When the Georgetown funding plan was announced, some representatives from the descendant community involved with the negotiations worried the effort would fall short and expressed concern that not enough input had been given by the wider descendant community. A year and a half after the plan's rollout, only about $180,000 had been raised. Descendants spoke out publicly expressing their frustration. "It is becoming obvious to all who look beyond words that Jesuits are not delivering in deed," Joseph Stewart, president and chair of the Descendants Truth and Reconciliation Foundation, wrote in a letter to Fr. Arturo Sosa, the Jesuit superior general in Rome. "The bottom line is without your engagement, this partnership seems destined to fail."[95]

Cheryllyn Branch's great grandfather was one of the 272 enslaved people sold by Georgetown. An infant at the time, Basil Ford was sold from St. Inigoes, the first plantation purchased by the Jesuits in Maryland, where enslaved Africans were forced to work the three thousand acres of land to produce tobacco crops, corn, wheat, apples, and peaches. Branch has visited the old plantation and told me she still gets chills thinking about her family's proximity to such an evil institution. "Slavery was not that long ago," the seventh-generation Catholic said. "These vestiges are with us in so many ways today."[96] The retired principal of Xavier University Prep, now St. Katharine Drexel Prep in New Orleans, Branch is past president of the GU272 Descendants Association, a group representing living and deceased descendants of the enslaved people sold by the Jesuits in 1838. She recalled following news reports about Georgetown University's history with slavery but was shocked when Richard Cellini, who founded the Georgetown Memory Project to track down descendants, called her in 2016. "He asked me if I was sitting down," Branch said. "It really has been a kind of spiritual awakening. I was rediscovering my roots and rediscovering who I am." Branch grew up watching her grandmother, a devout Catholic, attend Mass and pray the rosary every day. Her Catholic faith sustains her even as Branch acknowledges that she is sometimes frustrated that Georgetown and the Jesuits have not moved more quickly to grow from sincere expressions of repentance to concrete action. "There would be no Georgetown without what they did to African Americans," she said. "The Jesuits owe a debt to society and communities they have harmed. What we want the Jesuits to do is find ways they can begin to make communities whole. And that is a tall task."

While many people slow down in their seventies, Branch is a whirlwind of energy. After retiring as a Catholic school principal, she went back to the classroom at a charter school. As an activist and educator working with many low-income Black residents of New Orleans for more than three decades, she knows that the legacy of slavery and segregation impact current racial inequality. Branch has teamed up with a fellow parishioner at St. Gabriel the Archangel, Sister Helen Prejean, author of *Dead Man Walking*, to oppose the death penalty and mass incarceration, which Branch describes as "an extension of slavery." Branch sees persistent barriers to equal justice, including the US Supreme Court's 2023 ruling against affirmative action in higher education and legislative efforts to ban the teaching of "critical race theory," as a failure to honestly acknowledge the role that racism has played and continues to play in American life. "Why are we afraid of the truth?" she asks. "If we don't begin with the truth, if we don't begin with ways to reconcile our past with a present, with going forward, then we will not heal."

As Georgetown University's history became front-page news, the Society of the Sacred Heart of the United States and Canada Province—part of an international congregation of Catholic women religious founded in France—began to confront its own past involvement in slavery. "In spite of my repugnance for having Negro slaves, we may be obliged to purchase some," Rose Philippine Duchesne, who established the society in the United States, wrote in 1882.[97] A year later the Sacred Heart nuns in Grand Coteau, Louisiana, purchased their first person, an enslaved man named Frank Hawkins, for $550. Until the close of the Civil War in 1865, the Religious of the Sacred Heart (as members of the Society are called) owned 150 enslaved people in Louisiana, Missouri, and Kansas. This forced labor was used to build Catholic schools and to provide skilled trades and agricultural work. While this history was known as early as 1957 to some inside the religious congregation, the national attention focused on Georgetown University became a catalyst for the Society to publicly acknowledge its past. In 2016 as the Society prepared to celebrate its bicentennial in the United States, leaders launched a Committee on Slavery, Accountability and Reconciliation. "We sought to engage in deeper research with a view to telling the fuller story," said Carolyn Osiek, a sister who chaired the committee and is the provincial archivist for the Society. "We knew that this would mean both confronting a painful part of our legacy and committing to truth, healing and reconciliation for a better future."[98] Osiek spent months pouring over old handwritten documents, including five carefully labeled files identified as "slave records," as she compiled the research. The largest number of enslaved people owned by the Society were in Grand Coteau, Louisiana. Because the enslaved were baptized, married, and received other sacraments in the church, Osiek and a few other researchers cross-referenced sacramental records with house journals and financial records. A family tree was posted on Ancestry.com to help connect with possible descendants of the enslaved. Osiek acknowledged that publicly confronting such a horrific past was not easy for her and many of the predominantly white members of the Society. "I really had to go through a tough conversion to realize that bringing this history out in the open is a healing process, especially for African Americans," she said. "A lot of whites recoil and are afraid to look at this truth, but it has to be done. That is something I learned to understand. You think that the past is buried but it isn't."

The Society of Sacred Heart hosted an emotional ceremony on a Sunday in late September of 2018 that brought together about fifty descendants of those enslaved in Grand Coteau. Sheila Hammond, the provincial of the Society, stood near the altar inside St. Charles Borromeo Church and apologized for the "grievous evil and sin" that had caused "great suffering and harm for your ancestors and their children."[99] She acknowledged what had never been spoken out loud. "We recognize we would not be here today without the forced labor of your ancestors. As you and we gather to honor them, we Religious of the Sacred Heart are working to uncover our complicity in structural racism and to strengthen our commitment to counter the residual evils of slavery that continue to harm and deform far too many, especially the young." From the church, descendants and others who had gathered for the "We Speak Your Names" ceremony walked in a slow procession led by the steady beat of African drumming through a grove of southern oak trees to a new monument inscribed with the names of those enslaved who died at Grand Coteau and were buried in unmarked graves. The monument was blessed in the parish cemetery. Names of the known enslaved were read aloud. Descendants placed white roses on the monument and carried home soil from the land in glass jars.

Irma Dillard, who helped plan the ceremony with the descendants, is one of only two Black sisters in the Society of the Sacred Heart. The seventy-one-year-old has spent countless hours digging through the Grand Coteau records and meeting with ancestors. "If the Georgetown story didn't come out, we would have continued down this road of silent history," she told me. "This is difficult work because when you name racism, people feel they are being told they are bad. There is a lot of shame and guilt. Our church has erased and hidden so much of our history."[100] Dillard entered the Society in California when she was twenty-one and came of age as a young woman during the heady ferment of protest movements in the 1960s. For a time, she wore a dashiki and volunteered with breakfast programs run by the Black Panthers. She marched against the Vietnam War. In those early years after the Second Vatican Council, women religious were emerging from cloistered life. Nuns were getting arrested alongside Cesar Chavez and farm workers were organizing for better wages. Many sisters moved into low-income communities to put their faith into action. "It was a multiracial, multicultural movement for justice," Dillard recalls. The first time she traveled to the East Coast in 1975 was a culture shock. Most of the sisters she met were white, and many were from privileged backgrounds. "The racism and classism were shocking to me," she said. "It was a different world. If you didn't come from a certain background or go to the right school, you were treated as second class citizens." When it came to race, Dillard said many white people in the Society brought a "white savior" mentality to their work in low-income communities of color. In some ways, she thinks, this paternalistic attitude still lingers in the church. She now travels to Sacred Heart schools around the country urging students and administrators to make the connection between slavery, segregation, and contemporary manifestations of racism. She also leads antiracism workshops and Zoom meetings for her fellow sisters. In 2018 the Society of the Sacred Heart created a scholarship for African American students to attend the Society's schools in Grand Coteau. There has been some professional development for faculty and staff, and efforts to develop course curriculum for students in Sacred Heart schools that focus on diversity, equity, and inclusion. While she is grateful the Society is finally confronting its past and beginning to take action, Dillard is frustrated the process took so long and wants to see more comprehensive efforts "It has been baby steps," Dillard said. "I've been fighting this fight a long time. I do get tired. Lip service is not enough. We need honest conversations, and we have to look at racism and white supremacy head on in terms of reparations. And we have to make connections between racial justice and justice for LGBTQ people and anything that is against the message of liberation in the Gospels."

Megan Wilson-Reitz is a lay leader in the Society of the Sacred Heart's racial justice work at the Stuart Center for Mission. After fifteen years at John Carroll University in Cleveland, where she was an adjunct theology professor with research expertise in economic and racial justice, Wilson-Reitz came to the Stuart Center in 2022 as the Society was trying to better institutionalize its professed commitment to addressing racism. "I did not have a relationship with the Society before this job but for folks who have grown up in the Sacred Heart family, learning about this history of slavery has been very spiritually unsettling," said Wilson-Reitz, who is white. "The women who founded our order are revered saints, but they are also responsible for this terrible history. What does that mean? It's a question we are grappling with."[101] During workshops she leads for women religious and with the broader Sacred Heart community, she often finds hesitancy and discomfort among white people to look back. At one gathering of more than one hundred people, including nuns, teachers, lay members, and alumni of Sacred Heart schools, the conversation stalled. "People really didn't want to talk about the past, they wanted to talk about what we are doing now," she said. "They want to talk about policy, education and voting rights. That's all important, but we had to really back up and say, 'there is some healing to do here.' We need collective lament."

The Society sponsors a network of more than a dozen Sacred Heart schools, most of them in white, high-income communities. Active alumni include wealthy families who are not accustomed to interrogating systemic injustice. "This is a highly educated and sometimes elite and privileged community so there is a tendency to talk about issues of race and racism in an intellectual way rather to engage our emotions and even our bodies in ways that confront what has been broken," she said. "To do racial justice in a meaningful way means grappling with what our whiteness means and that includes facing this history. It's hard work and messy. It can't be done through a press release." More recent conversations in the Society have started to include discussions about the congregation's history of running boarding schools for Indigenous children. Pope Francis issued a historic apology in 2022 for the Catholic Church's role in perpetuating myriad physical and spiritual abuses in Canada's residential schools for Native peoples. In 2024 the US bishops' conference issued a formal apology for the abuse and history of trauma inflicted on Native Americans in church-run boarding schools that sought to force the assimilation of Native children into American culture. "The language of restorative justice is so important in all of this work," Wilson-Reitz said. "Restorative justice says a relationship has been broken, harm has been done, and we have a collective responsibility to repair it. There is so much trauma in our church, whether it's our history with racism or clergy sexual abuse. We have to confront this trauma in a way that brings healing and reconciliation."

HEALING THE WOUNDS OF CLERGY SEXUAL ABUSE AND INSTITUTIONAL HARM

Fr. Daniel Griffith was new to his role as the point person for ensuring a safe environment in the Archdiocese of St. Paul and Minneapolis when, in his words, "things really imploded." In 2014 Minnesota Public Radio broke a news story that revealed Archbishop John Nienstedt had allegedly authorized secret payments to priests who had sexually abused children and did not report alleged sex crimes to police.[102] A wave of damning investigative media reports followed over the next two years. Archdiocesan officials struggled to keep up with the clergy abuse revelations. Priests encouraged the archbishop to step down, but he refused. "We had failed in a lot of ways to protect children and adults," Fr. Griffith told me. "We missed so many things. It all came crashing down."[103] He uses the parable of the Good Samaritan to illuminate the church's failures. "Historically, the church has been the inn that welcomes those abandoned by the side of the road, but in our response to victim-survivors we were the robber and the priest who walked away." Ramsey County Attorney John Choi filed criminal charges against the archdiocese for failing to protect children from an abusive priest. Ten days later, Archbishop Nienstedt resigned along with his auxiliary bishop. The archdiocese filed for bankruptcy. Years of abuse and coverup had left Catholics in the archdiocese angry and exhausted. From those ashes, something new began to grow. As part of a 2016 settlement with the archdiocese that included new protocols to prevent and respond to clergy abuse, the reform-minded county attorney implemented a restorative justice approach that was quickly embraced and later expanded under the new leadership of Archbishop Bernard Hebda. The Archdiocese of St. Paul and Minneapolis is now viewed as a national model for its success in using restorative justice practices to help abuse survivors, priests, and other Catholics heal from the wounds of sexual abuse and systemic leadership failures.

In the wake of the criminal charges against the archdiocese, several parishes participated in a restorative justice pilot program where survivors of clergy abuse were invited to share their stories. Fr. Griffith led the programs at Our Lady of Lourdes in Minneapolis, where he served as pastor at the time. People came together in healing circles, where they listened, wept, shouted, and began the long journey to healing. “What really allowed our diocese to integrate restorative justice into our response to clergy abuse was to have victim-survivors leading the way,” he said. “They bring wisdom and a resolute determination.” At the same time, the priest began a period of personal discernment, what he described as “a call within a call”—a vocational tug leading him to focus on restorative justice as a core part of his ministry. In 2019 Archbishop Hebda named Fr. Griffith to be the Archdiocese Liaison for Restorative Justice and Healing. He traveled to parishes around St. Paul and Minneapolis, where he led intimate and often emotional meetings not only with abuse survivors but with other Catholics who felt betrayed by the abuse scandals. Clergy who never abused children but suffered the peripheral wounds of being the public faces of an institution that covered up crimes and sins have also found restorative justice a powerful way to address what Griffith calls “secondary trauma.” The priest is now frequently invited to speak in dioceses and other Catholic settings around the country about lessons learned in St. Paul and Minneapolis. He recalls a winter night in West Virginia when more than eighty people showed up in a snowstorm for a listening session he helped lead after the disgraced former bishop of Wheeling-Charleston faced credible accusations that he sexually harassed adults under his authority and spent church funds on lavish home renovations, liquor, and travel. “People want the opportunity to name the harms that have been done,” said Griffith, who is pastor and rector of the Basilica of Saint Mary. “The dynamism between Catholic social teaching and restorative justice holds so much potential. Sometimes we miss how the centrality of restoration is so foundational to our faith. There are deep and vast wounds that need to be addressed. Restorative justice is an important way to approach healing.” The county prosecutor who filed criminal charges against the Archdiocese of St. Paul and Minneapolis now lauds the archdiocese for its success in implementing restorative justice. "Sometimes better outcomes can happen when you think out of the box," the Ramsey County Attorney John Choi said as he shared a stage with Archbishop Hebda and other top leaders in the archdiocese during a 2019 event focused on restorative justice at the University of St. Thomas law school in Minneapolis.[104]

While Catholic restorative justice leaders are still part of a relatively small, fledgling movement, interest is growing. Fr. Griffith has been in conversation with several bishops about ways to adopt restorative justice practices in their dioceses. In a speech at the Catholic Mobilizing Network's conference in 2020, Cardinal Robert McElroy of San Diego touted its potential. "Restorative justice is a more expansive and demanding notion of justice than procedural justice can ever hope to be," McElroy said. "The beauty of the ethic of restorative justice is precisely that it breaks through the false order of the justice system as it currently exists in our country, our church, and our institutional life."[105] Catholic universities, in particular, are uniquely positioned to convene dialogues, build networks, and offer practical opportunities to apply restorative justice principles. The University of St. Thomas School of Law launched an Initiative on Restorative Justice and Healing in 2021. Fr. Griffith was named the founding director. A lawyer before he became a priest, Griffith acknowledges many lawyers tend to be wary about restorative justice. "Lawyers tend to be risk averse and often don't see how effective it can be," he said. Through the initiative future lawyers will be given in-the-field experiences and education in concepts of justice that provide an alternative to traditional punitive systems. Beyond the education of law students, the initiative is more broadly focused on responding to harm caused by racial injustice, sexual abuse by clergy and other institutional failures within the Catholic Church, and polarization in the church. Fr. Griffith has led listening sessions and healing circles with Black Catholics talking about their experiences with racism as part of a national effort promoted by the US bishops' conference after the police killing of George Floyd. The priest thinks the church could make more specific connections between how its own institutional norms and history often prevent a more systemic response to racism and clergy abuse. "The link there is abuse of power and exclusion," he said. "We have a closed culture in the church. One of the things restorative justice can do in an intersectional way is name the harm of this culture. We need to be asking how our ecclesial culture exacerbated these harms and injustices." Restorative justice, he emphasized, should be part of a continuum that leads to "transformative justice," which includes accountability for those who have caused harm and lasting structural changes.

Fr. Griffith works closely with a small but growing national network of leaders promoting the use of restorative justice. The group includes clergy abuse survivors, priests, deacons, psychologists, a handful of bishops, and scholars at Catholic universities. Bishop Shawn McKnight of the Jefferson City diocese in Missouri serves as an advisor to the group, which has met for an annual consultation at the University of Notre Dame since 2021. At those meetings, victim-survivors share their stories with church leaders, and practitioners have reflected on lessons learned from nations such as South Africa, Rwanda, and Canada that have used restorative justice to confront the wounds of apartheid, genocide, civil wars, and the abuse of Indigenous people. Recommendations developed at the meetings, which have been sent to the US bishops' conference, include establishing a national center led by experts who can train a broad array of church leaders to use restorative justice practices and creating a national healing garden as a permanent site of healing, prayer, and accompaniment for victim-survivors of sexual abuse. The group is also advocating for trauma-informed training to be made available for clergy, seminarians, and lay leaders. "One cannot overestimate the damage of trust that has been done within the Catholic community," Stephen J. Pope, a professor of theological ethics at Boston College who has participated in the national network's gatherings, wrote in *America* magazine. "Many younger Catholics I teach at Boston College believe the church pays only lip service to its professed moral standards of compassion for the vulnerable and fairness for all. Adopting the practices of the restorative justice movement could help re-establish the church's moral credibility on these pressing issues."[106]

Mike Hoffman, a clergy abuse survivor from Chicago, credits "RJ," as it's often called by practitioners, with helping him heal and remain active in the church. He speaks frequently in public forums about his abuse by a priest who was a trusted friend of his parents when he was a child. "Restorative justice starts with someone being heard, believed and listened to," Hoffman told me. "It's a healing process. But it's not always a straightforward path."[107] Hoffman chaired the Hope and Healing Committee in the Archdiocese of Chicago, and along with other abuse survivors and archdiocesan staff helped create the archdiocese's Healing Garden and the annual Hope and Healing Mass. Despite suffering abuse in the church, he is active in his parish and finds comfort in the liturgy and sacraments. "I believe in the community of believers," Hoffman said. "We all come to church as broken people. We're placing our pain at the altar. We're not alone. We're doing this together."

When Janine Geske first heard about restorative justice, she was skeptical. She had spent years presiding over homicide and sexual assault cases as a judge. "I really thought it was crazy," she said. "I thought 'what victim's family would want this?'"[108] But Geske, who is Catholic, eventually became convinced when as a circuit court judge she visited the Green Bay Correctional Institution to, in her words, "see where I was sending people." She participated in a three-day, intensive restorative justice circle that included more than two dozen incarcerated men listening to and dialoguing with survivors of crime. For Geske, the experience was transformative. She went on to lead the restorative justice program at the prison for fifteen years. After serving five years on the Wisconsin Supreme Court, Geske couldn't shake a nagging feeling that she wanted to integrate the values of her Catholic faith more deeply into her work. Married to a former Jesuit priest, she had developed an appreciation for Ignatian spirituality. She went on a retreat to discern her path. Those days of prayer and reflection led to her retirement from the Supreme Court so that she could focus on facilitating restorative justice work more comprehensively. Geske started the Restorative Justice Initiative at her alma mater, Marquette University, where at the law school she taught students to facilitate victim/offender dialogues and work with young offenders and those incarcerated in maximum-security prison through restorative practices. She believes incubating restorative justice training at Marquette, a Jesuit university, was an ideal fit given the alignment between Catholic values and restorative justice.

Geske has spent more than fifteen years using restorative justice practices to address the pain and trauma of clergy sexual abuse. Her work began at a time when she recalls some Catholics expressed frustration that the persistence of clergy abuse survivors was damaging the reputation of the church and draining financial resources from dioceses. "I would hear parishioners say, 'it was so long ago why don't they just get over it?' I knew how devastating the damage was so I wanted people in the pews, priests and seminarians to be able to see the impact," Geske said. She began working as an advocate for victim-survivors of clergy abuse in the Milwaukee archdiocese. Those experiences taught Geske about what she calls "the ripple effects" of clergy abuse that extend beyond the victim-survivor to the broader Catholic community. In an effort to make visible this wider trauma and potential for healing, Geske led a four-hour healing circle in 2006 that included survivors of clergy abuse, a priest who had abused a child, then Milwaukee Archbishop Timothy Dolan, a mother of a son who committed suicide after he was sexually abused by a priest, therapists, a woman who had left the church over the abuse crisis, and a woman who was still Catholic but struggling to stay in the church because of clergy abuse.[109] The edited session was filmed and made into a documentary, *The Healing Circle*, that over the past fifteen years has been screened at parishes, seminaries, Catholic universities, and other Catholic institutions around the world.

When leaders in the Archdiocese of St. Paul and Minneapolis began implementing restorative justice practices, they called Geske. She helped lead listening sessions and healing circles across the archdiocese. Geske recalls one Saturday morning in a church basement in St. Paul. She asked the group how the abuse crisis had impacted them. One lifelong Catholic who sent his children to Catholic schools and had never known anyone who was abused told Geske he could not enter a confessional because of his distrust of church leaders. Another man, a grandfather who was abused by a priest as a young man, said through tears that he had never been able to hug his grandson. Geske has also led sessions with seminarians and priests who talk about how the clergy abuse scandals have affected them. Some of the clergy have acknowledged not wearing their clerical attire outside of parish settings because of the stigma of the abuse crisis. Geske also travels to Rome, where she has taught restorative justice facilitation at the Pontifical Gregorian University's Center for Child Protection. Sisters, priests, diocesan leaders, and other Catholic ministry leaders from around the world have taken her classes.

The retired judge admits that her vocation takes a toll. There are times when her faith in the Catholic Church as an institution has reached a near breaking point, even as her own spirituality remains strong. The wounds she has tended to over the years radiate out far beyond those who were directly impacted by harm. "It's critical that the church rebuild its credibility and moral voice," Geske told me.

> Clergy abuse has been a tipping point for so many Catholics who have lost trust in the church, but even when I'm talking about abuse so many other issues always come up. Catholics want to talk about clericalism. They want to talk about how women are treated in our church. How do we listen to the laity and include LGBTQ people? How do we address these broader issues? If we can't do that it feels like the church is rearranging deck chairs on the Titanic.

In the final two chapters, I will explore why it is essential for the Catholic Church to discern new paths for reform and renewal. LGBTQ Catholics and women continue to be marginalized and wounded by church leaders in words and actions. Young people in particular recognize that the church's moral credibility is badly damaged by teachings and practices that push people to the peripheries. Listening sessions with Catholics from around the world during a global synod process offer unambiguous evidence that the faithful want meaningful reform that moves beyond symbol to real substance. The 2022 synod document, *Enlarge the Space of Your Tent*, which distills the feedback from Catholics, states this hunger in clear terms.[110] "What emerges is a profound re-appropriation of the common dignity of all the baptized," the document reads. "This starts from a desire for radical inclusion—no one is excluded."

NOTES

1. Meeting with the Bishops of the United States of America, *Address of the Holy Father*, Cathedral of St. Matthew, September 23, 2015, https://www.vatican.va/content/francesco/en/speeches/2015/september/documents/papa-francesco_20150923_usa-vescovi.html.
2. Robert W. McElroy, "Pope Francis Makes Addressing Poverty Essential," *America*, October 8, 2013, https://www.americamagazine.org/church-poor.
3. Cindy Wooden, "What Did Pope Francis Mean When He Said the Unborn and the Poor Are Equally Sacred?" *Catholic News Service*, April 18, 2018, https://www.americamagazine.org/faith/2018/04/18/what-did-pope-francis-mean-when-he-said-unborn-and-poor-are-equally-sacred.
4. Joshua J. McElwee, "Francis' New Exhortation a Call to Become Holy by Serving Others, Especially Migrants," *National Catholic Reporter*, April 9, 2018, https://www.ncronline.org/spirituality/francis-new-exhortation-call-become-holy-serving-others-especially-migrants.
5. Michelle Martin, "Czerny: Consistent Ethic of Life Includes Just Economic, Social Systems," *Catholic News Service*, October 9, 2022, https://cruxnow.com/cns/2022/10/czerny-consistent-ethic-of-life-includes-just-economic-social-systems.
6. Pope Francis, "Speech at World Meeting of Popular Movements," *Vatican Radio*, July 10, 2015, https://www.archivioradiovaticana.va/storico/2015/07/10/pope_francis_speech_at_world_meeting_of_popular_movements/en-1157291.
7. Junno Arocho Esteves, "Careful Engagement with Popular Movements Needed, Former Official says," *Catholic News Service*, September 25, 2019, https://cruxnow.com/vatican/2019/09/careful-engagement-with-popular-movements-needed-former-official-says.
8. Nate Tinner-Williams, "In Conference Address, Pope Francis Praises George Floyd Protestors as 'Collective Samaritans,' *Black Catholic Messenger*, October 17, 2021, https://www.blackcatholicmessenger.org/pope-francis-george-floyd-wmpm/.
9. Jack Jenkins, "Top Catholic Bishop Calls Social Justice Movements 'Pseudo-Religion,' *Religion News Service*, November 5, 2021, https://www.washingtonpost.com/religion/2021/11/05/catholic-bishop-gomez-social-justice/.
10. Most Rev. Jose H. Gomez, "Reflections on the Church and America's New Religions," Address Delivered by Video to Congress of Catholics and Public Life in Madrid, Spain, November 4, 2021, https://archbishopgomez.org/blog/reflections-on-the-church-and-americas-new-religions.
11. Michael Warsaw, "Beware of the 'Woke'?" *National Catholic Register*, November 13, 2021, https://www.ncregister.com/commentaries/beware-of-the-woke.

12. Statement: National Black Catholic Sisters' Conference on USCCB Head Gomez' Speech Against Social Justice Movements," *Black Catholic Messenger*, November 16, 2021, https://www.blackcatholicmessenger.org/nbsc-gomez-statement/.
13. "'Blessed Is the One Who Stays Awake'—Our Response to Criticism of Today's Movements for Social Justice," Pax Christi USA, November 9, 2021, https://paxchristiusa.org/2021/11/09/blessed-is-the-one-who-stays-awake-our-response-to-criticism-of-todays-movements-for-social-justice/.
14. "Laudato Si': On Care for Our Common Home, Encyclical Letter from Pope Francis," May 24, 2015. https://www.vatican.va/content/francesco/en/encyclicals/documents/papa-francesco_20150524_enciclica-laudato-si.html.
15. Marcus Mescher, interview with author.
16. Marcus Mescher, interview with author.
17. Joan Coaston, "The Intersectionality Wars," *Vox*, May 28, 2019, https://www.vox.com/the-highlight/2019/5/20/18542843/intersectionality-conservatism-law-race-gender-discrimination.
18. Lindsay Burke, Jennifer Plitsch, and Sarah Schuler, "President Trump Issues Executive Order Prohibiting 'Divisive Concepts' in Federal Contractor Trainings," *Inside Government Contracts*, September 29, 2020, Donald Trump issued an executive order in 2020 that prohibited federal agencies teaching what his administration described as "divisive concepts."
19. Taifah Natalee Alexander, "Efforts to Ban Critical Race Theory Have Been Put Forth in All but One State—and Many Threaten Schools with a Loss of Funds," *The Conversation*, April 7, 2023, https://theconversation.com/efforts-to-ban-critical-race-theory-have-been-put-forth-in-all-but-one-state-and-many-threaten-schools-with-a-loss-of-funds-200816.
20. "CRT Forward: Tracking the Attack on Critical Race Theory," report from CRT's Forward Tracking Project, UCLA School of Law Critical Race Studies, April 2023, https://crtforward.law.ucla.edu/wp-content/uploads/2023/04/UCLA-Law_CRT-Report_Final.pdf.
21. Letter from Fr. Mathias to St. Patrick Catholic Parish, July 11, 2021, https://www.stpatrickcatholicparish.org/pastoralnote-on-criticalracetheory.
22. Patrick Saint-Jean, S.J., "Critical Race Theory and Catholicism Go Hand in Hand," *U.S. Catholic*, July 20, 2021, https://uscatholic.org/articles/202107/critical-race-theory-and-catholicism-go-hand-in-hand/.
23. Michael S. Parker, M.D., "President's Letter," *The Pulse of Catholic Medicine*, Catholic Medical Association, Summer 2021, https://www.cathmed.org/pulse/2021-summer/presidents-letter-summer-2021/.
24. Cardinal Newman Society Staff, "Ten Ways Catholic Education and Critical Race Theory Are Incompatible," *Issues in Brief*, July 15, 2021, https://cardinalnewmansociety.org/10-ways-catholic-education-and-critical-race-theory-are-incompatible/.
25. Christine Firer Hinze, "The Drama of Social Sin and the (Im)Possibility of Solidarity: Reinhold Neibuhr and Modern Catholic Social Teaching," *Studies in Christian Ethics* (2009) https://www.luc.edu/media/lucedu/dccirp/pdfs/articlesforresourc/Article_-_Hinze,_Christine_1.pdf.
26. Gloria Purvis, "Yes, Critical Race Theory Is Compatible with Catholicism. Here's Why," *America*, July 6, 2021, https://www.americamagazine.org/faith/2021/07/06/critical-race-theory-catholic-teaching-240972.

27. Matthew Thompson, "The Elusive Quest for Black Progress," *New York Times*, July 3, 2023, https://www.nytimes.com/2023/05/26/headway/black-americans-racial-progress.html?smid=url-share.
28. Besheer Mohamad et al., "Faith among Black Americans," *Pew Research Center*, February 16, 2021, https://www.pewresearch.org/religion/2021/02/16/faith-among-black-americans/.
29. PRRI Staff, "Creating More Inclusive Public Spaces: Structural Racism, Confederate Memorials, and Building for the Future," September 28, 2022, https://www.prri.org/research/creating-more-inclusive-public-spaces-structural-racism-confederate-memorials-and-building-for-the-future/.
30. Robert P. Jones, "Racism among White Christians Is Higher among the Nonreligious. That's No Coincidence," *NBC News*, July 27, 2020, https://www.nbcnews.com/think/opinion/racism-among-white-christians-higher-among-nonreligious-s-no-coincidence-ncna1235045.
31. Rob McCann, "Message to Staff and Clients from Catholic Charities President and CEO Rob McCann," 2020, https://www.youtube.com/watch?v=lKRalTfFNDo.
32. Rob McCann, "Message to Staff and Clients from Catholic Charities President and CEO Rob McCann," 2020, https://www.youtube.com/watch?v=lKRalTfFNDo.
33. Sarah Salvadore, "Spokane Bishop Criticizes Catholic Charities' Leader on Racism Comments," *National Catholic Reporter*, July 8, 2020, https://www.ncronline.org/news/spokane-bishop-criticizes-catholic-charities-leader-racism-comments.
34. Erica Chenoweth and Jeremy Pressman, "Black Lives Matter Protests Were Overwhelmingly Peaceful, Our Research Finds," *The Spokesman Review*, October 20, 2020, https://carrcenter.hks.harvard.edu/publications/black-lives-matter-protesters-were-overwhelmingly-peaceful-our-research-finds.
35. Geneva Sands, "White Supremacists Remain Deadliest U.S. Terror Threat, Homeland Security Report Says," *CNN*, October 6, 2020, https://www.cnn.com/2020/10/06/politics/white-supremacists-anarchists-dhs-homeland-threat-assessment/index.html.
36. Sarah Salvadore, "Spokane Bishop Criticizes Catholic Charities' Leader on Racism Comments," *National Catholic Reporter*, July 8, 2020, https://www.ncronline.org/news/spokane-bishop-criticizes-catholic-charities-leader-racism-comments.
37. Fr. Bryan Massingale, interview with author.
38. John Gehring, "Becoming the Church We Say We Are: An Interview with Olga Marina Segura," *Commonweal*, March 12, 2021, https://www.commonwealmagazine.org/becoming-church-we-say-we-are.
39. Alisha Ebrahimji, "A Bishop in El Paso Kneeled in Prayer for George Floyd. Two Days Later, Pope Francis Called," *CNN*, June 5, 2020, https://www.commonwealmagazine.org/becoming-church-we-say-we-are.
40. John Gehring, "At the Crossroads of Migration: An Interview with Bishop Mark J. Seitz," *Commonweal*, January 28, 2023, https://www.commonwealmagazine.org/seitz-el-paso-migration-biden-border.
41. John Gehring, "At the Crossroads of Migration: An Interview with Bishop Mark J. Seitz," *Commonweal*, January 28, 2023, https://www.commonwealmagazine.org/seitz-el-paso-migration-biden-border.
42. Bishop Mark Seitz, "Night Will Be No More: Pastoral Letter to the People of God in El Paso," August 3, 2019,. https://www.hopeborder.org/nightwillbenomore-eng.

43. Office of the Texas Governor, Greg Abbott, "Governor Abbott Addresses National Catholic Prayer Breakfast," May 7, 2015, https://gov.texas.gov/news/post/governor_abbott_addresses_national_catholic_prayer_breakfast.
44. Melissa Chan, "A Year Before Uvalde School Shooting, Texas Expanded Gun Rights," *NBC News*, May 24, 2022, https://www.nbcnews.com/news/us-news/outrage-texas-gun-laws-follows-deadly-elementary-school-shooting-rcna30410.
45. Office of the Texas Governor, Greg Abbott. "Governor Abbott Champions Protecting Unborn at Texas Rally for Life," January 28, 2023, https://gov.texas.gov/news/post/governor-abbott-champions-protecting-unborn-at-texas-rally-for-life.
46. Zac Anderson, "Conservative Warrior DeSantis Not as Aggressive on Guns or Abortion," *Tallahassee Democrat*, June 10, 2022, https://www.tallahassee.com/story/news/2022/06/10/gov-ron-desantis-quiet-wake-uvalde-and-supreme-court-leak/7558345001/.
47. Gary Fineout, "Florida Lawmakers Hand DeSantis Political Win on Guns," *Politico*, March 3, 2023, https://www.politico.com/news/2023/03/30/desantis-florida-gun-laws-00089836.
48. Anthony Izaguirre, "DeSantis Signs Florida GOPs 6-Week Abortion Ban into Law," *Associated Press*, April 14, 2023, https://apnews.com/article/florida-abortion-ban-approved-c9c53311a0b2426adc4b8d0b463edad1.
49. Pope John Paul II, *Evangelium Vitae*, March 25, 1995, https://www.vatican.va/content/john-paul-ii/en/encyclicals/documents/hf_jp-ii_enc_25031995_evangelium-vitae.html.
50. Thomas Kika, "Nearly Half of GOP Accept Mass Shootings as Part of a Free Society: Poll," *Newsweek*, June 5, 2022, https://www.newsweek.com/nearly-half-gop-accept-mass-shootings-part-free-society-poll-1712960.
51. Ted Cruz, "Freedom Only Exists if Citizens Have the Means to Defend It," *Dallas Morning News*, May 3, 2018, https://www.dallasnews.com/opinion/commentary/2018/05/03/ted-cruz-freedom-only-exists-if-citizens-have-the-means-to-defend-it/.
52. Reuters staff, "U.S. Congressman Posts Family Christmas Picture with Guns, Days after School Shooting," *Reuters*, December 4, 2021, https://www.reuters.com/world/us/us-congressman-posts-family-christmas-picture-with-guns-days-after-school-2021-12-05/.
53. Kaitlin Lewis, "Republicans' AR-15 Lapel Pins Slammed in Wake of Nashville School Shooting," *Newsweek*, March 27, 2023, https://www.newsweek.com/republicans-ar-15-lapel-pins-slammed-wake-nashville-school-shooting-1790695.
54. Daniel Panneton, "How Extremist Gun Culture Is Trying to Co-Opt the Rosary," *Atlantic*, August 14, 2022, https://www.theatlantic.com/ideas/archive/2022/08/radical-traditionalist-catholic-christian-rosary-weapon/671122/.
55. Michael E. Diamond, "This Easter, Gun Control and Abortion Need Equal Priority from Pro-Life Catholics," *NBC News*, April 4, 2021, https://www.nbcnews.com/think/opinion/easter-gun-control-abortion-need-equal-priority-pro-life-catholics-ncna1262971.
56. Darreona Davis, "Firearms Now Number 1 Cause of Death for U.S. Children—While Drug Poisoning Enters Top 5," *Forbes*, October 5, 2023, https://www.forbes.com/sites/darreonnadavis/2023/10/05/firearms-now-no-1-cause-of-death-for-us-children---while-drug-poisoning-enters-top-5/?sh=5f5b2f29609e.

57. Kiara Alfonseca, "There Have Been More Mass Shootings Than Days in 2023, Database Shows," *ABC News*, December 4, 2023, https://abcnews.go.com/US/mass-shootings-days-2023-database-shows/story?id=96609874.
58. Richard Szczepanowski, "Panel: Gun Violence Is a Pro-Life Issue That Sensible Gun Laws Must Address," *National Catholic Reporter*, June 9, 2022, https://www.ncronline.org/news/politics/panel-gun-violence-pro-life-issue-sensible-gun-laws-must-address.
59. R. Szczepanowski, "Panel: Gun Violence Is a Pro-Life Issue."
60. Thomas Reese, "The Catholic Bishops Support Gun Control. Why Don't We Hear More About It?" *National Catholic Reporter*, June 14, 2022, https://www.ncronline.org/news/opinion/catholic-bishops-support-gun-control-why-dont-we-hear-more-about-it.
61. Scott Simon and Rina Torchinsky, "Chicago Archbishop Adds His Voice to the Calls for Gun Safety Legislation," *National Public Radio*, June 3, 2022, https://www.npr.org/2022/06/03/1102681056/chicago-archbishop-adds-voice-outcry-against-gun-violence.
62. Michael J. O'Loughlin, "Catholic Leaders React to Texas School Massacre: 'Don't Tell Me That Guns Aren't the Problem,'" *America*, May 25, 2022, https://www.americamagazine.org/politics-society/2022/05/25/catholic-udlave-texas-elementary-school-shooting-243056.
63. The Pillar staff, "Bishop Flores: 'Sacralized' Guns and 'Hope' after Darkness," *The Pillar*, May 26, 2022, https://www.pillarcatholic.com/p/bishop-flores-sacralized-guns-and.
64. US Conference of Catholic Bishops, *Letter to U.S. Congress*, June 3, 2022, https://www.usccb.org/sites/default/files/2022-06/Letter%20to%20Congress%20on%20Gun%20Violence%2C%20June%203%2C%202022_0.pdf.
65. Archdiocese of Dubuque, *A Message to the Faithful of the Archdiocese from Archbishop Michael Jackels*, May 25, 2022, https://files.ecatholic.com/23075/documents/2022/5/MJ_052522_RepairScandalThroughtheHealingoftheEucharist.pdf?t=1653512818000.
66. Ivana Saric, "Archbishop of San Antonio: 'We Have Made Guns an Idol in This Country,'" *Axios*, May 31, 2022, https://www.axios.com/2022/05/31/archbishop-san-antonio-guns.
67. Archbishop Gustavo García-Siller, interview with author.
68. Josephine Lopez Paul, interview with author.
69. US Conference of Catholic Bishops, Catholic Campaign for Human Development, *Recognizing the Stranger*, https://www.usccb.org/resources/recognizing-stranger.
70. Tom Roberts, "Report: Conservatives' Attacks Threaten Bishops' Anti-Poverty Organization," *National Catholic Reporter*, June 12, 2013, https://www.ncronline.org/news/justice/report-conservatives-attacks-threaten-bishops-anti-poverty-organization.
71. Pope Francis, *Fratelli Tutti*, October 3, 2020, https://www.vatican.va/content/francesco/en/encyclicals/documents/papa-francesco_20201003_enciclica-fratelli-tutti.html.
72. Joe Rubio, "The Day Pope Francis Welcomed Community Organizers from the Southwest to the Papal Residence," *America*, July 13, 2023, https://www.americamagazine.org/faith/2023/01/13/pope-francis-community-organizers-iaf-synod-southwest-244208.

73. Richard Woods, interview with author.
74. Lyla Youness et al., “Poison in the Air,” *ProPublica,* November 2, 2021, https://www.propublica.org/article/toxmap-poison-in-the-air.
75. Sharon Lavigne, interview with author.
76. Pope Francis, *Laudato Si': On Care for Our Common Home,* May 24, 2015. https://www.vatican.va/content/francesco/en/encyclicals/documents/papa-francesco_20150524_enciclica-laudato-si.html.
77. Kimberly Heatherington, “Despite New EPA Rule to Reduce Pollution, Catholic Activist Says Fight to Protect Communities Far from Over,” *National Catholic Reporter,* May 5, 2023, https://www.ncronline.org/earthbeat/justice/despite-new-epa-rule-reduce-pollution-catholic-activist-says-fight-protect.
78. James Bruggers, “Catholic Bishops in the U.S. Largely Ignore the Pope's Concern about Climate Change, a New Study Finds,” *Inside Climate News,* October 26, 2021, https://insideclimatenews.org/news/26102021/catholic-bishops-pope-francis-climate-change-laudato-si/.
79. Daniel DiLeo, interview with author.
80. Brian Roewe, “Creighton University to Divest Fully from Fossil Fuels within 10 years,” *National Catholic Reporter,* January 5, 2021, https://www.ncronline.org/earthbeat/justice/creighton-university-divest-fully-fossil-fuels-within-10-years.
81. Sharon Lavigne, interview with author.
82. James Bruggers, “‘Cancer Alley’ Residents’ Zoning Lawsuit Cites ‘Racial Cleansing,’” *Mother Jones,* March 26, 2023, https://www.motherjones.com/politics/2023/03/cancer-alley-zoning-lawsuit-environmental-justice-race/.
83. Fr. David Kelly, interview with author.
84. Krisanne Vaillancourt Murphy, interview with author.
85. Catholic Mobilizing Network, “AG Barr to Receive ‘Catholic’ Award Hours After Authorizing Execution,” September 23, 2020, https://catholicsmobilizing.org/in-the-news/ag-barr-receive-catholic-award-hours-after-authorizing-execution%C2%A0.
86. Robert P. Jones, “The Roots of Christian Nationalism Go Back Further Than You Think,” *Time,* August 23, 2023, https://time.com/6309657/us-christian-nationalism-columbus-essay/.
87. Becky Sindelar, “Society of Jesus Apologizes for the Sins of Jesuit Slaveholding at Georgetown University Liturgy,” Georgetown University, April 18, 2017, https://www.jesuits.org/stories/society-of-jesus-apologizes-for-the-sins-of-jesuit-slaveholding-at-georgetown-university-liturgy/.
88. Sindelar, “Society of Jesus Apologizes for the Sins of Jesuit Slaveholding.”
89. Rachel L. Swarns, “272 Slaves Were Sold to Save Georgetown. What Does It Owe Their Descendants,” *New York Times,* April 16, 2016, https://www.nytimes.com/2016/04/17/us/georgetown-university-search-for-slave-descendants.html.
90. Rachel Swarns, *The 272: The Families Who Were Enslaved and Sold to Build the American Catholic Church,* (Penguin Random House, June 2023) https://www.penguinrandomhouse.com/books/550959/the-272-by-rachel-l-swarns/.
91. Adam Rothman, interview with author.
92. Georgetown University, Office of Undergraduate Admissions. “Descendants,” September 1, 2016, https://uadmissions.georgetown.edu/applying/descendants/.
93. Georgetown University, “Georgetown Awards Funding to 5 Projects that Support Descendant Communities,” *University News.* April 28, 2023, https://www.georgetown

.edu/news/georgetown-awards-funding-to-5-projects-that-support-descendant-communities/?ref=blackcatholicmessenger.com.

94. Rachel Swarns, "Catholic Order Pledges $100 Million to Atone for Slave Labor and Sales," *New York Times,* March 15, 2021, https://www.nytimes.com/2021/03/15/us/jesuits-georgetown-reparations-slavery.html.
95. Rachel L. Swarns, "Catholic Order Struggles to Raise $100 Million to Atone for Slave Labor," *New York Times,* August 16, 2022, https://www.nytimes.com/2022/08/16/us/jesuits-reparations.html?smid=nytcore-ios-share&referringSource=articleShare.
96. Cheryllyn Branch, interview with author.
97. Rachel L. Swarns, "The Nuns Who Bought and Sold Human Beings," *New York Times,* August 2, 2019, https://www.nytimes.com/2019/08/02/opinion/sunday/nuns slavery.html.
98. Carolyn Osiek, interview with author.
99. Society of the Sacred Heart, "We Speak Your Names" ceremony, September 23, 2018. Grand Coteau, Louisiana. https://rscj.org/we-speak-your-names-september-23-2018.
100. Irma Dillard, interview with author.
101. Megan Wilson-Reitz, interview with author.
102. Tom Scheck, "Secret Accounts Paid for Clergy Misconduct but Left Church Open to Financial Abuse," Minnesota Public Radio, January 23, 2014, https://minnesota.publicradio.org/collections/catholic-church/2014/01/23/secret-accounts-kept-clergy-misconduct-quiet-but-left-archdiocese-finances-exposed/.
103. Fr. Daniel Griffith, interview with author.
104. Jean Hopfensperger, "St. Paul-Minneapolis Archdiocese Taps Restorative Justice to Heal Impact of Sex Abuse," *Star Tribune,* October 25, 2019, https://www.startribune.com/st-paul-minneapolis-archdiocese-taps-restorative-justice-to-heal-impact-of-sex-abuse/563888512/?refresh=true.
105. Tom Roberts, "Justice for All: Restorative Justice Goes Beyond Retribution," *National Catholic Reporter,* June 4, 2021, https://www.ncronline.org/news/justice-all-restorative-justice-goes-beyond-retribution.
106. Stephen J. Pope, "Can Restorative Justice Help the Church Heal from Sex Abuse Scandals?" *America,* December 6, 2018, https://www.americamagazine.org/faith/2018/12/06/can-restorative-justice-help-church-heal-sex-abuse-scandals.
107. Mike Hoffman, interview with author.
108. Janine Geske, interview with author.
109. Marquette Law School, "The Healing Circle." https://www.youtube.com/watch?v=zX8fBdmnOH8.
110. "Enlarge the Space of Your Tent," Working Document for the Continental Stage, General Secretariat of the Synod, 2022, https://www.synod.va/content/dam/synod/common/phases/continental-stage/dcs/Documento-Tappa-Continentale-EN.pdf.

6

RADICAL INCLUSION AND DIGNITY FOR LGBTQ CATHOLICS

Most Americans now broadly support equal rights for lesbian, gay, bisexual, and transgender people. More than 70 percent agree that same-sex marriage should be legal—including more than half of Republicans—a meteoric rise from 1996 when barely a quarter of the public supported civil marriage for same-sex couples.[1] Not only have a majority of Catholics consistently approved of gay marriage since 2011, US Catholics' support has exceeded the national average for two decades. It might be tempting to view those changes as inevitable from today's vantage point, but not long ago even many Democrats, including Barack Obama during his first presidential campaign, did not publicly support same-sex marriage. The speed at which LGBTQ equality became a mainstream issue represents a dizzying cultural transformation. What does this revolution mean for the Catholic Church—an ancient institution that measures change in centuries? Catholic leaders have been trying to answer that question in ways that demonstrate signs of both a hopeful openness to the development of church teachings and also a defensive retrenchment. What remains clear is that many LGBTQ Catholics and their allies now want more than symbolic gestures from the church. Data from Public Religion Research Institute finds that Catholics are more likely than people raised in any other religion to cite negative treatment of gay and lesbian people as a primary reason they left the church.[2] It is an inescapable reality that institutional structures that continue to exclude gay, lesbian, and transgender people remain a stumbling block to living out the church's own professed commitment to justice and human dignity.

TRADITION, DEVELOPMENT, AND THE FRANCIS PARADOX

When asked by a reporter during a 2013 in-flight press conference about the existence of a supposed "gay lobby" at the Vatican, Pope Francis responded with what is perhaps the most famous papal sound bite in history. "If someone is gay and he searches for the Lord and has good will, who am I to judge?" Francis said.[3] Even his use of the word "gay" (rather than homosexual) was viewed as radical and set off alarms for traditionalist Catholics. Only four months into his pontificate, Francis had signaled a refreshingly different approach than his predecessor Benedict XVI, who even before his election to pope wrote documents that included language that caused deep pain for gay Catholics and cracked down on sisters and priests who advocated for LGBTQ people during the more than two decades he led the Vatican's doctrinal office. The shift in tone and emphasis during the Francis pontificate has been lauded far beyond Catholic circles. In 2013 the oldest gay rights magazine in the United States, *The Advocate*, even named Pope Francis its "Person of the Year." Francis has expressed his support for civil union legal protections for same-sex couples and became the first pope in history to officially call for an end to laws that criminalize homosexuality in more than sixty countries. "Being a homosexual isn't a crime," Pope Francis said during an exclusive interview with the Associated Press in 2023, adding that Catholic bishops in countries who support punitive laws must go through "a process of conversion" and apply "tenderness, please, as God has for each one of us."[4]

The pope has met regularly with transgender people and LGBTQ advocates. "Before, the church was closed to us. They didn't see us as normal people, they saw us as the devil," Andrea Paola Torres Lopez, a Columbian transgender woman, told the Associated Press. "Then Pope Francis arrived and the doors of the church opened for us." In the fall of 2023, the Vatican's doctrinal office affirmed in a document that "a transsexual—even one who has undergone hormone treatment and gender reassignment surgery—may receive baptism under the same conditions as other faithful." One of the pope's friends and close advisors, the Chilean clergy abuse survivor and whistleblower Juan Carlos Cruz, is gay. Describing his initial meetings with the pope to CNN, Cruz said that Francis told him: "God made you like this. God loves you like this. The pope loves you like this and you should love yourself and not worry about what people say."[5] In 2021, Francis appointed Cruz to be a member of the Pontifical Council for the Protection of Minors, a notable move given that some conservative Catholics have sought to link the clergy abuse crisis to homosexuality (a claim not supported by independent research).

Pope Francis has also frequently praised Rev. James Martin, a prominent author, Jesuit priest, and editor at *America* magazine who is often targeted by conservative Catholic activists and some bishops in the United States for his ministry of fostering dialogue between the church and LGBTQ people.

In 2017, leaders at the Theological College at The Catholic University of America in Washington abruptly canceled a talk Martin was scheduled to give after right-wing Catholic activists flooded the seminary with ugly attacks against him.[6] But only a year later the Jesuit was invited to give a keynote address at the 2018 Vatican-sponsored World Meeting of Families. Pope Francis also personally endorsed the priest's ministry during a private audience in the papal library of the Apostolic Palace in 2019, a meeting that drew global headlines. The two met again for another meeting at the Vatican in 2022. The pope appointed Martin, who has served as an advisor to the Vatican's Dicastery for Communications, to be a member of the Synod on Synodality a year later. During a welcoming ceremony for hundreds of thousands of young people in Portugal gathered for World Youth Day in the summer of 2023, Pope Francis didn't specifically bring up LGBTQ people but again broadly emphasized a central theme of his papacy. "There is room for everyone in the church and, whenever there is not, then, please, we must make room," he said in Lisbon.[7] Earlier in the day, during a speech at the Catholic University of Portugal, the pope told students and young people to reject the kind of culture-war Catholicism that is a defining feature of many American Catholics leaders on the right. "Christianity cannot be lived as a fortress surrounded by high walls, one that raises the ramparts against the world," he said.[8]

For all of the important progress in shaping a more pastoral approach to gay, lesbian, bisexual, and transgender people during the Francis era—a reflection of the pope's theology of encounter and accompaniment—the church continues to marginalize LGBTQ Catholics in words and actions. Even sympathetic Francis observers have noted the often confusing, sometimes contradictory, messages the pope and Vatican statements have sent when it comes to homosexuality and the lives of LGBTQ people. In 2021 the Vatican's doctrine office issued a brief "responsum" to the question—"does the Church have the power to give the blessing to unions of persons of the same sex?"—with a curt one word answer: "Negative." In a brief explanatory note the statement acknowledged "the presence in such relationships of positive elements, which are in themselves to be valued and appreciated," but said that God "does not and cannot bless sin." The church, the note added, "cannot justify these relationships" because to do so would "approve and encourage a choice and a way of life that cannot be recognized as objectively ordered to the revealed plans of God."[9] The responsum, signed by Cardinal Luis Ladaria, who at the time served as prefect of the doctrine office, noted that Pope Francis "was informed and gave his assent" to its publication. Writing in *The New Yorker*, Paul Elie, a senior fellow with the Berkley Center for Religion, Peace, and World Affairs at Georgetown University, commented that while the substance of the statement was "no great surprise, its absolutizing language was, because it runs counter to Pope Francis's emphasis on the Church as an agent less of judgment than of mercy." The statement, Elie argued, "leaves L.G.B.T.Q. Catholics in limbo, trying to make sense of a Church that will not deign to bless their lives. And it suggests that, on matters of marriage and sexuality, Pope Francis's pontificate, too, is in a kind of limbo—unable to accompany people on the margins, because the Church itself is doing the marginalizing, and stymied by juridical formulas so heartless that the Pope winds up trying to distance himself from them."[10] After the document's publication Fr. James Martin tweeted: "Not since the anger over sex abuse in 2002 and 2018 have I seen so many people so demoralized, and ready to leave the church. And not simply LGBT people, but their families and friends, a large part of the church."[11] Belgian Bishop Johan Bonny of Antwerp said the statement caused "intellectual and moral incomprehension." In a commentary published in several Belgian and international newspapers, the bishop apologized for those who found the decree "painful and incomprehensible."[12] The bishop noted that he knows same-sex couples "who are legally married, have children, form a warm and stable family and actively participate in parish life. I'm immensely appreciative of their contributions." Archbishop Mark Coleridge, president of the Australian Bishops' Conference, told *The Tablet*, a weekly Catholic journal, the statement "isn't by any means the end of the conversation. I think it should give greater impetus to another kind of conversation about inclusion."[13]

Two years later Pope Francis issued an unexpected declaration at the end of 2023 that allowed priests to offer a non-liturgical blessing for same-sex couples. *Fiducia supplicans*: On the Pastoral Meaning of Blessings, was released by the church's highest-ranking doctrinal official, Cardinal Victor Manuel Fernández.[14] Francis DeBernardo, a gay Catholic and longtime advocate for LGBTQ Catholics, called the decision "a landmark and milestone in the church's relationship with LGBTQ people," and specifically pointed to a section in the document that states "an exhaustive moral analysis" should not be a precondition for conferring a blessing. The paragraph, he wrote, is "revolutionary" because "it overturns the dominant pastoral approach the Catholic Church has taken over the centuries, an approach which emphasized policing for doctrinal orthodoxy and demanding strict obedience over offering welcome and extending mercy."[15] Pope Francis, he added, is "bringing to an end the exclusionary practices of the previous two pontiffs by affirming that God's mercy is not something humans can limit, and which we may not always understand." The reaction from conservative Catholics around the world ranged from lukewarm to defiant. *LifeSiteNews* wrote that the decision was "in contradiction to the unchangeable Catholic teaching that the church cannot bless sinful relationships."[16] The US bishops' conference issued a muted reaction that downplayed the historic nature of the change by noting the church's teaching on marriage remained the same. Denver Archbishop Samuel Aquila said the blessings should be done "with discretion, preferably privately to avoid scandal and confusion."[17] German Cardinal Gerhard Müller, who led the Vatican's doctrine office under Pope Benedict XVI, called the decision "blasphemous."[18] The most critical reception came from Africa, the continent where the Catholic population is growing most rapidly. The Zambian bishops' conference said the Vatican document should be "taken as for further reflection and not for implementation in Zambia."[19] The Malawi bishops' conference responded that "blessings of any kind for same-sex unions of any kind are not permitted in Malawi."[20] A joint statement signed by Congolese Cardinal Fridolin Ambong, on behalf of African national bishops conferences, called same-sex unions "contrary to the will of God."[21]

The Vatican's doctrinal office in the spring of 2024 left many LGBTQ Catholics doubting how much Pope Francis is willing to move from pastoral gestures to more tangible reforms in how the church approaches issues of gender identity and sexuality. In *Dignitas Infinita*: On Human Dignity, the Dicastery for the Doctrine of the Faith reiterated centuries of church teaching about human dignity on a range of issues. The document also identified new "grave violations" that threaten human dignity, including gender theory and sex change operations. "Desiring a personal self-determination, as gender theory prescribes, apart from this fundamental truth that human life is a gift, amounts to a concession to the age-old temptation to make oneself God, entering into competition with the true God of love revealed to us in the Gospel," it said. A month later news broke that Pope Francis used a homophobic slur when referring to gay seminarians in a closed-door meeting with Italian bishops. In reiterating to the bishops that they should continue to refrain from admitting gay men to seminaries, "in order to prevent the risk that the gay person who chooses the priesthood could later end up living a double-life, continuing to practice homosexuality," the pope used an offensive slang word in Italian, *frociaggine*. "There is too much *frociaggine* in seminaries," the pope reportedly said. The Vatican issues a statement offering an apology from Pope Francis. Michael O'Loughlin, a prominent gay Catholic journalist who received a letter of appreciation from Pope Francis in 2021 for his book about Catholic responses to the AIDS crisis, reflected on the mix of heartbreak and hope the Francis papacy has left many LGBTQ Catholics grappling with over the years. "L.G.B.T.Q. Catholics, who are rightly disappointed, hurt and even angry today, are resilient enough to know better than to put the entirety of their faith in any one church leader," O'Loughlin wrote in *America* magazine after the remarks about the pope's slur became public. Unless the church "engages in the kind of deep theological reflection needed to understand what it means to welcome and integrate L.G.B.T.Q. people into the life of the church, in meaningful and concrete ways," he added, "the L.G.B.T.Q. community will continue to be left grasping onto gestures. Gestures alone, no matter how well meaning, are not enough."

CHURCH TEACHING AND CALLS FOR CHANGE

The Catechism of the Catholic Church teaches that gay people "must be accepted with respect, compassion, and sensitivity," and that "every sign of unjust discrimination in their regard should be avoided." At the same time, any sexual activity between people of the same sex is deemed "intrinsically disordered" and even an orientation toward homosexuality is described as "objectively disordered."[22] A 1986 document issued by the Vatican's doctrinal office, led by the future pope Cardinal Joseph Ratzinger, noted that "although the particular inclination of the homosexual person is not a sin, it is a more or less strong tendency ordered toward an intrinsic moral evil; and thus the inclination itself must be seen as an objective disorder."[23] The document, issued during the grim days of the AIDS crisis, described any gay sexual activity as "essentially self-indulgent" and argued that "homosexual activity prevents one's own fulfillment and happiness by acting contrary to the creative wisdom of God." In 2003, as political and cultural support for same-sex unions was growing, Ratzinger's doctrinal office denounced those civil laws as "gravely unjust" and emphasized that "legal recognition of homosexual unions or placing them on the same level as marriage would mean not only the approval of deviant behavior, with the consequence of making it a model in present-day society, but would also obscure basic values which belong to the common inheritance of humanity."[24] Allowing children to be raised by same-sex couples, the statement said, "would actually mean doing violence to these children." It is sickening to remember that the document was published at a time when the *Boston Globe*'s investigative Spotlight team had a year earlier uncovered evidence of widespread rape and sexual abuse of children by clergy, and revealed a culture of institutional coverup by diocesan officials. The lack of self-awareness didn't change much over the years for some church leaders. Bishop Thomas Tobin of Rhode Island tweeted in 2019 that Catholics should not attend LGBTQ Pride celebrations because the events are "especially harmful for children."[25]

US Catholic bishops have broadly opposed efforts to expand civil rights law to include sexual orientation and gender identity as protected classes. The US bishops' conference even quietly lobbied behind the scenes against 2020 legislation passed in the US Congress, the National Suicide Hotline Designation Act, that established a toll-free number for people facing mental health crises because the legislation included special funding for LGBTQ support.[26] The bishops argued it would infringe on religious liberty. LGBTQ people are more likely to report depression and are at a higher risk of committing suicide. Suicidal thoughts have trended upward among LGBTQ young people in the last several years, according to research from The Trevor Project. Nearly half of LGBTQ youth seriously considered suicide in 2022.[27]

A growing number of Catholic leaders in the United States have openly acknowledged the need for reevaluating church teaching, language, and institutional practices that marginalize LGBTQ Catholics. Cardinal Wilton Gregory of Washington, DC, when he was the archbishop of Atlanta in 2014, wrote that the distinction in church teaching between being gay and homosexual behavior "admittedly needs reexamination and development."[28] Bishop Robert McElroy of San Diego told *America* magazine in 2016 that language in the Catechism that describes gay sexual activity as "intrinsically disordered" is "very destructive language that I think we should not use pastorally."[29] The cardinal is on record saying the language of disorder "should be taken out of the catechism."[30] Chicago Cardinal Blase Cupich has also expressed support for revising the church's language about homosexuality. "Anytime language comes across as hurtful to people, the church has an obligation to examine that," he said in an interview with *America* magazine. "I would hope that the church would always be willing to examine the way it speaks, especially if it's made known to us that it's hurtful and that it is categorically exclusive of individuals."[31]

The Vatican used the acronym "LGBT" for the first time in a 2018 working document prepared for a synod focused on young people. "Some LGBT youths, through various contributions that were received by the General Secretariat of the synod, wish to 'benefit from greater closeness' and experience greater care by the church," the document read.[32] While not exactly a revolutionary statement, the use of a description often preferred by many lesbian, gay and transgender people themselves was an important sign of respect. Catholic teaching documents have typically used "homosexual" or referred to "homosexual tendencies," which reduce a person's multidimensional humanity to sexual acts. Backlash from conservative bishops ultimately succeeded in striking the use of "LGBT" from the synod's final report. Former Philadelphia Archbishop Charles Chaput told members of the synod that for the church "there is no such thing as an 'LGBTQ Catholic,' or a 'transgender Catholic' or a 'heterosexual Catholic,' as if our sexual appetites defined who we are."[33] Even as "LGBT" references were removed from the document, a surprisingly frank assessment appeared in the final text. "There are questions related to the body, to affectivity and to sexuality that require a deeper anthropological, theological and pastoral exploration, which should be done in the most appropriate way, whether on a global or local level," the statement read.[34] David Gibson, a veteran Catholic journalist and director of the Center on Religion and Culture at Fordham University, noted its importance in an analysis for *Religion News Service*. "The Catholic hierarchy is acknowledging that the church needs to update its understanding of the science of sex and gender, and that also means updating the church's theology on sexuality and its ministry to gay people," Gibson wrote. Such an approach, he added, could "help the church develop a more coherent and convincing theology for speaking about gay and transgender people, as well as a more pastoral approach in ministering to them."[35]

European bishops and clergy have been at the forefront of challenging the church to develop teaching and institutional practices in ways that more concretely affirm the dignity of gay people and same-sex couples. Only months after the Vatican's doctrine office rejected the blessing of gay partners as anathema to church teaching in 2021, German priests, deacons, and lay leaders at more than a hundred Catholic churches in the country openly defied that position and took part in public ceremonies organized under the motto #LiebeGewinnt (German for #LoveWins), that were open to "all loving couples, regardless whether they are gay, lesbian or straight."[36] During a 2023 gathering that brought together Germany's bishops and lay representatives as part of ongoing synodal meetings, a majority of bishops voted to officially approve blessings for same-sex couples beginning in 2026. German Cardinal Reinhard Marx has been particularly outspoken. "The catechism is not set in stone. One may also question what it says," he said in a 2022 interview with a German weekly newspaper. "Homosexuality is not a sin. It corresponds to a Christian attitude when two people, regardless of gender, stand up for each other, in joy and sorrow."[37] The cardinal said that he wants "to take church teaching forward," and questioned those who denigrate sexual relationships between committed same-sex partners. "People live in an intimate loving relationship that also has a sexual form of expression. And we want to say that this is not worth anything?" he asked. The bishops' conference of Belgium has also created a prayer liturgy for same-sex couples. The framework recommends that pastoral leaders use an "opening word, opening prayer and Scripture reading" as part of the blessing, according to the document, "Being Pastorally Close to Homosexual Persons: For a welcoming church that excludes no one."[38] While the bishops note that this "moment of prayer" is not the same as a sacramental marriage between a man and a woman, the framework includes a suggested community prayer asking that God "make their commitment to each other strong and faithful." Cardinal Jean-Claude Hollerich of Luxembourg, a Jesuit who Pope Francis appointed to the influential position of realtor general of the Synod of Bishops on synodality in 2023, told Germany's Catholic News Agency in 2022 that he believed the church's teaching that gay relationships are sinful is wrong. "I believe that the sociological-scientific foundation of this teaching is no longer correct," said Hollerich, who the pope also named to serve as an advisor on his nine-member Council of Cardinals helping reform church governance. "I think it's about time we did a fundamental revision of the doctrine here."[39] The cardinal's comments came in the wake of a campaign by more than a hundred Catholic Church employees in Germany who publicly came out as gay, saying they want to "live openly without fear." While Cardinal Hollerich later insisted in a press conference that he was not calling for a change in doctrine but "a change of attitude," the fact that a high-ranking figure in the church was even openly discussing these issues signals a significant change in church culture compared to previous years.[40]

SYNODAL ENCOUNTERS: A PATH OF DISCERNMENT

When the Vatican released a forty-five-page document in the fall of 2022 that summarized major themes distilled from synod listening sessions held with millions of Catholics around the world, the report included topics such as women's ordination and LGBTQ relationships that would have triggered formal investigations from Rome under John Paul II and Benedict XVI. The report, "Enlarge the Space of Your Tent," named after a biblical passage in Isaiah, reflects the voices of many Catholics who are calling for a deeper reform and renewal. "What emerges is a profound re-appropriation of the common dignity of all the baptized," the document reads. "This starts from a desire for radical inclusion—no one is excluded." The report specifically cites LGBTQ people as "among those who ask for a more meaningful dialogue and a more welcoming space."[41] Bishop John Stowe of Lexington, Kentucky, one of the most outspoken American bishops on issues of LGBTQ equality, views the synod process as "a new way of being church at every level." If the process is successful, the bishop said in 2023 at the Cardinal Joseph Bernardin Common Cause Lecture hosted by

Loyola University Chicago, its "impact will be comparable to that of the Second Vatican Council."[42] A listening church that goes to the peripheries, he believes, must learn from the experiences of LGBTQ people.

"Faith-filled LGBTQ persons whose Catholicism is just as much a part of their identity as their sexual orientation have made a profound impression on me," the bishop, who is a Franciscan, told me in an interview.[43] "I have spoken to too many individuals who have questioned their self-worth, questioned whether or not they are loved by God, questioned why they are alive at all, or questioned why they are uncomfortable in their own flesh to believe that sexual orientation is a choice or that God has somehow excluded them from his love. I struggle to understand why treating such persons with respect and taking their stories and struggles, along with their joys and accomplishments seriously, is such a threat to straight Christians." The bishop said that while he does not advocate for a change in the sacrament of marriage, "I do believe that we can support LGBTQ persons who need the same legal protection and rights for their committed relationships as marriage provides." He broke ranks with the US Conference of Catholic Bishops in 2021 when he supported the Equality Act, legislation that would prohibit discrimination in housing, employment, public accommodations, and health care by making sexual orientation and gender identity protected classes. The US bishops' conference opposed the bill on religious liberty grounds, arguing in a letter to Congress that provisions in the legislation would "discriminate against people of faith." Bishop Stowe contested that position and advocated for its passage. "LGBTQ people reflect the image of likeness of God, just as anyone else, and so it is our duty to love and defend them," Bishop Stowe wrote in a letter to Senator Dick Durbin and Senator Chuck Grassley, at the time the two highest-ranking members of the Senate Judiciary Committee.[44] "As a Catholic bishop, I hate to see any form of harmful discrimination protected by law, and it is consistent with our teaching to ensure that LGBTQ people have the protection they need." In a 2022 keynote address at Outreach, an annual LGBTQ Catholic Ministry Conference held at Fordham University, Bishop Stowe delivered a message that many LGBTQ Catholics rarely hear from a member of the hierarchy. "Don't let anyone tell you that you are not Catholic, that you are not part of the church, that you cannot be holy or that you are defined by sin," he said.[45]

Cardinal Robert McElroy of San Diego also grounds his frequent appeals for a more inclusive church in the context of synodal ecclesiology. "Since the call to synodality is a call to continuing conversion, reforming our own structures of exclusion will require a long pilgrimage of sustained prayer, reflection, dialogue and action—all of which should begin now," the cardinal wrote in 2023.[46] He cited the "Enlarge the Space of Your Tent" synod document, which concluded that "the vision of a church capable of radical inclusion, shared belonging and deep hospitality according to the teachings of Jesus is at the heart of the synodal process." Denying the Eucharist to divorced, heterosexual, or LGBTQ Catholics who are not celibate outside of marriage, he proposed, focuses "the Christian moral life disproportionately upon sexual activity." The heart of Christian discipleship, he writes, "is a relationship with God the Father, Son and Spirit rooted in the life, death and resurrection of Jesus Christ. The church has a hierarchy of truths that flow from this fundamental kerygma. Sexual activity, while profound, does not lie at the heart of this hierarchy. Yet in pastoral practice we have placed it at the very center of our structures of exclusion from the Eucharist. This should change." In some of the most pointed words used by a Catholic bishop to describe anti-LGBTQ discrimination, the cardinal called it "a demonic mystery of the human soul why so many men and women have a profound and visceral animus toward members of the L.G.B.T. communities." In the "face of this bigotry," he adds, "the dignity of every person as a child of God struggling in this world, and the loving outreach of God, must be the heart, soul, face and substance of the church's stance and pastoral action."

In a sign that the most reactionary culture warriors in the church refuse to engage with a spirit of goodwill even with their fellow brother bishops on these issues, Bishop Thomas Paprocki of Springfield, Illinois—at the time chairman-elect of the US bishops' committee on canonical affairs and church governance—responded to the essay by essentially calling Cardinal McElroy a heretic. "Until recently, it would be hard to imagine any successor of the apostles making such heterodox statements," Paprocki wrote in a *First Things* article entitled "Imagining a Heretical Cardinal." "Unfortunately, it is not uncommon today to hear Catholic leaders affirm unorthodox views that, not too long ago, would have been espoused only by heretics."[47] A month after his essay attracted widespread discussion and debate, Cardinal McElroy again framed his call for LGBTQ inclusion in the church in the context of the synod. "Pope Francis has called the whole of the church to a profound process of renewal through a synodal process that seeks to touch and transform every element of our ecclesial life and our outreach to the world," the cardinal told a conference hosted by the Franciscan School of Theology at the University of San Diego. "We believe we are approaching a real crisis in how to minister to the LGBT+ community," he said. "It is clear that the church in the U.S. must transform its outreach to LGBT+ persons if it seeks to be a truly welcoming presence in the world."[48]

In another positive sign, several dioceses in the United States held listening sessions with LGBTQ Catholics as part of the synod process. New

Ways Ministry, a Catholic outreach organization that advocates for equity, inclusion, and justice for LGBTQ people, also hosted three "Spiritual Conversations" in 2022 over Zoom with nearly a thousand people from the United States and more than two dozen other countries. Participants in the dialogue sessions met in small groups of six to eight people. While many who took part were lesbian, gay, bisexual, transgender, and nonbinary, participants also included parents of LGBTQ people, pastoral workers, and current or formerly vowed religious and clergy, including some of whom are LGBTQ themselves. A final report, entitled "From the Margins to the Center," summarized key themes participants raised during the discussions.[49] The findings provide both a bracing assessment of the difficulties many LGBTQ Catholics continue to face in the church as well as evidence that despite these challenges there are reasons for hope. "Almost all participants stated that they had been wounded by other Catholics because of sexual orientation and/or gender identity issues," the report found. "One participant was 'struck by the raw pain' that simply being affiliated with the church causes. The harm identified by participants comes in different forms: the denial of sacraments, employment and vocational discrimination, being forced to hide one's full self in church spaces, faith-based conversion therapy attempts, derogatory comments from some church leaders, and, in extreme cases, witnessing support for criminalizing homosexuality." At the same time the report noted that LGBTQ participants frequently cited the contributions of Catholic sisters in working to create a more inclusive church and spoke of their strong Catholic identity. "Most participants expressed an abiding love for the Catholic Church in spite of their doubts and challenges," the report found.

BUILDING A NETWORK FOR LGBTQ INCLUSION IN CATHOLIC SCHOOLS

David Palmieri knew he couldn't stay quiet any longer. During his more than two decades teaching theology at a Catholic high school outside of Boston, Palmieri watched a handful of students come out to friends and families. But in 2021 a student confided in the teacher that he was gay and told him the mental strain had driven him to attempt suicide. "At that point, I said I can't just be a passive ally," Palmieri told me. "I couldn't be silent. I needed to break this conversation open. The burden LGBTQ students carry in our Catholic schools is pretty heavy. Many times they are hiding and existing in the dark."[50] Palmieri spent months trying to find resources and support for LGBTQ students in Catholic schools. "There was very little out there. It was

Ezekiel's valley of dry bones," he said with a laugh. "There really wasn't any networking or dialogues happening." Palmieri came to realize he couldn't wait for someone else to act. Sitting on his couch one summer afternoon, he did a Google search and found a list of every Catholic high school in the United States. He picked the largest schools in each state and tracked down email addresses for theology teachers, campus ministers, and school counselors. "I sent hundreds of emails to people just asking them if they wanted to have this dialogue," he said. Most of those early emails went unanswered, which didn't surprise Palmieri considering what he calls the "culture of silence" around LGBTQ issues in Catholic schools. Eventually a few teachers wrote back, and then more began steadily trickling in. Teachers shared their own stories of frustration and desire to help LGBTQ students feel more visible and supported. By 2023 about four hundred people at Catholic secondary schools in forty-three states and seven countries were communicating with each other and sharing resources as part of a network Palmieri created called "Without Exception." The group describes its mission as "dedicated to discerning the art of accompaniment for LGBTQ + students in Catholic schools." Members share advice about starting LGBTQ support groups, navigating challenging conversations about how to create an inclusive culture when school administrators or bishops are indifferent or openly opposed, and encourage each other to be better advocates.

"LGBTQ+ kids are in our schools and we need to start with that reality," said Palmieri, who earned a doctorate in ministry in 2023 from Catholic University in Washington with a dissertation focused on LGBTQ ministry in Catholic schools. "It's a false choice to say we can either affirm our Catholic identity as a school or support these students. We can and should do both." He cites Pope Francis's preference for a "field hospital" theology that emphasizes encounter and accompaniment over a "desk-bound theology" as the foundation for his work. "We have to start with the real person, not a policy," he said. Palmieri is forty-nine, straight, and married with two children. He grew up in a Catholic family and teaches at the same high school he attended. When he was coming of age in Catholic school back in the 1980s and 1990s, there was plenty of adolescent joking about gay people, and it was not uncommon to hear the word "fag" casually tossed around on the playground or in the hallway. Attitudes reflected the broader culture at the time.

While same-sex marriage is legal today and outward expressions of homophobia are deemed less acceptable, a surge of legislation in states across the country have targeted LGBTQ people—transgender people most specifically. A growing number of Catholic bishops and dioceses in recent years have released policies focused on gender identity and transgender students that in many cases are insensitive and exclusionary. Palmieri noticed that many of those diocesan policies started coming out not long after the release of a 2019 document from the Vatican's Congregation for Catholic Education, entitled "Male and Female He Created Them: Towards a Path of Dialogue on the Question of Gender Theory in Education."[51] The thirty-page document, created as a resource for Catholic school leaders, was widely criticized for not consulting with any transgender people during its development. Cardinal Giuseppe Versaldi, a Pope Francis appointee who signed the document as head of the Vatican's Congregation for Catholic Education, acknowledged months after its release that there should have been wider consultation. While it encourages dialogue, opposes bullying, and calls for respecting "every person in their particularity and difference," the document also describes transgender people as representing "a provocative display" and says nonbinary identities reflect harmful ideologies that "annihilate the concept of nature." New policies on gender identity in US dioceses, Palmieri noted, not only send a harmful message to students who are lesbian, gay, bisexual, or transgender but have a chilling effect on teachers as well. "There is a tremendous amount of fear right now among people who work in Catholic schools that if you say or do the wrong thing, or are openly supportive of LGBTQ students, you can lose your job," he said. There are at least thirty-four gender identity policies and guidelines approved by Catholic dioceses across the country, according to Palmieri's research.

The Diocese of Sioux Falls, South Dakota, for example, now mandates that students and school staff use pronouns that they were assigned to at birth and threatens expulsion from school and termination of employment for teachers if they "advocate, celebrate, or express" same-sex attraction or "transgenderism" in a way that would "cause confusion or distraction in the context of Catholic school classes, activities, or events." In a letter addressed to the Catholic faithful of his diocese, Bishop Donald DeGrood wrote that "transgender ideology undermines the very basis for marriage and family, which are foundational to human society itself."[52] Under the policy trans people are also barred from serving as Eucharistic ministers or parish council members and are told not to receive Communion if they are "publicly living a transgender lifestyle or undergoing transition." The diocese acknowledges in the document that the policies are, in its own words, "intentionally exclusionary," but even though the policies are disproportionately focused on policing sexuality and gender identity, the diocese argues that the rules would apply to anyone in "a state of grave sin or public scandal."

In Denver, Colorado, the archdiocese's seventeen-page "Guidance for Issues Concerning the Human Person and Sexuality," warns that "the spread of gender ideology presents a danger to the faith of Christians."[53] The document tells school administrators they should not enroll transgender or gender-nonconforming students, prohibits students from using pronouns that are at "odds with the students biological sex," and bans transgender people from teaching in Catholic schools. The guidance also recommends that school leaders treat gay parents differently than heterosexual couples. On school forms same-sex couples are told to list only one mother or father, for example. "The other adult may be noted elsewhere as an additional emergency contact, but not listed as another parent," it reads. The guidance is intended to help Catholics "withstand" what it calls "the cultural current that threatens to unmoor our foundations." Denver Archbishop Samuel Aquila has also pointed to "transgender ideology" (along with critical race theory) as a reason for declining church attendance.[54] In Portland, Archbishop Alexander Sample released "A Catholic Response to Gender Identity Theory: Catechesis and Pastoral Guidelines" in 2023.[55] The document, which was shared with all Catholic school principals in the archdiocese, also instructs Catholic leaders to engage with students based on their "biological sex identity, rather than self-perceived gender identity." Catholic institutions are not permitted to display signs or symbols that support "gender identity theory." The guidelines are described as a "teaching and formation resource" for Catholic schools, religious education programs, sacramental preparation programs, and youth ministry activities. Hundreds of Portland families whose children attend Catholic schools have protested the guidelines, according to *The Oregonian*. At one Catholic school in the archdiocese, the newspaper reported, at least three faculty members refused to sign off on the archdiocese's guidance, and their contracts were rescinded.[56] Dozens of students responded by refusing to attend Mass and wearing pins and shirts in support of transgender rights. In an interview with the *California Catholic Daily*, Archbishop Sample called young people identifying as transgender "a tsunami coming at us."[57]

Palmieri sees that kind of hyperbole as emblematic of a defensive posture that hinders authentic listening and encounter. "What's driving this attitude is a fear that our schools will be overrun by a so-called ideology that will disrupt our Catholic understanding of the human person," he said. "The conservative movement is pushing that narrative and they have the ear of the bishops."[58] Even symbolic displays of inclusivity have sparked extreme reactions from some church leaders. In 2022 Bishop Robert McManus of Worcester, Massachusetts, stripped a Jesuit middle school of its Catholic status after the school flew flags representing the Black Lives Matter and LGBTQ pride movements.[59] The bishop declared that Nativity School, which is appealing the decision, could no longer use the title Catholic to describe itself and that Mass and the sacraments could no longer be celebrated on school grounds. Flying the flags, the bishop wrote, sends a "mixed, confusing and scandalous message to the public about the Church's stance on these important moral and social issues." In a follow-up letter, he specifically took issue with what he called the Black Lives Matter organization's "agenda for schools." Similar to the "gay pride movement," the bishop wrote, "those principles include, in their own words, to be 'queer affirming' and 'trans affirming.'"[60] Nativity School President Thomas McKenney said in a statement after the bishops' decree that the school's decision to fly the flags "simply state that all are welcome at Nativity and this value of inclusion is rooted in Catholic teaching."[61]

LGBTQ teachers in Catholic schools and other church institutions often face a difficult climate. Since 2007, according to New Ways Ministry, more than a hundred LGBTQ employees have lost their jobs in Catholic institutions.[62] The majority of those fired worked in Catholic schools. Margie Winters, a long-time religious education director at Waldron Mercy Academy in Philadelphia, was fired in 2015 after a parent outed her marriage to another woman. "I love and still love that community because it's part of my heart," she said in 2017. "It was like a death. This kind of firing is a trauma. The sense of exile has been hardest for me."[63] Archbishop Charles Thompson of Indianapolis, Indiana, declared in 2019 that Brebeuf Jesuit Preparatory School could no longer identify as a Catholic school after it refused to comply with the archdiocese's orders to fire a math teacher who is married to another man. The teacher's partner was fired from another Catholic school in the archdiocese. The Midwest Province of the Society of Jesus, which sponsors the Jesuit school, is appealing the archbishop's decision to the Vatican.[64] In another case in Indianapolis a female guidance counselor who worked for fourteen years at a Catholic high school was fired when her marriage to another woman became public. The teacher sued, claiming her work did not involve direct religious instruction, but a federal appeals court in 2023 ruled the archdiocese was within its rights to terminate the employee because of what is known as the "ministerial exception."[65] While religious denominations and churches have long had the legal right to decide who is hired and fired in positions typically filled by clergy, the US Supreme Court in 2012 broadly expanded the definition of what constitutes ministerial functions in ways that apply to more than ordained clergy. In 2023 the Archdiocese of Denver fired a technology teacher who had worked at All Souls Catholic School for six years after archdiocesan officials found a photo of her and her partner. "I know that choosing to work in a Catholic school as a lesbian, as someone within the queer community, might not make sense to everybody," Maggie Barton told Colorado Public Radio. "The reason why I did that is because of my faith. To feel my own faith being weaponized against me in this way, to be terminated and to lose this position is, it's heartbreaking."[66]

LGBTQ teachers who keep their sexuality hidden to avoid being fired also suffer. Emily Grad remembers her time working in a co-ed Catholic high school as a minefield of daily anxiety. "I was always afraid of someone catching me in public with my girlfriend," she told me. "I committed myself to hiding. I was living in shame. It was awful. It made me feel like I had no worth."[67] Grad told the principal at her Jesuit school that she identified as queer when she was hired. The principal assured her that would not be a problem. But Grad, who served as an administrator at the school, also knew that any public disclosure of her relationship with her partner could lead to her firing. The school's employee contract required staff to "adhere to Catholic values," and while the contract did not provide details about what that covered, Grad understood a public same-sex relationship would violate the terms of her employment. As psychologically debilitating as remaining in the closet was for her, the hypocrisy and selective policing of Catholic values made the experience even worse. Grad knew straight colleagues were dating while going through a divorce, living with unmarried partners, and even confiding in her that they were atheists. None of her colleagues seemed to worry those behaviors or beliefs would put their jobs at risk. She also faced open homophobia. A coworker she shared an office with insisted the word "fag" was not derogatory and spoke about a "gay agenda." For more than two years, Grad held her tongue. Eventually she complained to the principal about her colleague's behavior and was told to take it up with human resources. HR acknowledged the problem, but the teacher, who graduated from the school, had been on staff for forty years. His name was on a plaque in the school's athletic stadium. Grad was told the school was just waiting for him to retire. It was the last straw. She resigned. "I kept silent for years because of self-preservation and fear of having my sexuality and relationship disclosed," she said. "But I couldn't do it anymore." Spiritually and mentally exhausted, Grad used the stipend money she received from the school on her departure to take a pilgrimage to the famed Camino de Santiago in Spain. "My faith in God has never wavered but it's harder to forgive people who have done hurtful things," she said. "There are many members of the LGBTQ community who lose their faith because of what people have done to them or people who keep their faith but hold on to their anger. But I want to forgive and have hope that the church can change."

LGBTQ CATHOLIC PARENTS: AN EXPANSIVE UNDERSTANDING OF FAMILY

Marianne Duddy-Burke tears up and her voice still cracks with emotion almost two decades later when she thinks about how the same church that nurtures her faith turned her away from adopting children. The phone call from Catholic Charities of Boston on an early spring day two decades ago felt like a punch to the stomach. "The social worker called from her car during her lunch break and told me the reason we were not getting our calls returned about fostering a child was because we left our names and they knew we were a female couple," Duddy-Burke said. "It was horrendous. I was shaken to the core."[68] Duddy-Burke, the executive director of DignityUSA, a national advocacy organization for LGBTQ Catholics, eventually adopted two children, a daughter and son, with her spouse through a state agency in Massachusetts. Their mother marvels at the deep joy parenting brings even as she carries the scars of those experiences with a Catholic agency. For someone who once lived in a motherhouse with nuns, has a master's degree in theology, and is married to a former Sister of Mercy, the memories are painful. "With the connection we have to Catholicism, it was the hardest rejection we ever faced," Duddy-Burke said. Emily, her daughter, grew up steeped in Catholic culture as part of the affirming DignityUSA community. For a while as a child, she went to Catholic school. Her godparents are Catholic. She was baptized. But Emily no longer considers herself a member of the church. "A lot of kids don't get out of foster care," she said. "I was born addicted to drugs, but my mothers stepped up and gave me a chance. I will always be grateful for that. Being adopted, you always want love and you fear you're never going to get that. They showed me that I was worthy of love."[69]

Catholic Charities of Boston shut down its adoption programs in 2006. "In spite of much effort and analysis, Catholic Charities finds that it cannot reconcile the teaching of the church, which guides our work and the statutes and regulations of the commonwealth," Fr. J. Bryan Hehir, then president of the agency, said in a statement at the time.[70] The forty-two-member Catholic Charities board had voted unanimously to continue considering same-sex adoptions, and eight members of the board later stepped down in protest, according to the *Boston Globe*. Catholic agencies in several states have been embroiled in adoption controversies over the years. When the city council in Washington, DC, passed a measure legalizing same-sex marriage at the end of 2009, Catholic Charities in the nation's capital closed its doors for adoption services in 2010. The agency even stopped providing health insurance benefits to all of its employees to avoid giving benefits to a gay spouse. In 2011 Catholic Charities affiliates in Illinois shut down its more than four-decades-old adoption services rather than comply with a requirement that it could no longer receive state money if it turned away same-sex couples. Catholic Charities of Buffalo followed suit in 2018 after more than fifty years of hosting adoption and foster services. In a major change announced in 2021, the evangelical Bethany Christian Services—one of the nation's largest adoption and foster care agencies with offices in thirty-two states—changed its policy and started placing children with LGBTQ parents. "We will now offer services with the love and compassion of Jesus to the many types of families who exist in our world today," Chris Palusky, the organization's president and chief executive, wrote in an email to staff at the time. "We're taking an 'all hands on deck' approach where all are welcome."[71] Catholic agencies involved with adoption and foster care show no sign of following that lead.

The same year that Bethany Christian Services began placing children with LGBTQ parents, the city of Philadelphia argued that a Catholic social services agency in the city should be prohibited from continuing to receive city funding while refusing to place foster children with same-sex couples, which city officials argued is a violation of Philadelphia's nondiscrimination policy. Two Catholic foster parents and Catholic Social Services countered that the city's policy was religious discrimination. The US Supreme Court agreed in 2021, issuing a unanimous ruling in *Fulton v. Philadelphia*.[72] Chief Justice John Roberts wrote in the court's opinion that the Catholic social service agency "seeks only an accommodation that will allow it to continue serving the children of Philadelphia in a manner consistent with its religious beliefs." The unanimous decision reflected the fact that the case was decided on narrow grounds, specifically the terms of the city's contract with foster care agencies, rather than with broader questions raised by conflicts over religious liberty and LGBTQ rights. Several of the most conservative justices wanted a ruling that was broader in scope and that would have overturned a precedent set in the court's 1990 ruling, *Employment Division v. Smith*, which held that general laws that do not single out religion could not be challenged on the grounds that they violate the First Amendment's protection of the free exercise of religion. The conservative justice Samuel Alito Jr., who in his opinion wrote that "Smith was wrongly decided," argued that "the court has emitted a wisp of a decision that leaves religious liberty in a confused and vulnerable state." While she was relieved that more fundamental protections for LGBTQ rights were not struck down, Marianne Duddy-Burke called it "deeply problematic that some religiously-affiliated agencies continue to seek the ability to ban same-sex couples from opening their hearts and homes to children in need and undermine our hopes for expanding our families. The biases that lie at the heart of this case need to be eradicated."[73]

Interviews I have conducted with Catholic same-sex couples who adopted, moral theologians, former Catholic Charities directors, and case workers at adoption agencies help give a more personal understanding to the often contentious public battles that pit LGBTQ rights against religious liberty. Brian Cahill spent nearly a decade as the executive director of Catholic Charities in San Francisco before retiring in 2008. "If someone is in this kind of work you have to carefully manage the tension between church teaching and how a social service agency functions in a pluralistic society," Cahill told me.[74] While adoption services were never a large part of Catholic Charities' portfolio in San Francisco, the agency quietly helped facilitate the placement of a few children with same-sex couples each year. "I didn't expect many gays and lesbians to come to a Catholic agency, but if they did I wanted to make sure they were treated with dignity," Cahill said. This under-the-radar response became more tenuous to maintain in 2003 when the Vatican spoke in words that reverberated throughout Catholic institutions. The Congregation for the Doctrine of the Faith, or the CDF, then led by Cardinal Joseph Ratzinger, released a document responding to growing cultural and political support for same-sex civil unions. The document denounced those unions as "gravely unjust laws" and stated there were "absolutely no grounds for considering homosexual unions to be in any way similar or even remotely analogous to God's plan for marriage and family." Allowing children to be raised by same-sex couples, it stated, "would actually mean doing violence to these children."[75]

For a few years, Cahill acknowledged, his agency essentially ignored the document and continued placing a handful of children with same-sex couples. The city's archbishop at the time, William Levada, was not a liberal, but he preferred pragmatic solutions to fighting culture wars. In 1997 the archbishop had worked out a compromise after the San Francisco City Council enacted an ordinance requiring all agencies that contracted with the city government to extend health care benefits to people living in domestic partnerships, which included same-sex couples. In an effort to honor church teaching on both marriage and the moral right to health care, the "Levada Solution," as it became known, took root in the archdiocese. In a type of "don't ask-don't tell" maneuver, church employees in San Francisco would be allowed to designate anyone legally domiciled with them to share their benefits, whether an aging parent, unemployed sister, or gay partner. But when Archbishop Levada was picked to lead the Vatican's doctrine office in

2005, the cardinal who had crafted a deft solution over a thorny issue years earlier was now tasked to be an enforcer. Sparked by a press inquiry from *The Boston Globe*, the cardinal sent a statement back to his former archdiocese in San Francisco stating that "it has been and remains my position that Catholic agencies should not place children in homosexual households."[76] Cahill had a meeting with Archbishop George Niederauer, Levada's replacement, and told him he wanted to find a way forward that would not exclude same-sex couples seeking to adopt without violating church teaching. Niederauer, who Cahill described as a "traditional bishop but with a pastoral streak," didn't stop him.

Several theologians were brought in for consultation. Catholic Charities could not directly place children with same-sex couples without violating church teaching. Instead, the agency began working with Family Builders, a nonprofit organization that handled the placement. In the terminology used by moral theologians, the Catholic agency's participation now fell under the principle of "remote material cooperation," sufficiently removed from direct involvement and not intended to engage in activities contrary to church teaching. "I felt strongly about serving these families because we were a social service organization and that is what we did," Cahill said. "In California, some of the largest cohorts for potential adoptive parents are gay and lesbian couples. I was also the father of a gay son. I knew how he suffered so there was a personal part too." But when conservative Catholic media outlets began targeting Catholic Charities, the archdiocese was on the defensive. When Cahill retired in 2008, there was waning energy to continue threading the theological needle and maintaining the partnership with Family Builders. Catholic Charities ended its adoption work. Cahill views the current legal, cultural, and theological divides over gay adoption as part of broader church trends. "In the name of religious liberty bishops are trying to force their beliefs on others who don't share those beliefs," he told me. "It's not just the issue of foster care and adoption. You see it in their opposition to the Equality Act. Even some of the good bishops who are trying to do the right thing often gloss over the infuriating, destructive and hypocritical dichotomy of saying we love and respect LGBTQ people but also condemning them."[77]

Meli Barber supervises case workers at a nonprofit agency in Indianapolis that places foster children and youth with adopted parents. In a conservative red state, her agency has become a magnet for LGBTQ couples. "A common thread we see is people would do information sessions at other agencies and they may not be told 'no,' but they don't feel welcome or wanted," said Barber, formerly the director of religious education in the Archdiocese of

Indianapolis.[78] Same-sex couples have to be especially intentional about their decision to adopt, she said, and during visits with prospective parents Barber is impressed by how much care goes into preparing their homes. Same-sex parents are seven times more likely to raise adopted and foster children than straight couples, according to the Williams Institute at UCLA School of Law. LGBTQ children and youth are also overrepresented in the foster-care system, in many cases because they are rejected by family for their sexual orientation or gender identity. More than a third of New York City's young people in foster care, for example, identify as LGBTQ, according to a survey from the city's child welfare agency. These young people are placed more often in group homes or residential care rather than family homes, according to the survey, and are more likely to report having depression.[79] The Annie E. Casey Foundation also has found that nearly a quarter of young people in its foster care programs in seventeen states identify as LGBTQ. "A strength we see with queer couples is because many have experienced family rejection, they have a more expansive understanding of what it means to be a family and to choose a family," Barber said.

Jacob Kohlhaas, associate professor of moral theology at Loras College in Dubuque, Iowa, thinks church leaders can draw from Catholic tradition to embrace what he calls "a broader theological vision of parenthood."[80] He cites both secular and church history to make a case for why narrowly defining parental roles based on sexual complementarianism is shortsighted. The Rule of St. Benedict, he noted, includes instructions for myriad aspects of life, including accommodations for children in abbeys, which means in some cases monks were helping to raise children in community. Catholic nuns often led orphanages. Priests in recent years have adopted children. "When the church talks about parenting, it's really talking about sex," said Kohlhaas, author of *Beyond Biology: Rethinking Parenthood in the Catholic Tradition* (Georgetown University Press, 2021). "If the church is not opposed to single parenting and collective parenting, why are we opposed to same-sex parenting? It really all comes down to sex. My argument is we need to think more about parenting capabilities. Parenthood is essentially a commitment that involves a lot of work and shared roles." The church's restrictive views of gender roles and complementarianism, he adds, often creates a barrier to learning from contemporary research. "The church came to have a much healthier relationship with the natural sciences in the 20th century," he said. "But we have a tense relationship with the social sciences. We dismiss reliable research and call it ideology. There isn't any real indication there are developmental problems with kids raised by same-sex couples. To claim there is a problem without showing evidence makes the church look non-credible."

The shifting legal landscape surrounding religious liberty and LGBTQ rights, or the finer points of moral theology, are not what most same-sex parents are losing sleep over. Instead, they believe the real-life stories of struggle and success can humanize debates that too often feel abstract. John Freml and his husband, Rick, adopted a baby girl in 2016 through a private Illinois agency. It was a dream fulfilled, and they immediately bonded with their daughter. But when a few of the infant's biological family members found out the child had been placed with a same-sex couple, they took action to remove the baby. Experts made home visits. The Department of Children and Family Services seemed to favor keeping the child in Freml's home. But the painful process dragged on for over a year and cost the couple more than $30,000 in legal fees. They eventually lost in court. "It was heartbreaking," Freml said. "It took us a while to recover."[81] The couple later successfully adopted and now have a seven-year-old son, Riley, and a nine-year-old daughter, Jordan. They had planned to raise their children in a religious tradition. But Freml acknowledges his Catholic faith has been tested by the church's opposition to LGBTQ rights—from the firing of gay teachers in Catholic schools to bishops fighting the Equality Act and opposing same-sex couples adopting children. He drifted away from the church but eventually found his way back after his bishop, Thomas Paprocki of Springfield, Illinois, led prayers of "supplication and exorcism" to protest the state passing a marriage equality law in 2013.[82] Freml called the spectacle "egregious and hurtful." "I found a group of Catholic moms of LGBTQ kids protesting outside the cathedral," he said. "They hugged me and we cried and we sang. It really brought me back to the church. It showed me there was a place for me in the church." But in recent years, he has struggled to identify as Catholic. "My kids come from foster care and had such traumatic experiences in their lives even before they came to live with us so to think they might sit in Mass on a Sunday and hear a homily that calls their parents 'disordered' would only inflict more trauma on them," Freml said. He wants church leaders to hear a simple message. "LGBTQ families are no different from heterosexual families. We have the same desire to connect and to love."

TRANSGENDER CATHOLICS: "WE ARE NOT AN IDEOLOGY. WE ARE PEOPLE."

Christine Zuba walked into confession at a crossroads in her life. After feeling trapped in a man's body for decades, the fifty-eight-year-old told a priest at her Catholic church that she was transgender and had started her transition to becoming a woman. Back in 2014 not many people were talking about transgender experiences. The lifelong Catholic had no idea what to expect. At first, the priest brought up sex. She stopped him. "This has nothing at all to do with sex," she explained to him. "This is who I am. You can throw me out if you want, but if you do, I'm coming right back. This is my church too."[83] The priest assured her she was welcome. "Let's together say a prayer to our Blessed Mother to help guide you on your journey," he said. Zuba left confession with tears of relief running down her cheeks. About a month later, she returned to confession again and spoke with the church's monsignor. His first words were, "God loves everyone." The monsignor acknowledged that while he understood being gay, the transgender subject was relatively new to him. "I will need you to help me learn," he told her. Zuba was moved by his humility and acceptance. Not long afterward, the priest asked her to become a Eucharistic minister. Her parish, Saints Peter and Paul in Turnersville, New Jersey, also started a LGBTQ ministry. Zuba is grateful for her experience of welcome and respect. She understands many transgender Catholics never find that acceptance. "I know others are told they are sinners, that they are not Catholic," she said. "One of my best friends was even physically carried out of church after being refused Communion." If Zuba lived in the Diocese of Marquette in Michigan, for example, she would be prohibited from receiving the sacraments or serving in any church leadership positions unless she repented, under a policy instituted by the bishop in 2021 that excludes gay, transgender, and nonbinary Catholics from baptism, Communion, and confirmation.[84]

Zuba knew since the time she was four years old that she was different. She would go to bed praying that she would wake up a girl. As a male growing up in a traditional Polish American Catholic family, Zuba pushed those feelings down, dated, and eventually married in a Catholic church. She became a father of two children and was married for twenty-nine years. The decision to finally acknowledge her long suppressed identity, she said, felt existential. She prayed and went to therapy as she considered transitioning. "At first, I didn't think I could do it because I worried I would lose my faith, my family, my friends, everything," Zuba said. "But after a while it was something I had to do. I was prepared to lose everything." Her friends, family and church have embraced her in ways she never expected. Zuba also found out she wasn't alone. She began connecting with other gay, lesbian, and transgender Catholics across New Jersey who were active in LGBTQ ministries. A loose network formed over phone calls, events, and Zoom meetings. The group, Zuba said, "shares our joys and struggles." After she gave a talk in New York City, the executive director of Fortunate Families, a national Catholic ministry for LGBTQ Catholics, families, and allies invited her to become involved with the organization, and she eventually became chair of the group's transgender ministry. Zuba is now part of a small but expanding cohort of Catholics who are nationally known for speaking, writing, and advocating for transgender rights in the church. "It's so joyful to work with so many people who are trying to make our church more inclusive," she said. "There are parishes and priests that quietly reach out and minister to the LGBTQ community. Some of them don't make a big deal out of it because they are afraid. I do think there is a growing acceptance in our church, but a lot of bishops are afraid to speak out in this political environment." An exception has been Cardinal Joseph Tobin of Newark, New Jersey. The cardinal invited Zuba and more than a dozen LGBTQ Catholics and family members to dinner at his residence in 2018. "I was representing trans people and the cardinal just sat back, listened, and said 'tell me what you want me to know,'" she said. "It was just amazing." In 2022 Zuba had another experience she never could have imagined when she first decided to transition and worried everything in her life would shatter. Fr. Alex Santora, the pastor at Our Lady of Grace church in Hoboken, New Jersey, invited her to speak at the parish's annual Pride Mass in support of the LGBTQ community. "We are not disordered, confused or a fad," she told the congregation.[85] I asked Zuba what she most wanted church leaders to know about transgender people. "Just listen to our stories, our dreams, our hopes, and try to understand our lives as human beings and fellow Catholics," she told me. "Don't lump us into categories. We are not an ideology. We are people. I don't wake up in the morning thinking about being transgender. Our lives are no different than anyone else's. We live, we work, we pray. We have families. We ask simply to be accepted and to be a part of our church." Zuba said she is "cautiously and prayerfully optimistic" that the synod will bring more Catholics to a deeper discernment when it comes to understanding transgender people. "But we have to keep working," she said. "We can't stop being visible."

When Sister Luisa Derouen began ministering to transgender people in the late 1990s, she worked underground and even used a pseudonym to avoid drawing attention from what she calls "the orthodoxy police." At the time there was little if any public conversations about transgender rights in society. Few Catholic leaders were even thinking about ministry to lesbian and gay people. The legalization of same-sex marriage was still fifteen years away. Transgender people existed in the shadows. In New Orleans Sister Luisa started going to a support group meeting for LGBTQ people hosted by a secular gay rights organization. One day a woman walked in, and everyone started applauding. It was her first time at the meeting since her gender transition surgery. Sister Luisa reached out. "I told her I didn't know anything about this so I asked her if I could learn from her and told her I wanted to be an ally and be supportive," she said. "She was a deeply spiritual person and told me that for many transgender people a gender transition is part of a profoundly spiritual journey, but they don't have anyone to walk with them. I knew then that God was calling me to this ministry."[86] There were hardly any Catholics providing ministry to transgender people two decades ago. Sister Luisa recalls introducing herself at an international transgender conference in 2001 in Galveston, Texas, attended by several hundred transgender men and women, therapists, attorneys, and other advocates so she could connect with other religious advocates or clergy. She received a standing ovation from the crowd because she was the only faith leader in attendance. Since those early days, the Catholic sister has ministered to and accompanied more than 250 transgender people. She has listened to devoted Catholics who confess feeling worthless and sinful. Many have told her that God doesn't love them. More than a few have told her they fear going to hell. Some share their suicidal thoughts. Many are afraid of coming out but can't endure living a lie anymore. "Transgender people have made me a better Catholic and a better woman," Sister Luisa told me. "No ministry has shaped my own relationship with God the way this has. I have met so many holy people. They have taught me about courage and what it takes to live an authentic life and the price of that integrity."

In an effort to expand the number of Catholic leaders ministering to transgender and nonbinary people, Sister Luisa helped Fortunate Families start a "Transgender Ministry of Accompaniment" training course for pastoral ministers. In small groups, spiritual directors, therapists, ministry leaders, priests, sisters, and others receive resources and practical training for accompanying transgender people. Each trainee in the fifteen-week program is paired with a transgender person. A second track of workshops is designed for leaders in Catholic schools, dioceses, parish LGBTQ ministries, and Catholic schools. The ministry training launched in 2023, and within a few weeks seventy people applied. Session topics have included "Words Matter: Language and Terms," "Medical Realities for Trans People," "Parenting a Transgender Child," and "Spiritual Companioning and Counseling." While Sister Luisa stands out for her longtime advocacy for and ministry to the transgender community, Catholic sisters more broadly are some of the most vocal advocates for trans people and LGBTQ inclusion in the church. In 2023 more than six thousand sisters representing more than two dozen communities of women religious across the country endorsed a statement of solidarity with transgender people. "As members of the body of Christ, we cannot be whole without the full inclusion of transgender, nonbinary, and gender-expansive individuals," the statement reads. "We will remain oppressors until we—as vowed Catholic religious—acknowledge the existence of LGBTQ people in our own congregations. We seek to cultivate a faith community where all, especially our transgender, nonbinary, and gender-expansive siblings, experience a deep belonging."[87] The solidarity statement also challenged what it calls "harmful rhetoric from some Christian institutions and their leaders, including the Catholic Church," toward transgender people. The statement concludes with a call to "transform our hearts, our church, our politics, and our country" to ensure that the trans community is "acknowledged, boldly accepted, and celebrated."

When Sister Luisa reads statements from bishops who disparage advocacy for transgender rights—Oklahoma City Archbishop Paul Coakley claimed that "the trans movement is doing great damage to society," for example—she recognizes a profound lack of humility.[88] "I think bishops often listen in order to correct, but we also need to listen so we can learn," she told me. "When you listen to learn you also have to be willing to change. I think that terrifies some bishops." She wishes more church leaders would lead in the way that Bishop Thomas Zinkula has done in the Diocese of Davenport, Iowa. As bishops across the country were releasing policies that banned the use of pronouns that don't correspond to a person's biological sex and prohibited transgender people from teaching in schools or receiving Communion, Zinkula charted a different course. When the diocese formed a gender committee to study these issues, church leaders consulted widely with and listened to transgender people, parents of transgender children, and those like Sister Luisa who have accompanied transgender people. The committee also consulted with a pediatrician and a child and adolescent psychiatrist, both of whom acknowledged the complexities of the issues. "When we first met, the idea was to put together a policy on how to handle sexual and gender identity issues that were beginning to arise in schools and parishes," Bishop Zinkula told Davenport's diocesan newspaper. "But we didn't know enough about this topic yet, much less the people who would be affected by any policy we drafted and implemented."[89] Instead of a rigid policy of prohibitions, the diocese developed a guide for pastoral accompaniment of sexual and gender minorities in schools and parishes. The diocesan newspaper also published a series, "A Pastoral Approach to Gender," that received widespread praise and also some backlash from Catholics in Davenport. In one article written by the bishop, he addressed the criticism. "A few people consider it an imprudent use of time and space to address something that affects only a small minority of the population," Bishop Zinkula wrote. "It is true that the percentage of people experiencing gender dysphoria is small, but does that mean we don't need to minister to them? Jesus told a parable about the good shepherd leaving the 99 to go in search of the 1 lost sheep. We are obliged to seek out and minister to LGBTQ+ persons who are so often misunderstood and even vilified."[90] The bishop said that he had been "haunted" by a story a parent shared with the diocese's gender committee of a child who was told by a pastor how the youth had to dress at a confirmation Mass. Even after complying, the pastor didn't allow the young person to receive Communion. "The next Sunday the pastor preached that LGBTQ+ people will go to hell," the bishop wrote. "On Monday, the young person attempted suicide. This type of thing should never ever happen." The bishop acknowledged that some people are uncomfortable talking about transgender and nonbinary people but insisted that silence is unacceptable. "If the Church puts her head in the sand, closes her eyes, hopes this matter will simply go away and doesn't say anything about it, she would be making a huge statement to people experiencing gender dysphoria and those who love them. The silence would be deafening," he wrote. "Basically, the Church would be saying that she doesn't see you, hear you or care about you."

TRANSGENDER PATIENTS AND CATHOLIC HOSPITALS

One of the most contentious and complicated issues to emerge in recent years is how Catholic hospitals should approach particular types of medical care for transgender patients. More than one in seven US hospital patients receive treatment in a Catholic hospital, according to the Catholic Health Association, which includes more than six hundred hospitals and 1,600 long-term care and other health facilities. Catholic-affiliated health facilities are the largest group of nonprofit health care providers in the nation. When Jesse Hammons, a transgender man, went to a Catholic hospital in Maryland operated by the University of Maryland Medical System in 2019, a physician scheduled him for a hysterectomy as treatment for his diagnosis of gender dysphoria. The night before the surgery the doctor canceled the procedure. The hospital's chief medical officer decided the surgery could not be performed at a Catholic hospital because it would violate the US bishops' Ethical and Religious Directives for Catholic Health Services. The American Civil Liberties Union represented Hammons in court. A federal judge ruled in 2023 that the patient's rights were violated, and the medical system had to follow Maryland antidiscrimination law.[91] The Catholic hospital also receives federal Medicaid and Medicare funding. Section 1557 of the Affordable Care Act prohibits providers receiving federal funding from discriminating on the "basis of race, color, national origin, age, disability, or sex," and specifically includes provisions for "pregnancy, sexual orientation, gender identity, and sex characteristics."[92]

A few months after the ruling, the US bishops' conference released a document reaffirming that gender transition procedures should not take place at Catholic hospitals. In the fourteen-page doctrinal note, entitled "Moral Limits to the Technological Manipulation of the Human Body," members of the bishops' doctrine committee wrote that Catholic hospitals "must not perform interventions, whether surgical or chemical, that aim to transform the sexual characteristics of a human body into those of the opposite sex, or take part in the development of such procedures."[93] The Ethical and Religious Directives for Catholic hospitals, often called ERDs, were last revised in the mid-1990s and do not specifically address gender-transition procedures or gender affirming care more broadly, but according to the Catholic Health Association elective surgeries on reproductive organs where no pathology exists would be prohibited under the existing guidelines. When the US bishops' conference released the doctrinal note, Sister Mary Haddad, CEO of the Catholic Health Association, emphasized that "Catholic health care providers will continue to respect the dignity of our transgender patients and provide them with the same quality care we provide to all our patients." The "well-being of the whole person," she said in a statement, "must be taken into account in deciding about any therapeutic intervention or use of technology in caring for our patients."[94] Rev. Charlie Bouchard, the senior director of theology and sponsorship at the Catholic Health Association, told the Associated Press that the bishops' doctrinal note would not impact the care transgender patients receive at Catholic hospitals. "As we look at the document from the bishops, what we are mindful of is that we have a history of caring for the marginalized, and we see transgender people very much as a marginalized group," Bouchard said.[95] But Francis DeBernardo, a gay Catholic and executive director of New Ways Ministry, pointed out that the bishops' document does not reflect the lived experiences of transgender people and refuses to engage with or even acknowledge experts' guidance. "Nearly every major medical and psychological organization finds that gender-affirming medical interventions positively aid transgender people's human flourishing," he said. "This professional consensus about the best standards of care for transgender people is absent from the bishops' text." DeBernardo added that the document "relies on papal statements from the mid-20th century," but ignores that "the world has undergone an enormous transformation in understanding what is natural about gender."[96]

The US bishops' conference voted in June 2023 to start a process that could lead to a revision of the Ethical and Religious Directives. The section of the directives that the bishops voted to potentially revise has not been updated since 1994. "At that time," read the proposal the bishops approved, "it was not envisioned that it might be necessary to include specific guidance concerning radical modifications of the human body, such as are frequently advocated today for the treatment of the condition commonly known as gender dysphoria or gender incongruence."[97] Before the vote, several bishops spoke on the floor of the meeting and urged the doctrine committee to broaden its consultation before any revisions are made to the ERDs. "How do we help people who are wrestling with dysphoria?" San Diego Cardinal Robert McElroy asked. Cardinal Joseph Tobin of Newark urged the committee to consult a wide range of experts during the drafting process, "including people who are from the trans community." Archbishop Paul Etienne of Seattle called the issues involved in any revisions of Catholic health care directives "a delicate matter."[98] Therese Lysaught, a professor at the Neiswanger Institute for Bioethics and Health Policy at Loyola University Chicago, argued that the bishops' doctrinal note is fundamentally flawed. "The committee had an opportunity to open a real conversation both within the church and with our culture more broadly on these questions, and to begin to rebuild the credibility the U.S. bishops' conference has lost via the sexual abuse crisis and its role in the culture wars," wrote Lysaught, a member of the Pontifical Academy of Life.[99] "Instead, they chose a path that closed off further dialogue and further undermined the church's credibility. On the upside, the committee has demonstrated conclusively that the manualist method—the cold morality that persists as a remnant of another era—is intellectually, theologically and morally bankrupt." She contrasted the bishops' document with the approach Pope Francis encouraged during a 2023 address to Pontifical Alphonsian Academy. "I invite you to cultivate the patience of listening and exchange, as St. Alphonsus recommends for conflictual situations. Do not be afraid to listen," the pope said.

> It will be fundamental for the search for common solutions, that recognize and ensure respect for the sacrality of every life, in every condition. This listening will then be decisively enriched by the adoption of transdisciplinary research methods, which enables an approach to new challenges with greater competence and critical capacity, in the light of the Gospel and human experience. Only in this way will it be possible to develop reasonable and solid arguments in the bioethical

> field, rooted in faith, adapted to adult and responsible consciences and capable of inspiring socio-political debate.

The contrast between the US bishops and Pope Francis, Lysaught observed, "could not be more stark."

When the US bishops approved a proposal to begin considering a formal ban in Catholic hospitals of providing what is often described by advocates and doctors as gender-affirming care, I was at Fordham University in New York City covering the largest LGBTQ Catholic ministry event in the country. News of the bishops' action spread quickly through the Outreach conference, where several hundred LGBTQ Catholics, advocates, pastoral counselors, theologians, clergy, and allies from the United States and eight countries gathered for three days of dialogue, Masses, keynote speakers, and panel discussions. Pope Francis and New York Cardinal Timothy Dolan sent messages of support in the days leading up to the gathering. Ray Dever, a retired Catholic deacon from Florida who has a transgender daughter, seemed anguished by the bishops' vote that day. A soft-spoken man in his seventies, Dever has traveled around the country telling anyone who will listen that the church he loves can't be on the side of exclusion. "It's time for all of us—the people of God who are the church—to actively engage and not stand by passively while the words and actions of the church contribute to the stigmatization of transgender people," he told the audience during a panel discussion.[100] "At the heart of this issue is the Gospel. We're called to love our neighbor and those on the peripheries." Part of loving, respecting, and healing, he argued, is recognizing what he called "the pro-life nature of medically necessary gender-affirming care." When he watches bishops and other Catholics support the surge of legislation in states across the country that target transgender medical care and erode LGBTQ rights more broadly, Dever thinks of his transgender daughter Lexi, who attended Catholic schools and attempted suicide before finding a network of support and acceptance at Georgetown University. "As a church, we should be healers and life givers," he said. "It's time for the war on transgender people to stop and the church has a role to play in stopping it."

WHEN RELIGIOUS LIBERTY AND LGBTQ RIGHTS CLASH

Cardinal Blase Cupich of Chicago and New York Cardinal Timothy Dolan are often viewed as church leaders representing contrasting camps in the American hierarchy. The more "progressive" Cupich and the more "conservative" Dolan teamed up for a co-bylined article in *America* magazine in 2022 entitled, "Catholic Hospitals Welcome Transgender Patients—and Stand Firm in Their Religious Convictions."[101] In part the article was a response to efforts from the Biden administration to realign federal regulations with a 2020 Supreme Court decision that found discrimination against transgender people is a form of sex discrimination. In the wake of the ruling, the Biden administration announced it would prohibit discrimination on the basis of sexual orientation and gender identity at medical centers that receive federal funding—reversing a policy adopted under President Donald Trump. The US bishops' conference denounced the regulations as "a violation of religious freedom and bad medicine" that would force Catholic hospitals to perform gender transition surgeries.[102]

Cardinals Cupich and Dolan argued that Catholic hospitals serve all people, no matter their age, sex, racial or ethnic background, or religion. "It is also true for people who identify as transgender," the cardinals wrote. "They will receive the same treatment as any other patient. Catholic hospitals do not discriminate against anyone and to do so would be offensive to the embracing and expansive healing ministry of Jesus Christ. However, if health care facilities are to be places where the twin pillars of faith and science stand together, then these facilities and their workers must not be coerced by the government to violate their consciences." Objecting to performing gender transition procedures, they proposed, is not discrimination. "The focus of such an objection is completely on the procedure, not the patient," they wrote. "Prohibiting the removal of a healthy, functioning organ is not discrimination, provided that the same determination would be made for anyone of any sex or gender, which is true at Catholic hospitals."

Writing in *Commonweal* magazine, Jacqui Oesterblad, a civil rights attorney, affirmed that because "the Catholic healthcare tradition matters," the US bishops need a more convincing set of arguments to make their case in the public square. "Those who want Catholic institutions to remain substantively Catholic and to provide medical care within the constraints of Catholic medical ethics must articulate a more robust definition of pluralism and conscience rights," Oesterblad argued. Responding to the claim that Catholic hospitals do not discriminate against transgender patients, she observed:

> Many in Catholic health care argue that criticism over supposed discrimination against transgender patients is misplaced: Catholic hospitals will not perform certain procedures for *anyone* of *any* sex

> or gender. That's certainly true of some procedures, like vaginoplasties or tubal ligations. But the U.S. Health and Human Services antidiscrimination regulations are not referring to those. Doctors can choose the focus of their practice, and no law is going to force them to perform a procedure they don't have the skills and experience to perform. Instead, what is explicitly mentioned are hysterectomies, which Catholic hospitals can and *do* perform, in line with the Catholic ERDs. It's not true that Catholic hospitals decline to perform this specific procedure for everyone and for every reason. They perform this procedure for everyone with every medical diagnosis *except for* gender dysphoria. And this is the core of the disagreement.
>
> The only reason to perform a hysterectomy on a cisgender woman with endometriosis but not on a transgender man with gender dysphoria is if one has decided that gender dysphoria—a medical condition recognized in the DSM-5 and covered by insurance—is different from other medical conditions. That is a permissible distinction to draw in Catholic ethics. But legally, treating some diagnoses recognized by the broader medical community differently from others based on the gender associated with those diagnoses is the very definition of sex discrimination. Does this mean that Catholic practitioners and providers should be forced to violate their consciences and sincere religious beliefs? No. But it means Catholic hospitals are going to need an affirmative carve-out from nondiscrimination law. They need to *convince* lawmakers, and the voting public, that Catholic hospitals deserve an exception. It's no longer good enough, if it ever was, to argue that Catholic hospitals don't discriminate. Instead, Catholic hospitals need to argue that allowing them to remain substantively Catholic is good for American pluralism—and, crucially, that Catholic conscience rights don't have to interfere with anybody else's rights.[103]

Conscience always plays a role in the provision of medical care, Oesterblad added, but debates over conscience rights must not be framed simply. "The question is not whether conscience can be a limiting factor in health care," she writes, "but how to balance all the consciences at play. A basic starting principle is clear: A person who believes only in conscience rights for people who agree with them does not, by definition, believe in conscience rights. Conversations about conscience are fundamentally conversations about compromise."

Religious Liberty: From Consensus to Culture War

Beyond the complex tangle of theological, medical, pastoral, and practical questions at play in Catholic health care, broader societal debates over how to reconcile LGBTQ rights and religious liberty have turned increasingly rancorous. Not long ago religious freedom was largely viewed across the ideological and political spectrum as a bedrock value of American democracy that transcended partisanship. When the Religious Freedom Restoration Act passed Congress in 1993, Republicans and Democrats rallied to support the bipartisan legislation. The act came in response to a controversial 1990 US Supreme Court ruling, *Employment Division v. Smith,* that upheld the firing of two Native Americans who ingested peyote as part of religious ceremonies. In a 5–4 ruling, the late Justice Antonin Scalia wrote for the majority arguing that granting a religious exemption would "open the prospect of constitutionally required exemptions from civic obligations of almost every conceivable kind."[104] Legal decisions, politics, and cultural shifts have radically reconfigured the landscape since then. Religious freedom is now at the epicenter of the culture wars. In a 2014 US Supreme Court case brought by the evangelical Christian owners of the giant Hobby Lobby arts-and-crafts chain, justices ruled for the first time that even for-profit companies have religious conscience rights. In state legislatures across the country, GOP lawmakers attempted to pass narrowly defined religious freedom bills that offered sweeping exemptions for faith-based providers and that pitted the human rights of LGBTQ people against religious conscience—a false choice that serves neither important value.

At the federal level the Trump administration created a religious liberty task force housed in the Department of Justice to oversee legal directives on religious liberty cases. "A dangerous movement, undetected by many but real, is now challenging and eroding a great tradition of religious freedom," then Attorney General Jeff Sessions intoned ominously when announcing the task force.[105] "For many today, religious liberty is not a cherished freedom," Supreme Court Justice Samuel Alito Jr. told the Federalist Society in 2020. "It pains me to say this, but, in certain quarters, religious liberty is fast becoming a disfavored right."[106] That claim does not apply to the Supreme Court itself. According to a 2021 study published in *The Supreme Court Review* that considered seven decades of data, there has been a thirty-five-percentage point increase in the rate of rulings in favor of religion in orally argued cases, culminating in an 81 percent success rate in the court led by Chief Justice John G. Roberts Jr.[107] In cases involving the intersection of LGBTQ rights, religious liberty, and free speech claims, the court in recent years has often embraced an expansive reading of religious claims at the expense of protections for LGBTQ people. In 2018 the court ruled in favor of a Colorado baker who argued his Christian beliefs compelled him to refuse making a wedding cake for a gay couple. In 2023 the court sided with a Colorado web designer who argued she had a right to refuse to design wedding websites for same-sex couples despite a state law that prohibits discrimination against gay people by businesses open to the public. "We've seen a dramatic expansion of rights for conservative religious communities that has had a detrimental impact on equality rights, certainly for LGBTQ people," Elizabeth Platt, director of the Law, Rights and Religion Project at Columbia Law School, told *Reuters* after the decision.[108] High-profile Republicans such as Donald Trump's former Attorney General William Barr, have also defended religious liberty in highly selective ways. While Barr excoriated "militant secularists" for mobilizing "an unremitting assault on religion," his Department of Justice often dismissed religious liberty claims made by progressive advocates whose activism is inspired by their faith convictions. Under Barr's leadership the Justice Department prosecuted Scott Warren, a humanitarian aid volunteer arrested for leaving water for migrants crossing the Arizona desert. Warren argued his religious beliefs motivated his advocacy. As part of his 2019 acquittal the judge agreed with aspects of his legal arguments that the Religious Freedom Restoration Act applied to his case. Warren was one of dozens of people nationwide targeted by the Trump administration for acting on their religious beliefs on behalf of progressive and humanitarian causes, according to the Law, Rights, and Religion Project at Columbia Law School. The project's 2019 report, "Whose Faith Matters? The Fight for Religious Liberty beyond the Christian Right," chronicles the often-ignored religious liberty activism taking place outside of the conservative movement, including by those whose faith motivates them to assist immigrants, protect the environment, and protest capital punishment.[109]

While the conservative politicization of religious liberty is evident in court rulings, legislative efforts and right-wing victimization rhetoric that claims religion is under assault by the left, prominent liberal leaders have at times also contributed to growing polarization around questions of religious liberty. Along with other Catholic progressives, I have been critical of the leadership of the Knights of Columbus, a Catholic fraternal society whose top executives have been active in Republican political causes. But it was wrong when Democratic members of Congress, then Sen. Kamala Harris and Sen. Mazie Hirono of Hawaii, aggressively questioned a Catholic nominated for a federal judgeship in 2019 about his membership in the Knights during his confirmation hearings. The line of questioning implied that his membership might be considered an impediment to his nomination. Sen. Harris raised concerns about the Knights for the organization's opposition to abortion and same-sex marriage and for being "an all-male society." Sen. Hirono directly asked the nominee, "if confirmed, do you intend to end your membership with this organization to avoid any appearance of bias?"[110] After widespread criticism of the senators, including charges that the questions were anti-Catholic, the US Senate unanimously adopted a resolution "to reaffirm religious liberty and condemn religious tests for federal officials."[111] Melissa Rogers, the executive director of the White House Office of Faith-Based and Neighborhood Partnerships under President Biden who formerly served in the same position under President Obama, has pointed to language used in a 2016 report from the US Civil Rights Commission that framed religious liberty as a guise for discrimination, intolerance, and homophobia as an example of an insufficient appreciation for the value of religious freedom. "Some government officials have erred by presuming that religious beliefs and practices are insincere and that everything they would define as 'intolerance' can and should be eradicated by the state," Rogers, a church–state attorney, wrote in her book *Faith in American Public Life*.[112] The government at times "must reject some requests for religious exemptions," Rogers writes, "but they should do so without disparaging people's faith or appearing to call into question an entire First Amendment right." In *A Time to Heal, a Time to Build*, a Brookings Institution report authored by Rogers and E. J. Dionne Jr., the authors provide a series of recommendations for how to honor both religious freedom and pluralism. Rogers and Dionne write that "even the words 'religious freedom' have become toxic in recent years."[113] When I interviewed Rogers in 2020, she acknowledged that finding common ground on religious liberty issues has become harder. "At the same time," she said,

> I tend to agree with Supreme Court Justice Elena Kagan, who recently said that we can still often find common ground if we reframe the question or split off a smaller question. When I was in the Obama administration, we did that on some issues related to partnerships between government and faith-based organizations. We couldn't agree on some important issues like religious exemptions from certain civil-rights protections that apply to the use of taxpayer funds, but we looked at some other issues regarding protections for religious-liberty beneficiaries, and we found much more to agree about there.[114]

Douglas Laycock, an emeritus professor of law at the University of Virginia who is one of the most preeminent experts on religious liberty, thinks we have reached a stalemate in trying to strike a balance between respect for religious freedom and LGBTQ equality. Religious institutions that see a threat to their conscience rights and LGBTQ advocacy groups have become "deeply intolerant and have no respect for the rights of the other side," Laycock told me. "Both sides are dug in."[115] Laycock has advocated for same-sex marriage protections and also defended conscience exemptions for religious organizations. The Catholic Church and other religious institutions that hold traditional beliefs about marriage and sexuality face what Laycock calls "unprecedented demands" from city, state, and federal policies. At the same time, he noted, religious individuals and faith-based institutions have often overreached in making religious-liberty claims. A reasonable accommodation of religious-conscience concerns in a diverse public square, Laycock argues, is different from an absolutist understanding of religious liberty that has no limits. "Conservatives in Congress have introduced bills with names like the First Amendment Defense Act, which would provide absolute protection for religious beliefs and practices about marriage and zero additional protection for same-sex couples," he wrote in 2022. "Liberals have introduced bills with names like the Equality Act, which would prohibit sexual orientation or gender-identity discrimination in every area of federal regulation that protects individuals, provide zero protection for religious liberty, and actually repeal existing protections for religious liberty. Neither side can pass such one-sided legislation. But hardliners on both sides have opposed any compromise. They would rather do without legislative protection for their own rights than permit any protection for the other side's rights."[116]

Among those unwilling to compromise, he includes the US Conference of Catholic Bishops. The bishops opposed the Respect for Marriage Act, a bill designed to both protect same-sex marriage and protect religious liberty with respect to marriage. The legislation, which Laycock said is a model for showing that "legislative progress on gay rights requires corresponding protections for religious liberty," was supported by a range of conservative religious organizations such as the National Association of Evangelicals, the Council of Christian Colleges and Universities, and the Church of Jesus Christ of Latter-day Saints. Catholic bishops opposed the bill because of its "rejection of timeless truths about marriage is evident on its face and in its purpose," according to a letter from the US bishops' conference signed by Cardinal Timothy Dolan of New York and Bishop Robert Barron of Diocese of Winona-Rochester, Minnesota, who chaired the bishops' Committee on

Laity, Marriage, Family Life and Youth.[117] "If the Catholic view of marriage is the only true one and all other views are false, and if such falsehoods can never be enacted in legislation, then the adequacy or inadequacy of religious-liberty protections becomes irrelevant," Laycock wrote in response.[118] "The bishops will oppose any legislation that provides any protection for same-sex marriage, because such legislation rejects what is true and protects what is false. Compromise becomes impossible on this view, and if compromise is impossible, then legislative protection for religious liberty on these issues is also impossible. This intransigence, from the bishops and from many conservative Protestant groups as well, has done enormous damage to the cause of religious liberty in America." After a historic Supreme Court decision in 2020 found that the 1964 Civil Rights Act protects gay, lesbian, and transgender employees from discrimination based on sex—the majority ruling was written by conservative Justice Neil Gorsuch—the US bishops' official response from then president Archbishop José Gomez denounced the decision as "an injustice" that "redefined the legal meaning of 'sex' in our nation's civil rights law."[119] Before the court's ruling, workers in fewer than half the states had any established legal protections against sexual orientation and gender identity discrimination in employment.

A Catholic bishop who has tried to rescue religious liberty from the culture wars is San Diego Cardinal Robert McElroy, who as discussed earlier in the chapter is one of the most vocal leaders calling for LGBTQ inclusion in the church. During a speech at Georgetown University in 2017, he lamented that "the issue of religious liberty has become deeply enmeshed in the bitter divide which grips our nation and corrupts political and moral dialogue." He described two opposing ideological movements in conflict. "The first seeks to minimize the scope of religious liberty, and specifically reduce the freedom of religious communities to the freedom of worship," McElroy said. "The second seeks to maximize the exercise of religious conscience in society, undercutting the legitimate role that government has in advancing the common good."[120] The Catholic social tradition, he argued, rejects both approaches. "The Church must emphasize that a robust appreciation for the specifically religiously inspired works of faith communities in health care, social service and advocacy for the marginalized lie at the core of the Gospel imperative, and any realistic notion of religious liberty in the United States." At the same time there are religious liberty advocates who "seek to undermine the legitimate authority of the state by endorsing an ever expanding notion of individual rights of conscience in the public sphere without due regard for the governmental pursuit of the common good." "This, too," the cardinal said, "is a distortion of the Catholic doctrine of religious liberty."

The church "must defend absolutely the rights of conscience to internal belief, point to the moral warrants for the robust freedom of religious communities, and outline the nuanced Catholic teaching on the rights of believers to act upon their beliefs in society," McElroy said. "But the Church must be equally dedicated to defending the corresponding governmental right to—at times—restrict conscience-driven actions in pursuit of a genuine common good."

As a model for how Catholics might chart a better path forward on contentious religious liberty questions in a diverse society, the cardinal pointed to the contributions of the Jesuit priest John Courtney Murray. Once silenced by the Vatican for his writings on religious freedom, Murray later played a key role in drafting *Dignitatis Humanae,* the seminal document on religious liberty promulgated at the Second Vatican Council. Murray's 1960 book, *We Hold These Truths: Catholic Reflections on the American Proposition,* is widely regarded as helping Catholicism reconcile with American democracy. "The Catholic experience in the United States taught the world how to think about religious liberty in a new way," said Cardinal McElroy, noting that Murray helped to "reconcile what was the lived reality of the United States—namely, a vibrant, robust, constitutional order in which religious liberty was present." The cardinal proposed that a healthier understanding of religious liberty requires an ethic of solidarity that "will demand a rejection of the tribal element of politics" and "the increasing habit in our political culture of attributing all differences of opinion to ignorance or malice."

Catholics have a rich intellectual, theological, and social tradition that rejects the kind of false choices and binary arguments that fit neatly into partisan boxes and fuel the culture wars. Catholics should be leaders in reclaiming a more authentic, nonideological commitment to religious freedom that doesn't pit religion against LGBTQ rights. There is also room to find common ground between those who support and oppose same-sex marriage. As a 2021 statement from New Ways Ministry signed by more than 250 Catholic theologians, women religious, writers, and scholars noted, disagreement over "whether the current magisterial characterization of same-gender relationships and transgender identities is accurate or not" should not preclude a basic recognition that "Catholic social teaching presents a positive case for ending discrimination against LGBTQ people."[121] Among other sources, the statement cites the Second Vatican Council document *Gaudium et Spes,* which rejects "any kind of social or cultural discrimination." Catholic teaching, the New Ways Ministry statement argues, "should not be used to further oppress LGBTQ people by denying rights rooted in their inherent human dignity and in the church's call for social equality."

LEARNING FROM BLACK AND LATINX LGBTQ CATHOLICS

If Catholic leaders are going to be successful in disentangling religious liberty from any association with discrimination and exclusion, they should start by listening to and learning from the experiences of LGBTQ Catholics. In particular, Black and Latinx LGBTQ Catholics have stories of rejection and resilience that can bring wisdom to our church if we have the curiosity and humility to receive them.

Craig Ford is a Black Catholic who grew up attending a Baptist church as a kid. "I was raised in a tradition where being gay was a problem," he told me. "I wasn't exactly sure what kind of problem it was but I was more familiar with gay being a slur than being associated with anything good."[122] When Ford came out in 2006 at his predominately white Catholic high school in the suburbs of Philadelphia, he was the first openly gay student in the school. It suddenly became harder to navigate social groups. His conservative uncle couldn't accept the news. His anxious mother worried that her Black son now had to contend with his skin color *and* his sexuality, "two marks of mortal danger," as Ford described the dual challenges of racism and homophobia. Always drawn to religion and questions of theology, he started immersing himself in Catholic teaching about homosexuality. In his morality class, he read theologians and studied the Bible. He struggled with the layers of tension and contradiction he found himself trying to piece together as he considered the expansiveness of a loving God bumping up against what seemed like a rigidly narrow theology where his sexuality was deemed sinful and disordered. At the University of Notre Dame, where he majored in theology and philosophy, his hunger and youthful idealism to solve those riddles only grew. "In my zeal, I was going to fix everything in the church when it came to LGTBQ people," he said with a laugh. Later, as a student at Yale University's divinity school, he began to explore what it meant to be both Black and gay. Now a thirty-six-year-old professor at St. Norbert College in Wisconsin, Ford is a rising star in Catholic theological circles. Most Catholic conversations about the church and LGBTQ inclusion too often begin and end in white spaces, he observes, an environment that produces a myopic posture that brings cultural assumptions and societal experiences that fail to encompass complexity and diversity.

Ford has found that a common stereotypical perception is that most LGBTQ people are white and upper class. Many LGBTQ ministries are in liberal, white parishes where there are few people from low-income or even working-class backgrounds. What frequently gets lost in these spaces is any acknowledgement of economic inequality and the ways in which Black people who are gay, lesbian, bisexual, or transgender must navigate not only what it means to be a sexual minority but also a Black person in a society where racism degrades their humanity. Ford is trying to change those dynamics not only in his writing and lectures but through small steps in his own religious community, St. Norbert College Parish. After the murder of George Floyd, Ford put together a parish group called Out Loud, which he describes as an "intentional intersectional ministry." "LGBTQ inclusion, gender equality and racial justice are issues that often get separated in church ecologies," Ford said. "A lot of this work is about education and showing people how all these justice issues are connected. We can't have a Catholic ministry where gay people are in one area, trans people are in another, and Black Catholics are somewhere else."

A younger generation of diverse Catholics in their twenties and thirties are at the forefront of this movement to recognize intersectionality. This not only poses a challenge for white people, Ford notes, but also an older Black generation accustomed to leadership roles being assumed by only heterosexual men. "How do we expand our imagination and our circle of empathy within the Black community?" Ford asks. "Black women have been asking this for a long time. How do we love all of our people? How do we show deeper solidarity?" His generation is losing patience. "Gay Black Catholics used to hide their sexuality to stay in the church," Ford said. "But now people say I'm going to be me or I'm out and they are gone from Catholicism. This is a big generational threat the church is facing because the church is failing to have this multifocal, intersectional approach to justice for all people." Ford is active in a network called Queer Theologians of Color, a project founded in 2021 that seeks to bring more diverse LGBTQ Catholics into church conversations about inclusion and intersectionality. He edited a book, *All of Us*, that includes essays from scholars in the group. "I picked that title because God loves all of us in our complexity and if we don't reflect that in our church and in the way we think theologically then we're not going to survive." Ford is cautiously hopeful that if the synod process prioritized by Pope Francis can be institutionalized there will be an important shift. "The essential insight of the synod is that the locus of the magisterium is the people of God and that moves us away from a clerical model," he said. "For anything to be sustainable it has to come from people living and working in the parishes. It can't just be theologians." The urgency around these issues is pressing. "We are on a real time clock," he said. "Younger Catholics, in particular, are losing their connections to formal church institutions because they know it's possible to find community and spirituality elsewhere. If our churches don't step up, we will lose them."

Yunuen Trujillo knows what it's like to struggle to find a home in the Catholic Church. The thirty-seven-year-old immigration lawyer volunteered for a decade in Catholic youth ministry in the Los Angeles archdiocese without telling anyone she was gay. When she first came out as a high school student, Trujillo was an undocumented immigrant from Guanajuato, Mexico. Her mother, who was not a practicing Catholic but always loved liturgical music, insisted her daughter go to Mass with her that Sunday and made her attend a young adult spiritual retreat organized by a Catholic parish in the hope that she would change her mind about her sexuality. "A lot of people leave church when they come out of the closet, but in my case it was the other way around and I came in," Trujillo joked.[123] To her surprise she loved the retreat. Over the years her Catholic faith and spirituality deepened even as she continued to question how to navigate being Catholic and queer, the word she uses to describe herself. When she met the young adult ministry director for the Los Angeles archdiocese, he asked Trujillo to come help him with a program he had started on Guadalupe Radio, a popular Catholic Spanish language network. She volunteered there for five years, became a regional coordinator for young adult Hispanic ministry, and later taught religious formation classes in the archdiocese. During those years Trujillo spoke openly about her story as an undocumented immigrant and could easily connect that aspect of her life to her faith journey but kept quiet about her sexuality.

By 2014 she was done with hiding. "When I decided to come out again it was harder because at the time my entire network was Catholic," she told me. Trujillo was ready to leave the Catholic Church, but she met Catholic parents who had a gay son and had started a support group for Catholic parents with LGBTQ children. The parents urged her to stay. She had stumbled into a supportive community as an openly gay Catholic. Trujillo eventually became the religious formation coordinator for the Catholic Ministry with Lesbian and Gay Persons of the Archdiocese of Los Angeles, founded an Instagram account called @LGBTQ Catholics, and in 2022 wrote a book, *LGBTQ Catholics: A Guide to Inclusive Ministry*. She now speaks about LGBTQ Catholic ministry at conferences around the country, including at the annual Los Angeles Religious Education Congress, an event that draws more than 30,000 people from around the world. While Trujillo is glad to see a growing number of church leaders recognizing the importance of

LGBTQ inclusion, she worries that Latinx Catholics who are lesbian, gay, bisexual, or transgender are often missing from the discussion. "There isn't much LGBTQ ministry for Latinx people," she said. "Most of the outreach is being done in English so you have this real divide. There are hardly any resources for LGBTQ Catholics in Spanish. It can feel very lonely doing this work. Leaders in this ministry are usually white and male, which seems to fit with the stereotypes a lot of bishops have about LGBTQ people being financially secure and upper middle class, rather than a more complete picture that includes people of color who are more vulnerable." In her work as an immigration lawyer, Trujillo has represented a transgender Catholic woman from Guatemala who is seeking asylum, for example. "When I think about her and then I hear what some bishops are saying about who they think LGBTQ people are, there is a disconnect."

Catholic leaders also make a mistake by not acknowledging the many dimensions of LGBTQ people. "We have to be more intersectional," Trujillo said. "A lot of Latinx people come from families where at least one person is undocumented. But in the church we often separate that reality from LGBTQ ministry. Sometimes I feel like I have to hide aspects of who I am. If I'm doing LGBTQ ministry, I can't talk about the undocumented. If I am talking about the undocumented, I'm not expected to talk about LGBTQ people." Given the importance of family in Hispanic communities, Trujillo also wants to see more parishes incorporate family members into LGBTQ outreach and ministry.

> There is often more suspicion of LGBTQ ministry among Spanish-speaking Catholics, but if a parish leader says, "I want to start a support group for parents of LGBTQ young people," there is more openness. We have to start thinking of LGBTQ ministry as a family affair. Sometimes parents are the ones who can open the doors for this ministry. I watched my own mother go through her own journey, her own fears and process of discernment. LGBTQ ministry has to be for the family. If we are pro-family as a church, we have to recognize this.

Trujillo wants bishops and other Catholic leaders to understand that LGBTQ Catholics have gifts to share with the church. "It's such a missed opportunity if we don't get this right," she told me. "The church needs our vulnerability. Anyone who has faced their own wounds and fears and comes through all of that with a strong faith has something beautiful to share."

When Ish Ruiz was growing up in a devout Catholic family in Puerto Rico, there was church, family, and culture where swaggering machismo defined the blueprint for masculinity. A sensitive teenager attracted to other boys didn't fit into that mold. "I remember doing everything in my power not to be perceived as gay," Ruiz, thirty-six, told me.[124] But one day he shared a kiss with a fellow student at his all-boys Catholic school. He began a clandestine dating relationship that was at once thrilling and terrifying. When his parents caught him by listening in on a phone call, Ruiz found himself spiraling down a staircase of shame. His devastated parents forced him to see a therapist who tried to convince him that he would never live a happy and healthy life if he wasn't a heterosexual. "I wanted to fix myself and I tried really hard to date girls," he said. Ruiz never felt at home. "Liminality is characterized by the pain of not belonging," he said. "I didn't belong to Puerto Rico. I was queer so I wasn't a 'real' man. And so I wasn't a 'real' Catholic. The lack of belonging was hard but it forced me to enter into a space where I really had to think about what it meant for me to be Puerto Rican, gay and Catholic." When he left the island for college at the University of Dayton, he tried to play the part of a straight guy who loved football and chugged beer. "I tried to assimilate and not be as Puerto Rican," Ruiz recalls. He found himself feeling lost and miserable. He eventually started dating men and after a few relationships ended up falling in love. Ruiz's parents saw his newfound happiness, agreed to see a therapist to work through their own feelings, and finally came to accept their son. It wasn't until after college, when he moved to San Francisco to be a religion teacher in a Catholic high school, that Ruiz began to settle into an accepting community where he could integrate his Catholicism, his Puerto Rican identity, and his sexuality.

For the first time he realized that to be Latinx and gay wasn't the same as being white and gay. Raised to believe there was something wrong with him and that gay people go to hell, Ruiz never lost his faith. He pursued a theology degree. Ruiz acknowledges his Catholic journey has not always been easy. There were times when he stayed away from church, but he always found his way back. "My experience of God, the connection I feel on spiritual retreats. I couldn't imagine a life where I don't have that," he said. Ruiz is now an assistant professor of Latinx and Queer Decolonial Theology at Pacific School of Religion. "I continue to experience powerful grace in queer Catholic communities. It's really powerful. There is an indescribable joy and a sense of transcendence because of who we are together." In his writing, lectures, and conversations in parishes, Ruiz asks church leaders to rethink how they understand LGBTQ Catholics. He believes a more radically inclusive church won't come from the top down and reinforce a patriarchal paternalism. "LGBTQ inclusion is sometimes viewed as an exclusively pastoral matter," he said.

> But pastoral care is a low bar. We have communities and chosen families that support us. We're not these poor, queer brown people, the so-called marginalized who just need help. Pastoral care is a good starting point, but what can the church learn from the grace-filled witness of LGBTQ Catholics? Our experiences with navigating and conquering our shame requires us to be aware when we are mindlessly operating under some rules and norms that are oppressive. The church needs that lens. When people are used to surviving and challenging oppression it creates a way of looking at the world, an epistemology, that is very powerful. We are not only a white, heterosexual church. How can we learn to be a church that sees God in all of our diversity?

Ruiz is cautiously hopeful that the synod process can be the beginning of a paradigm shift.

"If the church is going to change, synodality is how it's done," he said. "Some people are waiting for the pope to change the church's teaching on LGBTQ issues, but that is not going to happen. You have to change the culture of the church and synodality is the way. It's about walking humbly and listening." But he cautions that synodal discernment and encounters can still operate under structures that shut down certain voices and start with a fixed destination before the conversations even begin. "There are ways we are willing to be transformed and ways we are not," Ruiz observed. "The church has not really answered the question of who we are listening to when we are listening. Synodality is an ecclesiology, not a process. It's a new way of being church. It's not a kumbaya moment. It can be messy."

NOTES

1. Justin McCarthy, "US Same-Sex Marriage Support Holds at 71% High," *Gallup*, June 5, 2023, https://news.gallup.com/poll/506636/sex-marriage-support-holds-high.aspx.
2. PRRI staff, "Exodus: Why Americans Are Leaving Religion and Why They're Unlikely to Come Back," *Public Religion Research Institute*, September 22, 2016, https://www.prri.org/research/prri-rns-poll-nones-atheist-leaving-religion/.
3. Nicole Winfield, "'Who Am I to Judge?' Pope Says of Gay Priests," *Associated Press*, July 29, 2013, https://apnews.com/general-news-7b465b60945f40deb3a68b3de742f84a.
4. Nicole Winfield, "The AP Interview: Pope Says Homosexuality Not a Crime," *Associated Press*, January 25, 2023, https://apnews.com/article/pope-francis-gay-rights-ap-interview-1359756ae22f27f87c1d4d6b9c8ce212.
5. Delia Gallagher and Hada Messia, "Pope Francis Tells Gay Man: 'God Made You Like That and Loves You Like That,'" *CNN*, May 21, 2018, https://www.cnn.com/2018/05/21/europe/pope-francis-gay-comments-intl/index.html.

6. John Gehring, "The Real Scandal: What Attacks on James Martin Say about the U.S. Church," *Commonweal*, September 19, 2017, https://www.commonwealmagazine.org/real-scandal.
7. Christopher White, "Make Room for Everyone in the Church, Pope Francis Tells Young People in Portugal," *National Catholic Reporter*, August 3, 2023, https://www.ncronline.org/vatican/vatican-news/make-room-everyone-church-pope-francis-tells-young-people-portugal.
8. White, "Make Room for Everyone in the Church."
9. Summary of Bulletin, Holy See Press Office. *Responsum of the Congregation for the Doctrine of the Faith to a Dubium Regarding the Blessing of the Unions of Persons of the Same Sex*, March 15, 2021, https://press.vatican.va/content/salastampa/en/bollettino/pubblico/2021/03/15/210315b.html.
10. Paul Elie, "The Vatican's Giant Step Backward on Same-Sex Unions," *New Yorker*, March 23, 2021, https://www.newyorker.com/news/daily-comment/the-vaticans-giant-step-backward-on-same-sex-unions.
11. James Martin (@JamesMartinSJ), "Not since the anger over sex abuse in 2002 and 2018 have I seen so many people so demoralized, and ready to leave the church. And not simply LGBT people, but their families and friends, a large part of the church," Twitter, March 18, 2021, https://twitter.com/JamesMartinSJ/status/1372588629458104325.
12. Raf Casert, "Belgian Bishop Lashes Out at Vatican over Gay Unions Decree," *National Catholic Reporter*, March 17, 2021, https://www.ncronline.org/news/belgian-bishop-lashes-out-vatican-over-gay-unions-decree.
13. Christopher Lamb, "Ruling on Same-Sex Blessings Is Not Last World," *The Tablet*, March 18, 2021, https://www.thetablet.co.uk/news/13965/ruling-on-same-sex-blessings-is-not-last-word-.
14. Dicastery for the Doctrine of the Faith, "Fiducia Supplicans: On the Pastoral Meaning of Blessings," December 18, 2023, https://www.vatican.va/roman_curia/congregations/cfaith/documents/rc_ddf_doc_20231218_fiducia-supplicans_en.html.
15. Francis DeBernardo, "Vatican Document Represents Pope Francis' Pastoral Revolution for Gay Catholics," *National Catholic Reporter*, December 28, 2023, https://www.ncronline.org/opinion/guest-voices/vatican-document-represents-pope-francis-pastoral-revolution-gay-catholics.
16. Ruth Graham and Amy Harmon, "American Catholics Split on Pope's Blessing for Gay Couples," *New York Times*, December 18, 2023, https://www.nytimes.com/2023/12/18/us/pope-francis-lgbtq-catholic.html?smid=nytcore-ios-share&referringSource=articleShare.
17. Archdiocese of Denver, "Archbishop Samuel J. Aquila Issues Statement on Fiducia Supplicans," December 20, 2023, https://archden.org/aquila-statement-fiducia-supplicans/.
18. Anthony Faiola, Michelle Boorstein, and Stefano Pitrelli, "'Anti-Pope' 'Blasphemous' Criticism of Francis Comes in Strident Terms," *Washington Post*, January 12, 2024, https://www.washingtonpost.com/world/2024/01/12/pope-francis-criticism-same-sex-blessings/.
19. Magdalene Kahiu, "Blessings for Same-Sex Couples 'Not for Implementation in Zambia': Catholic Bishops," *Association for Catholic Information in Africa* (Aciafrica),

December 20, 2023, https://www.aciafrica.org/news/9863/blessing-of-same-sex-couples-not-for-implementation-in-zambia-catholic-bishops.

20. Aci Africa/CNA staff, "Bishops in Malawi Declare 'Blessings for Same-Sex Unions of Any Kind Are Not Permitted,'" December 20, 2023, https://www.ncregister.com/cna/bishops-in-malawi-declare-blessings-for-same-sex-unions-of-any-kind-are-not-permitted.
21. Nicole Winfield, "Africa's Catholic Hierarchy Refuses Same-Sex Blessings, Says Such Unions Are Contrary to God's Will," *Associated Press*, January 11, 2024, https://apnews.com/article/vatican-lgbtq-blessing-africa-france-12ede13dec72ecdd9f6da1dd1877d7e5.
22. Catechism of the Catholic Church, US Conference of Catholic Bishops. https://www.usccb.org/sites/default/files/flipbooks/catechism/568/.
23. Joseph Cardinal Ratzinger, Prefect, Congregation for the Doctrine of the Faith, "Letter to the Bishops of the Catholic Church on the Pastoral Care of Homosexual Persons," October 1, 1986, https://www.vatican.va/roman_curia/congregations/cfaith/documents/rc_con_cfaith_doc_19861001_homosexual-persons_en.html.
24. Joseph Cardinal Ratzinger, Prefect, Congregation for the Doctrine of the Faith, "Considerations Regarding Proposals to Give Legal Recognition between Unions of Homosexual Persons," June 3, 2003, https://www.vatican.va/roman_curia/congregations/cfaith/documents/rc_con_cfaith_doc_20030731_homosexual-unions_en.html.
25. John Gehring, "The Case for Why Catholics Should March in LGBT Pride Parades," *Washington Post*, June 6, 2019, https://www.washingtonpost.com/religion/2019/06/06/case-why-catholics-should-march-lgbt-pride-parades/.
26. Christopher White, "For U.S. Bishops, LGBTQ 'Anthropology' Rules Out Equality Act Compromises," *National Catholic Reporter*, March 24, 2021, https://www.ncronline.org/news/us-bishops-lgbtq-anthropology-rules-out-equality-act-compromises.
27. Rina Torchinsky, "Nearly Half of LGBTQ Youth Seriously Considered Suicide, Survey Finds," *National Public Radio*, May 5, 2022, https://www.npr.org/2022/05/05/1096920693/lgbtq-youth-thoughts-of-suicide-trevor-project-survey.
28. Archbishop Wilton D. Gregory, "The Church Must Welcome All of Her Sons and Daughters," *The Georgia Bulletin*, October 16, 2014, https://georgiabulletin.org/commentary/2014/10/church-must-welcome-sons-daughters/.
29. Kevin Clarke, "Bishop McElroy Calls for a Practical 'Apology' to L.G.B.T. Catholics," *America*, https://www.americamagazine.org/faith/2016/07/07/bishop-mcelroy-calls-practical-apology-lgbt-catholics.
30. Zac Davis and Ashley McKinless, "Cardinal McElroy: Sex and Sin Need a New Framework in the Church," *Jesuitical*, February 3, 2023, https://www.americamagazine.org/faith/2023/02/03/cardinal-mcelroy-inclusion-sexualty-244650.
31. Michael J. O'Loughlin, "Cardinal Cupich on 10 Years of Pope Francis: Women, LGBT Catholics, Sex Abuse and What Comes Next," *America*, March 13, 2023, https://www.americamagazine.org/faith/2023/03/13/cardinal-cupich-pope-francis-10-years-244893#:~:text=%E2%80%9CAnytime%20language%20comes%20across%20as,is%20categorically%20exclusive%20of%20individuals.%E2%80%9D.
32. Joshua J. McElwee, "Synod Document Takes Inclusive Tone toward Youth Who Disagree with Church," *National Catholic Reporter*, June 19, 2018, https://www.ncronline.org/news/vatican/vaticans-synod-document-takes-inclusive-tone-towards-youth-who-disagree-church.

33. Cindy Wooden, "Archbishop Chaput Urges Synod to Use Care with Language, Especially on Sexuality," *Catholic News Service*, October 4, 2018, https://www.ncronline.org/vatican/archbishop-chaput-urges-synod-use-care-language-especially-sexuality.
34. David Gibson, "A Vatican Opening on Sexuality Worries Conservatives—and Cheers Reformers," *Religion News Service*, October 30, 2018, https://religionnews.com/2018/10/30/a-vatican-opening-on-sexuality-worries-conservatives-and-cheers-reformers/.
35. Gibson, "A Vatican Opening on Sexuality."
36. Associated Press staff, "German Catholics to Bless Gay Unions Despite Vatican Ban," *Associated Press*, May 12, 2021, https://www.nbcnews.com/feature/nbc-out/german-catholics-bless-gay-unions-despite-vatican-ban-n1267123.
37. Catholic News Service staff, "Cardinal Marx Calls for Change in Church Teaching on Homosexuality, Admits to Blessing Same-Sex Couples," March 31, 2022, https://www.americamagazine.org/politics-society/2022/03/31/cardinal-marx-germany-homosexuality-242735.
38. Michael J. O'Loughlin, "Belgian Bishops Create Prayer Liturgy for Same-Sex Couples," *America*, September 20, 2022, https://www.americamagazine.org/politics-society/2022/09/20/belgium-bishops-lgbt-blessing-243817.
39. Katholische Nachrichten-Agentur, "Top EU Cardinal Calls for Change in Church Teaching on Gay Relationships," *National Catholic Reporter*, February 2, 2022, https://www.ncronline.org/news/quick-reads/top-eu-cardinal-calls-change-church-teaching-gay-relationships.
40. Christopher White, "Top Synod Cardinal: Church Should Change Attitude, Not Teaching, on Gay Relationships," *National Catholic Reporter*, August 26, 2022, https://www.ncronline.org/vatican/top-synod-cardinal-church-should-change-attitude-not-teaching-gay-relationships.
41. "Enlarge the Space of Your Tent," Working Document for the Continental Stage, https://www.synod.va/content/dam/synod/common/phases/continental-stage/dcs/Documento-Tappa-Continentale-EN.pdf.
42. Michelle Martin, "Pope Francis Has Made Synods 'The New Way of Being the Church at Every Level,' Bishop Says," *Chicago Catholic*, April 20, 2023, https://www.chicagocatholic.com/chicagoland/-/article/2023/04/20/pope-francis-has-made-synods-the-new-way-of-being-the-church-at-every-level-bishop-says.
43. Bishop John Stowe, interview with author.
44. Michael J. O'Loughlin, "'It Is Our Duty to Love and Defend' LGBT Americans: Bishop Stowe Breaks with U.S. Bishops on the Equality Act," *America*, March 25, 2021, https://www.americamagazine.org/politics-society/2021/03/25/equality-act-usccb-bishop-stowe-religious-freedom-lgbt-240313.
45. "Bishop John Stowe to LGBTQ Catholics: 'I Love You,'" Address at Outreach conference, June 24, 2022. Fordham University, New York City, https://outreach.faith/2022/12/bishop-john-stowe-to-lgbtq-catholics-i-love-you/.
46. Robert W. McElroy, "Cardinal McElroy on 'Radical Inclusion' for L.G.B.T. People, Women and Others in the Catholic Church," *America*, January 24, 2023, https://www.americamagazine.org/faith/2023/01/24/mcelroy-synodality-inclusion-244587.
47. Thomas J. Paprocki, "Imagining a Heretical Cardinal," *First Things*, February 28, 2023, https://www.firstthings.com/web-exclusives/2023/02/imagining-a-heretical-cardinal.

48. Brynn Shaffer, "Inclusion, Conversion, Important for Synodality, Says Cardinal McElroy," *National Catholic Reporter*, February 2, 2023, https://www.ncronline.org/inclusion-conversion-important-synodality-says-cardinal-mcelroy.
49. "From the Margins to the Center: A Report on Spiritual Conversations Held with LGBTQ People and Allies as Part of the Synod on Synodality," New Ways Ministry, https://www.newwaysministry.org/wp-content/uploads/2022/06/Synodal-Report_FINAL.pdf.
50. David Palmieri, interview with author.
51. Congregation for Catholic Education, "Male and Female He Created Them: Towards a Path of Dialogue on the Question of Gender Theory in Education," Vatican City, 2019. https://www.vatican.va/roman_curia/congregations/ccatheduc/documents/rc_con_ccatheduc_doc_20190202_maschio-e-femmina_en.pdf.
52. Bishop Donald DeGrood, "Gifts of the Divine Creator: On Being Male and Female," August 4, 2022, https://s3.documentcloud.org/documents/22131509/gifts-of-the-divine-creator-1.pdf.
53. Elizabeth Hernandez, "Denver Archdiocese's Guidance to Catholic Schools: Don't Enroll Transgender Students Treat Gay Parents Differently," *Denver Post*, November 7, 2022, https://www.denverpost.com/2022/11/07/denver-catholic-archdiocese-lgbtq-guidance-transgender-gay-students/.
54. Ariell Simon and Robert Shine, "Denver Archbishop Blames Transgender Equality for Declining Church Attendance," *New Ways Ministry* (blog), March 8, 2023, https://www.newwaysministry.org/2023/03/08/denver-archbishop-blames-transgender-equality-for-declining-church-attendance/.
55. Archbishop Alexander Sample, *A Catholic Response to Gender Identity Theory*, Archdiocese of Portland, https://archdpdx.org/gender.
56. Julia Silverman, "Portland-Area Catholic Schools Are at a Crossroads over Transgender, Nonbinary Student Rights," *The Oregonian*, June 26, 2023, https://www.oregonlive.com/education/2023/06/portland-area-catholic-schools-are-at-a-crossroads-over-transgender-nonbinary-student-rights.html.
57. James Graves, "Portland Archbishop Sample Releases Gender Guidelines," *California Catholic Daily*, February 21, 2023, https://www.cal-catholic.com/portland-archbishop-sample-releases-gender-guidelines/.
58. David Palmieri, interview with author.
59. Brian Fraga, "Bishop Strips Middle School of Catholic Status for Flying BLM and Gay Pride Flags," *National Catholic Reporter*, June 16, 2022, https://www.ncronline.org/news/politics/bishop-strips-middle-school-catholic-status-flying-blm-and-gay-pride-flags.
60. Roman Catholic Diocese of Worcester, "Bishop Issues Letter Regarding Nativity School Flags," May 5, 2022, https://worcesterdiocese.org/news/bishop-issues-letter-regarding-nativity-school-flags.
61. Associated Press staff, "Bishop Punishes Worcester School over Black Lives Matter, Pride Flags," *Associated Press*, June 16, 2022, https://www.wbur.org/news/2022/06/16/pride-black-lives-matter-flags-worcester-catholic-school.
62. New Ways Ministry, "Employees of Catholic Institutions Who Have Been Fired, Forced to Resign, Had Offers Rescinded, or Had Their Jobs Threatened Because of LGBT Issues," https://www.newwaysministry.org/issues/employment/employment-disputes/.

63. John Gehring, "LGBT Catholics & the Francis Papacy," *Commonweal*, May 22, 2017, https://www.commonwealmagazine.org/lgbt-catholics-francis-papacy.
64. Arika Herron, "Brebeuf Jesuit Appeals Split from Catholic Church, Barred from Holding All-School Mass," *Indianapolis Star*, August 5, 2019, https://www.indystar.com/story/news/education/2019/08/05/brebeuf-jesuit-appeals-split-catholic-church-barred-holding-mass/1920187001/.
65. Elise Dubravec, "Indiana Court Rules against Fired LGBTQ Church Worker Citing Ministerial Exemption," *New Ways Ministry* (blog), August 21, 2021, https://www.newwaysministry.org/2021/08/21/indiana-court-rules-against-fired-lgbtq-church-worker-citing-ministerial-exception/.
66. Tony Gorman, "Denver Archdiocese Fires Catholic School Teacher after Discovering She Was in a Same-Sex Relationship," *CPR News*, February 4, 2023, https://www.cpr.org/2023/02/04/denver-archdiocese-fires-catholic-school-teacher-after-discovering-she-was-in-a-same-sex-relationship/.
67. Emily Grad, interview with author.
68. John Gehring, "LGBTQ Catholics Closely Watching Supreme Court Case on Adoption," *National Catholic Reporter*, April 12, 2021, https://www.ncronline.org/news/lgbtq-catholics-closely-watching-supreme-court-case-adoption.
69. Gehring, "LGBTQ Catholics Closely Watching."
70. Patricia Wen, "Catholic Charities Pulls Out of Adoption Business," *Boston Globe*, March 10, 2006, http://archive.boston.com/news/local/massachusetts/articles/2006/03/10/catholic_charities_pulls_out_of_adoption_business/.
71. Ruth Graham, "Major Evangelical Adoption Agency Will Now Serve Gay Parents Nationwide," *New York Times*, March 1, 2021, https://www.nytimes.com/2021/03/01/us/bethany-adoption-agency-lgbtq.html.
72. Supreme Court of the United States, *Fulton v. City of Philadelphia, Pennsylvania*, June 17, 2021, https://www.supremecourt.gov/opinions/20pdf/19-123_g3bi.pdf.
73. Robert Shine, "LGBTQ Catholics Express Relief, Disappointment at Supreme Court's Adoption Ruling," *New Ways Ministry* blog, June 21, 2021, https://www.newwaysministry.org/2021/06/21/lgbtq-catholics-express-relief-disappointment-at-supreme-courts-adoption-ruling/.
74. Gehring, "LGBTQ Catholics Closely Watching."
75. Joseph Cardinal Ratzinger, "Prefect, Congregation for the Doctrine of the Faith," *Considerations Regarding Proposals to Give Legal Recognition to Unions Between Homosexual Persons*. June 3, 2003, https://www.vatican.va/roman_curia/congregations/cfaith/documents/rc_con_cfaith_doc_20030731_homosexual-unions_en.html.
76. Steve LeBlanc, "Catholic Charities to Drop Adoption over Gay Issue," *Milford Daily News*, March 10, 2006, https://www.milforddailynews.com/story/news/2006/03/11/catholic-charities-to-drop-adoptions/41243336007/.
77. Brian Cahill, interview with author.
78. Meli Barber, interview with author.
79. Amanda Rosa, "What Happens to Some L.G.B.T.Q. Teens When Their Parents Reject Them," *New York Times*, November 11, 2020, https://www.nytimes.com/2020/11/11/nyregion/nyc-lgbtq-foster-care.html?smid=nytcore-ios-share&referringSource=articleShare.
80. Jacob Kohlhaas, interview with author.
81. John Freml, interview with author.

82. Brian Roewe, "Bishop Tries Exorcism as Illinois Legalizes Same-Sex Marriage," *National Catholic Reporter*, December 6, 2013, https://www.ncronline.org/news/parish/bishop-tries-exorcism-illinois-legalizes-same-sex-marriage.
83. Christine Zuba, interview with author.
84. Brian Fraga, "Marquette Diocese's LGBTQ Restrictions Blasted as 'Cruel Policy,'" *National Catholic Reporter*, December 14, 2021, https://www.ncronline.org/news/marquette-dioceses-lgbtq-restrictions-blasted-cruel-policy.
85. David Crary, "Rejection or Welcome: Transgender Catholics Encounter Both," *Associated Press*, February 26, 2022, https://apnews.com/article/religion-united-states-gender-identity-marquette-e88473adf85944f912511fc85d542d29.
86. Sister Luisa Derouen, interview with author.
87. Jack Jenkins, "In Letter, Thousands of Catholic Nuns Declare Trans People 'Beloved and Cherished by God,'" *Washington Post*, March 21, 2023, https://www.washingtonpost.com/religion/2023/03/31/letter-thousands-catholic-nuns-declare-trans-people-beloved-cherished-by-god/.
88. John Gehring, "Catholic Conservative Napa Institute's Profile Grows in Washington, DC," *National Catholic Reporter,* December 13, 2022, https://www.ncronline.org/news/catholic-conservative-napa-institutes-profile-grows-washington-dc.
89. Barb Arland-Fye, "Gender Committee Has Been Listening and Now Wants to Reach Out," *The Catholic Messenger*, August 18, 2022, https://catholicmessenger.net/2022/08/gender-committee-has-been-listening-and-now-wants-to-reach-out/.
90. Bishop Thomas Zinkula, "The Church Calls Us to Listen to People on the Margins," *The Catholic Messenger*, January 13, 2022, http://catholicmessenger.net/2022/01/the-church-calls-us-to-listen-to-people-on-the-margins/.
91. Liz Bowie, "Federal Court Rules that UMMS Discriminated against a Transgender Man," *Baltimore Banner*, January 7, 2023, https://www.thebaltimorebanner.com/community/public-health/federal-court-rules-umms-discriminated-against-a-transgender-man-XNDQEUMZPND5HDRSZENDL6WQLY/.
92. Section 1557 of the Patient Protection and Affordable Care Act, https://www.hhs.gov/civil-rights/for-individuals/section-1557/index.html.
93. US Conference of Catholic Bishops, *Doctrinal Note on the Moral Limits to Technological Manipulation of the Human Body*, March 20, 2023, https://www.usccb.org/resources/Doctrinal%20Note%202023-03-20.pdf.
94. Catholic Health Association, "CHA Statement on the United States Conference of Catholic Bishops' Decision to Revise the Ethical and Religious Directives for Catholic Health Care Services," June 16, 2023, https://www.chausa.org/newsroom/news-releases/2023/06/16/cha-statement-on-the-united-states-conference-of-catholic-bishops-decision-to-revise-the-ethical-and-religious-directives-for-catholic-health-care.
95. Deepa Bharath, "U.S. Bishops' New Guidelines Aim to Limit Trans Health Care," *Associated Press*, March 24, 2023, https://apnews.com/article/catholic-bishops-lgbtq-transgender-health-care-d840600deab56a681e02d16463322892.
96. Francis DeBernardo, "New Ways Ministry Criticizes New USCCB Guidance on Transgender Health Care," *New Ways Ministry* (blog), March 21, 2023, https://www.newwaysministry.org/2023/03/21/new-ways-ministry-criticizes-new-usccb-guidance-on-transgender-healthcare/.
97. Michael J. O'Loughlin, "Transgender Treatment at Catholic Hospitals: U.S. Bishops Vote to Begin Process That Could Formally Ban It," *America*, June 16,

2023, https://www.americamagazine.org/politics-society/2023/06/16/usccb-transgender-healthcare-catholic-hospitals-245508.

98. M. J. O'Loughlin, "Transgender Treatment at Catholic Hospitals."
99. Therese Lysaught, "U.S. Bishops' Transgender Document Fails Morally, Philosophically—and Is Poorly Argued," *National Catholic Reporter*, May 1, 2023, https://www.ncronline.org/opinion/guest-voices/us-bishops-transgender-document-fails-morally-theologically-and-poorly-argued.
100. Author reporting from 2023 Outreach conference at Fordham University. https://outreach.faith/conference-outreach-2023/.
101. Blase J. Cupich and Timothy Michael Dolan, "Catholic Hospitals Welcome Transgender Patients—and Stand Firm in Their Religious Convictions," *America*, September 26, 2022, https://www.americamagazine.org/politics-society/2022/09/26/catholic-hospitals-transgender-care-section-1557-243849.
102. U.S Conference of Catholic Bishops, "Bishop Chairmen Condemn Harmful Regulations Forcing Gender Ideology and Potentially Abortion on Health Care Workers and Religious Hospitals," July 27, 2022, https://www.usccb.org/news/2022/bishop-chairmen-condemn-harmful-regulations-forcing-gender-ideology-and-potentially.
103. Jacqui Oesterblad, "Conscience and Catholic Health Care," *Commonweal*, July 3, 2023, https://www.commonwealmagazine.org/conscience-and-catholic-health-care.
104. Pew Research Center, "The *Smith* Decision," October 24, 2007, https://www.pewresearch.org/religion/2007/10/24/a-delicate-balance6/.
105. Christopher Shea, "Why Jeff Sessions Thinks Christians Are under Siege in America," *Vox*, August 1, 2018, https://www.vox.com/the-big-idea/2018/8/1/17638706/religious-liberty-sessions-task-force-masterpiece-scalia-constitution.
106. Bill Chappell, "Justice Alito: Pandemic Has Brought 'Unimaginable Restrictions' on Freedoms," *National Public Radio*, November 13, 2020, https://www.npr.org/2020/11/13/934666499/justice-alito-pandemic-has-brought-unimaginable-restrictions-on-freedoms.
107. Adam Liptak, "An Extraordinary Winning Streak for Religion at the Supreme Court," *New York Times*, April 5, 2021, https://www.nytimes.com/2021/04/05/us/politics/supreme-court-religion.html?smid=nytcore-ios-share&referringSource=articleShare.
108. John Krunzel, "LGBT Rights Yield to Religious Interests at U.S. Supreme Court," *Reuters*, July 3, 2023, https://www.reuters.com/legal/lgbt-rights-yield-religious-interests-us-supreme-court-2023-07-01/.
109. "Whose Faith Matters? The Fight for Religious Liberty beyond the Christian Right," Columbia Law School, Law, Rights and Religion Project, November 2019, https://lawrightsreligion.law.columbia.edu/sites/default/files/content/Images/Whose%20Faith%20Matters%20Full%20Report%2012.12.19.pdf.
110. Valerie Richardson, "Kamala Harris, Mazie Hirono Target Brian Buescher Knights of Columbus Membership," *Washington Times*, December 30, 2018, https://www.washingtontimes.com/news/2018/dec/30/kamala-harris-mazie-hirono-target-brian-buescher-k/.
111. Catholic News Service staff, "No Place for 'Religious Test' in Government, Says Senate in Unanimous Vote," *Catholic News Service*, January 18, 2019, https://www.americamagazine.org/politics-society/2019/01/18/no-place-religious-test-government-says-senate-unanimous-vote.

112. Melissa Rogers, *Faith in American Public Life* (Baylor University Press, 2019).
113. E. J. Dionne Jr. and Melissa Rogers, *A Time to Heal, a Time to Build,* Brookings Institution, October 21, 2020, https://www.brookings.edu/articles/a-time-to-heal-a-time-to-build/.
114. John Gehring, "Rethinking Religious Liberty," *Commonweal,* January 6, 2020, https://www.commonwealmagazine.org/rethinking-religious-liberty.
115. John Gehring, "The Wrong Message," *Commonweal,* April 8, 2019, https://www.commonwealmagazine.org/wrong-message.
116. Douglas Laycock, "The Only Way Forward," *Commonweal,* November 29, 2022, https://www.commonwealmagazine.org/only-way-forward.
117. Brian Fraga, "Catholic Bishops a Religious Outlier in Opposing Bill to Protect Same-Sex Marriage," *National Catholic Reporter,* December 5, 2022, https://www.ncronline.org/news/catholic-bishops-religious-outlier-opposing-bill-protect-same-sex-marriage.
118. Laycock, "The Only Way Forward."
119. US Conference of Catholic Bishops, "President of US Bishops' Conference Issues Statement on Supreme Court Decision on Legal Definition of 'Sex" in Civil Rights Law," June 15, 2020, https://www.usccb.org/news/2020/president-us-bishops-conference-issues-statement-supreme-court-decision-legal-definition.
120. Thomas Reese, "Bishop McElroy Decries Extremism on Religious Freedom, Calls for Solidarity in American Politics," *National Catholic Reporter,* November 16, 2017, https://www.ncronline.org/opinion/signs-times/bishop-mcelroy-decries-extremism-religious-freedom-calls-solidarity-american.
121. *A Home for All: A Catholic Call for LGBTQ Non-Discrimination* (New Ways Ministry, August 9, 2021), https://www.newwaysministry.org/homeforall/.
122. Craig Ford, interview with author.
123. Yunuen Trujillo, interview with author.
124. Ish Ruiz, interview with author.

7

A LIVING TRADITION IN TRANSITION

As Catholics look to the future, the church again faces a familiar and fraught struggle over what it means for an ancient institution rooted in timeless truths to hold tradition, transition, and change in healthy tension. In a similar way that the Second Vatican Council sought to bring Catholicism into dialogue with the modern world—while also returning to the sources of wisdom from the early church—the Francis papacy has been characterized by an awareness that dialogue, discernment, and an openness to development in church teaching are not to be feared but are expressions of a living tradition. "Doctrine cannot be preserved without allowing it to develop, nor can it be tied to an interpretation that is rigid and immutable without demeaning the working of the Holy Spirit," the pope said in 2017.[1] The tradition of the church "is always in movement," as the pope described it two years later. "Tradition is the guarantee of the future and not the container of the ashes."[2]

The three-year synodal process, convened by Pope Francis in 2021, is one of the most significant developments in the church since Vatican II. Lay Catholics are now viewed as central protagonists in discerning future paths for the church. The process involved Catholics in dioceses around the world gathering to share their hopes, fears, anxieties, and joys. This grassroots engagement reflects the pope's desire for a listening church of encounter that walks with people and learns from their experiences. Synodality is a clunky, abstract-sounding word that doesn't exactly break through the noise in a social media age, but a church made up of people "capable of walking together, united in harmonious diversity, where everyone has something to contribute," as Pope Francis has described it, offers an inspiring vision for a style of Catholicism that is engaged, inclusive, and capable of managing the tensions and divisions that are inevitable in a global institution with more than a billion faithful. The synod offers a powerful model for building this hopeful church.

When some 450 Catholic leaders from around the world gathered in Rome in the fall of 2023 for the Synod on Synodality, Catholic women were recognized as voting-members for the first time since the establishment of the church's Synod of Bishops in 1965. In fact, nearly a fifth of the voting delegates were women. Pope Francis appointed a woman, Sister Nathalie Becquart, a member of the Xavière Sisters, Missionaries of Jesus Christ, in France, as an undersecretary of the General Secretariat of the Synod. Cardinal Robert McElroy of San Diego told the Religious Formation Conference in 2023 that the synod "was a stark contrast with past synods, where bishops alone voted, and the bulk of the sessions were spent listening to a seemingly endless series of speeches that left participants passive and disengaged."[3] Tensions were high leading into the first phase of the Synod on Synodality. A few days before the meeting opened, news broke that a group of retired cardinals, including the American Raymond Burke, wrote to Pope Francis several months earlier with concerns that the synod would lead to an undermining of church teaching, especially on the issues of same-sex marriage and women's ordination. The cardinals asked the pope to affirm that "Divine Revelation is binding forever, immutable, and therefore not to be contradicted." The pope's responses displayed his characteristic style of pastoral theology and desire to hold tradition and openness to change in balance. While Francis agreed with the cardinals that "the Divine Revelation is immutable and always binding," he emphasized that "the Church must be humble and recognize that she never exhausts its unfathomable richness and needs to grow in her understanding."[4] At the same time he affirmed the church's sacramental teaching of marriage as an "exclusive, stable and indissoluble union between a man and a woman," the pope added that "in our relationships with people, we must not lose the pastoral charity, which should permeate all our decisions and attitudes. The defense of objective truth is not the only expression of this charity; it also includes kindness, patience, understanding, tenderness, and encouragement. Therefore, we cannot be judges who only deny, reject, and exclude."

While many liberal Catholic advocates call for more tangible reforms, the pope's critics warn that the synod process itself poses a threat to the safeguarding of Catholic doctrine. "Synodality and its adjective, synodal, have become slogans behind which a revolution is at work to change radically the church's self-understanding, in accord with a contemporary ideology which denies much of what the church has always taught and practiced," Cardinal Burke wrote in a foreword to "The Synodal Process is a Pandora's Box," a book published on the eve of the 2023 synod by the Societies for the Defense of Tradition, Family and Property (TFP), an organization started in

Brazil in 1960 that is known for its opposition to the Second Vatican Council and support for right-wing political movements.[5] The book, which was published in eight languages and sent to several participants in the synod and Vatican officials, warned that the synodal process threatens "to demolish Holy Mother Church" through "neo-modernist" and "leftist" forces.[6] In a *First Things* essay written during the 2023 synod entitled, "The Church Is Not a Democracy," Cardinal Gerhard Müller, the former head of the Vatican's doctrine office, warned that "if the Synod is to keep the Catholic faith as its guide, it must not become a meeting for post-Christian ideologues and their anti-Catholic agenda."[7] The cardinal wrote that "any attempt to transform the Church founded by God into a worldly NGO will be thwarted by millions of Catholics," who "will resist to the death the transformation of the house of God into a market of the spirit of the age." At the conclusion of the synod, the cardinal told the *National Catholic Register*, a conservative publication in the United States, that "all is being turned around so that now we must be open to homosexuality and the ordination of women."[8]

It is unsurprising that many Catholics are impatient for change and others are defensively putting up barricades. Divisions over what constitutes authentic Catholic identity, and the proper role for the church in a modern world, are nothing new. Nearly sixty years after the conclusion of the Second Vatican Council, the council's legacy is still fiercely debated. The synod process, an affirmation and extension of the council, has inflamed old divisions. Pope Francis resisted attempts to view the synod through an ideological or political lens. The end goal is not a "plan of reformation," he insisted. The pope has asked the church to remember that the synod is "not a political gathering, but a convocation in the Spirit, not a polarized parliament, but a place of grace and communion."[9] While the documents of the Second Vatican Council ushered in historic changes in how the Catholic Church approached liturgy, modernity, and relationships with non-Christian religions, the council's emphasis on lay participation and responding to the "signs of the times" with social action never fully took root in the United States. A restorationist backlash reasserted hierarchical authority and centralized power in the decades after the council. "The current problem of the Church is precisely the non-acceptance of the Council," Pope Francis told the editors of European Jesuit magazines and Fr. Arturo Sosa, the superior general of the Jesuits, in 2022. "Restorationism has come to gag the Council. The number of groups of 'restorers'—for example, in the United States there are many—is significant."[10] In contrast, more church leaders in Latin America embraced the ecclesiology of the council. Latin American bishops meeting in Medellin, Columbia in 1968 famously called for a church that has a "preferential option for the poor." At a 2007 meeting of the Latin American and

Caribbean Bishops' Council (CELAM) in Aparecida, Brazil, the future pope, Cardinal Jorge Bergoglio of Buenos Aires, chaired the drafting committing for a final document that asserted the priorities of a missionary church of encounter that goes to the peripheries. Cardinal Christophe Pierre, apostolic nuncio to the United States, told *America* magazine in a 2023 interview that when he came to the United States in 2016 he was "astounded that many of the bishops didn't know what had happened in Aparecida."[11] The cardinal, who described the Aparecida conference as "a kind of synodal process of the South American bishops," remarked that US bishops "had not seen what had happened in their own continent, in South America." "This is very serious, because what has happened was not banal. It was the beginning of what we live today," he added. "They didn't know that the pope was one of the bishops at Aparecida, or that the whole South American church had made a tremendous effort of synodality."

The Catholic Church in the United States did have synodal experiences, even if many ultimately dissipated. As I described in an earlier chapter, the US bishops' Call to Action initiative responded to the Second Vatican Council by convening meetings and listening sessions around the country that led to a major grassroots conference in Detroit in 1976 that brought together some 1,300 Catholics. The two-year process was one of the most ambitious efforts to engage with lay Catholics ever undertaken by American bishops. It was nothing less than a "new way of doing the work of the Church in America," as Cardinal John Dearden of Detroit, the driving force behind Call to Action, described the effort at the time.[12] But when Catholics began raising questions about more democratic governance structures in the church, challenged bishops on why women were not given equitable ministerial roles, and asked for a reexamination of the church's positions on divorced and remarried Catholics, the process began to disintegrate amid mutual suspicion and acrimony. Bishops were willing to listen to lay Catholics, but when those conversations grew uncomfortable or were deemed too radical, the process unraveled. Nearly fifty years after the Call to Action conference—and more than ten years into Francis's papacy—many Catholics are still waiting for more concrete signs that church leaders can not only listen more closely but respond to calls for change. Catholic women are leading the way.

WOMEN'S LEADERSHIP AND SYNODALITY

Questions about power, patriarchy, and the role of women in Catholic institutions have only grown more urgent in recent years. When a Pennsylvania grand jury report was released in the summer of 2018, Katheen Sprows Cummings was furious. The report chronicled in painful detail seven decades of clergy sexual abuse in six Catholics dioceses in the state involving three hundred priests and a thousand victims.[13] A Pennsylvania native and historian of Catholicism at the University of Notre Dame, Cummings at the time directed the university's Cushwa Center for the Study of American Catholicism. For years, when she was asked to publicly comment about clergy abuse, she usually declined. Cummings mourned privately after a 2005 Philadelphia grand jury report had tainted the memories of her Catholic childhood when it named two sexually abusive priests who had served at her parish and several more who taught at her high school. But the latest grand jury report was released only a month after Theodore McCarrick—a celebrated Vatican diplomat and the former archbishop of Washington, DC—resigned from the College of Cardinals over sexual abuse allegations. The report and the McCarrick revelations were a tipping point for her.

Cummings wrote a commentary in *The New York Times* entitled, "For Catholics, Gradual Reform Is No Longer an Option," three days after the Pennsylvania report was published. "When it comes to the Roman Catholic Church, I have always been a 'place at the table' kind of feminist," Cummings wrote. "When asked how to integrate women more fully into the life of the church, I offer reasonable strategies. Bishops could, for example, recognize that the call for leadership might flow as much from the sacrament of baptism as from that of ordination, and appoint more women to leadership positions at all levels of church governance." But the "sickening revelations" from the grand jury report, she continued, "have propelled me directly to the center of the 'reset the table' camp. We need to rip off the tablecloth, hurl the china against the wall and replace the crystal with something less ostentatious, more resilient and, for the love of God, safer for children."[14] She acknowledged that "my once-polite requests for incremental reform have morphed overnight into demands that church leaders voluntarily relinquish their place at the head table."

Cummings worried about the reaction to her commentary, which drew nine hundred online comments and nearly three hundred personal emails, most of them positive. "As a woman in the church I was very well practiced at being careful and polite," she told me. "I often find myself as the only feminist in a group of Catholics or the only Catholic in a group of feminists. A priest once told me that he appreciated that I was not an 'angry feminist.' At the time I liked that but now I realize we should be angry."[15] More than five years after her *Times* commentary, Cummings still doesn't see a true reckoning with the deeper root causes that contributed to an institutional culture where abuse thrived. Some conservative bishops and other Catholics still blame the secular culture, especially the sexual revolution, rather than the church's own internal culture, as fostering the conditions that led up to the abuse crisis. "I think the way the Catholic Church developed in this country was to protect itself, for valid reasons, in the 19th century, when there was a lot of anti-Catholicism," she said. "And it looked inside itself and thought, 'it's us against them, and we have to be as strong as possible to fight what's coming from the outside.' Then, when that was no longer true—because you can't make an argument that Catholics are oppressed as a group anymore—those patterns still persisted."[16] Clergy sexual abuse and institutional coverup, she notes, are driven by abuse of power and a culture of secrecy. She credits journalists and victim-survivors for puncturing that self-protective bubble. "People throughout history almost never voluntarily relinquish power," she said. "It just doesn't happen. I'm still concerned that many bishops are hesitant to hire people who are willing to tell them hard truths."

There will be no lasting renewal and transformation in the church, Cummings believes, without more leadership roles for women. "The gravity of the abuse crisis would have been apparent far sooner, and the consequences far less devastating, if there had been women involved in these conversations," she said.[17] "If women were in positions of real power—and not just in positions of advising but given a real say in what happens next—things would look different now." She cautions that as important as the laity will be to change, there are also risks. "Clericalism is the 'father knows best' syndrome, but what I have learned is even women, the laity, can contribute to that culture by always thinking the priest or the bishop should have the final word," Cummings told me. "We do need lay empowerment, and I hope the synod can help, but how much will it really change things? I'm not always optimistic. It's still a very closed-door system." The historian takes a page from Catholic history to contextualize her skepticism. After Pope Paul VI convened a papal commission to study the question of whether the church should reaffirm its teaching against birth control, the pope ignored the advice of his own advisory commission to rescind the ban. The pope's 1968 encyclical, *Humanae Vitae,* affirmed the church's teaching that contraception is "intrinsically evil." Catholic married couples, including Patrick and Patty Crowley, served on the commission. Cummings has read the papers in the Crowley archives at the University of Notre Dame.[18] The couple, who were leaders in the Christian Family Movement, surveyed Catholic couples about their experiences with fertility, conception, and childrearing as part of information they collected for the papal commission. "Married Catholics wrote to them and poured out their personal travails and challenges with conceiving and childbearing," Cummings said. "Many of the letters are from people who were saying 'I'm so glad the church is finally listening to our experiences.' It reminds me of what we see with the synod now. Catholics are sharing their stories and experiences. So much of the language is the same. But will bishops really listen? Will it matter?"

Ellie Hidalgo is determined that the voices of Catholic women will matter. The co-director of Discerning Deacons, a project dedicated to engaging Catholics in conversations about the role of women and the diaconate, Hidalgo grew up in a vibrant Cuban American family in Miami where women were the backbone of a faith rich in culture and community. She moved to Los Angeles after college and learned about Dolores Mission Parish as a reporter for *The Tidings*, the archdiocese's newspaper. There she watched *madres* and *abuelas* in the East Los Angeles parish become courageous leaders in a community that at the time had the highest concentration of gang violence in the city. Fr. Greg Boyle, a Jesuit priest who served as pastor in the Boyle Heights church from 1986 until 1992, founded the now internationally renowned Homeboy Ministries, which has transformed the lives of ex-gang members. While Boyle wrote a bestselling book and became something of a religious celebrity, Hidalgo points to the quiet heroism of Latina Catholic women as the overlooked foundation of the parish.

"Fr. Greg had a really amazing group of women, mostly from Mexico, and he empowered them to go out into the community and make an impact," Hidalgo said. "I was captivated by this model of ministry where a priest and lay women were working side-by-side. It was a synodal way of being church long before people were talking about the synod."[19] Hidalgo moved from her newspaper job to become a pastoral associate at the parish, where she served for twelve years. When the coronavirus pandemic broke out in 2020, she moved back home to Miami to be with her elderly father. Her younger brother had recently died. While she sheltered in place, grieving the unexpected loss of her sibling and serving as a caregiver, Hidalgo found herself in a season of searching. She connected with Casey Stanton and a Jesuit priest, Luke Hansen, who put together a virtual workshop called "Discern, Dream & Scheme." Fifty people formed a cohort that met a few times a week to talk about their hopes for women in the church. The group took inspiration from conversations happening in the Amazon, where bishops and laity formed an ecclesial network to consult broadly about challenges, opportunities, and new pathways for the church. Under this innovative form of church governance, the issue of women's leadership emerged as a priority. A majority of bishops from the Amazon were in favor of ordaining women as deacons during the 2019 Synod of Bishops for the Pan-Amazon region. "I am going to take up the challenge that you have put forward, that women be heard," Pope Francis said in spontaneous remarks at the end of that synod.[20] The final document from the synod called for greater leadership roles for women but stopped short of calling for the ordination of women to the diaconate.

During her spiritual discernment in the early days of the pandemic, Hidalgo sensed what she called "a Holy Spirit moment," a time when her own yearnings to preach and serve seemed to be aligning with potential historic openings for women in the church. On the Feast of St. Phoebe, considered by many to be a deacon in the early church, Hidalgo organized a virtual prayer service, and to her surprise about five hundred people across the country participated. In April 2021, Stanton, Hidalgo, and Hansen formally started Discerning Deacons. A month later Pope Francis announced the beginning of a global synod process. Discerning Deacons, already built on a synodal style, began convening virtual meetings and hosting trainings for people who wanted to participate in the synodal process. During six months of synodal listening sessions organized by the group—led by Catholic educators, campus ministers, diocesan directors of religious education, and faith-based community organizers—more than 8,500 people in fifty dioceses across the country participated. Discerning Deacons shared its 2022 synthesis report with the US bishops' conference and the Vatican.

"The perceived refusal to welcome women's leadership and their vocational calls leaves many questioning the integrity of the Church's commitment to upholding human dignity and our common Baptism," the report noted.[21] Since the early days of Discerning Deacons, Hidalgo has been in dialogue with women in the Amazon. Discerning Deacons and women active in the Ecclesial Conference of the Amazon co-organized what they called an "intercontinental synodal encounter" and pilgrimage to the Basilica of Our Lady of Guadalupe in Mexico City in 2022. Archbishop Roque Paloschi of Porto Velho, Brazil, participated in the gathering. "Patriarchal and colonialist attitudes still persist among us, and in the face of this 'sin' we are invited to enter into a dynamic of conversion of mind, heart, and will, in order to recognize the service that women render to the Church, without making distinctions among men and women, but with dignity and equity in ministry," the archbishop wrote in a report published by the two organizations after the trip.[22]

Pope Francis first promised to convene a commission to study the question of whether women could be admitted to the diaconate when the topic came up during a 2016 meeting with the International Union of Superiors General, an organization that represents heads of women's religious orders from around the world. In 2019, the pope said the twelve-member commission was unable to reach consensus about the historical role of women deacons in the early church. A final report was never made public. The pope formed a second commission to study the question in 2020 following the Synod of Bishops from the Amazon, and that remains ongoing. For years, scholars such as Phyllis Zagano of Rutgers University, who served on the first commission convened by the pope, have argued there is compelling evidence that there were women deacons in the early church and that modern acceptance of women as deacons would be a return to church tradition rather than a break from the past. In the spring of 2024, Pope Francis appeared to close the door on the idea. "I understand you have said no to women as priests, but you are studying the idea of women as deacons," the CBS News correspondent Nora O'Donnell said to Pope Francis during an hourlong interview in the spring of 2024. "Is that something you're open to?" The pope responded: "If it is deacons with Holy Orders, no," he said, referring to the sacrament by which deacons, priests, and bishops are ordained to ministry. "For a little girl growing up Catholic today, will she ever have the opportunity to be a deacon and participate as a clergy member in the church?" O'Donnell asked. "No," the pope said bluntly.

Ellie Hidalgo still remains hopeful. "One media interview does not close the door on a bold vision the pope himself initiated," she said. In past decades, church leaders shut down conversations. Pope John Paul II's 1994 apostolic constitution, *Ordinatio Sacerdotalis,* declared "the Church has no authority whatsoever to confer priestly ordination on women."[23] But now a culture of silence has been broken, Hidalgo said, and a new "spiritual practice for listening" is beginning to emerge. She calls the pope's decision to include women delegates who were able to vote in the synod "a seismic shift in the way the Catholic Church walks in the world." But Hidalgo is worried that without more formal roles in place to allow women's leadership to flourish, much is left to chance. "We need stable ministries for women because women's participation in ministerial roles expands and contracts depending on who the bishop happens to be," she said. "Structures are built and structures are dismantled. The bishops themselves are often not in agreement about what authority women should have and what women's roles should be. If women could be admitted to the diaconate, we would no longer fight about this expansion and contraction. There would be a structure in place that meets pastoral needs." The challenge is far bigger than the issue of women deacons. Hidalgo sees the Catholic Church losing a generation of young women. "Women play a vital role in passing on the faith to the next generation," she wrote in a *Miami Herald* commentary.

> But when 99% of Catholic churches will have a male preacher this Sunday in a world where 50% of the Catholic population are women, it's time for our daughters and granddaughters—and sons and grandsons—to see us naming out loud a problem we've endured quietly in our hearts. What seemed normalized to my devout Catholic Cuban grandmothers, and became uncomfortable for my mother and has become unacceptable for me, is now unbearable for my nieces and many of our daughters. This will have untold consequences for the future of Catholic ministries.[24]

* * *

Sister Carol Zinn thinks that even many well-intentioned Catholics calling for change are stuck having the wrong conversations about women, reform, and the future of the church. The executive director of the Leadership Conference of Women Religious, whose member congregations make up about two-thirds of the nearly 40,000 Catholic sisters in the United States, Zinn wants to see a more expansive paradigm shift at a time when the established structures of political, economic, and religious institutions are disintegrating. "The institutional church brought itself down with the sex abuse crisis and six miles from my office the U.S. Congress, the infrastructure of our government, is also imploding from within," Zinn said. "The environment and the planet are imploding. All of these Western institutions that have held us together for the last four or five centuries are fraying. When that happens, something else needs to be born."[25]

Zinn became a Sister of St. Joseph after the Second Vatican Council, a time when many women religious and other lay Catholics were awakening to what the council called the "universal call to holiness," a responsibility shared by all Catholics through baptism. Zinn is grateful there are Catholics advocating for women in the diaconate, but she believes the starting point should be different. "When we talk about women in the church, most people go right to the ordination question. I'm not interested in the conversation of ordination from a gender perspective. I am more interested in it from a purpose perspective," Zinn told me.

> What does it mean to be ordained? Vatican II reminded us that all the people of God have a role. The culture of the institutional church is not inclusive so even if you put another gender in an ordained role, it doesn't necessarily mean something systemically and constitutively is going to change. Will it make a contribution? Perhaps. But only if it is at the front end of this deeper conversation about what it means to

> be a baptized member of the Catholic Church. For me, the women's ordination question is not about gender because the gender conversation isn't even about gender, it's about power.

To describe the myopic vision that can grow from a patriarchal institution, Zinn uses the analogy of race. "Looking at the role of women in the church is just as difficult as a white person like me confronting my unexamined whiteness and privilege," she observed.

> I have no idea what it's like to be in the world with dark skin. In a similar way, the institutional, hierarchical church does not really understand how to be in the church other than as a male. So until the institutional church is ready to engage in these more essential conversations, until we're ready to deconstruct and rebuild from a much more inclusive base, ordaining women as deacons or having a few women walking around as cardinals won't change things. When you hang ornaments on a Christmas tree, the tree is still a tree.

As she thinks about the future of religious congregations and the future of the church more broadly, Zinn draws on her experience guiding the Leadership Conference of Women Religious (LCWR) through a tumultuous period. In 2012, the Vatican's doctrine office released a report that reprimanded LCWR for espousing "radical feminist themes incompatible with the Catholic faith."[26] The product of a two-year investigation, the report described the doctrinal situation as "grave," and criticized the US sisters for failing to speak out against same-sex marriage and abortion. The conference responded that the report was "based on unsubstantiated accusations and the result of a flawed process that lacked transparency."[27] The Vatican appointed an American bishop to oversee LCWR as part of a reform process. The crackdown angered many Catholics in the United States who hold great affection for sisters. The Vatican's rebuke came only two years after LCWR joined other Catholic sisters to support President Obama's healthcare reform law, which the US bishops opposed over concerns about abortion funding. Zinn was soon shuttling between LCWR headquarters outside of Washington, DC, and Rome for meetings at the Vatican. The oversight ended in 2015 after a three-year process. What she called "a very hard journey" holds lessons for a divided church today. "We really stayed committed to having respectful dialogue," Zinn said. "It was a transformation because we learned that before all this we were not really talking. One of the graces that came out of all this is a determination to come to the table together—bishops, priests, laity—and LCWR is trying to do that. As a church, we have to be in conversation with each other. We can't be in silos."

Catholic sisters are known for valuing consultation, collaboration, and inclusive leadership models that emerge from deep listening and discernment. Zinn believes that if the synodal process promoted by Pope Francis can be embedded in the culture of the church—rather than simply viewed as a series of meetings—there is potential for lasting renewal. "This does not start with talking about theology or doctrine," she explained. "It starts with people. It starts with encountering and walking with people. The interesting thing to me about Pope Francis is he is not changing church teaching, and yet absolutely *everything* has changed. But the real transformation is not going to come from Rome or the U.S. bishops' conference. It's going to come at those small group tables, in conversations of five or seven people. It's going to come when people are in conversation with each other." She expects continued resistance from Catholics who cling to old models and structures that no longer serve people. During her thirteen years working at the United Nations, where she represented Sisters of St. Joseph in ministry around the world, Zinn often saw the most powerful nations resist change because the status quo benefited their interests. Powerful forces in the Catholic Church will do the same. But a church that will look different from the one we have today is inevitable. "As Pope Francis says, we are not in an era of change, but a change of era," Zinn said. "This happens about every 500 years. What is happening in the Roman Catholic Church is part of a larger cultural shift across the West at the institutional level of infrastructure. New things are being born even if we can't see what they are yet." Zinn argues that conversations about "church reform" miss the mark because the process of transformation runs deeper.

"The simplest image I have in my mind is that of a caterpillar becoming a butterfly," she said.

> A caterpillar is not reformed into a butterfly. It's transformed. Everything about it, everything that it was, is given over to the process of metamorphosis. Once it's all decomposed in the chrysalis, it begins to transform. That chrysalis environment may be what we're entering into today in the church. And this is true across all sectors, not just religion. Every institution from education to health care to government to politics is in a process of dying, of being transformed and reborn.

While many church leaders lament the declining numbers of vocations and the closure of churches, Zinn remains hopeful.

> The change happens slowly but we know from cosmology that when something new in the universe is born, it takes pockets of energy to line up and when enough pockets of energy line up, then transformation happens. I think we are in that mode. The people of God are fine. I am not worried about getting people back. I *am* concerned people do not have a home in their faith. But I see people finding places where meaning making can happen, where meaningful conversations can take place, and that is not always in a church, mosque or a synagogue.

NUNS & NONES: A HOME FOR SEEKERS

Katie Gordon is one of those seekers who was raised Catholic yet is finding a home outside the church. She left at fourteen when, in her words, the "lukewarm" Catholicism she experienced as a child growing up in a suburban parish in western Michigan wasn't feeding her searching intellect and spiritual restlessness. The big questions she wanted to explore in science and secular philosophy didn't feel compatible with the Catholic faith. Adding to her angst, the revelations of clergy sexual abuse became national news when she was twelve. She remembers listening to news stories about the scandals on National Public Radio while driving in the car with her mother. In her teenage years she immersed herself in reading secular and atheist writers. But despite her skepticism of religion, Gordon was drawn to social justice and fascinated by the intersection of faith and politics. By her mid-twenties, she was becoming more curious about spirituality, even if institutional religion held no appeal. Gordon took a job at an interfaith organization and started meeting Catholic sisters from the Dominican congregation in Grand Rapids. "I would see the sisters at interfaith events and at climate justice marches. I got more curious about their lives," Gordon told me.[28] One day she nervously told a sister that she was agnostic or maybe even an atheist. "The sister looked at me and said, 'that's ok, 'I am too on some days.' I was so surprised and relieved. That led to conversations with other sisters who wrestled with doubt and faith their entire lives. The fact that they stayed a part of the Catholic tradition while also searching and struggling really made an impression on me."

Most of Gordon's friends were similar to her: spiritual but not religious. They were part of a growing demographic the researchers call "nones"—people who are not affiliated with any religious denomination. A 2022 Pew Research Center report, "Modeling the Future of Religion in America," found that "nones" now make up 30 percent of the US population. If current trends continue, the report found, the number of Christians could fall below 50 percent of the US population by 2070. "The decline of Christianity and the rise of the 'nones' may have complex causes and far-reaching consequences for politics, family life and civil society," the report noted.[29] In the US religious landscape, "the most important story without a shadow of a doubt is the unbelievable rise in the share of Americans who are nonreligious," Ryan Burge, a political science professor at Eastern Illinois University and author of *The Nones*, told the Associated Press in 2023.[30] About four in ten religiously unaffiliated Americans are under thirty, a group that expresses high levels of distrust toward a wide range of institutions.

"My friends and I wanted to be part of some intentional spiritual conversations and create community, but traditional religion didn't quite fit," Gordon said. She began introducing her friends to the sisters she had gotten to know, and sixteen of the young people started meeting for biweekly conversations with the sisters in the living room of the sisters' retreat center. They gave themselves a cheeky name: Nuns & Nones. Gordon prefers the term "seekers" or "spiritually complicated" over "nones," but the catchy name had an undeniable appeal. Conversations often started with a reflection prompt. The group sat in a circle facing each other, a physical and symbolic posture Gordon preferred to looking up at a priest on an elevated altar. Several of the millennials in the group identified as queer and grew up in Catholic homes and parishes where their sexuality became a source of pain and shame. The sisters' welcome was a relief, even a form of healing. "The more time we spent with the sisters, we learned about their fifty, sixty-year commitment to social justice, prayer and action, all of these beautiful things over the long haul," Gordon said. "Trump had just been inaugurated. My friends and I were in despair about how we could make change. The sisters showed us how to model these countercultural commitments over a lifetime. This is what we wanted to do and they had done it for so long."

Gordon and the sisters in Grand Rapids were not alone. The idea of bringing sisters and nones together in more formal ways began to take shape at a meeting of women religious and religiously unaffiliated millennials at Harvard Divinity School in late 2016. Nuns & Nones launched that same year as an organization dedicated to creating what it calls "a new imagination for what spiritual community can be for our times."[31] Local groups began popping up across the country. The gatherings look different depending on the location. In some places there are occasional weekend retreats. Others have a more consistent, congregational feel with weekly meetings. There are also webinars, Zoom gatherings, and online communities. In one pilot experiment in a suburb south of San Francisco, five millennials in their early thirties spent six months living with Mercy sisters in a convent.[32] Gordon is a co-founder and was a national organizer for Nuns & Nones for six years. The thirty-three-year-old graduate of the Harvard Divinity School views movements like Nuns & Nones as filling a void left when people no longer find a home in a formal religious denomination but are still seeking community, religious wisdom, and spiritual paths. Rather than discarding the Catholic tradition, Gordan says the groups provide a creative balance to hold tradition and experimentation together. "The Catholic flavor of Nuns and Nones helped me reconnect to my origin tradition in a way that was life-giving," she explained. "The parish I was raised in represented one aspect of the Catholic tradition and the institutional church. I felt when I went to my parish that I was part of the hierarchical structure of the church. With the sisters, I found a radically different model of what it means to be spiritual and what it means to be church. In a way, I was really getting a more complete picture of what the Catholic tradition is all about." She references the phrase "on the edge of the inside" from the Franciscan priest, writer, and contemplative leader Richard Rohr to explain how sisters, in her words, are "solidly within the tradition and institution, but are not part of the hierarchy and open to movements on the ground." At the same time millennials and other young seekers are often "on the edge of the outside," Gordon says, because while they have left a particular denomination, they "remain with open hearts and hands to religious traditions."

As a student at Harvard Divinity School, Gordon read about the stories of early monastic communities. In the lives of the desert fathers and mothers, Saint Benedict, and other monastics, she found parallels for challenges and opportunities facing the church and society today. "The monastics were ordinary people who saw society in its brokenness, corruption, and oppression and sought to live in a different way," she wrote for the Harvard Divinity Bulletin.[33] "There are many moments at the founding of Christian monasticism that ring deeply resonant with our own social, spiritual, and political moment today. The Roman Empire was collapsing. The systems that people used to depend on were no longer functional, and alternatives were needed." After graduating from divinity school, Gordon moved into a monastery in Erie, Pennsylvania, where she lives in a small intentional community called Pax Priory. She admits it might seem like a strange decision for someone who entered divinity school as a self-identified "non-religious seeker" to live with Benedictine sisters, many of whom are more than double her age. But Gordon said she was drawn to the sisters' connection to "a deeper lineage of Christianity and monasticism," and finds meaning in reclaiming the "early roots of the tradition" that she believes have often been forgotten or lost in the institutional church.

When she thinks about the growing number of young Catholics leaving the church and the decline of institutional religious structures, Gordon believes that hope can be found in what she calls "the possibility between the old and the not-yet, the ancient and the emergent." An example of this synthesis between tradition and new forms of spiritual experimentation is Monasteries of the Heart, an online community (or "monastery without walls") that has grown to 26,000 members since 2011. The Benedictine sisters who Gordon lives with started the online movement to share Benedictine spirituality in a new era when the decline of traditional religious observance has not meant a loss of spiritual yearning. Sister Joan Chittister, a prominent author and sought-after speaker, came up with the idea. Her book, *The Monastery of the Heart: An Invitation to a Meaningful Life*, serves to anchor the community. Members participate in online courses and retreats, Zoom conversations, and book discussions.

While Gordon appreciates that Pope Francis's emphasis on synodality and pastoral theology has "instigated a very long process of change for the church," she does not anticipate what she calls more "radical changes" when it comes to how the church views women and LGBTQ people. "I sense that he is shifting the culture of the church so those changes might happen one day, but in the meantime, I spend my time and energy invested in more local, radical Catholic experiments rather than waiting for the Vatican," she said. "To me that is where hope is more alive." She knows that many Catholic leaders in dioceses across the country are anxious about the closing of churches, the lack of young people coming to Mass, and the decline in religious vocations. But Gordon argues we need a "narrative reframe" in how we think about those losses. She notes that "many religious teachings speak to a sacred cycle of collapse and innovation." In the Jewish story, "there is exodus, struggle and renewal." Christians are anchored in "the life, death and resurrection of Jesus." Gordon thinks that framework can serve as a narrative that could help Catholic leaders appreciate that assessing the present and future of Catholicism can't simply be a numbers game.

> We talk about decline and diminishment of religious orders and religious life, but while the numbers are shrinking there is also growth. We see more and more people, especially young people, drawn to Benedictine spirituality or the Ignatian spirituality of the Jesuits. We need a wider vision of what growth and decline means for the church that goes beyond how many people are ordained and who is showing

> up at Mass on Sunday. We're still stuck in these old institutional paradigms. We need to be asking new questions that lead us into the future.

* * *

Even as alternative forms of religious communities and Catholic spirituality such as Nuns & Nones will continue to develop in the coming decades, Catholics are also working to renew the church from the inside. At thirty-three, Nicole Perone is already a seasoned Catholic professional. The national coordinator of ESTEEM, a leadership formation program for Catholics at more than a dozen university campuses across the United States and the Caribbean, Perone previously served as the director of adult faith formation for the Archdiocese of Hartford, chairs the National Institute for Ministry with Young Adults, and is on the board of the All Africa Conference: Sister to Sister. She also teaches a class in Catholic social teaching at Sacred Heart University in Connecticut. While almost everyone seems to be talking about young people leaving the church, Perone has found that many Catholic leaders are not always eager to have young people at tables where decisions are made. "Young people are leaving as young as 13, so if we wait until they're old enough to 'pay their dues,' they are not going to be here to participate," said Perone, a graduate of Yale Divinity School.[34] When it comes to conversations about young people and the church, Perone acknowledges she finds it frustrating that attention is most often focused on either the nones or ultra-traditionalists, or "rad-trads," as they are often called. "Those are the poles, but there is also a big swath in the middle we don't talk about and when we don't, we miss an important demographic," she told me. "Most young Catholics are on a spectrum in terms of their relationship with the church. There is a lot of complexity. But we like tidy boxes in how we categorize people."

Young adult Catholics in this overlooked middle are not usually obsessed with the politics of the church or following every battle in the culture wars. In Perone's experience, young adult Catholics are more likely to drift away because they face what she calls "the slow burn of the church becoming irrelevant" in their lives. "This crisis of authority is the real issue," she said.

> A lot of young Catholics who were told as children that the church is an authority figure, and the church can help you sort out these fundamental questions of life, have struggled with what they perceive as the church's hypocrisy on sexual issues and the abuse crisis. They are not going to church every Sunday, but they go to get married or baptize a child and they have a bad experience with the parish secretary or priest who makes them feel unwelcome. If a young person is reaching

> out to the church in some capacity in these gateway moments, and we slam the door, we miss an opportunity and probably lose them.

The way many parishes are structured presents additional barriers. "We still have a very outdated model of parish life," Perone told me. "In many ways, our culture and practices are designed for a church that doesn't exist anymore. The idea that all Catholics are going to be there Sunday morning, or the mother stays at home raising the kids while the man works, and we have a parish fish fry on Friday night, that's just not the life most people have today." Research backs up that observation. Springtide Research Institute, which surveys the attitudes of young people about their religious experiences, has found that many young Catholics report finding spiritual and sacred meaning outside of traditional parish settings. The pandemic only further exacerbated the disconnect between young Catholics and the church. Only 6 percent of young Catholics said a faith leader reached out to them personally during the first year of the pandemic, compared to 18 percent for Protestants.[35]

Perone grew up in what she describes as a "fairly standard" Catholic family in suburban New Jersey. There was church on Sunday, and the cultural Catholicism of her Italian American family was ever present at baptisms, first communions, funerals, and weddings. But Perone didn't think much about her faith until she became involved with service and social justice projects at her parish. That led to her transferring from a public school to a Catholic high school. "The inflection point in my faith were these experiences with service and social justice," she said. "It wasn't just about volunteering or building houses. It was asking these bigger questions about income inequality and food insecurity." At a Jesuit college in Maryland, Perone jokes that she was "ruined for life" as Ignatian spirituality and learning more about Catholic social teaching fueled an even deeper commitment to the justice demands of her faith. When she arrived at Yale Divinity School, Perone was at a crossroads. She saw women pursuing ministerial roles in Protestant churches. What some have called the "stained glass ceiling" in Catholicism felt more ever present to her in a diverse religious environment. "I wrestled with a lot of questions and I was a case study in someone struggling with all these issues related to women and young people in the church," she said. Perone knows talented Catholic women who didn't see a role for themselves in the Catholic Church pursue careers where there were less barriers to advancement. "I watched these really great women who were raised Catholic, women I loved and respected, leaving the church or feeling they were pushed out because they thought their voices didn't matter," she said.

But Perone found a supportive Catholic community at Yale's St. Thomas More Catholic Chapel and Center. Catholic women mentors she met at Yale through ESTEEM (where she now serves as national coordinator) had a major influence on keeping her connected to the church and allowed her to see a future inside Catholic institutional spaces. Only a few months before graduating, Perone was invited to speak on a panel discussion at the Vatican on International Women's Day that featured Catholic women from around the world talking about women's leadership in the church. "I was surrounded by brilliant and passionate women who, like me, love the Church and want to see it reach its fullest potential," she said. "It was the first Catholic space I was invited in to speak with authority. I saw lay people, women, doing these amazing things in the church. I saw that our voices could be really powerful."

Perone was invited back to the Vatican in 2018 for a week-long gathering of three hundred young Catholics from around the world who participated in a Pre-Synod on Young People, the Faith, and Vocational Discernment. In his opening address Pope Francis told the group, who ranged in age from sixteen to twenty-nine, that the contributions of young people are vital. "We need to dare to have new sentiments, even if it means taking risks," the pope said.[36] "A man or woman who does not risk does not mature. An institution that chooses not to risk remains a child, it does not grow up. That's why we need you young people, living stones of a church with a young face. You provoke us to break free of the logic of 'it has always been done this way,' which is a sweet poison that tranquilizes the soul." Perone served on the writing committee for the youth synod's final report. "One part of the story that doesn't fully get told is how young people reclaimed the synodal process," she told me. Vatican officials had a methodical plan charted out that was heavy on process—meetings, readings, and note taking. "We knew we had to reframe to really focus on the most pressing thoughts on the minds of young people. We made sure this was something driven by the young people." Perone also learned a valuable lesson in how big the global church really is when young Catholics from Russia, China, and Syria, some of whom took risks just to be at the meeting, spoke of life-and-death issues in their countries. "Some of the more traditionalist Catholics participants from the United States wanted to talk about social issues and the Latin Mass," Perone said. "I'm not saying those issues aren't important, but hearing from young Catholics in other countries really puts things in perspective."

Perone is not pollyannaish about the challenges facing the church. "My daughter will be told she can be anything she wants in life with a couple of asterisks and that is hard to swallow," she said about the church's prohibition on women's ordination. She called it shameful that some US bishops have been "ambivalent at best and openly hostile at worst" toward the synod. And she laments that in too many institutional Catholic settings there can be a culture of fear and silence around topics that are deemed too progressive or radical. "As a woman and a young adult, it's really disheartening to me that so many topics cause a reaction of closing ranks and purging people for thinking differently. It makes me sad as someone who loves the church and who has studied the Catholic intellectual tradition," she said. But Perone chooses hope for herself, her husband, and her young daughter. "I believe there is something rich and beautiful in our Catholic identity," she said.

> I've seen so much of the good of Catholic life. Young adults are here now. My daughter is here now. The church I want to see on the other side of the synod is a church that is not afraid to be radically hospitable and to grapple and discern together. We can't let fear of change, fear of the new, fear of the secular world, hold us back. I'm hopeful for a church that is less afraid and more courageous.

* * *

Tracey Lamont remembers feeling adrift as a young adult Catholic. In her mid-twenties she helped lead Confirmation classes at a large Catholic parish in Florida. "I had a real hunger and restlessness to explore my faith in a much deeper way and create community, but except for the occasional theology-on-tap event, there was really nothing for my age group in the church," she recalled.[37] Lamont carried her frustration to graduate school at Fordham University in New York, where she wrote a dissertation that challenged sociological scholarship on millennials that in her mind erroneously pointed at young people—rather than religious institutions—as the primary source of religious disaffiliation. Lamont now directs the Loyola Institute for Ministry at Loyola University in New Orleans. She leads an innovation hub at the university backed by an initial $1.5 million grant from the Lilly Endowment that is focused on helping parishes listen and accompany young adults in more effective ways. A lot of people talk and write about synodality. Lamont is helping the church put it into practice. She has a straightforward message for clergy and other parish leaders.

"Young adults are not a problem to be solved," said Lamont, who at forty-three is a member of Generation X. "We hear it with the millennials and we're hearing it even more with Gen Z, that there's something problematic because they're leaving the church. Maybe what's problematic is the way the church is accompanying them. If we flip the script and look internally and say, 'maybe it was us.' What would look differently in our parishes?

How would ministry change?" The key is moving from what Lamont calls a "problem-solution" mindset to a "practical theology" that starts from the reality of young people's lives. "The solution is not more catechesis or moral education," said Lamont, who has advised the US Conference of Catholic Bishops on young adult outreach since 2017. "Young people know what the church teaches. What they need is someone to accompany them and have real conversations with them as they ask hard questions. They don't live in a black and white world. It's absolutely developmentally appropriate for them to challenge authority and try to find their identity as they move from adolescence into young adulthood. We need to be there with them. There is no program or pre-packaged solution. It's about listening."

As part of the innovation project at Loyola University, Lamont has partnered with more than a dozen Catholic parishes across the country to develop structured listening sessions with young adults in their twenties. To prepare, Lamont and her team spend four weeks providing the pastor (and at least one other staff person at the parish) with context and research about psychological development, the impact of social media culture, and the rising rates of loneliness among young people. When the listening sessions begin, young adults are encouraged to speak candidly. It can take a while for participants to settle in enough to feel comfortable speaking honestly. Lamont says she is amazed by the breakthroughs that eventually come. The most frequent topic brought up is how the church's perceived lack of welcome toward LGBTQ people is a source of pain. In one predominantly Latino parish, a young person spoke about feeling torn between the love for her faith and a gay friend who felt rejected by the parish. Instead of growing defensive, a church leader in the listening session admitted he didn't know how to effectively accompany an LGBTQ person but wanted to learn. Other participants acknowledged how unusual it was to even be asked by church leaders to share their views and opinions.

"What I've found to be transformative is in these groups the young people are building community and connection, and they feel seen and heard, often for the first time," Lamont said. The hardest step is the follow up. It's one thing to listen to young people, but adopting a leadership style of "co-responsibility," she says, means that pastors must see lay people, including young adults, as collaborative partners in shaping the vision and practice of a parish. Listening requires vulnerability, acknowledging when harm has been done, and being open to criticism that is hard to hear. Lamont thinks the most significant roadblock to embracing a synodality rooted in a culture of listening, discernment, and accompaniment come from those priests and bishops who are afraid to wade into an often messy process. She does not see many US dioceses prioritizing synodal leadership. "Fear is at the heart of the pushback." she said. "We're talking about changing a massive power dynamic." When I asked Lamont what it would take to scale up the kind of breakthroughs she is seeing in her work with parishes, her answer came without hesitation. "We need to change seminary formation," she said. "The biggest barrier we find is clergy. Seminarians are not being taught how to develop the skills needed for synodality. It's still a very didactic model. We're operating seminaries out of fear and pride. If we can't create a church where there is true co-responsible leadership, we're in real trouble."

* * *

The steady erosion of institutional Catholic life, as evidenced in clergy shortages, anemic Mass attendance, and the shuttering of churches built for bygone eras, is by now a familiar, decades-old narrative not unique to Catholicism. Other Christian denominations are also rapidly shedding institutional infrastructure amid cultural and demographic changes. "We are currently in the middle of the largest and fastest religious shift in the history of our country," write Jim Davis, Michael Graham, and Ryan Burge in their 2023 book, *The Great Dechurching: Who's Leaving, Why Are They Going and What Will It Take to Bring Them Back?* "No theological tradition, age group, ethnicity, political affiliation, education level, geographic location or income bracket escaped the dechurching in America."[38] There are signs that the Catholic Church faces some especially strong headwinds. "American Catholics in particular have seen a significant shift in the number who say religion is *not* important in their lives," a 2023 report from Public Religion Research Institute noted.[39] "White Catholics are now twice as likely to say religion is not important (16% in 2022 vs. 7% in 2013) compared to ten years ago, and this shift is even larger among Hispanic Catholics (13% in 2022 vs. 2% in 2013)."[40] The Catholic Church has experienced a greater net loss due to religious switching than any other religious tradition in the United States. There are now more "nones" than Catholics in the United States.[41] This Catholic decline would be far more extreme without the influx of Latino immigrants who in recent decades have shifted the demographic growth engines of American Catholicism from the Northeast to the South and West. Hispanics account for nearly 71 percent of the growth of the Catholic population in the United States since 1960. The majority of Catholics younger than twenty-five today are Latino.

Hosffman Ospino, a professor of Hispanic ministry and religious education at Boston College, describes Hispanics as "the largest force transforming American Catholicism."[42] Nearly half of all US Catholics now self-identify as

Hispanic. "The present and the foreseeable future of American Catholicism are intimately linked with the Hispanic experience," said Ospino, a native of Colombia who is a leading expert on Hispanics and the church.[43] But in recent years Ospino has watched Hispanic Catholics, especially in their twenties and thirties, become increasingly detached from Catholicism. "Is the Hispanic Catholic hope slipping through the Church's fingers?" he asked in a 2023 *Our Sunday Visitor* article.[44] In 2022, 43 percent of Hispanic adults identified as Catholic, down significantly from 67 percent in 2010, according to the Pew Research Center.[45] Even as Latinos remain about twice as likely as US adults overall to identify as Catholic, the share of Latinos who are religiously unaffiliated (describing themselves as atheist, agnostic, or "nothing in particular") was 30 percent in 2022, compared to only 10 percent in 2010. US-born Latinos are now more likely to identify as "nones" than Catholics. Ospino points to several factors at work. The US-born Hispanic population, the children or grandchildren of immigrants, are now reaching adulthood without making Catholicism a part of their identity. Immigrant Hispanic adults coming to the United States are also more likely to leave the faith than earlier generations of immigrants. For Hispanic Catholics who do stay, Ospino says they often don't see their culture and contributions appreciated by the wider church. And when it comes to Latinos in positions of Catholic leadership, the percentage of Hispanic bishops, theologians, clergy, and administrators is still small.

The US Catholic bishops' primary effort to engage Latino Catholics is an Encuentro that brings together Hispanic ministry leaders, clergy, bishops, diocesan directors, and young Hispanics for a series of gatherings at the local, regional, and national level. There have been five Encuentros since 1972. Some 250,000 people participated in the most recent Encuentro in 2018, the culmination of four years of consultation and workshops across the country. The goal is to better understand, and encounter, the needs of Latino Catholics and support Hispanic ministry by listening to those on the front lines. Ospino, who serves on Encuentro leadership teams, describes the gatherings, which involve dialogue sessions, workshops, training, and liturgy, as a successful example of synodality. "The Latino Catholic community has been doing synodal dialogue for fifty years," Ospino said. "This is at the core of Latin American theology and ecclesiology." As important as the Encuentro process has been in supporting Hispanic Catholic ministry, Ospino knows that many Latino Catholics have little if any formal attachments to diocesan or parish life. The church has to find more creative ways of reaching these Catholics. "There is a new way of being Catholic and a new way of being Latino in the U.S.," Ospino, who is forty-nine, told me.

> We need to figure out how to have these Catholics find their ways into the structures and service and the life of the church. We need to understand they are not going to be Catholic like their immigrant parents or as white Catholics. Many of the models that served Latino communities in past decades are not working. There is always resistance to change, but either we come up with new ways to engage them, and give them opportunities to be leaders, or we lose them.

It is also imperative that church leaders become more responsive to Black Catholics, especially at a time when a long overdue reckoning with white supremacy and racism in the church and society is drawing more attention. Despite representing only 4 percent of the Catholic population in the United States, Black Catholics have a proud history and serve the church today in vital ways. A 2022 analysis from the Pew Research Center found that only 54 percent of Black Catholics who were raised in the faith remained Catholics as adults, compared to 61 percent of white Catholics and 68 percent of Hispanic Catholics.[46] At the end of 2023 there were only five Black bishops (out of 266 active bishops), and one Black cardinal, Wilton Gregory of Washington, the first African American to be elevated to the College of Cardinals. While 77 percent of Black Catholics said that "opposition to racism is essential to what being Christian means to them," only 41 percent reported having heard a homily focused on race in the twelve months prior to completing the survey. (Most of the data was collected before the murder of George Floyd in 2020.) The findings in the study "will add up to losing Black Catholics if we don't see our church fighting with, and for, us for racial equality," wrote Tia Noelle Pratt, a Villanova University sociologist of religion whose research focuses on systemic racism and African American Catholic identity. "This study is a call to action for scholars and church leaders alike."[47]

There are signs of hope. Young Black Catholics, by some measures, are more connected to their faith tradition and express more religious satisfaction than their white Catholic peers, according to survey responses and analysis from the Springtide Research Institute. In a 2022 report from the institute, 39 percent of young Black Catholics say they are "flourishing" in their faith lives, compared to 21 percent of young white Catholics.[48] The study also found young Black Catholics are more likely to trust organized religion, attend religious services and youth groups, pray daily and study scripture, and consider themselves to be a religious or spiritual person. Young Black Catholics are also far more likely than young white or Hispanic Catholics to seek help from their faith community when they are overwhelmed or experience stress in life. Researchers cite the resilience of Black Catholics' family bonds as one reason why younger Black Catholics seem to be more rooted in their Catholic identity. "Black Catholic faith is still an intergenerational phenomenon," Josh Packard, the executive director of Springtide Research, and Byron Wratee, a doctoral candidate in systematic theology at Boston College, wrote in *Religion News Service*.[49] "Grandparents, parents, aunties and uncles are encouraging younger Black Catholics to attend church. While the numbers of churchgoing Black Catholic millennials and Gen Zers is decreasing, they have maintained a higher connection to church because their family stresses the importance." Packard and Wratee note that while "traditional markers for determining one's religiosity—like how often they attend religious services—tend to result in overgeneralizations about Gen Z's curiosity about religion and spirituality," there "could just as well be an exciting future for young Black Catholics in America, a group that is growing, flourishing and rooted in traditional religious practices more than their peers."

RECOVERING TRADITION, FINDING "FRESH PATHS"

The future of Catholicism in the United States will likely be an evolving story of loss and decline, along with new opportunities for reform, renewal, and innovation. The characterization is not as contradictory as it may sound. In his insightful essay, "What Happens Now?" David Gibson, director of the Center on Religion and Culture at Fordham University, references the opening line of Peter Steinfels's essential 2004 book, *A People Adrift: The Crisis of the Roman Catholic Church in America*, in which Steinfels writes that "the Roman Catholic Church in the United States is on the verge of either an irreversible decline or a thoroughgoing transformation." Two decades after Steinfels summarized what he saw as the church's existential crossroads, Gibson attempts to hold the tension together. "Maybe it's both," Gibson writes.

> Maybe the decline is a form of transformation, one that is shifting American Catholicism away from the model of American Christendom—the default view of the Catholic Church as a static community that practices the faith reflexively and is accorded an equally reflexive degree of respect, if not reverence, that has prevailed for so long. That paradigm has prevailed in Church infrastructure and institutions and, most important, in the ecclesial mindset that starts from the notion that "we've always done it this way," and anything to the contrary is a threat. A poisonous logic, Pope Francis has called it.[50]

Transformation requires a kind of death. We hold on to structures, habits, and institutional ways of being that are familiar and comfortable. But there will be no vibrant future for American Catholicism if nostalgia and reflexive resistance to any change shrinks the Catholic imagination. This does not mean succumbing to the broader ambient culture and tossing aside tradition. The radical demands of the Gospels *are* counterculture. Catholic Christians should stand apart from and challenge society with our rejection of hyper-individualism, the worst excesses of consumer capitalism, the deification of markets, and extreme inequalities that literally kill people. We should reclaim for our age the most authentic expressions of the Catholic tradition by defending human dignity, standing in solidarity with the poor, and welcoming refugees. The Catholic who refuses to do so does not fail a political or partisan test but ignores the unambiguous requirements of Christian discipleship. It is this tradition, following in the footsteps of Jesus and developed over centuries in the light of Catholic social teaching, that remains timeless—ancient but always new.

Over the centuries, and still today, many have distorted faith and orthodoxy in the name of their defense. Reclaiming Catholicism will require a change in church cultures and practices that bury the essence of faith under a harsh legalistic theology that fails to see and walk with people in the complexities of their lives. "If the Christian is a restorationist, a legalist, if he wants everything clear and safe, then he will find nothing," Pope Francis said early in his papacy.[51] "Tradition and memory of the past must help us to have the courage to open up new areas to God." Several years later Francis was even more pointed in his description. "A church that does not develop its thinking in an ecclesial way is a church that goes backward," the pope said. "That is the problem of many today who claim to be traditionalists. They are not traditionalists, they are 'backwardists.' Tradition is the root of inspiration in order to go forward in the church."[52] Can the Catholic Church be "open to fresh paths and new ways of speaking," as the pope encouraged in a 2021 homily to start the synod?[53] The reactionary impulse to label any change and development as dangerous or even heretical contrasts with the church's own tradition of development. In the centuries before the Second Vatican Council, the church was disfigured by its association with slavery and antisemitism. Modernism and democracy were regarded as evils. Popes and other church leaders rightly renounced those earlier teachings and saw in them folly, arrogance, and sin. In our own time many Catholics wrestling with questions about the church's teachings and practices as they relate to women, human sexuality, dignity for LGTBQ people, and new expressions of family life are also engaging in forms of faithful discernment and calls for development that are authentically Catholic. We must rediscover yet again an appreciation for what a living tradition means.

Yves Congar, the French Dominican priest who served as a theological advisor at the Second Vatican Council and helped shape many of the council's seminal documents, described tradition as "like the Church itself: it comes from the past but looks forward to the future." Tradition "grows and renews itself," Congar said, adding that "nothing is more foolish than to think everything has been said in the past."[54] Pope Francis has quoted Congar's memorable line from his book *True and False Reform in the Church* that there is "no need to create another church, but to create a different church." A church open to reform and renewal does not mean, Congar warned, "trying to invent a new synthesis from scratch."[55] Instead the *ressourcement* theology that Congar espoused, and that Vatican II embraced, represents a return to the roots of early Christianity to rediscover wisdom that had been lost. When Pope John XXIII convened the council, he saw the integration of *ressourcement* with *aggiornamento*, "updating," as the complementary pillars that could hold up an ancient church as it sought to thrive in a modern world. "Since change is part of the human condition, it cannot be something un-Catholic," observed the late Jesuit priest John O'Malley, a renowned historian of the twentieth-century church and an expert on the council who died in 2022. "Change, moreover, does not necessarily entail loss of identity. In fact, it is sometimes necessary to assure identity, especially of a living organism."[56]

* * *

In this book I have explored the landscape of US Catholicism, particularly as it relates to the church's profile in politics and public life. There is widespread recognition that the church's capacity to speak with moral credibility and prophetic insight about the most urgent issues of our time has been severely damaged by the ongoing fallout from the clergy abuse crisis, and the perception that significant swaths of the American hierarchy have aligned with the Republican Party. Even beyond the Catholic Church, the conflation of religion with conservative politics has turned a generation of Americans away from institutional religion. "It is not just that the United States is becoming a more secular nation," writes David Campbell, a University of Notre Dame political scientist who has documented declining religious affiliation for more than a decade. "It is that Americans' secularization is, at least in part, a backlash to the employment of religion for partisan ends." Campbell, the author (with Jeff Layman and John Green) of *Secular Surge: A New Fault Line in American Politics*, argues that the "politicization of religion and the attendant secular backlash" does "not bode well for the state of religious tolerance in contemporary America" and "diminishes the ability of religious leaders to speak prophetically about issues of public policy."[57]

This does not mean that US bishops and other Catholic leaders should withdraw from the public square and stop speaking about contentious issues such as abortion, marriage, and sexuality. It does mean that if Catholic leaders want to more effectively communicate in a diverse society that is becoming less Christian and more distrustful of institutional religion, there must be a greater commitment to speak with humility, an acknowledgement that disagreement is not always fueled by animosity, and a genuine search for common ground. Chicago Cardinal Blase Cupich has modeled this posture in ways that other church leaders might learn from and emulate. After the US Supreme Court ruled in favor of same-sex marriage in 2015, Cupich took a notably different approach than many of his fellow bishops and other conservative Christian leaders who denounced the decision using language that only further inflamed divisions. "The proposed reason for the ruling is the protection of equal rights for all citizens, including those who identify themselves as gay," he wrote. "The rapid social changes signaled by the Court ruling call us to mature and serene reflections as we move forward together. In that process, the Catholic Church will stand ready to offer a wisdom rooted in faith and a wide range of human experience." He added that "respect must be real, not rhetorical" and urged Catholics to "extend support to all families, no matter their circumstances, recognizing that we are all relatives, journeying through life under the careful watch of a loving God."[58] In his response to the Court's 2022 abortion decision overturning *Roe*, the cardinal showed a similar instinct to bridge divides. He applauded the ruling but also said the decision "underscores the need to understand those who disagree with us, and to include an ethic of dialogue and cooperation."[59]

Cathleen Kaveny, a scholar of theology and law at Boston College, has observed that contemporary public discourse is often characterized by rhetoric that is "skewed much more toward contempt and exclusion than repentance, rehabilitation, and reconciliation."[60] We see this rhetorical style in effect daily, if not hourly, on social media, in dueling partisan salvos in the press, when Catholic clergy denounce President Biden as a "fake Catholic," and in the maximalist rhetoric of pro-life and pro-choice activists. In her 2016 book, *Prophecy Without Contempt: Religious Discourse in the Public Square*, Kaveny offers a detailed cross-disciplinary analysis of how the style of biblical prophets and the Puritan preachers have been weaponized today in service of decimating political and ideological opponents. "The jeremiad only works if all parties agree on the fundamental premise," Kaveny observed in an interview with the Boston College Law School Magazine. "You can't call people to task for straying from a premise they don't believe in. So topics like abortion or same-sex marriage don't respond to a legalistic indictment like a jeremiad. It just doesn't work in the highly emotive world of the culture wars."[61] Instead Kaveny argues for what she calls a "compassionate and humble truth-telling" and suggests that examples can be found in Abraham Lincoln's Second Inaugural and the Bible. "If the rhetoric of prophetic indictment is going to have a place in an increasingly pluralistic society such as our own, I argue that its practitioners must develop some humility, particularly with respect to their knowledge of God's will," she writes.[62]

Catholic leaders have become too dependent on a prophesy of contempt (to borrow from Kaveny's language) to reflexively denounce secularism as the primary source of societal ills and even the church's own struggles. While there are indeed strains of secularism that are hostile to any religious expressions in the public square, a church that perpetually portrays itself as a victim—a dour church of "gloom-and-doom"—does not engage, persuade, and inspire. Catholics can instead draw from the resources of the church's own rich intellectual and social tradition—a commitment to faith and reason, the prudence to reject false choices—to navigate secularization in less defensive and ultimately more effective ways. Charles Taylor, the renowned Canadian philosopher who is Catholic, has been lauded by Pope Francis and other leaders for providing insights into how to make sense of a dramatically changed cultural landscape in which Christianity is no longer the default worldview in the West. Taylor distinguishes between a secularism that is animated by a sharp-edged ideological opposition to religion, and a less antagonistic secularity he views as most at play in a modern world where spiritual seekers, skeptics, traditionally religious believers, agnostics, and atheists are all, in his words, continually "cross-pressured" in an environment where identity and belief are often evolving. "Secularization represents a challenge for our pastoral imagination, it is 'an occasion for restructuring the spiritual life in new forms and for new ways of existing'," Pope Francis said in 2019, quoting from Taylor's widely acclaimed book *A Secular Age*.[63] Taylor's scholarship, Francis added, "allows us to deal with Western secularization in a way that is neither superficial nor given to fatalistic discouragement." This equilibrium is crucial, the pope observed, "in order to adopt the spiritual attitudes suitable for living, witnessing, expressing and proclaiming the faith in our time."[64]

A renewed Catholicism for our time will be a hopeful faith, unafraid to engage the wider secular culture, rooted in tradition while open to development, and always moving outward into the world. A church closed in on itself, as Pope Francis reminds us, becomes self-referential, static, and sick. A fortress church has no future. The Catholic imagination that will carry us into the next century will have to be expansive, creative, and agile enough to adapt as some institutional structures wither away or are transformed for a new era. "In the church of the past, you had people coming to Mass out of habit," Bishop Joseph Tyson in Yakima, Washington, told me. "The church of the future is people don't come to us, we go to them."[65] As part of priestly formation in the Yakima diocese, Bishop Tyson requires seminarians to spend time working in the fields with migrants who pick cherries and other fruits in sweltering heat. The bishop rolls up his sleeves and joins them. For the first time, in 2021 the seminarians and bishop spent several weeks living in the same residence with the migrants, a former hotel that serves as a temporary home for the seasonal workers. "We're really creating mobile parishes for people on the move," the bishop said. "That's a missionary church." The migrant ministry in Yakima is a small but powerful example of how the church can find new ways to live out gospel values in a contemporary context. "My hope is the skill set the seminarians learn in the fields will be replicated inside the parish structure and renew those parish structures," Bishop Tyson explained. "Parishes can be very self-referential and turn inward. It's not about trying to convince people to come to a building or a program. This is about flipping our understanding and going out into the world."

* * *

I started my initial reporting and research for this book in 2022 as an admittedly restless Catholic. The elation I and many others felt in 2015 after Pope Francis's election had given way to unease as the backlash to his papacy was hardening. When a vocal minority of bishops began clamoring to deny President Biden communion in 2020, the hypocrisy and selective policing of Catholic identity put the American church in an unflattering spotlight. The divisive politics and culture wars that came to define the Catholic narrative in the United States often left me demoralized. These years of reporting and listening to the stories of Catholics who love our faith and want the church to reflect the best of its teachings and tradition leave me more hopeful. When I'm pulled toward cynicism and doubt, I remember Black Catholics on the front lines of racial and climate justice; LGBTQ Catholics calling our church to a wider, more inclusive love; those overlooked bishops who are true pastors; Catholic advocates working to heal the wounds of clergy abuse and advance restorative justice; and the courage of Catholic women chipping away at stained-glass ceilings that are slowly but inevitably starting to crack. I have been reminded again that the soul of the Catholic Church will always be the diverse pilgrim people of God—faithful, flawed, complex, and creative. I am also more grateful than ever that Pope Francis, in the face of outsized expectations from the left and bitter opposition from the far right, has succeeded in staying the course. His remarkable pastoral gifts and big-hearted humanity have opened the windows of the church to a world we need not fear. Pope Francis's legacy should inspire us to chart a hopeful Catholic future where the church can hold tradition and change together as part of a living faith that is a source of mercy, healing, and justice.

NOTES

1. *Address of His Holiness Pope Francis to Participants in the Meeting Promoted by the Pontifical Council for Promoting the New Evangelization*, Synod Hall, October 11, 2017. https://www.vatican.va/content/francesco/en/speeches/2017/october/documents/papa-francesco_20171011_convegno-nuova-evangelizzazione.html.
2. Joshua J. McElwee, "Francis Criticizes Traditionalist Catholics Who 'Safeguard the Ashes' of the Past," *National Catholic Reporter,* June 2, 2019, https://www.ncronline.org/vatican/francis-criticizes-traditionalist-catholics-who-safeguard-ashes-past.
3. Dan Stockman, "Cardinal McElroy: Women and Men Religious Can Lead Synodal Shift," *National Catholic Reporter,* November 10, 2023, https://www.ncronline.org/news/cardinal-mcelroy-women-and-men-religious-can-lead-synodal-shift.
4. "Pope Francis Responds to Dubia Submitted by Five Cardinals," *Vatican News,* October 2, 2022, https://www.vaticannews.va/en/pope/news/2023-10/pope-francis-responds-to-dubia-of-five-cardinals.html.
5. Cindy Wooden, "Retired Cardinal Burke Claims Synod Causing 'Grave Harm' to Catholic Church," August 23, 2023, https://www.ncronline.org/news/retired-cardinal-burke-claims-synod-causing-grave-harm-catholic-church.
6. Christopher White, "Behind the Synod Opposition: Far-Right Groups, Political Activists and Cardinal Burke," *National Catholic Reporter,* September 11, 2023, https://www.ncronline.org/vatican/vatican-news/behind-synod-opposition-far-right-groups-political-activists-and-cardinal.
7. Gerhard Cardinal Müller, "The Church Is Not a Democracy," *First Things,* October 27, 2023, https://www.firstthings.com/web-exclusives/2023/10/the-church-is-not-a-democracy.
8. Edward Pentin, "Cardinal Muller Says Synod on Synodality Is Being Used by Some to Prepare the Church to Accept False Teaching," *National Catholic Register,* October 27, 2023, https://www.ncregister.com/interview/cardinal-mueller-says-synod-on-synodality-is-being-used-by-some-to-prepare-the-church-to-accept-false-teaching.
9. Justin McLellan, "Pope Addresses Fears around Synod: 'Not a Political Gathering,'" *Catholic News Service,* October 4, 2023, https://www.usccb.org/news/2023/pope-addresses-fears-around-synod-not-political-gathering.
10. Christopher Lamb, "Pope Says Refusal to Accept Vatican II Is 'Problem' for Church," *The Tablet,* June 14, 2022, https://www.thetablet.co.uk/news/15592/pope-says-refusal-to-accept-vatican-ii-is-problem-for-church.
11. Gerard O'Connell, "Cardinal Pierre on Why the U.S. Bishops are Struggling to Connect with Pope Francis," *America,* November 2, 2023, https://www.americamagazine.org/faith/2023/11/02/cardinal-christoph-pierre-interview-246416.

12. Francis J. Butler, "Cardinal John Dearden Wanted to Give Lay Catholics Influence after Vatican II. Pope Francis' Vision for Synods Could Finally Do It," *America*, October 8, 2021, https://www.americamagazine.org/faith/2021/10/08/cardinal-dearden-1976-synodality-vatican-241578.
13. Office of Attorney General, "Commonwealth of Pennsylvania," *Pennsylvania Victims Report*, https://www.attorneygeneral.gov/report/.
14. Kathleen Sprows Cummings, "For Catholics, Gradual Reform Is No Longer an Option," *New York Times*, August 17, 2018, https://www.nytimes.com/2018/08/17/opinion/catholic-church-reform.html.
15. Kathleen Sprows Cummings, interview with author.
16. Kerry Temple, "Having Coffee with Kathleen Sprows Cummings," *Notre Dame Magazine*, Winter 2018–19, https://magazine.nd.edu/stories/having-coffee-with-kathleen-sprows-cummings/.
17. Temple, "Having Coffee with Kathleen Sprows Cummings."
18. University of Notre Dame, *Patrick and Patricia Crowley Papers*, 1964, https://archives.nd.edu/findaids/ead/html/RWL.htm.
19. Ellie Hidalgo, interview with author.
20. Joshua J. McElwee, "Amazon Synod Calls for Married Priests, Pope to Reopen Women Deacons Commission," *National Catholic Reporter*, October 26, 2019, https://www.ncronline.org/earthbeat/amazon-synod-calls-married-priests-pope-reopen-women-deacons-commission.
21. "Discerning Deacons for a Synodal Church: Synthesis Report of Consultations Conducted from January—June 2022 for the first phase of the global Synod on Synodality for U.S. Region XVI," https://discerningdeacons.org/wp-content/uploads/2022/08/DD-Synod_Final-Web-EN.pdf.
22. "An Intercontinental Synodal Encounter," Discerning Deacons and Conferencia Eclesial de la Amazonia. Mexico City, August 31–September 5, 2022, https://discerningdeacons.org/wp-content/uploads/2023/05/Pilgrimage-Synthesis-Final-Web-En.pdf.
23. *Ordinatio Sacerdotalis,* Apostolic Letter of John Paul II to the Bishops of the Catholic Church on Reserving Priestly Ordination to Men Alone, May 22, 1994, https://www.vatican.va/content/john-paul-ii/en/apost_letters/1994/documents/hf_jp-ii_apl_19940522_ordinatio-sacerdotalis.html.
24. Ellie Hidalgo, "Young Women Want to Know the Church Supports Them," *Miami Herald*, June 16, 2023, https://www.miamiherald.com/opinion/op-ed/article276443591.html.
25. Sister Carol Zinn, interview with author.
26. Congregation for the Doctrine of the Faith, *Doctrinal Assessment of the Leadership Conference of Women Religious*, April 18, 2012, https://www.vatican.va/roman_curia/congregations/cfaith/documents/rc_con_cfaith_doc_20120418_assessment-lcwr_en.html.
27. Leadership Conference of Women Religious, "LCWR Board Meets to Review CDF Report," June 1, 2012, https://www.lcwr.org/news/lcwr-board-meets-to-review-cdf-report.
28. Katie Gordon, interview with author.
29. Pew Research Center, "Modeling the Future of Religion in America," September 13, 2022, https://www.pewresearch.org/religion/2022/09/13/modeling-the-future-of-religion-in-america/.

30. Peter Smith, "The Nones: United States," *Associated Press,* October 5, 2023, https://projects.apnews.com/features/2023/the-nones/the-nones-us.html.
31. Nuns & Nones, "Our Story," https://www.nunsandnones.org/about.
32. Soli Solgado, "For Nuns and Nones Six-Month Pilot Program, Millennials Move In," *National Catholic Reporter,* June 10, 2019, https://www.ncronline.org/nuns-and-nones-six-month-pilot-program-millennials-move.
33. Katie Gordon, "Nuns and Nones Meet on the Edge," *Harvard Divinity Bulletin,* Autumn/Winter 2019, https://bulletin.hds.harvard.edu/nuns-and-nones-meet-on-the-edge/.
34. Nicole Perone, interview with author.
35. Springtide Research Institute, "Sacred Experience Benefits Gen. Z Spirituality, Wellbeing," October 25, 2023, https://springtideresearch.org/post/news/sacred-experience-benefits-gen-z-spirituality-wellbeing.
36. Joshua J. McElwee, "Church Must Take Risks to Grow, Francis Tells Pre-Synod Meeting of Youths," *National Catholic Reporter,* March 19, 2018, https://www.ncronline.org/news/vatican/church-must-take-risks-grow-francis-tells-pre-synod-meeting-youths.
37. Tracy Lamont, interview with author.
38. Jim David and Michael Graham with Ryan P. Burge, *The Great Dechurching: Who's Leaving, Why Are They Going, and What Will It Take to Bring Them Back* (Zondervan, 2023).
39. Public Religion Research Institute, "Religion and Congregations in a Time of Social and Political Upheaval," May 16, 2023, https://www.prri.org/research/religion-and-congregations-in-a-time-of-social-and-political-upheaval/.
40. Public Religion Research Institute, "Divergent Perspectives: The Unique Views of White and Hispanic Catholic Americans," October 11, 2023, https://www.prri.org/spotlight/divergent-perspectives-the-unique-perspectives-of-white-and-hispanic-catholic-americans/.
41. Mark Pattison, "Pew Poll Shows 'Nones' Exceeding Catholics in U.S.," *Catholic News Service,* October 18, 2019, https://catholicphilly.com/2019/10/our-changing-church/pew-number-of-nones-now-tops-catholics-in-american-society-2/.
42. Hoffsman Ospino, "Is the Hispanic Catholic Hope Slipping through the Church's Fingers?" *Our Sunday Visitor,* September 15, 2023, https://www.oursundayvisitor.com/is-the-hispanic-catholic-hope-slipping-through-the-churchs-fingers/.
43. Hoffsman Ospino, interview with author.
44. Hoffsman Ospino, "Is the Hispanic Catholic Hope Slipping through the Church's Fingers?" *Our Sunday Visitor,* September 15, 2023, https://www.oursundayvisitor.com/is-the-hispanic-catholic-hope-slipping-through-the-churchs-fingers/.
45. Jens Manuel Krogstad, Joshua Alvarado, and Beesher Mohamed, "Among U.S. Latinos, Catholicism Continues to Decline but Is Still the Largest Faith," *Pew Research Center,* April 13, 2023, https://www.pewresearch.org/religion/2023/04/13/among-u-s-latinos-catholicism-continues-to-decline-but-is-still-the-largest-faith/.
46. Jeff Diamant, Beesher Mohamed, and Joshua Alvarado, "Black Catholics in America," *Pew Research Center,* March 15, 2022, https://www.pewresearch.org/religion/2022/03/15/black-catholics-in-america/.
47. Tia Noelle Pratt, "Why Pew's New Study on Black Catholicism Is Critical for U.S. Church Leaders," *National Catholic Reporter,* March 16, 2022, https://www.ncronline.org/news/opinion/why-pews-new-study-black-catholicism-critical-us-church-leaders.

48. Springtide Research Institute, *The State of Religion & Young People 2021—Catholic Edition*, https://springtideresearch.org/product/catholic-edition-2021.
49. Josh Packard and Byron Wratree, "Young Black Catholics Are Still Here and Flourishing More Than Their Peers," *Religion News Service*, April 1, 2022, https://religionnews.com/2022/04/01/young-black-catholics-are-still-here-and-flourishing-more-than-their-peers/.
50. David Gibson, "What Happens Now?" *Notre Dame Magazine*, Winter 2021–2022, https://magazine.nd.edu/stories/what-happens-now/.
51. Antonio Spadaro, S.J, "A Big Heart Open to God: An Interview with Pope Francis," *America*, September 30, 2013, https://www.americamagazine.org/faith/2013/09/30/big-heart-open-god-interview-pope-francis.
52. Christoper White, "Pope Francis Says Catholic Church Committed 'Cultural' Genocide of Canada's Indigenous Peoples," *National Catholic Reporter*, July 30, 2022, https://www.ncronline.org/news/vatican/pope-francis-says-catholic-church-committed-cultural-genocide-canadas-indigenous.
53. *Homily of His Holiness Pope Francis*, St. Peter's Basilica, October 10, 2021, https://www.vatican.va/content/francesco/en/homilies/2021/documents/20211010-omelia-sinodo-vescovi.html.
54. Patrick Granfield, "From 1967: An Interview with Yves Congar," *America*, originally published on May 6, 1967, https://www.americamagazine.org/faith/2023/12/05/vantage-point-yves-congar-246643.
55. Granfield, "From 1967: An Interview with Yves Congar."
56. John W. O'Malley, "The Style of Vatican II," *America*, February 24, 2003, https://www.americamagazine.org/issue/423/article/style-vatican-ii.
57. David E. Campbell, "The Perils of Politicized Religion," *Daedalus*, Summer, 2020.
58. Archdiocese of Chicago, "Statement of Archbishop Blase J. Cupich, Archbishop of Chicago," June 28, 2015, https://dig.abclocal.go.com/wls/documents/2015/062815-wls-cupich-statement.pdf.
59. Archdiocese of Chicago, "Statement of Cardinal Blase J. Cupich, Archbishop of Chicago, on the Supreme Court's Decision in *Dobbs v. Jackson Women's Health Organization*," June 24, 2022, https://www.archchicago.org/statement/-/article/2022/06/24/statement-of-cardinal-blase-j-cupich-archbishop-of-chicago-on-the-supreme-court-s-decision-in-dobbs-v-jackson-women-s-health-organization.
60. Katharine Whittemore, "Prophesy Without Contempt: A Q & A with Libby Professor Cathleen Kaveny," *Boston College Law School Magazine*, April 25, 2016, https://lawmagazine.bc.edu/2016/04/prophecy-without-contempt-a-qa-with-libby-professor-cathleen-kaveny/.
61. Whittemore, "Prophesy Without Contempt."
62. Cathleen Kaveny, "Understanding the Rhetorical Forms of the Culture Wars," *Political Theology Network*, June 30, 2016, https://politicaltheology.com/book-preview-understanding-the-rhetorical-forms-of-the-culture-wars-cathleen-kaveny/.
63. Michael Sean Winters, "Pope Francis Is Right. The Catholic Church Can't Go Backwards," *National Catholic Reporter*, August 3, 2022, https://www.ncronline.org/news/opinion/pope-francis-right-catholic-church-cant-go-backwards.
64. Cindy Wooden, "Pope Francis Gives Ratzinger Award to Philosopher Charles Tayor and Jesuit Fr. Paul Bere," *Catholic News Service*, November 11, 2019, https://www

.americamagazine.org/faith/2019/11/11/pope-francis-gives-ratzinger-award-philosopher-charles-taylor-and-jesuit-father.

65. John Gehring, "Seminary Immersion Program Yields a Harvest of Pastoral Experience," *National Catholic Reporter*, August 30, 2021, https://www.ncronline.org/news/justice/seminarian-immersion-program-yields-harvest-pastoral-experience.

INDEX

ABOUT THE AUTHOR

JOHN GEHRING is the author of *The Francis Effect: A Radical Pope's Challenge to the American Catholic Church.* His writing and commentary have appeared in *The New York Times, The Washington Post, CNN, National Catholic Reporter, America, National Public Radio,* and *Commonweal.*